Lecture Notes in Computer Science   **9738**

Commenced Publication in 1973
Founding and Former Series Editors:
Gerhard Goos, Juris Hartmanis, and Jan van Leeuwen

More information about this series at http://www.springer.com/series/7409

Margherita Antona · Constantine Stephanidis (Eds.)

Universal Access in Human-Computer Interaction

Interaction Techniques and Environments

10th International Conference, UAHCI 2016
Held as Part of HCI International 2016
Toronto, ON, Canada, July 17–22, 2016
Proceedings, Part II

 Springer

Editors
Margherita Antona
Foundation for Research & Technology –
Hellas (FORTH)
Heraklion, Crete
Greece

Constantine Stephanidis
University of Crete / Foundation for
Research & Technology – Hellas
(FORTH)
Heraklion, Crete
Greece

ISSN 0302-9743   ISSN 1611-3349   (electronic)
Lecture Notes in Computer Science
ISBN 978-3-319-40243-7   ISBN 978-3-319-40244-4   (eBook)
DOI 10.1007/978-3-319-40244-4

Library of Congress Control Number: 2016941076

LNCS Sublibrary: SL3 – Information Systems and Applications, incl. Internet/Web, and HCI

Printed on acid-free paper

This Springer imprint is published by Springer Nature
The registered company is Springer International Publishing AG Switzerland

Foreword

The 18th International Conference on Human-Computer Interaction, HCI International 2016, was held in Toronto, Canada, during July 17–22, 2016. The event incorporated the 15 conferences/thematic areas listed on the following page.

A total of 4,354 individuals from academia, research institutes, industry, and governmental agencies from 74 countries submitted contributions, and 1,287 papers and 186 posters have been included in the proceedings. These papers address the latest research and development efforts and highlight the human aspects of the design and use of computing systems. The papers thoroughly cover the entire field of human-computer interaction, addressing major advances in knowledge and effective use of computers in a variety of application areas. The volumes constituting the full 27-volume set of the conference proceedings are listed on pages IX and X.

I would like to thank the program board chairs and the members of the program boards of all thematic areas and affiliated conferences for their contribution to the highest scientific quality and the overall success of the HCI International 2016 conference.

This conference would not have been possible without the continuous and unwavering support and advice of the founder, Conference General Chair Emeritus and Conference Scientific Advisor Prof. Gavriel Salvendy. For his outstanding efforts, I would like to express my appreciation to the communications chair and editor of *HCI International News*, Dr. Abbas Moallem.

April 2016   Constantine Stephanidis

HCI International 2016 Thematic Areas and Affiliated Conferences

Thematic areas:

- Human-Computer Interaction (HCI 2016)
- Human Interface and the Management of Information (HIMI 2016)

Affiliated conferences:

- 13th International Conference on Engineering Psychology and Cognitive Ergonomics (EPCE 2016)
- 10th International Conference on Universal Access in Human-Computer Interaction (UAHCI 2016)
- 8th International Conference on Virtual, Augmented and Mixed Reality (VAMR 2016)
- 8th International Conference on Cross-Cultural Design (CCD 2016)
- 8th International Conference on Social Computing and Social Media (SCSM 2016)
- 10th International Conference on Augmented Cognition (AC 2016)
- 7th International Conference on Digital Human Modeling and Applications in Health, Safety, Ergonomics and Risk Management (DHM 2016)
- 5th International Conference on Design, User Experience and Usability (DUXU 2016)
- 4th International Conference on Distributed, Ambient and Pervasive Interactions (DAPI 2016)
- 4th International Conference on Human Aspects of Information Security, Privacy and Trust (HAS 2016)
- Third International Conference on HCI in Business, Government, and Organizations (HCIBGO 2016)
- Third International Conference on Learning and Collaboration Technologies (LCT 2016)
- Second International Conference on Human Aspects of IT for the Aged Population (ITAP 2016)

Conference Proceedings Volumes Full List

1. LNCS 9731, Human-Computer Interaction: Theory, Design, Development and Practice (Part I), edited by Masaaki Kurosu
2. LNCS 9732, Human-Computer Interaction: Interaction Platforms and Techniques (Part II), edited by Masaaki Kurosu
3. LNCS 9733, Human-Computer Interaction: Novel User Experiences (Part III), edited by Masaaki Kurosu
4. LNCS 9734, Human Interface and the Management of Information: Information, Design and Interaction (Part I), edited by Sakae Yamamoto
5. LNCS 9735, Human Interface and the Management of Information: Applications and Services (Part II), edited by Sakae Yamamoto
6. LNAI 9736, Engineering Psychology and Cognitive Ergonomics, edited by Don Harris
7. LNCS 9737, Universal Access in Human-Computer Interaction: Methods, Techniques, and Best Practices (Part I), edited by Margherita Antona and Constantine Stephanidis
8. LNCS 9738, Universal Access in Human-Computer Interaction: Interaction Techniques and Environments (Part II), edited by Margherita Antona and Constantine Stephanidis
9. LNCS 9739, Universal Access in Human-Computer Interaction: Users and Context Diversity (Part III), edited by Margherita Antona and Constantine Stephanidis
10. LNCS 9740, Virtual, Augmented and Mixed Reality, edited by Stephanie Lackey and Randall Shumaker
11. LNCS 9741, Cross-Cultural Design, edited by Pei-Luen Patrick Rau
12. LNCS 9742, Social Computing and Social Media, edited by Gabriele Meiselwitz
13. LNAI 9743, Foundations of Augmented Cognition: Neuroergonomics and Operational Neuroscience (Part I), edited by Dylan D. Schmorrow and Cali M. Fidopiastis
14. LNAI 9744, Foundations of Augmented Cognition: Neuroergonomics and Operational Neuroscience (Part II), edited by Dylan D. Schmorrow and Cali M. Fidopiastis
15. LNCS 9745, Digital Human Modeling and Applications in Health, Safety, Ergonomics and Risk Management, edited by Vincent G. Duffy
16. LNCS 9746, Design, User Experience, and Usability: Design Thinking and Methods (Part I), edited by Aaron Marcus
17. LNCS 9747, Design, User Experience, and Usability: Novel User Experiences (Part II), edited by Aaron Marcus
18. LNCS 9748, Design, User Experience, and Usability: Technological Contexts (Part III), edited by Aaron Marcus
19. LNCS 9749, Distributed, Ambient and Pervasive Interactions, edited by Norbert Streitz and Panos Markopoulos
20. LNCS 9750, Human Aspects of Information Security, Privacy and Trust, edited by Theo Tryfonas

Universal Access in Human–Computer Interaction

Program Board Chairs: **Margherita Antona, Greece, and Constantine Stephanidis, Greece**

- Gisela Susanne Bahr, USA
- João Barroso, Portugal
- Jennifer Romano Bergstrom, USA
- Rodrigo Bonacin, Brazil
- Ingo K. Bosse, Germany
- Anthony Lewis Brooks, Denmark
- Christian Bühler, Germany
- Stefan Carmien, Spain
- Carlos Duarte, Portugal
- Pier Luigi Emiliani, Italy
- Qin Gao, P.R. China
- Andrina Granić, Croatia
- Josette F. Jones, USA
- Simeon Keates, UK
- Georgios Kouroupetroglou, Greece
- Patrick Langdon, UK
- Barbara Leporini, Italy
- Tania Lima, Brazil
- Alessandro Marcengo, Italy
- Troy McDaniel, USA
- Ana Isabel Paraguay, Brazil
- Michael Pieper, Germany
- Enrico Pontelli, USA
- Jon A. Sanford, USA
- Vagner Santana, Brazil
- Jaime Sánchez, Chile
- Anthony Savidis, Greece
- Kevin Tseng, Taiwan
- Gerhard Weber, Germany
- Fong-Gong Wu, Taiwan

The full list with the program board chairs and the members of the program boards of all thematic areas and affiliated conferences is available online at:

http://www.hci.international/2016/

HCI International 2017

The 19th International Conference on Human-Computer Interaction, HCI International 2017, will be held jointly with the affiliated conferences in Vancouver, Canada, at the Vancouver Convention Centre, July 9–14, 2017. It will cover a broad spectrum of themes related to human-computer interaction, including theoretical issues, methods, tools, processes, and case studies in HCI design, as well as novel interaction techniques, interfaces, and applications. The proceedings will be published by Springer. More information will be available on the conference website: http://2017.hci.international/.

General Chair
Prof. Constantine Stephanidis
University of Crete and ICS-FORTH
Heraklion, Crete, Greece
E-mail: general_chair@hcii2017.org

http://2017.hci.international/

Contents – Part II

Universal Access to Mobile Interaction

Virtual Reality, 3D and Universal Access

Intelligent and Assistive Environments

Multimodal and Natural Interaction
for Universal Access

A Human-Computer Interface
and an Analysis on the Drawing
of Curves with a Face Tracker Mouse

Ivana S. Bandeira[1]([✉]) and Fernando Henrique G. Zucatelli[2]

[1] Institute of Mathematics and Statistics (IME-USP),
R. do Matão 1010, São Paulo 05508-090, Brazil
ivana@ime.usp.br
[2] Center of Engineering, Modeling and Applied Social Sciences (CECS-UFABC),
Av. dos Estados 5001, Santo André, São Paulo 09210-580, Brazil
fernando.zucatelli@aluno.ufabc.edu.br

Abstract. Recent research on interactive electronic systems, like computers, can improve the quality of life of many researchers, students, professors, etc. In the case of disabled people, technology helps them to engage more fully into the world. Our study aims to evaluate interfaces for curves drawing with movements of the face. This article discusses about motivations to build such software, how the software works, iterative development of the software, and user testing by people with and without disabilities.

Keywords: Curves · Computer graphics · Design · User experience and usability · HCI

1 Introduction

In general, we often refer to curves only as a set of points on the plane or in space. Nevertheless, the formal definition is given by the concept of function. In this case, we describe curves three-dimensionally in the space as polygonal curves. In other words, a polygonal curve is a finite sequence of line segments, called edges joined end to end. The endpoints of the edges are named vertexes. Let $v_0, v_1, ..., v_n$ denote the set of $n + 1$ vertexes, and $e_0, e_1, ..., e_n$ designate a sequence of n edges, where $e_i = v_i v_{i+1}$. Here, we consider closed curves where the last endpoint is equal the first $v_n = v + 0$.

It is possible to find several applications in many areas of knowledge like Mathematics, Physics, Engineering, Computing and, specially, in computer graphics [1–4]. Besides, the concept of curves allows us to define subsequent ideas of curvature, torsion, surface, and area, which are fundamental in any topics whose applications involve three-dimensional geometry. This fact allows further expansion to the applications of this work.

This present discussion is particularly devoted to *Physically Challenged People* (PCP) who cannot use their hands when working on a computer.

© Springer International Publishing Switzerland 2016
M. Antona and C. Stephanidis (Eds.): UAHCI 2016, Part II, LNCS 9738, pp. 3–14, 2016.
DOI: 10.1007/978-3-319-40244-4_1

Their participation in academia has been growing steadily, and as such their access to such programs enabling performing physical experiments in a virtual way is highly desirable. Overall, there is a few software has been specifically designed to attend these users' needs of usability to these users. Exceptions include software for typing with the eyes and head by moving the gaze across a keyboard displayed on the computer screen [5]. However, software systems controlled by the these movements is not available for the most of the activities, for example, drawing. One of the biggest problems when designing on a computer is clicking and dragging to obtain the desired figure.

Despite not being so scientific, art is a form of communication. A possibility of using it relies on the digital art, a practice that uses digital technology as an essential part of the creative or presentation process. The images in the visual arts consist of points, lines, shapes, colors, textures that we call elements of visual language. There have recently been solutions with eye-gaze technology, which enables people without hand movements to draw with their eyes [6].

Since the beginning of the project, our focus has been on understanding the users needs and identifying the usability goals and the user's experience. Furthermore, we present a graphical user interface (GUI) implemented to work with the *HeadMouse*® [7], which allows the computer mouse functions to be carried out through movements of the head and face by the person. The clicking and the movements of the cursor are performed by software, which identifies the users movements of head, eyes, and mouth via a web cam.

In terms of digital accessibility, we hope to contribute to people with disabilities as well as to works by many other researchers in the literature [8–11].

2   Methodology

The current objective is to investigate temporal requirement and performance, but the most important point is the experience of the users, such as: how they feel about their performance using a face tracker, paying attention to mental and physical requirements, effort and frustration. Our interface is programmed in *MatLab*® as seen at Fig. 1, with the commands being activated by a mouse click on virtual buttons via the face tracker. The main view of the interface and buttons are described as follows:

1. **Draw**: Start the point-picking routine by clicking the mouses left button in the correct location for a valid coordinate. The program shows the coordinate in the grid and stores it to the variable "pts", plotting the points after each correct click. If the click is on a wrong location, then nothing is done. A click with the mouses right button finishes the sub-routine and stops the clock. During this operation no other action is allowed. The next Draw command will start at the last point and the clock is resumed.
2. **Read**: Open a file window searching for a *.mat* file previously stored with the "pts" data. After choosing the file, the grid points are updated.

3. **End Curve**: This command closes the curve by connecting the last point taken with the first one. The number of picked points is incremented. Attention is need as it doesnt have any restrictions to get more points.

4. **Undo**: Clean the last point and decrement the actual "Current Number of Points" at the information panel. It is possible to "Undo" all the points.

5. **Redo**: Redraw the next point if there is a next point. If more than 1 point has been undone, but not all of them has been re-picked, then "Redo" will redraw the previously points until the "Current Number of Points" reaches the "Maximum Number of Points".

6. **Save next**: Stores the "pts" data at a *.mat* file, saves the actual view as a *.png* file and creates a *.tex* file with these data. Each file has some prefix to identify it, which is identified by the extension "file_save_name". This *.mat* file is exactly the one to be read at the "Read" button.

7. **Restart**: Refresh the variable "pts", the clock, and the Open/Closed curve option.

8. **Exit**: Close the interface.

The **Save next** function has a very important task, it enables a fast data analysis because variable "pts" has all points and the time used to select them, so there is no need to make manual notes during the test and on the other hand the *.tex* file organizes it together with the set of figures for every test, therefore a simple *.tex* base file calls every single *.tex* file from the tests by using an input function from LATEX. It is simple to insert all of the same tests because their names change only by the number from the "Save Counter", and show the results. In addition to providing a useful tool for saving data to users, it facilitated the collection of data in the test sessions. Figure 2 shows the interface while choosing a point. Buttons stays disabled until the right button is clicked, which warrants that the function gets the points needed. Figure 3 presents the possibility to rotate the view and check the picked points, it can be stored as it is by clicking the "Save next" button.

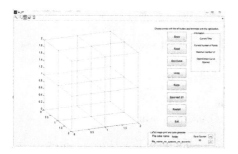

Fig. 1. Interface view

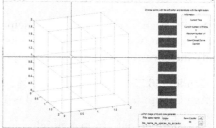

Fig. 2. Collecting points on screen

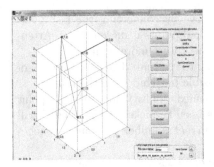
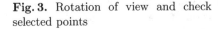

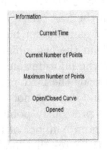

Fig. 3. Rotation of view and check selected points

Fig. 4. Information panel

Figure 4 is the information panel, exhibiting the time when the last point was picked, the current point to be picked and the maximum point number. This is especially useful to know how many times a "Undo" commands have been made and therefore how many "Redo" can be done forwards.

The interface is designed to prevent the user from committing unintentional errors. With this proposal, the drawing region is enabled only when the "Draw" button is pressed. In addition, the user has access again to other options when the curve drawing ends.

For a scheme of a richer characterization of how people with physical disabilities are adopting devices for interaction, we asked: Which devices are being used for on a daily basis? Which adaptations are users making to improve accessibility?

We noticed some non-commercial adaptions created by the participants, such as the use of a pen in the mouth to guide the mouse and the use of cheek movements to press buttons. Although there are many advances in technology, accessibility challenges still exist.

2.1 Users Characteristics

Typically, each of the 16 users participated in at least one session. For the rest of this article, we will use the word "user" to refer to the primary subject. Our study includes the following demographic breakdowns:

– Gender: 56.25 % male and 43.75 % female;
– Age Group: 6.25 % teenagers ($13 \sim 17yrs$) 93.75 % adults ($18 \sim 64yrs$).

We collected data from 4 mobility impaired users including three painters and two web designers (one participant being both) and 12 able-bodied participants involving undergraduate students. Of these, one was undergraduate student, one was master student, eight were doctoral students and one was post-doctoral student. The areas of study were the following: Geology, Applied Mathematics, Bioinformatics, Statistic and Differential Geometry.

Among the participants who have disabilities, there were two women with the Charcot-Marie-tooth disease (CMT is a hereditary motor and sensory neuropathy affecting both motor and sensory nerves, with weakness and muscle atrophy affecting arms and hands), a man who became quadriplegic after car accident, and two people with atrophy in the upper limbs. Two participants were virtually tested with a remote control software according to our evaluation criteria.

2.2   Survey Respondents

Twelve participants responded to our survey. We wanted to investigate about the experience in drawing using a computer, the needs, benefits and difficulties doing this action.

Twelve participants answered our survey. We wanted to investigate the users experience of drawing through a computer along with needs, benefits and difficulties regarding this action. All participants use the computer more than once a week. But, just 37.5 % were expert computer users and only 25 % were programmers.

In the group of mobility impaired users there also was one undergraduate student, one master student in a French language program, one doctoral student in applied mathematics, one programmer, and seven participants who use software to draw.

Of these, three are mobility impaired users and they are able to use professional applications. They reported that the most effortful task was to learn commands to get started with these programs, followed by the difficult to control the conventional mouse.

The others told that they do not use software to draw because they know no software that can meet their needs, such as plotting graphics, in an easy way easy without having to spend time training it.

2.3   Interaction Styles

The concept of interaction styles refers to all the ways by which an user can interact with a computer. In our study, we had considered the followings: conventional mouse/mouse-pad by hand (Fig. 8), chin (Fig. 5), thumbs, feet (Fig. 7); trackball by chin; face tracker (Fig. 6). An experimental restriction was that the participant needed to be seated. Because of the condition of being lying in bed, a young man had difficulties in positioning the camera in order to get good calibration, thus he did not participate in the research.

Only two participants had experience in the field. One did it by curiosity, whereas the other had already used an eye and facel tracking device at the same university. One participant said to have used some kind of tracker, not just facial, for a game. In Fig. 8, the participant is a painter and he told that he would use our interface in his digital painting classes. Interaction with the fingers was by far the most common direct interaction method for people with and without disabilities. A boy and one woman use their toes to point and it is noteworthy

Fig. 5. Trackball by chin

Fig. 6. Virtual mouse with face tracker

Fig. 7. Conventional mouse by foot

Fig. 8. Mousepad by hand

that this boy and other girl used thumbs to interact. We observed that motor impairments did not interfered with their ability to perform. Our attentiveness to the surrounding issues of human-computer interaction is in the sense to ensure system functionality and usability, providing effective user interaction support, and enhancing a pleasant user experience. Thus, the user performance is so important as the user experience. In this sense our present work is also devoted to impaired people that cannot use the upper limbs. Their participation in academia has been growing steadily and their access to programs that allow the access to draw in each interaction style is crucial.

3   Discussion

The experiment was divided into three sessions of about 40 min, with each participant working individually.

In the **first session**, the users created eight curves freely with three four, five, six, seven, eight, nine, and ten points, respectively (Fig. 9). The time of each action was estimated and it is showed in Fig. 10.

The average time was 53.3862 s. In general, all users were satisfied with their performance and told that the interface was easy to use and the learnability of the

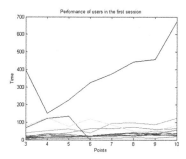

Fig. 9. Free draw

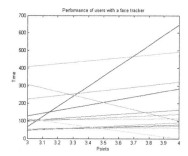

Fig. 10. Repeating first and second curve

commands was not difficult to understand because of the buttons and the grid. Performance and estimated time were similar between impaired users and able-bodied participants. One boy who has problem in his arms tried to manipulate the mouse with the two thumbs initially, but he had a lot of difficulties and then he tried it with his right foot, which was the easiest way to him.

When asked if they had ever experienced other method of interaction besides the conventional mouse and keyboard, only four of them had used touch screen technology in their personal computer. The colored lines on the graph represent the performance of the participants in the sessions, which measured the time spent in relation to the amount of points in the curves.

In the first session (Fig. 11), the users made the first attempt of moving the mouse with head movements. The participants should redraw the first and second curves created in the free-drawing session. The time increased by 90 s. Being out of the comfort zone can be pointed as a possible cause, since it is arduous to perform a new task in the beginning. Other reason is related to the users personality: some participants were worried because they could not click where they wanted and this influenced their results. They aimed to have the same performance as the first attempt with the methods they were used to.

After the user detected and located the virtual mouse by means of the head mouse, the click actions can be emulated. With regard to the interface, the targets may be small, leftover, unexpected clicks generated by involuntary movements resulting from lack of practice in controlling the face. In order to alleviate such a problem, a routine was established to attract the click to the desired target even if the click is done with 0.5° of distance.

In the **second session**, the participants should redraw five opened curves with three (2), four (2) and five points selected from the database captured in the first session. The average time was reduced by 30 s. Some users reported during the validation experiments that they did not feel so stressed in the second session as in the first one because they knew what they should do and their performance was better. By comparing head movements to natural movements, it was found that the users had similar performance, as can be seen Fig. 13.

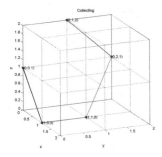

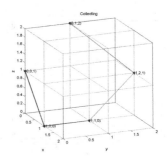

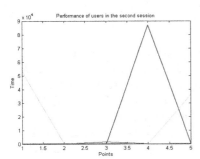

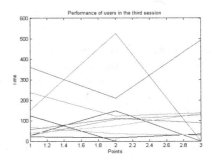

Fig. 11. Correct example   **Fig. 12.** Wrong curve

Fig. 13. Performance of second session   **Fig. 14.** Performance of third session

However, the members being tested committed minor errors when starting the curve as points were clicked wrongly or accidentally. The participants felt more satisfied with controlling better the head. In the following two pictures we compare a wrong curve (Fig. 12) to a correct one (Fig. 11). This participant could have used the "Undo" button, but she had to use it twice and so she preferred not get bored and tired doing it.

In the **third session**, the participants were expected to draw closed curves selected from the database captured in the first session. The experiment was divided into two parts:

(i) It was required to join the last point to the first one, thus closing the curve.
(ii) It was necessary to press the "End Curve" button to close the curve.

The average time between both parts was increased by 50 s, even for a lower amount of points (Fig. 14). The same deviation was observed between the first and second sessions. One possible reason for these results was the fatigue caused during the development in the first part of the session. However some participants who had given up presented a better performance compared to the first one.

In this study, in addition to evaluating the performance of input interfaces for drawing curves with face tracking mouse, we were interested in understanding the users' experience, more specifically the "work load" experienced by the participants. Notwithstanding, some concepts regarding mental demand or effort are difficult to measure. Some comments cited by the participants helped identify changing needs in the physical components, which improved the users experience. For example, if we could enlarge the target area, it would be much more convenient to click on a button. Other suggestion was to replace the direct click on the grid for access via a virtual keyboard with large buttons.

The issues related to each users perception are shown in Table 1. They were requested to describe the feelings experienced while performing the task with respect to mental demand, physical demand, temporal demand, own performance, effort and frustration. The performance ranged from "very good" to "very bad", whereas the other five scales from "very low" to "very high". We can estimate the experienced work load described by the participants in the first and last sessions.

Table 1. Results of session 1 and 3

item		Session 1					Session 3				
		very low	low	medium	high	very high	very low	low	medium	high	very high
		1	2	3	4	5	1	2	3	4	5
1st	Mental demand	3	7	2	0	1	4	3	1	0	0
2nd	Physical demand	1	6	0	3	2	5	3	0	0	0
3rd	Temporal demand	0	2	1	5	4	4	4	1	0	0
4th	User performance	3	3	0	3	5	6	2	1	0	0
5th	Effort demand	0	5	1	3	3	5	4	0	0	0
6th	Frustation	1	1	6	1	3	4	5	0	0	0

Mental requirement has to do with remembering to click, which enables the region by pushing the draw button. Then, in order to have access to virtual buttons again it is needed to simulate the conventional mouses right button with the functionality of a face tracker. After the third time, it became a natural process for the participants.

The use of a different tool can have caused stress and fatigue because the users wanted to avoid making mistakes. Maybe personality traits, such as those of scientists and artists, make the participants to strive to be perfect at the tasks and they end up forgetting the time. In fact, no error occurred in the first attempt with the head mouse. As a consequence, as shown in the time bar chart, the time spent was longer than the expected.

Due to the slow process of moving the cursor and clicking on a small target to achieve good performance, some participants were angry and insecure, besides the tiredness. Although there is no error, the majority of the participants felt some kind of disappointment due to thoughts that they could do better. However, almost all participants (two had given up - one with impairment and an able-bodied one) reported that it was a challenging situation and they would eventually become an expert.

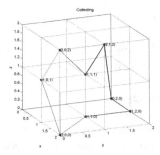
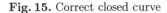
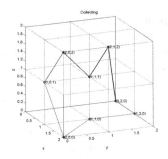

Fig. 15. Correct closed curve   **Fig. 16.** Wrong closed curve

In general, the feeling of frustration is associated with the time spent to perform the task. There is no difference of opinion between the users with or without disabilities. If the participants thought it was taking too much time in comparison to the time spent in their usual interaction style, frustration would be higher and performance rated as poor. The controlling of the face tracking mouse was improved with the inclusion of a button for closing the loop and an attractor for the target, which changed the situation, as can be seen in Table 1.

The mental activity, including the physical demand, became so simple that sometimes the participant had to be reminded about what should be done.

After two sessions, the users found the best way to control the facial movements to achieve the desired performance. This fact reduced both time spent and frustration significantly.

All participants had improved their performance by using less effort, which can be seen at their choice in the fourth and fifth items of the Table. Most of them managed to reach performance rates similar to those in the form of interaction they were used to, either by using conventional mouse or individual adaptations.

The users noticed that the combination of our interface with *HeadMouse*® is useful when they have awareness about their own hands or when they are continually busy with other tasks. Then, they were interested in improving their performance.

The frustration was lower when a button was included to end a curve. Clicking on a button is one standard form of interaction, and for this reason they can feel comfortable and less stressed. Other consideration is about the button size, which was larger than the target area.

Time demand, physical demand and efforts decreased. Also, the users were satisfied with their performance. Some comments indicate that the interface allowed them to create prototypes rapidly as well as examples of curves and polygons. However, error rates increased too.

We highlight the examples of Figs. 15 and 16, which had the highest error rates because of the curve begins and ends with the same color.

We highlight the examples of Figs. 15 and 16, which had the highest error rates because of the curve begins and ends with the same color. We did not expect such a mistake because the previous session was clear, with change in color sequence being normal on the edge every click. When closing the curve, the user noticed it was wrong because of the difference in the color sequence. This fact was interesting for some participants who play a memory game, where the player has to follow an aleatory sequence. It was suggested to create a game using the idea of this development to curves associated with a face tracker, something like the 80's game called Simon Says or Genius in Brazil. Additionally, there is a significant area for development in accessibility, ranging from custom-made interaction styles, for people with limited mobility through support for indirect interaction methods, thus allowing personalization of interactions that can be adapted over time.

4   Conclusion

One of our goals by using a high-level language such as $MatLab^{®}$, was to reduce as much as possible the verbosity and provide rapid prototypes to understand issues about interaction styles and users experience. As a consequence, we have also provided better maintenance, usability and understanding of the method to draw curves with a face tracking mouse. One of the best results of this research was to find that if equal conditions are provided for people with or without physical disabilities, their performances are equivalent. There are also essential advantages in using interaction methods, such as prevention from repetitive strain injuries and progressive degenerative diseases (*e.g.* CMT). It is better to create long-term skills, as seen in the first session, since a new method of interaction can be stressful and cause the participant to the drop out from the trial. Further studies are necessary to study the possibility of enlarging the target point and creating a virtual keyboard to access the coordinates in the grid. We have also intended to create an indicator to show where the curve begins. By applying these concepts, we aim to generalize the idea to surfaces in the space. Also, we can implement the game as cited above. Another possible work is to obtain access via an eye tracker where the user can make less effort to perform actions more quickly, since the eye is the organ moving faster. Therefore, we could associate it with the face tracker for a finer adjustment. Developing these technologies is not just a matter of wanting to help others, but also a question of giving tools to people with reduced mobility so that they can fulfill their potential. And for people without physical problems, these technologies can provide alternative methods of interest.

References

1. Maheshwari, A., Sack, J.R., Shahbaz, K., Zarrabi-Zadeh, H.: Staying close to a curve. In: CCCG (2011)
2. Krantz, S.G., Parks, H.R.: The plateau problem. In: Maurin, K. (ed.) A Mathematical Odyssey, pp. 111–135. Springer, Heidelberg (2014)

3. Zhang, X., Zhang, H.: Experimental and numerical investigation on crush resistance of polygonal columns and angle elements. Thin-Walled Struct. **57**, 25–36 (2012)
4. Pan, H., Choi, Y.K., Liu, Y., Hu, W., Du, Q., Polthier, K., Wang, W.: Robust modeling of constant mean curvature surfaces. ACM Trans. Graphics (TOG) **31**(4), 85 (2012)
5. Majaranta, P., Rih, K.-J.: Twenty years of eye typing: systems and design issue. In: Proceedings of the Symposium on Eye Tracking Research and Applications: ETRA 2002, pp. 15–22. ACM Press, New York (2002)
6. Studios, T.: Art of Francis Tsai. http://francis001.deviantart.com/
7. Palleja, T., et al.: Implementation of a robust absolute virtual head mouse combining face detection, template matching and optical flow algorithms. Telecommun. Syst. **52**(3), 1479–1489 (2013)
8. Hornof, A., Cavender, A., Hoselton, R.: Eyedraw: a system for drawing pictures with eye movements. In: ASSETS 2004 ACM SIGACCESS Conference on Computers and Accessibility, pp. 86–93, ACM Press (2004)
9. Perini, E., Soria, S., Prati, A., Cucchiara, R.: FaceMouse: a human-computer interface for tetraplegic people. In: Huang, T.S., Sebe, N., Lew, M., Pavlović, V., Kölsch, M., Galata, A., Kisačanin, B. (eds.) ECCV 2006 Workshop on HCI. LNCS, vol. 3979, pp. 99–108. Springer, Heidelberg (2006). doi:10.1007/11754336_10
10. Chau, T., Memarian, N., Leung, B., Treherne, D., Hobbs, D. Worthington-Eyre, B., Lamont, A., Pla-Mobarak, M.: Home-Based Computer Vision Access Technologies for Individuals with Severe Motor Impairments, Handbook of Ambient Assisted Living (2012)
11. Jian, Y., Jin, J.: An interactive interface between human and computer based on pattern and speech recognition. In: Proceedings of the 2012 International Conference on Systems and Informatics (ICSAI), pp. 505–509. IEEE, Yantai (2012). doi:10.1109/ICSAI.2012.6223047, 56978531

The Common Characteristics
of User-Defined and Mid-Air Gestures
for Rotating 3D Digital Contents

Li-Chieh Chen[1], Yun-Maw Cheng[2](✉), Po-Ying Chu[1],
and Frode Eika Sandnes[3]

[1] Department of Industrial Design, Tatung University, Taipei, Taiwan
{lcchen, juby}@ttu.edu.tw
[2] Graduate Institute of Design Science, Department of Computer Science
and Engineering, Tatung University, Taipei, Taiwan
kevin@ttu.edu.tw
[3] Oslo and Akershus University College of Applied Sciences, Oslo, Norway
Frode-Eika.Sandnes@hioa.no

Abstract. Recently, the technology of mid-air gestures for manipulating 3D digital contents has become an important research issue. In order to conform to the needs of users and contexts, eliciting user-defined gestures is inevitable. However, it was reported that user-defined hand gestures tended to vary significantly in posture, motion and speed, making it difficult to identify common characteristics. In this research, the authors conducted an experiment to study the intuitive hand gestures for controlling the rotation of 3D digital furniture. Twenty graduate students majored in Industrial Design were invited to participate in the task. Although there were great varieties among different participants, common characteristics were extracted through systematic behavior coding and analysis. The results indicated that open palm and D Handshape (American Sign Language) were the most intuitive hand poses. In addition, moving hands along the circumference of a horizontal circle was the most intuitive hand motion and trajectory.

Keywords: Mid-air gesture · User-defined gesture · 3D digital content rotation

1 Introduction

Manipulating 3D digital contents through mid-air gestures is a new experience for most people. In many applications, such as interactive product virtual exhibition in public and medical image display in a surgery room, the tasks may include translation, rotation, and scaling of 3D components. In order to facilitate the natural mapping between controls and displays, eliciting intuitive gestures from a group of user-defined gestures is necessary. However, due to individual differences in the experiences of using 3D applications and relative input devices, it is extremely difficult to develop consensus gestures. Given the potential difficulty, identifying the common characteristics of intuitive gestures is still important to inform the development process of

M. Antona and C. Stephanidis (Eds.): UAHCI 2016, Part II, LNCS 9738, pp. 15–22, 2016.
DOI: 10.1007/978-3-319-40244-4_2

gesture recognition algorithms. Therefore, the objective of this research is to study the common characteristics of intuitive gestures through a pilot experiment of 3D digital content manipulations.

2 Literature Review

Since 3D and mid-air hand gesture controls are natural, intuitive and sanitary [1–3], the number of applications have increased significantly. The contexts include interactive navigation systems in museum [4], surgical imaging systems [1, 2], interactive public displays [5], and 3D modelling [6]. Based on the number and trajectory of hands, mid-air gestures could be classified as one or two hands, linear or circular movements, and different degrees of freedom in path (1D, 2D, or 3D) [7]. If the context is not considered, mid-air gestures could be pointing, semaphoric, pantomimic, iconic, and manipulation [8]. The types of control tasks could be select, release, accept, refuse, remove, cancel, navigate, identify, translate, and rotate [8]. Since the characteristics of contexts could influence gesture vocabularies [9], the gestures for short-range human computer interaction [10] and TV controls [11, 12] were reported to be different. Even for the same task in the same context, users may prefer different gestures, which could be influenced by previous experiences in using different devices. While choosing an intuitive mid-air gesture for a specific task, it is necessary to consider and analyze the common characteristics of user-defined gestures.

3 Experiment

In order to explore the characteristics of hand gestures for manipulating 3D digital contents, a pilot experiment was carried out. The context of an interactive exhibition system for 3D product virtual models was considered. In a laboratory with illumination control, each participant stood on the spot in front of a 50-inch TV, with a distance of 200 cm. During the experiments, the images simulating the rotating products were displayed on the TV, which was controlled by a laptop computer with a computer mouse. In order to obtain gesture characteristics, the motions of the body and hand joints were recorded by one overhead camera and two 3D depth cameras. Each participant conducted two trials of experiments to offer self-defined gestures for rotating product models with respect to the vertical axis (Fig. 1). The participants were encouraged to provide with separate gestures for start or stop rotations, respectively. In the first trial, a Microsoft Kinect for Windows (v2) sensor was mounted on the top of the TV. The sensor could extract 25 joints per person. The motion of the arms and hands was recorded by the Kinect Studio program running on a desktop computer. The images of body tracking were displayed on a 23-inch monitor, which was placed on the right hand side of the TV. In the second trial, an Intel RealSense 3D Camera (F200) was used to extract the position and orientation of 22 joints on a hand. It was placed between the participant and the TV. The distance to the participant was adjusted with respect to the arm length. The height was adjusted to the shoulder height of each participant. The motion of each hand gesture was recorded by the Hands Viewer program. The program was running on a laptop computer with a 15-inch display, which was placed on the lower right hand side of the TV. Therefore, each participant performed the tasks of user-defined gestures by facing two 3D depth cameras with different distances. In addition, offering different gestures between two trials was encouraged.

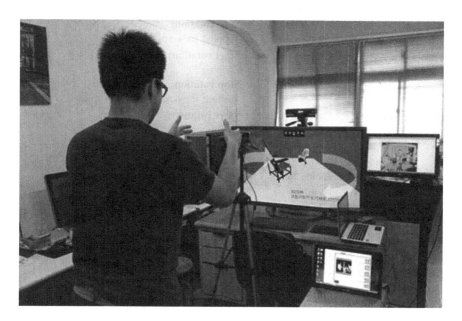

Fig. 1. Experiment setup

4 Results and Discussions

Twenty students, majored in the Master Program of Industrial Design, were invited to participate in the experiment. From two trials of user-defined gestures, forty gestures were recorded. In the first trial, the numbers of one-hand and two-hand gestures were 8 and 12, respectively. In the second trial, the numbers of one-hand and two-hand gestures were 11 and 9, respectively. There were no significant differences in the numbers of one-hand and two-hand gestures. For systematic behavior coding and analysis, the gestures were categorized based on hand poses, orientations, motions and trajectories. Fourteen types of one-hand gestures were identified (Table 1). Fifteen types of two-hand gestures were identified (Table 2). Although many types of gestures were identified, common characteristics could be extracted. Open palm and D Handshape (American Sign Language) were the most intuitive hand poses. For one-hand gestures, moving along the circumference of a horizontal circle was the most intuitive hand

Table 1. User-defined gestures with one hand

Type	Hand pose	Hand orientation	Hand motion and trajectory	Count
1-1	Open palm	Facing up	Rotating with respect to the vertical axis at the center of the palm	2
1-2	Open palm	Facing forward	Moving in a 3D smiling curve from left to right (or right to left)	2 (SP)
1-3	D Handshape	Index finger pointing forward	**Start rotation:** Moving along the circumference of a horizontal circle **Stop rotation:** Tapping forward	2
1-4	Open palm	Changing	**Start rotation:** Swiping **Stop rotation:** Pushing forward	2 (SP)
1-5	Open palm	Facing forward	**Start rotation:** Swiping (from left to right; or from right to left), **Stop rotation:** Grabbing	2 (SP)
1-6	Pinch	Facing forward	Moving in a 3D smiling curve from left to right (or right to left)	1
1-7	D Handshape	Pointing forward		1
1-8	D Handshape	Pointing up	Moving along the circumference of a horizontal circle	1
1-9	Open palm	Facing down		1
1-10	Open palm	Facing down	**Start rotation:** Moving along the circumference of a horizontal circle; **Stop rotation:** Fist	1
1-11	Grab	Facing forward		1
1-12	D Handshape	Index finger pointing forward		1
1-13	Open palm	Fingers pointing forward	**Start rotation:** Rotating with respect to the vertical axis at the center of the palm **Stop rotation:** Pushing forward	1
1-14	Open palm	Facing down	**Start rotation:** Moving along the circumference of a horizontal circle; **Stop rotation:** Palm facing down and moving downward	1

Note: SP (Same Participant)

Table 2. User-defined gestures with two hands

Type	Hand pose	Hand orientation	Hand motion and trajectory	Count
2-1	Open palm	Facing to each other; Fingers pointing up	Moving relatively with a constant distance along the circumference of a horizontal circle	3
2-2	Open palm	Facing down		3
2-3	Open palm	Facing to each other; Fingers pointing forward		2
2-4	Open palm	Facing to each other; Fingers pointing down		2
2-5	D Handshape	Facing down; Index finger pointing forward		1
2-6	D Handshape	Facing to each other; Index finger pointing up		1
2-7	Open palm	Raising arms to around 45 degrees, with fingers pointing down naturally,		1
2-8	L Handshape	Facing down; Index finger pointing forward		1
2-9	Open palm	Facing up	Rotating with respect to the vertical axis at the center of the palm	1
2-10	First hand – open palm; Second hand – free pose	First hand - facing forward; Second hand – changing	Raising one hand with the palm facing forward, Moving the second hand circularly with respect to the raising hand	1
2-11	Holding a virtual steering wheel,	Facing to each other	**Start rotation:** Moving relatively with a constant distance along the circumference of a horizontal circle; **Stop rotation:** Moving two hands downward similar to holding a disc and then putting it down	1

(Continued)

Table 2. (*Continued*)

Type	Hand pose	Hand orientation	Hand motion and trajectory	Count
2-12	Open palm	Facing to each other; Fingers pointing forward	**Start rotation:** Moving relatively with a constant distance along the circumference of a horizontal circle **Stop rotation:** Moving downward quickly	1
2-13	Left hand open palm; Right hand changing	Left hand facing down and stay still,	Left hand stays still. **Start rotation:** Right hand moving circularly under left hand **Stop rotation:** Right hand fist	1
2-14	Changing	Changing	**Start rotation:** Moving single hand circularly along the circumference of a horizontal circle; **Stop rotation:** Two Hands, Palm pushing forward	1
2-15	Changing	Changing	**Start rotation:** Two Hands, Fist, moving circularly with respect to the vertical axis **Stop rotation:** Single Hand, Palm pushing forward	1

motion and trajectory. For two-hand gestures, moving two hands relatively with a constant distance along the circumference of a horizontal circle was the most intuitive hand motion and trajectory. Sample gestures recorded by the Hands Viewer program were displayed in Fig. 2.

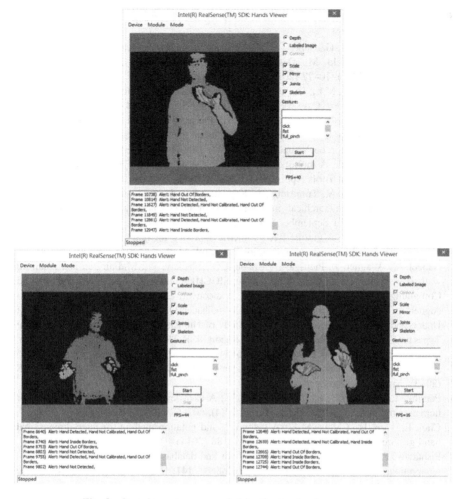

Fig. 2. Sample gestures recorded by the hands viewer program

5 Conclusion

In this research, a systematic behavior coding scheme was developed to analyze and decompose user-defined gestures. In addition, the most intuitive hand pose and trajectory of gestures for rotating 3D virtual models with respect to the vertical axis were identified. These results could be used to inform the development team of mid-air gestures and serve as the references for 3D digital content manipulations.

Acknowledgement. The authors would like to express our gratitude to the Ministry of Science and Technology of the Republic of China for financially supporting this research under Grant No. MOST 104-2221-E-036-020.

References

1. O'Hara, K., Gonzalez, G., Sellen, A., Penney, G., Varnavas, A., Mentis, H., Criminisi, A., Corish, R., Rouncefield, M., Dastur, N., Carrell, T.: Touchless interaction in surgery. Commun. ACM **57**(1), 70–77 (2014)
2. Rosa, G.M., Elizondo, M.L.: Use of a gesture user interface as a touchless image navigation system in dental surgery: Case series report. Imaging Sci. Dent. **44**, 155–160 (2014)
3. Hettig, J., Mewes, A., Riabikin, O., Skalej, M., Preim, B., Hansen, C.: Exploration of 3D medical image data for interventional radiology using myoelectric gesture control. In: 2015 Eurographics Workshop on Visual Computing for Biology and Medicine (2015)
4. Hsu, F.-S., Lin, W.-Y.: A multimedia presentation system using a 3D gesture interface in museums. Multimedia Tools Appl. **69**(1), 53–77 (2014)
5. Ackad, C., Clayphan, A., Tomitsch, M., Kay, J.: An in-the-wild study of learning mid-air gestures to browse hierarchical information at a large interactive public display. In: UBICOMP 2015, 7–11 September 2015, Osaka, Japan (2015)
6. Vinayak, Ramani, K.: A gesture-free geometric approach for mid-air expression of design intent in 3D virtual pottery. Comput. Aided Des. **69**, 11–24 (2015)
7. Nancel, M., Wagner, J., Pietriga, E., Chapuis, O., Mackay, W.: Mid-air pan-and-zoom on wall-sized displays. In: Proceedings of the SIGCHI Conference on Human Factors and Computing Systems, CHI 2011, May 2011, Vancouver, Canada, pp. 177–186 (2011)
8. Aigner, R., Wigdor, D., Benko, H., Haller, M., Lindlbauer, D., Ion, A., Zhao, S., Koh, J.T.K.V.: Understanding Mid-Air Hand Gestures: A Study of Human Preferences in Usage of Gesture Types for HCI, Microsoft Research Technical Report MSR-TR-2012-111 (2012). http://research.microsoft.com/apps/pubs/default.aspx?id=175454
9. LaViola Jr., J.J.: 3D gestural interaction: the state of the field. ISRN Artif. Intell. **2013**, 1–18 (2013). Article ID 514641
10. Pereira, A., Wachs, J.P., Park, K., Rempel, D.: A user-developed 3-D hand gesture set for human-computer interaction. Hum. Factors **57**(4), 607–621 (2015)
11. Choi, E., Kim, H., Chung, M.K.: A taxonomy and notation method for three-dimensional hand gestures. Int. J. Ind. Ergon. **44**(1), 171–188 (2014)
12. Pisharady, P.K., Saerbeck, M.: Recent methods and databases in vision-based hand gesture recognition: A review. Comput. Vis. Image Underst. **141**, 152–165 (2015). Pose & Gesture

Evaluating Somatosensory Interactions: Designing a Handheld Tactile Acoustic Device for Mobile Phones

Maria Karam[1(✉)] and Patrick M. Langdon[2]

[1] Kings College London, London, UK
maria.karam@kcl.ac.uk
[2] Department of Engineering, University of Cambridge, Cambridge, UK
pml24@cam.ac.uk

Abstract. We present the details of preliminary development efforts to create a tactile acoustic device (TAD) for the hands. The Model Human Cochlea (MHC) is a method for conveying sound to the body in a chair form factor, and originally developed as a sensory substitution system to provide some access to sounds from movies or music to deaf and hard of hearing people. We present initial design research on modifying the MHC system from a chair to a mobile handheld tactile device, towards improving mobile-phone speech comprehension in noisy environments. Scaling the MHC from the back, which has the least sensitive skin on the body, to the highly sensitive skin on the hands, requires an understanding of the physiology, psychology, electronics, and software applicable to this kind of sensation. This research addresses factors critical to expanding the design of tactile acoustic devices for somatosensory system interactions to different areas of the body.

Keywords: Interactive displays · Somatosensory systems · Crossmodal systems · Mobile phone interaction · Multimodal HCI systems · Sensory substitution · Tactile acoustic devices

1 Introduction and Background

The system described in this paper is a sensory augmentation approach to displaying sound on the body, modeled on the workings of the human cochlea and the sense of hearing. The Model Human Cochlea (MHC) (Karam et al., 2009) is applied to the body using the back of the torso and thighs as contact points for an array of transducers that register sound on the body. This work focuses on extending the MHC to other areas of the body, specifically the hands, where speech sounds may be experienced as tactile signals that could enhance mobile phone communications.

1.1 The MHC

The MHC is a chair-based system that provides an alternative means of experiencing entertainment-related sound vibrations, focusing on the enigmatic characteristics such as emotion, prosody, and even timbre, through the back (Russo et al., 2012). The MHC

© Springer International Publishing Switzerland 2016
M. Antona and C. Stephanidis (Eds.): UAHCI 2016, Part II, LNCS 9738, pp. 23–31, 2016.
DOI: 10.1007/978-3-319-40244-4_3

emulates certain functions of the human cochlea on the body by using sounds as the vibrations mapped onto a tactile display, rather than using representations of sounds based on haptic stimulation (Gemperle et al., 2001, Wall and Brewster, 2006). The MHC was developed for use on a chair as an effective form factor and delivery system for watching movies or entertainment forms requiring seats. Because the back is one of the least sensitive areas of the body (non-glabrous or hairy skin), we hypothesize that applying a TAD on more sensitive area of the body can potentially improve tactile acoustic perception towards the identification of speech sounds. Mobile phones represent an obvious application for delivering sound to the body, where tactile acoustics can improve speech access for deaf and hard of hearing people, or even hearing people in noisy environments. To begin modifying the tactile sound system for use as a handheld device, we explored some of the critical factors identified in previous work on human somatosensory interactions (HSI) to help inform and extend the design of the existing entertainment seating MHC device for the hands (Karam and Langdon, 2015).

2　Human Somatosensory System Interactions (HSI)

The skin is an organ that can detect many types of sensations, including but not limited to heat, pressure, stretch, pain, and vibrations from sound. Research on the substitution and augmentation of sounds as vibrations dates back to the 1920s (Gault, 1927) towards developing a new way for deaf people to access and comprehend speech. There are two main types of layouts used in these kind of systems based on the literature: grid formation, or linear (spectral) array. The grid approach is very effective at communicating spatial information, while the spectral approach separates sound frequencies into bands, expressed on the body in a linear arrangement as vibrations. Different tactile devices can also lead to different effects to create the the desired sensations. Such approaches have been slow in uptake as everyday devices, as they often require extensive training and large, expensive equipment to process and power the signals. Further considerations that influence the design of HSI systems include the sensitivity of different parts of the skin to vibration, and the need to explore more than just haptic vibrations when designing tactile displays for the body.

Mechanical haptic vibrations stimulate more than just the cutaneous receptors, and are commonly used as notifications, semaphoric messages, spatial vibrational patterns (Gemperle et al., 2001, Back-y-Rita et al., 1969, Bach Y Rita et al., 1987, Wall and Brewster, 2006), and tactile speech communications (Brooks and Frost, 1983). This type of discrete haptic signal may not however be sufficiently complex to exploit the full potential of the somatosensory system in speech comprehension. While there has been some success in mapping word elements to vibrations (Brooks and Frost, 1983, Gault, 1927), sound vibrations may potentially be more effective at stimulating cutaneous sensors with more complex yet subtle vibrations (Russo et al., 2012).

2.1 HSI Framework

The somatosensory system is a complex network of neural mechanisms, cognitive processes, and responses that are connected to all human physical perceptions (Gault 1927; Gallace and Spence 2014) and represent an abundance of potential sensations to explore for HSI. The HSI framework is next applied to help expand the design of the MHC for mobile phone interactions on the hands (Karam and Langdon 2015).

Interaction Scenario. The HSI framework led us to initially consider a mobile phone case as the housing for the new design. While headphones and hands free interactions are commonly used for phone communications, this work considers a mobile phone interface as a practical approach to initial investigations of the MHC for the hands. Size and power constraints influenced the design of this project, which influenced our use of the existing processing system designed for the theatre to drive this research, which will primarily explore different transducer array layout, sizes, and positioning.

Physiology. The front part of the hand is one of the most sensitive areas of the body, (glabrous or non-hairy skin) capable of detecting fine details of texture and Vibratory discrimination thresholds for touch sensors are dependent on both frequency and amplitude of stimulation. Sensations are dependent on rapidly adapting and slow adapting mechanoreceptors (RA I, SA I, RA II, SA II), embedded in skin sensitive to frequencies between 0.50 and 1000 Hz and with receptive field sizes varying from 1–1000mm2. Touch sense has been identified with Pacinian Corpuscles, the RAII receptors, but in fact is known to be associated with all the glabrous skin afferents including Meissner corpuscles, Ruffini corpuscles and the Merkel complex cells. Amplitude in such studies is measured in mm of displacement rather than work done (power), and thresholds vary from 0,01 to 40 mm. The contact discrimination threshold (receptive field size) on the body varies from 0.7 to 100 mm, but this is undoubtedly modified by amplitude or vibratory power in psychophysical functions, as has been described (Gallace and Spence 2014; Karam and Langdon 2015).

Cognition. Using sound as vibrations may improve comprehension and detection of speech on the hands using the multimodal integration of speech and vibration, which may be easier to identify than haptic signals that represent sounds. Based on the familiarity of sound vibrations, we hypothesize that speech comprehension on the MHC will improve tactile sound detection and identification when it supports an audio signal that is distorted or masked. The higher levels of tactile sensitivity of the glabrous skin on the hand may also reveal additional signals that could not be detected on the non-glabrous parts of the body, potentially increasing comprehension of tactile sound.

Technology. Characteristics of the transducer size, number, arrangement, power requirements, form factors, materials, drivers, and processing characteristics pose technological challenges when scaling the MHC. Several prototypes were developed during this design process to help us explore the different transducer sizes and layout options, however, we did not develop new processing hardware for this work, but use the existing processing drivers and algorithms to evaluate the mobile devices.

3 Design Considerations

The smaller area of skin on the hands represents a challenge to designing multi-user form factors that support multi-channel transducer arrays, which must not disrupt the hand. Additionally, the variation in size and shape of different hand size limits the layout of spectral array, as does the number of channels we explore in this work. The original TAD system uses 16 voice coils, aligned along 2 rows on either side of the spine. Placement of the transducers aims to maximize the contact points to increase tactile acoustic resolution, while avoiding bone conduction or deep tissue vibrations used in haptic displays.

3.1 Interaction Design

The initial 8-transducer design was first considered using 1 cm diameter contact point transducers to fit into the phone case (Fig. 1a). A breakdown of the MHC chair suggests that the 8 × 2 spectral layout represents left and right sides of the spine, with upper and lower segments. This suggested 4 discrete segment mappings to consider when translating the system from the back to the hand, where the segments are closer together, (fingers, palm, wrist palm…), limiting the linear placement of the array of transducers. Additional layouts considered are shown below (Fig. 1b, c).

Fig. 1. a: 8-channel layout; b: 4-channel case; c: Right hand edge design

3.2 Physiology: Sizing the Transducers

Transducers that support multi channel arrays for the hand were optimal at 1 cm to 2 cm in contactor diameter, leveraging the higher sensitivity of the hand, but using less power, but posing interesting questions in determining an optimal layout.

Body Segments. Early studies on the MHC suggested that sound 'chunks' or perceptual units of sounds, like a musical composition, had to be located on the same linear segment of the body for users to easily map sounds to the vibrations, for example, arms, legs, torso (Karam et al., 2009). The current work further identifies segments based on skin type: glabrous or non-glabrous skin, and joint separations. The segments - left/right, skin type, and position - are critical factors in determining optimal configurations of transducers to body segment. Further breakdown of the body can reveal additional design challenges, as with the fingers, where the segments are small, and required freedom of movement, unlike the larger, less functional arms and torso.

3.3   Form Factor

The mobile phone was chosen to support real time mobile phone interactions with the transducers. However, while we aimed to provide both sounds and vibrations to a user, this was not easily accomplished in a working mobile phone, where the headphone jack does not permit the sound to be split to another channel within the phone. A workaround was to use headphones and a signal splitter to allow us to use the sound for both audio and tactile displays.

3.4   Technology: Signal Processing and Power Requirements

Our unique design opportunities lie in understanding and leveraging the different sensitivities of the skin, enabling us to explore new designs of transducers that could be very low profile. However, for this work, we are focusing on supporting form factor, layout, and comprehension testing rather than designing new hardware. With the glabrous skin's higher sensitivity to vibrations, we can leverage the hands to support decreasing the power levels for the transducers, while maintaining enough vibration to effectively stimulate the skin. This will be explored next.

3.5   Cognition: Evaluating User Perceptions

While strong vibrations may be easily detected on the body, the finer vibrational information that relate to speech sounds are not detectable to all parts of the skin. Perceptual effects that are also found in audio perception appear to be present in the tactile acoustic domain: masking, individual tastes, and amplitude preferences still occur in the perception of tactile sound. Different frequencies may also have to be placed on the body in an optimal location to achieve maximum detection and perception.

To conduct a first set of tests, we selected a 4-channel setup, allowing us to use the minimal configuration of transducers, while still delivering the multi-channel MHC signal to the hand. We tested this initial prototypes for signals strength, layout, and resolution, to determine if there any feature of speech could be perceived on the hand. 14 volunteers were asked to try the system, and to provide initial user feedback using a mobile phone in a TAD case (Fig. 1b). Participants were asked to place one hand on the mobile TAD, which was initially set up on a table. An audio signal from the phone was redirected to the tactile transducers, which was not audible.

A radio talk show segment was used as the sound sample, with the vibrations divided up along the four-transducer array along the side of the phone case. The show featured a calm male host, speaking with an excited female caller. Each participant re-ported that they could feel voices, with most indicating that they could detect the sex of the voice, and many indicating that they could the emotion of argument or persuasion. Some observed behavior we observed during the sessions included moving the phone around their hands to feel all the transducers, and placing the device by the ears to try and hear the vibrations. All participants also identified that the signal was speech.

4   Design Challenges

Participants tended to hold the phone prototype along the edges, possibly a reflection of the poorly designed form factor that requires the fingers to ensure the device doesn't slip out of the hands: this suggested that moving the transducers to the edges of the case would be more in consonance with the natural way that people hold their phones. Three transducers were moved to the one side, with a fourth set on the opposite side to improve contact with the fingers in a new prototype design (see Fig. 1c).

We had to consider handedness in this case, resulting in versions of the new device. This was deemed impractical, and the prototype was abandoned for the remainder of this study. The next prototype was a block of wood, which was modeled as a phone with both audio and tactile signal outputs (Fig. 2).

Fig. 2. Early prototyping showing non-finger handed design

For this version, we used a stereo signal to drive the transducers, which was somewhat limited in its use, but it did reveal that two channels alone have some effect, but constraining the transducers to different form factors did not allow us to properly gauge tactile perception of speech, nor to evaluate individual transducers and their effects on different areas of the hand.

Several other two-transducer versions were developed to support left-right hand interactions, and to isolate transducer size, number, and placement on the body without the physical constraints of a mobile phone form factor. These prototypes were secured in putty or silicone to protect the connections from the stress that mobile interactions placed on the transducers (Fig. 3a, b). Further studies can be run, but the system requires a more effective design to support a more functional form factor that won't constrain the hand movements or functionality.

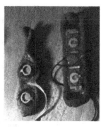

Fig. 3 a and b. Early prototyping showing transducer pair in silicone

5   Discussion

After considering the current form factors and transducer sizes, the mobile phone form factor was abandoned for several reasons: First, people increasingly use headsets with Bluetooth connections to interact with their phones, reducing the amount of time holding the phone while in use. Second, it is impractical, from an engineering perspective, to embed transducers into phones as they already struggle with power consumption and additional hardware would further reduce battery life. Third, although the smaller sized transducers were somewhat effective at communicating some speech information to the hands, individual differences in behavior and approaches to mobile phone interactions suggested that a more universally accessible form factor would need to be developed to support multi-channel vibrations for the hand while on the move. Fourth, the shapes and sizes of mobile phones are not designed to ergonomically fit in the hand, and it became apparent that we would have to find an alternative form factor to better support tactile perception. Fifth, implementing a commercial TAD into a mobile phone would require a drastic modification in the hardware, and sound sources to be distributed to multiple channels to support the multi-modal interactions required by the TAD.

The current tests suggested that the vibrations provide some level of recognizable speech information to the hands, but did not work out as an effective form factor to support and effectively test the multichannel TAD for mobile phone interactions.

Shifts in the zeitgeist of end-user devices are suggesting that mobile phones may soon be replaced by more practical devices, in support of wireless, wearable devices that provide better ergonomics and usability for interactions with the somatosensory system. Further electronic processors and drivers will also be developed and designed into the system to improve HSI, and the design of these devices must be reimagined to enable them to utilize skin contact as a way to help offload some of the attention demands placed on the ears and eyes to the body without interfering with primary tasks. Some new models we are developing are shown in Fig. 4.

Fig. 4. 1 New form factors that are being developed to support future experiments

6   Conclusions and Future Work

We have begun to explore the extension of the MHC to include the hands, and other areas on the body, where the higher sensitivity of cutaneous receptors could increase tactile acoustic perception and offer more of the body's surface as locations for tactile information displays. The design exercise presented in this paper suggests that the MHC has the potential to communicate similar information to the hands, using smaller and fewer transducers than is required for the back. Adding more channels can also potentially lead to an increase in tactile acoustic resolution, further expanding on the principles behind the MHC. New prototypes will be developed to help explore different interaction paradigms and devices that are now being designed into fashion, jewelry, and other accessories, towards increasing access to and availability of the somatosensory system and the continued development of the study of HSI in new applications including wayfinding, navigation, communication, and intimacy.

References

Bach-y-Rita, P., Webster, J.G., Tompkins, W.J., Crabb, T.: Sensory substitution for space gloves and space robots. In: Space Telerobotics Workshop, Jet Propulsion Laboratory, Pasadena, CA, 20–22 1987, pp. 51–57 (1987)

Bach-Y-Rita, P., Collins, C.C., Saunders, F.A., White, B., Scadden, L.: Vision substitution by tactile image projection. Nature **221**(5184), 963–964 (1969)

Brooks, P.L., Frost, B.J.: Evaluation of a tactile Vocoder for word recognition. J. Acoust. Soc. Am. **74**(1), 34–39 (1983)

Gallace, A., Spence, C.: In touch with the future: The sense of touch from cognitive neuroscience to virtual reality. OUP, Oxford (2014)

Gault, R.H.: Hearing through the sense organs of touch and vibration. J. Franklin Inst. **204**(3), 329–358 (1927)

Gemperle, F., Nathan O., Siewiorek, D.: Design of a wearable tactile display. In: Proceedings of the 5th IEEE International Symposium on Wearable Computers ISWC 2001. IEEE Computer Society, Washington (2001)

Karam, M., Langdon, P.: Seeing, hearing and feeling through the body: the emerging science of human-somatosensory interactions. In: Antona, M., Stephanidis, C. (eds.) UAHCI 2015. LNCS, vol. 9176, pp. 205–216. Springer, Heidelberg (2015)

Karam, M., Russo, F.A., Fels, D.I.: Designing the model human cochlea: an ambient crossmodal audio-tactile display. IEEE Trans. Haptics **2**(3), 160–169 (2009)

Meenowa, J., Hameed, M., Furner, S., Langdon, P.M.: Using haptic displays for workload reduction and inclusive control. In: 11th International Conference on Human Computer Interaction (HCII 2005), 2005-7-22 to 2005-7-27, Las Vegas, Nevada, USA (2005)

Russo, F.A., Ammirante, P., Fels, D.I.: Vibrotactile discrimination of musical timbre. J. Exp. Psychol. Hum. Percept. Perform. **38**, 822–826 (2012)

Wall, B., Brewster, S.: Feeling what you hear: tactile feedback for navigation of audio graphs. In: Proceedings of the SIGCHI Conference on Human Factors in Computing Systems (CHI 2006), pp. 1123–1132. ACM, New York (2006)

Withana, A., Koyama, S., Saakes, D., Minamizawa, K., Inami, M., Nanayakkara, S.: RippleTouch: initial exploration of a wave resonant based full body haptic interface. In: Proceedings of the 6th Augmented Human International Conference (AH 2015), pp. 61–68. ACM, New York (2015)

Body Motion Analysis for Emotion Recognition in Serious Games

Kyriaki Kaza, Athanasios Psaltis, Kiriakos Stefanidis, Konstantinos C. Apostolakis,
Spyridon Thermos, Kosmas Dimitropoulos[✉], and Petros Daras

Information Technologies Institute,
Centre for Research and Technology Hellas, Thessaloniki, Greece
{kikikaza,at.psaltis,kystefan,kapostol,
spthermo,dimitrop,daras}@iti.gr
http://www.iti.gr

Abstract. In this paper, we present an emotion recognition methodology that utilizes information extracted from body motion analysis to assess affective state during gameplay scenarios. A set of kinematic and geometrical features are extracted from joint-oriented skeleton tracking and are fed to a deep learning network classifier. In order to evaluate the performance of our methodology, we created a dataset with Microsoft Kinect recordings of body motions expressing the five basic emotions (anger, happiness, fear, sadness and surprise) which are likely to appear in a gameplay scenario. In this five emotions recognition problem, our methodology outperformed all other classifiers, achieving an overall recognition rate of 93 %. Furthermore, we conducted a second series of experiments to perform a qualitative analysis of the features and assess the descriptive power of different groups of features.

Keywords: Body motion analysis · 3D body movement features · Emotion recognition · RBM · Serious games

1 Introduction

One crucial component of games design and development is the accurate measurement of user's experience and undoubtedly, the most important aspect of user's experience is their affective state. Particularly in serious games, the inference of player's affective state could provide not only valuable information for player's engagement and entertainment level, but also indications of whether or not the desirable educational objectives are reached. The majority of state of the art emotion recognition frameworks capitalize mainly on facial expression or voice analysis; however, research in the field of experimental and developmental psychology has shown that body movements, body postures, or the quantity or quality of movement behavior in general, can also help us differentiate between emotions [1, 2].

In particular, specific qualities and characteristics of body movements, such as velocity, direction, turning away/forwards, body expansion/contraction has been examined in the inference of different emotions and combinations of these qualities are

© Springer International Publishing Switzerland 2016
M. Antona and C. Stephanidis (Eds.): UAHCI 2016, Part II, LNCS 9738, pp. 33–42, 2016.
DOI: 10.1007/978-3-319-40244-4_4

suggestive of specific emotions [3, 4]. For example, expressions of joy are characterized by fast, upward directed movements with the arms raised. Similarly, movements indicative of grief tend to be slow, light, downward directed, with the arms closed around the body. Body turning away and body contraction, as an attempt to appear as small as possible is shown to be a strong indicator of fear, while body turning towards is typical of happiness and anger.

As more and more game companies and research centers move towards low cost RGB-depth sensors, a growing interest emerges considering the role of body movement in games, not only in terms of natural user interaction, but of emotion recognition during gameplay as well. Bodily expression provides a means for emotion recognition from a distance [5], and therefore motion analysis is crucial in generating multi-modal data in gameplay environments where players' facial analysis data are either too remote or partially obstructed (e.g. children wearing glasses, hats or other headwear). Additionally, the inclusion of bodily expression as an additional channel for affect communication can help resolve ambiguity observed in the identification of certain basic mental states, such as anger and fear [6].

Over the last years, different approaches have been proposed for emotion recognition based on body movements, gestures and postures [7–11]. These studies obtained quite interesting results, highlighting the importance and feasibility of using body expressions for affect recognition. Specifically regarding affect recognition in games, Piana et al. [12] presented a method that uses features derived from 3D skeleton data and a multi-class SVM classifier for the recognition of six emotions, which was integrated in a platform of serious games for children with Autism Spectrum Condition. This method achieved a 61.3 % recognition rate when evaluated at a dataset of recorded body movements of actors who were asked to express freely the six basic emotions. Savva et al. [13] proposed an automatic recognition method of affective body movement in the context of a Nintendo Wii tennis game which feeds dynamic movement features to a Recurrent Neural Network (RNN) algorithm. This method was tested at a dataset of non-acted movements captured with Animazoo IGS-190 during gameplay and reached a recognition rate of 57.46 %, comparable with the 61.49 % accuracy of human observers' recognition.

Our focus at this paper is to present a method for emotion recognition based on body motion analysis that will be incorporated in serious games that aim at helping children aged 7–10 acquire prosocial skills. Using a set of 3D features, we decided to test the recognition performance of deep learning architectures, such as neural networks (NNs) and Restricted Boltzmann Machines (RBMs), in an emotion recognition task, as well as the descriptive power of different groups of features. This study led to the design of a deep learning network classifier with stacked RBMs. In the following sections, we will briefly analyze the groups of features used (Sect. 2); then, we will present the proposed classifier (Sect. 3); finally, we will evaluate and compare the recognition accuracy of different classifiers and different groups of features, using a dataset of acted movements associated with five emotions (Sect. 4) and will conclude with a discussion about results and future work (Sect. 5).

2 Body Motion Analysis

In this section, we will present a set of movement features which we utilize in our method and which are proven crucial in the process of emotion recognition [14]. The 3D body movement features are extracted from joint-oriented skeleton tracking using the depth information provided by Kinect sensor [15]. We divide the set of features into the following groups: kinematic related, spatial extent related, smoothness related, symmetry related, leaning related and distances related.

2.1 Kinematic Related Features (G1)

Velocity and Acceleration. The velocity and acceleration features per frame are calculated as the mean velocity and acceleration of all frame joints. The velocity and acceleration can be approximated in our case by considering finite differences of position divided by the sampling time interval ΔT [16].

Kinetic Energy. Kinetic energy provides an estimate of the overall energy spent by the user during movement. The amount of movement activity has been shown to be relevantly important for differentiating emotions [17]. The kinetic energy is proportional to the square of velocity. We ignore the mass term in kinetic energy as it is not relevant [16]. So the proportional amount of the kinetic energy of each joint K_i is calculated as:

$$K_i = \frac{1}{2}v_i^2 \tag{1}$$

Then, the kinetic energy of the entire body is calculated as the sum of all joints' kinetic energies.

2.2 Spatial Extent Related Features (G2)

The following features provide an estimate of how the body occupies the 3D space surrounding it. According to research in experimental psychology, the contraction index can be used to infer specific emotional states; people are considered to usually spread out when they are happy, angry or surprised, and similarly reduce their size when in fear [3].

Bounding Box Volume. A bounding box is the minimum cuboid containing the body. Given the 3D positions of the user's limbs' end effectors, we can approximate this volume as the minimum parallelepiped surrounding the user's body.

Contraction Index. Contraction index in 3D is defined as the normalized bounding volume containing the user's body and is related to the definition of ones' "personal space" [14]. The 3D contraction index is then calculated by comparing this bounding volume and an approximation of the volume of the density (DI) of the 3D coordinates calculated as follows:

$$DI = \frac{3}{4}\pi \cdot DI_x \cdot DI_y \cdot DI_z \tag{2}$$

where DI_x, DI_y, DI_z are the approximated density indices calculated respectively on x, y and z axes as described in the following Equations:

$$DI_x = \frac{1}{n}\sum_{i=1}^{n} dx_i \tag{3}$$

$$DI_y = \frac{1}{n}\sum_{i=1}^{n} dy_i \tag{4}$$

$$DI_z = \frac{1}{n}\sum_{i=1}^{n} dz_i \tag{5}$$

in which dx_i, dy_i and dz_i are the distances between the center of mass and the ith joint. The 3D Contraction Index is then calculated as the normalized ratio between DI and the Bounding Volume.

Density. A different measurement of body spatial extent is represented by the density index. Given the center of mass of the user's tracked skeleton C, the density index is calculated as the average sum of Euclidean distances of all tracked joints from C:

$$DEI = \frac{1}{n}\sum_{i=1}^{n} d_{Ci} \tag{6}$$

2.3   Smoothness Related Features (G3)

Curvature (k) measures the rate at which a tangent vector turns as a trajectory bends and provides an indication of joints' trajectories' smoothness. According to Wallbott [2], "a smooth movement seems to be large in terms of space and exhibit a high but even velocity", so it will have low curvature value; by contrast, a sharp trajectory movement will have a high curvature.

The smoothness index for three dimensional curvatures is computed as follows:

$$k_i = \frac{\sqrt{(\dot{x}_i \cdot \ddot{y}_i - \dot{y}_i \cdot \ddot{x}_i)^2 + (\dot{z}_i \cdot \ddot{x}_i - \dot{x}_i \cdot \ddot{z}_i)^2 + (\dot{y}_i \cdot \ddot{z}_i - \dot{z}_i \cdot \ddot{y}_i)^2}}{(\dot{x}_i^2 + \dot{y}_i^2 + \dot{z}_i^2)^{\frac{3}{2}}} \tag{7}$$

In our features set, we include right and left wrist curvature, head curvature and torso curvature.

2.4 Symmetry Related Features (G4)

It has been shown that asymmetry of movements can be related to emotion expression [18]. Each symmetry (SI_x, SI_y, SI_z) is computed from the position of the barycenter and the left and right joints (e.g., wrists, shoulders, feet, knees) as described below:

$$SI_{Xi} = \frac{(x_B - x_{Li}) - (x_B - x_{Ri})}{x_{Ri} - x_{Li}} \qquad (8)$$

where x_B is the coordinate of the center of mass, x_{Li} is the coordinate of a left joint i (e.g., left hand, left shoulder, left foot, etc.) and, x_{Ri} is the coordinate of a right joint. In the same way, we compute SI_y, SI_z. The three partial indices are then combined in a normalized index that expresses the overall estimated symmetry:

$$SI = \frac{SI_{Xi} + SI_{Yi} + SI_{Zi}}{3} \qquad (9)$$

In our features set, we include wrists, elbows, knees and feet symmetry.

2.5 Leaning Related Features (G5)

Head and body movement and positions are relied on as an important feature for distinguishing between various emotional expressions [13]. The amount of forward and backward leaning of a torso and head joint is measured by the velocity of the joint's displacement along its z component (depth) respective to the body position and orientation, while the amount of right and left leaning is measured by the velocity of joint's displacement along its x component.

2.6 Distance Related Features (G6)

The distances between hands can be indicative of expansion or contraction of gestures, while the distance between hand and head as well as hand and torso could provide estimation for the existence of specific movements (e.g. touching head with one hand in case of grief).

The aforementioned features are extracted per frame and then, their mean value is calculated for the sequence of frames. The total of the mean values for all features constructs the feature vector used as a movement descriptor. Distances and coordinates used in calculations are normalized with respect to height.

3 Deep Learning Network Classifier

In this section, we propose a deep learning network classifier consisting of stacked RBMs, which proved to outperform other classic classifiers at the emotion recognition task, as we will see in Sect. 4.

A Restricted Boltzmann Machine [19] is a parameterized generative model representing a probability distribution. Given some observations, the training data, learning a Boltzmann Machine (BM) means adjusting the BM parameters such that the probability distribution represented by the BM fits the training data as well as possible. Boltzmann machines consist of two types of units, so called visible and hidden neurons, which can be thought of as being arranged in two layers. The visible units constitute the first layer and correspond to the components of an observation. The hidden units model dependencies between the components of observations (Fig. 1).

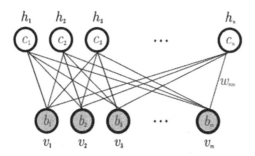

Fig. 1. The undirected graph of an RBM with n hidden and m visible variables

For our emotion recognition task, aiming at a network architecture that will handle independently each group of features, we designed the architecture depicted at Fig. 2.

At our two-layer network, we stacked seven RBMs, six at the first layer and one at the second layer, and train them layerwise, starting at the base layer and move up to the second, with no feedback from the higher layer to the lower layer. Each RBM of the

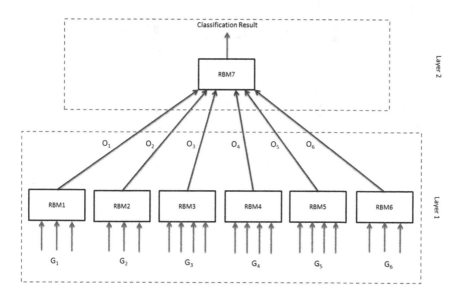

Fig. 2. Deep learning network classifier with 7 stacked RBMs

first layer receives as input the features of a different group of features and it is trained in an unsupervised (since unsupervised pre-training guides the learning towards basins of attraction of minima that support better generalization from the training data set [20]) and afterwards in a supervised way. Then, the output probabilities of the first layer are fed as input to the second layer and the seventh RBM is trained. The output probabilities of the second layer constitute the classification result.

4   Experimental Results

4.1   Dataset

In order to evaluate the performance of our methodology, we created a dataset with Kinect recordings of body movements expressing the 5 basic emotions (anger, happiness, fear, sadness and surprise) which are likely to appear in a gameplay scenario. The predefined set of movements (Fig. 3) associated with these emotions was selected based on social psychology research that identified body movements and postures which, to some degree, are specific for certain emotions [1, 2, 8]. Each emotion was represented with two different types of movements and each recording had duration of 4 s. 14 subjects (5 women and 9 men) participated in the recording session. They were shown a short video with the aforementioned movements and afterwards, they were asked to perform each movement, according to their personal style, 5 times, in front of a Kinect sensor.

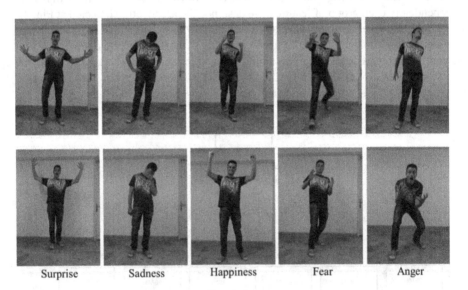

| Surprise | Sadness | Happiness | Fear | Anger |

Fig. 3. Dataset movements expressing five emotions

4.2 Classification Results

The purpose of the experiments conducted was to evaluate the recognition rate of deep learning network classifiers at the problem of emotion recognition from body motion analysis. For this purpose, we compared the recognition rates of classic classifiers (Naïve Bayes, Linear MultiClass SVM, Non Linear SVM) with the recognition rates of deep learning network classifiers (multilayer perceptron MLP, RBM, our proposed architecture with stacked classifiers) at a Leave-One-Subject-Out cross validation (LOSO cv) training the classifiers over 13 subjects and testing them with the data of the 14th left out subject. The results of these experiments are shown at Table 1. As we can see, the three DL network classifiers achieved higher classification accuracy than classic classifiers, with the proposed classifier outperforming all others with a recognition rate of 93 %.

Table 1. Classification results

Algorithm	Method	Recognition Rate
Naïve Bayes		77.21%
Linear MultiClass SVM	Crammer and Singer (CS)	77.78%
	Weston and Watkins (WW)	78.35%
	one-versus-all (OVA)	79.78%
Non Linear SVM	Crammer and Singer (CS)	84.5%
	Weston and Watkins (WW)	84.71%
	one-versus-all (OVA)	84.78%
MLP		85.53%
RBM		88.9%
Stacked RBMs Classifier		93%

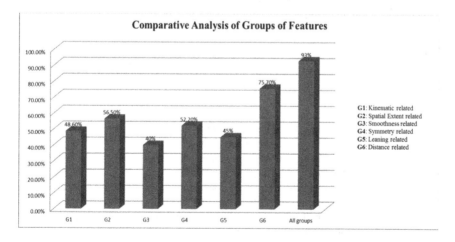

Fig. 4. Recognition rates with different groups of features

4.3 Comparative Analysis of Different Groups of Features

Furthermore, we conducted a second experiment to perform a qualitative analysis of the features and assess the descriptive power of the different groups of features. Our purpose was to examine the contribution of each group of features to the classification process. For the experiments, we trained six different RBMs, each with a different group of features. As it is shown at Fig. 4, only the distances related features, although being quite simplistic, can provide a decent recognition accuracy of 75.7 %, constituting the only group that could be practically used in a recognition task. This means that all groups of features have a significant contribution and are necessary in order to achieve high classification accuracy.

5   Conclusions and Future Work

In this work, we have presented a complete method for affect recognition from body movements that are likely to appear at a gameplay scenario. We have confirmed that a set of geometric and kinetic features can act as adequate descriptors for movements related to emotions and that deep learning classifiers can provide better recognition rates than classic classifiers at this recognition task. Additionally, we have proposed a classifier with stacked RBMs that outperformed all other classifiers in recognition accuracy. Our next goal is to test our method at non-acted emotion expressions recordings during gameplay of prosocial game Path of Trust [21] and as a following step; the affective information derived from body expression analysis will be fused with facial and audio analysis information, in order to further increase the robustness of the algorithm. The final recognition module will be incorporated in Path of Trust game and other serious games for children.

Acknowledgement. The research leading to this work has received funding from the EU Horizon 2020 Framework Programme under grant agreement no. 644204 (ProsocialLearn project).

References

1. Ekman, P.: Differential communication of affect by head and body cues. J. Pers. Soc. Psychol. **2**(5), 726 (1965)
2. Wallbott, H.G.: Bodily expression of emotion. Eur. J. Soc. Psychol. **28**, 879–896 (1998)
3. Boone, R.T., Cunningham, J.G.: Children's decoding of emotion in expressive body movement: The development of cue attunement. Dev. Psychol. **34**, 1007–1016 (1998)
4. de Meijer, M.: The contribution of general features of body movement to the attribution of emotions. J. Nonverbal Behav. **13**(4), 247–268 (1989)
5. de Gelder, B.: Why bodies? twelve reasons for including bodily expressions in affective neuroscience. Philos. Trans. R. Soc. B Biol. Sci. **364**(1535), 3475–3484 (2009)
6. Gunes, H., Shan, C., Chen, S., Tian, Y.: Bodily expression for automatic affect recognition. In: Emotion Recognition A Pattern Analysis Approach, pp. 343–377 (2015)

7. Castellano, G., Villalba, S.D., Camurri, A.: Recognising human emotions from body movement and gesture dynamics. In: Paiva, A.C., Prada, R., Picard, R.W. (eds.) ACII 2007. LNCS, vol. 4738, pp. 71–82. Springer, Heidelberg (2007)

8. Coulson, M.: Attributing emotion to static body postures: recognition accuracy, confusions, and viewpoint dependence. J. Nonverbal Behav. **28**, 117–139 (2004)

9. Kleinsmith, A., De Silva, R., Bianchi-Berthouze, N.: Cross-cultural differences in recognizing affect from body posture. Interact. Comput. **18**(6), 1371–1389 (2006)

10. Camurri, A., Mazzarino, B., Ricchetti, M., Timmers, R., Volpe, G.: Multimodal analysis of expressive gesture in music and dance performances. In: Camurri, A., Volpe, G. (eds.) GW 2003. LNCS (LNAI), vol. 2915, pp. 20–39. Springer, Heidelberg (2004)

11. Kleinsmith, A., Fushimi, T., Bianchi-Berthouze, N.: An incremental and interactive affective posture recognition system. In: Carberry, S., De Rosis, F. (eds.) International Workshop on Adapting the Interaction Style to Affective Factors, in Conjunction with the International Conference on User Modeling (2005)

12. Piana, S., Stagliano, A., Odone, F., Verri, A., Camurri, A.: Real-time automatic emotion recognition from body gestures. In: Proceedings of IDGEI (2014)

13. Savva, N., Bianchi-Berthouze, N.: Automatic recognition of affective body movement in a video game scenario. In: Camurri, A., Costa, C. (eds.) INTETAIN 2011. LNICST, vol. 78, pp. 149–159. Springer, Heidelberg (2012)

14. Piana, S., Stagliano, A., Camurri, A., Odone, F.: A set of full-body movement features for emotion recognition to help children affected by autism spectrum condition. In: IDGEI International Workshop (2013)

15. Kinect for windows (2013). http://www.microsoft.com/en-us/kinectforwindows/

16. Shan, J., Akella, S.: 3D human action segmentation and recognition using pose kinetic energy. In: 2014 IEEE Workshop on Advanced Robotics and its Social Impacts (ARSO), pp. 69–75 (2014)

17. Camurri, A., Lagerlöf, I., Volpe, G.: Recognizing emotion from dance movement: comparison of spectator recognition and automated techniques. Int. J. Hum Comput Stud. **59**(1), 213–225 (2003)

18. Roether, C.L., Omlor, L., Giese, M.A.: Lateral asymmetry of bodily emotion expression. Curr. Biol. **18**(8), R329–R330 (2008)

19. Smolensky, P.: Information processing in dynamical systems: foundations of harmony theory. In: Rumelhart, D.E., McClelland, J.L. (eds.) Parallel Distributed Processing: Explorations in the Microstructure of Cognition, vol. 1, pp. 194–281. MIT Press, Cambridge (1986)

20. Erhan, D., Bengio, Y., Courville, A., Manzagol, P.-A., Vincent, P., Bengio, S.: Why does unsupervised pre-training help deep learning? J. Mach. Learn. Res. **11**, 625–660 (2010)

21. Apostolakis, K., Kaza, K., Psaltis, A., Stefanidis, K., Thermos, S., Dimitropoulos, K., Dimaraki, E., Daras, P.: Path of trust: a prosocial co-op game for building up trustworthiness and teamwork. In: B Games and Learning Alliance: Fourth International Conference, GALA (2015)

Design and Evaluation of an Authoring Tool and Notation System for Vibrotactile Composition

Somang Nam[✉] and Deborah Fels

Ryerson University, 350 Victoria St., Toronto, Canada
{somang.nam, dfels}@ryerson.ca

Abstract. Vibrotactile stimulation can be used as a substitute for audio or visual stimulation for people who are deaf or blind. This can enable some media content to be made more accessible to audiences with disabilities because the vibrotactile sense can be engaged. Artists have become interested in creating vibrotactile art as a new and exciting art form. In order to do this, new tools and a notation must be developed and evaluated that support the creation and experience of vibration on the skin. The Beadbox tool, along with a supporting notation system, was developed for the purpose of composing vibrotactile art. The main findings in the evaluation suggest that the Beadbox has a good usability with a low learning barrier, has direct functionality, and aesthetically pleasing.

Keywords: Vibrotactile · Human-computer interaction · User interface

1 Introduction

Art and technology are consistently related to each other in many aspects throughout history. Both share a core creative process. With the advent of technology for creative activities, the process of creative expression has been propelled to new heights. One of the newest additions to the suite of creative tools and techniques is vibrotactile art. Vibrotactile technologies enable vibration patterns to be composed so that audiences can experience/feel those patterns through the tactile sense rather than through audio/visual media. Currently there are a number of vibrotactile output devices (i.e. Emoti-chair [1]) but there are few methods for inputting the data to express those vibrations (e.g., [2–4]) and other methods for other media (e.g., music notation and music composition tools) are used. Artists have recently become interested in creating vibrotactile compositions as a new art form. However, in order to do this, new tools are needed so that the unique elements of vibrotactile stimuli can be expressed. In addition, there is no standard notation system for vibrotactile stimuli in which these expressions can be recorded and/or shared with audiences and other artists. This paper presents a vibrotactile time-based notation system and a software tool called Beadbox, which embodies this notation system. Artists use the vibrotactile notation system though the Beadbox software to compose vibrotactile expressions. In doing so, other artists can reproduce those vibrotactile compositions, and they can be represented on a variety of

© Springer International Publishing Switzerland 2016
M. Antona and C. Stephanidis (Eds.): UAHCI 2016, Part II, LNCS 9738, pp. 43–53, 2016.
DOI: 10.1007/978-3-319-40244-4_5

output devices. The Beadbox is evaluated with user studies where participants are asked to use the software to create a vibrotactile composition. For each user study session, pre and post questionnaire are used to gather subjective data regarding their impressions and opinions. Qualitative and quantitative data are analyzed to determine system elements of the usability of Beadbox and its user interface.

2 Background

2.1 Human Vibrotactile Perception

The basic mechanics of the human vibrotactile system are made possible by mechanoreceptor cells in the skin, which convert the frequency, amplitude, and duration of vibration applied to the skin into an electrical signal that travels to the person's brain [5]. Many researchers have claimed that there are four essential parameters of a vibrotactile stimulation: frequency, intensity (amplitude), spatial information, and temporal information [3]. A vibrotactile notation system then must be able to provide the information relating to these four parameters. The human sense of touch is limited to discerning frequencies between 20 Hz and 1000 Hz (the human ear can perceive frequencies between 20 Hz and 20,000 Hz) [6]. However, several studies warned about the negative effects of low frequency vibration on the human body so care must be taken when applying low frequencies to the body [7]. For the temporal coding, Cohen et al. [8] conducted experiments to find out how the duration of vibrotactile stimuli influences frequency discriminability. The results indicated that the minimum duration of vibration to determine tactile presence is 50 ms. For the intensity of vibration, Verrillo [9] interpreted that the derived curves of vibrotactile intensity change similarly to the equal loudness contours in audition. Displaying these maximum and minimum vibrotactile values where empirically derived and assisting artists in understanding how to work within them is one goal of the compositional tool developed for this research.

2.2 Existing Vibrotactile Authoring Tools

Several authoring tools that allow for vibrotactile compositions exist in the literature. The posVibEditor [10] allows prototyping for vibrotactile pattern by using a timeline with graphical representation of waveforms. Users can edit the frequency patterns of the stimulus in detail. Also, the multichannel timeline interface uses sample clips of frequency patterns with different durations created in the pattern editor. The VibScoreEditor [11] uses a western music notation score as the user interface where each musical note has a single frequency associated with it. However, it can be complex to use if the user does not have background knowledge of music composition structure and format. The minimum duration of a note is about 1 ms, which is hard for a human to perceive. The frequency range does not have a maximum limit meaning that composers could use frequencies that are not detectable by the skin. In addition, the developers of the VibScoreEditor did not conduct any user studies so it is difficult to determine how usable and useful the tool is. The TactiPEd [12] provides a visualization of spatial information as well as frequency, duration and intensity in a histogram format via a timeline. The interface provides a visualization of output orientation, which can be rearranged by users to fit their output device. Each sequence has its own visualization for its output, which is coloured in a different hue. However, there is no visualization for the intensity level and the timeline measure is difficult to match with the actual frequency samples. These existing authoring tools take different approaches to their interface designs, each with advantages and disadvantages. The vibrotactile composition tool developed in this research will consider the advantages provided by these tools and attempt to avoid their pitfalls.

3   System Overview of the Beadbox

The purpose of the Beadbox is to facilitate the creation of vibrotactile interactive art by controlling four essential variables: (1) frequency, (2) intensity, (3) spatial distribution of the signal among the vibrotactile actuators and (4) temporal information. All of these components are the foundation of a vibrotactile signal and can be controlled by a user to produce patterns over time and space that can be felt by human skin [13]. The Beadbox proposes a unique notation system in order to allow users to control these variables and produce these patterns. Users can record a vibrotactile composition, play the piece while they are creating, edit the file, and save the finished piece. Figure 1 displays an overview of the Beadbox with each component labeled. The Beadbox was implemented in Java 1.8 and uses an Audio Stream Input/Output (ASIO) API with the

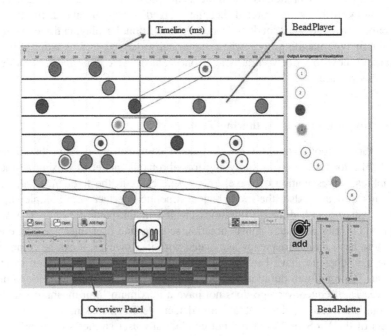

Fig. 1. An overview of the Beadbox.

ASIO4ALL driver and jASIOhost library. The output device for the user study is the Emoti-Chair [1] with a Firepod™ soundcard connection. Each Bead can be created from the Bead Palette and adjusted with a corresponding frequency and intensity slider. The created Bead can be placed on the BeadPlayer timeline. Each track of the Bead-Player represents an output contactor, with specific colour hue. The overview panel displays each page, while a page has duration of 1 s. The output arrangement visualization on the right column has interactivity; the user can drag to arrange the visualization icons to be in the same form as the output device.

3.1   Vibrotactile Notation

The notation design is the major component of the interface design. To build up a notation system, a basic information unit must be defined. The basic unit in this system is called a "Bead". A Bead is developed to deliver essential information for vibrotactile art composition. It is similar to a "note" in music notation, providing composers with a mechanism to express and record their ideas. In order to devise a visualization of a Bead, the basic unit of the Emoti-chair output, a voicecoil, was used as an underlying metaphor as seen in Fig. 2. A Bead then is represented by two concentric circles where the outermost circle is described by darker, heavier line.

Fig. 2. Simple voice coil visual metaphor.

Prior research has been carried out to investigate models of sensory substitution where different properties of perceptual systems can be used to represent various physical parameters such as frequency. These models were used to inform the representation of the vibrotactile parameters. The first mapping that has been explored was colour as a visual representation of auditory frequencies [14]. The second model was the relationship between the visual brightness of a colour and the audio frequency [15]. The researchers found that if a colour is brighter, then people tend to indicate that the sound stimuli would be higher pitch, and louder volume. If two variables have an overlapping information it is possible that users would be confused compared with a one-to-one mapping. Therefore, brightness was assigned to visualize the frequency level of vibrotactile stimuli. Figure 3 depicts a sample scale of the notation with different frequency level information.

100 Hz   300 Hz   500 Hz   800 Hz   1000 Hz

Fig. 3. Colour brightness gradation (dark to light as frequency increases) by sample frequency level.

Other researchers have found that there was a relationship between audio loudness and the size of a visual object. Louder sounds were seen to be related to the visual looming object by [16] where looming signals cause an avoidance response, resulting in a similar effect both in visual and auditory stimulations. For the Beadbox, the output intensity may be relative to the operating systems volume control (in logarithmic scale), or the size of output actuator. The Beadbox limits the maximum intensity to 50 dB to prevent any discomfort to the audience. The intensity coefficient scales linearly in the Beadbox from 0 to 100. The diameter of the inner circle of the Bead then represents amplitude whereby a smaller diameter would represent the lower intensity coefficient level. Figure 4 shows an example of the changes in diameter of the inner Bead circle showing lowering intensity coefficient.

Fig. 4. Sample Bead showing lower intensity coefficient.

The last factor is timing information. To control the timing of the note, the user can drag and drop the Bead in the desired location along the timeline. The default duration of a Bead is set as 50 ms, which is the minimum stimulus duration a human needs to discriminate different frequencies [8]. From this point, the duration of each Bead can be controlled by connecting a start point to an end point. As seen in Figs. 5, 6 and 7, the pattern is interpreted as a single connected Bead which will be expressed without pause or cut. Duration can be assigned to two Beads on different tracks or two notes from different intensity or frequency levels. When there is a connection between different tracks, there will be constant decrement (or increment) at a linear rate on either frequency or intensity over time from the start Bead to the end Bead (Fig. 6). Similarly, a connection between two different intensities or frequencies will give a transition as well (Figs. 5 and 7).

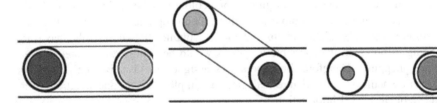

Fig. 5. A Bead with a certain duration changing from a low frequency to high frequency.

Fig. 6. A Bead with a certain duration changing from one track to another track

Fig. 7. A Bead with certain duration from a low intensity to a high intensity.

4 User Study

4.1 Methodology

A user study was carried out to evaluate the general usability of the Beadbox as a vibrotactile pattern authoring tool. Thirty people (20 female, 10 male) participated in the Beadbox user study. They ranged in ages between 18–64, with 19 in 18–24 age category, eight in 25–34 and one in each of the other three older age ranges (35–44, 45–54, 55+). Twenty-two participants were amateur artists; three participants were full-time professional artists; three participants were part-time professional artists; and two were non-artists. For types of creative practices, participants could select more than one specialization. There were four main categories of art practice: Group 1 = "Visual Artists: including Painting, Photography, Printmaking, Sculpture, Performing Art or Installation", Group 2 = "None", Group 3 = "Musical Artists: Music", and Group 4 = "Combined art specialists: participants who specialize in multiple genres." Six participants were in Group 1; six participants were in Group 2; five participants were in Group 3; and thirteen participants fell in Group 4.

For the study, participants completed a pre-study questionnaire, demonstration tutorial, a main composition session using Beadbox, and a post-study questionnaire. The pre-study questionnaire consisted of six forced-choice questions on demographics and artistic background of the participant. Basic instructions for the Beadbox were given in the 15 min demonstration where participants could practice, ask questions and discover the interface capabilities. In the main composition session, participants were asked to create a 5–10 s vibrotactile composition using the system. During the composition session, the participants were allowed to test and play their composition while sitting on the Emoti-chair. While participants were composing, the screen was being recorded, as was their verbal commentary. After the composition session ended, participants were asked to complete a post questionnaire. It consisted of ten questions from the System Usability Scale (SUS) [17], four questions regarding the interface and controls of each vibrotactile factor, and five open ended questions regarding their enjoyment of their composition when they played it on the Emoti-chair. The Likert-scale rating ranged from 1-strongly disagree to 5-strongly agree. We also asked what their intentions were for their composition, what were their expectations were, and what they liked and disliked about the Beadbox. Quantitative results were then analyzed with statistical methods and qualitative data with thematic analysis. Six themes were identified, defined and then subjected to a reliability test (see Table 2). Reliability was established by having two independent raters code about 20 % of the data randomly sampled, while including examples from each theme. The Intra-class Correlation statistic showed that there was agreement at a level of 0.84 and above. A single rater then completed the coding for the remaining data.

4.2 Results

4.2.1 Forced-Choice Questions from the Post-Study Questionnaire

A chi-square test was carried out for all forced-choice post-study questions to compare the participant responses to questions with chance. There was a significant difference

Table 1. Results of chi-square test and descriptives for all significant Likert-scale type questions (p < 0.05). A rating of 1 is strongly disagree and 5 is strongly agree.

Question	Chi-Square	Mean	S.D.	Mode	p-Value
A.1. I think that I would like to use this system frequently	16.00	3.43	0.971	4	0.003
A.2. I found the system unnecessarily complex	30.33	1.63	0.718	1	0.000
A.3. I thought the system was easy to use	29.33	4.33	0.711	5	0.000
A.4. I think that I would need the support of a technical person to be able to use this system	17.00	2.10	0.995	2	0.002
A.5. I found the various functions in this system were well integrated	35.67	3.63	0.809	4	0.000
A.6. I thought there was too much inconsistency in this system	14.67	2.13	0.973	1	0.005
A.7. I would imagine that most people would learn to use this system very quickly	33.33	4.37	0.928	5	0.000
A.9. I felt very confident using the system	21.00	4.00	0.871	4	0.000
A.10. I needed to learn a lot of things before I could get going with this system	13.33	2.07	1.015	1	0.01

between responses and chance for nine of seventeen questions (see Table 1 for all significant questions). The p-value was set at p < 0.05 and N was 30 for all questions. A Kruskal-Wallis non-parametric test was applied to the art practice groupings to determine whether there was a difference in the ratings between these groups. The result of the test showed that there was a significant difference in the complexity rating between the different artist specializations, $X^2(3) = 7.94$, $p = 0.047$, with a mean rank of 10.17 for Group 1, 22.25 for Group 2, 12.10 for Group 3, and 16.15 for Group 4.

4.2.2 Qualitative Data

All comments from participant's responses to the open ended questions and audio/video recordings were coded into the defined themes (see Table 2). The number of occurrences for each theme is depicted in Fig. 8. A one-way analysis of variance (ANOVA) was used to find any significant differences between the themes for the number of comments participants made. There was a statistically significant difference between groups (F (8,111) = 3.166, p = 0.003). A post hoc Tukey's HSD test was performed to determine the significant between the different pairs. There was a significant difference between the Interface Elements theme (M = 1.69; SD = 0.736) and the Creativity Positive theme (M = 1.00; SD = 0) (p < 0.05). There were no significant differences in other paired themes.

Table 2. Themes and definitions used for thematic analysis.

Themes	Definition / Examples
Music Concepts	The Beadbox interface is related to the music concepts such as rhythm, sound output as melody, intensity as accent, etc. *"I want the audience to feel like they're at a party where the music is ridiculously loud and you can feel the bass drop."*
Interface Elements	User interface and interaction components influence the work process; simple design; easy to use; visual aspects; *"It's quite colourful and visual."*
Functionality	The quality of being suited to serve a purpose well or not; Having a way to perform certain functions. *"I didn't like the fact that I couldn't align the notes automatically."*
Creativity	It affects to the creativity when users using the Beadbox to compose. *"It expanded my creativity."*
Technical Issue	Bugs or other technical issues. *"I didn't like the screen setup, and minor glitches."*
Emoti-Chair	Related to the Emoti-Chair rather than the Beadbox. *"I liked the chair vibrations."*

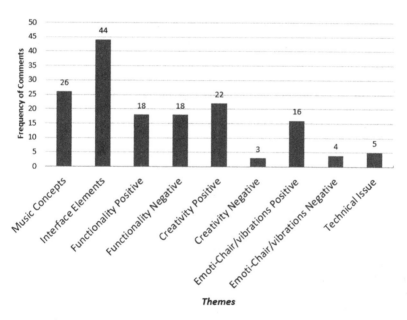

Fig. 8. Frequency of comments from participants in each theme.

5   Discussion

5.1   The Usability of Beadbox

The definition of usability according to the ISO/IEC 9126-1 standard is "the capability of the software product to be understood, learned, used and attractive to the user, when used under specified conditions" [18, p. 7]. This definition can be evaluated using three factors: learnability, functionality and its aesthetic. This discussion section focuses on these three aspects of the Beadbox. Responses to the three learnability questions (A.4, A.7, and A.10) showed that participants thought Beadbox was easy to learn. Given the relatively short amount of time participants were given to learn the concept of vibro-tactile art (30 ± 10 min.), each participant learned how compose rapidly, and said that their composition was created as intended. According to Maguire [19], a usable system allows the user to concentrate on the task, which also means it is functional with reduced errors and reinforces learning for reduced training time. Some related comments mentioned:

"It was easy to learn how to use and flexible."

"I like how it has a low learning curve for a relatively new art form"

For functionality, participants also agreed that the Beadbox was easy to use and that is was not unnecessarily complex. The notion of complexity, however, was related to the level of artistic knowledge and practice. Participants who specialized in some artistic practices thought that using the Beadbox was less complex than those who had no specialization. Although not significant, participants in visual art and music thought it was less complex than those from other fine arts, including performing art, and dance. In addition, fifteen out of forty-four comments in the *Interface Elements* theme related to Beadbox being easy to use. Participants' responses to open-ended questions included that Beadbox was very easy to use, exemplified by:

"Very easy to use, instant results on what you've made."

"I like how simple the program is to use, generally. It is very easy to understand and fairly intuitive. After a little trial and error, it was pretty easy to create a track."

Participants also agreed that they wanted to use the Beadbox frequently and that the various Beadbox functions were well integrated. Out of eighteen comments, seven were listed under the *Functionality Positive* theme, and mentioned that the Beadbox was able to function so that each participant could create a vibrotactile art piece as they intended. Even though it was eventually achieved, some functions needed to be modified during the study cycles in order to address technical issues that arose during the studies. In addition to functionality, participants also made comments on the visual aspects of Beadbox. Thirteen of forty-four of the comments contained in the *Interface Element* theme were related to visual appeal. Participants liked that they could interact with a variety of simple shapes and colours. Participants said they really appreciated the colour arrangement and aesthetics, for example:

"The colour coding system for the intensity, different tracks, etc. was very helpful."

"The colourful circles were most appealing to me."

"It wasn't solely for the aesthetic value, but an interactive piece that allows the participants to be part of an immersive space."

Some participants mentioned that the circular-shaped design of a Bead and its simple layout on the Beadplayer improved learnability of the Beadbox. It also enabled multiple approaches to the compositional process. For example, participants who specialized in visual art commented that they focused more on the visual display of the Bead patterns rather than thinking about the vibration output. They tried to draw something using Beads, even after they knew that vibrations would result from those patterns. From the screen recordings and their composition piece, it seemed that they tried to draw a gun, stairs, a house or a smiley face. A future research direction could be exploration of the relationship between visually appealing compositions and their vibrational impact on audiences. Artists from different genres may be able to connect their specializations and the creation of vibrotactile art.

6   Conclusion

In this paper, a standalone vibrotactile composition tool, the "Beadbox" and its notation system was explained. The user study results on its usability showed that the tool is easy to learn and has good usability, with an attractive visual interface that is also functional. The Beadbox still can be improved by having options to provide different types of waveforms, or having secondary functionalities such as a detailed numeric frequency editor and a better navigation interface for the overview panel. The future research direction can be focused on further exploring the relationship between visual-tactile domains using the Beadbox as a drawing tool to output tactile stimulation.

Acknowledgements.   Funding was graciously provided by the Social Sciences and Humanities Research Council. We gratefully acknowledge all of the participants in the study. In addition we thank The Vibrafusion Lab and David Bobier, and Maria Karam of TAD Inc for their valuable advice and assistance in this research.

References

1. Karam, M., Branje, C., Nespoli, G., Thompson, N., Russo, F.A., Fels, D.I.: The emoti-chair: an interactive tactile music exhibit, pp. 3069–3074 (2010)
2. Branje, C.: The Vibrochord - Investigating a Vibrotactile Musical Instrument. University of Toronto (2015)
3. Brown, L.M.: Tactons: Structured Vibrotactile Messages for Non-visual Information Display (2007)
4. Gunther, E., O'Modhrain, S.: Cutaneous grooves: composing for the sense of touch. J. N. Music Res. **32**(4), 369–381 (2003)

5. Verrillo, R.T., Bolanowski, S.J.: Tactile responses to vibration. In: Havelock, D., Kuwano, S., Vorländer, M. (eds.) Handbook of Signal Processing in Acoustics, pp. 1185–1213. Springer, New York (2008)
6. Brown, L.M., Brewster, S., Purchase, H.C., et al.: A first investigation into the effectiveness of tactons, pp. 167–176 (2005)
7. Moore, B.C.: An Introduction to the Psychology of Hearing. Emerald Group Publishing, Bingley (2012)
8. Schust, M., et al.: Effects of low frequency noise up to 100 Hz. Noise Health **6**(23), 73 (2004)
9. Griffin, M.J.: Handbook of Human Vibration. Academic Press, London (2012)
10. Cohen, B., Kirman, J.H.: Vibrotactile frequency discrimination at short durations. J. Gen. Psychol. **113**(2), 179–186 (1986)
11. Verrillo, R.T.: Subjective magnitude functions for vibrotaction. IEEE Trans. Man Mach. Syst. **11**(1), 19–24 (1970)
12. Who.int, Guidelines for Community Noise – Chap. 4 (2015)
13. Ryu, J., Choi, S.: posVibEditor: graphical authoring tool of vibrotactile patterns, pp. 120–125 (2008)
14. Lee, J., Ryu, J., Choi, S.: Vibrotactile score: a score metaphor for designing vibrotactile patterns, pp. 302–307 (2009)
15. Panëels, S., Anastassova, M., Brunet, L.: TactiPEd: easy prototyping of tactile patterns. In: Kotzé, P., Marsden, G., Lindgaard, G., Wesson, J., Winckler, M. (eds.) INTERACT 2013, Part II. LNCS, vol. 8118, pp. 228–245. Springer, Heidelberg (2013)
16. Gescheider, G.A.: Psychophysics: The Fundamentals (2013)
17. Caivano, J.L.: Color and sound: physical and psychophysical relations. Color Res. Appl. **19**(2), 126–133 (1994)
18. Marks, L.E.: On cross-modal similarity: the perceptual structure of pitch, loudness, and brightness. J. Exp. Psychol. Hum. Percept. Perform. **15**(3), 586 (1989)
19. Walker-Andrews, A.S., Lennon, E.M.: Auditory-visual perception of changing distance by human infants. Child Development, pp. 544–548 (1985)

Active-Wheel Mouse
for Human-Computer Interface

Slippage-Perception Characteristics on Fingerpad

Yoshihiko Nomura[(⊠)] and Satoshi Oike

Mie University, Tsu 514-8507, Mie, Japan
nomura@mach.mie-u.ac.jp

Abstract. This paper presents an active wheel mouse that can present slippages to the fingertip skin. The active wheel mouse is a mouse device that embeds a wheel actively rotating in any directions, with any speeds and duration times. Here, raised-dots of 4.5 and 10.5 mm intervals were especially introduced to the peripheral surface of the wheel. As a result of a pilot study by psychophysical experiments, it was suggested that, from the viewpoint of the perceived lengths, the active wheel mouse was effective enough to provide the slippage information and that is superior to the flat surface without raised dots, i.e., non-bumpy surface.

Keywords: Active-wheel mouse · Man-machine interface · Motion · Slippage perception · Fingerpad · Raised dot

1 Introduction

The objective of this study is to develop "an active wheel mouse" that can present slippages to the fingertip skin. The active wheel mouse is a mouse device that embeds a wheel: the wheel actively rotates in any directions, with various speeds and duration times. Here, as a way to enhance the perceptual characteristics, raised-dots were introduced to the peripheral surface of the wheel. Touching on the wheel surface, the users can perceive the slippages of the wheel surface via one's cutaneous sensation on finger-pad: the instantaneous directed velocities of the slippages can be recognized as the instantaneous directed velocities of the moving surfaces, and, the integrations of the instantaneous directed velocities over some duration time result in the lengths of the slippages. Thus, we can be recognized motion trajectories of the moving surfaces. This function can be utilized for various situations. For example, we can employ one of the so-called "stop and go" schemes as in the following.

- ["Stop" phase] Computer rotates a wheel in some direction with a speed and for a duration time. Then, we can recognize a directed line segment from the presented slippage.
- ["Go" phase] Regarding the directed line segment as hand motion, and, actively moving the mouse, we recognize a hand movement, i.e., a stroke, through the motion.

© Springer International Publishing Switzerland 2016
M. Antona and C. Stephanidis (Eds.): UAHCI 2016, Part II, LNCS 9738, pp. 54–61, 2016.
DOI: 10.1007/978-3-319-40244-4_6

Furthermore, by consecutively iterating the "stop and go" phase, we can learn a series of hand movements. The hand movements could be brush strokes of line drawings such as calligraphies and route maps. This function, as it were, can be regarded as a computer-to-human communication. Needless to say, the active wheel mouse inherits the hand positioning and the clicking function as in ordinary mouse devices. These functions can be regarded as a computer-to-human communication.

Beside the stop and go scheme, we can employ an on-line feedback schemes between computer and user as in the following. If we recognize the perceived slippage velocities presented by wheel as the hand-motion velocities, we are momentarily able to be instructed how to move our hand. By accepting the momentary instructions continuously, we would be able to learn curved hand movements. This hand motion instructing function would be helpful for with visually impaired persons.

Thus, the active wheel mouse is expected to work as a novel interfaces enabling us to communicate by motions with computer in a mutual way. This paper presents a result of a pilot study by a psychophysical experiment on the cutaneous sensory characteristics of the slippages of the wheel surface on a fingertip.

2 Design of Active-Wheel Mouse

2.1 Previous Works

Tsagarakis et al. proposed a slip displaying device made of a pair of cones [1]. The effects of the tangential contact displacement were studied by Salada et al. [2]. For the use of the raised dot for slip speed perception, Dépeault et al. (2008) studied the slip-speed scaling. They dealt with the perception of the slip-speeds not by absolute values, but by relative ones, i.e., the ratios of the test speed against a standard one [3]. As for mouse type fingertip tactile devices, Gleeson et al. proposed a fingertip-mounted tactile display reflecting a tangential skin displacement feedback [4]. Moscatelli et al. proposed a sphere-based slippage presenting device [5].

2.2 Purpose and Solution

The purpose is to develop a mouse which presents displacement vectors, i.e., line segments via cutaneous slippage sensation on the human fingerpad. Aiming at the purpose, as a human-computer information channel, we employ cutaneous slippage sensation on the fingerpad. That is, as shown in Fig. 1, we developed an *"active wheel mouse"*: it embeds two stepping motors that rotate the wheel of 20 mm in diameter with respect to the orthogonal two axes, i.e., one rotates the wheel of 20 mm in diameter, and the other changes the direction of rotation (see Fig. 2). Especially, we introduced raised dots on the wheel peripheral surface (see Fig. 3). Practically, in order to clarify the effectiveness of the raised dots, we employed three kinds of wheels: the first and the second wheel have surfaced with the raised dots of intervals, 4.5 and 10.5 mm, and the third wheel has a flat surface without raised dot.

Fig. 1. Active wheel mouse

Fig. 2. Two stepping motors (M25SP-6NK and M15SP-2 N, MITSUMI ELECTRIC CO., LTD., Tokyo, Japan)

Fig. 3. Wheel with raised dots

3 Experiment

3.1 Experimental Conditions

The factors and their corresponding factor levels employed in an experiment were as follows:

Control factor to be optimized
- Surface factor: (3 levels) two kinds of dotted surfaces of intervals, 4.5 and 10.5 mm and a flat surface without dot

Signal factors being related to presented slippages
- Length factor: (6 levels) 25, 50, 75, 100, 125, 150 mm.
- Angle factor: (12 levels) 0, 30, ~ , 300, 330 degrees (30 degree steps)
- Speed factor: (3 levels) 30, 60, 120 mm/s

Error factor
- Subject factor: (2 levels) 2 people aged 22 and 26, right handedness
- Repetition number: (2 levels) 2 times repeated

3.2 Experimental Procedures

As for the conditions described in the former section, we employed an orthogonal array of 72 runs based on the experimental design scheme. For each of the run, subjects were asked to perform the following procedures.

Step 1:   Subjects closed their eyes and touched the wheel surface on their fingerpad through an opening (see Fig. 4)

Step 2:   Subjects perceived the slippage length and angle by using their fingerpad cutaneous sensation

Step 3:   When the wheel stopped, subjects answered their perceived length and angle by touching a start and an end point on a touch panel display (see Fig. 5)

Fig. 4. Active wheel viewed from an opening through which users put their fingertip on the wheel peripheral surface.

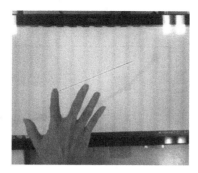

Fig. 5. Subjects answered their perceived slippages by using a touch panel display

3.3   Experimental Results

The relative errors, i.e., the ratios of the absolute errors against the true lengths, were examined, and were summarized from the viewpoints of the systematic error, i.e., sample mean of the error, and the standard error of the random error. To evaluate the perceived length quantitatively, a relative error measure, e_l, was employed as follows.

$$e_l = (l - L)/L \tag{1}$$

where l and L denote the perceived and actual length, respectively.

Before explaining the experimental results, it should be noted that the sample number was too small to make the conclusion statistically legitimate.

Perceived length. For the three kinds of surfaces, the systematic errors are shown in Fig. 6 together with the standard errors being proportional to the random errors. Length factor effect with perceived length relative errors was also shown in Fig. 7.

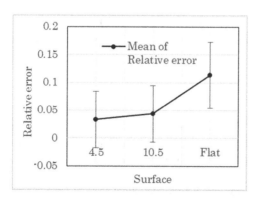

Fig. 6. Surface factor effect with perceived length relative errors (Error bar: standard error)

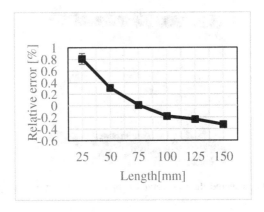

Fig. 7. Length factor effect with perceived length relative errors (Error bar: standard error)

For the perceived length data, statistical tests were applied to confirm the significances of the factor effects, and the test results are shown in Table 1: the systematic errors were test by ANOVA, and the random errors were by Bartlett's test.

As for the perceived length relative errors, it seems to be that the raised dots are superior to the flat surface, especially from the viewpoints of the systematic errors from Fig. 6. We can see a lengthening effect in short lengths of presented slippages, and the shortening effect in long lengths of presented slippages from Fig. 7 as in the previous works [6–9].

Table 1. Statistical test results of the factor effects on the perceived lengths

Factor	Systematic error (by ANOVA)		Random error (by Bartlett's test)	
	Significance probability $P(F)$	Decision	Significance probability $P(\chi^2)$	Decision
Surface	0.037	*	0.204	NS
Speed	0.301	NS	0.006	**
Direction	0.000	***	0.030	*
Length	0.000	***	0.000	***

* $P < 0.05$, ** < 0.01, *** < 0.001, NS = Not Significant

Perceived direction. For the three kinds of surfaces, the systematic errors are shown in Fig. 8 together with the standard errors being proportional to the random errors. Direction factor effect with perceived directional errors was also shown in Fig. 9.

For the perceived direction data, statistical tests were also applied to confirm the significances of the factor effects, and the test results are shown in Table 2.

As for the perceived directional errors, it seems to be that the raised dots didn't show any significant difference among the three surfaces from the viewpoints both of

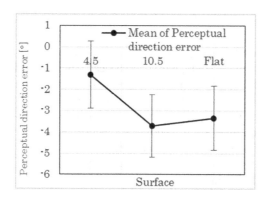

Fig. 8. Surface factor effect with perceived directional errors (Error bar: standard error)

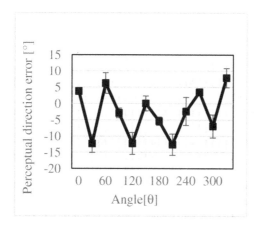

Fig. 9. Direction factor effect with perceived directional errors (Error bar: standard error)

Table 2. Statistical test results of the factor effects on the perceived directions

Factor	Systematic error (by ANOVA)		Random error (by Bartlett's test)	
	Significance probability $P(F)$	Decision	Significance probability $P(\chi^2)$	Decision
Surface	0.411	NS	0.758	NS
Speed	0.098	NS	0.657	NS
Direction	0.000	***	0.000	***
Length	0.705	NS	0.979	NS

* $P < 0.05$, ** < 0.01, *** < 0.001, NS = Not Significant

the systematic and of the random errors. There were only a significant difference with the directional factor effect: the systematic error shows the tendency of perceiving the directions as orthogonal angles as in the previous work [7] (Table 2).

4 Conclusions

An active wheel mouse that can present slippages to the fingertip skin was developed, and a pilot study was conducted by a psychophysical experiment. Here, we, especially, introduced the raised dots of 4.5 and 10.5 mm intervals to the wheel surface together with the flat surface without raised dots for comparison.

As a result of the pilot study, it was suggested that, from the viewpoint of the perceived lengths, the active wheel mouse was effective enough to provide the slippage information and that is superior to the flat surface.

In the future, the sample size should be increased enough, and the results are used for acquiring line drawing information with visually impaired persons.

Acknowledgement. This work was supported by KAKENHI (Grant-in-Aid for scientific research (B) 19H02929 from JSPS).

References

1. Tsagarakis, N.G., Horne, T., Caldwell, D.G.: Slip aestheasis: a portable 2D slip/skin stretch display for the fingertip. In: Eurohaptics Conference, 2005 and Symposium on Haptic Interfaces for Virtual Environment and Teleoperator Systems, World Haptics 2005, First Joint. IEEE (2005)
2. Salada, M., et al.: An experiment on tracking surface features with the sensation of slip. In: Eurohaptics Conference, 2005 and Symposium on Haptic Interfaces for Virtual Environment and Teleoperator Systems, World Haptics 2005, First Joint. IEEE (2005)
3. Dépeault, A., Meftah, E.M., Chapman, C.E.: Tactile speed scaling: contributions of time and space. J. Neurophysiol. **99**(3), 1422–1434 (2008)
4. Gleeson, B.T., Horschel, S.K., Provancher, W.R.: Design of a fingertip-mounted tactile display with tangential skin displacement feedback. IEEE Trans. Haptics **3**(4), 297–301 (2010). IEEE
5. Moscatelli, A., Naceri, A., Ernst, M.: Navigation in the fingertip. In: 2013 World Haptics Conference (WHC). IEEE (2013)
6. Syed Yusoh, S.M.N., Nomura, Y., Sakamoto, R., Iwabu, K.: A study on the duration and speed sensibility via finger-pad cutaneous sensations. Procedia Eng. **41**, 1268–1276 (2012)
7. Nomura, Y., Syed Yusoh, S.M.N., Sakamoto, R.: Hand-motion perception by four haptic modes: active/passive and with/without fingerpad cutaneous sensation. J. Adv. Mech. Des. Syst. Manufact. **7**(4), 560–575 (2013)
8. Nomura, Y., Iwabu, K.: Length perceptual characteristics on raised-dot slippages. In: Human-Computer Interfaces and Interactivity: Emergent Research and Applications, pp. 286–308. IGI Global (2014)
9. Nomura, Y., Kato, H.: Raised-dot slippage perception on a fingerpad using an active wheel device. In: Recent Advances on Using Virtual Reality Technologies for Rehabilitation. Nova Science Publishers (2015)

BCIs for DOC Patients: Assessment, Communication, and New Directions

Rupert Ortner[1(✉)], Jitka Annen[2], Tim von Oertzen[3], Arnau Espinosa[4],
Javi Rodriguez[4], Brendan Z. Allison[5], Günter Edlinger[1,5],
Steven Laureys[2], Martin Hamberger[3], Andrea Kammerhofer[3],
Florian Guttmann[3], and Christoph Guger[1,5]

[1] G.tec medical engineering GmbH,
Sierningstrasse 14, 4521 Schiedlberg, Austria
{ortner, edlinger, guger}@gtec.at
[2] Coma Science Group, Cyclotron Research Centre and GIGA Research,
University of Liège, GIGA(B34), Quartier Hopital,
Avenue l' Hopital 11, 4000 Sart-Tilman, Belgium
{jitka.annen, steven.laureys}@ulg.ac.be
[3] Department of Neurology, Neuromed Campus,
Kepler Universitätsklinikum, Linz, Austria
{Tim.vonOertzen, Martin.Hamberger, Andrea.Kammerhofer,
Florian.Guttmann}@gespag.at
[4] G.tec medical engineering Spain, C/l'Acer 32, 08038 Barcelona, Spain
{espinosa, rodriguez}@gtec.at
[5] Guger Technologies OG, Herbersteinstrasse 60, 8020 Graz, Austria
allison@gtec.at

Abstract. Recent work has sought to extend brain-computer interface (BCI) technology to persons diagnosed with a disorder of consciousness (DOC). This new approach can use real-time measures of brain activity to facilitate assessment of conscious awareness, and potentially provide communication for some users. We present the mindBEAGLE system, a hardware and platform for these goals, results from two patients, and future directions.

Keywords: Brain-computer interface (BCI) · Disorder of consciousness (DOC) · Mindbeagle · P300 · Motor imagery

1 Introduction

1.1 BCIs for DOC Patients

During most of the history of brain-computer interface (BCI) research, the main goal was to develop new tools that could provide communication for patients who could not communicate otherwise due to severe motor disabilities [1–3]. Patients with late-stage amyotrophic lateral sclerosis (ALS, also called Lou Gehrig's disease) were a classic target user group, since they often have little or no reliable control of voluntary muscle activity, but do exhibit signs of consciousness and the desire to communicate. While helping such patients remains important, some newer review/commentary articles have

© Springer International Publishing Switzerland 2016
M. Antona and C. Stephanidis (Eds.): UAHCI 2016, Part II, LNCS 9738, pp. 62–71, 2016.
DOI: 10.1007/978-3-319-40244-4_7

identified new directions to extend BCI technology to help different patient groups, including persons diagnosed with disorders of consciousness (DOCs) [2–4].

Recently, several groups have presented work that extends BCI technology to DOC patients. Results have shown that 17–42 % of these patients do exhibit activity reflecting that they are conscious, and may even be able to communicate using a BCI, despite a medical diagnoses suggesting communication is impossible [5–10]. Thus, in addition to providing communication, BCI technology could be adapted to a wholly new capability: assessment of consciousness. This new use of BCI technology, not just for communication but also to determine whether someone is mentally capable of communication, could have a tremendous impact on patients and their families.

This new research direction requires innovative approaches to human-computer interaction (HCI). Conventional BCIs assume that target users are conscious and have sufficient cognitive function to communicate. Thus, there has been very little work focused on using BCI technology for assessment of consciousness. BCIs also usually assume intact visual function. It is often unknown whether DOC patients have intact vision, therefore, BCI's for this population should provide specialized task instructions and new paradigms working independently from vision. Furthermore, user-friendly interaction is even more important than in other BCIs, since confusing or ambiguous instructions could hamper a patient's only chance at re-assessment and, if possible, communication.

The new mindBEAGLE system was developed to meet these needs. Last year, we presented a paper at the HCI International conference series that introduced our new mindBEAGLE system, its unique HCI protocols, and results from initial evaluation. The current paper reviews the mindBEAGLE approach (including hardware and software), presents new results from patients, and concludes with discussion of future directions and unique HCI-related issues with DOsC patients.

1.2   MindBEAGLE

The mindBEAGLE system shown in Fig. 1 uses auditory stimuli to present task instructions, and auditory or vibrotactile stimuli to present cues and feedback. The left panel shows the hardware components; a laptop running the mindBEAGLE software, an electrode cap, amplifier, earbuds, and a vibrotactile stimulator. Although this system is being sold and used by research partners, it is still in development, primarily to improve portability without sacrificing signal quality in real-world settings.

The mindBEAGLE system can use four general approaches: based on motor imagery (MI); auditory P300 s; vibrotactile P300 s with 2 stimulators (placed on the left and right wrists); and vibrotactile P300 s with three stimulators (placed on the wrists and one ankle). These four approaches are available across three usage modes: assessment, quick test and communication. We are currently developing two additional modes, which provide rehabilitation and prediction.

Assessment Mode. The goals of this mode are: (1) to determine whether a patient can produce reliable, distinct EEG signals that are adequate for BCI-based communication; and (2) to identify which approach is most effective for that patient. For example, with

Fig. 1. The left panel shows the mindBEAGLE system. The right panel shows a close-up of the vibrotactile stimulators attached to the wrists. The right panel also shows the optional anti-static grounding straps. Usually, mindBEAGLE obtains adequate quality signals without any grounding strap, however in rare settings they can be used to reduce noise.

MI, auditory cues instruct the subject to imagine left or right hand movement. If the resulting EEG activity indicates successful task performance, then the patient may be able to communicate using a BCI based on MI.

Quick Test Mode. This mode is designed to provide a quicker means of checking for indicators of consciousness than assessment mode. It is available with the auditory approach and the vibrotactile approach with two stimulators. The quick tests are essentially the same as the tests in assessment mode.

Communication Mode. Communication mode can currently provide YES/NO communication through left vs. right hand motor imagery or through left wrist vs. right wrist vs. either ankle vibrotactile stimuli. In communication mode, the experimenter can pre-record questions that mindBEAGLE presents within a synchronous BCI paradigm, such as "Do you want us to change your bed position?" or "Do you want to change the temperature?" Since the communication is binary, additional questions are often needed to gather more information, such as whether the temperature should be increased or decreased, and by how much.

Rehabilitation Mode. This mode will allow cognitive, sensory, and/or motor rehabilitation. Because of the challenges of conducting rehabilitation with this patient population, and the many types of rehabilitation they may seek, developing and improving rehabilitation mode should be an ongoing effort over many years. This mode may leverage some developments from g.tec's RecoveriX system, which is currently designed to provide motor rehabilitation for persons affected by stroke.

Prediction Mode. If rehabilitation is available, patients may want to learn about the most likely outcome, and how much training is needed to achieve optimal rehabilitation. Prediction mode will help predict rehabilitation outcomes, which could not only help patients consider the effort involved but might also facilitate decisions relating to long-term care, insurance, expected costs, and other factors. Prediction mode will also identify which parameters (such as target frequencies for MI) should be most effective, which could be used to automatically update parameters used in the classification mode. Unlike the preceding three modes, prediction mode may not entail distinct runs or sessions. Instead, prediction mode may operate by re-analyzing data collected during other modes.

2 Methods

2.1 Subjects

We present data from two patients who exhibited promising EEG signals during mindBEAGLE assessment. Both patients had been diagnosed as minimally conscious. Persons in the minimally conscious state (MCS) are considered aware of themselves, emotions and their environment in a fluctuating manner [11]. Medical experts typically attempt to communicate, but communication on the behavioral level is impossible, perhaps because of motor disabilities and aphasia. Because these patients cannot provide informed consent, consent was obtained through a legally authorized person, and all procedures were approved by an ethical review board at the relevant hospital partner.

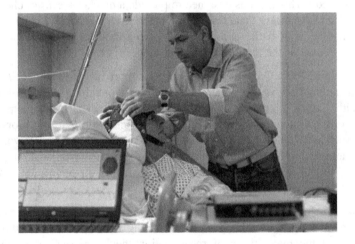

Fig. 2. This picture simulates a physician working with a DOC patient. The laptop in the foreground presents the user's free-running EEG (top left), brain map (top right), and evoked potential activity (bottom right).

Patient 1 was a 61-year-old male. Patient 2 was a 40-year-old female, and a patient at the Sart Tilman Liège University Hospital in Liège, Belgium.

2.2 Procedure

Before working with each patient, we tried to identify autobiographical questions relevant to each patient. This could involve reviewing the anamnesis and/or speaking with family members. We developed YES/NO questions such as "Is your father named Jose?" or "Were you born in Austria?"

Each recording session began with mounting a cap on the patient, affixing the vibrotactile stimulators, and inserting earbuds into the ears. Each session involved a variable number of "assessment" runs. We now use all four of the approaches presented above. However, during the data collection presented in this paper, we did not use all four approaches, since they were still in development. In all tasks, chance accuracy was 12.5 %. Patients had a short break after each run, and each session lasted 45-60 min. Patient 1 exhibited the indicators of awareness shown in the following section during the third recording session. Patient 2 exhibited these indicators in the first session. A simulation of a session with the mindBEAGLE is shown in Fig. 2.

3   Results

3.1   Patient 1

Figure 3 shows results from Patient 1, who participated in AEP and MI assessments. The MI assessments did not reveal indicators of consciousness, which may stem from challenges in MI BCIs that have been widely recognized in the BCI community.

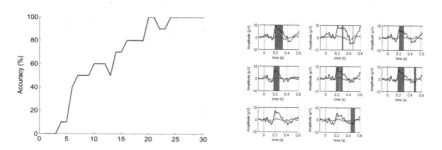

Fig. 3. Data collected from Patient 1 during the AEP paradigm. The left panel shows how accuracy increases to 100 % with sufficient repetitions. This is typical of healthy users as well; communication with fewer trials is challenging. The right panel shows the topographic distribution of brain activity elicited by the task, which was selective attention to one of eight tones. The green shaded areas indicate areas with a statistically significant difference. Six channels show a P300 to target tones only, reflecting that the user was able to silently count target tones while ignoring other stimuli. This confirms that the user could process stimuli and understand instructions. Thus, this patient might be able to communicate. However, patients who can process auditory and/or vibrotactile stimuli and follow the basic instructions in the assessment paradigm might not be willing and/or able to communicate.

3.2   Patient 2

Figure 4 shows results from Patient 2, who participated in AEP, VT2, and VT3 assessments.

4 Discussion

4.1 Results Summary

Based on the work presented above, and very new data still being analyzed, we have four observations that are generally consistent with other recent work. First, in some users, the P300 BCI approaches relied largely on non-P300 activity. Second, the P300 BCI approaches were generally more effective than the MI approach. This, patients exhibited substantial within- and across- subject variability. Fourth, effective BCI performance was possible for persons with severe disabilities, but often required more data than with healthy users.

4.2 Future Directions

Because of the novelty of this research field and patient group, we see considerable opportunity for new research. Our highest priority is validation. We need to evaluate mindBEAGLE and emerging technologies with many more patients. The challenges with the MI approach can only be addressed through further research, along with several other future directions.

From an HCI perspective, DOC patients introduce several challenges that merit future study. Visual stimuli, which are vital in most interfaces, cannot provide reliable interaction. DOC patients have cognitive and/or attentional deficits that may create difficulty understanding the tasks, remembering instructions, maintaining attention to task demands, or focusing on the different cues. They may also have sensory deficits, such as difficulty hearing or feeling, which could render auditory and/or vibrotactile

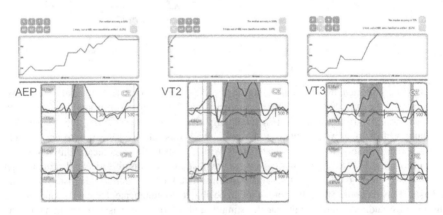

Fig. 4. Data collected from Patient 2 across the auditory evoked potential (AEP) paradigm (left panels), vibrotactile stimuli with two stimulators (VT2, middle panels), and vibrotactile stimuli with three stimulators (VT3, right panels). All three of these protocols led to clear differences in the evoked EEG (bottom panels), and the classifier could successfully identify the target (top panels). The VT2 protocol was especially effective, leading to 100 % classification accuracy after only three trials. The VT3 protocol also led to high accuracy, suggesting that the patient possibly could communicate. (Color figure online)

modalities ineffective. These challenges have long been recognized within the HCI community, such as within the design of assistive technologies (ATs) designed for persons with disabilities [12]. However, DOC patients introduce another challenge that is unique within HCI. Many of these patients fade in and out of consciousness, with no a priori way to determine whether they are in an up or down state before beginning a session. Thus, we need to attempt assessment several times, since assessments that do not reveal indicators of consciousness may simply mean that we need to try again. Furthermore, we currently have no way to know how many assessments are appropriate before concluding that a patient could never communicate. Even if many prior assessments were unsuccessful, there is always a chance that the patient could pass an assessment if medical or research experts try one more time. This may create a heart wrenching dilemma: given the limited resources in a medical environment, when is it appropriate to give up with one patient and move on to the next one to possibly change his/her life?

This is a serious challenge, and we currently have no solution. Behaviorally, there is no known way to determine when patients may be sufficiently aware for a mind-BEAGLE session. It may be possible to use EEG or other measures to identify indicators of awareness more quickly than we can right now, which is an important future direction we are now exploring. In some cases, administering medications may increase the chance that a patient will be aware prior to a session, although this solution introduces further ethical challenges.

Another unique challenge involves "BCI inefficiency". This phenomenon, also called "BCI illiteracy", means that a user is unable to use a particular BCI approach. A BCI used for communication should ideally provide communication for all users who need it. However, this is not always possible, just like conventional interfaces; some people cannot use keyboard or mice due to motor disabilities or other reasons. Moreover, given this unique patient group, it is not realistic to expect high literacy. Many patients who are diagnosed as unable to communicate really are unable to communicate. If they are not able to use a BCI for communication, this may not reflect a failure by the BCI designers. Rather, it may indicate that the BCI is performing as well as can be expected for a patient who is indeed unable to reliably produce EEG differences. Many patients diagnosed with DOC are indeed unable to understand instructions, maintain attention, develop and implement goal-directed behavior required to answer questions, etc. These patients are presumably unable to communicate with any known technology, and could not be helped without major advancements in medical technology. Nonetheless, we are exploring improved protocols and signal processing approaches that could improve BCI literacy. Additional data from DOC patients should help us identify relevant EPs and other EEG characteristics could lead to improved classification accuracy and literacy.

Furthermore, the MI approach usually requires training, and has been recognized within the BCI community as more prone to BCI inefficiency [13, 14]. While most healthy people can attain effective communication with the MI approach, MI BCIs are not able to detect reliably discriminable brain signals in a minority of users. The training requirements in most MI BCI approaches are more daunting for DOC patients for at least three reasons. First, training sessions are pointless if the patient cannot understand instructions and follow the task. With this target patient group, a P300 BCI may be needed to assess these mental capabilities. However, some healthy people can attain effective MI-based communication with fairly brief training [15], even with a limited electrode montage [16]. Second, any session with this patient group is much less casual than with healthy persons. Third, it is unknown whether this target population is capable of producing clear differences between left and right hand MI that a BCI could detect. Research has shown that persons with late-stage ALS can produce MI signals adequate for BCI control [17]; therefore, the inability to produce certain movements, even for an extended time, does not necessarily prevent people from imagining movement in a way that an MI BCI could detect. Patients with DOC have different disabilities than late stage ALS patients, and thus this question remains open for further study.

So far, we have focused on EEG activity. Within the BCI community, there has been some attention to "hybrid" BCIs [18] that might combine EEG-based signals with other tools to image the brain (such as fMRI) or other biosignals (such as activity from the heart, eyes, or muscles). These methods may be less promising as tools to provide communication for persons diagnosed with DOC. Aside from high cost and low portability, fMRI imaging requires a very strong magnetic field that is difficult or impossible to use with the electronic and metal devices that DOC patients need. Deriving information from other biosignals can be helpful for diagnosis, but is not especially helpful when trying to provide communication to persons with little or no ability to voluntarily modulate these signals.

Like many BCI researchers, we are interested in improving software, including better HCI-based and user-centered software to interact with users. In addition to the unique challenges of working with DOC patients, we also need to present information to system operators in an engaging, informative manner. Figure 2 shows how system operators can view the EEG, brain maps, and ERPs in real-time. We need additional testing to determine whether this is indeed the most informative and effective way to present information to system operators. We also need to consider differences among system operators, who might be medical doctors, nurses, research professors, postdocs, graduate students, technicians, or other people with different backgrounds and skills. The most effective interface components may differ for different users based on their expertise.

Hardware development is another important future direction. Figures 1 and 2 show systems that used wired, active, gel-based electrodes embedded in a cap. A wireless system might be easier to use while eliminating the risk of snagging cables on equipment. Dry electrodes might provide adequate signal quality while reducing preparation and cleanup time. New electrode montages and mounting hardware could enable electrodes that do not require a cap, such as electrodes embedded in headphones, headbands, or other head-mounted devices.

In summary, the results obtained so far from our group and other groups have clearly shown that some patients diagnosed with DOC do exhibit indicators of consciousness with BCI technology and might be able to communicate, even though they do not exhibit indicators of consciousness on a behavioral level. On the other hand, the majority of DOC patients do not exhibit such indicators with BCIs. This is still a new research direction with many unanswered questions and very serious challenges, and we do not know which approaches will be most effective. Drawing on lessons from

BCI research, the most effective approach will probably vary across different users, which underscores the importance of providing different approaches through different sensory modalities to increase the chance that at least one of them will be effective. We are excited about the prospect of helping some people within this unique patient population, and both hope and expect that future research will lead to more universal and effective solutions.

References

1. Allison, B.Z., Wolpaw, E.W., Wolpaw, J.R.: Brain computer interface systems: Progress and prospects. British review of medical devices 4(4), 463–474 (2007)
2. Wolpaw, J.R., Winter Wolpaw, E. (eds.): Brain-Computer Interfaces: Principles and Practice. Oxford University Press, Oxford (2012)
3. Allison, B.Z., Dunne, S., Leeb, R., Millan, J., Nijholt, A.: Recent and upcoming BCI progress: overview, analysis, and recommendations. In: Allison, B.Z., Dunne, S., Leeb, R., Millan, J., Nijholt, A. (eds.) Towards Practical BCIs: Bridging the Gap from Research to Real-World Applications, pp. 1–13. Springer-Verlag, Heidelberg (2013)
4. Brunner, C., Birbaumer, N., Blankertz, B., Guger, C., Kübler, A., Mattia, D., Millán, J.D.R., Miralles, F., Nijholt, A., Opisso, E., Ramsey, N., Salomon, P., Müller-Putz, G.R.: BNCI Horizon 2020: towards a roadmap for the BCI community. Brain-Comput. Interfaces 2(1), 1–10 (2015)
5. Schnakers, C., Vanhaudenhuyse, A., Giacino, J., Ventura, M., Boly, M., Majerus, S., Moonen, G., Laureys, S.: Diagnostic accuracy of the vegetative and minimally conscious state: clinical consensus versus standardized neurobehavioral assessment. BMC Neurol. 9, 35 (2009). doi:10.1186/1471-2377-9-35
6. Lugo, Z.R., Rodriguez, J., Lechner, A., Ortner, R., Gantner, I.S., Kübler, A., Laureys, S., Noirhomme, Q., Guger, C.: A vibrotactile P300-based BCI for consciousness detection and communication. Clin EEG and Neurosci (2014)
7. Ortner, R., Aloise, F., Prückl, R., Schettini, F., Putz, V., Scharinger, J., Opisso, E., Costa, U., Guger, C.: Accuracy of a P300 speller for people with motor impairments: a comparison clin. EEG Neurosci. 42(4), 214–218 (2011)
8. Ortner, R, Prückl, R, Guger, C.: A tactile P300-based BCI for communication and detection of awareness. Biomed Tech (Berl). (2013)
9. Risetti, M., Formisano, R., Toppi, J., Quitadamo, L.R., Bianchi, L., Astolfi, L., Cincotti, F., Mattia, D.: On ERPs detection in disorders of consciousness rehabilitation. Front Hum. Neurosci. 20(7), 775 (2013)
10. Lulé, D., Noirhomme, Q., Kleih, S.C., Chatelle, C., Halder, S., Demertzi, A., Bruno, M.-A., Gosseries, O., Vanhaudenhuyse, A., Schnakers, C., Thonnard, M., Soddu, A., Kübler, A., Laureys, S.: Probing command following in patients with disorders of consciousness using a brain–computer interface. Clin. Neurophysiol. 124, 101–106 (2013)
11. Giacino, J.T., Ashwal, S., Childs, N., Cranford, R., Jennett, B., Katz, D.I., Kelly, J.P., Rosenberg, J.H., Whyte, J., Zafonte, R.D., Zasler, N.D.: The minimally conscious state: definition and diagnostic criteria. Neurology. 58(3), 349–53 (2002)
12. Cook, A., Hussey, S.: Assistive technologies: principles and practice. Mosby: St. Louis, Missouri (2002)
13. Vidaurre, C., Blankertz, B.: Towards a cure for BCI illiteracy. Brain Topogr. 23(2), 194–8 (2010)

14. Allison, B.Z., Neuper, C.: Could anyone use a BCI? In: Tan, D.S., Nijholt, A. (eds.) Applying our Minds to Human-Computer Interaction. Brain-Computer Interfaces. Human-Computer Interaction Series, pp. 35–54. Springer Verlag, London (2010)

15. Ortner, R., Scharinger, J., Lechner, A., Guger, C. How many people can control a motor imagery based BCI using common spatial patterns? In: Seventh Annual International IEEE EMBS Conference on Neural Engineering Montpellier, France, April 2015

16. Guger, C., Edlinger, G., Harkam, W., Niedermayer, I., Pfurtscheller, G.: How many people are able to operate an EEG-based brain-computer interface (BCI)? IEEE Trans. Neural Syst. Rehabil. Eng. **11**(2), 145–7 (2003)

17. Kübler, A., Nijboer, F., Mellinger, J., Vaughan, T.M., Pawelzik, H., Schalk, G., McFarland, D.J., Birbaumer, N., Wolpaw, J.R.: Patients with ALS can use sensorimotor rhythms to operate a brain-computer interface. Neurology **64**, 1775–1777 (2005)

18. Pfurtscheller, G., Allison, B.Z., Brunner, C., Bauernfeind, G., Solis-Escalante, T., Scherer, R., Zander, T.O., Mueller-Putz, G., Neuper, C., Birbaumer, N.: The hybrid BCI. Front Neurosci. **21**(4), 30 (2010)

The Improvement of Cognitive Maps of Individuals with Blindness Through the Use of an Audio-Tactile Map

Konstantinos Papadopoulos[✉], Marialena Barouti, and Eleni Koustriava

University of Macedonia, Thessaloniki, Greece
kpapado@uom.gr, k.s.papado@gmail.com

Abstract. The aim of the present study was to examine the impact of audio-tactile maps on the improvement of cognitive maps of individuals with blindness. The area mapped on the aid was known and familiar to the participants. Twenty adults with blindness (total blindness or only light perception) took part in the research. The age ranged from 20 years to 52 years (M = 37.05). The subjects participated in two experiments. During the first experiment the participants depicted their cognitive maps of a familiar city route on a haptic model using the materials materials given. In the second experiment the participants read the audio-tactile map of this route, and then they were asked to depict anew their cognitive map of the same route on a haptic model. The findings highlight the positive effect of the use of audio-tactile maps from individuals with blindness on the knowledge of a familiar city area.

Keywords: Blindness · Spatial knowledge · Audio-tactile map · Cognitive map

1 Introduction

People often need to move toward an unseen goal, and to manage this they have to plan their movements by gathering and organizing all the available knowledge about the environment [1]. In other words, they need to form a mental picture or a cognitive map that in turn supports their movement within the environment. The procedure of forming a mental picture is very significant for every day life activities (e.g. go for shopping, go to work) [2].

Individuals with visual impairment are required to rely on all their senses, other than sight, for the perception of spatial information and objects' attributes, such as (e.g., shape, dimensions) [3]. Although visual input is indeed necessary for spatial coding, lack of it can be compensated for through the development of another sensory modality. For instance, part of this research underlines the effectiveness of touch in specific tasks, which individuals with visual impairments performed as well as or even better than their sighted counterparts [4–6]. Although spatial information are received in a slower rhythm when relying on touch than in the case of visual reception, this does not have necessarily an impact on the quality of representation produced [7].

Cognitive mapping is in effect a process of mental representation of spatial knowledge [8], during which an individual acquires, stores, recalls, and decodes information about the relative locations and attributes of the phenomena in his/her environment [9].

© Springer International Publishing Switzerland 2016
M. Antona and C. Stephanidis (Eds.): UAHCI 2016, Part II, LNCS 9738, pp. 72–80, 2016.
DOI: 10.1007/978-3-319-40244-4_8

While cognitive mapping of spaces is a prerequisite to develop adequate orientation and mobility skills [10], most of the information required for cognitive mapping is gathered through the visual channel [11].

Individuals with blindness are facing significant difficulties during their orientation and mobility in space. The majority of the researchers that examined spatial performance of individuals with visual impairments and sighted individuals came to the conclusion that visual experience influences decisively spatial behavior [12–14]. Moreover, blindness has a negative impact on the development of blind people's spatial skills [14–16]. However, cognitive maps of individuals with visual impairments appear to contain basic environmental features as streets, buildings, parks, fixed obstacles, bus stops etc. [17] and show that they understand spatial relationships between places when presented on a tactile map [18]. Knowing how individuals with visual impairments understand space and what are the features that their cognitive maps contain could help planning the environment appropriately, make the right information available to them and improve their wayfinding [18].

The study of spatial knowledge seems to be a complex process, especially considering that cognitive maps are dynamic entities which continuously change and evolve [8]. The evaluation of spatial knowledge for individuals with blindness uses techniques divided into route-based techniques and configurational techniques [19]. A widely used technique for examining configurational knowledge is reconstruction tasks, where individuals with blindness are asked to build a haptic model [18]. However, Kitchin and Jacobson [19] revealed a highly interesting dimension of evaluation techniques for spatial knowledge, indicating that the restrictions each evaluative process sets as well as the skills of individuals with blindness related to the performance of knowledge [18] may induce specific cognitive results [20].

Supporting the relative localization of objects, maps lead to the acquisition of survey knowledge; a knowledge than can be obtained more quickly and with less effort than direct experience either from sighted individuals [21] or from individuals with visual impairments [22].

Researchers have pointed out that raised-line graphics of the spatial environment prepare individuals with visual impairment to travel an unfamiliar space more safely and efficiently than work with a verbal description or a sighted guide [23], demanding a smaller cognitive load than direct experience [24]. Thinus-Blanc and Gaunet [24] stated, also, that when an individual with blindness read a haptic map has the ability to maintain a stable reference point. Using points of reference during spatial learning enables allocentric coding which leads to better spatial performance and knowledge [12, 25].

In the case of individuals with visual impairments, maps contribute to the handling of daily living problems inducing autonomy, independence and a better quality of life [23, 26, 27]. Tactile maps are important for spatial awareness [28] of close or distant places supporting wayfinding [29] and orientation and mobility of individuals with visual impairments [30], as well as improving spatial cognition in the long-term [31].

Research on the optimum support that could be offered to individuals with visual impairments, propose the conjunction of the haptic modality with the audio/vocal one [3]. It is undisputable that the amount of information perceived through touch is significantly restricted compared to the amount of information perceived through sight [3]. In order to enhance the amount of information, multi-modal approaches for individuals with visual impairments are being into research [3]. Hence, multimodal interactive maps could enable the access of people with visual impairment to spatial knowledge [32].

Zeng and Weber [33] give an overview of different type of maps used by people with blindness. The authors also mention audio-tactile maps which combine audio with tactile information. In case of Audio-Tactile maps, information can be represented by tactile graphics, audio symbols, tactile symbols, audio-tactile symbols (combined e.g. a tactile symbol that when a user touches it, he can hear additional information) and Braille labels. Audio-tactile maps become available with the use of a touchpad.

Touchpad offers at the same time access to the benefits of tactile maps and verbal aids. The combination of auditory and tactile information may result in a more complete concept [34]. Landau and his colleagues [34] found that individuals with visual impairments can enjoy control and independence coming from the ability to make choices between tactile and auditory information used through a touchpad.

Moreover, touch pads give the ability to use environmental auditory cues, incorporating, in a way, the soundscape into the tactile map. Including auditory cues in a map may promote an individual's orientation, since individuals with visual impairments are proved to use auditory cues to determine and maintain orientation within an environment [35, 36] and to associate the soundscape with the structural and spatial configuration of the landscape and create cognitive maps [37].

2 Study

The aim of the present study is to examine the impact of audio-tactile aids on the improvement of cognitive maps of individuals with blindness with reference to a familiar area. Specifically, the aim is actually the comparison of the cognitive maps of individuals with blindness before and after the use of the audio-tactile map.

2.1 Participants

The sample of the study consisted of 20 individuals with blindness, (11 males and 9 females). The age ranged from 20 years to 52 years (M = 37.05, SD = 10.35). Seventeen participants were blind or had severe visual impairments and 3 had the ability to detect very large objects. The visual impairment was congenital for 10 participants and acquired for the rest 10 participants.

The participants were asked to state the way of their daily move in outdoor places, by choosing one of the following: (a) with the assistance of a sighted guide, (b) sometimes myself and sometimes with the assistance of a sighted guide, and (c) myself, without any assistance. Moreover, the participants were asked to indicate the frequency of their independent movement using a 5-point likert scale: always, usually, sometimes, seldom, or never. In addition, these two questions were answered from orientation and mobility (O&M) specialists, who were familiar with the participants and could assess the latter's ability of independent movement. Tables 1 and 2 present the answers of the participants and O&M specialists.

Table 1. Ability of independent movement according to the answers of participants and O&M specialists - the score represent the number of participants in each group.

	With the assistance of a sighted guide	With and without the assistance	Without the assistance
Participants	1	6	13
O&M specialists	3	4	13

Table 2. Frequency of independent movement according to the answers of participants and O&M specialists - the score represent the number of participants in each group.

	Seldom	Sometimes	Usually	Always
Participants	0	1	13	6
O&M specialists	3	5	8	4

2.2 Instruments

The main research instrument was audio-tactile maps of a familiar city area. An audio-tactile map was created to represent each of the three different routes. These routes had approximately the same length and the same number of turnings.

Researchers visited each route, recorded the spatial information (as far as absolute location and kind of information are concerned) and selected 30 of them to be mapped out. The choice of spatial information was made in a way that the existence of spatial information on every street of the route was assured.

Moreover, sound recording for each route was made at a certain time, during evening hours and for 20 s at each point. Sound was recorded at the beginning and the end of each route, at all intersections and at some places with special auditory information, such school, café, car wash etc. For the recording a Telinga Stereo Dat-Microphone was used with the recording system Zoom H4n-Handy Recorder.

Adobe Illustrator CS6 was used for the creation of digital tactile maps. These maps were then printed on microcapsule paper and the 3 tactile maps (one for each route) were developed. On each tactile map dots were placed at the locations of spatial information and short length vertical lines were placed on the locations where sounds were recorded. Moreover, the street names and the spatial information were presented through synthetic speech; there were no Braille labels.

The software application Iveo Creator pro 2.0 together with the device touchpad, were used to develop the audio-tactile maps. Both of them are products of "ViewPlus® Technologies" company. The files produced by the software are saved in Scalable Vector Graphics (SVG) format. The touchpad device is a pointing device consisting of specialized surface that can translate the position of a user's fingers to a relative position on the computer screen. When used in combination with a tactile image, this device has the potential to offer tactile, kinaesthetic and auditory information at same time [38].

A laptop, a touchpad device and headphones through which participants listened to audio information (street names, spatial information and sounds) were used by them to read the audio-tactile maps.

In the phase where their cognitive map was depicted, a range of different materials were used by the participants. The materials included a kappa fix carton on which an A3 sheet was fastened. Moreover, a string was placed in the position of roads, thumb-tacks to fasten the laces and twist them when there were turnings were used, and different type of thumbtacks were placed in the position of obstacles.

2.3   Procedures

The examination procedure was carried out individually in a quiet environment. Initially, participants were informed about the procedure of the experiment and the haptic model they should create at the end.

The subjects participated in two experiments. During the first experiment the participants depicted their cognitive maps of a familiar city route on a haptic model using the materials given. In the second experiment the participants read the audio-tactile map of this same route, and then they were asked to depict anew their cognitive map of the route on a haptic model. This means that each participant was examined in the same route before and after the reading of the audio-tactile map.

The experiments were not conducted all in one day to prevent the effect of fatigue impinging on the results. A circular design was applied with reference to routes. For instance, the first participant was examined on the cognitive map of the first route, the second participant was examined on the cognitive map of the second route, the third participant was examined on the cognitive map of the third route, the fourth participant was examined on the cognitive map of the first route, and so on. This design was applied in order to avoid any error resulting from differences in the areas' degree of difficulty.

In the second experiment the examination included participants reading the audio-tactile map through the use of a touchpad device and then depicting their cognitive map. Initially, the tactile map was placed on the touchpad device and a familiarization process took place. Then the audio-tactile map reading phase followed. Each participant read the audio-tactile map using he/her using touch, and by tapping the streets he/she listened to their name, by tapping the dots he/she listened to the information they represent, and finally by tapping the small vertical lines he/she heard the sounds of the particular area.

The maximum time that was offered for the map reading was 15 min, in which participants had to learn the route, street names and 30 pieces of spatial information. They could refer to the map and listen to the information as many times as they wish during the 15 min, while they could stop reading before the time span of 15 min was completed. A five-minute pause followed. Then the participants used the materials given by the researcher to depict their cognitive map.

At the end of each experiment, the participants created a haptic model representing their cognitive map of the route under examination. There was no time limit for the creation of the haptic model. Each time a participant touched an item on the haptic model, the researchers pointed out what this item stood for so that he/she could make a review.

After the completion of the haptic model, the researchers were drawing the maps, by drafting the outline of the materials of the haptic model on the A3 sheet. The recording of the data on the cognitive maps and their analysis followed.

During the processing of the cognitive maps (haptic models), the following variables were recorded and calculated by the researchers as to their accuracy: (a) the number of the streets, (b) the names of the streets, and (c) the number of spatial information participants placed on the haptic model. Specifically, with respect to streets, variables that were examined included how many streets participants placed properly and how many names of streets were indentified right. Regarding the amount of spatial information, the variable "correct information" was calculated; correct was considered the piece of information that was defined accurately with reference to its kind as well as location on the street.

3   Results

The findings have arisen after the comparison of the cognitive maps of the participants before and after they had read the audio-tactile map, with reference to 3 variables: "number of streets-correct," "street names-correct", "information-correct". The mean and standard deviation (SD) of scores are presented in Table 3. Moreover, repeated-measures ANOVAs were conducted for the 3 variables: number of streets-correct, street names-correct, and information-correct.

Table 3. Mean (M), and standard deviation (SD), of correct answers regarding the number of streets, street names, and spatial information.

	Before the audio-tactile map reading		After the audio-tactile map reading	
	M	SD	M	SD
Number of streets-correct	6.05	2.01	7.55	1.05
Street names-correct	5.35	2.64	5.95	2.50
Information-correct	2.25	1.20	6.95	6.89

The implementation of repeated-measures ANOVAs revealed significant differences for the variables: number of streets-correct [$F (1, 19) = 9.000$, $p < .01$], and information-correct [$F (1, 19) = 9.408$, $p < .01$].

4   Conclusions

The results of the present study highlight the contribution of audio-tactile maps to the improvement of the existing spatial knowledge of individuals with visual impairments. In this case it could be assumed that sound and/or soundscape have a supportive role for memory, while in combination with touch lead an individual to better organize the storage and recall of spatial information. Theorists have already suggested that combining tactile and auditory information may lead to a more complete concept [34].

It should be noted that the assessment tool used in the present study might have influenced the results. Transferring a cognitive map on a haptic model implies no special scale adaptations, while transferring a cognitive map created through walking experience in the physical environment on haptic model could possibly entail an inherent difficulty relative to scale adaptations. Future research should try to examine and compare the cognitive maps of individuals with visual impairments with multiple-scale tools or methods, for instance monitoring walking behavior in the physical environment.

Moreover, it is worth noting that the divergence between the cognitive map before and the cognitive map after the audio-tactile map could be greater if the participants were skillful users of the touchpad and the audio-tactile map. The repeated use of the aid could result in the improvement of individuals with blindness regarding the coding of information in cognitive maps.

The results of the present study provide a new dimension on orientation and mobility training. Audio-tactile maps appear to be quite a supportive tool in the cognitive mapping of an area, and therefore significant aid for orientation and mobility within familiar areas.

The research presented in this paper constitutes part of an extended research completed in the context of the Research Funding Project: "THALIS - University of Macedonia - KAIKOS: Audio and Tactile Access to Knowledge for Individuals with Visual Impairments". From this project a series of publications have arisen, some of which may resemble with each other. Several similarities exist between the present paper and the paper "The contribution of audio-tactile maps to spatial knowledge of individuals with visual impairments" [39]. However, both the research aim and the research area were different in each study. Moreover, the participants were not the same in each research. Papadopoulos and Barouti [39] studied the ability of individuals with blindness to create cognitive maps of a city area through the use of audio-tactile maps. This area was unfamiliar to the participants and, thus, there was no previous spatial knowledge with reference to the area. On the other hand, the aim of the present study was the comparison of the cognitive maps of individuals with blindness before and after the use of the audio-tactile map. That means that we examined the impact of audio-tactile aids on the improvement of cognitive maps that the participants had already developed for a familiar area. Furthermore, the main research instrument of the present study was audio-tactile maps of a familiar city area, while on the research of Papadopoulos and Barouti [39] the main research instrument was audio-tactile maps of an unknown city area.

References

1. Péruch, P., Chabanne, V., Nesa, M.P., Thinus-Blanc, C., Denis, M.: Comparing distances in mental images constructed from visual experience or verbal descriptions: the impact of survey versus route perspective. J. Exp. Psychol. **59**(11), 1950–1967 (2006)
2. Steyvers, F.J.J.M., Kooijman, A.C.: Using route and survey information to generate cognitive maps: differences between normally sighted and visually impaired individuals. Appl. Cogn. Psychol. **23**, 223–235 (2009)
3. Ghiani, G., Leporini, B., Paterno, F.: Vibrotactile feedback to aid blind users of mobile guides. J. Vis. Lang. Comput. **20**, 305–317 (2009)
4. Heller, M.: Picture and pattern perception in the sighted and the blind: the advantage of late blind. Perception **18**, 379–389 (1989)
5. Heller, M.A., Brackett, D.D., Scroggs, E., Allen, A.C.: Haptic perception of the horizontal by blind and low-vision individuals. Perception **30**, 601–610 (2001)

6. Postma, A., Zuidhoek, S., Noordzij, M.L., Kappers, A.M.L.: Differences between early-blind, late-blind, and blindfolded-sighted people in haptic spatial-configuration learning and resulting memory traces. Perception **36**, 1253–1265 (2007)
7. Morash, V., Pensky, A.E.C., Alfaro, A.U., McKerracher, A.: A review of haptic spatial abilities in the blind. Spat. Cogn. Comput. **12**, 83–95 (2012)
8. Kitchin, R.M.: Cognitive maps: what are they and why study them? J. Environ. Psychol. **14**, 1–19 (1994)
9. Downs, M.R., Stea, D.: Image and Environment: Cognitive Mapping and Spatial Behavior. Edward Arnold, London (1973)
10. Lahav, O., Mioduser, D.: Construction of cognitive maps of unknown spaces using a multi-sensory virtual environment for people who are blind. Comput. Hum. Behav. **24**(3), 1139–1155 (2008)
11. Loomis, M.J., Klatzky, L.R., Golledge, G.R., Cicinelli, G.J., Pellegrino, W.J., Fry, A.P.: Nonvisual navigation by blind and sighted: assessment of path integration ability. J. Exp. Psychol. Gen. **122**(1), 73–91 (1993)
12. Papadopoulos, K., Koustriava, E.: The impact of vision in spatial coding. Res. Dev. Disabil. **32**(6), 2084–2091 (2011)
13. Papadopoulos, K., Koustriava, E., Kartasidou, L.: The impact of residual vision in spatial skills of individuals with visual impairments. J. Spec. Educ. **45**(2), 118–127 (2011)
14. Papadopoulos, K., Barouti, M., Charitakis, K.: A university indoors audio-tactile mobility aid for individuals with blindness. In: Miesenberger, K., Fels, D., Archambault, D., Peňáz, P., Zagler, W. (eds.) ICCHP 2014, Part II. LNCS, vol. 8548, pp. 108–115. Springer, Heidelberg (2014)
15. Koustriava, E., Papadopoulos, K.: Mental rotation ability of individuals with visual impairments. J. Vis. Impair. Blin. **104**(9), 570–574 (2010)
16. Koustriava, E., Papadopoulos, K.: Are there relationships among different spatial skills of individuals with blindness? Res. Dev. Disabil. **33**(6), 2164–2176 (2012)
17. Papadopoulos, K.: A school program contributes to the environmental knowledge of blind. Br. J. Vis. Impair. **22**(3), 101–104 (2004)
18. Jacobson, R.D., Kitchin, R.M.: Assessing the configurational knowledge of people with visual impairments or blindness. Swansea Geogr. **32**, 14–24 (1995)
19. Kitchin, R.M., Jacobson, R.D.: Techniques to collect and analyze the cognitive map knowledge of persons with visual impairment or blindness: issues of validity. J. Vis. Impair. Blin. **91**, 360–376 (1997)
20. Golledge, R.G., Smith, T., Pellegrino, J.W., Doherty, S., Marshall, S.: A conceptual model and empirical analysis of children's acquisition of spatial knowledge. J. Environ. Psychol. **5**(1), 25–52 (1985)
21. Thorndyke, P.W., Hayes-Roth, B.: Differences in spatial knowledge acquired from maps and navigation. Cogn. Psychol. **14**(4), 560–589 (1982)
22. Caddeo, P., Fornara, F., Nenci, A., Piroddi, A.: Wayfinding tasks in visually impaired people: the role of tactile maps. Cogn. Process. **7**(1), 168–169 (2006)
23. Espinosa, M.A., Ungar, S., Ochaita, E., Blades, M., Spencer, C.: Comparing methods for introducing blind and visually impaired people to unfamiliar urban environments. J. Environ. Psychol. **18**(3), 277–287 (1998)
24. Thinus-Blanc, C., Gaunet, F.: Representation of space in blind persons: vision as a spatial sense? Psychol. Bull. **121**(1), 20–42 (1997)
25. Papadopoulos, K., Koustriava, E., Kartasidou, L.: Spatial coding of individuals with visual impairment. J. Spec. Educ. **46**(3), 180–190 (2012)

26. Jacobson, R.D.: Navigating maps with little or no sight: an audio-tactile approach. In: Proceedings of the Workshop on Content Visualization and Intermedia Representations, Montreal, Canada, pp. 95–102 (1998)

27. Papadopoulos, K., Karanikolas, N.: Tactile maps provide location based services for individuals with visual impairments. J. Locat. Based Serv. **3**(3), 150–164 (2009)

28. Habel, C., Kerzel, M., Lohmann, K.: Verbal assistance in tactile-map explorations: a case for visual representations and reasoning. In: 24th AAAI Conference on Artificial Intelligence, pp. 34–41. AAAI Publications, Atlanta (2010)

29. Passini, R., Duprés, A., Langlois, C.: Spatial mobility of the visually handicapped active person: a descriptive study. J. Vis. Impair. Blin. **80**(8), 904–907 (1986)

30. Lawrence, M.M., Lobben, A.K.: The design of tactile thematic symbols. J. Vis. Impair. Blin. **105**(10), 681–691 (2011)

31. Ungar, S.: Cognitive mapping without visual experience. In: Kitchin, R., Freundschuh, S. (eds.) Cognitive Mapping: Past Present and Future, pp. 221–248. Routledge, Oxon (2000)

32. Brock, A., Truillet, P., Oriola, B., Jouffrais, C.: Usage of multimodal maps for blind people: why and how. In: ITS 2010 ACM International Conference on Interactive Tabletops and Surfaces, pp. 247–248. ACM, New York (2010)

33. Zeng, L., Weber, G.: Accessible maps for the visually impaired. In: IFIP INTERACT Workshop on ADDW, Lisbon, Portugal, pp. 54–60 (2011)

34. Landau, S., Russell, M., Erin, J.N.: Using the talking tactile tablet as a testing accommodation. Review **38**(1), 7–21 (2006)

35. Jansson, G.: Spatial orientation and mobility of people with visual impairment. In: Silverstone, B., Lang, M.A., Rosenthal, B., Faye, E.E. (eds.) The Lighthouse Handbook on Visual Impairment and Rehabilitation 2000, vol. 1, pp. 379–397. Oxford University Press, New York (2000)

36. Koutsoklenis, A., Papadopoulos, K.: Auditory cues used for wayfinding in urban environments by individuals with visual impairments. J. Vis. Impair. Blin. **105**(10), 703–714 (2011)

37. Papadopoulos, K., Papadimitriou, K., Koutsoklenis, A.: The role of auditory cues in the spatial knowledge of blind individuals. Int. J. Spec. Educ. **27**(2), 169–180 (2012)

38. Jansson, G., Juhasz, I.: The reading of virtual maps without vision. In: XXIII International Cartographic Conference, ICC, Moskow (2007)

39. Papadopoulos, K., Barouti, M.: The contribution of audio-tactile maps to spatial knowledge of individuals with visual impairments. In: Kouroupetroglou, G. (ed.) Proceedings of International Conference on Enabling Access for Persons with Visual Impairment - ICEAPVI, Athens, pp. 141–146 (2015)

Evaluation of the Use of Eye and Head Movements for Mouse-like Functions by Using IOM Device

Andréia Sias Rodrigues[1,2(✉)], Vinicius da Costa[1,2],
Márcio Bender Machado[1,2], Angélica Lacerda Rocha[2],
Joana Marini de Oliveira[2], Marcelo Bender Machado[2],
Rafael Cunha Cardoso[1,2], Cleber Quadros[2],
and Tatiana Aires Tavares[1]

[1] Pós Graduação em Ciências da Computação,
Universidade Federal de Pelotas (UFPel),
Caixa Postal 15.064-91.501-970, Pelotas, RS, Brazil
{Andreia.sias, tatianaaires}@ufpel.edu.br,
viniciusdacosta@gmail.com, {marciomachado,
rafaelcardoso}@pelotas.ifsul.edu.br
[2] South Rio-Grandese Federal Institute for Education, Science and Technology,
Praça Vinte de Setembro, 455 - Centro, Pelotas, RS CEP 96.015-360, Brazil
angelicalacerdarocha@gmail.com,
joana.marinideoliveira@gmail.com,
cleber.smquadros@gmail.com, marcelo@ifsul.edu.br,

Abstract. This paper describes a process of assistive technology evaluation using the eye and head movements as a CHI - Computer Human Interaction. In order to collect the data, it was used the Glasses Mouse Interface (IOM - Interface Óculos Mouse), device in development at the Federal Institute of Science, Education and Technology (IFSUL) which has been evaluated according to principles of user experience and usability testing.

Keywords: Accessibility · Assistive technologies · Computer human interaction · Glasses mouse · Assistive technologies evaluation

1 Introduction

People with disabilities generally do not have the same access to health care, education and employment opportunities. It is known that, very often, they do not receive the support they need, and end up experiencing the taste of exclusion to perform their daily activities. Analyzing the overall rates of people with disabilities, it is possible to perceive that social inclusion of minorities is not a simple task. One of these daily activities is the use of information technology. Although it can be considered a basic activity, for a population that is affected by a motor disability, the search for technological means enabling access to computer use, it becomes a necessity, especially in educational institutions.

M. Antona and C. Stephanidis (Eds.): UAHCI 2016, Part II, LNCS 9738, pp. 81–91, 2016.
DOI: 10.1007/978-3-319-40244-4_9

The problem arises when access to technological resources is denied due to the high cost. Several initiatives, in many areas of knowledge, try to adopt the full use of various computer tools for people with motor disabilities through the use of what is called assistive technologies (ATs), which allow accessibility and inclusion of users with those needs.

There are already many projects involving different areas of knowledge developing new applications of Computer Human Interaction (CHI) on Assistive Technologies.

A kind of project in this area regards to the creation of Interface Glasses-Mouse called IOM [19] in the South Riograndense Federal Institute at Pelotas (RS). Such device aims to allow the use of the computer by people with motor paralysis (without compromised intellectual capacity), including the use of Information and Communication Technologies (ICTs), to control the mouse movements through the head the movement and the action of mouse click, by the blinking of the eyes. The project is still under development of its features. In the other hand, it is already patented, having ready and tested prototypes for its posterior industrialization. That will enable an affordable lower cost device when compared to many existent devices with the similar purpose.

To validate the development of the IOM project a systematic mapping of assistive technology for the same purpose is required, mainly to enable the user with motor disabilitiesto manipulate graphical computer interfaces. The purpose of this mapping is to understand the state of the art in this scenario and confirm that the research is moving in the right direction.

The tests of User eXperience (UX) and usability evaluation have also been implemented and are aimed, through the analysis of their results, to generate inputs in how to establish the interaction of this device with these interfaces, describing difficulties and opportunities for improvement of the IOM project.

2   Glasses Mouse Interface (IOM - Interface Óculos Mouse)

The IOM system, represented in Fig. 1, is composed by a glasses with two sensors (gyroscope and accelerometer) that allow people use head and eyes movements to control the computer tasks. The IOM enables an alternative interaction style to mouse and keyboard controls. Hence, such solution can be very useful for users to perform hands-free control tasks.

This device is characterized as glasses that, may or not, contain the ocular lenses, according to the user needs. It basically presents two types of sensors which are responsible for the capture of voluntary eye blinking, the positioning, and inclination of the head. According to the user's motor disability, software control routines, such as calibration of inertial position and cursor speed, may be adapted by the user using the computer interface device to increase the comfort and performance.

Besides making possible the interaction with the computer hands-free, other goals of the IOM project is to develop a low-cost, lightweight and comfortable assistive technology. At this purpose we use prototypes in preliminary design stage to evaluate their performance according to these requirements.

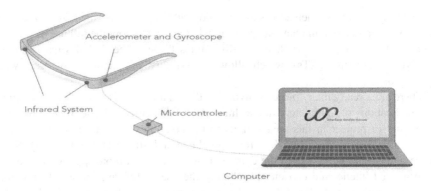

Fig. 1. The structure of IOM System

3 Related Works

Several projects in HCI area are under development or have already been developed in order to facilitate and enable users with disabilities to access the computer, as shown in Table 1.

Some examples of these devices are switches, joysticks and pointing devices activated by the body movements; computer screen vitual keyboard simulator softwares; speech recognition systems; eye movement controlled by computer vision systems; devices that control head movements; and more sophisticated devices employing the electric potential of the brain using EEG signals - electroencephalography, signals received by the eye movements using EOG - electrooculography [4] or contraction signals of voluntary muscles using EMG - electromyography [12] and even interfaces controlled by the brain, and brain-computer interface (BCI) together with a combination of brain sensors [3].

The detection of head movements can be done through video cameras, defined as video-based or camera-based, or by a device attached to the head with sensors that capture these movements, called head-based or head-track. Other motion capture method, is the face monitoring, which detects the region of the nose and mouth to control the mouse pointer. Alternatively, eye tracking (eye-based or gaze tracking) positions the mouse cursor at the estimated position of the user's eyes.

Eye tracking interfaces obtained even better performance than the traditional mouse (hand motion) in the speed aspect, however, the accuracy of current eye trackers is not sufficient for a satisfactory pointing in real time [6]. In [6], it proposed a more than one movement use technique to capture the cursor movement, head movement and eye tracking, called HMAGIC (Head Movement And Gaze Input Cascaded Pointing). The mouse pointer is activated by the direction of gaze and head movements the user makes for fine-tuning. The idea is to combine the advantages of speed of eye movements with the precision of the head movements.

Other related works use the camera-mouse software [23] to capture movements of the head, by recognizing the face and using the user nose as a central point. In [1] was added a feature to the camera-mouse to avoid accidental clicks, a pop up window allows the user to confirm the click, if it is inside a period of time that you can not be sure that you really wanted click the object in focus.

An overview of these assistive technology devices in CHI for motor disability users was made, like a comparative table, using as a tool the systematic mapping, show in Table 1.

Table 1. Assistive Technologies to mouse control for users with motor disabilities

Assistive technology	Movements	Ref.	Based	Tests with people with motor disabilities	Evaluation methods	System description
Click Control	Interacts with another pointer controller. Uses the camera mouse	[1]	video-based an gesture-based	yes, one student with cerebral palsy	User eXperience observation, a type of communicability as well.	Prevents accidental clicks (involuntary movements) through a screen to cancel the click. Can work with any mouse controller system.
User Tracking	face (head, nose, eyes and mouth)	[2]	video-based (remote - kinect sensors)	No	Usability (task-oriented) measurement time, precision and comfort	Natural movements using kinect in recognition of the face, eyes, nose, mouth (open, closed) and diferents sounds to click.
HMagic	head and eyes	[6]	video-based + eye track	No	Usability and UX	Cascading eye movements (speed) + head movements for precision
Tongue drive	tongue	[7]	movements based	yes	Usability	This system consists of a headset that transmits (wireless) data captured by sensors on the user's mouth. Managing to capture the rotary movements of the tongue.
AsTeRICS	head and speech (adaptive)	[8]	video-based	yes	Usability and UX	Adjustable platform depending on the user's disability. Web Cam + Plug in, facial recognition.
Snap Clutch	eye tracking captured by Tobii X120 and implemented by Tobii SDK	[9]	eye-based	yes	Task-Oriented, Usability (OS 9241-9) and Fitts Law interface, and think-loud technique.	Move the eyes to pointer control in games. For entertainment purpose.
Mouth switch	Head and mouth	[10]	video-based	no	Task-Oriented, Usability	Detects the head and mouth movements both vertically and horizontally

(*Continued*)

Table 1. (*Continued*)

Assistive technology	Movements	Ref.	Based	Tests with people with motor disabilities	Evaluation methods	System description
Eye-Gaze	eyes	[13]	Gaze-tracking - oculography	yes	Task-Oriented, Usability and UX	Hardware to be used in parallel with the mouse.
2D cursor-to-target	voluntary contraction of facial muscles	[12]	Capture face signals muscles (sEMG)	no	UC, Davis IRB Protocol 200513697-3. Usability	Two EMG sensors capture two muscles of the face to be the X and Y coordinates on the screen
Wiimote	head and speech	[14]	head-tracking pointer and speech	–	–	Windows API, the WiiLab and also the SAPI (speech recognition) and software that includes the Wii and Glasses LED control (IR) and captures the head movements
Camera Mouse	face (head, nose, mouth and eyes)	[23]	video-based, face track	yes	Task-Oriented, Usability and UX	Capture of the head movements to move and stop at certain objects to select time (dwell click).
FaceMouse	nose	[26]	video-based	yes	UX	Capture the face image and uses the nose as a reference for pointing on the screen
Head-Tracking Pointer (HTP)	head	[27, 28]	video-based	yes	Task-Oriented, Usability	Head movement to control the cursor
Blink and wink Detection	head and eye blink	[29]	video-based	No	Usability and precision tests	Head movements to control and blink to click
Haptic Glove Leap Motion	captures hand movements	[15]	gesture-based	No	UX	Device is like a glove that captures hand movements. Uses the Leap Motion.
The Eyebrow Switch	eyebrow	[16]	video-based	Noo	UX	Device that checks the movement of the eyebrow, works like pointer.
Head Track	head	[30]	video-based	No	Usability	Device that captures the movement of the head through a web cam
Head tracking, and the virtual keyboard interface	face	[18]	video-based	yes	Usability	Used in mobile devices, captures the image with a camera and an overlay keyboard image, where the user can see more clearly where the nose points.

4 Evaluation Methodology

Many tests have been applied, as a way to quantify and qualify the IOM User eXperience in relation to its control of the GUI (Graphic User Interface). A qualitative approach, in order to evaluate the device's UX and usability with oriented tasks, resulted in the quantitative data analysis for continual improvement of the IOM. Although the project focuses on the development of AT for people with motor disabilities, it was decided at that time to apply the tests in typical users (without restricted mobility). This is done due to the fact that when we test this device directly with people with motor disabilities, it generates an expectation of immediate use of a product that is still in its initial development cycle. These users get high expectations that can influence the evaluation of aspects of UX, while the typical users are completely "disengaged" and without risk of frustration.

It was also considered that the feedback from a typical user, with respect to IOM's user experience, will be approximated in basic concepts of cognitive ergonomics and the utilization of the tool in computer use will approximate the user with motor disabilities since the tests there is a restriction only use the IOM as CHI device without any other apparatus. According to Brade [20], the test of driving process follows the steps below, which were used in evaluation methods: Test planning, Organization of material, Local preparation, Pilot test, Choice of users, Test driving, Result analysis. The intended audience for the evaluation tests was composed by students of the institution and the operating system used in the test (Microsoft Windows) for activities development. As explained before, the intention was not to assess the IOM interface specifically for disabled users (despite the central bias of the project predict that) but the general public, and this may give general contributions that are useful for the use of IOM in a specific context. If we think of features that include people with motor disabilities to use the IOM would have two most common usage scenarios. The first one would be the use at home, in different postural positions, some of which can compromise the efficiency of the usability testing and operation of the device (e.g. a lying person using computer). Another scenario, which was planned for the tests environment, it was the classroom environment, or work location in which through the IOM would be possible to include this user in a real scenario with accessibility purposes education and work, for example. We have opted for this second condition by the ease of using the actual project development educational environment. For verification in terms of usability, it was applied a script of predefined tasks consisting in a user interaction with some graphic elements arranged in the interface. This script was explained in real time to users at the moment of development of tasks, and to complete a task was revealed the next step. Uptake of these tasks listed below where the time interval was quantify between each of the tasks as well as the errors made (clicking in an inappropriate spot for example) using the formula: **time in seconds / wrong clicks**.

List of WIMP (Windows Icons Menus and pointers) tasks:

1. Click on the icon (open file manager); 2. Clicking on an icon (maximize window); 3. Make a scrolling (scroll to the bottom of the screen); 4. Clicking on an icon to open ".doc" file; 5. Clicking on an icon to changing tools tab; 6. Clicking on an icon to close

software; 7. Clicking on an icon to open file manager menu; 8. Clicking on an icon to close file manager.

The listed tasks generate quantitative data, the time of the task execution was logged by the video recording, whereby it is possible to identify some usage patterns and constant errors in the use of IOM in which usability becomes evident. In order to qualifying the user experience we apply our observations in the records recorded on video, aind in which bodily expressions and audios were collected about IOM use. It were also applied two questionnaires, one focused on the general perception of use and the the other focused use of the AttrakDiff [21] online tool which generates a User eXperience chart from opposite pairs of adjectives attributed by users to the tested device.

5   Results and Discuss

A total of 9 volunteers, 3 women and 6 men aged between 18 and 45 years, were recruited in IFSUL - campus Pelotas to develop planned tests which were applied. Most of them were students and had never used any device or eye movements based software and head pointer control in the GUI. Half of them uses glasses for visual disability and almost use the mouse as the primary interaction tool with the computer. As the testing protocol already established, at first the typical users made a routine tasks with the common mouse and then using the IOM device. This whole routine was recorded in both the GUI and through facial and body registration of users. They were also asked to answer a use experience questionnaire. Some ergonomic aspects were raised in this questionnaire about the IOM's usage on a possible fatigue generated by its use in the eyes and overall comfort.

Some of results about the questionnaire applied of the users:

- Most users stated that the use of IOM caused a little eye fatigue, or no fatigue;
- In relation to the neck comfort, which needs to be moved to control the pointer on the GUI through the IOM, three users felt a moderate to high fatigue.
- About general physical effort the data also points for most users with low or no fatigue. Only two users reported a moderate to high fatigue, which was confirmed by good comfort appointed by a majority of IOM users;
- In addition to the ergonomic aspects that generate important axes of analysis, especially regarding the IOM design principles, the functional aspects of the same interaction with the computer were answered by users, who, in general, indicated that their difficulties and overall experience of use IOM. Most users indicated difficulties both in the control of the mouse pointer's movement speed and the accuracy of the same as the charts below.

This qualitative analyse about questionnaire is confirmed as shown in Table 2, average time of tasks development in usability testing, which demonstrated the highest time spent with the IOM and the recurring errors to perform each of the tasks regarding the use of the mouse.

Table 2. Average times in the tasks in seconds /total errors numbers

User average	1	2	3	4	5	6	7	Average/errors
Mouse	3.8/1	5.3/0	4.2/0	4.3/0	5.7/1	4.6/0	2.8/0	31/4
IOM	13/1	29.5/3	19.7/2	33/1	23.4/3	54.6/14	19.6/2	186.7/24

In general terms the average time for development tasks using the traditional mouse is around 17 % faster than with the IOM. Although comparatively the mouse as a device that allowed greater flexibility (smaller tasks runtime) and a lower error rate in the context of this research, the majority of users indicated a satisfactory user experience with the IOM regarding the first use of it.

6 Discussion

Through the comparative Table 1 of systematic mapping, we can see that several studies show the use of the head and eyes movements as good techniques to be used as a control in HCI devices, especially considering the scenario of assistive technology focused on people with motor disabilities.

Even the capture of eye movements have less physical movement of the heads movements, still this movements have spent less physical effort than the employee to move arms or hands. However the results of usability evaluation with the IOM were significantly worse than the average mouse which leads us to consider some aspects. One hypothesis is that the learning curve for users, when faced to a new device, is larger, requiring of the user more time to use the same to get more consistent comparative results of IOM in relation to the mouse that is already widely used. We will require new testing devices that actually use this same technique of interaction to establish standards for more calibrated comparisons according to the device rated in the issue in here, just like as those ones listed in systematic mapping. These tests must also follow more specific protocols and be refined as established by Morimoto [6] whereby the tabulated data have higher accuracy, and this method already applied in tests with some other devices such as the Camera Mouse [4], which allows a good degree of comparison.

We evaluated the implementation of Communicability Evaluation Method (CEM), or the think loud method, on the tests and this has not established a direct relationship with the aim of testing since our goal was not to assess semantic aspects of graphic elements of the interface, but the usability and user experience with the IOM device. In terms of user experience, these tests showed that users found some difficulty in evaluating this new device because it has characteristics of objects reference (glasses and mouse) used in a new context of use, like HCI device. The estrangement in the use of this should be evaluated as normal if we consider that this new apparatus has no other similar already widespread, which makes it a product with innovative features to intended audience of people with motor disabilities. Through a questionnaire Attrak-Diff tool was qualified friendly and attractive as the IOM is. The results show how the IOM is a desirable and self-oriented device.

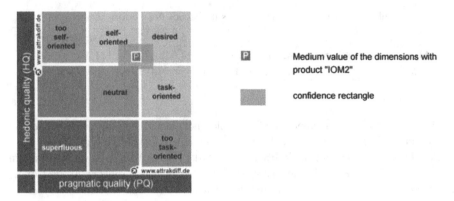

Fig. 2. Evaluation use generator perceived by IOM (Color figure online)

7 AttrakDiff Tool

In Fig. 2 the axis of the average value of the product dimensions is well on the threshold between self-directed and desirable product. There is, therefore, the interpretation of these results, the perception of space for development both in terms of usability as in hedonic quality. The user is clearly stimulated by the product, but it is at least this power valence threshold, and you can say the same regarding the perception that the product gives to self-solve. The results of usability tests confirms the need of improvement of the IOM especially in some specific points such as: cursor movement speed control; accuracy and the the click itself controlled by eye blinks presented some usability issues. Suggestions collected by users and implementation for group perceptions by IOM and its testing compared to other devices with the same purpose (some of which are already being implemented software): control from the head movement speed; implementation of graphical interface element that facilitates the control on the accuracy of the click; new click control modes, such as longer blink or time without moving the cursor to activate the action. For further work is necessary to apply new tests with these protocols and an increasing systematization of the results of the IOM compared to other assistive technologies that use the same principle of interaction, in order to generate a final product more enjoyable and usable by users with motor disabilities.

References

1. Kwan, C., Paquette, I., Magee, J.J., Lee, P.Y., Betke, M.: Click control: improving mouse interaction for people with motor impairments. In: The Proceedings of the 13th International ACM SIGACCESS Conference on Computers and Accessibility (ASSETS 2011), pp. 231–232. ACM, New York (2011)
2. Martins, J.M.S., Rodrigues, J.M.F., Martins, J.A.C.: Low-cost natural interface based on head movements. Procedia Comput. Sci. **67**, 312–321 (2015)

3. Hakonen, M., Piitulainen, H., Visala, A.: Current state of digital signal processing in myoelectric interfaces and related applications. Biomed. Signal Process. Control **18**, 334–359 (2015)

4. Naves Jr., E., Pino, P., Losson, E., Andrade, A.: Alternative communication systems for people with severe motor disabilities: a survey. BioMedical Engineering OnLine 2011

5. Feng, W., Chen, M., Betke, M.: Target reverse crossing: a selection method for camera-based mouse-replacement systems. In: PETRA 2014: Proceedings of the 7th International Conference on PErvasive Technologies Related to Assistive Environments, May 2014

6. Kurauchi, A., Feng, W., Morimoto, C., Betke, M.: HMAGIC: head movement and gaze input cascaded pointing. In: PETRA 2015: Proceedings of the 8th ACM International Conference on PErvasive Technologies Related to Assistive Environments, June 2015

7. Huo, X.: Tongue drive: a wireless tongue-operated assistive technology for people with severe disabilities, 03 November 2011. https://smartech.gatech.edu/handle/1853/45887. Accessed 02 Dec 2015

8. Ossmann, R., Thaller, D., Nussbaum, G., Pühretmair, F., Veigl, C., Weiß, C., Morales, B., Diaz, U.: AsTeRICS, a flexible assistive technology construction set. Original Res. Art. Procedia Comput. Sci. **14**, 1–9 (2012)

9. Vickers, S., Istance, H., Hyrskykari, A.: Performing locomotion tasks in immersive computer games with an adapted eye-tracking interface. ACM Trans. Access. Comput. **5**(1), Article 2, 33 p. (2013)

10. Su, M., Yeh, C., Hsieh, Y., Lin, S., Wang, P.: An image-based mouth switch for people with severe disabilities. Recent Pat. Comput. Sci. **5**, 66–71 (2012)

11. Zhu, D., Gedeon, T., Taylor, K.: Head or gaze? Controlling remote camera for hands-busy tasks in teleoperation: a comparison. In: Proceedings of the 22Nd Conference of the Computer-Human Interaction Special Interest Group of Australia on Computer-Human Interaction, OZCHI 2010, pp. 300–303. ACM, New York (2010)

12. Perez-Maldonado, C., Wexler, A., Joshi, S.: Two-dimensional cursor-to-target control from single muscle site sEMG signals. IEEE Trans. Neural Syst. Rehabil. Eng. **18**, 203–209 (2010)

13. Biswas, P., Langdon, P.: Multimodal intelligent eye-gaze tracking system. Int. J. Hum.-Comput. Int. **31**(4), 277–294 (2015)

14. Azmi, A., Alsabhan, N.M., AlDosari, M.S.: The wiimote with SAPI: creating an accessible low-cost, human computer interface for the physically disabled. IJCSNS Int. J. Comput. Sci. Netw. Secur. **9**(12), 63–68 (2009)

15. Nguyen, V.T.: Enhancing touchless interaction with the leap motion using a haptic glove. Comput. Sci. (2014)

16. Su, M.C. et al.: Assistive systems for disabled persons and patients with parkinson's disease. Lecture Notes on Wireless Healthcare Research: 105

17. Manresa-Yee, C., Varona, J., Perales, F.J., Salinas, I.: Design Recommendations for Camera-Based Head-Controlled Interfaces that Replace the Mouse for Motion-Impaired Users. Springer-Verlag, Berlin Heidelberg (2013)

18. Montanini, L., Cippitelli, E., Gambi, E., Spinsante, S.: Low complexity head tracking on portable android devices for real time message composition. Received: 1 April 2014 / Accepted: 25 February 2015 / Published online: 8 March 2015 © OpenInterface Association 2015

19. Machado, M.B., Colares, A., Quadros, C., Carvalho, F., Sampaio, A.: Oculos Mouse: Mouse Controlado pelos movimentos da cabeca do usuario, Brazilian Patent INPI n. PI10038213, Brazil (2010)

20. Brade, A.N.: Shaping Web Usability, 304 p.. Addison-Wesley, Boston (2002)

21. Hassenzahl, M., Burmester, M., Koller, F.: AttrakDiff: Ein Fragebogen zur Messung wahrgenommener hedonischer und pragmatischer Qualität. In: Mensch and Computer 2003, pp. 187–196. Vieweg + Teubner Verlag
22. World Health Organisation. World Report on Disability. Geneva: World Health Organisation (2011). http://whqlibdoc.who.int/publications/2011/9789240685215_eng.pdf? ua=1 Accessed on 20 July 2015
23. Betke, M., Gips, J., Fleming, P.: The camera mouse: visual tracking of body features to provide compute access for people with severe disabilities. IEEE Trans. Neural Syst. Rehabil. Eng. **10**(1), 1–10 (2002)
24. Alonso-Valerdi, L.M., Salido-Ruiz, R.A., Ramirez-Mendoza, R.A.: Motor imagery based brain–computer interfaces: an emerging technology to rehabilitate motor deficits. In: Original Research Article. Neuropsychologia, In Press, Corrected Proof, Available online 14 September 2015
25. Feng, W., Chen, M., Betke, M.: Target reverse crossing: a selection method for camera-based mouse-replacement systems. In: PETRA 2014: Proceedings of the 7th International Conference on PErvasive Technologies Related to Assistive Environments, May 2014
26. Perini, E., Soria, S., Prati, A., Cucchiara, R.: FaceMouse: a human-computer interface for tetraplegic people. In: Huang, T.S., Sebe, N., Lew, M., Pavlović, V., Kölsch, M., Galata, A., Kisačanin, B. (eds.) ECCV 2006 Workshop on HCI. LNCS, vol. 3979, pp. 99–108. Springer, Heidelberg (2006)
27. Kjeldsen, R.: Improvements in vision-based pointer control. In: Proceedings of ACM SIGACCESS Conference on Computers and Accessibility, pp. 189–196. ACM Press (2006)
28. Kjeldsen, R., Hartman, J.: Design issues for vision-based computer interaction systems. In: Perceptual User Interfaces 2001, Orlando, Fla (2001)
29. Missimer, E., Betke, M.: Blink and wink detection for mouse pointer control. In: Makedon, F., Maglogiannis, I, Kapidakis, S. (eds.) Proceedings of the 3rd International Conference on PErvasive Technologies Related to Assistive Environments (PETRA 2010). ACM, New York, Article 23, 8 p. (2010). doi:http://dx.doi.org/10.1145/1839294.1839322
30. Goncalves, C., Padilha Lanari Bo, A., Richay, R.: Tracking Head Movement for Augmentative and Alternative Communication

Usability Evaluation of a Wheelchair Virtual Simulator Controlled by a Brain-Computer Interface: Lessons Learned to the Design Process

Anderson Schuh[1(✉)], Marcia de Borba Campos[1], Marta Bez[2], and João Batista Mossmann[2]

[1] Faculty of Informatics (FACIN),
Pontifical Catholic University of Rio Grande do Sul (PUCRS), Porto Alegre, Brazil
anderson.schuh@acad.pucrs.br, marcia.campos@pucrs.br
[2] Faculty of Informatics (FACIN), Feevale University, Novo Hamburgo, Brazil
martabez@gmail.com, mossmann@gmail.com

Abstract. This paper presents the design, implementation and evaluation of a wheelchair simulator, which is controlled by a noninvasive Brain-Computer Interface device. We use the eye blink to control the control interface. Two experiments were conducted to evaluate the Simulator's utilization quality. The results showed that it is important to have a training phase or eye blink calibration, and a module for recognition of voluntary and involuntary blinking. The adopted scanning system for the wheelchair driving and the collision system were well accepted by the participants.

Keywords: Brain computer interfaces · Usability · Human computer interaction

1 Introduction

This article presents lessons learnt from the project, implementation and evaluation of a wheelchair virtual simulator operated by a noninvasive and low cost brain-computer interface (BCI). A BCI measures the brain activity related to the user's intention and translates into control signals, which are detected and decoded by applications [1–5]. The noninvasive BCIs can base themselves on electroencephalogram signals (EEG), device which distributes electrodes within the scalp and through them makes the electrophysiological brain activity log [1, 4, 6]. In this article, the user moves a virtual wheelchair through a blink of an eye. Therefore, the portable EEG was chosen, Neurosky Mindwave (MW) [7], which allows identifying a blink of an eye and through the strength, defines if they were voluntary or involuntary.

In this sense, [8] developed a noninvasive BCI based on motion envisioned engines, capable of controlling in a real environment, an unmanned aerial vehicle. In the training phase, this study also used a real vehicle simulator.

This is justified, since "simulation is the process of designing a computational model of a real system and conducting experiments with this model in order to understand its behavior and/or evaluate strategies for its operation".

© Springer International Publishing Switzerland 2016
M. Antona and C. Stephanidis (Eds.): UAHCI 2016, Part II, LNCS 9738, pp. 92–101, 2016.
DOI: 10.1007/978-3-319-40244-4_10

In addition, the simulation can be used when the real system does not exist yet as part of the real model planning [9]. [10] already investigated the potential use of the teaching simulations in situations where natural demonstrations were impossible to be carried out or potentially dangerous, as in a case of accidents. These factors contribute to our motivation in developing the simulator.

The simulator was developed using the game engine Unity3D. There are two scenarios, wheelchair control and drive system, detecting possible collisions system. In the simulator, the wheelchair speed is increased while it moves frontwards, being considered its weight, wheels friction with the ground and, any unevenness existing in the existing scenarios. The scenarios have targets, which appear on a predetermined manner, they may be collected by the users.

The evaluation's goal was to establish the EEG MW and the wheelchair's simulator usability. Nevertheless, the following questions were set, related to the usability goals.

- Be effective and efficient: the Simulator must allow the wheelchair to be conducted through a blink of an eye, recognized by a BCI. Questions: Is the user able to conduct the wheelchair efficiently, and collect the objects which are in a route, in the shortest time possible? Is the use of EEG MW efficient to recognize voluntary and involuntary blinks?
- Be safe on the use: the Simulator detects a possible wheelchair collision in the scenario and it disables the command which would take to such collision. Question: Was it necessary the use of the collision system?
- Be useful: the Simulator has commands which allow using the wheelchair, as well as indicators of location of the next object to be collected. Question: does the wheelchair drive and control systems allow the user to move in a desired manner in the best way possible?
- Be easy to learn how to use it: the Simulator has simple commands to move the wheelchair and spin it round, which are triggered by a BCI. Questions: Was it easy to use the BCI to conduct the wheelchair? Was it easy to learn how to conduct the wheelchair and collect the objects?
- Be easy to remember how to be used: there was a stage of experimentation/BCI adjustment to recognize the simulator and experiment the EEG MW. Question: Is it important a user training phase, so the user interacts with BCI as well as with the wheelchair's conducting system, before its use per se?

The Simulator's evaluation was performed with users in a controlled environment who had to collect objects which appeared on the scenarios. Two experiments were performed, they varied in type and size of samples, implementation stages (BCI adjustment, simulator training, object collection, object stage), time for collecting (free or determined), wheelchair control system (forward, right, left; or forward, right, left, rear), collision system (forward, right, left; or forward, right, left, rear), measure of strength which identifies a voluntary blink (fixed or customizable). These variations aimed to reduce negative aspects of the use experience identified on Experiment 1 as well as tried to improve the positive aspects to Experiment 2.

To obtain efficiency and effectiveness measures, all participants received the same tasks in each experiment. Data collection took part from the use and questionnaires observation. There were also recording logs of user's actions in which with the rest of the collected data enabled to answer questions related to the simulators and EEG MW usability as well as discuss about the participants felt regarding these resources.

There were positive results regarding the time used to perform tasks, decrease error rate, high acceptance of the wheelchair moving systems, reference of routes and collision prevention. However, the observation of the users behavior, confirmed by some given opinions showed that the use of the BCI did not respond to some participants commands, with such needed accuracy, which caused discomfort and dissatisfaction with BCI and with the manner of the commands collection to interact with the Simulator.

These issues, with the detail of project's stages, implementation and Simulator's evaluation, virtual wheelchair simulator, discussion of associated projects and lessons learnt are presented and discussed in this paper.

2   Related Papers

There are different tasks that relate the BCI use to control the wheelchair. Some studies use real wheelchairs [11–13] and others do it through virtual wheelchair [14, 15] in a computing environment. There are studies in which the chair's control is by the blink of an eye [16], movement's imagination [17] and selective attention [18]. There are systems that use mechanisms to prevent accidents involving wheelchairs [19]. Some studies use the BCI calibration sessions [20]. In addition to these, they are related to the wheelchair's control through BCI and BCI hybrid use [21, 22].

3   The Simulator

3.1   Applied Technologies

It was chosen the portable EEG NeuroSky Mindwave (MW) [7], which has an electrode disposed in the prefrontal region, Fp1 in the 10–20 pattern and a reference electrode in the ear clip. Whereas it is unlikely possible to modulate the attention and relaxation levels with precision and control, it was decided to use the blink of an eye as a way to move and rotate the wheelchair in the Simulator. The MW is capable of measuring the strength with which it is carried out a blink and pass on this information on integral values, which may vary from 1 to 255, respectively from a light blink to a strong blink, or an involuntary blink to a voluntary blink. Within the simulator system, it is possible to configure a threshold to aim a voluntary blink. As an engine to the application, it was used Unity 3D, which besides being free, has a large user community. In order to model objects, it was used Autodesk 3DS Max, which features easy integration with Unity 3D.

For this study it was developed two scenarios:

- Scenario A1: consists of a room with four sides and three creeping obstacles (Fig. 1A and B).
- Scenario A2: it is based on an open recreational area of the university campus (Fig. 1C and D). It has a "mesh" object, which prevents the wheelchair to collide with other objects while being displaced or rotated.

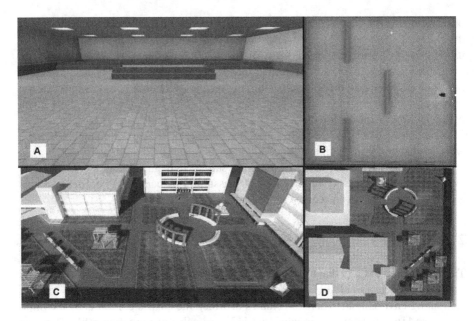

Fig. 1. Scenarios

To carry out the tasks in the scenarios, it was instantiated objects of the "Target" type, which appear in serial form inasmuch they are collected. The Simulator features an "Arrow" object, which indicates the direction of the next target to be collected, as these are not always in the active viewing area of the scenario.

The wheelchair was modeled as a reference [23]. There are two central wheels, which are responsible for the torque force that moves the chair, two rear wheels that support the central wheels with the directional control, and two front wheels, which help in the balance of the chair. In the wheelchair implementation it was defined its weight in addition to the approximate weight of a person between 18 and 34 years [24], in a total of 105 kg.

The virtual wheelchair has two maximum speed, 3.5 km/h and 7 km/h. The chair's speed is increased while it is moved forward. The speed increase also considers the wheelchair's total weight, the friction of the wheels with the ground and the existing gaps in the ground.

From the based command definition at the blink of an eye it was developed an arrows-based control system, which allows the user to control the wheelchair (Fig. 2). This follows a scanning system classified as simple, automatic and independent [25]. In this way, the scanning starts automatically and the moving and rotation arrows are highlighted by an interval of time, going to the next arrow, if it has not been chosen by the user. When the user blinks, the arrow is chosen and carries out its action immediately. To stop it, the user should blink again. The control system starts until the user selects the next action.

Fig. 2. Target indication arrow and scanning system.

As error prevention, it was developed a sensors system to avoid collisions of the wheelchair with the scenario objects. Three sensors were included in each active side of the wheelchair. When a sensor detects a possible collision, the motion of the wheelchair is interrupted and the actions that led to this collision are disabled. Returning to a state of security, the controls are reactivated.

4   Usability Evaluation

4.1   Experiment 1

Profile of the Participants. The sample was intentional and the experiment was carried out with students from a discipline of the 7th semester of an undergraduate course of Feevale University. The sample consisted of four students aged between 22 and 25 years, all male, healthy, who have not had previous contact with BCIs.

Data Collecting Tools. It was observed the use, application of questionnaires and the events record logs. The log stores the date of usage, execution starting time, the scenario that is being executed (A1 or A2), maximum speed (3.5 km/h or 7 km/h), targeted collection time, total number of avoided collisions and ending time execution.

Methodology. The experiment involves a period of Training and a Test phase, in that order. The objectives of the training phase were to experiment the EEG MW control modes and interact with the virtual wheelchair in the scenario A1. The test phase aimed to collect the targets of scenario A2 through the BCI usage.

In the training phase, there was an explanation of the functioning of the EEG MW and of the Simulator as well, and the participants had to collect 4 targets in the shortest possible time with the wheelchair's maximum speed at 3.5 km/h.

The test phase consists of two sessions, with no time limit, with intervals of two minutes between them. The task was to collect 8 targets in the shortest possible time with the wheelchair's maximum speed at 3.5 km/h in Session 1 and 7 km/h in Session 2. The targets were placed in the same positions in the two sessions. It was configured the blink threshold amounting to 75 for all users at all stages.

Findings. To analyze the results it was defined a better time, which consisted in the shortest time by target, taking into account the participants logs. Figure 3 shows the graph of the participants performance in collecting the targets in Sessions 1 and 2 of the Test phase.

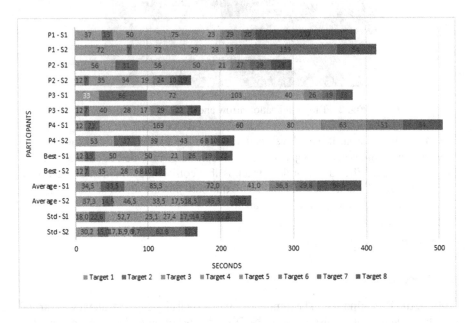

Fig. 3. Experiment 1: participants performance in Sessions 1 and 2 (Color figur online)

From this experiment, it can be noted that:

- (Be effective and efficient in the use) The scanning system which moves the wheelchair proved to be efficient, although there were difficulties related to the modulation of the blink of an eye. It is worth to emphasize that even though there is the blink threshold calibration, the EEG MW algorithm (and not of the Simulator) may encounter problems in detecting the blink as voluntary or involuntary. Still, there have been speed increasing in collecting the targets between the sessions, which may be due to the increasing of the wheelchair's speed, of the training in the BCI use, in the applicant's scanning system usage, in the prior knowledge of the scenario and location of the targets.
- (Be safe in the usage) The collision system was activated by 2 participants who had recognition difficulties of their voluntary blink by the EEG MW.
- (Be of good usage) There was no problem in the scanning system usage. There were suggestions to include a back arrow to facilitate maneuvers with the wheelchair.

- (Be easy to learn) The performance improvement between the sessions may indicate a facility to learn how to use the Simulator, which can be due to the Training stage or the sequential collection targets. Despite the initial difficulties to interact with the EEG MW, the participants indicated that the Simulator is easy to use intuitively.
- (Be easy to remember how to use) Users remembered how they should use the scanning system, how to prevent the activation of the collision system and how to adjust the blink. However, it cannot be observed if the improvement in the time was given by the training with EEG MW, knowledge of the scenario and targets location and/or continuous usage of the wheelchair's Simulator.

In order to evaluate the need for a training phase and the refinement of the scanning system, it was carried out the Experiment 2.

4.2   Experiment 2

Profile of the Participants. The sample was composed of nine volunteers, healthy, between the ages of 19 to 42, being that eight were male and one was female, without prior knowledge with the BCI.

Methodology. Experiment 2 differs from Experiment 1 mainly due to the substitution of the Training phase by the EEG MW Calibration phase for voluntary blinks training without using the Simulator scenarios. There have also been changes in the scanning and in the motion systems of the virtual wheelchair, which now has a fourth arrow to allow the chair to be moved backwards. The test phase was similar to Experiment 1.

Findings. Data were treated and represented similarly to Experiment 1. Figure 4 presents the participants' performance graph to collect the targets in Sessions 1 and 2 of the Test phase.
From the findings, the following questions are answered:

- In order to have a better user performance, it is necessary to have a training phase in the wheelchair's Simulator or is it satisfactory to have a BCI calibration phase? This experiment showed that the continuous usage of the Simulator and consequently of the EEG MW, brings improvement in the participants performance. When comparing the data collected from the initial two experimental sessions of the two experiments, it is clear that there was no gain in the performance that there has been training.
- A customization of the blink of an eye threshold would facilitate the Simulator's usage instead of using a fixed value? Yes, in general, participants reported that they had ease of use after understand the pattern of the blinks. However, some participants reported difficulties of interaction, even though they have calibrated the EEG.
- Backwards favors the replacement of the chair in the scenario to replace the use of the rotating arrows? Yes, the inclusion of this arrow allowed reducing the amount of avoided collisions and of the time while conducting the chair to collect the targets.

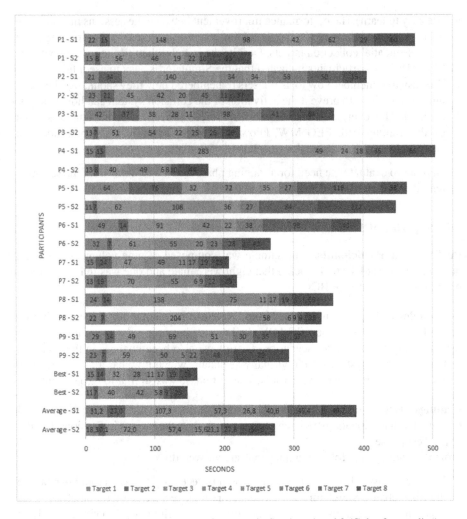

Fig. 4. Experiment 2: participants performance in Sessions 1 and 2 (Color figur online)

5   Final Considerations

This paper presented the design, implementation and evaluation of a wheelchair simulator. To interact with the simulator it was chosen the EEG MW and the commands were activated by the blink of an eye. Two experiments with different samples were carried out. The studies showed that it is important to have an EEG calibration phase in order that the users can establish which blinks should be recognized as voluntary and involuntary. The Simulator interface to conduct the wheelchair was based on a scanning system, which did not present difficulties to the participants. It is noteworthy that in the second experiment the wheelchair could be moved backwards, which optimized the chair conduction process.

From this study, the following issues have been identified for future work:

- Customization: the escalation time between the Scanning System arrows must be configured by the user. It is also considered the configuration possibilities for scenarios, targets, total time limit for collection and time target for collection.
- Vision mode of the virtual camera: the third-person perspective should be changed to the first person.
- User actions registration: for a better analysis, it is planned the threshold registration, the path traveled by the chair, being possible to check the collisions and the time that the chair moved around the scenario and the speed in which the wheelchair was at the moment.
- Improve the collision system in order to recognize objects which are not only at the sensors height.
- Carry out an evaluation with real wheelchairs users and include other interaction possibilities, besides the blink of an eye.
- Disengage the Simulator's control, making it independent from the control interface. Currently, the simulator is functional only with the use of MW. To expand the possibilities of simulator's usage, a communication protocol control will be created, being possible the use different types of control interface.

References

1. Graimann, B., Allison, B., Pfurtscheller, G.: Brain-computer interfaces: a gentle introduction. In: Graimann, B., Pfurtscheller, G., Allison, B. (eds.) Brain-Computer Interfaces. Springer, Heidelberg (2010)
2. Levine, S.P., et al.: Identification of electrocorticogram patterns as the basis for a direct brain interface. J. Clin. Neurophysiol. **16**, 448–455 (1999)
3. Leuthardt, E.C., et al.: Evolution of brain-computer interfaces: going beyond classic motor physiology. Neurosurg. Focus **27**, 4 (2009)
4. Nicolas-alonso, L.F., Gomez-gil, J.: Brain computer interfaces, a review. Sensors **12**, 1211–1279 (2012)
5. Wolpaw, J.R.: Brain-computer interfaces as new brain output pathways. J. Physiol. **579**, 613–619 (2007)
6. Lebedev, M.A., Nicolelis, M.A.L.: Brain-machine interfaces: past, present and future. TRENDS in Neurosci. **29**(9), 36–546 (2006)
7. Neurosky. Neurosky Mindwave (2015). http://www.neurosky.com/Products/MindWave.aspx. Access in: Jun 2015
8. Lafleur, K., et al.: Quadcopter control in three-dimensional space using a noninvasive motor imagery-based brain-computer interface. J. Neural Eng. **10**, 046003 (2013)
9. Filho, P.J. de F. Introdução à Modelagem e Simulação de Sistemas - com Aplicações em Arena, 1st ed. Visual Books, Florianópolis (2001)
10. Akpan, J.P.: Issues associated with inserting computer simulations into biology instruction: a review of the literature. Electronic Journal of Science Education, Southwestern University **5**(3) (2001)
11. Diez, P.F., et al.: Commanding a robotic wheelchair with a high-frequency steady-state visual evoked potential based brain–computer interface. Med. Eng. Phys. **35**, 1155–1164 (2013)

12. Iturrate, I., Antelis, J., Miguez, J.: Synchronous EEG brain-actuated wheelchair with automated navigation. In: Robotics and Automation, pp. 2318–2325 (2009)
13. Teymourian, A., Lüth, T., Gräser, A., Felzer, T., Nordmann, R.: Brain-controlled finite state machine for wheelchair navigation. Proceedings of 10th International ACM SIGACCESS Conference on Computers and Accessibility, pp. 257–258 (2008)
14. Gentiletti, G.G., et al.: Command of a simulated wheelchair on a virtual environment using a brain-computer interface (2009)
15. Grychtol, B. Lakany, H. Bernard, A. A virtual reality wheelchair driving simulator for use with a brain-computer interface. Proceedings of the 5th UKRI PG Conference in Biomedical Engineering and Medical Physics. (2009)
16. Rani, J.A.B., Umamakeswari, A.: Eletroencephalogram-based Brain Controlled Robotic Whellchair. Indian J. Sci. Technol. **8**, 188–197 (2015)
17. del R. Millán, J. et al.: Asynchronous Non-Invasive Brain-Actuated Control of an Intelligent Wheelchair (2009)
18. Ahn, S., et al.: Achieving a hybrid brain-computer interface with tactile selective attention and motor imagery. J. Neural Eng. **11**, 066004 (2014)
19. Millán, J.D., et al.: Combining brain-computer interfaces and assistive technologies: state-of-the-art and challenges. Front. Neurosci. **4**, 161 (2010)
20. Galán, F., et al.: A brain-actuated wheelchair: Asynchronous and non-invasive Brain-computer interfaces for continuous control of robots. Clin. Neurophysiol. **119**, 2159–2169 (2008)
21. Alisson, B.Z., et al.: Toward a hybrid brain-computer interface based on imagined movement and visual attention. J. Neural Eng. **7**, 026007 (2010)
22. Diez, P.F., et al.: Attention-level transitory response: a novel hybrid BCI approach. J. Neural Eng. **12**, 056007 (2015)
23. Jazzy. Product Specifications Sheet (2011). http://www.pridemobility.com/jazzy/jazzyselectelite.asp. Access in out/2013
24. IBGE. Dados amostrais e estimativas populacionais das medianas de altura e peso, por situação do domicílio e sexo, segundo a idade e os grupos de idade Brasil – período 2008–2009. 2009. http://www.ibge.gov.br/home/estatistica/populacao/condicaodevida/pof/2008_2009_encaa/tabelas_pdf/tab1_1.pdf. Access in: out/2013
25. Browning, N.: Recursos de acessibilidade ao computador. In: Schirmer, C. et al. (eds.) Atendimento Educacional especializado: deficiência física. Brasília: SEESP-SEED-MEC. http://portal.mec.gov.br/seesp/arquivos/pdf/aee_df.pdf (2007)

Long-Term Evaluation of a Modular Gesture Interface at Home for Persons with Severe Motor Dysfunction

Ikushi Yoda[1(✉)], Kazuhiko Ito[2], and Tsuyoshi Nakayama[2]

[1] National Institute of Advanced Industrial Science and Technology (AIST),
Tsukuba, Japan
i-yoda@aist.go.jp
[2] Research Institute, National Rehabilitation Center for Persons
with Disabilities (NRCD), Tsukuba, Japan
{itoh-kazuyuki-0923,nakayama-tsuyoshi}@rehab.go.jp

Abstract. We have researched gesture interfaces for persons with motor dys-function who could not use normal interface switches. The users have cerebral palsy, quadriplegia, or traumatic brain injury, and they have involuntary movement, spasticity, and so on. The purpose is to provide these users with easy and low-priced interfaces for operating PCs. To develop a low-priced interface, we used a commercially available image range sensor and developed a non-contact and non-constraint interface. For this purpose, we have collected various gestures of many persons with motor dysfunction and classified them into three types of users. We have developed seven types of gesture interfaces for users and applied three different modules to three subjects. We describe the basic structure of the gesture interfaces and their long-term evaluations.

Keywords: Gesture interface · Gesture recognition · Alternative input device · Persons with motor dysfunction

1 Introduction

Some individuals with severe motor dysfunction are unable to use existing computer interfaces due to spasticity, involuntary movements, limited range of arm motion, or diminished muscle strength. The interfaces available to these individuals, if any, are limited to customized switch interfaces, which makes it impossible for them to operate a computer with any degree of ease [9]. In their daily life, they are reliant on their caregivers to perform all but the most basic operations with household appliances such as televisions and air conditioners. Providing an environment in which these individuals can operate a personal computer with ease and use home appliances without restriction is essential for allowing them to live fulfilling and rewarding lives. Yet for disabled individuals who are only able to use simple switch-based devices, these more sophisticated operations are all but impossible. It is also very expensive to develop an interface capable of responding to changes in the individual's movements caused by physical deterioration as a result of disease progression and aging.

© Springer International Publishing Switzerland 2016
M. Antona and C. Stephanidis (Eds.): UAHCI 2016, Part II, LNCS 9738, pp. 102–114, 2016.
DOI: 10.1007/978-3-319-40244-4_11

In the present study, we conducted research and development on a gesture interface to enable simpler operation of computers and home appliances among the many individuals with motor dysfunction who have difficulty operating a standard keyboard and mouse. Specifically, we developed a contactless, non-restrictive interface using a commercially-available imaging range sensor with the aim of making it affordable to all users.

The most important factor in developing this interface was that it had to involve technology that could easily be customized to a diverse range of individual users at low cost. To this end, we collected data on the movements of various disabled individuals, classified each of these movements according to body part, and developed a modularized gesture recognition engine [1]. We then utilized the results to start a basic, long-term experiment. In this paper, we describe the framework, methods, and specific conditions of this long-term experiment.

The authors have previously developed an interface based on head gestures for individuals with severe cerebral palsy who are unable to operate a motorized wheelchair, as part of a project to assist severely disabled persons [8]. In this project, we applied high-end technologies to provide an interface required by individuals with severe motor dysfunction who were incapable of operating existing interfaces due to their intense involuntary movements. Our research focused primarily on actual clinical use in order not to deviate from how disabled individuals actually use the devices. As a result, we succeeded in developing an interface that enabled users to independently operate their wheelchairs within a secure park environment.

However, two major hurdles remained, namely the high cost of the proprietary stereo vision sensor hardware that we developed to generate range images in real time, and the high cost of adapting the interface to various disabled individuals.

In response to the first problem, the commercial release of active range image sensors leveraging the pattern projection method has meant that the hardware can now be made for around JPY20,000, making it affordable for most disabled individuals, although with the limitation that it can only be used indoors. Resolving the remaining cost issue would enable the supply of an interface that has been keenly awaited by various disabled persons. Provided that it is only used indoors, the remaining issue of adapting the interface to various disabled individuals would be resolved.

To this end, we developed an interface based on an image range sensor for cerebral palsy patients who had difficulty using existing devices due to involuntary movements outside the target recognition site or spasticity, despite the fact that their gestures could be understood by a caregiver or other experienced individual [3]. Based on the concept of promoting harmony between the human operator and device, we conducted research and development over an expedited 1-year time frame on a single cerebral palsy patient (selected as a user who would typically have difficulty operating a conventional interface) to create a customized interface focusing primarily on this user's finger gestures, as well as head (i.e., nodding) and mouth (i.e., opening and closing) gestures.

A similar research project known as "OAK" ("Observation and Access with Kinect") is being conducted to develop a solution for assisting the activities of severely disabled persons [4]. The research aims to enable disabled users to operate a computer more intuitively through the combined use of software developed with a Windows software development kit. However, this project was primarily intended for the children of disabled parents, and it is not intended as a system for classifying adaptable gestures for the disabled community as a whole. The research is also based on libraries of existing video games, which raises a fundamental problem in that there is no corresponding library for images of the user that are not taken from a frontal aspect. Another issue is that the device does not work without a particular type of sensor.

In the present study, we assume that all of the gesture recognition modules can be implemented using any available stereo vision (range image)-based human sensing technology, such as a real-time gesture recognition system [5], shape extraction based on 3D data [6], or data extraction based on long-term stereo range images [7]. We also assume that replacing the range sensor will not affect the usability of the interface. Our ultimate objective is to develop an interface that can automatically adapt to a wide range of body gestures, as well as long-term changes in how users perform these gestures.

2 Processing Structure

2.1 Collecting Data on Body Positions

Using the range image sensor, we recorded different voluntary gestures that the subjects from disability support groups and other organizations would like to see integrated into the interface. All subjects exhibited spasticity, spastic or involuntary movements, or were quadriplegics with severe motor dysfunction. Despite being able to move some parts of their body at will, all subjects had some form of motor dysfunction characterized by a constant impediment in the form of spastic or involuntary movements that made it difficult to use conventional switch-based interfaces and that severely restricted the parts of their body that they could move voluntarily. We used the range image sensor to gather data on the types of gestures that these severely quadriplegic subjects would like to use in an interface.

Focusing on these subjects who have great difficulty using a standard keyboard or mouse, we targeted the following body sites for gesture-based input.

- Hands and arms (arms, elbows, forearms, hands, fingers)
- Head (whole head movement, tongue extension/retraction, eye movement)
- Legs (exaggerated foot or leg movements)
- Shoulders

To date, we have collected gesture data for these body sites from 36 subjects over a period of about 2 years, while also listening to the opinions of the disabled users and their caregivers. In total, we have gathered data on 125 body site movements, including gestures that can be made with multiple body sites.

Before conducting the study, we obtained the informed consent of the subjects based on the approval of the Ergonomic Experimental Committee of the National Institute of Advanced Industrial Science and Technology and the Ethical Review Committee of the National Rehabilitation Center for Persons with Disabilities.

Three-dimensional (3D) movement data collected from the disabled subjects were classified and systematized based on the assumption that the movements could be recognized from the range images. In this context, the term "systematize" essentially means classifying similar movements as gestures that can be recognized by a single underlying recognition module. In other words, we assume that a module can be created that can recognize gestures for each region of the body based on the collected data. Because this approach focuses on operating a computer in a static indoor environment with no movement [2], providing high-resolution range images should enable high-precision imaging of the body region of interest without the need for a sophisticated object model or image properties requiring significant computational resources. The results are shown in Table 1.

Table 1. Classifications of gestures

	Moving one finger	17
Hand	Moving wrist	12
	Moving hand	16
	Moving entire head	19
Head	Sticking out/retracting tongue	15
	Eyes (eye movement, blinking, opening eyes wide)	17
Legs	Moving one leg from the knee down	3
	Extending/retracting knee	5
Shoulder	Up/down, forward/backward	7
Other	Currently unclassified	17
	Total body sites	125

Based on the data collected from the 36 subjects, we classified 3 types of gestures for the hands and arms, 3 types of gestures for the head, 2 types of gestures for the legs, and 1 type of gesture for the shoulders. The camera is positioned so as not to hinder the subject and is ideally located to recognize gestures, so the classification is done on the assumption that gestures can be recognized with a single model. Movements that were classified as other types of gestures were those that clearly differed from the above-mentioned gestures, even when they originated from 1 of the 4 body sites, or those that originated from a distinct body position such as the ear.

2.2 Approach Based on the Extent of Voluntary/Involuntary Movements

We have collected and classified gestures obtained from people with severe motor function disabilities, and then developed a basic prototype recognition module capable of recognizing and identifying the gestures. We have classified all subjects into three basic types.

Type 1: Little involuntary movement and small voluntary movement

Type 2: Large involuntary movement and clear and large voluntary movement

Type 3: Large involuntary movement and small voluntary movement (the most difficult type)

If we investigate the gesture interfaces for the three types, the strategies for each type are obviously different. Because the type 1 users cannot move themselves, their recognition areas are not moving. If the system can detect the recognition areas exactly, it monitors only the small movements.

On the other hand, in types 2 and 3, the recognition areas are moving, and the methods of detecting and tracking the areas are the most important. The recognition of voluntary movement is the next step in processing.

We focus on type 1 users in this paper, and we have developed a gesture interface without a body part model. Our method is detecting the recognition area by 3D data exactly and recognizing the movement by the learning method. We consider that the method will be applied to the same type of users at low cost.

2.3   Developing Site-Specific Recognition Modules

Based on the data categories shown in Sect. 2.1, we tested a series of prototype recognition modules based on the assumption that a single module could be adapted to suit multiple subjects by manually adjusting the default settings. Below is a list of body parts that have been tested thus far. Based on the above categories, the interface has now been equipped with 2 types of hand modules, 2 types of head modules, and 1 type of leg module (Table 2).

Table 2. Recognition modules

Part of body	Recognition module	Model or not
Hand	Finger gesture recognition module	Model
	Arm gesture recognition module	Model
Head	Head recognition module	Model
	Tongue recognition module	Model
Legs	Knee gesture recognition module	Model
Any part	Closest part recognition module to camera	No model
	Simple differential recognition module	No model

Although the research was initially conceived based on body site-specific recognition modules, we subsequently conceived 2 types of recognition modules without site-related models in consideration of the size and nature of the movements. These modules are shown below, specifically the module for tracking the area closest to the camera and the module for extracting subtle movements.

Recognition Module for the Site Closest to the Camera. This module tracks the movement of the most proximal part of a recognition site situated closest to the camera. For subjects in whom site-specific classification (modeling) proves difficult, this module captures the target site as accurately as possible using distance data (shape data) and then learns to recognize that portion's movements (i.e., simple properties based on differences between frames).

Simple Differential Recognition Module. For subjects in whom site-specific classification (modeling) proves difficult, this module captures the target site as accurately as possible using distance data (shape data) and then learns to recognize that portion's movements (i.e., simple properties based on differences between frames).

In summary, we have developed 5 model-based site recognition modules and 2 recognition modules without models.

3 Long-Term Evaluation

We have gathered and classified the site-specific data of numerous disabled individuals and have developed individual recognition models corresponding to the data. While we will continue to gather and classify data, our main emphasis from now on will be to develop the techniques to adapt the recognition modules to individual users. This will involve both initial personalized adaptations and adaptations to long-term subtle changes. The long-term objective is that these adaptations will be implemented semi-automatically with only the caregiver's assistance. We therefore conceived the following experiment with 3 phases in order to develop adaptive techniques for these initial and long-term changes.

3.1   Phase I: Gathering Basic Data

In the initial adaptation to individual subjects, the data requested by the subject will be recorded for a period of about 2 weeks. While the ultimate aim is to automate the personal adaptation process, the aim in this phase is to gather abundant data on subtly different wheelchair and bed positions each day. The data will then be fed into the recognition modules developed thus far so that they can acquire the various parameters.

3.2   Phase 2: Gathering Supervised Data with Recognition Functions

In the phase after completing basic personal adaptation to the recognition modules, a recording system with recognition functions will be used to collect semi-supervised signal data. Specifically, the user will be instructed to play a general music video game (such as "*Taiko Drum Master*") while evaluating the recognition performance and gathering additional data.

This approach is not 100 % accurate, because the expected timing of the user's drum beat is presumed to occur within a certain time frame, and it will likely result in the acquisition of supervised signals exceeding a certain probability. We will spend approximately 2 weeks gathering the data and will then conduct adaptive processing of the various parameters, etc., to further enhance recognition performance.

Figure 1 shows the screen of a web-based application using gesture gymnastics. The application has the same basic architecture as the above-mentioned percussion rhythm game. The parts are designed to respond to gestures from up to 4 different body sites. Each part is matched to a gesture selected by the user, which the user then performs to operate the application.

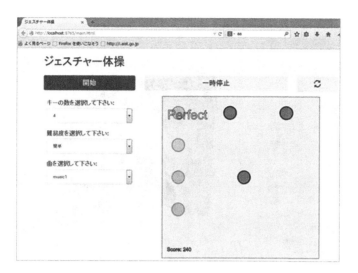

Fig. 1. Gesture gymnastics

3.3 Phase 3: Testing in Long-Term Operation

In this phase, we are conducting validation testing of an actual application upon further enhancing the recognition performance based on data such as daily changes in the relative position of the camera and user, and daily changes in the user's movements. The application used the same gesture gymnastics content as in Phase 2, with each user operating the application for 2 to 3 months. Users were asked to use the application every day if possible. The music and operating selections were based on methods best suited to each user. The aim of this testing was to assess the application's ability to handle actual long-term use after adjusting the parameters based on data acquired over a period of about one month.

4   Experiment

We have started long-term testing in 3 individuals with severe motor dysfunction. The target body sites, the level of motor function at each body site, and the extent of involuntary movements all differ among these subjects.

4.1   Subject with Multiple Target Body Sites with Minimal Involuntary Movement

The main subject in this experiment had little involuntary movement and small voluntary movement. Figure 2 indicates the monitoring image of the subject by the RGB-D camera. He is lying in his bed and basically cannot change his body positon by himself.

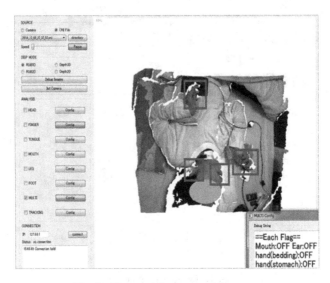

Fig. 2. User and four recognition areas

The four rectangles indicate four recognition parts. The system is able to monitor the specific movement of his mouth, the movement of his right ear, and the movements of his right and left forefingers individually. We are now setting first positions and their parameters manually. On the other hand, the daily parameters are set automatically by the user's particular actions. For applying to the daily positon changes of the camera and the user, the user performs the music game for one to two minutes, and the system adjusts all parameters automatically.

The cables in Fig. 2 are for the one-switch device and the trackball. The user could use his right and left forefingers for the interface. Our system uses one RGB-D camera, which monitors his whole upper body, and four switch interfaces can be used simultaneously. We consider that this user is suitable for our interface system to improve it though our experiments.

The long-term evaluation testing targeted a combination of 2 recognizable body sites selected by the user (Fig. 3).

4.2 Subject with Typical Head Movements

This test targeted a subject with a high cervical spine injury who was able to operate a wheelchair but required the assistance of a caregiver to operate remote control switches and a personal computer. Head movement was selected as the target recognition site. The subject exhibited almost no involuntary movements and, although he did not have the range of head motion available to a healthy individual, the level of difficulty required for gesture recognition was not high. While simple estimation of head inclination can be performed with existing 2D recognition engines, this experiment was conducted using range images with the aim of not only estimating head inclination, but

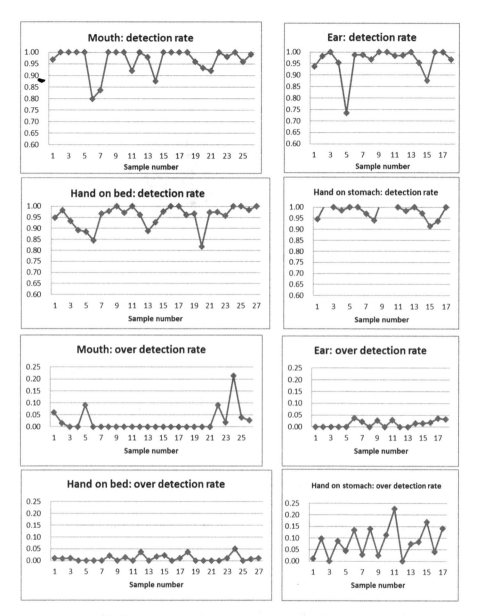

Fig. 3. Parts: simple detection rate and over detection rate

also enabling combined recognition of other sites on the subject's upper body, and adapting to users whose sideways and vertical movements differed in magnitude.

The test was conducted by assigning 3 channels according to the user's preferred gestures, namely a frontal → right-facing → frontal gesture, a frontal → left-facing → frontal gesture, and a frontal → downward-facing → frontal gesture. The evaluation testing also obtained results on these 3 operating methods (Figs. 4 and 5).

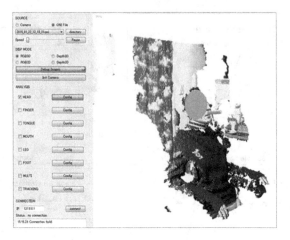

Fig. 4. Gesture recognition for subject 2

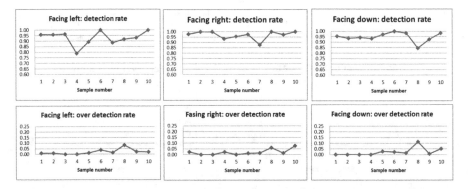

Fig. 5. Facing left, right, and down: simple detection rate and over detection rate

4.3 Finger Recognition Subject with Frequent Involuntary Movements

This test targeted a subject with cerebral palsy who had the highest level of difficulty in terms of large involuntary movements and limited recognizable voluntary movements. The subject's only voluntary movement was the middle finger on one hand, while his arms exhibited significant involuntary movements that prevented his hands from remaining still, thus necessitating constant tracking of hand position. The subject's constantly-moving hands also made it necessary to perform recognition of the fingers regardless of whether they were facing forward, left, or right (recognition was simply not possible when images of the subject's fingers could not be captured).

The actual recognition process is depicted in Fig. 6. The red rectangle indicates the target recognition site. A colored sack was attached to enhance the resolution of the range images and to offset the intensity of the subject's involuntary movements.

There was only 1 type of operation, so the evaluation test was conducted every day, and the test music was changed where appropriate (Table 3).

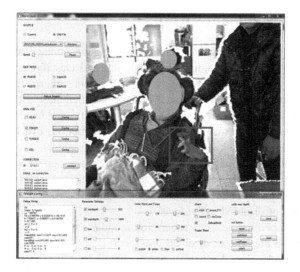

Fig. 6. Gesture recognition for subject 3

Table 3. Finger: simple detection rate, over detection rate, and involuntary gesture numbers

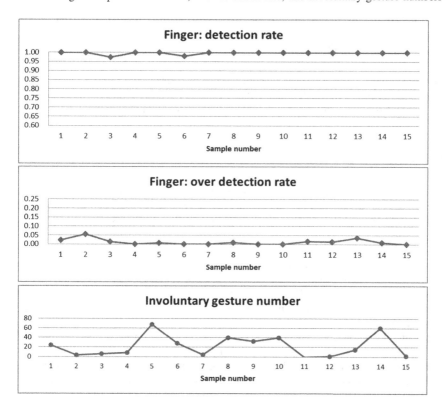

5   Conclusions and Future Work

In the present study, we attempted to adapt an inexpensive, contactless, non-restrictive sensor to various disabled individuals by gathering and classifying 3D data on the diverse movements of actual disabled users. Using the data gathered from 36 users, we obtained gesture data from 125 body sites. We then classified these data into a total of 9 body sites capable of voluntary movement, namely the arms and hands (fingers, wrists, forearms), head (head movement, tongue extension/retraction, eye movement), legs (swinging and opening and closing of the knees), and shoulders.

At the same time, we classified disabled users by focusing on the size and nature of target site movements. This classification was based on the extent of involuntary movements, as well as voluntary movements, at target sites. As a result, we were able to classify 3 types of disabled individuals.

We then developed the gesture recognition modules based on the classification of target body site and the type of disabled user.

Specifically, we developed a head recognition module, a finger recognition module, and a simple differential recognition module without a target model, and conducted long-term testing on 3 disabled individuals. The testing was divided into 3 phases, and the recognition results were presented. In terms of basic testing, useful recognition results were obtained in 3 subjects.

In the future, we intend to continue long-term testing by conducting the third test phase involving the use of an actual application and the automatic acquisition of routine data on recognition parameters.

Acknowledgment.   This work was supported in part by a Health and Labor Sciences Research Grant: Comprehensive Research on Disability Health and Welfare in 2014. The authors grate-fully acknowledge the many who have supported and encouraged this work.

References

1. Yoda, I., Itoh, K., Nakayama, T.: Collection and classification of gestures from people with severe motor dysfunction for developing modular gesture interface. In: Antona, M., Stephanidis, C. (eds.) UAHCI 2015. LNCS, vol. 9176, pp. 58–68. Springer, Heidelberg (2015)
2. Yoda, I., Tanaka, J., Raytchev, B., Sakaue, K., Inoue, T.: Stereo camera based non-contact non-constraining head gesture interface for electric wheelchairs. In: Proceedings of International Conference of Pattern Recognition ICPR 2006, vo. l4, pp. 740–745 (2006)
3. Yoda, I., Nakayama, T., Ito, K.: Development of interface for cerebral palsy patient by image range sensor. Grant Program Report Tateishi Sci. Technol. Found. **22**, 122–125 (2013). (in Japanese)
4. Iwabudhi, M., Guang, Y., Nakamura, K.: Computer vision for severe and multiple disabilities to interact the world **37**(12), 47–50 (2013) (in Japanese)
5. Monekosso, D., Remagnino, P., Kuno, Y.: Intelligent environments: methods, algorithms and applications (Advanced Information and Knowledge Processing). In: Yoda, I., Sakaue, K. (eds.), Chapter 6 Ubiquitous Stereo Vision for Human Sensing, pp. 91–107. Springer-Verlag, Heidelberg (2009)

6. Hosotani, D., Yoda, I., Sakaue, K.: Wheelchair recognition by using stereo vision and histogram of oriented gradients, in real environments. IEEE Workshop Appl. Comput. Vis. **2009**, 498–503 (2009)
7. Onishi, M., Yoda, I.: Visualization of customer flow in an office complex over a long period. In: Proceedings of International Conference on Pattern Recognition (ICPR), pp. 1747–1750 (2010)
8. Tanikawa, T., Yoda, I., et al.: Home environment models for comfortable and independent living of people with disabilities. J. Hum. Life Eng. **12**(1), 23–27 (2011). (in Japanese)
9. "Survey on persons with physical disability 2006," Department of Health and Welfare for Persons with Disabilities, Social Welfare and War Victims' Relief Bureau, MHLW (2006)

Universal Access to Mobile Interaction

How to Achieve Design for All:

"List", "Focus" and "Multimodality" as Minimal Requirements

Denis Chêne[(✉)], Éric Petit, and Sophie Zijp-Rouzier

Orange Labs, 28 Ch du Vieux Chêne, 38243 Meylan, France
{denis.chene,eric.petit,sophie.zijprouzier}@orange.com

Abstract. This paper introduces basic principles for "design for all". List, focus, multimodal feedbacks and several action means are the keys. A generic touch-based interface component (MenuDfA) was designed, offering hierarchical navigation with continuous and secure gestures along with a high level of flexibility. A novice user profile was set. A comparative test to a classical tactile interface shows that the optimized interface for novice users solves difficulties, but generates also some issues. These latter have been easily resolved through parameters adjustment.

Keywords: Design for all methods techniques and tools · Access to mobile interaction · Design for all best practice · Accessibility guidelines · Universal design methodology · Touch-based interaction · Continuous manipulation · Menudfa · Handheld device

1 Introduction

Reverse of the traditional way of adjusting afterward standard interfaces to diversity (the Assistive Technologies way), "Design for all" methodology aims at providing continuity between accessibility features and standard ones [2]. But user interfaces (UI) are mainly visually oriented and rely on absolute positioning, whereas some accessibility profiles need exclusively relative positioning (pointless interface). Closing this gap is both a social and technical challenge with the objective of designing interfaces for all kind of users in different contexts of use.

The interface elements organization, types of menus, kinds of controls, and in case of a touch-based interface, kinds of gestural commands, are all the questions this paper tries to cater to. First we explore user needs and basic user interface requirements to reach design for all purpose. By extracting common interaction patterns we underline that simple "List" (or "Menu") and "Focus" are prerequisite elements to achieve universal approach, along with minimal commands and multimodal feedbacks. On this basis, a user interface for hand-held device has been designed. His architecture is described. An optimized profile dedicated to novice users is defined. It has been assessed in a controlled user study. Experimental results highlight some useful improvements that result in an enhanced profile well suited for novice users. Discussion follows on

© Springer International Publishing Switzerland 2016
M. Antona and C. Stephanidis (Eds.): UAHCI 2016, Part II, LNCS 9738, pp. 117–128, 2016.
DOI: 10.1007/978-3-319-40244-4_12

how core interaction patterns and "list" and "focus" elements are likely useful for other interaction profiles.

2   User Needs Overview

2.1   Design for All Methodology: First Resolve Borderline Issues

Norman's interaction model [9] details human-machine interaction loop into two main phases, execution and evaluation. Physical, sensory and cognitive affordances [18] are the first basic levels of the interaction loop. They all need to be adjusted to each kind of user, as such content themselves.

Human Centered Design approach requires defining user needs and context of use [4, 14] and to identify common interaction patterns that may be extracted from user needs. In his dimensions dedicated to set priorities, Vanderheiden [17] defines a level 1 with the condition to be compliant to each kind of interaction specificities. But some interaction situations are easier to solve than others. For instance, resolving a low zoom level user need is easier to achieve, as it is not so far away from a standard interface, than resolving a very high zoom level that is significantly different from standard interaction schema. This gap from standard interaction has to be taken into account because it has great consequences on design effort.

This paper argues for coping first with interaction logics that are far away from the standard one. Those interaction logics should be the first design starting point. Indeed, when they are lately taken into account in a subsequent design, it's really hard, costly and times consuming to treat them. Those interaction specificities are well known and clearly detailed in [5]. They consist of sequential interaction, pointless interaction, secure navigation, minimal commands, refined design, and various mono-modalities. Afterwards, other interaction logics should be easily handled.

2.2   Interaction Basic Components to Design for All

Rendering for All. On the interaction level, users need that interface elements are rendered in many suitable ways. It addresses texts, colors, images, tactile, sounds and type of voices. These elements should be available through a single modality, and also through multimodality. They should be sequentially available or rendered in parallel way as some users are restraint to sequential perception (audio, tactile, restricted visual display) or can use parallel one (mainly vision). There are also some needs about rendering information rhythm. Indeed user may need slow down information or accelerated one. All this range of rendering aspects should be handled by the user interface.

Actions for All. Regarding the action part, some users need step by step actions (sequential actions, and/or selection separated from validation) or direct access (short-cuts, selection-validation fusion). But some of them have only monotask capacity or some other are able to deal with multitasks. Some of them need totally pointless interface, and other need to point at, which implies visual-motor or audio-motor coordination (deictic, head or finger). Finally there may be some needs of "uncolocated" actions (to act somewhere whereas the selected object is elsewhere) or colocated ones (to act where the selected object is). All this range of action means has to be available.

Adaptability. As seen previously, at the interface level those actions and rendering effects need to be adjustable from preset profiles to personalized one. Adjustment of the perception and action means should be available at the interaction level (a blind user will need a slow synthesis at the beginning but will quickly ask for a speedy one). They also should be available at the task/functional level (a novice user needs less available functions than an expert user).

Contents for All. Content needs address linguistic and cultural diversity (written and oral languages, signed languages). This is valuable for text but also for images. Indeed some images or icons are relevant in a certain context but may be not in a different culture [13]. Some contents need to be slightly reworded or simplified (for novice user, or in case of other cognitive constraints). Again, users need sometimes augmented contents (audio description for the blind or close caption for the deaf). All this range of contents should be available for each kind of user.

In the following part a generic navigation component is presented [10, 11]. This component aims at catering previous requirements of rendering, actions, adaptability, and contents for all. It is a set of consistent interaction techniques which demonstrates effective alternatives to visual-centric interface designs on mobile devices.

3   Implementation of a Generic Component for Touchbased Interfaces

In most graphical user interfaces (GUI), there are too many objects and it's really a mess for novice or disabled user to deal with them. Several innovative approaches about how to design "menus" were explored [3, 8, 12]. But those menus are still limited to a single usage and are not able to embrace the diversity of context of use. Moreover as they often rely on pointing, they generate accessibility limitations. Those complex objects are difficult to adapt to user or context limitations. But they all have in common to offer to make a choice among several proposals. Reducing interaction to this basic task, leads us to consider a string of elements usually displayed as a list.

3.1   Interface Objects Simplification to a Vertical List

A list is a basic interface element that enables to make choices. It can be displayed globally, or sequentially, it has a well-known spatial and linear organization, it can be adjusted to each modality, and can be easily warped to many visual adjustments. It's a generic container for colors, texts, images. It is suited to reading optimization provided that it's displayed vertically. A succession of tabs is also a list, but horizontally displayed. Those are not really optimized for rapid reading and are not adapted in case of numerous items. These are the reasons why vertical lists are the primary requisite. Starting from a *vertical list* doesn't prevent the use of more complex components as they can be recomposed afterwards for other interaction profiles. Thereby, a mosaic can be considered as a spatially spread list that still can be browsed sequentially through a Z logical path, from left to right. So starting from list and expand it to mosaic (more adapted to pointing interfaces) is still feasible. Even a slider can be considered as a list of items. Actually, most complex graphical components can be simplified in a listview, intrinsically sequentially browsable. This approach centered on the list element involves that the whole application is a cascading hierarchy of list elements.

3.2   Navigation Commands and Focus

To navigate easily through this hierarchy and inside each list is an important point for accessibility. Indeed user needs to learn the interface without the risk of missed validations. Secure navigation can be achieved through selection and validation dissociation. And pointless navigation can be achieved with focus manipulation. If a focus is materialized on the interface (visually, auditively and tactilely) and manipulated by the user, then selecting an item can be differentiated from validating it, with or without the need to point at it. Navigation through nested lists involves only four commands even if other ones may be added for other profiles (as shortcut commands). It can be achieved through Next-Previous navigation inside the current list, and through going In or Out hierarchy levels. Those commands can be achieved through many types of different gestures or other controls (as vocal), but the major point is that only four navigational commands are mandatory. Another command is useful for some users that don't have immediate feedback about the ongoing focused item. This command is called "get info" command. It enables to inform the user about the current focused item or the UI state. Rendering effect of current manipulation is expressed visually with a focus. As for vertical list rendering, it may be displayed through vocal, audio, visual, and tactile modalities.

3.3   MenuDfA Component

MenuDfA is a generic navigation component for touch-based interfaces under Android OS which implements principles mentioned above along with several interaction profiles optimized to each kind of user. So, MenuDfA focused on overcoming difficulties faced by part of the population when operating touch-based interfaces, especially smartphones [6, 7, 15]. In particular, standard pointing gestures, such as "tap" pose several usability problems: they require high positioning accuracy and temporal control and imply strong visual-motor coordination. Beyond being prone to manipulation error, they are not suited to all users (e.g. a person with low vision). This is exacerbated by the fact that standard touch interaction does not separate selection and validation: you just brush the screen and the item underneath finger is triggered. In fact, there is no means to safe explore the interface before using its features. In addition, modern touchscreen interfaces embed various interface elements (e.g. icons, tabs, grids, vertical and horizontal lists, widgets, ...) which provide rich but heterogeneous layouts and behaviors. The consequence is twofold, on one hand, this generates cognitive load for the user, and on the other hand, this prevents incorporating appropriate navigation mechanisms for achieving usability for all.

MenuDfA component combines following principles. Firstly, it organizes the various items of the intended application in the form of a set of hierarchical lists where the items of each list are displayed vertically. Secondly, MenuDfA provides a sequential access to the interface elements, as well as a direct access. In both cases selection and validation may be set to two separated operations. Interaction mode can be set to pointless or pointed at, and thus allowing uncolocated or colocated actions. Therefore it covers a large diversity of user needs and situations.

Sequential navigation relies on the use of a selection focus that the user manipulates by means of slide gestures. Thus, the user can navigate the entire application just by moving the focus in the four directions: Vertical displacements for moving through the on screen items, and horizontal displacements for moving through the hierarchy of lists. The mapping of the gestures is chosen to be aligned with the displacement of the focus (up, down, right and left). Note, that contrary to classical touch screen interfaces; here the gestural interaction doesn't rely anymore on absolute positioning as all the gestures make use of relative positioning (they can begin anywhere on the screen). Moreover, gesture can be discrete or continuous. A discrete mapping means that, between the moment the finger touch the screen and the moment it leaves the surface, a gesture triggers a unique command (e.g. move the focus to the next item). This is the most current in sequential interfaces. Continuous mapping consists in a continuous gesture control of the focus. In that case, the detection criterion relies on the distance traveled by the finger during gesture, combined with the movement direction. This implies to define a special transfer function (similar to a CD-gain [1]) between the motor space and the visual space. In that case, appropriate feedbacks have to be designed in order to ensure a smooth coupling between perception and action, as implemented in MenuDfA.

Direct access to interface elements (classical way), is still available with MenuDfA in order to allow pointing when it is more appropriate for the user. So, the user can choose to "Press & Hold" onto the intended item. In that case, validation consists in two phases: firstly selection (i.e. the focus comes underneath finger on the intended item), then validation of the selected item after a given time. It is different from classical interfaces where the both are merged. Note, that here, depending on the setting value of the time duration between selection and validation, these two phases are more or less separated. To summarize, MenuDfA provides separate selection and validation operations both through direct access and sequential access. This feature is then combined with appropriate feedback (e.g. vocal and tactile feedback) to ensure secure exploration of the interface, meaning the possibility for the user to get prior information on a given function before to trigger it. In the case of sequential access it allows furthermore to use "relative positioning", eliminating the need to point at a precise place, thus relaxing constraints on absolute positioning and on visual control. Those properties are fundamental to address usability for all.

The third characteristic of MenuDfA is related to the flexibility of interaction, both in terms of feedback and gestures. Regarding gestures, Table 1. gives the whole set of gestures managed by MenuDfA. In addition, a set of parameters is provided along with these various gestures allowing to finely customize each type of interaction according to the user needs. The next part deals with MenuDfA's architecture and design.

Table 1. Gestures available in MenuDfA component

Vertical navigation ("selection" command) or Information feedback ("get info")		
Gesture description	**Associated Command**	**Targeted profiles**
↑↓ Vertical slides, with inertia and continuous mapping without colocation constraint	- the focus moves up or down.	- novice - elderly - standard/expert
↑↓ Vertical slides (discrete mapping if fast and continuous if slow), without inertia nor colocation	- the focus moves up or down.	- blind - motor1
● located Press&Hold (direct access)	- Selection (the focus jump underneath finger)	- customized
◉ Tap without colocation constraint (anywhere on the screen)	- get information (vocal, visual tooltip) on the current selection	- low vision, blind - illiterate, cognitive - motor1
◉ Tap without colocation constraint	- the focus moves to the next item	- motor2 - blind
Gestures for horizontal navigation (only validation or back command)		
Gesture description	**Associated command**	**Targeted user profiles**
→ Right slide without colocation constraint	- validation of the selected item.	- standard/expert - blind
← Left slide without colocation constraint	- back to the upper level	- all profiles
● Press&Hold without colocation constraint	- validation of the selected item	- motor1&2 - blind
◉ ◉ Double tap without colocation constraint	- validation of the selected item - zoom in/out	- customized
Combined gestures for vertical and horizontal navigation (selection and validation)		
Gesture description	**Associated command**	**Targeted profiles**
└▼ Spatial compound gesture without colocation constraint	- selection, then validation, then selection, then validation	- standard/expert - blind
●→ located Press&Hold then slide Right	- selection (the focus jump underneath finger) then validation	- standard/expert
● located Press with a very short delay (almost Tap)	- selection and immediate validation	- near-usual tactile interface
● located Press&Hold with a medium delay	- selection then validation	- standard/expert - novice
● located Press&Hold with a long delay	- selection then validation	- illiterate - cognitive
⌐↵ Symbolic gesture without colocation constraint	- launch of a specific command	- expert

3.4   Architecture

Design for all in the field of HCI results in complex software systems, primarily because it relies on a global design approach which must cope with various human and technical factors. Among these factors, we find: multimodal rendering (visual, audio, tactile), navigation logic, gesture recognition, and customization capabilities. When considered together it poses a great technical concern. For example, making a simple sequential, circular and re-sizable item list with standard API (e.g. Android 5.0) is already a problem in itself because such mechanisms are not originally supplied. Likewise, manipulating a selection focus with slide gestures is not common (and thus available) and requires implementing a dynamic transfer function along with a gesture recognition engine. And also, designing a flexible event-driven program that allows hot-changing the interaction mode is not so common. That's why MenuDfA's software architecture involves several modules and frameworks. In particular, it consists of the following pieces: a gestural interaction framework named DGIL as a C ++/Java library, an event-driven programming framework named AEvent as a Java library, a graphical sequential list view named DfAList as a Java Class, a graphical "pager" named DfAPager as a Java Class to handle the lists hierarchy and a central module based on a Model-View-Controller architecture (MVC).

In this schema, DGIL provides a syntactic description of the gesture during its articulation, in the form of a sequence of gestural primitives. They chunk the gestural dialog into meaningful units, allowing a one-to-one correspondence between desired operations and gesture. For example, in a particular mode of DGIL, a "Press & Hold" gesture gives rise to the following sequence:

PRESS → SHORT_PRESS → LONG_PRESS → RELEASE → END_GESTURE

A vertical slide leads to a richer one:

PRESS → SHORT_PRESS → START_MOVE →EARLY_MOVE_DOWN
(1   %,2   %,4   %,9   %,17   %,30   %,53   %,
90 %) →MOVE_DOWN→ EARLY_MOVE_DOWN
(0 %,4 %,13 %,25 %,48 %,73 %)→CANCEL_EARLY_MOVE→END_GESTURE

In this example, the MOVE_DOWN primitive indicates (and causes) an effective change of item selection. But before it occurs, a series of EARLY_MOVE_DOWN primitives is emitted. This series of events is in charge of continuously moving the focus during the transient phase. This primitive has a parameter which indicates the percentage of distance to travel before triggering the change. In fact, this parameter is used to implement the transfer function that drives the motion rendering of the focus. More specifically it ensures that it works at all scales, that the CD-gain is correct (equal to 1 on average), and that the motion direction is always taken into account. Actually, within the software architecture, DGIL's primitives are converted into events of type AEvent.

Regarding AEvent, firstly it provides a means to implement flexible coupling between events and commands, allowing changing the gesture mapping at run-time. Secondly, it handles memory persistence of the parameters, facilitating customization. With AEvent framework, one can create "Handlers" that contain each a collection of event-command pairs, and then create a "Profile" that gathers several handlers which determine a particular user profile. Concerning the central module, it integrates DGIL-AEvent with an MVC design pattern, as a key point to reduce and master complexity in order to handle multi-profile.

4   Test of the Profile for "Novice User"

Even if the different profiles were built upon user needs analysis, a user centered design methodology requires checking continually that needs are still met. A controlled study was conducted to evaluate novice and expert tactile interaction modes. Those profiles where defined from studies underlying elderly people difficulties with tactile interfaces [7] and also the opportunity to use thumb interaction [6, 16] knowing that single-handed device is a very current context of use.

An interaction profile for novice users (N interface) was designed. Touch-based interaction in the N interface was designed to cater to novice constraints. As they need time to ask for information and to feel confident, selection time was separated from validation time. Thus, focus manipulation (selection) is followed by validation. This means that standard tap cannot be used and must be replaced by continuous manipulation: either using "Press & Hold" with a long delay of 800 ms (●) or using vertical and horizontal slides (∧∨ ←→). As they need support for pointing with inaccuracy then large items were designed and pointing with tolerance zone was added. As they need access to any screen area through the thumb, then selection and validation were available without colocation constraint. Thus it means that the user can manipulate the focus while pointing at another location (see Fig. 1) as well as on the same (Fig. 2).

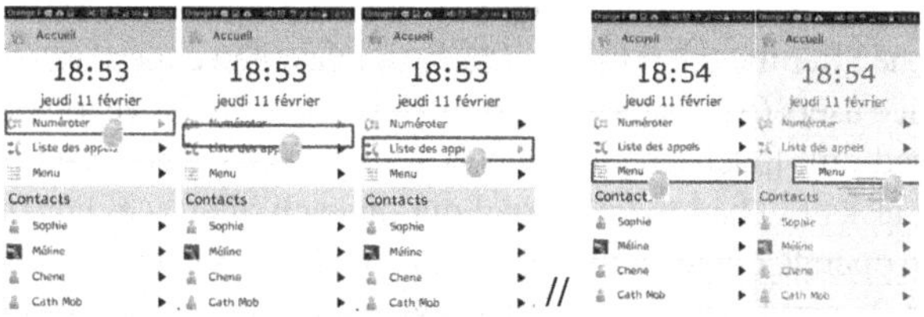

Fig. 1. Colocated continuous Up-Down focus manipulation (selection) and colocated Right gesture (validation).

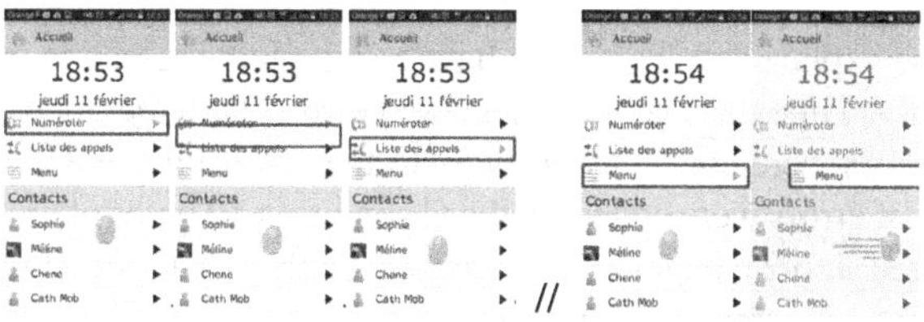

Fig. 2. Uncolocated continuous Up-Down focus manipulation (selection) and uncolocated Right gesture (validation).

To sum up, in the N interface, selection can be performed either by a continuous vertical slide or by a Press & Hold (under 800 ms). In the latter case, selection occurs during the first stage of the press and gives rise to the vocalization of the current focused item.

Validation follows as a second stage only if the user holds his press after 800 ms (⬤). Otherwise, the user can validate with a slide towards right (➔). Similarly, the back command is a continuous gesture to the Left, also without colocation constraint (⬅), which implies that no back button is displayed on the N interface. When an uncolocated Tap ◉ is executed (anywhere on the screen), then it repeats vocalization of the focused item. It enables user to ask for information as much as he wishes. In order to perform a meaningful comparison of the two tactile interaction modes, an equivalent Classical tactile interface was also designed (C interface). On the C interface only the standard Tap is available to achieve selection/validation in a unique phase. Hence, it implies colocation constraint. Back action is available on the screen with a back button on the top left part of the screen. C and N interfaces were designed with the same functionalities enabling making a phone call from number dialing, or from contact selection, or from call log history. Contact list is available and contacts are editable. The only visual differences between these two interfaces are the existence in the N interface of a focus element (a rectangle), some visual feedbacks associated to continuous manipulation, and the lack of any back button.

4.1 Comparative User Test

This novel interface optimized for novice user (N) was compared to its classical version (C). Experimental plan was the following: S10 < I2*T5 >. N and C interfaces (I factor) were both used one after the other by 10 elderly touchscreen expert users and 10 elderly touchscreen novice users (S). Users were from 70 years old to 74 years old. Novice users had never touched any touchscreen devices. Expert users were used to use a tactile mobile phone. 5 tasks (T) had to be carried out on each interface. For one of them the user was asked to operate device with only one hand. Experimentation duration was one and half an hour. N and C interfaces order was counterbalanced. And before each of them some explanations about the tactile interaction mode were given to user. For the N interface the explanation was: «you have to move the focus in order to select the item you want. Then validate it doing a right gesture». If the user had some difficulties to execute this pre-test, then it was added: «you can also do a long press to validate». For the C interface the explanation was: «you have to tap on the screen in order to validate the item you want». Time, task achievement, and errors were recorded in log files, and on videotapes. Errors were coded accordingly to the type of generated errors. In the N condition 9 types of errors were coded. In the C condition 10 types of errors were coded. They were gathered into 2 categories: pointing inaccuracies, focus adjustment difficulties, non-actable items (*common pointing* errors named *CP*) and some specific N condition errors about *laterality confusion* (very few) and *missed validations due to uncolocation* (named *MVU*).

Results. A Wilcoxon signed ranks test shows that in N condition novice global errors were as numbered as in C condition (novice N errors M = 1.75, SD = 2.37 and C errors M = 1.78, SD = 2.34) whatever was the task. This was not expected as in the N condition uncolocation and Selection-Validation dissociation were here to solve gesture inaccuracies and careless mistakes. Further analysis shows that this is due to the specific errors that appear in N condition (*MVU*). Indeed, novice users are constantly stuck to direct pointing. It was awaited for expert users of standard tactile pointing interfaces as they are used to directly point at items, but it wasn't for novice users. Actually, uncolocated validation makes the user to validate another item without realizing that it is not the focused one. The Right gesture without colocation constraint ($\rightarrow$) is a trap for novice and expert users until they have acquired that the focus can be used in an uncolocated manner. On the contrary the Left gesture ($\leftarrow$) doesn't generate error at all as it is never dependent on location (it just goes back to the previous level).

Details results show that if one focuses on *CP* errors only, then the N condition fulfills its goal. Indeed Mann-Whitney test shows, that *CP* errors (gesture inaccuracies and pointing located errors) are significantly fewer in number (z = 2.42, p < .01) for novice in N condition (*CP* errors M = 0.31, SD = 0.77) than for novice in C condition (*CP* errors M = 1.78, SD = 2.34). To sum up, these usual errors due to short press gestures and tight coupling between validation and selection (classical Tap) are mainly done on C prototype but very few on N prototype, as expected (Fig. 3). Hence, N condition with its "Selection & Validation" dissociation and its numerous facilitations has served its purpose to substantially reduce expected usual errors.

One of the tasks asked users to operate one-handed with the thumb. Similarly, if one focuses on *CP* errors, results show that in N condition novice users (M = 0.5, SD = 0.93) are doing quite as much errors as expert users (0), i.e. almost zero. In thumb interaction mode, N condition made the glass ceiling disappear between novice and expert users. It is not the case in the C condition where novice users (M = 3.75, SD = 3.54) are doing significantly more errors (z = 2.383, p < .02) than expert users (M = 0.625, SD = 1.06). Usual pointing interface (C) is still a trap for novice users, and also for expert users that make errors in such one-handed situation. On the contrary, N condition is well suited both for novice and expert users in a one-handed situation, considering *CP* errors.

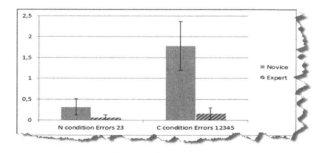

Fig. 3. Mean of expected errors (without *MVU* errors) in N condition vs C condition

Novice Profile Adjustment. According to this study, we have adjusted the novice interaction profile in disabling the Right gesture validation, which was the cause of missed validation due to uncolocation errors (*MVU*). This was done easily just by setting an option, taking advantage of our flexible architecture. Other adjustments are planned in order to improve display specifications (size, contrast, and legible "Accessible DfA" font[1]), audios and tactile feedbacks synchronization.

5   Discussion and Conclusion

Through this experimental study, an innovative touchscreen interaction optimized to novice users was defined, tested and adjusted. Right validation gesture, as source of many uncolocation errors wasn't kept in the final novice profile. Selection-Validation phases dissociation was confirmed as appropriate. Left, Up and Down gestures, and Simple Tap for getting information about the current focused item turned out to be well suited to novice users. Improvement of the novice profile was easily made after the test thanks to the general great flexibility offered by MenuDfA's architecture. A multimodal interface built upon list and focus, enabling continuous commands (gestures, vocals) enables to plainly deal with many profiles. Blind user profile is not so far from the novice one. The only difference is that they don't need colocated Press & Hold but need uncolocated Right gesture that is totally suitable in their case. Some motor impaired users using the back of their hand (fingers up) may be glad to use it in the same way. For them, Left and Right gestures may be an easy way to navigate inside the list hierarchy. Novice profile is also interesting in case of illiterate users because these latter are often novice in technology. The main difference is that they are not able to read the nature of the item, thus they need to ask for information more frequently. For them located Press & Hold with a long delay will certainly be useful. Other cognitive, expert, and low vision profiles are under study.

References

1. Casiez, G., Vogel, D., Balakrishnan, R., Cockburn, A.: The impact of control-display gain on user performance in pointing tasks. In: HCI 2008, vol. 23, pp. 215–250 (2008)
2. Constantine, S.: Adaptive techniques for universal access. User Model. User Adap. Inter. **11**, 159–179 (2001)
3. Francone, J., Bailly, G., Lecolinet, E., Mandran, N., Nigay, L.: Walvet menus on handheld devices: stacking metaphor for novice mode and eyes-free selection for expert mode. In: ACM AVI (2010)
4. Guide 71. Guide for addressing accessibility in standards. ISO/IEC Guide 71 (2014)
5. ISO/IEC 29138-1: User needs summary. To be published 2017. ISO/IEC/SC35/WG6
6. Karlson, A.K., Bederson, B.B., Contreras-Vidal, J.L.: Understanding single-handed mobile device interaction. In: Lumsden, J. (ed.), Handbook of Research on User Interface Design and Evaluation for Mobile Technologie, pp. 86–101 (2008)

---

[1] Available at https://github.com/Orange-OpenSource/font-accessible-dfa.

7. Kobayashi, M., Hiyama, A., Miura, T., Asakawa, C., Hirose, M., Ifukube, T.: Elderly user evaluation of mobile touchscreen interactions. In: Campos, P., Graham, N., Jorge, J., Nunes, N., Palanque, P., Winckler, M. (eds.) INTERACT 2011, Part I. LNCS, vol. 6946, pp. 83–99. Springer, Heidelberg (2011)

8. Lee, D.S., Yoon, W.C.: Quantitative results assessing design issues of selection-supportive menus. Int. J. Ind. Ergon. **33**(1), 41–52 (2004)

9. Norman, D.A.: The design of everyday things. Doubleday, New York, NY (1988)

10. Petit, É., Chêne, D.: MenuDfA: vers une navigation gestuelle tactile conçue pour tous. < hal-01188978 > (2015)

11. Petit, É., Chêne, D.: 27ème conférence francophone sur l'Interaction Homme-Machine., Oct 2015, Toulouse, France. IHM-2015, pp. d03 (2015)

12. Roudaut, A., Bailly, G., Lecolinet, E., Nigay, L.: Leaf menus: linear menus with stroke shortcuts for small handheld devices. In: Gross, T., Gulliksen, J., Kotzé, P., Oestreicher, L., Palanque, P., Prates, R.O., Winckler, M. (eds.) INTERACT 2009. LNCS, vol. 5726, pp. 616–619. Springer, Heidelberg (2009)

13. Singh, N., Pereira, A.: The culturally customized web site. Ed. Routledge, NY (2012)

14. Song, K., Lee, S.: Mapping user accessibility needs systematically to universal design principles. In: Lee, S., Choo, H., Ha, S., Shin, I.C. (eds.) APCHI 2008. LNCS, vol. 5068, pp. 446–456. Springer, Heidelberg (2008)

15. Trewin, S., Pettick, D.: Physical accessibility of touchscreen smartphones. In: Proceedings of the 15th International ACM SIGACCESS Conference on Computer and Accessibility, vol. 19, pp. 1–8 (2013)

16. Trudeau, M.B., Young, J.G., Jindrich, D.L., Dennerlein, J.T.: Thumb motor performance varies with thumb and wrist posture during single-handed mobile phone use. J. Biomech. **45**, 2349–2354 (2012)

17. Vanderheiden, G.: Fundamental principles and priority setting for universal usability. In: ACM (ed.) CUU 2000 Arlington VA USA (2000)

18. Vermeulen, J., Luyten, K., van den Hoven, E., Coninx, K.: Crossing the bridge over Norman's Gulf of execution: revealing feedforward's true identity. In: CHI 2013, April 27 − May 2, Paris, France (2013)

VoxLaps: A Free Symbol-Based AAC Application for Brazilian Portuguese

Karla de Oliveira[1(✉)], Jefferson Junior[1], Jefferson Silva[1],
Nelson Neto[1], Marcelle Mota[1], and Ana Oliveira[2]

[1] Faculdade de Computação, Universidade Federal do Pará, Belém, Brazil
`karla.santoli@gmail.com`, `jefjr2504@gmail.com`,
`jeffkd35@gmail.com`, `dnelsonneto@gmail.com`,
`cellemota@gmail.com`
[2] Núcleo de Desenvolvimento em Tecnologia Assistiva e Acessibilidade,
Universidade do Estado do Pará, Belém, Brazil
`anairene25@gmail.com`

Abstract. This paper aims to highlight the need for access to assistive technologies focused on augmentative and alternative communication (AAC), especially those available for the Brazilian Portuguese language, and the problems involved, as well as provide answers to these difficulties through the VoxLaps software, a free graphical symbol-based AAC application for the Android platform, developed under the supervision and support from a multidisciplinary rehabilitation team. This group of students and professionals evaluated the software functionality and usability, as well as other ACC tools, in order to compare their performances through the observation-based method and usability tests.

Keywords: Assistive technology · Augmentative and alternative · Communication · Voice synthesizer and Human-Computer interaction

1 Introduction

Assistive technology (AT) is an interdisciplinary area of knowledge, encompassing products, resources, methodologies, strategies, practices and services aimed at promoting quality of life and social inclusion for people with special needs (PSNs) [1]. In recent years, the branch of AT has made substantial progress consolidating theoretical approaches, scientific methods and technologies, as well as exploring new fields of application. Recent developments in mobile technology field, especially the introduction of tablets, smartphones and mobile applications, created new opportunities in the field of AT. These advances have influenced the behavior of consumers of this technology, impacting on their participation and everyday life [2]. However, despite this development, the AT access is still restricted.

Indeed, current statistics [3] reveal that although Android and iOS stores have 3 million mobile applications, the research process of these applications to AT is still a difficult task, considering that the app stores do not use appropriate IDs, such as categories and classification of AT by disability. Furthermore, the descriptions of these

M. Antona and C. Stephanidis (Eds.): UAHCI 2016, Part II, LNCS 9738, pp. 129–140, 2016.
DOI: 10.1007/978-3-319-40244-4_13

applications do not always include appropriate keywords and in many cases, users do not know the right keywords to use for searches in the app stores. Allied to these questions there are other factors that restrict this access, such as the language, reliability, stability, functionality and usability of applications, issues which according to [4] can only be properly addressed by a team of AT experts through appropriate evaluation methodologies. In addition to these factors, in developing countries like Brazil, the cost is also relevant because, according to the 2010 Census, about 60 % of the population lives with an monthly income of less than one minimum wage per capita and 23.9 % of total Brazilian population has at least one of the investigated disabilities: visual, hearing, motor, mental or intellectual.

Considering the market and current researches [5], a noticeable trend is the growing supply of AT products for communication, especially given the proliferation of mobile devices. As a result, individuals with disabilities, including those with complex communication needs, are also rapidly adopting augmentative and alternative communication (AAC) applications [6]. An inventory of several AAC applications is presented in [7]. In order to develop their own AAC tool, the authors analyzed approximately 40 applications available in the market, and among them only eight were chosen, using as criteria the number of resources, best practices and level of innovation. Among the selected set, only two provided support for the Portuguese language, which is an important aspect in the context of this work, since the effectiveness of visual communication using AAC symbols is also influenced by cultural differences, although to a lesser extent than language [8].

In response to these needs, we developed a free symbol-based AAC application for mobile devices using the Android platform, with support for the Brazilian Portuguese language, called VoxLaps, presented in this work through the following sections: Sect. 2 Augmentative and Alternative Communication: deals with the definition of AAC and presents well-know AAC tools and their main characteristics; Sect. 3 VoxLaps: details the development process, design and features of the proposed software; Sect. 4 Usability Tests: describes the applied usability testing procedure and participants; Sect. 5 Obtained Results: discusses the results obtained from the usability experiments; Sect. 6 Conclusion and Future Works.

2 Augmentative and Alternative Communication

According to [9], alternative communication is any form of communication other than speech and used by a person in face-to-face communication contexts. Gestural and graphic signs, Morse code, among others, are alternative forms of communication for individuals who lack the ability to speak.

According to American Speech-Language-Hearing Association, AAC includes all forms of communication that are used to express thoughts, needs, wants, and ideas. Then, AAC provides to individuals with several speech or language problems special augmentative aids, in order to replace or supplement insufficient communication skills or abilities. It helps these people to communicate interactively, to gain better education, and to increase self-worth and self-esteem. In [10], the authors suggested the following terminology for AAC systems: no tech – rely on the user's body to convey messages;

low tech – these systems do not use electronics, but involve objects outside the individual's body; and high tech – based on electronic devices that allow the use of picture symbols and words to create messages. The message is activated by touch or any accessible external switch to produce a printout and synthesized (or digitized) speech.

Most AAC systems are based on the principle of communication boards with symbols associated to words (or buttons), as shown in Fig. 1. These boards are organized into categories, such as actions, feelings, people, places and other subjects, extracted from pictographic collections (or libraries) allowing people with difficulties in communicating to create their message by tapping the buttons and then transforming it to voice and text message. There are many pictographic libraries, among these we quote: Picture Communication Symbols (PCS) [11], Pictogram Ideogram Communication Symbols (PIC) [12], Blissymbols [13] and the ARASAAC project [14], which is free distributed under the Creative Commons license. Figure 1 shows examples of words represented by such collections.

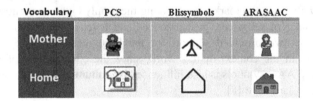

Fig. 1. Representing a vocabulary through different pictographic libraries

Some of the main AAC tools for Portuguese are described below:

1. **Livox – Liberdade em Voz Alta (Loud Voice Freedom)** – is a successful AAC product for tablets. It has communication boards organized by categories, allows the scanning of symbols to be enabled or disabled, and supports multiple users [15]. The acquisition of this product is subject to purchase of a tablet with the software pre-installed or the acquisition of the license agreement.
2. **Que-Fala** is a Web solution available for tablets, smartphones and desktops, to replace the former paperboards [16]. After purchasing one of the single use packages, the user must enter the boards to be used, considering that the application comes empty. In addition, for enabling speech synthesis, the user must click exactly on the sound icon over the figure, which may be a stress point, considering some groups of PSNs.
3. **Vox4All** is available for tablets and smartphones using Android and iOS operating systems. It is a commercial application, but its developers have provided one trial version for very limited use. The commercial version includes several features: create, edit and delete boards; and enabling or disabling the figure scanning system. Based on communication networks that enable the interconnection between boards, the application allows the use of the device's camera, image gallery and voice recorder, aiming to extend the graphic symbols database [7]. Despite offering many features and support for three languages, including Portuguese, the tool was

considered little intuitive by rehabilitation professionals who participated in the tests carried out through this work, according to Sect. 4. Cost is also important, considering that rehabilitation institutions need to acquire a sizeable number of licenses.

4. **Adapt** is a free tool available on the Google Play Store [17]. It has limited features, for example, the creation of new users and automatic scan of boards and buttons are not supported. However, it allows creating and editing communication boards. It uses only the images that are pre-defined in the application, i.e. not allow the use of the device's camera or gallery to acquire new symbols.

5. **Araboard** is divided into two distinct parts, called Constructor and Player. According to the authors [18] the part identified as Constructor allows tutors to create, edit and delete communication boards, enter pictographic from the system libraries or through the use of the device camera. The user accesses the boards through the Player module. The solution is free and available in the Google Play Store, but the Constructor module was experiencing failure during the process of creating boards, preventing its use because the application comes with no board option previously set, hence it was not used in our tests.

3   VoxLaps

VoxLaps is an application that has been developed for tablets and smartphones using the Android platform. It will be published under the Creative Commons license. This AAC software focuses on the Brazilian Portuguese language and its development process was divided into three phases. The goal was to start with an application that turns symbolic message into synthesized speech. Next, we extended the tool with the features present in different AAC software. The last step was the tool validation by rehabilitation professionals and students. The methodology consisted of:

- *Learning about the user:* Comprises of meeting relevant aspects of the individual with special needs, their environment and the AT used for supporting the activities of his daily routine. The implementation of this phase took place through the participation of professionals in the field of rehabilitation of the Development Center for Assistive Technologies and Accessibility (NEDETA), Brazil, who acted as the requirement providers.
- *Project execution:* Based on user needs, a survey was conducted for AAC applications in mobile app stores, databases, websites and blogs related to AT. From this research free and commercially tools were selected, which had relevant characteristics for the project.
- *Testing selected tools:* The selected tools were tested in order to identify strengths, weaknesses and opportunities for improvement. This analysis generated a list of initial requirements, which was evaluated and modified as requested by the requirements suppliers until its final approval.
- *Initial prototype:* System prototypes were developed based on the set of the collected requirements. The initial prototype consisted in boards arranged into categories called person, question, expression, verb, adjective, action, feeling, food,

letters and numbers. These categories were composed of images with texts, which when activated, transformed the text into synthesized speech.

- *User rating:* The developed prototypes were presented and evaluated by the requirements supplier, i.e. rehabilitation professionals. The problems identified were corrected, noting the user-identified considerations. Through this iterative process, all the highlighted requirements have been implemented.

- *Current prototype:* The involvement of users throughout the development process enabled a better understanding of the needs and goals of the target audience, favoring the use of strategies such as, for example, the Fitzgerald Key. Based on colors code, the Fitzgerald Key aims to understand the importance of ordering the words in the sentence and the implications of any change into the meaning. Thus, we have: Person - yellow, Verbs - green, Adjectives and Adverbs - blue, Nouns - orange, Miscellaneous - white and Social (signs that feature words facilitating social interaction) - pink [19]. Figure 2 illustrates the application of this concept.

(a)　　　　　　　　　　　　　　　(b)

Fig. 2. (a) Initial screen of VoxLaPS with 10 categories, identified by text and color, as well as "yes" and "no" buttons. (b) Communication board to express emotions. (Color figure online)

The current version of VoxLaps consists of 10 boards, distributed in the following categories: Individual, Questions, Expression, Verb, Adjective, Action, Feeling, Food, Letter, Number and the Yes/No buttons. The used symbols are works of Sergio Palao to CATEDU and published under the Creative Commons license [14]. The key features of VoxLaps are presented below:

- *Manage users:* This feature allows creating, editing and deleting user profiles to which can be created multiple and different patterns of communication boards, being this one of the innovative features of the tool, since it helps adapt the tool to the needs of different users on the same device.

- *Manage boards:* This feature allows creating, editing and deleting communication boards for different user profiles. Through it, the tutor can set the number of rows and columns that will compose each board and the system will adapt the buttons to screen size, noting the amount reported.

- *Manage buttons:* This feature allows creating, editing and deleting buttons that will compose a communication board. To create and edit buttons, the user can use the device's sensors (camera and voice recorder) and gallery.

- *Automatic scan of boards and buttons:* This feature allows the user to dispense with the mouse and use the application as a trigger. When the user activates this function, the buttons present on the graphical interface are visited sequentially, and the system will synthesize the message corresponding to the visited item by touch any part of the screen. The user can adjust the scan speed.
- *Message transcription:* This feature keeps the selected words in a text box located at the top of the tool's interface. So, the user can repeat (i.e. synthesize) the formed phrase through activation of the Play button, reuse the content, in whole or in part, and navigate between the boards during the message composition.
- *System settings:* This feature allows setting the border color of the visited item and the scan speed.

4   Usability Tests

The evaluation experiments have compared the current version of VoxLaps with the free software Adapt and two commercial applications: Vox4all and Que-Fala. Brazilian rehabilitation students and professionals, unrelated to the development process, were invited to perform seven tasks using one of the chosen AAC tools. The selected applications were evaluated through observation-based method and usability tests. Table 1 presents the activities associated with the preparation and execution of these tests.

Table 1. Activities for the usability tests [20]

Activity	Task
Preparation	✓ Set tasks for participants to perform. ✓ Define the participants' profile and recruit them. ✓ Prepare material for observing and recording. ✓ Run a pilot test.
Data collection	✓ Observe and record the performance and opinion of the participants during controlled use sessions.
Interpretation and consolidation of results	✓ Collect, account for and summarize the data collected from participants.
Reporting results	✓ Report performance and opinion of the participants.

The testing team was composed by 12 Brazilian evaluators recruited as follows: (a) **two** speech therapists; (b) **three** occupational therapists; (c) **one** psychologist; (d) **one** educational psychologist; (e) **one** neuropsychologist; (f) **three** undergraduate students in occupational therapy; (g) **one** master student of postgraduate studies in linguistics.

Each task describes a situation that allows the user to explore the tools' features. The tests were recorded and observed on-site. At the end, the volunteers answered a questionnaire that evaluates user satisfaction, user profile and user perception related to the employed tools. Table 2 presents the tasks used with a simple description and related goals.

Table 2. Description and goals of the tasks

Task	Description	Goal
1. Pre-recorded phrase reading	The professional wants to use the speech synthesizer to demonstrate to the patient, how he must proceed to transmit a pre-recorded message from the device. To accomplish this task, the professional accesses the desired category and clicks on the corresponding image to select the message to be transmitted, which is expected to be emitted by speech synthesizer.	It evaluates the performance of a basic functionality of vocalizers, comprising the voice synthesizing of messages formed by selection of images or symbols.
2. Enabling automatic scan of buttons	You want to make available to a patient with multiple disabilities, the automatic scan of buttons feature. In this feature, the system visits each button on a board, in constant speed, highlighting it in order to allow the impaired user to select a button at the time of its scan by tough or click on suitable trigger. Based on this information, activate the system scan.	It comprises enabling/disabling the automatic scanning feature, functionality that allows buttons in a particular category to be automatically visited, simplifying the user selection.
3. Creating new user for a new patient	The institution receives constantly new patients, so it is necessary to provide the appropriate boards as treatment support. These boards are individual and personalized. Currently, these boards are made manually, grouped by categories and identified with the name of the patient. In this way, using the tools listed, create a new user (patient) called "Johnny".	It includes the insertion of new users (PSNs) into the system.
4. Creating new communication boards	During the treatment, you realize the need to create new communication boards appropriated to the patient's stage of evolution. This board must contain a name that	It comprises the insertion of new categories of communication boards for patients registered in the system.

(*Continued*)

Table 2. (*Continued*)

Task	Description	Goal
	identifies its category, as well as a related image. Several buttons may be included on it, which will facilitate the communication process. So, using the indicated tool, create a new custom board for your new patient, named "Family".	
5. Inclusion of buttons in communication boards	The boards are composed of buttons, which have an image and a text. When a button is selected, the associated text is synthesized. After you create a new board, you must insert the buttons relating to the created category. Now that you have created a new user and a new board named "Family", insert a new button with the text "I'm Johnny" and use the mobile device's camera to take a picture of the patient to be used as identification of the new button.	It includes the insertion of buttons (images) into categories of existing boards.
6. Recording new messages on buttons	The speech synthesizers use TTS, i.e. a text-to-speech system that converts natural language text to voice. However, that voice is not familiar to the patient. In order to let the patient better suited to the use of the tool, you want to insert, in the "Family" board, new buttons that perform the voice of the patient's mother as well. To create these new buttons, you should use the device's voice recorder. In this way, you should record a new message in a button.	It comprises recording the message (voice) for the message to be transmitted.
7. Editing buttons and boards	You have already created a new button on the "Family" board, named "godmother", and after performing the whole process, you realize the word was	It comprises performing changes of boards and buttons present in the tool.

Table 2. (*Continued*)

Task	Description	Goal
	misspelled and you want to fix it. Using the Edit feature, change the message of an existing button and then change the name of the board, which contains the button that was changed.	

5 Obtained Results

For carrying out the tests, each of the 12 participants used only one tool and they were distributed as follows: Adapt (2); Que-Fala (2); Vox4All (4); and VoxLaps (4). Due to restrictions in the number of volunteers, the tools with more features were privileged. Table 3 shows the tasks performed and the hit percentage for each tool. The features not covered are identified by DNE (i.e. does not exist).

Table 3. Comparing the selected tools through seven tasks

Tasks	Tools			
	Adapt	Que-Fala	Vox4All	VoxLaps
	%	%	%	%
1. Pre-recorded phrase reading	100	100	100	100
2. Enabling auto scan of buttons	DNE	DNE	25	75
3. Creating new user	DNE	DNE	DNE	75
4. Creating new communication boards	0	50	0	50
5. Inclusion of buttons in communication boards	50	50	25	50
6. Recording new messages on buttons	DNE	DNE	25	75
7. Editing boards and button	50	50	25	75

- **Task 1:** all the selected tools come with this functionality and all participants were able to satisfactorily perform the task.
- **Task 2:** Vox4All offers this functionality, but the users felt difficulties to locate it and considered the screen polluted, making it hard the perception of the desired information. Considering VoxLaps, the users' justification was the ease to locate the functionality at the interface.
- **Task 3:** among the selected applications, only VoxLaps introduces support for this functionality.
- **Task 4:** all the selected tools support this functionality, however, the results were almost non-satisfactory, considering that: participants who tested Adapt managed to locate this feature within the application, but could not complete the task, giving up from it after a few tries. The justification presented was the low intuitiveness of the

interface and the lack of labels indicating the function of important icons on the screen, such as "insert image". In Que-Fala, the user who did not complete this task reported that the application was uninviting, as it started blank, leaving to the user the responsibility of populating the tool with images for communication, i.e. the user spends much time trying to figure out and configure the tool. Vox4All presents a rich configuration area, which allows the creation of boards, linking them with other existing boards, and the use of available resources on the device, such as camera and voice recorder, among others. Nevertheless, none of the four participants who tested Vox4All managed to complete the task, because of the following reasons: difficulties to understand the icon represented by a pencil, on the top of the screen, indicated the "setup area"; those who understood it and were able to access this area, passed through the option of creating a new board without noticing it, or performed the task inserting images into existing boards, believing to be performing the task correctly. In the end, all participants evaluated the tool as little intuitive. Among the 4 participants who used VoxLaps, only two were able to complete the task. The justification presented was the tool needed labels to identify the icons on screen, as they were not intuitive. Moreover, the closeness of the create button and board icons, caused confusion to the user, that executed the action of create button instead of create board. Another problem pointed was the lack of identification of the user location during navigation in the tool.

- **Task 5:** this task reflects the results of the previous activity, because to create buttons it is required a board inserted on the tool, thus, the failures that occurred in the previous step are reflected in this task. In Adapt, the participants were unable to insert new boards, however, as the tool came with some native boards, they allowed the execution of this task. In Que-Fala, only the user who has succeeded in task 4 performed this activity, as there is a dependency between boards and existing buttons in this application. In Vox4All, the justification for the results is similar to that of Adapt, considering that despite task 4 not been carried out, the fact that this application has native boards allowed the completion of the task. In VoxLaps, the results obtained in previous step reflected in the current task.
- **Task 6:** Considering Vox4All, the users felt it difficult to find this functionality, and only one participant completed this task. In VoxLaps, one of the participants was unable to perform the task, for the same reason pointed by the Vox4All users.
- **Task 7:** This task is similar to task 5 and was inserted in order to validate the results obtained there. Note that the results were similar.

6   Conclusion and Future Works

Based on the tests with students and rehabilitation professionals, there are relevant factors that restrict or even inhibit the use of AAC tools for some of the users, who often end up opting for manual boards. Although these boards are useful during the treatment sessions, they are restricted to the training environment, because patients do not feel the urge to use such boards in other social environments, like school, cinema, parks and others.

Therefore, the development of robust and intuitive tools is essential in this context, because the tutors (rehabilitation professionals, parents, teachers, etc.) need to expand communication boards according to the patient evolution, and this activity should be carried out in a simple and objective way, so there is no waste of time or too much effort from tutors, and consequently from the PSNs. Through the usability tests, it was possible to demonstrate that the user-centered development favored the increase of user satisfaction levels compared with other tools used in our tests, with a decrease in errors occurrence being observed during the execution of the proposed scenarios.

Furthermore, our tests also identified new features, and items to be improved for a next version of the VoxLaps software. Tests with patients are being conducted and for future works, we propose the presentation of these evaluation results, together with comparisons with other tools, in order to identify negative and positive points and opportunities for improvement. Another work intends to adapt VoxLaps to recognize Bluetooth devices in order to expand the target audience that can be benefited.

References

1. Brasil, 2009. Subsecretaria Nacional de Promoção dos Direitos da Pessoa com Deficiência. Comitê de Ajudas Técnicas. Tecnologia Assistiva. Brasília: CORDE, 138 p (2009)
2. Kouroupetroglou, G., Kousidis, S., Riga, P., Pino, A.: The mATHENA Inventory for Free Mobile Assistive Technology Applications. In: Ciuciu, I., et al. (eds.) OTM 2015 Workshops, LNCS. vol. 9416, pp. 519–527. Springer, Switzerland (2015). doi:10.1007/978-3-319-26138-6_56
3. Statista: Number of apps available in leading app stores as of, May 2015. http://www.statista.com/statistics/276623/number-of-apps-available-in-leading-app-stores/
4. Billi, M., Burzagli, L., Catarci, T., Santuci, G., Bertini, E., Gabbanini, F., Palchetti, E.: A unified methodology for the evaluation of accessibility and usability of mobile applications. Univ. Access Inf. Soc. **9**, 337–356 (2010)
5. Rodrigues, P.R., Alves, L.R.G.: Tecnologia Assistiva – Uma Revisão do Tema. Rev. HOLOS, Ano 29, Vol. 06 (2013)
6. Rehabilitation Engineering Research Center on Communication Enhancement (2011) Mobile Devices and Communication Apps: An AAC-RERC White Paper. http://aac-rerc.psu.edu/documents/RERC_mobiledevices_whitepaper_final.pdf
7. Quintela, M.A.; Correia, S., Mendes, M.: Augmentative and alternative communication: Vox4all® presentation. In: Proceedings of the 8th Iberian Conference on Information Systems and Technologies (CISTI), Lisboa, pp. 1–6 (2013)
8. Car, Z., Vukovic, M., Vucak, I., Pibernik, J., Dolic, J.: A platform model for symbol based communication services. In: Proceedings of the 11th International Conference on Telecommunications. ConTEL 2011, pp. 141–148. IEEE (2011)
9. Gândara, R.I.V.: A Utilização das TIC como Meio de Aprendizagem na Educação Especial. Dissertação – Escola Superior de Educação João de Deus. Lisboa (2013)
10. Hanline, M.F., Nunes, D., Worthy, M.B.: Augmentative and alternative communication in the early childhood years. Young Child. **62**(4), 78–82 (2007)
11. Clik.: PCS – Picture Communication Symbos – Simbolos de Comunnicação Pictórica (2016). http://www.click.com.br/mj_01.html#pcs

12. Pitane.: PIC – Pictogram Ideogran Communication (2016). http://www.contagem.pucminas. br/pitane/index.php?option=com_content&view
13. Blissymbol (2016). http://bliss.ideia.me/#header_0
14. ARASAAC.: Portal Aragonês de Comunicação Aumentativa e Alternativa. Centro Aragonés de Tecnologías para la Educación (2016). http://catedu.es/arasaac/index.php
15. Agora Eu Consigo Tecnologias de Inclusão Social Ltda (2016) Livox. http://www.livox. com.br/
16. Métodos Soluções Inteligentes Que-Fala! (2016). http://www.quefala.com.br
17. Abacore Adapt (2016). https://play.google.com/store/apps/details?id=com.argulu.adapt&hl= pt_BR
18. Baldassarri, S., Rubio, J.M., Azpiroz, M.G., Cerezo, E.: AraBoard: A multiplatform alternative and augmentative communication tool. Procedia Comput. Sci. **27**, 197–206 (2014). 5th International Conference on Software Development and Technologies for Enhancing Accessibility and Fighting Info-exclusion, DSAI 2013
19. Campos, F.H.B., Costa, M.E.: Vitória, Vitória: Contou-se Uma História: Usando um Sistema Aumentativo e Alternativo de Comunicação. Atas do XII Congresso Internacional Galego-Português de Psicopedagogia. Braga: Universidade do Minho (2013). ISBN: 978-989-8525-22-2
20. Barbosa, S.D.J., Silva, B.S.: Interação Humano-Computador, pp. 92–106. Elsevier, Rio de Janeiro (2010)

Three Text Entry Methods Based on Smartphone Discrete Tilting: An Empirical Evaluation

Sandi Ljubic[(✉)]

Faculty of Engineering, University of Rijeka,
Vukovarska 58, HR-51000 Rijeka, Croatia
sandi.ljubic@riteh.hr

Abstract. Tilt can be used as an input modality for mobile devices, providing possibility for touch-free text entry implementations. This paper builds on previous research on modeling three text entry methods that utilize discrete tilt concept and rely on tilt-only interaction. These methods are analyzed a priori in theory, however, they have not yet been comparatively assessed by empirical approach. The work presented herein offers a contribution in that respect, as methods are evaluated against efficiency, learnability, and users' satisfaction in a study involving 20 participants. The efficiency of tilt-based text entry is inspected by observing performance metrics through repetition and practice time. Required physical and mental demands are also investigated, as well as are perceived frustration and overall effort. The results obtained from controlled text-entry experiment supported a detailed comparative analysis of methods' characteristics, and revealed a relation between theoretical predictions of upper-bound text entry speeds and real efficiency of the presented methods.

Keywords: Text entry · Tilt-based interaction · Mobile devices · Empirical evaluation

1 Background

Dominant interaction techniques used for text entry across the most of the contemporary on-screen soft keyboards utilize direct touch (*tap*), sliding gestures (*swipe*), or a combination of both (*tap-and-swipe*). Apart from the touchscreen, motion sensors integrated into modern mobile devices can also be used for input control, providing a possibility to augment mobile text entry with new tilt-based methods.

Tilting has been initially analyzed as an input support for special hardware prototypes (*Unigesture* [1]), small watch-like devices (*TiltType* [2]), and feature phones with 12-button multitap-based keyboards (*TiltText* [3], *Vision TiltText* [4]). *Unigesture* approach prevents inputting individual letters, relying on an inference engine able to predict complete words based on the device tilting sequence. *TiltType* does not support single-handed text entry, and requires a combination of both button pressing and device tilting for character selection. *TiltText* technique allows for one-hand texting wherein tilt gestures are used to resolve character disambiguation after initial key press. *Vision TiltText* is functionally equivalent to the original *TiltText* method, but uses the built-in

© Springer International Publishing Switzerland 2016
M. Antona and C. Stephanidis (Eds.): UAHCI 2016, Part II, LNCS 9738, pp. 141–152, 2016.
DOI: 10.1007/978-3-319-40244-4_14

camera for detecting both movement and tilt of the phone. None of the aforementioned methods operates using standard QWERTY, as zone-based character layouts are favored in those designs instead.

More recent motion-based solutions support text entry on present day mobile devices, namely touchscreen smartphones and tablets. *WalkType* [5] is an adaptive text entry system which uses accelerometer data to improve touch typing on a soft QWERTY keyboard, by compensating imprecise input while walking. *The Dasher* [6] is a text entry system in which a probabilistic predictive model and zoom-and-point interaction are simultaneously used for character selection. It supports multiple platforms and input modalities, here including continuous tilt as a way of pointing on a mobile device. Tilt-based target selection, enabled by continuous tilting of a tablet device, has been empirically investigated by Fitton et al. [7]. The proposed input technique was intended for text entry, however, experimental interface did not implement full-layout keyboard and procedure did not involve real text entry tasks.

Continuous tilting of a mobile device generally demands a high level of visual attention to select targets, i.e. characters accurately. The main emphasis of the author's previous research is put on a discrete tilt concept which, on the contrary, supports interaction less relying on visual feedback. Discrete tilt is an input primitive which is actually comprised of two movements: (i) device leaves the neutral position zone, rotating along the longitudinal or the lateral axis; (ii) after reaching a predefined threshold angle, device returns to the neutral position zone by an immediate backward movement. Altogether four basic input commands can be defined using discrete tilt: Roll Left, Roll Right, Pitch Down, and Pitch Up (depicted in Fig. 1).

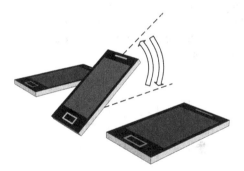

Fig. 1. Pitch *Up* input command invoked by discrete tilt. The device needs to be twisted up-then-down against its lateral axis. *Pitch Down* is invoked in the same way, only down-then-up tilting sequence is used instead. A neutral position is assumed when the device is parallel to the horizontal plane.

Discrete tilt concept is initially introduced in [8], along with the respective text entry method called *Keyboard Bisection* which uses an extended QWERTY-based layout and specially designed input scheme for character selection. This method subsequently motivated the implementation of two additional text entry solutions also relying on discrete tilt: *Single Cursor*, and *Quad Cursor* [9]. Basic concepts of the proposed methods are briefly described in the following.

Keyboard Bisection (KB). The tilt-based method in question uses discrete tilts for visual enlargement of a particular part of the keyboard. For example, Roll Left command will cause keyboard bisection resulting in the display of the left half of the current character layout. This way text entry is enabled with tilt movements exclusively, as particular character can be entered using step-by-step layout reduction (see example in Fig. 2). The KB method facilitates touch typing as well, since keyboard buttons are touch-enabled and their ever-increasing size allows for more precise selection. Nevertheless, in this paper the tilt-only interaction is of particular concern.

Buttons with different background color represent placeholders for frequently used characters/actions. These four common options can be alternatively selected using tilt-and-hold (or *long tilt*), a special interaction case when discrete tilt is extended by retaining the device position for 2 s before returning to the neutral position zone. Within the KB method, character selection involves exactly five discrete tilts, with the exception of shortcuts that can be selected either with one long tilt or four regular tilts.

Single Cursor (SC). This method abandons changeable layout concept and provides a consistent design with QWERTY alignment in three rows. It uses a specially visualized character (cursor) for marking the current position within the keyboard layout. Character selection is thus performed by tilting, i.e. moving the cursor in the appropriate direction. Input confirmation is achieved by dwelling in the neutral position zone (for a predefined amount of time) after successful discrete tilt execution. An example of character entry procedure using the SC method is shown in Fig. 3.

The efficiency of SC text entry method heavily depends on the cursor's path between the initial position and the location of the following character/symbol. In that respect, the method supports circular navigation: a single discrete tilt can switch the cursor between the first and the twelfth column, as well as between the first and the third row. Additionally, long tilts can be used for shortcut activations, thus bypassing the need for constant cursor switching.

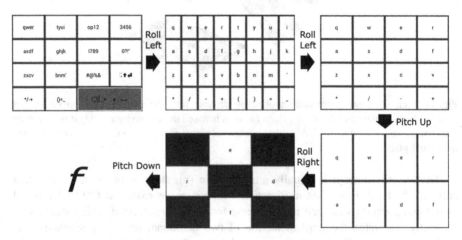

Fig. 2. Inputting character **f** by making use of tilt-only interaction within the *Keyboard Bisection* method. Different bisection strategies can be used for character selection.

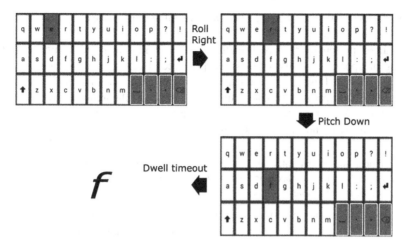

Fig. 3. Inputting character **f** using *Single Cursor* method, assuming that cursor initially marks letter *e*.

Quad Cursor (QC). Finally, the QC method uses the same character layout as the SC method, but in addition virtually divided into quad-based zones. These zones are accessible via quad cursor, a group of four adjoining characters from the same row. Both tilting and dwelling are used for text entry, as shown in example in Fig. 4.

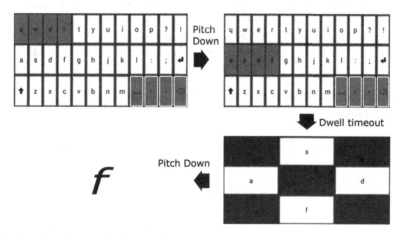

Fig. 4. Inputting character **f** using *Quad Cursor* method, assuming that cursor initially marks the letter group, i.e. the quad *q-w-e-r*.

The QC method requires three actions for character input: (i) navigating the cursor to the target quadruple, (ii) selecting the respective quadruple by dwelling, and (iii) making a final discrete tilt in order to choose among four presented characters. The third step is equal to the final letter resolving within the KB method. Circular navigation of quad cursor is allowed, as well as is shortcut activation using long tilts. While the QC method supports faster positioning than the SC, it additionally requires one extra tilt for the final 4-letter disambiguation.

The three presented tilt-based methods are already analyzed using predictive modeling of upper-bound text entry speed [9]. Predictions are derived from a combination of a tilt-based movement model, and a linguistic model (digraph frequencies in English). Obtained results, presented in Table 1, refer to theoretical expert-level text entry performance. More details on the respective modeling procedure, results, and discussion can be found in author's previous work [9].

Table 1. Upper-bound text entry speed predictions for presented tilt-based methods (*cf.* [9]). Predicted values hold for the maximum text entry expertise, as error-free input is assumed and all cognitive activities are ignored.

Text entry method	Text entry speed predictions (WPM_{max})	
	Long tilts not enabled	Using long tilts
Keyboard bisection	5.79	5.46
Single cursor	4.21	4.42
Quad cursor	5.16	5.15

Low text entry rates are predicted for discrete-tilt-based input methods. This is reasonable to expect, as the related input procedures assume several discrete tilts (and some dwell time) for a single character entry. Nevertheless, tilt-based input could provide support when typing on small screens becomes problematic, and/or in situations when visual contact with the smartphone display is obstructed. The presented methods can be furthermore enhanced using word prediction algorithms, but this research focuses solely on interaction aspects of tilt-based text entry. Real efficiency and workload demands of the presented methods were inspected by conducting a user study.

2 Empirical Evaluation: Participants, Apparatus, and Procedure

Twenty users were involved in text entry experiment (18 males, 2 females), their age ranging from 21 to 37 with an average of 25.25 years (SD = 5.17). While all participants were regular users of a touchscreen smartphone (85 % were owners of an Android device), 18 of them had already been interacting with tilt-based mobile applications (mainly games). Users reported their preferred hands posture while holding smartphone as follows: 40 % for two-thumbs typing, another 40 % for single-handed usage, i.e. one-thumb typing in portrait orientation, and 20 % for cradling – a case where one hand is holding the device, while the other (usually the dominant one) performs the text entry. Only one participant was left-handed.

All three tilt-based text entry methods were tested on a Samsung Galaxy S5 smartphone (SM-G900F) running Android Lollipop OS. This device is 142 × 72.5 × 8.1 mm large and weighs 145 g. A simple Android application was developed, able to support tilt-based input methods, as well as to gather tilt actions, text entry events and the corresponding timing data. The application implements transcription-based text entry tasks, meaning that each trial requires rewriting a displayed text phrase randomly selected from a 500 instances set developed by MacKenzie and Soukoreff [10]. All phrases in question consist exclusively of lowercase letters and space character, without any punctuation symbols. A single task was considered completed when a particular phrase was fully and correctly transcribed, so a distinct cognitive load for error checking was inherently involved. Data logging for a task instance began with the first discrete-tilt event and ended after entering the last correct character in a given phrase. All network-based services on the smartphone were turned off during the experiment. Regarding input methods' basic settings, threshold angles for pitch and roll movements were set to 30° and 45° respectively, while 1.2 s was assigned for dwell timeout. These values correspond to those used in modeling of upper-bound text entry speeds.

Before the testing, participants were informed about the main research goals. Participants' basic information about age, mobile device usage, and previous experience with tilt-based interaction was collected afterwards. This initial survey was followed by a detailed demonstration of text entry methods, in order to familiarize users with supported tilt-based character input schemes. Participants had no training sessions whatsoever. In the actual experiment, participants were instructed to enter three different text phrases, each one five times in a row, using available tilt-based methods (KB, SC, QC). The repetition part was applied in order to enhance users' skill acquisition, as well as to boost up the level of text entry performance. Single-handed interaction with the smartphone was obligatory, hence users had to hold the device in their dominant hand Fig. 5. Text entry tasks could have been accomplished while sitting or standing, so each user had to make a choice of respective position in regard to her/his own preference. Participants were furthermore instructed to input text "as quickly as possible, while trying to avoid errors", and to use long tilts for both space and backspace activations. Breaks were allowed between text entry tasks, as well as before shifting to another text entry method. A repeated measures (i.e. within-subjects) design was utilized, and the order of text entry methods was properly counterbalanced.

After the testing of each tilt-based text entry method, users were asked to estimate perceived workload by completing a questionnaire based on the rating part of the NASA-TLX (NASA Task Load Index). Namely, subjective opinions had to be reported on a 20-point Likert scales for five factors: mental demand, physical demand, frustration, performance, and effort.

Finally, at the end of the experiment, participants completed a short post-study survey, providing their concluding remarks on ease of use, perceived learnability, and overall satisfaction.

Fig. 5. A participant doing the text entry task using *Keyboard Bisection* method

3 Results and Discussion

Given that task iteration (of the same phrase) was not considered an independent variable in the experiment, the effect of repetitive entry was observed from the descriptive statistics standpoint only. Figure 6 presents achieved input performances averaged across five trials related to text entry iterations of a particular phrase. It can be seen that text entry performance generally improves with repetition, irrespective of the used tilt-based method. It is expected and understandable as task replication allowed for learning by means of inherently involved practice. Text entry speeds and total error rates are highly negatively correlated, which is a direct consequence of implemented tasks that required fully correct transcription.

Participants entered 900 phrases in total. After averaging data across unique phrases, altogether 180 text entry performance records were obtained: 20 participants × 3 methods × 3 unique phrases. Figure 7 shows levels of text entry performance, achieved using three tilt-based methods, for three different phrases. Unsurprisingly, performance enhancement through time can be observed once again.

To analyze the obtained data, a 3 × 3 repeated measures ANOVA was used, with *Method* (KB, SC, QC) and *Phrase* (1st, 2nd, 3rd) being the within-subjects factors. The Greenhouse–Geisser ε correction for the violation of sphericity was applied when appropriate. In cases where significant effect was found, post-hoc pairwise comparisons with Bonferroni adjustment were utilized. As text entry speed (i.e. WPM metric) is of particular concern in this paper, error rates are reported in graphs only.

The analysis revealed a significant effect of tilt-based entry *Method* on text entry speed ($F_{1.208,22.956} = 87.647$, $\varepsilon = 0.604$, $p < .001$). The effect of *Phrase* (i.e. practice through time) was also statistically significant ($F_{1.391,26.437} = 51.833$, $\varepsilon = 0.696$, $p < .001$). Finally, the effect of *Method*Phrase* interaction was found statistically significant as well ($F_{4,76} = 3.787$, $p = .007$).

As for the pairwise comparisons, the differences between text entry methods, as well as between phrases, are reported in the following.

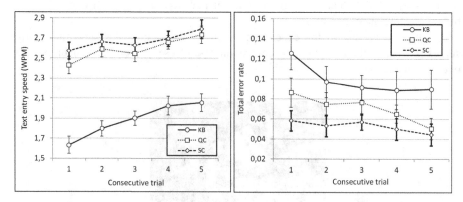

Fig. 6. Input performance averaged across five repetitive trials. The graphs show mean text entry rates and mean error rates, along with error bars with ± 1 standard error of the mean.

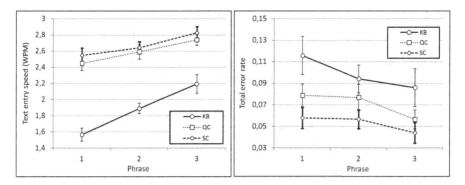

Fig. 7. Text entry performance averaged across three different phrases. The graphs show mean text entry rates and mean error rates, along with error bars with ± 1 standard error of the mean.

- SC vs. KB: (2.670 ± 0.073 WPM) vs. (1.884 ± 0.078 WPM), p < .001
- QC vs. KB: (2.592 ± 0.071 WPM) vs. (1.884 ± 0.078 WPM), p < .001
- SC vs. QC: (2.670 ± 0.073 WPM) vs. (2.592 ± 0.071 WPM), p = .886, ns

- Phrase 3 vs. Phrase 1: (2.585 ± 0.075 WPM) vs. (2.187 ± 0.064 WPM), p < .001
- Phrase 3 vs. Phrase 2: (2.585 ± 0.075 WPM) vs. (2.373 ± 0.063 WPM), p = .001
- Phrase 2 vs. Phrase 1: (2.373 ± 0.063 WPM) vs. (2.187 ± 0.064 WPM), p < .001

The KB was the slowest of the three tilt-based text entry methods. The SC appeared to be the fastest one, with a less prominent difference when compared with the QC. Concerning text entry performance through time, participants achieved the best results when entering the third, i.e. the last phrase. In that respect, it was decided to use that level of text entry performance in the further investigation. Namely, the participants' third-phrase performance was compared with theoretical predictions of upper-bound text entry speeds. The respective relations are shown in Fig. 8.

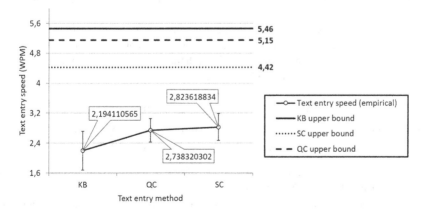

Fig. 8. The comparison of text entry speeds between empirical evaluation results and theoretical predictions. The graph shows mean text entry speeds and standard deviations, as well as upper-bound values (long tilts usage is assumed).

Interestingly, text entry speeds obtained from user testing are ordered just the opposite from what theoretical predictions suggest. While predictive models assume that bisection principle maintains the highest entry rate potential, in conducted experiment both the SC and the QC showed to be significantly faster than the KB method. In addition, real text entry speeds of the presented methods seem to be rather low when compared to their upper-bound limits. This discrepancy between theoretical predictions and empirical outcomes may raise the questions about validity of the modeling procedure. However, more detailed inspection of the obtained results can put a new light on the respective relation.

Upper-bound text entry speed predictions hold for total-expert behavior, which assumes all mental activities ignored and error making completely avoided. Experimental results revealed the largest error rate for the KB method (8.59 %), what makes accuracy improvement more promising for the KB than for the other two methods (5.64 % error rate with QC, 4.40 % for SC). It must be noted here that KB method implementation has one severe limitation in handling wrong bisections. Namely, bisection command has no undo option, thus causing errors to be even more time consuming. According to the aforementioned, error-free text entry would further benefit KB-method's performance the most.

Regarding mental activities involved when using tilt-based methods, the KB seems to be more demanding because of its ever-changing appearance. This especially applies to novice users usually accustomed to positional consistency of keyboard characters. Reaching the text entry expert level with QC or SC requires "shortest path" continuous utilization when navigating cursor within an otherwise well-known character layout. On the other hand, expert usage of the KB method assumes mastering the bisection principle, i.e. learning and remembering character layouts invoked by particular bisection commands.

Given that the KB method offers more room for improvement, text entry speed can be expected to further increase at the greater pace for KB than for the other two methods. To corroborate this argument, efficiency improvement was analyzed basing on the difference between input speeds achieved while entering the first phrase (at the beginning of the experiment) and the third phrase (at the end of the experiment). The results are presented in Fig. 9.

Users improved their text entry speed over three phrases in such way that, in comparison with both the SC and the QC, KB improvement was more than twofold. The presented values correspond to 3.21 CPM (characters per minute) enhancement for KB, 1.57 CPM for QC, and 1.35 CPM for SC. Mean text entry speed enhancement differed significantly between observed methods ($F_{2,38} = 6.524$, $p < .05$). Post hoc pairwise comparisons confirmed statistical significance of the following differences:

- KB vs. QC: (0.627 ± 0.091 WPM) vs. (0.290 ± 0.070 WPM), $p < .05$,
- KB vs. SC: (0.627 ± 0.091 WPM) vs. (0.278 ± 0.067 WPM), $p < .05$.

Text entry speeds converge to their upper bounds at different paces. If such improvement trends would hold for longer period, the relation between methods' real efficiencies would become in line with the ranking of the theoretical predictions. Predicted limits seem more convincing in that respect, regardless of initial divergence from empirical outcomes. Nevertheless, a more longitudinal study should be carried out to confirm such presumptions. To put things into perspective, it should be noted that

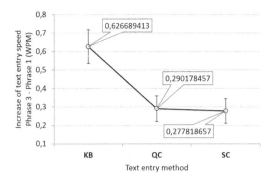

Fig. 9. An increase of text entry speed between entering the first phrase and the third phrase (mean values ± 1 standard error).

real text entry speeds were obtained from the experiment wherein users spent no more than 50 min per method. It is therefore reasonable to expect higher levels of text entry expertise on the longer run.

The qualitative evaluation of the presented methods was based on two questionnaires. The first one aimed for comparative rating of perceived workload, and was constructed using the "Raw TLX" format. The goal of the second one was to assess users' final impressions on general usability attributes of the three different input techniques.

The box plots derived from the first questionnaire are shown in Fig. 10. The Friedman test was used to assess TLX-based scores. In cases where significant effect was confirmed, post hoc analysis was conducted by making use of Wilcoxon signed-rank tests with a Bonferroni correction applied (i.e. significance level set at $p < .017$).

The type of text entry method being used had a significant effect on three factors: perceived mental demand ($\chi^2(2) = 18.329$, $p < .001$), physical demand ($\chi^2(2) = 7.892$, $p = .019$), and overall performance ($\chi^2(2) = 8.778$, $p = .012$). Statistically significant differences were not confirmed for perceived frustration ($\chi^2(2) = 1.848$, $p = .397$) and overall effort ($\chi^2(2) = 5.688$, $p = .058$). Post hoc analysis revealed the following facts:

- The KB method required considerably higher mental activity than both the SC method ($Z = -3.708$, $p < .001$) and the QC method ($Z = -3.247$, $p = .001$);
- Regarding physical activity, the SC method was significantly more demanding than the QC ($Z = -2.468$, $p = .014$);
- Participants were more satisfied with their performance while using the QC than while using the KB ($Z = -3.013$, $p = .003$).

The workload assessment results confirmed the issues previously discussed. As opposed to cursor navigation concept, transformable character layout clearly imposed extra mental efforts. When it comes to physical demand within cursor-based methods, the SC involved much lengthier tilt-based distances between two characters, thus higher wrist fatigue in comparison with the QC is no surprise. The KB had the lowest level of perceived efficiency, which can in turn be contributed to the highest obtained error rate.

Ease of use, learnability, and overall satisfaction were the usability attributes inspected in the concluding survey. Participants rated three text entry methods against these attributes on a 7-point Likert scale. The results are shown in Fig. 11.

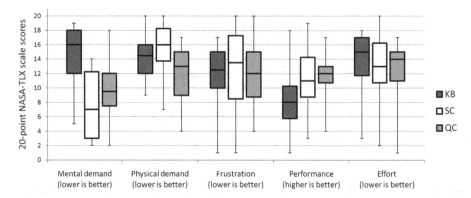

Fig. 10. Users' opinions on perceived workload of tilt-based input methods. For each factor, the corresponding box plots show minimum and maximum, 25 percentile (Q1), 75 percentile (Q3), and median value (M).

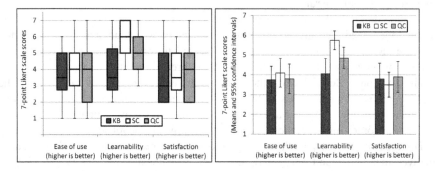

Fig. 11. Usability attributes: box plots (left), mean values and confidence intervals (right)

The methods were equally rated for ease of use, as well as for overall satisfaction. However, Friedman test revealed a statistically significant difference in perceived learnability ($\chi^2(2) = 16.551$, p < .001). Post hoc Wilcoxon signed-rank tests confirmed that the SC method was the easiest to learn. From the perceived learnability standpoint, it significantly outperformed both the KB (Z = −2.932, p = .003) and the QC (Z = −2.807, p = .005). There was no significant difference in learnability between the KB and the QC (Z = −1.811, p = .07). Cursor-based methods include a typical QWERTY layout and somewhat simpler input schemes than the mentally demanding KB method. In addition, the SC design is completely straightforward and does not involve any layout changes. In that respect, the obtained learnability ratings seem fully justified.

4   Conclusion

Three tilt-based methods that utilize discrete tilt concept and rely on tilt-only interaction were comparatively evaluated in a user study involving twenty participants. Empirically obtained text entry speeds were compared with their theoretical upper bounds, previously derived by predictive modeling. The observed discrepancy between empirical results and theoretical predictions was discussed in detail. In addition, the results of qualitative assessment were presented, thus providing the insight into methods' workload demands and usability attributes.

In general, tilt-only interaction proved to be a viable option for text entry in the mobile domain. Input efficiency may not be as high as needed, but discrete-tilt concept could provide support in some specific use cases. Namely, tilt-based input offers a possibility for blind typing, as well as texting on particularly small devices where touch typing is unsuitable (e.g. smartwatches). As shown in this paper, a simpler character input scheme would be a better choice for securing initial acceptance.

References

1. Sazawal, V., Want, R., Borriello, G.: The unigesture approach. In: Paternó, F. (ed.) Mobile HCI 2002. LNCS, vol. 2411, pp. 256–270. Springer, Heidelberg (2002)
2. Partridge, K., Chatterjee, S., Sazawal, V., Borriello, G., Want, R.: TiltType: accelerometer-supported text entry for very small devices. In: Proceedings of 15th ACM Symposium User Interface Software and Technology (UIST 2002), pp. 201–204. ACM Press, New York (2002)
3. Wigdor, D., Balakrishnan, R.: TiltText: Using tilt for text input to mobile phones. In: Proceedings of 16th ACM Symposium User Interface Software and Technology (UIST 2003), pp. 81–90. ACM Press, New York (2003)
4. Wang, J., Zhai, S., Canny, J.: Camera phone based motion sensing: interaction techniques, applications and performance study. In: Proceedings of 19th ACM Symposium User Interface Software and Technology (UIST 2006), pp. 101–110. ACM Press, New York (2006)
5. Goel, M., Findlater, L., Wobbrock, J.: WalkType: using accelerometer data to accommodate situational impairments in mobile touch screen text entry. In: Proceedings of 2012 ACM Conference Human Factors in Computing Systems (CHI 2012), pp. 2687–2696. ACM Press, New York (2012)
6. Ward, D.J., Blackwell, A.F., MacKay, D.J.C.: Dasher – a data entry interface using continuous gestures and language models. In: Proceedings of 13th ACM Symposium User Interface Software and Technology (UIST 2000), pp. 129–137. ACM Press, New York (2000)
7. Fitton, D., MacKenzie, I.S., Read, J.C., Horton, M.: Exploring tilt-based text input for mobile devices with teenagers. In: Proceedings of 27th International BCS Human Computer Interaction Conference (BCS-HCI 2013), pp. 1–6. British Computer Society, London (2013)
8. Ljubic, S., Kukec, M., Glavinic, V.: Tilt-based support for multimodal text entry on touchscreen smartphones: using pitch and roll. In: Stephanidis, C., Antona, M. (eds.) UAHCI 2013, Part III. LNCS, vol. 8011, pp. 651–660. Springer, Heidelberg (2013)
9. Ljubic, S., Glavinic, V., Kukec, M.: Predicting upper-bound text entry speeds for discrete-tilt-based input on smartphones. J. Interact. Sci. 2(3), 1–15 (2014)
10. MacKenzie, I.S., Soukoreff, R.W.: Phrase sets for evaluating text entry techniques. In: Proceedings of Extended Abstracts on Human Factors in Computing Systems (CHI EA 2003), pp. 754–755. ACM Press, New York (2003)

Braillet the Wristwatch-Style Refreshable Braille Display

Its Hardware, User Interface and Benchmarks

Kazunori Minatani[✉]

National Center for University Entrance Examinations,
Komaba 2-19-23, Meguro-ku, Tokyo 153-8501, Japan
minatani@rd.dnc.ac.jp

Abstract. There is a demand for a way for blind persons to receive information at any time and in any place, however that is impossible to realize with an existing user interface: voice output. Thus the author had developed a wristwatch-style refreshable braille display which is named the Braillet. It has 8 braille cells and 16 input switches. It is controlled from a host computer via the Bluetooth. An user interface which enable an appropriate interaction with host computer using the Braillet is explained. There is no standardized benchmark test to evaluate the performance of refreshable braille displays. The author developed a test that measures the response speed of them. It shows the Braillet can display braille characters with sufficient quick response for users. Executing the heaviest kinds of workload, the Braillet can work during 2 h with the Wristband Battery 2.

Keywords: Braillet · Refreshable braille display · Wearable device · Blind persons · Benchmark test

1 Introduction

There is no fully appropriate user interface for blind persons' mobile use. Until now, while standing, blind persons must use mobile computer devices with voice output. It is in standing situations in outdoor or public spaces that mobile devices demonstrate their advantages. Taking account of environmental noise, voice output is not a comfortable user interface in these places. Moreover, for blind persons who recognize circumstances with the auditory sense, the dispersion of attention between environmental sound and voice output from a device may result in reduced recognition ability.

Refreshable braille displays have been used as output devices for computers for blind persons as well as voice synthesis software. The size and weight of such refreshable braille displays are too large and heavy for mobile use [1].

A wearable refreshable braille display in the shape of a wristwatch which is named Braillet has been developed to realize more comprehensive support for mobile use (Fig. 1). [2] Blind persons can use it in a standing situation.

The development policies given below were decided on.

© Springer International Publishing Switzerland 2016
M. Antona and C. Stephanidis (Eds.): UAHCI 2016, Part II, LNCS 9738, pp. 153–161, 2016.
DOI: 10.1007/978-3-319-40244-4_15

Fig. 1. Braillet's appearance mounted on the arm of a Japanese adult male

- Downsizing: because of the device must be wearable on the arm.
- Proper functions for mobile use: for versatility this refreshable braille display presents information by communicating with a host computer like a smartphone.
- Wireless communication: for the wearability the and flexibility, the communication between this device and a host computer must be a wireless one (Bluetooth).

2   Hardware Implementation

Considering the wearability and the readability, the number of columns (characters) for this refreshable braille display is determined to be 8. The smallest-sized braille cell unit that the author has been able to purchase is the SC11 supplied by KGS Corporation. The SC11 is supplied as a component assembled with a power supply backplane board for 8 cells.

Braillet also has totally 16 input switches. Namely, it has 8 touch cursors corresponding to each braille cell and 3 buttons laid out to the left of the braille cells (Fig. 2) and a five directional navi-stick is mounted on the wristband.

The 1,500 mAh Wristband Battery 2 [3] is adopted. Using this product, a battery unit can be loaded in the wristband part of a watch.

A high voltage power supply is required to drive piezoelectric elements. With this refreshable braille display, using a DC-DC converter a 200 V voltage is generated from the 5 V voltage supplied by the battery.

The Microchip PIC24FJ64GB002 was adopted as micro computer, on which a pic24f_btstack which is a Bluetooth stack ported to the PIC24F series, and control firmware were loaded on it. The layout of the main board is shown in Fig. 3.

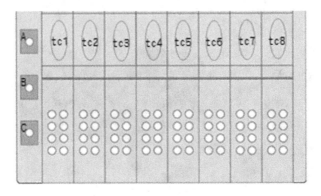

Fig. 2. The layout of the wristwatch-style refreshable braille display's buttons and cells

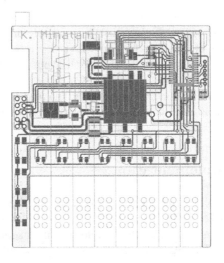

Fig. 3. The layout of the main board

3   Components of a Proposed User Interface

3.1   Command Input Display and Content View Display

Topics discussed in this and next sections are fully explained in elsewhere [4].

User interface displays are divided into two classes: *command input display*, and *content view display*. [4] A user selects aimed content on a command input display and browses it on a content view display.

The command input display lists commands that can be executed using *one-character icons*. For example, the watch function to display the current time can be represented as "w", the date function to display today's date as "d" and the music player function as "m". A user can directly select a command by pressing a touch cursor that corresponds to each one-character icon. An intuitive interface is achieved when the one-character icons are appropriately chosen.

When the touch cursor corresponding to each one-character icon is pressed, the presentation of the refreshable braille display is then switched to the content view display. For example, the watch function displays the current time. When the back button (now assigned to the B button) is pressed in the content view display, the display's presentation is returned to the command input display.

The series of display transitions and operations described above is shown in Fig. 4. In this paper, 8-dot North American Braille Computer Code [5] is used as a braille system.

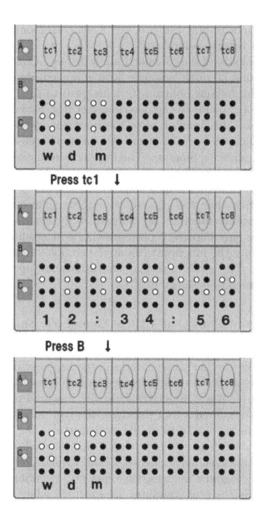

Fig. 4. An example of the series of display transitions and operations

3.2   Assistance of Operation by Guidance

The usability of an interface that displays one-character icons on the command input display is dominated by the intuitiveness of the one-character icons and the user's memory. For example, let us consider placing a one-character icon that represents a function for displaying a weather report on the command input display in addition to the three one-character icons mentioned above. If the rule of using the first character of a function's name as the one-character icon is followed as intuitive, the one-character icon for a weather report function must be "w". To use this command input display appropriately, the user must correctly understand and memorize how the two "w" icons correspond to each function (watch and weather report) beforehand.

To assure the usability of the command input display, a guidance function for indicating the function of a one-character icon is implemented. If a user simultaneously presses the guidance button (now assigned to the C button) and the touch cursor that corresponds to the one-character icon for which he/she wants to know the function, the description of the function represented by the one-character icon is indicated. Users confirm functions represented by one-character icons by using this guidance function. The display is returned to the command input display by pressing the back button (now assigned to the B button) when the description of the function is indicated.

If the touch cursor that was pressed with the guidance button is pressed again, the corresponding function is executed. With this arrangement, when users confirm that a one-character icon represents a function they want to execute, they can execute the function without the trouble of returning to a command input display. The series of display transitions and operations related to the guidance functionality is shown in Fig. 5.

3.3   One-Character Icons that Utilize Geometric Shapes

We considered a way for the Braillet to be utilized by a person who does not recognize braille. The Braillet's user interface, the usability of which is highest by using braille as characters, mainly focuses on braille users as a target. However, braille users are not the majority of visually impaired persons. Therefore, we experimentally considered a user interface that can be available for visually impaired persons who do not know braille as characters.

A music player interface has been developed that displays one-character icons not as characters, but as geometric shapes. Braille symbols have similar geometric shapes to the pictograms used in music players. Functions of music player software operating on the host computer are executed when touch cursors corresponding to each braille symbol are pushed.

The series of display transitions to execute the music player and the music player interface, which displays one-character icons as geometric shapes, are shown in Fig. 6.

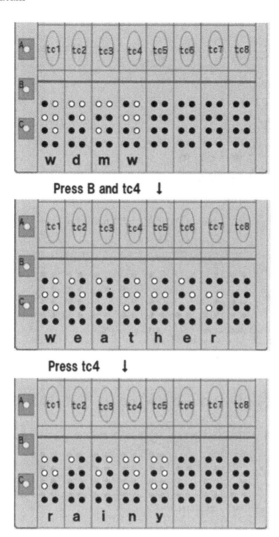

Fig. 5. The series of display transitions and operations related to the guidance functionality

4 Benchmarking

To evaluate the applicability of the Braillet, the author developed a benchmark test and software to execute it and carried it out with the Braillet.

4.1 Considerations of a Standardized Benchmark Test to Evaluate the Performance of a Refreshable Braille Display

There is no standardized benchmark test to evaluate the performance of refreshable braille displays. Here, the word "performance" means the quality of a

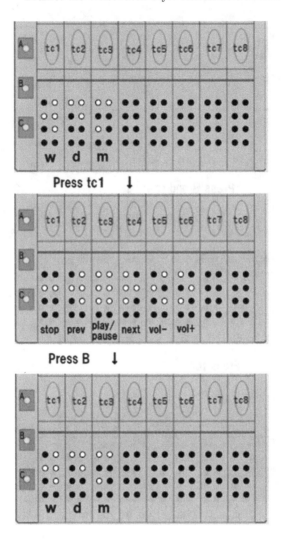

Fig. 6. The series of display transitions to execute the music player and the music player interface

display device as a user interface, and response speed in particular. Measured values of such performance are not indicated in the product specifications of refreshable braille displays released by their manufacturers. This may be due to manufacturers and consumers sharing a belief that the necessary performance is satisfied. However, it is not obvious that such a conviction is correct. This is a particularly serious issue in confirming the performance of non-traditional and experimental refreshable braille displays like the Braillet.

4.2 Method

The author developed a test that measures the response speed of a refreshable braille display and compares it with the reading speeds of visually impaired persons. An accurate measurement of reading speeds of visually impaired persons has indicated a median speed of 7.5 characters per second (cps) and a maximum of 14.4 cps. [6] These values can function as a benchmark. If the response speed of a refreshable braille display achieves a speed that is necessary to display 14.4 cps, it can be judged that its speed is sufficient.

Software called BrailleBench has been prepared, which sends commands to display a set of characters to a refreshable braille display at freely selectable intervals. To communicate with the refreshable braille display, it uses the BRLTTY [7] driver software for refreshable braille displays on Linux and its external API BrlAPI. [8] The set of characters to be sent is generated at random from uppercase or lowercase letters of the alphabet, digits and blank spaces. The length of the set is coordinated with the capacity of the refreshable braille display output (i.e., for Braillet it will be 8 characters).

A test involving sending a command to display a set of characters 100 times at 0.3-s intervals was carried out with the Braillet and the Baum VarioConnect 40. The Baum VarioConnect 40 [9] was tested for comparison. It is a standard portable 40-cell refreshable braille display, and it can be connected to a host computer via USB or Bluetooth. To check the results, the evaluation is recorded by a commercially available digital movie camera.

The reasons for sending the command to the refreshable braille displays at 0.3-s intervals are as follows. First, if the Braillet is functioning properly, a sufficient response speed (over 14.4 cps) can be confirmed. Secondly, reliable verification can be performed using videos recorded by the digital movie camera (30 fps).

4.3 Results

The test finished in 30.1 s with the Braillet (26.6 cps), and in 30.2 s with the VarioConnect 40 connected via USB (132.5 cps). The test also finished in 30.2 s with the VarioConnect 40 connected via Bluetooth (132.5 cps). The recorded videos confirmed the proper operation of the refreshable braille displays.

4.4 Battery Run Time

The battery run time of the Braillet was measured using a simple test. The watch function was executed, and the battery run time of the Braillet with a 1,500 mAh Wristband Battery 2 was measured. It has been confirmed that the Braillet can operate for 2 h with this arrangement.

It is reasonable to expect that the battery run time can be extended from this measured value. The watch function sends a command to display characters representing the time every second. In practical use, displaying characters with such frequency may be one of the heaviest kinds of work for a refreshable braille display. The Braillet operates using 5 V voltage, so it can operate using USB standard compliant high-capacity batteries instead of the Wristband Battery 2.

5   Conclusion

The size of the Braillet is 60 mm wide, 64 mm deep, and 28 mm in height. Taking account of the fact that an 8-cell SC11 unit has a width of 51.2 mm and depth of 67.45 mm, it can be judged to have been sufficiently minimized in size. Its unit's measured weight is 73 g and total weight, including the Wristband Battery 2, is 155 g.

An user interface which enable an appropriate interaction with host computer is contrived.

It can display braille characters with sufficient quick response for blind persons' braille reading speed. It can work during 2 h with the Wristband Battery 2.

Acknowledgment. The author would like to thank to The Telecommunications Advancement Foundation.

This work was partly supported by JSPS KAKENHI Grant Number 25750096.

References

1. HandyTech: Braille Star 80 - HandyTech.de. https://handytech.de/en/products/braille-displays-and-note-takers/braille-displays/braille-star-80. Accessed 12 February 2016
2. Minatani, K.: A wristwatch-shaped wireless refreshable braille display which realizes augmented mobile access for blind persons. In: Proceedings of 2014 IEEE 3rd Global Conference on Consumer Electronics, pp. 206–210 (2014)
3. Thanko Inc.: Wristband Battery 2. http://www.thanko.jp/product/4707.html. Accessed 12 February 2016. (in Japanese)
4. Minatani, K.: A proposal for a user interface with a several-cell refreshable braille display. In: Proceedings of The 5th International Conference on Information and Communication Technology & Accessibility, pp. 21–25 (2015)
5. The Braille Authority of North America: Code for Computer Braille Notation, American Printing House for the Blind (2000)
6. Legge, G.E., Madison, C., Mansfield, J.S.: Measuring braille reading speed with the MNREAD test. Vis. Impair. Res. **1**(3), 131–145 (1999)
7. BRLTTY Team: BRLTTY - Official Home. http://mielke.cc/brltty/. Accessed 9 February 2016
8. Hinderer, S., Thibault, S.: BrlAPI Reference manual. http://mielke.cc/brltty/doc/Manual-BrlAPI/English/BrlAPI.html. Accessed 9 February 2016
9. BAUM Retec AG: BAUM Retec AG - VarioConnect12. http://www.baum.de/en/products/brailledisplay/vconnect12.php. Accessed 9 February 2016

Evaluation of Non-visual Zooming Operations on Touchscreen Devices

Hariprasath Palani[1,2], Uro Giudice[1], and Nicholas A. Giudice[1,2(✉)]

[1] Spatial Informatics Program, School of Computing and Information Science,
University of Maine, 348 Boardman Hall, Orono, ME 04469, USA
{hariprasath.palani, nicholas.giudice}@maine.edu,
uro@vemilab.org
[2] Virtual Environments and Multimodal Interaction (VEMI) Laboratory,
University of Maine, Carnegie Hall, Orono, ME 04469, USA

Abstract. The limited screen real estate of touchscreen devices necessitates the use of zooming operations for accessing graphical information such as maps. While these operations are intuitive for sighted individuals, they are difficult to perform for blind and visually-impaired (BVI) people using non-visual sensing with touchscreen-based interfaces. We address this vexing design issue by investigating the perceptual and cognitive factors involved in: (1) non-visual zooming operations, and (2) integrating information across multiple zoom levels to build a global cognitive map. A behavioral study compared map learning performance between two zoom-mode conditions and a no-zoom control. Results revealed that non-visual zooming operations are not only possible, but actually lead to improved efficiency of touch-based non-visual learning. Findings provide compelling evidence for the efficacy of incorporating zooming operations on touchscreen-based non-visual interfaces and have significant broader impacts for improving the accessibility of a wide range of graphical information for BVI people.

Keywords: Interaction design · Assistive technology · Haptic information access · Haptic interaction · Multimodal interface

1 Introduction

Gaining access to graphical information such as maps, graphs, and diagrams represents a longstanding challenge for blind and visually-impaired (BVI) people. Efforts to address this challenge can be traced back for centuries beginning with raised tangible graphics [1, 2]. Many approaches have endeavored to provide non-visual access to graphical information, with techniques ranging from simple paper-based tactile graphics to complex refreshable haptic displays (see [3–5] for detailed reviews). However, the majority of these approaches have not made significant inroads in reaching blind end-users because of a number of factors, including that they are static, expensive, have limited portability, are cumbersome to author, and require a steep learning curve to master [6, 7]. With the recent advancement in touchscreen technologies, we have estimated (based on informal surveys of participants in our lab and through discussion at blindness-related social/advocacy organizations) that 70–80 % of

© Springer International Publishing Switzerland 2016
M. Antona and C. Stephanidis (Eds.): UAHCI 2016, Part II, LNCS 9738, pp. 162–174, 2016.
DOI: 10.1007/978-3-319-40244-4_16

BVI people who use a cell phone are using touchscreen-based smartphones. As a result, many researchers and developers are employing touchscreen devices to provide BVI users with access to graphical information by capitalizing on the device's built-in vibration and auditory features [8–10]. Touchscreen-based solutions suffer from unique challenges due to the perceptual limitation imposed by both haptic perception (e.g., low haptic resolution and lack of cutaneous information) and the hardware (e.g., a featureless glass surface display with limited screen real estate). Our previous work addressed these limitations through development of a touchscreen-based solution, called a Vibro-Audio Interface (VAI) and demonstrated that the VAI is a viable multimodal solution for learning various formats of graphical information such as graphs, polygons, and maps [7, 11–13]. Studies have also shown that simulating haptic feedback on touchscreen interfaces using additional hardware such as mounting vibro-tactors on the fingers [14, 15, 17] and using electro-static screen overlays [16, 18] can be used as a potential solution for providing BVI people with non-visual access to graphical information.

Although promising, a major limitation with the VAI, and all other touchscreen-based solutions, is that the underlying devices have a limited screen real estate (ranging from $\sim$ 3 to 18 in.), which constrains the amount of graphical information that can be simultaneously presented. A common method for presenting complex large-format graphical information (such as maps) is to group information based on its spatial proximity and relevance, and then to allow users to access this grouped information at different spatial and temporal intervals. These intervals are usually termed as zoom levels and the process of navigating between these zoom levels is termed as a zoom-in operation (navigating deeper into the rendering) or a zoom-out operation (navigating towards the top layer). For example, choosing Toronto as a location in Google maps will yield different information granularity based on its representation at different zoom levels (see Fig. 1). Zoom level 0 (lowest zoom level) will yield the overview of the globe, and as one zooms in to level 10, city names around Toronto will be accessible, and by further zooming in to level 17, finer (deeper) details such as street names within the city will become accessible. For the purpose of this paper, this scenario of navigating between different levels of information content is referred to as *information-zooming*.

Fig. 1. Google maps displaying Toronto at zoom levels 0, 7, and 18

Zooming operations are also used for magnifying (scaling-up) or shrinking (scaling-down) the graphical renderings without affecting their topology. In general, magnifying is termed as a zoom-in operation, and shrinking is termed as a zoom-out operation. For the purpose of this paper, this alternative zooming scenario is referred to as *image-zooming*. *Image-zooming* does not involve navigating between different levels of information content, as is the case with *information-zooming*; instead, a single level of information content is either magnified or shrunk based on a fixed-step or a variable-step scale factor. With both these scenarios, it is essential for the users to integrate the different pieces of graphical information conveyed across zoom levels into a consolidated whole, i.e., the cognitive map. This information integration is especially important for BVI users as challenges in non-visual environmental sensing often limit their access to information that is necessary for cognitive map development [6]. To overcome this issue it is vital that BVI people can access spatial products such as maps to learn environmental relations. However, for this to work with touchscreen devices, they must be able to accurately integrate information between different zoom levels.

Sighted individuals can intuitively perform this integration process by using various zooming techniques (e.g., pinch gestures) as rapid saccadic eye movements and a large field of view makes the top-down grouping of map information relatively easy [3, 19]. By contrast, touch-based non-visual interfaces cannot directly employ these techniques as haptic exploration is a slow, serial, and highly cognitively demanding process. In addition, finger-based gestures are the primary mode of accessing and learning the graphical elements, so cannot be simultaneously used for performing zooming operations [20]. Moreover, haptic exploration requires investigating the map using a contour following technique to determine whether to zoom in or out [21]. This process can be extremely inefficient and frustrating depending on the complexity and structure of the graphic [22, 23] and how the zoom levels are implemented [24]. To appreciate this challenge, the reader is invited to try learning a map using zooming operations with your eyes closed. To overcome this challenge you must learn graphical elements at each zoom level independently and then integrate the levels to build a comprehensive mental representation of the map. To ease this non-visual integration process, the information across levels (at least the adjacent levels) should have meaningful relations [24], and include prominent features (landmarks) such that users can easily relate and integrate the levels [25]. The question remains open as to how non-visual graphical elements can be best learned at each zoom level and then integrated to build a global cognitive map. To our knowledge, no work to date has addressed this issue. Our motivation is to fill this gap in the literature by experimentally evaluating *whether users will be able to employ non-visual zooming operations to build a global cognitive map by integrating and relating graphical elements presented across multiple zoom levels.*

2   Current Research

Many researchers have evaluated the use of traditional zooming techniques (known to work with visual displays) with non-visual interfaces. Some notable work with haptic displays include the use of fixed-step zooming for enhancing or shrinking virtual graphical images at a fixed linear scale [26, 27], identifying the number of steps (zoom levels) for optimal handling in haptic zoomable interfaces [28], and the use of logarithmic step zooming that enhances or shrinks the graphical image via electronic haptic displays [29]. Studies have also made comparisons between zoom levels with audio-tactile map exploration [10], and studied zooming operations using auditory cues to learn virtual environments [30]. While each of these projects demonstrated the users' ability to perform traditional zooming techniques to achieve a particular task, they did not evaluate whether users were able to learn and develop a cognitive map of the given graphical material, which is our focus here. Another major limitation of these studies is that they did not address *information-zooming scenarios*; rather, evaluations were only made with *image-zooming applications*, which results in graphical elements being cropped or partially displayed while zooming from one level to another. Work by [31] addressed these issues with *image-zooming* scenarios and found that use of — what is called — an intuitive zooming approach was more effective than the traditional fixed step-zoom approach [21] and that maintaining meaningful relations across zoom levels benefits tactile learning [24]. However, these studies did not evaluate whether users were able to develop a global cognitive map of the graphical renderings being apprehended. For a zooming method (or algorithm) to be truly useful, in addition to being intuitive and robust, it should also support exploration and integration of graphical elements across different zoom levels. With this logic, a behavioral study was conducted to evaluate whether non-visual zooming methods support users in development of cognitive maps by facilitating non-visual exploration, and integration of graphical elements across multiple zoom levels.

3   Experimental Evaluation

This study extends the use of our Vibro-Audio Interface for investigating graphical access and map reading as evaluated in previous work [7, 12] by employing complex large-format graphical materials such that the use of zooming or panning operations is necessary to perceive the layouts in their entirety. Twelve blindfolded-sighted participants (five males and seven females, ages 19-30) were recruited for the study. All gave informed consent and were paid for their participation. The study was approved by the Institutional Review Board (IRB) of the University of Maine. It is important to note that use of blindfolded-sighted participants is justifiable here as we are testing the ability to learn and represent non-visual material that is equally accessible to both sighted and BVI groups. In support, an earlier study with the VAI found no differences between blindfolded-sighted and BVI participants [7]. Indeed, inclusion of blindfolded-sighted participants is generally accepted as a normal first step in the preliminary testing of assistive technology (see [32] for discussion).

3.1   Experimental Conditions

Three different zoom-mode conditions were compared as part of this study, namely: (1) Fixed zoom, (2) Functional zoom, and (3) No zoom (control).

Fixed zoom. This method is where a single level of information content is either magnified (zoomed-in) or shrunk (zoomed-out) based on a fixed-step scale factor. The advantage of adopting a fixed step zoom methodology is the redundancy of the graphical elements across zoom levels, which facilitates the integration process as users can relate graphical elements by maintaining references (i.e., landmarks) between the zoom levels. Since touchscreens have a limited screen real estate (i.e., viewport), information content will inevitably extend beyond the viewport as one zooms in using this method. To facilitate access to the information beyond what is directly perceivable on the display, it is necessary to incorporate panning operations. From earlier work with the VAI, we found that a technique called two-finger drag was an intuitive and efficient approach for performing non-visual panning [12]. With this technique, users can explore and learn graphical elements with their primary finger and when panning is necessary they initiate or stop the panning-mode by placing or removing a second finger on the screen. Once in panning mode, users could pan the map in any direction by dragging it with the two fingers synchronously. The advantage of this panning method is that users can stay oriented and maintain their reference as their primary finger is constantly in contact with the map (Fig. 2).

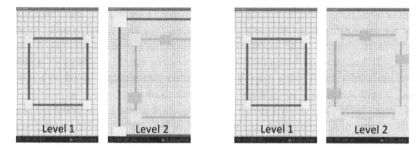

Fig. 2. Fixed zoom demo (left), functional zoom demo (right)

Functional zoom. The functional zoom method implemented here is adopted from what is termed "intuitive zooming" implemented on a tactile mouse-based display [24, 31], where the different zoom levels are based on an object hierarchy (see [24] for details). This zooming algorithm involves two rules: (1) objects that are close to each other are considered as meaningful groupings and are selected as a whole to be represented in a sub-graphic; otherwise, (2) individual objects are represented in each sub-graphic. By adopting this algorithm the redundancy of graphical elements across zoom levels was avoided in this condition. For instance, zooming in to level 2 with functional zoom will only show the corridor segments and landmarks. Whereas level 2 in the fixed zoom condition will show the corridor segments and landmarks along with the boundary (redundant from level 1). While the spatial relations between the two levels are explicit in the fixed zoom condition, they must be interpreted between levels with the functional zoom technique. The redundancy was purposefully avoided in this condition to assess whether users would be able to interpret these spatial relations when they are not explicitly specified.

No-zoom control condition. To assess the influence of using zooming operations and their effect on spatial and temporal integration of graphical elements across zoom levels, a no-zoom condition was included as a control. In this condition, the entire indoor layout was presented to the user at a single zoom level using the VAI.

To facilitate access to the complete map, which extended beyond the contours of the display, the two-finger drag panning method was also incorporated into this condition.

3.2   Experimental Stimuli and Apparatus

For all three conditions, the Vibro-Audio Interface was implemented on a Samsung Galaxy Tab 7.0 Plus tablet, with a 17.78 cm (7.0 in.) touchscreen serving as the information display. Three building layout maps were used as experimental stimuli (with two additional maps used for practice). Each map was composed of corridors, landmarks, and junctions. Each map had three levels of information: (1) a layer containing the exterior wall structure of the building, (2) a layer showing the corridor structure with position of important landmarks indicated, and (3) a layer showing landmarks (e.g., an Exit). The three maps were carefully designed such that they had the same complexity but different topology. Each map required the user to zoom into each of the three different levels (and/or to pan in all four directions) in order to access the map in its entirety. The complexity was matched in terms of: (1) Boundary structure, (2) Number and orientation of corridor segments, (3) Number of junctions, and (4) Landmarks. Each of the maps had 3 landmarks with names based on a standard building layout theme, e.g. entrance, exit, and rest room.

The maps were all rendered using previously established vibro-tactile parameters (7). Line widths of 8.9 mm (0.35 in.) were used, which corresponded to 60 pixels on the 7.0 in. touchscreen. The vibration feedback was incorporated using Immersion Corp's universal haptic layer (UHL) (Immersion, 2013). The exterior walls were given a constant vibration, based on the UHL effect "Engine1_100" which uses a repeating loop at 250 Hz with 100 % power. A pulsing vibration based on the UHL effect "Weapon_1" (a wide-band 0.01 s pulse with a 50 % duty cycle and a 0.02 s period) indicated the junctions. The corridors were rendered with a fast pulsing vibration based on the UHL effect "Engine3_100" which uses a repeating loop at 143 Hz with 100 % power. The landmarks were indicated by an auditory cue (sine tone) coupled with a fast pulsing vibration, based on the UHL effect "Engine3_100". In addition, speech output (e.g., name of the landmark) was provided for the junctions and landmarks upon tapping the vibrating region. Similarly, the zoom levels were indicated by speech output. For example, zooming-in to level 2 from level 1 was indicated by a speech message "at corridor level".

3.3   Procedure

A within-subjects design was used in the experiment. In each condition, participants learned a building layout map and performed subsequent testing tasks. The condition orders were counterbalanced and individual maps randomized between participants. The study consisted of a practice, learning, and testing phase for each condition. The first practice trial in each condition was a demo trial where the experimenter explained the zooming technique, task, goal, and strategies. The participant explored the stimuli with corrective feedback from the experimenter. In the second practice trial, they were blindfolded and were asked to learn the complete map, and perform a test sequence without a blindfold. The experimenter evaluated the practice test results immediately to ensure they correctly understood the tasks before moving on to the learning phase. During the learning phase, participants were first blindfolded and were instructed to explore and learn the map. While learning, they were allowed to switch back and forth between the zoom levels without restriction. They were asked to indicate to the experimenter when they believed that they had learned the entire map. Once indicated, the experimenter removed the device and proceeded to the testing phase, which consisted of three tasks: (1) landmark positioning, (2) inter-landmark pointing, and (3) map reconstruction.

In the landmark positioning task, blindfolded participants were asked to mark the position of a landmark by either zooming-in or zooming-out from one level to another level. The task assessed the accuracy of participants' mental representation of the physical map, as correct performance required them to infer the spatial relations from their cognitive map. As an example, "from the landmark level (level 3), zoom-out to the exterior wall level (level 1) and mark the position of "Exit" with reference to its position on the exterior wall of the building". This task was excluded from the no-zoom control condition, as there was only one zoom-level. The inter-landmark pointing task assessed the accuracy of participants' cognitive map by asking them to indicate the allocentric direction between landmarks using a physical pointer affixed to a wooden board. Since participants never learned the straight-line direction between landmarks, they could only perform this Euclidean task by inferring the spatial relations from their cognitive map. Three pointing trials were tested for each map (e.g., indicate the direction from the entrance to the restroom) covering all three pairs of landmarks. Finally, in the reconstruction task, participants drew the map and labeled the landmarks on a template canvas of the same size as the original map. To provide them with a reference frame of the map's scale, the reconstruction canvas was matched with the device screen size. From this design, seven experimental measures were evaluated as a function of zoom-mode condition.

3.4   Experimental Measures

Learning time.   The learning time represents the level of cognitive effort imposed on the user while learning the map with each zoom-mode condition. The Learning time is the time taken from the moment they first touched the screen until they confirmed that they had completed learning of the map. The learning time ranged from ~ 1.5 min to ~ 11 min (Mean = 304 s, SD = 153 s).

Positioning accuracy.   As discussed earlier, participants were asked to mark the position of landmarks from one zoom level onto another zoom level and accuracy was measured by comparing the marked position to its actual position. The no-zoom control condition was excluded for this measure, as there were no zoom levels.

Positioning Time.   For the three positioning tasks, the time taken to identify a landmark using zooming operations was measured. Similar to positioning accuracy, this time was only compared between the functional zoom and fixed zoom conditions.

Pointing accuracy. Angular errors were measured by comparing the reproduced angle to the actual angle between landmarks and were then analyzed in two ways: Unsigned (absolute) error and Signed (relative) error (under-estimation represents a negative bias and over-estimation represents a positive bias).

Reconstruction accuracy. The reconstructed maps were analyzed in terms of whether the maps reflected the correct spatial configuration of the exterior walls and corridor segments using a bi-dimensional regression method [33]. Thirteen anchor points (3 landmarks and 10 junctions) were chosen on each reconstructed map. Their degree of correspondence with the actual map were analyzed based on three factors: (1) Scale (i.e., magnitude of expansion or contraction), (2) Theta (i.e., rotation), and (3) Distortion Index (i.e., overall difference considering both scale and theta).

Landmark labeling accuracy. Landmark labeling accuracy was measured from the reconstructed map and discrete scoring was applied based on their correctness, ranging from 0 to 3 (i.e., 1 for each correct label, 3 if all three labels were correct).

Subjective preference. Participants were asked to order the three conditions based on their preference (with one being most preferred). These data were analyzed to gauge what conditions were most liked.

4   Results

Performance data for each of the measures described above were analyzed and compared between the three zoom-mode conditions using a set of repeated measures ANOVAs and post-hoc paired sample t-tests. The f, t and p values of these analyses are given in Table 1, along with significant group comparisons. Overall results demonstrated that there were no significant differences between conditions across all measures tested except for learning time.

Table 1. ANOVA and paired sample t-tests results along with significant group comparisons

Measures	Significant Group Comparisons	Anova		Fixed vs. Functional		Fixed vs. Control		Functional vs. Control	
				paired-sample t-tests					
		f	sig.	t	sig.	t	sig.	t	sig.
Learning Time	Fixed vs. Functional, Functional vs. Control	8.591	0.002	4.044	0.002	0.787	0.448	3.694	0.004
Positioning accuracy	None	1.044	0.329	-1.022	0.329	*	*	*	*
Positioning time	None	0.363	0.559	-0.457	0.650	*	*	*	*
Pointing accuracy	None	1.261	0.303	1.989	0.072	-0.74	0.48	-1.34	0.207
Reconstruction accuracy	None	0.186	0.831	-0.432	0.674	0.000	1.000	0.561	0.586
Landmark labeling	None	0.000	1.000	0.000	1.000	0.000	1.000	0.000	1.000

Learning time. Results showed that participants took less time to learn using the functional zoom condition (M = 222.33 s, SD = 99.35) as compared to the fixed zoom condition (M = 335.83 s, SD = 145.95) or the no-zoom condition (M = 368.92 s, SD = 175.47). Learning time with functional zoom was significantly faster than the other two conditions ($ps < 0.05$), which demonstrates the intuitiveness of this method. However, no significant differences were observed between the fixed and no-zoom conditions. This is interesting because participants performed both zooming and panning operations in the fixed zoom condition, whereas they performed only panning in the no-zooming condition. This suggests that incorporation of a zooming operation did not impose any additional measurable cognitive load on the learning process.

Positioning Task. Results showed that there was no significant difference between fixed and functional zoom conditions for either the relative positioning accuracy or the positioning time. This similarity is an important outcome, as fixed zoom (M = 27.55 s, SD = 6.6) was expected to perform better than the functional zoom (M = 25.44 s, SD = 5.11) as it had the advantage of providing a clear reference between corridors and landmarks at a single zoom level. The similarity of performance demonstrates that participants were able to accurately relate graphical elements and reference them even when presented independently across zoom levels.

Pointing Task. No significant differences (all $ps > 0.05$) were observed between the three zoom-mode conditions in pointing accuracy (for both signed & unsigned error), indicating that learning from all three conditions led to the development of a similar cognitive map. This outcome also suggests that none of the conditions led to reliably different cognitive biases (signed error) in the mental representation of the map.

Reconstruction Task. Results of the bi-dimensional regression analysis also revealed no significant differences between zoom-mode conditions (all $ps > 0.05$) for the three factors evaluated: Scale, Theta and Distortion Index. A numerical difference in the scale factor suggests that participants generally perceived the map to be of smaller size when apprehended from the zooming conditions (Fixed M = 0.983, SD = 0.15, Functional M = 0.975, SD = 0.11) but not when perceived from the no-zoom control condition (M = 1.05, SD = 0.16). This is likely because when they started learning the map, the rendering was within the display frame for zooming conditions (level 1) but extended beyond the frame in the no-zoom control condition. This difference might have created an illusion that maps rendered in this condition were bigger than the maps in the zooming conditions. However, this difference was not statistically significant, so should be taken with a grain of salt. In addition, overall performance with the theta and DI factors suggested that all three conditions led to the development of a similar cognitive map.

Subjective preference. Participants preferred the zooming conditions over the no-zoom condition, with an equal level of preference for the two zooming conditions. We attribute this outcome to the fact that graphical elements were less cluttered in the zooming conditions as compared to the no-zoom condition. In parallel with our interpretation, seven (out of twelve) participants self reported that it was easier to learn graphical elements as groups (zoom levels) rather than learning them all at once.

5   General Discussion

It is necessary to incorporate zooming operations for accessing complex graphical information such as maps within the limited screen real estate of touchscreen devices. However, implementing and performing zooming techniques with non-visual interfaces is difficult owing to the perceptual and cognitive challenges underlying touch-based exploration. Furthermore, in situations with complex graphical information such as maps, the various graphical elements are often disconnected and rendered across multiple zoom levels. This paper addressed these challenges and investigated whether users could perform non-visual zooming operations and subsequently integrate graphical elements across zoom levels to form a globally coherent spatial representation in memory. A usability study was conducted to assess users ability to perform two different zooming methods when learning indoor layout maps by integrating map information presented across three zoom levels. Accuracy in cognitive map development was evaluated by comparing performance in exploration, learning, and spatial behaviors between three zoom mode conditions, namely: (1) fixed-step zoom, (2) functional zoom, and (3) a no-zoom control condition. All six measures tested required development and accessing of cognitive maps to infer various spatial relations between graphical elements. We postulated that if users were able to effectively integrate and relate graphical elements across zoom levels in the zooming conditions, the resulting cognitive maps should be similar to the one developed from the no-zoom control condition.

The most important outcome of the study is the similarity of performance observed across pointing, positioning, and map reconstruction tasks between the three zoom-mode conditions, demonstrating that all three conditions led to development of a similar cognitive map. It is important to note that the performance with the no-zoom control condition was not negatively influenced by the incorporation of a panning operation as the fixed zoom condition also incorporated panning and exhibited similar (even numerically better) performance. Furthermore, the error performance found here across all conditions is consistent with previous work on touchscreen-based graphical access [7, 11–14], suggesting that learning from all three zoom-mode conditions led to development of an accurate cognitive map.

Learning time with functional zoom was significantly faster than the other two conditions. Although not statistically different, the overall trend of the data suggests that the functional zoom technique exhibited superior performance in all measures tested. This superior performance for functional zoom demonstrates that users were able to integrate and relate graphical elements even when the inter-element relations are not explicit. These findings are congruent with earlier work on intuitive-zooming [24] and suggest that avoiding redundancy and maintaining meaningful graphical relations between adjacent zoom levels is critical for effective non-visual exploration and learning of complex graphical information using zooming operations.

One limitation of the current study procedure was that the design did not require participants to perform zoom-out operations during the learning phase and only one of the three positioning trials during testing involved zoom-out operations. Although the positioning performance did not significantly differ between the three trials, enforcing equal use of zoom-in and zoom-out operations during learning would likely strengthen users' ability to integrate graphical elements. Future work should address this limitation and compare more than 3 zoom levels to generalize the findings, which would also be more representative of complex graphical materials.

In conclusion, incorporating zooming and panning operations are an important first step in making digital graphics accessible to BVI people using touchscreen interfaces. We contribute to this effort by demonstrating that touch-based non-visual zooming operations support learning of complex large-scale graphical materials and aid the development of accurate cognitive maps. As discussed earlier, a major challenge in providing traditional tactile map access to BVI users is the size of the physical maps and the expense and effort of authoring these products for non-visual access. We believe touchscreen-based multimodal interfaces are a viable solution to overcome these challenges. Providing map access via such interfaces could have significant broader impacts on increasing BVI independence by offering a new tool to promote environmental learning and wayfinding behavior.

Acknowledgements. We acknowledge support from NSF grants CHS-1425337 and CDI-1028895 on this project.1

References

1. Eriksson, Y.: Tactile Pictures. Pictorial representations for the blind, pp. 1784–1940 (1998)
2. Perkins, M.: Perkins Museum (2015). http://www.perkinsmuseum.org/. Accessed 01 Jan 2015
3. O'Modhrain, S., Giudice, N.A., Gardner, J.A., Legge, G.E.: Designing media for visually-impaired users of refreshable touch displays: possibilities and pitfalls. Trans. Haptics **8**(3), 248–257 (2015)
4. Rowell, J., Ungar, S.: The world of touch: an international survey of tactile maps. Part 1: production. Br. J. Vis. Impair. **21**(3), 98–104 (2003)
5. Rowell, J., Ungar, S.: The world of touch: an international survey of tactile maps. Part 2: design. Br. J. Vis. Impair. **21**(3), 105–110 (2003)
6. Giudice, N.A., Legge, G.E.: Blind navigation and the role of technology. In: Engineering Handbook of Smart Technology for Aging, Disability, and Independence, pp. 479–500. Wiley (2008)
7. Giudice, N.A., Palani, H.P., Brenner, E., Kramer, K.M.: Learning non-visual graphical information using a touch-based vibro-audio interface. In: Proceedings 14th International ACM SIGACCESS Conference on Computers and Accessibility, pp. 103–110 (2012)
8. Hoggan, E., Brewster, S.A., Johnston, J.: Investigating the effectiveness of tactile feedback for mobile touchscreens. In: Proceeding Twenty-Sixth Annual CHI Conference Human Factors Computer Systems - CHI 2008, p. 1573 (2008)
9. Hoggan, E., Brewster, S.A.: Designing audio and tactile crossmodal icons for mobile devices. In: Proceedings of the 9th International Conference on Multimodal Interfaces ICMI 2007, p. 162 (2007)

10. Poppinga, B., Pielot, M., Magnusson, C., Rassmus-Grohn, K.: TouchOver map: audio-tactile exploration of interactive maps. In: Proceedings of 12th International Conference of Human Computer Interaction with Mobile devices ACM, Stock. Sweden, pp. 545–550 (2011)

11. Raja, M.K.: The development and validation of a new smartphone based non-visual spatial interface for learning indoor layouts, University of Maine (2011)

12. Palani, H.P., Giudice, N.A.: Evaluation of non-visual panning operations using touch-screen devices. In: Proceedings of 16th International ACM SIGACCESS Conference on Computers & Accessibility (2014)

13. Gershon, P., Klatzky, R.L., Palani, H.P., Giudice, N.A.: Visual, tangible, and touch-screen: comparison of platforms for displaying simple graphics. Assist. Technol. **28**, 1–6 (2015)

14. Goncu, C., Marriott, K.: GraCALC: An accessible graphing calculator. In: Proceedings of 17th International ACM SIGACCESS Conference on Computers & Accessibility, pp. 311–312 (2015)

15. Goncu, C., Marriott, K.: GraVVITAS: generic multi-touch presentation of accessible graphics. In: Campos, P., Graham, N., Jorge, J., Nunes, N., Palanque, P., Winckler, M. (eds.) INTERACT 2011, Part I. LNCS, vol. 6946, pp. 30–48. Springer, Heidelberg (2011)

16. Mullenbach, J., Shultz, C., Colgate, J.E., Piper, A.M.: Exploring affective communication through variable - friction surface haptics. In: Proceedings of SIGCHI Conference on Human Factors in Computing Systems, pp. 3963–3972 (2014)

17. Noguchi, T., Fukushima, Y., Yairi, I.E.: Evaluating information support system for visually impaired people with mobile touch screens and vibration. In: Proceedings of 13th International ACM SIGACCESS Conference on Computers and Accessibility, p. 243 (2011)

18. Xu, C., Israr, A., Poupyrev, I., Bau, O., Harrison, C.: Tactile display for the visually impaired using TeslaTouch. In: Proceedings CHI EA 2011, pp. 317–322 (2011)

19. Klatzky, R.L., Giudice, N.A., Bennett, C.R., Loomis, J.M.: Touch-screen technology for the dynamic display of 2D spatial information without vision: Promise and progress. Multisens. Res. **27**(5–6), 359–378 (2014)

20. Jones, L.A., Lederman, S.J.: Human Hand Function. Oxford University Press, Oxford (2006)

21. Rastogi, R., Pawluk, T.V.D., Ketchum, J.: Intuitive tactile zooming for graphics accessed by individuals who are blind and visually impaired. IEEE Trans. Neural Syst. Rehabil. Eng. **21**(4), 655–663 (2013)

22. Casey, S.M.: Cognitive mapping by the blind. J. Vis. Impair. Blind. **72**(8), 297–301 (1978)

23. Wijntjes, M.W.A., van Lienen, T., Verstijnen, I.M., Kappers, A.M.L.: Look what i have felt: unidentified haptic line drawings are identified after sketching. Acta Psychol. (Amst) **128**(2), 255–263 (2008)

24. Rastogi, R., Pawluk, D.T.V.: Toward an improved haptic zooming algorithm for graphical information accessed by individuals who are blind and visually impaired. Assist. Technol. **25**(1), 9–15 (2013)

25. Passini, R., Proulx, G.: Wayfinding without vision: an experiment with congenitally totally blind people. Envi. Behav. **20**(2), 227–252 (1988)

26. Schloerb, D.W., Lahav, O., Desloge, J.G., Srinivasan, M.A.: BlindAid : virtual environment system for self-reliant trip planning and orientation and mobility training. In: Haptic Symposium, pp. 363–370 (2010)

27. Schmitz, B., Ertl, T.: Making digital maps accessible using vibrations. In: Miesenberger, K., Klaus, J., Zagler, W., Karshmer, A. (eds.) ICCHP 2010, Part 1. LNCS, vol. 6179, pp. 100–107. Springer, Heidelberg (2010)

28. Ziat, M., Gapenne, O., Stewart, J., Lenay, C., Bausse, J.: Design of a haptic zoom: levels and steps. In: Second Joint EuroHaptics Conference and Symposium on Haptic Interfaces for Virtual Environment and Teleoperator Systems, pp. 102–108 (2007)

29. Magnuson, C., Rassmus-Grohn, K.: Non-visual zoom and scrolling operations in a virtual haptic environment. In: Proceedings of Eurohaptics, pp. 6–9 (2003)

30. Walker, S., Salisbury, J.K.: Large haptic topographic maps: marsview and the proxy graph algorithm. ACM Siggraph, pp. 83–92 (2003)

31. Rastogi, R., Street, W.M., V Pawluk, D.T.: Automatic, intuitive zooming for people who are blind or visually impaired. In: Proceedings of 12th International ACM SIGACCESS Conference on Computer Accessibility, pp. 239–240 (2010)

32. Chae, S., Yim, S.-B., Han, Y.: Flight simulation on tiled displays with distributed computing scheme. In: Kim, J.-H., Lee, K., Tanaka, S., Park, S.-H. (eds.) AsiaSim 2011. PICT, vol. 4, pp. 1–6. Springer, Heidelberg (2012)

33. Tobler, W.R.: Bidimensional regression. Geogr. Anal. **26**, 186–212 (1994)

Proposal of an Alternative HMI Mechanism for Blind Android Users Based on Media Headsets as Input/Output Peripherals

Miguel Páramo Castrillo[(✉)], Silvia de los Ríos[(✉)],
Juan Bautista Montalvá Colomer,
María Fernanda Cabrera-Umpierrez, and María Teresa Arredondo

Life Supporting Technologies,
Universidad Politécnica de Madrid, Madrid, Spain
{mparamo,srios,jmontalva,chiqui,mta}@lst.tfo.upm.es

Abstract. This paper introduces an alternative method of interaction over Graphical User Interfaces (GUIs), using a button enabled headset as a main Input/Output (IO) peripheral. This paper is focused on the underlying basis which is based on the results and implementation of an Android prototype once the viability for this system has been remarkably proven. Being blind Android users the initial target beneficiaries does not restrict the scope of this solution since its conceptual approach is scalable to other various systems and may be applied to mainstream users. Hence, the main objective is to create an alternative, effective and low cost mechanism for blind users or eyes free scenarios by means of the buttons built in modern media headsets; or in other words, the main motivation of this article is to present this solution as an alternative Human Machine Interaction (HMI) mechanism with the objective of proposing an elegant and comfortable way of interaction over specifically designed software; resulting in a plausible better solution for many use cases where the eyes free approach may be beneficial.

Keywords: Interaction · Eyes-free · HMI · Android · Blind · Headset · Accessibility · UX · UI

1 Introduction

There are close to 40 million blind persons and 285 million of visual impaired worldwide [1]. A fraction of these people uses a smartphone on their daily basis and in any case, no one should be excluded from using it. Blind people face the challenge of using a mobile device that is designed for the non visual impaired and integrates a touch screen as the main input hardware. Blind users tend to interact with their devices with the assistance of a voice synthesizer or TTS (Text To Speech) combined with an "Explore by Touch" mode in detriment of the usage of traditional output to Braille accessories. This assistive solution is integrated by default on the main mobile operating systems (Android [2] and iOS [3]) and relies on a software that recognizes a set of gestures the user can "draw" with their fingers over the touch screen; enabling the navigation across the GUI, the identification of the different elements within it and the interaction with

M. Antona and C. Stephanidis (Eds.): UAHCI 2016, Part II, LNCS 9738, pp. 175–184, 2016.
DOI: 10.1007/978-3-319-40244-4_17

them while providing spoken feedback through the TTS at the same time. According to the general opinion of blind users, this current accessibility implementation has still slight room for improvement but is solving the obvious challenges they face and is satisfactory, especially the iOS implementation.

Despite the viability of the current solutions, they attempt to adapt the GUIs instead of doing the inverse process: not forcing the people to operate with an input hardware that was not originally conceived for them.

Some hypotheses are proposed: interaction based on gestures is not so intuitive and may lack precision; while the feedback given by the headset buttons themselves feels instead more accurate and precise. Apart of that, some Explore by Touch gestures are not natural or intuitive and require some training and learning [4]. Finally, the screen is also one of the major battery drainers of the smartphones (according to independent tests, on average it takes at least 30 % of the total or a regular usage) so this alternative system would certainly save power (using the screen to display any GUI is optional).

Modern mobile headsets have evolved and may integrate a built-in microphone for hands-free calls, up to three buttons for media player controlling [5] or even radio antennae. They keep the same size of a traditional headset and are retro compatible with standard jack plugs; meaning they can be plugged directly into a compatible jack port without requiring alternative hardware or further setup (Fig. 1).

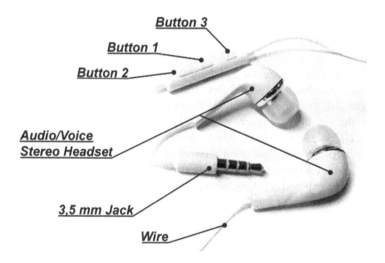

Fig. 1. A three-buttoned media headset by Samsung

2 Methodology

This proposal has been conceived following steps: Analysis, high level design, proof of concept implementation, prototype implementation and tests. As a prototype or Minimum Viable Product (MVP), the initial phase consisted on planning the solution and the HMI mechanism; this step also implied the analysis of use cases and potential benefits for the users. After that, the initial proof of concept (alpha) version was coded over a simple and function-less app in order to ensure that the implementation was feasible for the target system. Once the initial prototype was created and polished, then a full demo newsreader app with several functions was created. This second MVP (beta) was the solution subjected to evaluation with several users: 14 users: 12 non blind users and 2 blind users. All the feedback given was analyzed and conclusions were taken afterwards.

The track to achieve the proposed solution had two fundamental pillars which are the Software Development Methodology (SDM) and the User Centered Design (UCD) methodology [6]. Due to the cyclical SDM process and the also cyclical nature of the UCD methodology, both were combined into a single development process were users would participate and guide the successive iterations of the product. At the current state of the proposed solution, technical viability was granted and the proof of concept was made, hence not requiring a second iteration.

3   Implementation

This HMI implementation requires either a software layer built on top of some OS (Operating System) interaction mechanisms (acting as a hook for certain input events) or a custom made application that handles the behavior of the input events. Both solutions are feasible (at the moment this paper was written) but the first one relies much more on the Android OS and may not have granted stability and maintenance in the future, plus, it is less flexible and powerful since it limits the hooked events for security reasons and the hooking mechanism is more complex and slower, presumably lagging the response time and jittering the interaction. So for those reasons, the MVP was created following the second paradigm as described as follows. In any case, the specific implementation for Android can essentially be adapted to other systems.

When pressed, those headset buttons feed the device with a signal that is directly mapped by the OS into a keystroke as if generated directly from a keyboard. The Android API [7, 8] legitimately allows capturing and managing these input events directly from a foreground application (that could be the main launcher but for security reasons, not a third party app). Developers can use this eases in order to build apps based on the here exposed solution; where tactile exploration is not required and their users can control the whole application even keeping the device into their pocket.

When the prototype is launched, the Text To Speech engine is activated so it is ready to be called from the interface anytime. It operates in "Flush" mode, meaning that any message sent will not be queued but played immediately instead; even "cutting" the previous pending utterance if any. This way any user that has gain expertise with the system can interact far more quickly and also there are no problems of synchronization or delay among the focused element with the spoken feedback. Each time an element gains focus or is selected (both events are treated as the same) the TTS provides a description of it.

The given implementation considered different input events that are mapped to trigger certain actions depending on the operating mode of the user interface.

3.1   Input Events

Given a single commutable signal, there is a chance of extending the input it feeds into the system by controlling the intervals and duration of the "clicks". An extra degree of freedom (the time variable) allows a single input signal to "expand" into the following three:

- **Single click (S):** The user clicks on the button for a short time. The interval where the switch is commuted is shorter than the one established for the "long press" event.
- **Double click (D):** The user clicks twice times the commuter in a short period of time. The interval between the two clicks is shorter that the window time established for two separated "single click" events.
- **Long press (L):** The user presses the button for a time longer than the defined for a "single click".

3.2   Actions

On the other hand, the plausible actions that can be carried out are the following:

- **Activation (A):** It will activate the focused element. The response of the element will likely provide a description of it, navigate to another menu, modify its state or trigger a certain predefined action.
- **Next element (N):** Action that navigates to the next element in the UI. It will un-focus the current element and focus/select the next one. The TTS will speak the description of the element being now focused automatically. As stated before, the interface is linear and cyclical so the last element will be concatenated with the first and vice versa.
- **Previous element (P):** The exact opposite of "Next", it gives focus to the previous element in the UI.
- **Back (B):** Action that returns back to the previous menu. If the user switched to another menu, since they are stacked, this event will "close" the current menu and enter back into the one where the current was coming from (Fig. 2).

3.3   UI Setups

There are certain particularities of the interface's behavior that must be considered. These HMI mechanisms are based on a sequential (linear) and cyclical UI. Cyclical means that it "chains" in both directions (next and previous) the first and last element within the interface. Also, being linear makes each menu to position the UI components in just one dimension (vertical or horizontal). Apart of those two important characteristics, the UI can also function under those following setups based on the way they handle the inputs, the logic within the UI or the UI design principles (Fig. 3).

- **Default (D):** Each action has a direct input which is triggered on the release of the input event. Interface that only responds to input events without any other internal behavior.

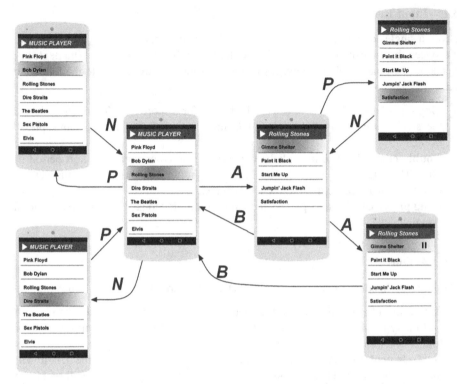

Fig. 2. Example of a diagram of inputs and its transitions under default (D) or continuous (C) GUI setup.

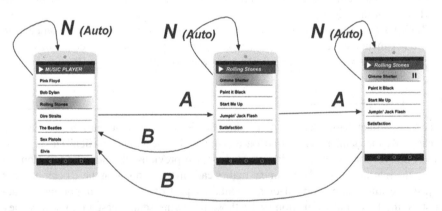

Fig. 3. Auto-scan (S) mode. There are no "Previous" actions and the scanner inputs "Next" automatically.

– **Continuous input (C):** Particular case of the default mode. An input signal that is kept in time (by definition, only applicable to long presses) can be kept acting even after the initial treatment of the input. Unlike the default mode, it delivers events instead of waiting for a release of the commuter. This continuous "Long press" input is interesting and supposed to be limited to generate a continuous flow of "Next" events (it would be similar to a manual auto-scan that stops when the user releases the button) or "Back" events (similar to going quickly from the hierarchy of menus to the root).

– **Auto-Scan (S):** The "Next" (or "Previous") action is automatically triggered at regular pulses by a timer; so the UI is continuously and automatically advancing from one element to the next. This mode is opened to other exclusive actions (these actions for scan control are referred as **R** from now on) such reverting the scanning direction, halting/un-halting it or even slowing it down briefly (Fig. 4).

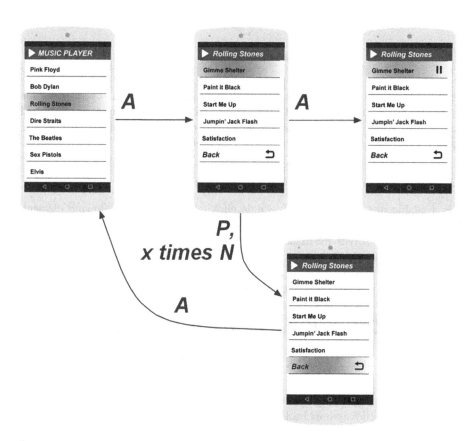

Fig. 4. Back as an element (E) mode. There are no Back actions since the UI includes an element that triggers this action.

- **Back as Element (E):** Design principle that includes the "Back" action as a focusable element within the UI. This setup is complementary to the rest (Fig. 5).

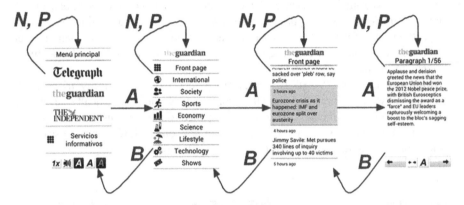

Fig. 5. Newsreader prototype on continuous mode

It is possible to define the behavior of **1 to 3** buttoned headsets by mapping the inputs (**S**ingle, **D**ouble, **L**ong) with the actions (**A**ctivate, **N**ext, **P**revious, **B**ack and scan control **R**) working under certain setups (operation modes) of the UI (**D**efault, **A**uto-Scan, **C**ontinuous input and with Back as Element).

3.4 Single Buttoned Headset Viable Configuration Mappings

It is available just a single button. Single click advances to the following element, double activates and long press returns. No previous action can be performed but the cyclical interface solves the issue. A variant integrates the "Back" as a focusable element at the end of each menu. In this second case, either double click, long press or both can be used to activate (these optional configuration is represented as -/symbol in all tables, where at least one of the inputs must handle the event):

Mode D	Input		
Button	**S**	**D**	**L**
1	N	A	B

Mode DE	Input		
Button	**S**	**D**	**L**
1	N	-/A	

Other alternatives; click activates while long press moves continuously to the next element. Double click returns back:

Mode C	Input		
Button	**S**	**D**	**L**
1	A	B	N

Its variation including the "Back" element can avoid using the double click:

Mode CE	Input		
Button	S	D	L
1	A	-/A	N

Mode CE	Input		
Button	S	D	L
1	N	A	N

Finally, under auto-scan, the button just activates the focused element since the logic behind the interface is responsible of the automatic and sequential navigation. Flux control of the scanner is optional as well:

Mode S	Input		
Button	S	D	L
1	A	-/R	B

Mode SE	Input		
Button	S	D	L
1	A	-/R	

3.5 Double Buttoned Headset Viable Configurations

Under those kind of headsets mappings for button 1 or 2 can be reverted. One button goes previous and its long press returns back. The second button goes next and its long press activates:

Mode D	Input		
Button	S	D	L
1	P	-	B
2	N	-/A	

Mode DE	Input		
Button	S	D	L
1	P	-/A	
2	N		

Also other configurations are viable without mapping the "Previous" action. One button activates and when long pressed it returns back. The second button navigates sequentially and optionally in continuous mode:

Mode D	Input		
Button	S	D	L
1	A	-	B
2	N	-	-

Mode C	Input		
Button	S	D	L
1	A	-	B
2	N	-	N

Under auto-scan, the first button controls activation and the second just the scanner flux. Long press returns. In case of "Back" element implemented, activation on other events apart from single click is optional:

Mode S	Input		
Button	S	D	L
1	A	-/A	-/B
2	-/R	-/R	

Mode SE	Input		
Button	S	D	L
1	A	-/A	
2	-/R		

3.6 Triple Buttoned Headset Viable Configurations

Headsets with more than three buttons can avoid "complex" interactions such the double click and can be set in a natural an easy way of interaction. Also, having such variety of inputs, there is no need to implement the auto-scan or the "Back" despite they can be set that way. The two main configurations are the same under default or continuous mode. It can be used one button for each next/previous event while the third button activates and its long press returns:

Mode D	Input		
Button	S	D	L
1	A	-	B
2	P	-	-
3	N	-	-

Mode C	Input		
Button	S	D	L
1	A	-	B
2	P	-	P
3	N	-	N

Other mappings for those three buttons may not feel much natural. Also any UI in auto-scan or with the back element over-complex or redundant since there is enough control capability with those 3 buttoned headsets.

4 Results

A first prototype was made for the Android platform and tested with 12 non blind users and two blind users, as mentioned above. In the test sessions they attempted to complete a variety of uses cases just using the buttons on the media headset and not being able to either touch or watch the screen. The observation of the trials and the focus groups taken afterwards for a preliminary evaluation were very positive and increased the interest of deeper research in order to improve the yet promising results. The prototype consisted on a GUI integrating a complete news reader among other functionalities. Users could consult a given newspaper, navigate among its categories and the latest news published in each and also control the article presentation paragraph by paragraph. The prototype was based on the continuous mode setup under a three buttoned headset and the previously detailed mapping.

The results were very promising since all of the users were able to interact with the prototype application without being able to see the screen and also without any training apart of a brief explanation. After few seconds they could interact naturally, quickly and with an extreme accuracy. There were no errors or misunderstandings as long as the TTS information was also enough descriptive. Also, two of the users were technically limited and never had used a smartphone before. One of them was a blind woman used to work with a Nokia device with a built in voice synthesizer. Even though they could complete all the trial use cases at its first attempt and even started using the system by themselves freely. This blind woman was totally impressed and delighted with the solution and demanded for a complete system based on this method of interaction.

5   Conclusions and Future Lines

The technique detailed in this paper is a viable alternative for eyes free control of UIs and has the potential of being extremely useful for blind users. It is yet pending to evaluate the solution with a wider sample of blind users and with a more sophisticated and improved prototype and also to test it in terms of satisfaction, accuracy, speed and power consumption against the commercial solutions (Touch to explore and Voice over). However the initial tests were promising and the feedback gathered during the trials will be considered in future iterations of the product despite those considerations are more related to the UI itself than the HMI mechanism.

Finally, the conclusions of this experiment put into manifest that other techniques involving accessible design, an ontology of interactive components and layout definitions of the UI are not mandatory but extremely relevant in order to achieve an excellent user experience when a GUI-less is meant to be designed under following this HMI mechanism. Those fields, along with a deep analysis and specification of the setup modes are beyond the scope of this paper but will be considered on future lines for an eventual development of a commercial solution under the precepts of Universal design.

References

1. WHO: Visual impairment and blindness fact sheet N°282. http://www.who.int/mediacentre/factsheets/fs282/en/
2. Google Inc.: Explore by touch in talkback. https://support.google.com/accessibility/android/answer/6006598?hl=en
3. Apple Inc.: Voice over getting started. https://www.apple.com/voiceover/info/guide/
4. Kane, S., Wobbrock, J., Ladner, R.: Usable gestures for blind people: understanding preference and performance. In: Proceedings of 2011 Annual Conference Human factors Computer System - CHI 2011, pp. 413–422 (2011)
5. US Patent: US20110263303, Multi-button control headset for a mobile communication device (2011)
6. Abras, C., Maloney-Krichmar, D., Preece, J.: User-centered design. In: Bainbridge, W. (ed.) Encyclopedia of Human-Computer Interaction, vol. 37 pp. 445–456. Sage Publications (2004)
7. Google Inc.: Android Activity (onKeyDown) (2016) http://developer.android.com/reference/android/app/Activity.html#onKeyDown%28int,%20android.view.KeyEvent%29
8. Google Inc.: Android KeyEvent http://developer.android.com/reference/android/view/KeyEvent.html

LOVIE: A Word List Optimized for Visually Impaired UsErs on Smartphones

Philippe Roussille[✉] and Mathieu Raynal

CNRS, IRIT, F31 062 Toulouse, France
philippe.roussille@irit.fr

Abstract. On mobile devices, most text entry systems offer assistance through the means of prediction or correction word lists. These lists can hardly be used by visually impaired users in a short time. In this paper, we present three studies to find an interaction which minimizes the time required to select a word from a list without knowing its elements *a priori*. First, we explored the various possible item layouts, to conclude that a linear spatial arrangement is preferable. Then we studied the audio feedback, and we have determined that providing on-demand audio feedback is enough. Finally, we proposed four validation interactions to retain a validation based on the principle of a press-release gesture.

1 Introduction

Smartphones are difficult to use for visually impaired people due to their big touchscreen presenting no physical buttons, hence presenting no tactile cues. Consequently, their daily uses are difficult, especially for text input. However, there exist techniques allowing the visually impaired to use a traditional soft keyboard (VoiceOver for Apple, TalkBack for Android, DUCK). Since the visually impaired know the character layout, they can type fast relying on that knowledge.

Yet, soft keyboards are often enhanced by a completion, prediction or correction system. Such a system usually offers a word list to the user. That list is made of the most probable words given the input context. As a consequence, every proposed word differs on each time the list is being displayed. The users can neither learn nor anticipate the word list that appears. Such lists are thus problematic for the visually impaired as they lack a global vision of the list when it appears. They have to browse it entirely to see the proposed words. Selecting a word in such a list is usually a time loss for the user.

This article aims to facilitate access towards different words within a list as well as selecting the wanted word. As such, we carried out three studies on three problems linked to list interaction. The first study focuses on how to present the different words of a list to a visually impaired user. The second study aims to find the best vocal feedback to the user whilst he uses the list. Finally, the third study was made to find the best interaction allowing to select the word chosen by the user.

© Springer International Publishing Switzerland 2016
M. Antona and C. Stephanidis (Eds.): UAHCI 2016, Part II, LNCS 9738, pp. 185–197, 2016.
DOI: 10.1007/978-3-319-40244-4_18

2   Items Presentation

The first problem at hand is to correctly present the items to the user. Indeed, since visually impaired users have no access to visual information, they should have little to no time lost finding all the elements they need to select.

When it comes to lists and layouts, the usual design is made through a balance between depth and breadth, turning most of the selective operations into a hierarchical browsing. Hierarchy is very common on small devices, as it allows a logical organization and presentation of a large number of items through a tree-like structure [10].

Usually, when browsing a list, selecting an item determines what will be presented next, since browsing is made in a linear fashion. As such, hierarchical browsing is sometimes a challenge, even more when it grows deeper and wider. Different strategies and trade-offs have been studied and modeled [4]. It appears that broader and wider presentations are more efficient [8,12]. However, since the efficiency depends on screen size and the complexity of the task [3], Users actually prefer a deeper hierarchy on a mobile phone, which has a small screen size [5]. However, due to the serial quality of audio-enhanced lists, a broad list might result in information overload for the user.

The items or options in a visual menu are often ordered in some logical fashion. Alphabetical, numerical, and chronological ordering are all examples of ordering techniques that can reduce menu selection times if used appropriately [10]. Ordering menus by frequency of use is another technique that has been found to significantly reduce performance times [11], although it results in dynamic menus that also lead to poorer performance due to the lack of consistency [9]. Even it's preferable to offer a display that order elements under a hierarchy to increase learning. it is however impossible for us to use that approach due to the extreme changing nature of our content: we cannot establish a stable hierarchy that the user could remember or use easily without increasing his cognitive load more than necessary.

For modern screen readers, there exist different strategies to avoid these problems. According to Borodin [1], modern screen readers often read the number of available items, then open an auxiliary window for the user to navigate within the list (like JAWS). Again, the main approach is a vocalization of the list content to the user, which takes time and is not really usable on a mobile environment.

As it is not possible to build a solution effective to quickly run through the elements in a preferred order, giving the smallness of our screen, we chose to focus on a simple set of layouts that an user could easily browse efficiently.

2.1   Proposed Presentations

During our first experimental study, we wanted to know what item presentation would best meet the needs of users. Therefore, we proposed three different presentations.

The first presentation displays the whole word list on the screen. The screen is used entirely and divided so that every item has an identical size. This presentation is called "absolute" presentation. Using this as a principle, we studied three different layouts:

- **line**: the elements are placed on a horizontal line,
- **column**: the elements are arranged in a vertical column,
- **grid**: the elements are arranged in several columns comprising an even number of elements.

The second presentation describes a more dynamic arrangement. Unlike the "absolute" presentation, the elements are dynamically linked to the position of the user's finger. The first element is positioned at the location where the user places his finger, and the following items are achieved when the user moves away from that point. The user can confirm the item he is looking for releasing his finger from the screen. This presentation will be called the "relative" presentation.

In these two presentations, the main interaction is to press finger onto the screen to select an item, move finger on the screen to navigate among the different items and then release the finger to validate the last selected item. On the other hand, the user can cancel by pressing with two fingers onto the screen.

In this last presentation, the items are not all visible on the screen at the same time. Only one word is available. The user can browse the list by sliding his finger left or right, validate by sliding down and cancel by sliding up. This presentation will be called the "list" presentation.

2.2   Method

Participants. 12 participants (3 women and 9 men, mean age = 25) with normal or corrected-to-normal vision participated in our study. They were all blindfolded to ensure they couldn't see the screen at all.

Apparatus. Participants used a Samsung Galaxy SIII smartphone. The device has a resolution of 306 ppp for a 136.6 mm × 70.6 mm screen, a ARM Cortex-A9 MPCore Quad core set at 1.4 GHz and uses Android 4.3. They used their finger to navigate through the items. The items were synthesized from text using the Google Translate service. The audio was trimmed to provide feedback as fast as possible, reducing any possible delay. Nothing was displayed onto the screen during the experiment, making the grids and items invisible to the users.

Procedure. The task was to find a word in the available items as fast as possible. The task went as follow: first, the participant was read the instruction, he was then given the word to search, then he had to browse the items to find the correct one, and ultimately validate it. If he answered a different item, we considered his answer to be wrong. Once a session was completed, the participant was asked to answer a SUS test for each technique, and state his preference among the layouts he went through.

Design. Each participant had to go through two sessions. One session comprised only four elements per list, while the other comprised only six elements per list. Both sessions were run one after the other. The twelve participants were then split at random into two even groups. The first group started with four items lists, while the second started with six items lists. For every session, the participant had to go through five blocks of tasks, one for each presentation. The blocks were balanced through a Latin square. Each block was made of three series of tasks, each run one after the other. Each series comprised as many tasks as there were positions in the list (4 or 6). For each task, the position of the word to select was picked at random. However, in each series, every possible position in the list is tested through a selection task. This leads us to a total of 1,800 trials.

Collected Data. In order to study the different presentations, we collected various data during the experiment: we collected the number of items seen by the user, the time taken for the participant to make his selection, the distance (in pixels) he traveled, the errors he made and the answers he gave to the SUS questionnaire.

2.3   Results and Discussion

Figures 1 and 2 show the main results of the first study. The vertical bars depict the items arranged in a line (yellow), a grid (orange), a column (red), using a relative arrangement (green), and using a list (blue). The hatched bars correspond to the 6 items results, while the clear bars are used for the 4 items lists.

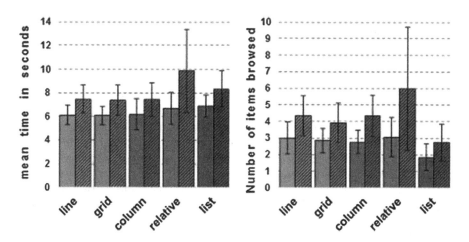

Fig. 1. Mean time in seconds (left), and error rate (right) to select an item with each presentation. (Color figure online)

Number of Items. In the first place, we can see that the number of items browsed depends on the number of items within that list. Indeed, when the user has six items in the list, he goes through more items to find the one he wants. On average, the user browses 1.5 additional items when there are six items rather than four. This is also visible on the time measured, which takes 1.7 s (about 120 %) longer to find the desired word. This increase is not due by the two items that are additionally present at the end of the list : indeed, no matter what the desired item's position is, there is always a significant increase in the time spent for a six items list.

Items Browsed. Items browsed (Fig. 1 - Right) is the number of items covered participants browsed before he validated his selection. The validated word itself is included. The "list" presentation is the one needing the least browsed items to reach the desired word : for a list of 4 items, the "list" presentation only needs 1.85 items, while the "relative" presentation needs 3. For the "absolute" presentations, this number is of 2.9 items on average, no matter the layout used. The differences between relative and absolute are not significant ($p > 0.05$), but the differences between the list and the absolute and relative layout are ($p < 0.04$) significant. This notable difference can be explained by the fact that all the items are shown at the same time on screen for the absolute and relative presentations. The user, while browsing the list, can pass through the desired item and not stop on it. As a consequence, he has to go through more items to select the correct one. On the "list" presentation, the items are shown one at a time. Thus, the user can pass through less easily, and therefore selects the needed item in a shorter time.

Time Selection. Time selection (Fig. 1 - Left) is the time required to select the desired item. It is computed between the moment the user presses his finger on the screen to point the first item and the moment when he validates his choice by releasing his finger.

There is not a significant difference between the absolute and relative presentation.

There is no significant difference between the absolute and the list presentation. However, there is a visible difference on the item level. This is due to the time spent interacting: swiping on the screen is an easy gestures, but it takes more time than absolute selection.

The relative layout is longer than the two others, especially in the context of a list with six items. This is due to the smallness of the items in the list, requiring slow gestures to compensate the needed high precision. Thus, the relative presentation takes longer.

Similarly, there is no significant difference within the absolute layout (line, grid and column are similar time-wise speaking).

Accuracy. The precision is given by the error rate in the selection task for each presentation type (Fig. 2 - Left). It is computed through the ratio of incorrectly selected items divided by the total number of selected items.

There is no significant difference in terms of error rate between the absolute layouts and the list layout. When it comes to lists of six items, the relative layout becomes significantly more error-prone compared to the others (9.7 % compared to 3 % on average, $p < 0.05$ given by a Friedmann analysis). This can be explained to the required precision to interact with the relative layout: the more elements there are on the screen, the smaller they become. Shall the user selects a starting point in a corner, the elements are going to be harder to select. These cumulative problems cause a higher error rate.

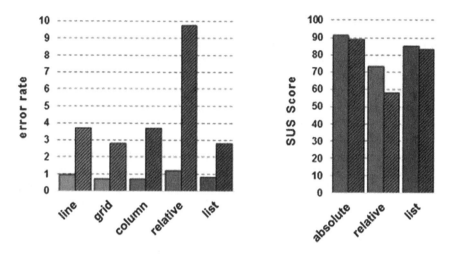

Fig. 2. Error rate to select an item with each presentation (left), and SUS Score for the three presentations (right) (Color figure online)

User Satisfaction. User satisfaction was evaluated through the obtained results collected in the SUS questionnaire (Fig. 2 - Right). Subjects gave the "usable" rating for all presentations when there were only four elements: in fact, every presentation has obtained a score of at least 70. The absolute presentation was the one preferred. For presentations involving six elements, scores were lower, showing that the dynamic one was unusable in this case (score 58). This reflects the user's preference : users prefer to use our presentation for small lists than large lists, and if possible absolute presentations interactions.

In summary, the absolute layout appears to be the most appropriate. Indeed, it is the one necessitating the least time while yielding a small error rate. The list layout shows less browsed items, but takes more time. Finally, the relative layout is inappropriate. Indeed, it's longer to use than the other two, and yields more errors. Besides, depending on the initial position, items can be of smaller sizes, leading to precision problems. Therefore, for the two following studies, we have retained the "line" layout of the "absolute" presentation. On the other hand, we saw that the time spent selecting and browsing an item is directly linked to the size of the list. Since it is faster with four elements and better rated by the participants. So we kept only four items for our list in the two last studies.

3 Audio Feedback

Beyond the way the items are arranged for an easy navigation, the offered audio feedback must also be efficient for the visually impaired users : it should allow them to have a fast and efficient knowledge about the possible words along with their position in the list; and as a consequence, on the screen as well.

Concerning parsimony, Brewster [2] indicates that for small devices such as connected phones or watch, interactions should reduce the number of modalities. Indeed, for them, it's more efficient to use different and distinguishable gestures than to rely on provided tactile or audio feedback to guide the user to validating an option. As such, if there is no need for audio feedback beforehand, it would be better to limit it to just during the selection. Being cautious to the quantity of the feedback is thus important : we must not overload the user with information.

When the word list is known beforehand, sound-based techniques can be used. This allows to shorten the necessary time for audio feedback. Zhao presents an approach of continuous audio feedback through the Earpod [16]. The earPod provides users with audio feedback that is synchronously linked to touch input. It is intended to allow users to discover menus and lists at their own pace. Each interaction made by the user is sonified, making audio feedback more precise than visual feedback. This system, according to them, gets less efficient when imbrication appears or menus and list grew bigger. Finally, when the elements are different in meaning but small in numbers, one of the most common choices is the use of earcons (according to Helle [6]) : an earcon, similarly to an icon, uses a distinctive sound to allow a quick finding of the information (e.g. an alarm beep for an error, a noise of torn paper to notify a deletion. A study made by Walker [13] compares the earcons alongside a text-to-speech approach : given the results, text-to-speech is more efficient when it is coupled with earcons and spearcons. Spearcons, like their earcons counterparts, are sounds that are made to distinguish between different items. Unlike earcons, though, they are made up of synthesized speech that is speeded up to the point of being too fast to be fully recognizable. However, the designers must be cautious: sonification methods and earcons are often regarded as being distracting, and are not always appreciated by the majority of the users. However, in a context of text-input, this solution is quite impracticable : indeed, the proposed lists of words offered by a prediction system depends on the user's own input. As such, we chose not to use a sound-based solution. Ordering menus by frequency of use could potentially be very beneficial, especially since auditory menus are usually conveyed serially. In most cases the user would probably be able to make a selection after listening to just a few menu items [15]. In our case, since words are sorted by their usage frequency, the desired word is highly likely too be in one of the first positions in the list. Given this observation, this second study was made to assess whether it would be beneficial for the user to be given the whole set of words before he starts making his selection within the list.

3.1   Considered Feedback

In this experiment, we assess and compare two types of feedback :

- **item**: as in feedback produced when the user selects an element, and only there;
- **context**: feedback played before the user makes any selection, in which the entire list is being read to the user, in addition to the "item" feedback provided to the user as he selects.

3.2   Method

Hypothesis. With the absolute layout, the user can easily learn and know the on-screen position of each item. As such, if the list of words is announced beforehand, the user may point directly to where he expects to find the desired word. Therefore, he won't have to go through all the items to find the one he wants. Our first hypothesis (H1) is that the user browse through fewer items if the items in the list are announced beforehand, and during their selection. Our second hypothesis (H2) is thus that if the user browses fewer items, he will select the desired word faster.

Participants. 12 participants (3 women and 9 men, mean age = 25) with normal or corrected-to-normal vision participated in our study. They were all blindfolded to ensure they couldn't see the screen at all.

Apparatus. Participants use the same smartphone that in the first study. They used their finger to navigate through the items. The items were made from random fruit names that were synthetized from text using the Google Translate service. The audio was trimmed to provide feedback as fast as possible, reducing any possible delay. Nothing was displayed onto the screen during the experiment, making the grids and items invisble to the participants.

Procedure. The task was to find a word in the available items as fast as possible. The task went as follow: first, the participant was read the instruction, he was then given the word to search, then he had to browse the items to find the correct one, and ultimately validate it. If he answered a different item, we considered his answer to be wrong. The participants had then to state his preference through a SUS questionnaire. These tests were done after each combination was played.

Design. The experiment was made into one single session. Each participant had to go through two blocks. The twelve participants were then split at random into two even groups. The first group started with "context" feedback while the other group started with "item" feedback. Each block was made of six series of tasks, each run one after the other. Each series comprised five tasks, one for each position in the list, including its absence. Each item position (including its absence) was made to be selected three times in the list. Similarly to our first experiment, the positions were randomized. The users gave us a total of 660 trials.

Collected Data. In order to study the different feedbacks, we collected various data during the experiment: we collected the number of items seen by the user, the time taken for the user to make his selection, the errors he made and the answers he gave to the SUS questionnaire.

3.3   Results

The main result of our second experiment concern the number of items browsed to reach the desired word. When the user is given "context" feedback, he browses 1.9 items on average, versus 3.6 items on average with "item" feedback when he has no help for the selection ($p < 0.05$). This result hence confirms our first hypothesis H1.

For the item feedback, the position of the desired word in the list has an influence. Indeed, the more the word is located far away in the list, the more items the user browses: when the word is located in the first position of the list, the average number of items browsed is 2.3, while it is respectively of 2.8, 3.3 and 3.6 for the following three positions. For the context feedback, there is no such effect : no matter the position of the desired item is, the number of items browsed is between 1.6 and 1.8. This means that the user has a knowledge of the layout when he knows the words in advance, and can thus point the words faster on screen.

However, the participants averaged a higher time when the list was announced before (5.56 s) compared to when the list was not given at the beginning (5.26 s). Yet this difference is not significant. Our hypothesis H2 is not verified. This result is verified no matter what the position of the word in the list is. In all the cases, the user takes a bit less time with item feedback than context feedback. This can be explained by the time taken to pronounce the list initially, in the case of context feedback, which is not compensated by the time saved by the user to select the desired word.

In both cases, the error rate is low (1.8 % for "context" feedback and 1.2 % for "item" feedback) and therefore has no impact. Finally, the scores for SUS questionnaire are almost similar for both conditions (79 for "context" feedback and 77.6 for "item" feedback).

4   Validation Technique

Once the user has selected one word, he must validate it. Here, in this third study, we focus on what gesture would be best suited to validate a word, as opposed as its simple selection.

When it comes to validation, for Kane et al. [7], the solution must rely on gestures which use multiple fingers. In their study, they designed such interactions to be used within list driven environment (for example, checking a contact within the list, browsing through a musical playlist, etc.) by focusing on a "swiping" approach, like a "one-finger-scan", coupled with a "second-finger-tap". In this context, the lists are browsed as the finger draws onto the list with the first finger, and validated using a second finger without releasing the first finger. Such an approach simplifies the exploration while offering the user an easier selection. For Kane, it is vital to use multi-finger exploration to enhance accessibility towards visually impaired users.

For Wilson et al. [14], selection is made through a pressure-detection solution. They studied two main validation strategies : holding the finger temporally on an item to validate it, or release the finger from the screen. According to their studies, error-wise, it's more efficient to hold temporally than to release the finger, but at the expense of a longer interaction time.

4.1   Considered Feedback

We studied four different validation interactions which can be used to select an item from a list:

- **release**: the user slides his finger on the screen to select a word, and release it to confirm his choice.
- **dual tap**: the user presses finger onto the screen to select an item, moves finger on the screen to navigate among the different items and then types the screen with two fingers simultaneously to validate the item placed at this location.
- **double tap**: the user select an item in the same way that the "dual tap", and validate its choice by performing a double tap with one finger (similar to a double-click).
- **broken line**: the user slides his finger on the screen to select a word. To validate his selection, the user must perform a 90 angle on his route.

We retain, according to our observations of the two previous studies, a line layout containing four elements, with the "item" feedback.

4.2   Method

Participants. 12 participants (3 women and 9 men, mean age = 32.5 years) participated in our study. They all had normal or corrected-to-normal vision. They were all blindfolded to ensure they couldn't see the screen at all.

Apparatus. Participants use the same smartphone that in the first two studies. They used their finger to navigate through the items. The items were made from random fruit names that were synthetized from text using the Google Translate service. The audio was trimmed to provide feedback as fast as possible, reducing any possible delay. Nothing was displayed onto the screen during the experiment, making the grids and items invisible to the participants.

Procedure. The task was to find a word in the available items as fast as possible. The task went as follow: first, the participant was read the instruction, he was then given the word to search, then he had to browse the items to find the correct one, and ultimately validate it. If he answered a different item, we considered his answer to be wrong. Once a session was completed, the participant was asked to answer a SUS test for each technique, and state his preference among the layouts he went through.

Design. The whole experiment was conducted in one single session for all the participants. Every session constituted of four blocks, run one after the other. Each block was made to test one validation interaction. The block order was balanced through a Latin square. Each block was made of two series of tasks, each run one after the other. Each series comprised four selection tasks. For each task, the position of the word to select was picked at random. However, in each series, every possible position in the list is tested through a selection task. At the end of each block, the participants had to fill in a SUS questionnaire. The users gave us a total of 384 trials.

Collected Data. In order to study the different interactions, we collected various data during the experiment : we collected the number of items seen by the user, the time taken for the user to make his selection, the errors he made and the answers he gave to the SUS questionnaires.

4.3   Results

Quantitative Results. We first computed the time taken to validate an item using a specific gestures, this is to say the time spent between the moment the instructions finish and the moment the users validate his input.

The users took 5.6 s on average for release, 6.16 s for double tap, 5.66 s for dual tap and 6.75 s for broken line.

There is no significant difference between the dual tap and the release gestures ($p > 0.1$), nor between the broken line and the double tap gestures ($p > 0.1$). There is however a significant difference between the two groups dual tap/release and double tap/broken line ($p < 0.01$).

Finally, we computed the error rate for each validation technique. They are 4,2 % for drag and release, 6 % for double tap, 6 % for dual tap, and 9 % for broken line.

Here, there is no significant difference between the dual tap/drag and release/double tap gestures (p = 0.34), but they are about one half compared to the broken line gesture (p = 0.03). In any case, release seems to be the better suited in terms of efficiency.

Qualitative Results. According to the users' answers, they found broken line and dual tap to be unsatisfactory (both ranked under 70), whereas they ranked double tap and release to be their favourite interactions (they scored 81 and 85 respectively). The overall ranking gave release the first position (selected 1st by nine users on the twelve), followed by dual tap, broken line, while dual tap was ranked last by our users.

4.4 Discussion

As we saw in this study, the validation gesture is something that should be thought carefully. Indeed, offering an easy approach to items must go in par with a clearly well defined method to distinguish selection from validation. Timed validation (via double tap) or pattern validation (via drawing lines) can be used effectively to split the interaction between selection and validation, but it's slower and might take more time to be accurate. Given our users' feedback, it also helps to have an unmistakable way which is resistant to mistypings: as such, a drag-and-release approach is better suited for validation.

5   Conclusion

In this article, we showed the importance of adopting a practical approach to design interactions for selection and validation in a dynamic context accessible by the visually impaired. Since there is little learning or memorization available, information must be directly accessible, preferably arranged linearly (possibly a grid with many elements). The audio feedback is only required when selecting elements (no significant gain in terms of time). Finally, the validation must be fast and accurate, if possible in one simple gesture, such as a drag-and-release approach.

In this study, we restricted ourselves to a list of words. However, in the case of text input, a possible improvement can use some context analysis solutions to sort the list of suggestions or corrections to be as fast and accurate as possible. We see this technique as a result of our ongoing work to improve the efficiency of our system.

References

1. Borodin, Y., Bigham, J.P., Dausch, G., Ramakrishnan, I.V.: More than meets the eye: a survey of screen-reader browsingstrategies. In: Proceedings of the 2010 International Cross Disciplinary Conference on Web Accessibility (W4A), W4A 2010, pp. 13:1–13:10. ACM, New York (2010)

2. Brewster, S., Lumsden, J., Bell, M., Hall, M., Tasker, S.: Multimodal 'eyes-free' interaction techniques for wearable devices. In: Proceedings of the SIGCHI Conference on Human Factors in Computing Systems, CHI 2003, pp. 473–480. ACM, New York (2003)

3. Chae, M., Kim, J.: Do size and structure matter to mobile users? an empirical study of the effects of screen size, information structure, and task complexity on user activities with standard web phones. Behav. Inf. Technol. **23**(3), 165–181 (2004)

4. Eberts, R.: Cognitive modeling. In: Handbook of Human Factors and Ergonomics, pp. 1328–1374 (1997)

5. Geven, A., Sefelin, R., Tscheligi, M.: Depth and breadth away from the desktop: the optimal information hierarchy for mobile use. In: Proceedings of the 8th Conference on Human-Computer Interaction with Mobile Devices and Services, MobileHCI 2006, pp. 157–164. ACM, New York (2006)

6. Helle, S., LePlâtre, G., Marila, J., Laine, P.: Menu sonification in a mobile phone a prototype study. In: ICAD 2001, pp. 255–260 (2001)

7. Kane, S.K., Bigham, J.P., Wobbrock, J.O.: Slide rule: making mobile touch screens accessible to blind people using multi-touch interaction techniques. In: Proceedings of the 10th International ACM SIGACCESS Conference on Computers and Accessibility, Assets 2008, pp. 73–80. ACM, NewYork (2008)

8. Kiger, J.I.: The depth/breadth trade-off in the design of menu-driven user interfaces. Int. J. Man Mach. Stud. **20**(2), 201–213 (1984)

9. Mitchell, J., Shneiderman, B.: Dynamic versus static menus: an exploratory comparison. ACM SigCHI Bull. **20**(4), 33–37 (1989)

10. Norman, K.L.: The Psychology of Menu Selection: Designing Cognitive Control at the Human/Computer Interface. Intellect Books, Oxford (1991)

11. Sears, A., Shneiderman, B.: Split menus: effectively using selection frequency to organize menus. ACM Trans. Comput. Hum. Interact. (TOCHI) **1**(1), 27–51 (1994)

12. Shneiderman, B.: Designing menu selection systems. J. Am. Soc. Inf. Sci. **37**(2), 57 (1986). (1986–1998)

13. Walker, B.N., Kogan, A.: Spearcon performance and preference for auditory menus on a mobile phone. In: Stephanidis, C. (ed.) UAHCI 2009, Part II. LNCS, vol. 5615, pp. 445–454. Springer, Heidelberg (2009)

14. Wilson, G., Brewster, S.A.: Pressure-based menu selection for mobile devices. In: Proceedings of the 12th International Conference on Human Computer Interaction with Mobile Devices and Services, pp. 181–190 (2010)

15. Yalla, P., Walker, B.N.: Advanced auditory menus. Georgia Institute of Technology Technical report, Atlanta, October 2007

16. Zhao, S., Dragicevic, P., Chignell, M., Balakrishnan, R., Baudisch, P.: Earpod: eyes-free menu selection using touch input and reactive audiofeedback. In: Proceedings of the SIGCHI Conference on Human Factors in Computing Systems, CHI 2007, pp. 1395–1404. ACM, New York (2007)

Design of a Mobile Augmented Reality Application: An Example of Demonstrated Usability

Tsai-Hsuan Tsai[1(✉)], Hsien-Tsung Chang[2], Ming-Chun Yu[1], Huan-Ting Chen[2], Chun-Yi Kuo[3], and Wei-Hung Wu[3]

[1] Department of Industrial Design, Chang Gung University, Taoyuan, Taiwan
ttsai.cgu@gmail.com
[2] Department of Computer Science and Information Engineering, Chang Gung University, Taoyuan, Taiwan
[3] Metal Industries Research & Development Centre, Kaohsiung, Taiwan

Abstract. Mobile augmented reality (MAR) services allow a user to interact with virtual information in the real word through the user interface (UI) of his/her mobile device. However, it is necessary to introduce augmented reality (AR)-related usability principles when developing and designing MAR services to ensure that they conform to the usability principles and provide user experiences that meet users' expectations. On this basis, the present study designed an MAR application aimed at product marketing and providing an interactive experience based on the usability principles. In addition, experts were invited to measure the usability of the system based on a mobile-specific heuristic evaluation checklist. The results demonstrated that the MAR application designed in the present study met the system usability requirements and could provide users with a positive experience during their interactions with it.

Keywords: Mobile augmented reality application · Experiential marketing · Usability · Mobile-specific heuristic evaluation

1 Introduction

Augmented reality (AR) is a technology that integrates computer-generated digital information into the physical world using real-time computing techniques to provide users with an interactive experience of a combined virtual and physical world. In addition, AR provides experiences and sensations that cannot be perceived or imagined in normal natural environments by enhancing users' sensory perceptions (e.g., visual, auditory or tactile perception) using digital technologies [1]. With the rapid popularization of smart phones and tablet computers, the video cameras, graphics processing capabilities, wireless communication functions and global positioning system (GPS) capabilities with which these smart systems are equipped have significantly improved the usability and practicality of AR technology. In other words, a user's personal smart mobile device, which acts as another set of visual and auditory sense organs, can perceive virtual information embedded in the real world and integrate this information into the interface that is displayed to the user. When the user aims the

M. Antona and C. Stephanidis (Eds.): UAHCI 2016, Part II, LNCS 9738, pp. 198–205, 2016.
DOI: 10.1007/978-3-319-40244-4_19

camera on his/her mobile device at an object or a marker, the virtual information is directly superimposed and displayed on the user interface (UI) via the camera's lens, and the user can interact with the system through a new UI that integrates virtual and real information [2, 3]. As a result, experiential marketing combined with AR technology has become the model application of this technology that is currently the most popular. An introduction by means of AR technology can not only can provide consumers with effective service experiences but can also improve brand value and consolidate long-term customer loyalty [4]. For example, the Japanese personal care company Shiseido allows consumers to experience different makeup effects in real time using the Magic Makeup Mirror makeup simulator [5]. The German shoe chain Goertz allows consumers to try on different styles of shoes virtually using Kinect motion-sensing technology. Consumers can upload photographs to Facebook and make purchases directly using Quick Response codes displayed on the monitor [6]. IKEA's AR catalog, which is based on a similar concept, allows consumers to directly bring various types of virtual exhibits home and to easily try to match various furniture styles at home using markers in the AR catalog without having to move any furniture at home. These practical applications demonstrate that the use of AR technology has been gradually expanding from exhibitions and physical stores to personalized mobile experiences.

Good systems cannot be created using advanced hardware and technology alone. Mobile AR (MAR) applications can create more realistic and innovative experiences, but they also cause MAR services to face more usability-related challenges. However, when mobile applications and AR technology are being used and developed extensively, the focus is often on technological development, and the user experience and usability are not considered. As a result, there are few MAR applications on the market that are user-friendly and satisfy users' expectations [7]. Therefore, to optimize the usability of AR applications and provide user-friendly interactive experiences, the present study first investigated the usability of mobile applications and AR technology. Then, based on suitable AR UI design usability principles, the present study designed a MAR application that satisfied the requirements of product marketing and interactive experiences. Finally, the present study measured the usability of the UI based on a mobile-specific heuristic evaluation checklist.

2 Usability Issues for MAR Applications

MAR allows the real world to become part of the overall interactive UI. Therefore, the timeliness of the display of virtual information, the way the information is visualized, the accuracy of marker recognition and the ability to interact with the user all affect the overall interactive experience of MAR [8]. Ko et al. [9] summarized the usability issues that a user faces when operating an MAR application. (a) Small display size – Interactions with MAR applications are based on mobile devices. Therefore, the size of the screen of the mobile device creates a usability issue when the user receives information. In addition, AR displays real and virtual information simultaneously. Therefore, it is necessary to avoid displaying an excessive amount of information and requiring complex UI operations when the UI is being designed. (b) Multimodal interface – MAR discovers virtual information in the real environment through a mobile device. Therefore, it is necessary to consider the properties and usability of two types of UI: tangible UIs and conventional graphical UIs. (c) Limited manipulation – The touch screen of a mobile device is its main input terminal. Gesture operations can generate a direct link between the user and a virtual object. In addition, suitable gesture operations can improve operability and the understanding of the information. On this basis, Ko et al. [9] proposed five usability principles for AR applications in a smart phone environment. (a) User-information – MAR applications need to provide users with suitable visual information and a clearly classified menu structure. In addition, MAR applications need to conform to users' expectations in how they express information; (b) User-cognition – MAR applications need to be able to minimize users' memory loads, allow users to react as expected and enable users to learn applications easily; (c) User-support – MAR applications should provide users with useful information, reduce errors, handle tasks and perform personalizing tasks; (d) User-interaction – MAR applications focus on the interaction between the user and the application, e.g., MAR applications provide feedback with minimum manipulation; and (e) User-usage – MAR applications emphasize actual usage, i.e., operations that are suitable for the situation and the degree of freedom of operation. These five usability principles all have corresponding evaluation conditions. The present study first designed an MAR application with the MAR usability principles comprising the design rationale and then measured the usability of this MAR application.

3 Design and Development of an MAR Application that Is Aligned with the Usability Principles

In view of the current lack of user-friendly MAR applications, the present study designed an MAR application, the Sakura three-dimensional (3D) MAR application, that conforms to Ko et al.'s MAR principles in terms of usability and the user experience. The Sakura 3D MAR application was jointly developed by the Digital Media Lab and WIDE Lab of Chang Gung University in Taiwan and the Metal Industries Research and Development Center in Taiwan to help Taiwan's Sakura Corporation, a professional manufacturer of kitchen appliances and systems, break out of traditional marketing strategies and create a more realistic interactive experience for consumers using AR technology and thereby improve the benefits of marketing products and the quality of service. The MAR application designed in the present study supported all the smart phones and tablet computers that run the Android system (version 4.4 or later) and was released in the Android Market (Google Play) (https://play.google.com/store/apps/details?id=com.ming.SAKURA3D&hl=en) for consumers to download and use in September 2015. The main design functions of the Sakura 3D MAR application are discussed in detail in the following sections.

3.1 Virtual Information Display

To allow consumers to fully understand the form and external design details of a newly launched exhaust hood, the exhaust hood is displayed in the form of a 3D virtual model. Users can freely and directly operate this 3D virtual model using designed gestures (Fig. 1). Users can rotate this product model freely through 360° and enlarge and shrink it using two fingers to see its details. When the red arrow button on the outer ring is tapped, the corresponding product function and its innovative technology are displayed. When the illustration button is triggered, it becomes semi-transparent to provide users with visual cues during its operation. It is worth mentioning that the circular operation of the UI helps guide users to the proper locations and that each of the four triangular buttons points to information on one of the four major features. When a triangular button is tapped, the outer ring rotates back to the corresponding location to guide the user to a new position.

Fig. 1. Design of the guided interactive interface

3.2 Brochure and the AR Marker

Traditional marketing is based on paper or digital catalogs or brochures, which do not allow consumers to easily imagine what a product will look like in their homes. An AR brochure is a physical paper brochure with augmented content, which is used as an AR marker. A user can display a virtual product in a real space (e.g., the consumer's home) by aiming his/her smart phone at the number of the product in the paper brochure. In addition, size is often an important consideration in cookware purchases. The MAR application designed in the present study provides a one-to-one product experience (Fig. 2). Before purchasing cookware, consumers can use the paper catalog as an AR anchor point and the size of the catalog as a reference to display the actual product in real space on a one-to-one scale. AR catalogs allow consumers to visualize the size of a product in their homes and provides them with more diverse and convenient ways of shopping.

Fig. 2. One-to-one experience of different product models

3.3   User-Friendly Interface Design

The user-friendly interface allows users to easily obtain the most important information through the UI's layout and to understand the available options and the connections between different functions. Because the MAR application designed in the present study provided an interactive experience by superimposing digital content directly on real space on the mobile device after recognizing a marker image via the camera's lens, the maximum visual range of the user was considered. In the UI's design, in addition to considering top-to-bottom and left-to-right reading habits, emphasis was placed on ensuring that the user would still be able to easily tap and switch with his/her thumbs when holding the device with both hands. Therefore, the most frequently used main function menu was placed in the lower left part of the UI, and the title function was fixed in the upper left part of the UI. Through simple visual focusing, users were guided as they completed the main task (Fig. 3). All the interactive functions were included in the main function menu, and all the experience functions were switched by tapping.

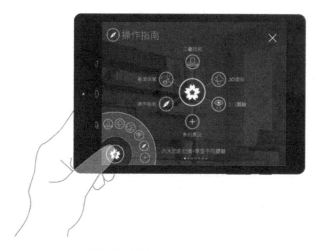

Fig. 3. Main function menu

4   Validation of the Developed AR Application Design

The present study used the mobile-specific heuristic guidelines proposed by Gómez et al. [10] for mobile UIs as a usability checklist for the MAR application that was designed. The 10 usability heuristics proposed by Nielsen were used as the heuristic evaluation (HE) method. HE not only has an extensive coverage of and a high explanatory power for usability but is also efficient, accurate and low-cost. Therefore, HE is widely used to measure the usability of system UIs. Here, the usability of the UIs of mobile devices is considered as an example. With the development of new technology and updated devices, Gómez et al. [10] noted that it is necessary to develop heuristic guidelines for mobile environments. Therefore, they adapted traditional usability heuristics, rearranged them into a new heuristic classification and developed a compilation of heuristic evaluation checklists for mobile interfaces. Then, the resulting mobile-specific HE checklist was used to verify the usability of the UI of the MAR application developed in the present study.

In the present study, three experts in the field of digital media design and three experts in the field of information engineering were invited to measure the UI's usability. These six experts all had knowledge and experience relating to system development and UI usability and could effectively identify potential problems in the usability of a system's UI. In addition, some subheuristics from the mobile-specific HE checklist, such as searching, inputting data, shopping, banking and privacy were not included in the functions of the MAR application designed in the present study. Therefore, two subheuristics were moved from the original 13 heuristics. The results of the evaluation based on 11 usability heuristics were as follows:

- Visibility of the system's status: Feedback and the system's status were provided in a timely fashion, and the UI provided sufficient clues to help users operate it.
- Match between the system and the real world (mental model accuracy): Proper analogies and content conforming to the mental models of users were used to help users fully understand the UI's functions, menus and operational guidelines.
- User control and freedom: Straightforward gestures provided users with high operability during the interaction. The permanent main function menu allowed users to switch between front and back functions at any time.
- Consistency and standards: The overall design of the UI was highly consistent. Visual displays, such as icons, could also convey the meanings of their functions.
- Error prevention: The occurrence rate of potential errors was minimized through simple and visual operational procedures.
- Recognition rather than recall: The title of each function page was displayed in the form of an icon complemented by text, which efficiently improved the level of recognition of the system and reduced the knowledge burden on the user.
- Flexibility and efficiency of use: Interactive switching via the main function menu complemented by image icons provided users with a visual and fast interactive interface design.
- Aesthetic and minimalist design: The simple and easy-to-understand visual design of the interface allowed users to have a clear and highly immersive interactive experience in the interactive AR environment.

- Help users recognize, diagnose and recover from errors: The instruction page provided allowed users operating the system for the first time to more rapidly understand its operation. However, there were no auxiliary illustration functions such as interaction cues on the actual interactive pages. Therefore, the experts recommended that auxiliary illustration functions be added to the design of the functional interactive interface.
- Skills: The overall operation of the system was quite intuitive and within the range of general users' abilities.
- Pleasurable and respectful interaction: Operations could be performed using gestures, giving users a higher degree of freedom of control. In addition, system feedback with the user as the center could improve the level of satisfaction with interactions.

5   Conclusion

With the rapid popularization of mobile carriers and the increasing maturation of AR technology, MAR applications can create more realistic and personalized interactive experiences and marketing services for consumers. MAR services allow a user to interact with virtual information in the real word through the UI of his/her mobile device. However, it is necessary to introduce AR-related usability principles when developing and designing MAR services to ensure that they conform to the usability principles and provide user experiences that meet users' expectations. On this basis, the present study designed an MAR application aimed at product marketing and providing an interactive experience based on Ko et al.'s MAR usability principles. In addition, experts were invited to measure the usability of the system based on Gómez et al.'s mobile-specific HE checklist. The results demonstrated that the MAR application designed in the present study met the system usability requirements and could provide users with a positive experience during their interactions with it. In the future, we will conduct further usability evaluations involving users and investigate their acceptance of and satisfaction with this MAR application.

Acknowledgements. We thank all of the individuals who participated in the study. This research was funded by Taiwan Metal Industries Research & Development Centre, Chang Gung University, and Taiwan Ministry of Science and Technology Ministry (MOST103-2221-E-182-051-MY2).

References

1. Daponte, P., De Vito, L., Picariello, F., Riccio, M.: State of the art and future developments of the augmented reality for measurement applications. Measurement **57**, 53–70 (2014)
2. Carmigniani, J., Furht, B., Anisetti, M., Ceravolo, P., Damiani, E., Ivkovic, M.: Augmented reality technologies, systems and applications. Multimedia Tools Appl. **51**, 341–377 (2011)

3. Linaza, M.T., Marimón, D., Carrasco, P., Álvarez, R., Montesa, J., Aguilar, S.R., Diez, G.: Evaluation of mobile augmented reality applications for tourism destinations. In: Fuchs, M., Ricci, F., Cantoni, L. (eds.) Information and Communication Technologies in Tourism 2012, pp. 260–271. Springer, Heidelberg (2012)
4. Krieger, C.: Empirical study of the effects of mobile augmented reality marketing as a communicative marketing vehicle with particular focus on consumer behaviour, brand value and customer retention. Dublin Business School (2013)
5. http://www.lifestyleasia.com/hk/en/wellness/beauty/feature/mirror-mirror-digital-makeup-simulators-at-shiseido/
6. http://www.goertz.de/
7. Olsson, T.: Concepts and subjective measures for evaluating user experience of mobile augmented reality services. In: Huang, W., Alem, L., Livingston, M.A. (eds.) Human Factors in Augmented Reality Environments, pp. 203–232. Springer, New York (2013)
8. Kourouthanassis, P.E., Boletsis, C., Lekakos, G.: Demystifying the design of mobile augmented reality applications. Multimedia Tools and Applications **74**, 1045–1066 (2013)
9. Ko, S.M., Chang, W.S., Ji, Y.G.: Usability principles for augmented reality applications in a smartphone environment. Int. J. Hum. Comput. Interact. **29**, 501–515 (2013)
10. Yáñez Gómez, R., Cascado Caballero, D., Sevillano, J.-L.: Heuristic evaluation on mobile interfaces: a new checklist. Sci. World J. **2014**, 1–19 (2014)

Task Performance of Color Adaptation on the Screen Display

Fong-Gong Wu$^{(\boxtimes)}$, Carlos Cheang, and SuHuey Tan

Department of Industrial Design,
National Cheng Kung University, Tainan, Taiwan
fonggong@mail.ncku.edu.tw,
caxrlxos@gmail.com, sh030265@gmail.com

Abstract. Smart devices have been gaining importance in our lives during the recent years, causing the human beings to spent increasingly more time on the electronic screen. Screens simultaneously act as an interface for both input and output. Therefore, the use of colors on screens have become an important topic. The experiment records the reaction time of each task after color adaptation. Color samples used in this study include the three primary colors and the three complex colors; the size of the stimulus shown in the experiments was a controlled factor, allowing participants to discriminate between each. Results of the experiments showed that the average reaction time after color adaptation is shorter than that of before color adaptation. The background color Blue showed the best performance each time. In other words, the human visual ability reaches a steady level after a very short time period. The results of this study can be applied on user interface design.

Keywords: Chromatic adaptation · Complex color · Primary color · Landolt C · Screen · Performance

1 Introduction

With the advances in technology, smart phones and tablets are playing an increasingly important role in our daily lives, resulting in us spending more and more time on these devices [1]. The most frequently performed activities on smart devices are social networking, online games, and E-commerce. Screens, and the colors appearing on them are closely related to our lives. Inferring from the current trend of social development, it is very likely that humans and websites are going to develop a closer interaction, therefore the design principle of use of color on screen will be highly valued. It not only enhances the aesthetics of appearance, but also improves the interaction between people and things. [2].

Along with the trend of electronic devices, the practice of reading has also transformed from printed books to e-book, which strengthens the fact that screens are linked to our lives in every possible way. Research also show that the digital version of books is able to provide more information than traditional books, at the same time showing higher comprehensive scores [3, 4]. Since the most commonly used output interface for these devices are monitors, the research on color adaptation on screens are exceptionally

© Springer International Publishing Switzerland 2016
M. Antona and C. Stephanidis (Eds.): UAHCI 2016, Part II, LNCS 9738, pp. 206–216, 2016.
DOI: 10.1007/978-3-319-40244-4_20

important in terms of enhancing the usability and efficiency of mobile applications, such as improving reader comprehensive level of digital books.

Cone cells are divided into three types, each responsible for the three different range of color lights respectively. People can only discriminate color in the photopic vision because rod cells are unable to discriminate different colors. When people got used to a certain color of stimulation, the human eyes will consider it as white. This process is called color adaptation. Current studies on color adaptations are mostly on primary colors. However, people use complex color more often in daily lives. In order to achieve greater contribution, this study has set the following goals: First, the sample of colors would include the primary colors as well as the complex colors of each primary color, in order to discriminate the differences between them. Second, to investigate is difference between each time point after color adaptation.

From Belmore and Shevell [5], the authors did an experiment to determine the cumulative effect of very-long-term and short-term chromatic adaptation on color perception. The results indicated that short-term chromatic adaptation caused the most shift on color perception, very-long term caused the least shift on color perception, and both chromatic adaptations have a cumulative effect on color perception. Werner [6] pointed out the focus of color research is how the color and spatial analysis of an image interact. His experimental results suggested a close relationship between color and form analysis during chromatic adaptation. This result disproved the theory proposed by previous predecessors that there is no influential relationship between different stimulus, and that chromatic adaptation is not only processed at the retina, but attributed to a temporal integration process during eye movements.

Based on Shevell [7], the participants in this experiment viewed an annulus composed of a mixture of green and red monochromatic lights and they were instructed to adjust the radiance of either green or red so that the annulus appeared a perfect yellow. The results of the experiments deduced a two-process theory. In the first process, a person will receive a changing signal when he or she is adapted to chromatic light. In the second process, a restoring signal that tends to drive back toward equilibrium the opponent response resulting from the adapting light.

Kuller [8] was a study on the effects of red and blue scheme offices on performance efficiency. The results demonstrated that there was no common influential factor between the two tasks on performance efficiency, but it showed that red color could trigger negative emotions. Meanwhile, the authors speculated that red had the most influence on proofreading, a tedious task, and blue had the most influence on writing essays, a creative task. Oetjen and Ziefle [9] proceeded with their experiment using Landolt C for the directional determination task. The position of participants and screen were fixed by a chin-rest, which allowed precise control of viewing distance and angle. Participants used the customized five cross positioned buttons to interact with the screen. The target appeared on screen when participants pressed the central button and the other four buttons were pressed for directional determination of the target gap. This two-step input approach effectively determines and records visual discrimination and motor reaction time from the participants. Although this input device can intuitively correspond to the direction of target stimulus, the cross positioned buttons resulted in inconsistent reaction times.

Therefore, the purpose of this study was to investigate the impact of adaptation between different colors during screen operation.

2   Method

Due to the increasing popularity of mobile devices and the topic of this study on color adaptation on screen based visual tasks, our experiment will simulate a visual search task done on the screen, with an aim to explore the impact of color adaptation on screen based visual tasks. The experiment consists of a pre-test and a post-test.

Independent variables include background color, color adaptation time, and stimulus color; Controlled variables include stimulus pattern size and ambient light; Dependent variables include reaction time and error rate.

2.1   Participants

There are 30 participants between the ages of 20 and 30 years old (14 male, 16 female). To ensure each subject's ability to distinguish colors, the Ishihara color blindness test is done before participation. During the experiment, participants are required to use both eyes during the discrimination task of the ring pattern of Landolt C, so a limit of vision acuity of at least 0.8 is set as a boundary for the choice of participants.

2.2   Equipment and Environment

The test book consists of a series of colored plates, called the Ishihara plates. Each of contains a circle of dots appearing in slight differences of colors and sizes. Dots within the pattern form a number or shape clearly visible to those with normal color visions, however, are invisible, or difficult to process for those with a red-green color vision defect, or vice versa.

The display and operation interface used is an Acer notebook of screen size 14 inches, resolution 1440 by 900 pixels, a Inter i3 Processor, and color setting on 32-bit color system. The color calibrator used in this study is Eye-One Display 2, which is a world leading brand of color calibrator, to ensure the color displayed in every trail of experiment is precise and consistent. E-Prime Professional Software, which is currently one of the most recognized experiment software worldwide with accurate timing and easy operation, is employed for this study.

Landolt C ring settings used refer to the previous Wu [10] and Schrauf and Stern [11] study results and recommendations. We have reduced the low visual acuity notch directions, keep the upper left oblique, lower the left, upper right, and lower right oblique notches. In addition, to ensure that the pattern type subjects to focus observation and reduces knee-jerk answer questions, the experiment will add no-gap patterns. Considering that ruse task (no-notch pattern) was added in this experiment, the index finger and middle finger will hit the response of four oblique notch direction, and the thumb will hit the response of no-gap stimulus. The middle fingers are placed on F and J, the index fingers are placed on V and N, and the thumbs are placed on the space bar.

The background colors chosen for the experiment are red, blue, green, and mixture of the three primary colors cyan, magenta, and yellow. The reason for the choices is to find out the differences between moonlight and complex colors. Stimulus pattern color is another independent variable. The colors used are black, red, green, blue, cyan, magenta, and yellow. The reason for the choices is to explore the color combinations which produce better task performance results and interface usability.

2.3 Procedure

In order to simulate the environment for the general use of computer operation, the experiment space, color temperature, and illumination simulation of the lighting are controlled. Luminance is set to about 700lux, and color temperature to about 6000 K. Table and chairs are maintained in a fixed position, with only the height of chair adjustable before the experiment in order to ensure the vision line is perpendicular to the computer screen. After introducing this study, an exercise is given to all participants to familiarize with the operation. All participants are instructed to place their fingers on the corresponding keyboards before pre-test started.

When the pre-test started, a stimulus is shown on the screen. Participants are required to determine the direction of the stimulus as soon as possible and press the corresponding direction keys. Reaction time is recorded by E-Prime software. Every participant has to complete 250 trials for the test given in random order. At the end of the pre-test, participants will take a rest for 3 min before proceeding to the post-test.

The difference between the pre-test and the post-test is the existence of a color adaptation phase in the post-test. The experiment program is set to arrange six background colors randomly in order at the beginning of every set of test, after that a two-minute long color adaptation begins. Two minutes later, a series of color stimulus, Landolt C in this experiment, start to appear. The color of the stimulus do not change until the next period of color adaptation begins. The program will then use another background color and stimulus color. After every trial of the test, a black screen will display for 1.5 s before the next stimulus appears. Participants are required to finish 25 questions with the same background color. After the completion of 25 questions, there will be a rest period, in which the whole screen will display black and the participant is told to look away from the screen. 1.5 min later, the program will proceed to the next color adaptation phase with another background color automatically. Each set of the test is composed of six different background colors, and each of the participants are required to complete a total of 3 sets of tests. The order of all tasks in the experiment will be generated randomly to prevent a learning effect during the experiment to ensure the accuracy of the results. The process of the post-test is shown as Fig. 1.

2.4 Analysis

The reaction time for the different combination of colors in the pre-test was used as a comparison baseline to the post-test. Incorrect responses in the test will be disregarded. All data will be rearranged in Microsoft Excel, and analyzed with SPSS statistics.

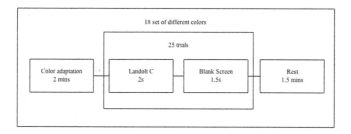

Fig. 1. Process of the post-test

Within subjects effects and Repeated measures will be conducted in SPSS, to discriminate the difference of each colored light. As the six stimulus colors that would appear in each background color are not entirely the same, these two factors will be analyzed respectively. First, Repeated measures of the background color; second, Repeated measures of the stimulus color in different background colors. Mauchly's sphericity test is conducted. Finally, the simple main effect test will be conducted when there is a statistically significant difference in the within subjects effects.

3   Result

3.1   Repeated Measures of Background Color in Pre-Test

As shown in Table 1, the results of Mauchly's test showed a background color $W = 0.346$, $p = 0.012 < 0.05$, reaching a significant level. However, it did not match sphericity assumption and is modified with Epsilon.

Table 1. Within subjects effects of bgColor without color adaptation

Tests of within-subjects effects

Source		Type III Sum of Squares	df	Mean Square	F	Sig.
bgColor	Sphericity Assumed	227568.838	5	45513.768	49.652	.000
	Greenhouse-Geisser	227568.838	3.562	63889.348	49.652	.000

After modifying, pair wise comparison of background color is conducted and summarized in Table 2. The result showed that background color of Blue is significantly different from all the other background colors. The difference between background colors Cyan and Green did not reach significant level. Finally, the difference between Magenta, Red and Yellow did not reach significant level either.

3.2   Repeated Measures of Background Color and Time in Post-Test

The results of Mauchly's Test of repeated measures of background color and time after color adaptation show that, neither of them (background color $W = 0.085$,

Table 2. Pair wise comparison of background color without color adaptation

Mean difference (I-J)						
(I) bgColor	(J) bgColor					
	Blue	Cyan	Green	Magenta	Red	Yellow
Blue		−94.226[*]	−89.266[*]	−29.974[*]	−23.976[*]	−22.005[*]
Cyan	94.226[*]		4.960	64.251[*]	70.249[*]	72.221[*]
Green	89.266[*]	−4.960		59.292[*]	65.290[*]	67.261[*]
Magenta	29.974[*]	−64.251[*]	−59.292[*]		5.998	7.969
Red	23.976[*]	−70.249[*]	−65.290[*]	−5.998		1.971
Yellow	22.005[*]	−72.221[*]	−67.261[*]	−7.969	−1.971	

[*] The mean difference is significant at the .05 level.

$p < 0.0001 < 0.05$; time point $W = 0.000$, $p < 0.0001 < 0.05$) had matched sphericity assumptions and need to be modified with Epsilon.

Amongst the six background colors, Cyan and Green showed a similar performance, the difference of Magenta, Red and Yellow was not significant, while the difference between Blue and Yellow was not significant either. Finally, Red and Yellow background colors showed similar performance. Pair wise comparisons between the rest of the pairs were all significant. Data in details is shown in Table 3.

Table 3. Pair wise comparisons of each background color after color adaptation

Pairwise comparisons						
Mean difference (I-J)						
(I) bgColor	(J) bgColor					
	Blue	Cyan	Green	Magenta	Red	Yellow
Blue		−75.343[*]	−83.135[*]	−26.135[*]	−37.350[*]	−19.653
Cyan	75.343[*]		−7.792	49.208[*]	37.993	55.690[*]
Green	83.135[*]	7.792		57.000[*]	45.785[*]	63.483[*]
Magenta	26.135[*]	−49.208[*]	−57.000[*]		−11.215	6.483
Red	37.350[*]	−37.993	−45.785[*]	11.215		17.698
Yellow	19.653	−55.690[*]	−63.483[*]	−6.483	−17.698	

[*] The mean difference is significant at the .05 level.

3.3 Repeated Measure of Stimulus Color in Post-Test

The results of Mauchly's test show that, stimulus colors (red background color $W = 0.133$, $p < 0.0001 < 0.05$; green background color $W = 0.201$, $p < 0.0001 < 0.05$; blue background color $W = 0.334$, $p = 0.009 < 0.05$; magenta background color $W = 0.161$, $p < 0.0001 < 0.05$; cyan background color $W = 0.142$, $p < 0.0001 < 0.05$; and yellow background color $W = 0.112$, $p < 0.0001 < 0.05$) reached a significant level, it doesn't match sphericity assumption and need to be modified with Epsilon.

In Red background color, Magenta and Yellow stimulus are significantly different with respective to all the others color. The difference between Blue and Cyan was not significant, but Blue was significantly different from the others. Black, Cyan and Green performed in a similar way. According to the descriptive statistics, Yellow is the only one that showed outstanding performance, while Magenta showed unsatisfactory performance.

In Green background, with an exception to Blue and Red, pair wise comparison of all the others showed significant results. According to the descriptive statistics, Black is the only stimulus color that showed outstanding performance; while Cyan is the only stimulus color that showed unsatisfactory reaction time.

In Blue background, performance of stimulus colors of Yellow and Cyan did not reach significant level. All the others were pairwise significantly different. According to the descriptive statistics, Yellow and Black are the colors that showed best performance, and Magenta, Red and Black are the colors with the most unsatisfactory performance.

In Magenta background, Red is the only stimulus color that showed significant difference in performance, while the rest of the stimulus colors showed no significant difference. According to the descriptive statistics, Black, Blue, Cyan, Green and Yellow have the best and similar performance, while Red is the only color showing an unsatisfactory performance.

In Cyan background, Green, Magenta and Yellow showed significant difference to the rest of the stimulus colors, while Black, Blue and Red showed no significant difference and acted in similar ways. According to descriptive statistics, Black, Blue and Red showed the best performance, and Green is the only stimulus color that showed unsatisfactory performance.

In Yellow background, Cyan and Green showed significant difference to the rest of all stimulus colors. The following three pairs of stimulus colors, Black and Blue, Magenta and Red, Blue and Red, all showed no significant difference in between. According to the results of descriptive statistics, Black and Blue showed the best response performance, and Cyan is the only stimulus color that showed unsatisfactory performance. The descriptive statistics of different color combinations of the post-test is summarized in Table 4.

Table 4. Descriptive statistics of different color combination of the post-test

Descriptive statistics								
Background Color	Stimulus color							
	Black	Blue	Cyan	Green	Magenta	Red	Yellow	Total
Blue	638.25		579.94	602.68	650.12	621.45	567.84	607.27
Cyan	567.30	559.69		1137.36	629.08	592.92	711.89	679.87
Green	575.89	608.01	1105.58		645.70	586.18	704.86	686.85
Magenta	604.24	628.11	606.30	624.47		751.14	608.46	633.37
Red	618.91	647.80	629.77	629.39	782.12		567.45	644.40
Yellow	562.49	586.86	753.46	653.94	609.46	595.06		626.53
Total	593.86	608.31	714.10	720.90	668.27	622.75	624.34	646.10

3.4   Summary

Before adaptation, Blue has the shortest average response time amongst all 6 background colors, and it is significantly different to all the other colors. Cyan background color showed the longest average response time, and the background color green showed no significant difference with it. After adaptation, Blue background color has the shortest average response time compared to all the other colors, and is also significantly different. Cyan background color has the longest average response time, an the background colors of green with Cyan was not significant. Overall, it showed same results without color adaptation, but the average response time after color adaptation is shorter than without.

Before adaptation of Red background color, the black, cyan, green, yellow stimulus showed better performances, while magenta showed an unsatisfactory performance. After adaptation of Red background, yellow showed the best performance, and magenta showed the most unsatisfactory results. Before adaptation of Green Background, black, blue, magenta, red, showed better performance, while cyan showed an unsatisfactory performance. After adaptation, black showed the best performance, while cyan showed the most unsatisfactory performance.

In Blue background, cyan, green, magenta, red, and yellow, showed better performance, while black showed the most unsatisfactory performance before adaptation. After adaptation, cyan and yellow performed better, while black, magenta, and red showed unsatisfactory performance. In Magenta Background, black, blue, cyan, green, and yellow showed better performance, while red showed the most unsatisfactory performance before adaptation. Black, blue, cyan, green, yellow performed well, while red showed the most unsatisfactory performance after adaptation.

Before adaptation with a Cyan background, black, blue, magenta, and red performed well, while green showed the most unsatisfactory performance. After that, the black, blue, and red, performed better, while green showed the most unsatisfactory performance. In Yellow background, black, blue, magenta, and red showed better performance, while cyan and green showed the most unsatisfactory performance before adaptation. On the other hand, black and blue performed better, while cyan and green showed the most unsatisfactory performance after adaptation.

Stimulus colors with the most satisfactory and unsatisfactory performance against each background color before and after adaptation had been concluded as Table 5.

4   Discussion

The results of the pre-test show that amongst the 6 background colors, Blue presented the shortest average reaction time, following by Yellow, Red, Magenta, Green, and Cyan. From the results of the pair wise comparison, these 6 background colors can be divided into 3groups by performance. The first group consists of Blue, it is significantly different to all the other background colors. The second group consists of Yellow, Red and Magenta. These 3 background colors showed similar performance. Finally, in the third group are Green and Cyan, which also showed similar performance.

Table 5. Color combination that have better performance

Background color	Better performance (no color adaptation)	Worst performance (no color adaptation)
	Better performance (after color adaptation)	Worst performance (after color adaptation)
Red	Black, Cyan, Green, Yellow	Magenta
	Yellow	Magenta
Green	Black, Blue, Magenta, Red	Cyan
	Black	Cyan
Blue	Cyan, Green, Magenta, Red, Yellow	Black
	Cyan, Yellow	Black, Magenta, Red
Magenta	Black, Blue, Cyan, Green, Yellow	Red
	Black, Blue, Cyan, Green, Yellow	Red
Cyan	Black, Blue, Magenta, Red	Green
	Black, Blue, Red	Green
Yellow	Black, Blue, Magenta, Red	Cyan, Green
	Black, Blue	Cyan, Green

None of these 6 background colors showed outstanding performance with a stimulus color combination, but most of them did show unsatisfactory performance with a certain stimulus color. These unsatisfactory combinations are: Magenta background with Green stimulus, Blue background with Black stimulus, Magenta background with Red stimulus, Cyan background with Green stimulus, and finally, Cyan stimulus and Green stimulus showed the worst performance with a Yellow background. The color combinations listed above were difficult to distinguish from appearance.

In the post-test, Blue performed the best amongst the 6 background colors. Listing from the shortest time to the longest, they are Yellow, Magenta, Red, Cyan, and Green respectively. Quite similar to the results of the pre-test, the 6 background colors can be divided into 3 groups by their performance. Cyan and Green have similar performance, Blue and Yellow can be put into the same group, and finally, Red and Cyan background colors showed similar performance.

With regard to the effects of the stimulus colors against these 6 background colors, not all of them showed a significant performance with the stimulus-background color combinations, but several stimulus colors did show similar performance. Comparing the results of the two tests, we can see that the process of color adaptation amplifies the difference between the stimulus colors.

5   Conclusion

According to past literature, color adaptation phenomena is very common in our daily lives. Most of the current studies are on the field of color contrast or color and design. Since smart phones, tablets and portable computers are the most common types of display today, this study aims to find out the effects of color adaptation on screens.

Participants in this study fixate the screen to achieve the adaptation of colors. The task of participants is to discriminate the direction of the Landolt C while the reaction time before and after color adaptation was recorded. The effects of the different color combinations are discussed.

Pre-test was set up by using the experience gained from other researchers, including the notch size and direction of the Landolt C. There are a total of 6 background colors and 7 stimulus colors. The reaction time of each trial of task was recorded to evaluate the performance and compare the difference between each background color. With an addition of a color adaptation phase in the post-test, the rest of settings are based on the pre-test. The length of the color adaptation is 2 min in total, and the reaction time at the following 25 time points are recorded.

Magenta is the only background color that showed the same result before and after color adaptation. The four background colors Red, Green, Cyan and Yellow showed parts of the same results before and after color adaptation, with the differences of stimulus colors amplified. The most outstanding performance occurred with background color Blue. Against background color Blue, a stimulus color that performed well showed unsatisfactory results after color adaption. According to the results of the analysis, some background colors had less choices of desirable stimulus colors after color adaptation. These changes were caused by color adaptation unquestionably. In other words, when you have a specific background color, you can choose a stimulus color that works better, but in another situation, when the background color was not decided beforehand, a background with a good stimulus color may perform less desirable than another background with a bad stimulus color, because background color itself like Blue has the shortest average reaction time amongst all background colors.

According to the performance summary of all color combinations, color scheme suggestions for an interface may vary under different conditions. First, if there is no color image preferences, we can consider using Blue as the background color, because it showed the best performance score amongst the 6 color samples in the study. Next, if we had a specific color image determined, in other words, we had a background color decided beforehand, then we can simply apply the stimulus colors with the best performance shown in Table 5. For example, in Cyan background color, Black, Blue and Red stimulus would be the best choices.

Acknowledgement. The authors would like to thank the Ministry of Science and Technology in Republic of China for financially supporting this research under Contract no. NSC 101-2221-E-006-007-MY3.

References

1. Kim, T., et al.: Optimal control location for the customer-oriented design of smart phones. Inf. Sci. **257**, 264–275 (2014)
2. Smith, D.: Environmental colouration and/or the design process. Color Res. Appl. **28**(5), 360–365 (2003)
3. Miller, E.B., Warschauer, M.: Young children and e-reading: research to date and questions for the future. Learn. Media Technol. **39**(3), 283–305 (2014)

4. Grimshaw, S., et al.: Electronic books: children's reading and comprehension. Br. J. Educ. Technol. **38**(4), 583–599 (2007)
5. Belmore, S.C., Shevell, S.K.: Very-long-term and short-term chromatic adaptation: are their influences cumulative? Vis. Res. **51**(3), 362–366 (2011)
6. Werner, A.: The spatial tuning of chromatic adaptation. Vis. Res. **43**(15), 1611–1623 (2003)
7. Shevell, S.K.: Color perception under chromatic adaptation: equilibrium yellow and long-wavelength adaptation. Vis. Res. **22**(2), 279–292 (1982)
8. Kuller, R., et al.: Color, Arousal, and Performance-A comparison of three experiments. Color Res. Appl. **34**(2), 141–152 (2009)
9. Oetjen, S., Ziefle, M.: A visual ergonomic evaluation of different screen types and screen technologies with respect to discrimination performance. Appl. Ergon. **40**(1), 69–81 (2009)
10. Wu, F.-G., et al.: Influence of primary screen color Landolt-C rings on vision consistency differentiation ability. Procedia Manufact. **3**, 4520–4527 (2015)
11. Schrauf, M., Stern, C.: The visual resolution of Landolt-C optotypes in human subjects depends on their orientation: the 'gap-down' effect. Neurosci. Lett. **299**(3), 185–188 (2001)

Virtual Reality, 3D and Universal Access

Human Performance and Cognitive Workload in Multi-sensory Virtual Environments

Mortaja AlQassab[(⊠)] and David Wang

Electrical and Computer Engineering Department,
University of Waterloo, Waterloo, ON, Canada
{malqassa, dwang}@uwaterloo.ca

Abstract. In this paper, we present the results of an experiment evaluating human performance and cognitive workload by examining the response time and accuracy in a multi-sensory virtual environment. This study examines Haptic, Audio and Visual Environments (HAVEs). The results of this study indicate that there exists a combination of senses that increase performance and decrease workload.

Keywords: Human performance · Cognitive workload · Multi-model virtual environment · Collaborative virtual environments · Human-Machine Interaction

1 Introduction

Communication is linked to different sensory modalities. In Collaborative Virtual Environments (CVE) and Human-Machine Interaction (HMI), communication is normally limited to audio-visual communication. Current research suggests that including more channels of communication through added sensory modalities could, to some extent, enhance performance, increase the ability of an individual or a group to accomplish a task, or increase tele-presence [1]. Integrating another sensory modality to the communication model could also convey information for operators whose other senses are preoccupied in a demanding task.

A primary task can be thought of as a physical task a human operator performs with minimal cognitive loading and a secondary task is a cognitive task where the human operator receives and processes data. For example, a car driver performs a primary task by steering the car in the correct direction. A secondary task would be receiving direction information from a GPS.

In this paper, an experiment is designed and conducted to evaluate the performance of participants for a combination of two sensory feedback modes in a primary task. The combined sensory modalities for the primary task are audio-visual, haptic-visual or audio-haptic. A secondary task is also designed to evaluate workload of each feedback mode and the effect of different levels of workload on task completion time and task accuracy. The sensory modalities the participants are exposed to in the secondary task are audio, haptic or visual.

© Springer International Publishing Switzerland 2016
M. Antona and C. Stephanidis (Eds.): UAHCI 2016, Part II, LNCS 9738, pp. 219–230, 2016.
DOI: 10.1007/978-3-319-40244-4_21

2   Related Work

Haptic, Audio and Visual Environments (HAVEs) involve the reproduction of sensory cues via computer peripherals. HAVEs range from simple single-sensory environments to sophisticated multi-sensory and multi-dimensional environments. Complex HAVE systems usually consist of three modalities: haptic technology, binaural sound, and 3D visuals. Each component has different effects that should be handled to build a virtual environment that is efficient and realistic. Additionally, virtual systems usually involve various kinds of navigation and selection tasks.

There has been significant research to quantitatively and qualitatively evaluate single-modality and human performance in HAVEs. In [2], auditory sensory feedback was evaluated in a collaborative visual and haptic environment quantitatively by measuring the task completion time and also qualitatively by interviewing subjects. It has been shown that adding auditory feedback has enhanced the performance of participants in an object manipulation application. In [3], a standard Fitts` task was used to evaluate human performance in a selections task with and without haptic feedback. Researchers in [4] have evaluated the addition of visual feedback in haptic-enabled Virtual Environment (VR) in the influence of visually observing object deformation in the user perception of static and dynamic friction. Recently, haptic feedback has received a wide attention from researchers. In a motion tracking application, for example, where a vibro-tactile feedback is provided for users if they deviate from the desired trajectory, performance was studied [5]. Although the addition of haptic feedback in [5] has not reduced motion errors, it enhanced user experience reported by survey responses. Haptic feedback has also been recruited in training simulators. The ability of trainees to learn faster by adding haptic feedback to computer simulation for coursework teaching and driving training was evaluated in [6, 7] respectively. Haptic feedback has also been used as an assistance in a writing training application between an expert and a beginner [8]. In a tele-operated tasks, the added haptic feedback has improved the user`s performance to remotely manipulate objects using a robotic arm [9].

Additionally, a few studies have looked into the evaluation of dual-sensory-modality performance in HAVEs. In a collaborative environment, verbal communication and haptic feedback were evaluated in a navigation task as well as a combined haptic and verbal in terms of task completion time [10]. Results show that participants under haptic only condition take longer to complete the task. A hockey game was tested using different combinations of dual-sensory-modality and three-sensory-modality in a collaborative environment. Dual-sensory modality and three-sensory-modality combinations were also studied in [11] by presenting stimuli and the user responds by pressing the corresponding button.

Most of the current research focuses on evaluating quantitative task performance [9, 12–18], tele-presence and social presence [12, 19–21], subjective performance [22–25], user experience [1, 6, 26] and subjective perceived safety [1]. In this paper, subjective measures and objective measures are used to assess different combined sensory-modality. This paper also evaluates the amount of cognitive workload for different single-sensory modalities investigates the effects of workload on task performance.

3 Methods

3.1 Participants

Twenty-nine participants volunteered for this experiment. All participants are male and female undergraduate and graduate students from the University of Waterloo. All participants were regular computer users. Demographic data has not been collected from participants.

3.2 Experimental Design

A between-subject design is utilized in this experiment. There are three trials; the first trial consists of a primary task only, the second trial adds a secondary cognitive, and the third trial is conducted under the same conditions as the second trial. The independent variables are the indications sent to the participant. The indications differ according to the trial in which the participant is volunteering. There are three different trials with differing primary tasks; Audio-Visual (AV), Haptic-Visual (HV) and Audio-Haptic (AH). The dependent variables are the time it takes the participants to press the virtual button (response time measured) and the number of times the participant presses the correct button (accuracy).

3.3 Procedure

The implementation of this experiment includes two different tasks: a primary task and a secondary task. During each experiment, each participant has to perform three trials. The first trial includes the primary task only. The second and the third trials include the primary task and the secondary task. The purpose of the third trials is to indicate the learning effect for each condition.

The primary task includes three different feedback modalities; they are auditory, visual and haptic. In the primary task, two of the modalities are combined to form the indications to press the virtual buttons; the combined modalities are Audio-Visual (AV), Haptic-Visual (HV) and Audio-Haptic (AH). During each primary task, every participant is introduced to only one of the combinations.

When the first trial is started, the participant has a one-minute training to get familiar with the operation of the haptic device. The participant also has a one-minute training in the second trial. For each primary task, each participant presses the virtual button that is indicated by the feedback combination. Depending on the combined feedback modes, the participant receives a flash of light from the button itself, a tone from the headset or a force from the haptic device.

The direction of the light, tone or force indicates the button to press. For instance, in the AV condition, if a participant receives a flash of light from the up button and a tone from both earbuds, the participant is required to press the up button. Figure 3(A), (B) and (C) shows the all possible visual, auditory and haptic feedback modes for this experiment. For each trial, a button is chosen randomly at 3 s interval. Participants are required to press all indicated buttons in the first trial. In the second and third trials, participants are required to press the buttons while performing a secondary task which is described below. All trials are 5 min long with 1 min of training prior to the first and second trial.

The secondary task includes three different feedback modalities; auditory, visual and haptic. In the secondary task, one of the modalities is used to form the information channel. The only trials that include the secondary task are the second trial and third trial.

After the first trial is completed, the participant has a one-minute training to get familiar with the operation of the haptic device and the procedure of recognizing and writing the codes. For the secondary task, each participant performs the primary task (pressing a virtual button) while a Morse code (e.g. •— •• — — •) is conveyed to the participant through other remaining sensory feedback. Depending on the feedback mode, the participant receives flashes of light from the button itself, tones from the headset or vibrations from the haptic device. For example, a participant receives flashes of flight from the virtual button when the visual feedback is chosen. All codes are between two to six bits of size. For the secondary task, a code is chosen randomly every 60 s. Participants are required to recognize and write the code by pausing the experiment (pressing the space bar). The experiment is automatically paused every 60 s to give the participant a chance to write the code on the paper provided to the participant.

The quantitative data collected in this experiment are the primary task response time (the time it takes a participant to press the appropriate button), response time accuracy (the number of correct button presses), the secondary task response time (the time it takes a participant to recognize the correct code), the secondary task accuracy (the number of correct codes) (Fig. 1).

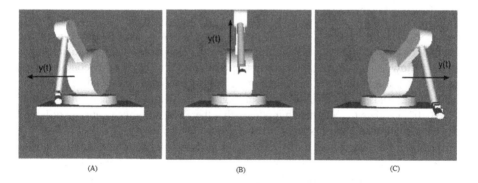

Fig. 1. Haptic feedback mode (A) A force to the left (B) A force Up (C) A force to the right

4 Results

The results are analyzed using a between-subject Analysis of Variance (ANOVA) and multiple two-sample t-tests. The analysis is done at 0.05 significance level. In some cases, the analysis is done at 0.10 or 0.15 significance level. The significance level is stated when it is higher than 0.05. The average response time, accuracy, and subjective performance and subjective workload are calculated for all trials and conditions after eliminating all outlying data points (Fig. 2).

Fig. 2. Auditory feedback mode (A) A tone from the left earbud (B) A tone from both earbuds (C) A tone from the right earbud.

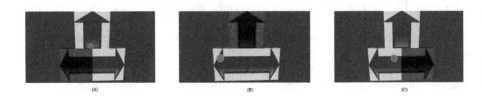

Fig. 3. The graphical user interface (GUI) and visual feedback mode (A) Left virtual button flashing (B) Up virtual button flashing (C) Right virtual button flashing.

4.1 Human Performance

In this section, the results of human performance analysis are presented. Figure 4 summarizes average primary task response time and standard deviation among trials. Figure 4 shows a significant difference in response time between the AH condition and the HV condition in the Trial 1. A slight difference between the HV condition and AV condition in trial 1 can also be seen in Fig. 4. The results of the ANOVA test, p = 0.0102, validate the alternate hypothesis that there is a difference between different sensory modalities for the first trial involving only the primary task.

Because of the introduction of secondary task, there is a slight increase in response time especially apparent in AV condition and HV condition. In the second trial, the null hypothesis is also rejected at 0.05 alpha level. P-value of 0.0148 confirms that there is a difference in response time between conditions

According to Fig. 4, there is a difference in response time between the AH and AV conditions in the third trial at a significance level of 0.15. The ANOVA test p-value is 0.1364, and the two-sample t-test p-value for the difference between the AH and AV conditions is 0.0290. It is worthwhile to note that the response time considerably increased for the HV condition from the second trial to the third trial. The two sample t-test does not show any evidence for a difference between the AV and HV conditions (p > > 0.05) and HV and AH conditions (p > > 0.05).

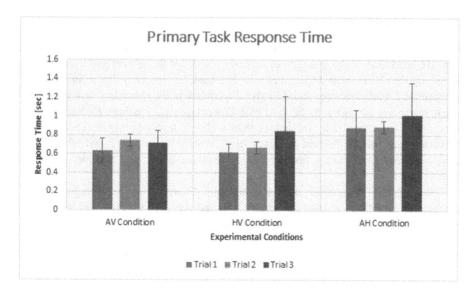

Fig. 4. Average primary task response time

Figure 5 shows the average primary task accuracy among all trials. The accuracy for all conditions in the first trial is considerably high. The accuracy for the AV and AH are 97 % and 98 % with a negligible increase of 1 %. The accuracy in the second trial is consistent for all conditions. 97 % accuracy is achieved for all conditions in trial 2.

In the third trial, only the AV condition decreased to 93 %. ANOVA tests and multiple two-sample t-tests does not reveal any difference in accuracy between conditions.

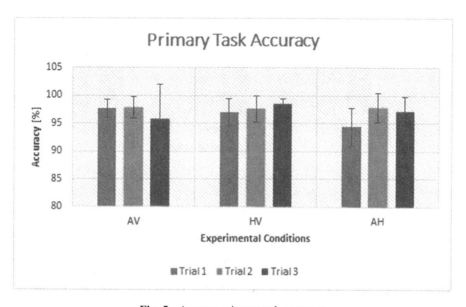

Fig. 5. Average primary task accuracy

4.2   Cognitive Workload

This section discusses the second part of the experiment which evaluates the human cognitive workload. Response time of secondary task for the second and third trials is plotted in Fig. 7. In both trials, auditory feedback is generally faster in terms of response time. Participants exposed to visual feedback in the secondary task take more time to recognize the codes. In the third trial, however, visual feedback response time is faster than haptic feedback, yet higher than auditory feedback mode. The auditory feedback mode has the highest accuracy of all conditions in trial 2 and trial 3. The visual feedback mode has a faster accuracy than the haptic and auditory feedback modes.

One-way ANOVA analysis does not show any differences in the average response time among conditions in both the second trial and the third trial (p-value > > 0.05). Figure 8 depicts the secondary average task accuracy between feedback modalities for all trials. As can be seen from the figure, there is a difference between the visual condition and the auditory condition in terms of accuracy in identifying the codes (p-value = 0.0224). The auditory condition shows a higher accuracy than the visual condition. A difference is not detected between the visual and haptic conditions or between the auditory condition and the haptic condition. In the third trial, the ANOVA test shows the same trend at a 0.10 significance level (p = 0.0709).

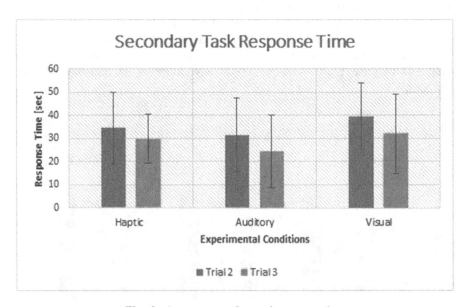

Fig. 6. Average secondary task response time

Two-sample t-test analysis of the secondary task accuracy supports the one-way ANOVA. The two-sample t-test shows that there is a difference between the haptic and auditory conditions (p-value = 0.0223) and the visual and auditory conditions (p-value = 0.0183).

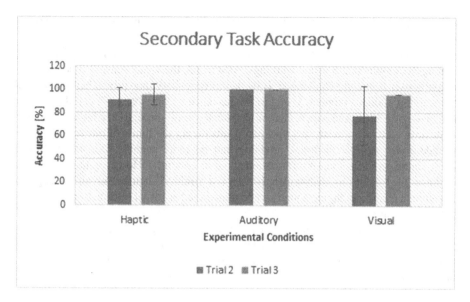

Fig. 7. Average secondary task accuracy

5 Discussion

5.1 Human Performance

The lack of effective feedback is arguably one of the most common problems in the designing of interfaces. The results of this study provide some of the basic foundations on the design for human-in-the-loop applications. Most of the current implementations either utilize visual only or auditory only sensory modalities to provide feedback to users. Moreover, some studies has shown that only using one sensory modality is inadequate [10, 27]. To address these problems, sensory modality replacement or sensory modality addition to current and future interfaces may be adapted. This research study can potentially be used in HCI, tele-operation, collaboration, communication and medical applications (Fig. 6).

Many researchers find that only using audio and visual communication is ineffective. In [27], it is found that haptic communication increases presence and enhances user experience. Similarly, it is can be seen that haptic coupled with visual feedback has the lowest response time in the primary task. Although haptic feedback can increase human performance, the absence of visual feedback can be problematic [1].

In terms of tele-operation, the aviation industry is a promising area for multi-model feedback to be implemented. For instance, the ground control station of an Unmanned Aerial Vehicles (UAVs) can also be enhanced with an added haptic feedback. While most commercial and military airplanes provide haptic feedback by nature (except some fly-by-wire airplanes) since they are mechanically operated, UAVs do not have haptic feedback. The addition of haptic feedback to a UAVs' ground controller can enhance the user experience and increase the performance. It has been proven that virtual forces increase the accuracy and decrease the time to complete the tele-operated task [9] in an assembly task.

The results of this research study can also be used in the design of HMI. Most of the warning in computers are visual warnings. As a result, the visual sensory modality of a computer user is already challenged. If the auditory sensory modality is being reserved for receiving auditory content, visual messages, such as "low battery", can disturb the user. To solve this, messages can be haptically sent through available computer peripherals such as a mouse or a trackpad. Considering the limits of our senses, using one additional sensory feedback modality can be more suitable. For example, car engine sound provides a lot of information about its condition. However, humans might not have the ability to distinguish between a healthy engine and an ill engine. Therefore, a change in engine sound can be transmitted as visual information for the car operator to examine.

Our findings support the use of more than one sensory feedback in virtual environments to improve task performance. These findings complement existing findings in literature. For example, results from a collaborative virtual environment study show that participants under haptic only condition take longer to complete the task than haptic and verbal condition [10].

5.2   Cognitive Workload

Recent research supports the use of haptic as a communication medium [28–30]. Instead of overloading the visual and auditory communication mediums, haptic cues are conveyed to users fixated in a demanding task. For instance, a haptic turn-taking protocol is suggested by [30].

Additionally, utilizing visual feedback poses more cognitive workload as graphical user interface become more complex [31]. It is found that increasing the dimensionality from 2D to 3D in visual interfaces decreases the ability for participants to locate, interact and manipulate objects. To address this problem, the implementation of another feedback mode is necessary to reduce the amount of cognitive workload and ensure effective communication.

This study also investigates the effects of cognitive loading on users' judgement and the ability of users to recognize an encoded message when they are engaged in another demanding task. The results of the study on workload can specifically be used on communication. In other words, the type of sensory modality used to communicate can, depending on the context, be chosen to effectively convey a message. For instance, a pilot crew is frequently engaged with multiple communications at a time; they communicate with a pilot, in a multi-crew setting, and they communicate with Air Traffic Control (ATC) using an auditory channel. Therefore, a haptic turn-taking protocol, similar to the turn-taking protocol defined in [30], can be used for pilots to relinquish control of the airplane and to acknowledge control of the airplane.

6 Conclusion and Future Work

The information age has inundated communities with information. Thus, humans have to make more decisions very rapidly. Many tools, such as notepads, personal digital assistance (PDAs), and cellphones, have been invented to improve the brain or off-load some of its resources to external functions. Despite the fact that the human brain capacity can store much information, humans have retrieval limitations. Consequently, in highly-demanding safety-critical tasks, a proper feedback and communication model should be implemented to increase human performance and decreased the perceived workload. Our goal in this study is to find the ultimate feedback and communication model. The results of this study supports the hypothesis that there exists combined sensory modalities that has a higher response time and higher accuracy. However, there were some drawbacks in this experiment. The experiment only investigated 2D environments, the second level of collaboration, and a limited range of codes. In the next stage, the environment will be modified to include higher dimensions, higher levels of collaboration and an extended range of code. The future system will provide more information about the differences on different feedback and communication modes.

References

1. Kjölberg, J., Sallnäs, E.: Supporting object handling and hand over tasks in haptic collaborative virtual environments. In: EuroHaptics 2002 Conference Proceedings, pp. 71–76 (2002)
2. Huang, Y.Y., Moll, J., Sallnäs, E.L., Sundblad, Y.: Auditory feedback in haptic collaborative interfaces. Int. J. Hum Comput Stud. **70**, 257–270 (2012)
3. Teather, R.J., Natapov, D., Law, F.: Evaluating haptic feedback in virtual environments using ISO 9241-9. In: Virtual Reality Conference, VR 2010, pp. 9–10. IEEE (2010)
4. Srinivasan, M.A., Beauregard, G.L., Brock, D.L.: The impact of visual information on the haptic perception of stiffness in virtual environments. In: Proceedings of the ASME Dynamics Systems and Control Division (1996)
5. Bark, K., Khanna, P., Irwin, R., Kapur, P., Jax, S.A., Buxbaum, L.J., Kuchenbecker, K.J.: Lessons in using vibrotactile feedback to guide fast arm motions. In: 2011 IEEE World Haptics Conference, pp. 355–360 (2011)
6. Young, J.J., Stolfi, C., Tan, H.Z., Chevrier, J., Dick, B., Bertoline, G.: Learning force concepts using visual trajectory and haptic force information at the elementary school level. In: 2011 IEEE World Haptics Conference, pp. 391–396 (2011)
7. Mulder, M., Abbink, D.A., Boer, E.R.: The effect of haptic guidance on curve negotiation behavior of young, experienced drivers. In: 2008 IEEE International Conference Systems, Man and Cybernetics, pp. 804–809 (2008)
8. Ullah, S., Liu, X., Otmane, S., Richard, P., Mallem, M.: What you feel is what i do: a study of dynamic haptic interaction in distributed collaborative virtual environment. In: Jacko, J.A. (ed.) Human-Computer Interaction, Part II, HCII 2011. LNCS, vol. 6762, pp. 140–147. Springer, Heidelberg (2011)
9. Boessenkool, H., Abbink, D.A., Heemskerk, C.J.M., van der Helm, F.C.T.: Haptic shared control improves tele-operated task performance towards performance in direct control. In: 2011 IEEE World Haptics Conference, pp. 433–438 (2011)

10. Wang, J., Chellali, A., Cao, C.G.L.: A study of communication modalities in a virtual collaborative task. In: Proceedings - 2013 IEEE International Conference Systems, Man and Cybernetics, SMC 2013, pp. 542–546 (2013)

11. Hecht, D., Reiner, M.: Sensory dominance in combinations of audio, visual and haptic stimuli. Exp. Brain Res. **193**, 307–314 (2009)

12. McLaughlin, M., Sukhatme, G., Peng, W.P.W., Zhu, W.Z.W., Parks, J.: Performance and co-presence in heterogeneous haptic collaboration. In: 11th Symposium Haptic Interfaces Interfaces for Virtual Environment and Teleoperator Systems, HAPTICS 2003. Proceedings (2003)

13. Zahariev, M.A., MacKenzie, C.L.: Auditory, graphical and haptic contact cues for a reach, grasp, and place task in an augmented environment. In: Proceedings of 5th International Conference Multimodal Interfaces, ICMI 2003, p. 273 (2003)

14. Pinho, M.S., Bowman, D.A., Freitas, C.M.D.S.: Cooperative object manipulation in immersive virtual environments. In: Proceedings of ACM Symposium on Virtual Reality Software and Technology, VRST 2002, p. 171 (2002)

15. Moll, J., Pysander, E.-L.S., Eklundh, K.S., Hellstrom, S.-O.: The effects of audio and haptic feedback on collaborative scanning and placing. Interact. Comput. **26**, 177–195 (2013)

16. Sallnäs, E.: Collaboration in multi-modal virtual worlds: comparing touch, text, voice and video. J. Endod. **28**, 172–187 (2002)

17. Chellali, A., Milleville, I.: Haptic communication to enhance collaboration in virtual Environments. In: Proceedings of European Conference on Cognitive Ergonomics, ECCE 2010, pp. 83–90 (2010)

18. Girard, A., Bellik, Y., Auvray, M., Ammi, M.: Visuo-haptic tool for collaborative adjustment of selections. In: Oakley, I., Brewster, S. (eds.) HAID 2013. LNCS, vol. 7989, pp. 40–49. Springer, Heidelberg (2013)

19. Sallnäs, E., Rassmus-Grohn, K., Sjostrom, C.: Supporting presence in collaborative environments by haptic force feedback. ACM Trans. Comput. Interact. **7**, 461–476 (2000)

20. Nam, C.S., Shu, J., Chung, D.: The roles of sensory modalities in collaborative virtual environments (CVEs). Comput. Hum. Behav. **24**, 1404–1417 (2008)

21. Ullah, S., Richard, P., Otmane, S., Naud, M., Mallem, M.: Haptic guides in cooperative virtual environments: design and human performance evaluation. In: Haptics Symposium 2010 IEEE (2013)

22. Bailenson, J.N., Yee, N.: Virtual interpersonal touch: Haptic interaction and copresence in collaborative virtual environments. Multimed. Tools Appl. **37**, 5–14 (2008)

23. Oguz, S.O., Kucukyilmaz, A., Sezgin, T.M., Basdogan, C.: Haptic negotiation and role exchange for collaboration in virtual environments. In: 2010 IEEE Haptics Symposium, HAPTICS 2010, pp. 371–378 (2010)

24. Smith, J., MacLean, K.: Communicating emotion through a haptic link: Design space and methodology. Int. J. Hum Comput Stud. **65**, 376–387 (2007)

25. Mason, A.H., MacKenzie, C.L.: The effects of visual information about self-movement on graspforces when receiving objects in an augmented environment. In: Proceedings of 10th Symposium Haptic Interfaces Virtual Environment Teleoperator System, HAPTICS 2002 (2002)

26. Sallnäs, E., Zhai, S.: Collaboration meets Fitts' law : passing virtual objects with and without Haptic force feedback. In: INTERACT, pp. 97–104 (2003)

27. Oakley, I., Brewster, S., Gray, P.: Can you feel the force? an investigation of haptic collaboration in shared editors. In: Proceedings of EuroHaptics (2001)

28. Levitin, D.J., Maclean, K., Mathews, M., Chu, L.: The perception of cross-modal simultaneity. Int. J. Comput. Anticip. Syst. **5**, 323–329 (2000)

29. MacLean, K.E.: Haptic interaction design for everyday interfaces. Rev. Hum. Factors Ergon. **4**, 149–194 (2008)
30. Chan, A., Maclean, K., McGrenere, J.: Learning and identifying haptic icons under workload. In: First Joint Eurohaptics Conference Symposium Haptic Interfaces Virtual Environment Teleoperator Systems, World Haptics Conference (2005)
31. Cockburn, A., Mckenzie, B., Zealand, N.: Evaluating the effectiveness of spatial memory in 2D and 3D physical and virtual environments. In: CHI 2002 (2002)

The Impact of Tactile Sensations on Virtual Reality Impairment

Mortaja AlQassab[1], Adam Gomes[1(✉)], Maria Karam[2], David Wang[1],
Zhechen Du[1], Orion Bruckman[1], and Richard Bustos[1]

[1] Electrical and Computer Engineering,
University of Waterloo, Waterloo, ON N2L 3G1, Canada
adam_gom@live.com
[2] Tactile Audio Displays Inc., 454 King St. W., Toronto, ON M5V 1M1, Canada

Abstract. In this paper, an initial pilot study is conducted in order to ascertain the impact of adding tactile sensations to audio-visual (AV) environments. It is well known that adding more realism to virtual reality environments can cause a decrease in performance or even impairment. In this pilot study, participants experience a virtual roller coaster with a fully immersive AV simulator. The impact of adding tactile sensations through the addition of tactile actuation is studied. Although the subjects perceived no difference in presence or motion sickness, quantitative measurements of anterior body sway seem to indicate that there is less impairment with the tactile haptic sensations. Additional subjects will be added to ascertain the statistical significance of this finding in the future.

Keywords: Virtual reality · Impairment · Tactile sensation · Haptics

1 Introduction

Virtual reality environments are a growing application area, with fully immersive haptic-audio-visual environments (HAVE) being employed in diverse areas such as training and gaming. However, it is possible that adding more realism can create a decrease in performance [1] or even cause impairment [2]. With the increasing popularity of HAVE environments, it becomes crucial to study how adding different modalities of sensory input can impact the user's ability to carry out tasks. In an extreme case, the impact on the user could be severe enough that they should be discouraged from activities such as operating heavy equipment or even driving.

In this study, the impact of tactile feedback in HAVE environments will be examined. The HAVE environment consists of a fully immersive head-tracking Oculus Rift to provide the visual. The sound is played through headphones and tactile feedback is supplied by a haptic chair from TADs Inc.

Section 2 gives the background. A brief description of the experimental apparatus is described in Sect. 3 and Sect. 4 describes the VR environment that the subjects are immersed in. Section 5 will present an analysis of the pilot study, while the last chapter will present conclusions and future research.

© Springer International Publishing Switzerland 2016
M. Antona and C. Stephanidis (Eds.): UAHCI 2016, Part II, LNCS 9738, pp. 231–240, 2016.
DOI: 10.1007/978-3-319-40244-4_22

2   Background

Although the technology exists to increase realism in virtual reality (VR) environments, it can come with a cost. In [1], it was demonstrated that, in taking a 2D visual display to a 3D display, a demonstrable decrease performance in a command and control application was measured. In attempting to create more realism using immersive VR, nausea and other side effects can be introduced [2].

There are many ways to leverage the somatosensory system to create a more immersive experience for the user in VR environments, including vibrations, motion, and force feedback, which help the user to suspend disbelief and increase the realism of the experience. These devices come in different forms, and use a variety of touch-based sensations to create physical sensations and feedback from the VR world for the user.

The TactaVest [3] is a wearable system that uses tactors (tactile transducers) to provide the user with specialized information to enhance VR interactions. Events taking place in the scene can be translated to the user through vibrations in respective locations on the body. Wearable systems are an effective way to provide full body haptic experiences to the user, but these may also be problematic when developing systems for multiple users. For example, sizing devices for different body types, housing the cables, providing enough power to drive the system, and ensuring the transducers are properly positioned on the body. Wearable haptic devices in VR may also provide mobility to the user, but can also pose safety issues for users who are not able to see the actual environment, which can lead to tripping on or disconnecting cables. The Surround haptics system [4], developed by Disney Labs is a chair-based tactile display that uses tactors to create haptic sensations. This system uses a 4×3 array of tactors to create a variety of haptic sensations for the user, which are used to increase the connection a user has to a game or VR environment by leveraging the different illusions that can be created through haptic vibrations. Another approach to improving the VR experience is to create motion for the user. While motion actuators can be used to provide the user with the sense that they are moving along with the action taking place in VR, this can often be expensive, and also lead to motion sickness in some users. While this is a problem inherent in the use of VR displays [5], motion in the seat may increase nausea in users, despite the potential benefits it may have for the user experience. An alternative approach to using actual motion actuators to move a chair was developed for the HapSeat system [6]. This approach leverages the kinesthetic and vestibular mechanisms of the somatosensory system to provide the user with a sense of movement, without actually moving the seat. This is accomplished by applying force feedback to the arms and head, which may effectively trick the user into believing that they are moving simply through the displacement of their limbs. By placing force feedback devices on the arms and head rest of the chair, the force feedback sensations can cause the user to feel like they are moving, but with potentially less risk of causing motion sickness. Since most of the haptic systems described rely on the use of mechanical vibrations and force feedback sensations that are not linked to real world experiences, it is necessary to create mappings of vibrations onto the events or experiences they are linking to in the virtual world. While researchers are discovering and developing new sensations and libraries of different haptic sensations [7], it is challenging to create more naturalistic experiences that the user can feel and intuitively map onto the events they are intended to be feeling.

In a different approach to providing real time tactile feedback to users, sound originating from the virtual world or scene can be used as tactile vibrations on the body. The Emoti-Chair was first developed in 2008 to provide deaf and hard of hearing people with access to sounds from movies and music entertainment [8]. Studies into this type of sensation showed that sounds could be communicated to the body as a natural form of input, and effectively identified and linked to the source of the sound. In addition, information pertaining to the emotional expression and quality of the sound could naturally be detected by users, who in most cases were deaf and may never have heard sounds before, but could still interpret the emotional content [9].

Tactile acoustic devices (TADs) are based on the model of the human cochlea, which theorizes that by presenting sounds on the skin in a similar manner that the human cochlea uses to process sounds one can effectively turn the skin into a hearing organ [10]. Because of the ability to directly communicate sound to the body, it is possible to create tactile sensations that can lead to an immediate recognition of the mappings between the vibrations and the sounds.

Given the often sound-rich environments associated with VR, the TAD system may be a natural extension to the existing haptic devices and systems gaining traction within the VR domain. While this is a novel application for the TAD technology, its ability to integrate into the content of most VR scenarios increases its potential to quickly provide relevant and important tactile information to the user, and to possibly increase and enhance the overall experience of virtual world interactions.

Extending this technology to the VR world could potentially offer more interesting and naturalistic sensations to users, which may also work in combination with other haptic and tactile devices to provide a richer experience for the user.

3   Experimental Method

In this pilot study, subjects are asked to sit in a fully immersive audio-visual environment and go through a realistic computer simulated roller coaster simulation (see Fig. 1). All subjects will experience an identical ride. The 3D visual component is enabled through head-tracking VR Oculus Rift goggles, and the stereo sound component is supplied via stereo headphones. All tests will be run with the subjects sitting in a system developed by Tactile Audio Displays Inc. (TADsInc), which combines an X-Rocker Pro 4.1 gaming seat [11,12] that has been augmented with an 8-channel TAD (Tactile Acoustic Device) and a low frequency bass transducer (as well as speakers) built into the seat. This is a chair that has 12 tactile sound transducers situated along the back and seat, with half situated to the left or right of the spine (see Fig. 2). The tactile sensations are generated using sound to simulate the vibrations that sounds generate and

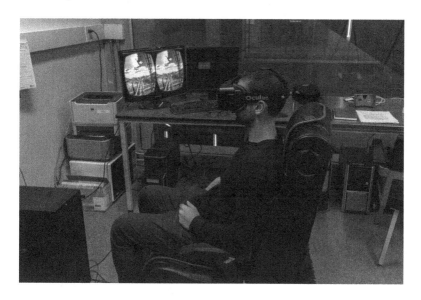

Fig. 1. Setup of roller coaster experiment

transmit through the seat of a roller coaster. This is based on providing tactile sound to the body as an approach to creating a sense of enhanced realism for the user, who can experience the 'feeling' of the sound of the roller coaster on their body.

Participants in the study are first asked to sit down in the Haptic chair while one of two scenarios (tactile sensation on, tactile sensation off) are chosen for them at random. The participant will then watch a black screen on the Oculus Rift display for 3 min 14 s. After the time has elapsed, the participant is asked to move into the viewing space of the NaturalPoint OptiTrack motion capture system [15], and is told to stand as still as possible for one minute as their motion sway is recorded (see Fig. 3). This consists of recording the relative position of 3 infra-red markers placed on the back of the subject's head. After the recording is complete, the participant is told to sit back down in the chair, and is fitted with headphones. The participant then experiences the roller coaster simulator with either the haptic sensation on or off. After watching the simulation for 3 min 14 s, the participant is told to move into the OptiTrack viewable area. The participant is once again told to stand as still as possible for one minute as their sway is recorded. After the experiment is complete, the participant is told to complete two questionnaires; the IPQ Presence Questionnaire [16] and the Motion Sickness Assessment Questionnaire [18]. The IPQ Presence Questionnaire is used to measure the sense of presence experienced in a VR environment, and the Motion Sickness Questionnaire asks the participant to qualitatively rate their impairment from the study. After the completion of the experiment and questionnaires, the participant is told to come back for a second session where they will perform the experiment with haptics off, if they did the first experiment

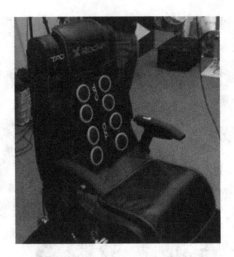

Fig. 2. TAD X-Rocker chair

with haptics on, or vice versa. The second session follows the same procedure as the first, including the completion of the same questionnaires.

4   VR Environment

To study the effects of VR impairment, a roller coaster simulator was chosen as the VR content for this study. This simulator virtually places the participant in the front cart of a roller coaster while the cart moves at a predetermined rate along the tracks. The ride repeats itself continuously until the program is closed automatically by a timer. An image of the roller coaster environment in shown in Fig. 4. This VR environment was created in the Unity game engine platform using assets from the asset store [13,14], and the Oculus Rift Unity plugin. As the environment was created in a game engine, the user has an immersive, spherical view of the environment. Additionally, due to the head-tracking hardware of the Oculus Rift, the user can move their head around in the virtual environment. The simulator is run on an Intel Core i5 CPU and a Nvidia GeForce GTX 980Ti GPU. A high performance GPU is being used to minimize lag effects which may be present when using the Oculus Rift. The audio from the VR environment is fed into the TAD haptic chair's audio mixer, using a 3.5 mm audio cable, to create tactile sensations. Headphones are also connected to the chair to allow the participant to hear the sounds coming from the roller coaster. The Oculus Rift is connected to the computer using an HDMI cable and is integrated with the VR environment using the aforementioned Oculus Rift Unity plugin.

5   Pilot Study

Six participants were recruited for this pilot experiment. Of the six participants, 5 are male and 1 is female, and all University of Waterloo students. All participants

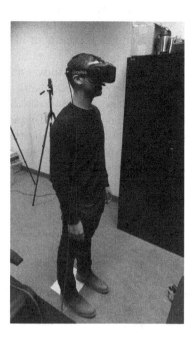

Fig. 3. Capturing motion sway using optitrack

Fig. 4. Roller coaster VR environment through Oculus Rift

are regular computer users, however, their experience with VR environments varied greatly. This study was approved by the Office of Research Ethics at the University of Waterloo who allowed the recruitment of participants using both posters and university administered e-mails.

The quantitative data collected in this study consists of the time-series recording of the anterior motion sway of participants. This is done capturing the position of three infra-red markers, placed on the back of the participants' heads, using the NaturalPoint OptiTrack system. To qualitatively assess motion sickness, data is collected from two Likert-type questionnaires. One being the Igroup Presence Questionnaire (IPQ) to assess perceived presence, and the other being the Motion Sickness Assessment Questionnaire (MSAQ), which allows participants to express how sick they felt. Linear regression is conducted for time series position data (x, y, z). Mean Square Error (MSE) is calculated for the residual values from the line of best fit corresponding to the subject's motion sway in the anterior direction, i.e. $\frac{1}{n}\sum_{i=1}^{n}(z - z_0)^2$. Only movement in the z-direction is used for the MSE calculations; however, due to the alignment of the participant with the OptiTrack system, anterior motion is not always solely in the z-direction. As a result, these calculations do not fully encapsulate total motion sway. A sample graph of a participant's motion with the line of best fit is shown in Fig. 5. Figure 6 depicts the average MSE for six participants. There is a difference between the Haptics ON condition and the Haptics OFF for all markers. The Haptics ON to the Haptics OFF average ratios (Eq. 1) are 0.76, 0.86, 0.84 for Marker 1, Marker 2 and Marker 3 respectively. As can be seen in Fig. 6, the MSE for Marker 1 in the Black 1 experiment is quite large at 1.5×10^{-4}mm^2. This is due to an outlier data point. Instead, using only 5 participants' data in the MSE calculations, the MSE for Marker 1 drops to 1.03×10^{-4}mm^2, which is more in line with the other results.

$$MSE_{ratio} = \frac{1}{n}\sum_{i=1}^{n}\frac{MSE_{i\,HapticsON}}{MSE_{i\,HapticsOFF}} \tag{1}$$

The questionnaire data supports the hypothesis that there is no difference between the Haptics ON and Haptics OFF experimental conditions although differences are quantitatively confirmed by the position data analysis. As can be seen in Fig. 7, there an insignificant difference in Motion Sickness between the Haptics OFF and Haptics ON. The results use only the raw data from the questionnaires.

5.1 Sample Size

The sample size of this study is estimated using an t-statistic iterative method [17]. An initial z-test is conducted to estimate the initial degrees of freedom by replacing the t-statistic power and confidence level with z-statistic coefficients. Multiple t-tests were computed to refine the degrees of freedoms at each iteration for the smallest difference between the obtained value and desired true value to be detected. For the second iteration, the degrees of freedom of the first iteration

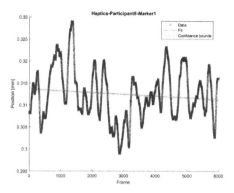

Fig. 5. Pilot study participant's anterior sway and corresponding line of best fit

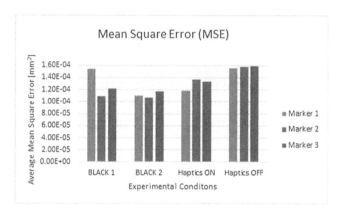

Fig. 6. Average Mean Square Error (MSE) for each condition: position is recorded for infra-red markers attached to the Oculus Rift VR goggles (Color figure online)

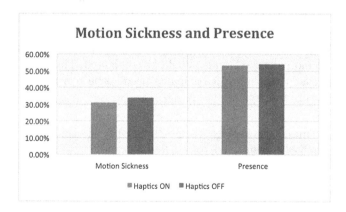

Fig. 7. Average Motion Sickness and average Presence: data collected from Igroup Presence Questionnaire (IPQ) presence questionnaire and Motion Sickness Assessment Questionnaire (MSAQ) (Color figure online)

is used to look up the value of the level of confidence and statistical power. Since each participant volunteers for two sessions, the number of participants required to achieve statistical significance is approximately 37 using Eq. 2. The results of the calculations are shown in Table 1.

$$n = \frac{2(t_\alpha + t_\beta)^2 s^2}{d^2} \tag{2}$$

Here, α is the confidence level (95 % for the study), β is the statistical power (80 % for the study, s is the standard deviation, d is the smallest difference detected between the obtained and desired true values, t_α is two-sided t-statistic for α-value of 0.05, and t_β is on-sided t-statistic for β-value of 0.2.

Table 1. Sample size calculation based on a pilot study involving 6 participants

Iteration	INITIAL (z-stat)	1	2
t_α	1.96	1.99	1.99
t_β	0.84	0.84	0.84
s	5.0×10^{-5}	5.0×10^{-5}	5.0×10^{-5}
d	2.25×10^{-5}	2.25×10^{-5}	2.25×10^{-5}
$df = n - 1$	75 sessions	77 sessions	77 sessions

6   Conclusion and Future Work

This pilot test is an initial study into the impact of tactile sensations on HAVEs. The preliminary results indicate that the addition of tactile sensations in this application, in order to increase realism, does appear to decrease impairment when the tactile haptic sensations are on. This is despite the fact that the subjects' perceived presence and motion sickness, captured through questionnaires, seem to indicate no difference between the haptics on and off scenarios. This indicates that a more detailed study should be conducted. The calculations indicate that over four times more participants need to be recruited. This will be conducted in future research.

Acknowledgements. This research was greatly aided by the assitance of Mr. Shi Yao Liu and Mr. Nikesh Mandhan.

References

1. Van Der Meulen, J., Smith, J.R.: The effect of 2-dimensional and 3-dimensional perspective view displays on situation awareness during command and control. In: 2015 IEEE International Inter-Disciplinary Conference on Cognitive Methods in Situation Awareness and Decision Support (CogSIMA), pp. 89–95. IEEE (2015)

2. Regan, C.: An investigation into nausea and other side-effects of head-coupled immersive virtual reality. Virtual Real. **1**(1), 17–31 (1995)

3. Lindeman, R.W., Page, R., Yanagida, Y., Sibert, J.L.: Towards full-body haptic feedback: the design and deployment of a spatialized vibrotactile feedback system. In: Proceedings of the ACM Symposium on Virtual Reality Software and Technology, VRST 2004, pp. 146–149. ACM, New York (2004)

4. Israr, A., Kim, S.C., Stec, J., Poupyrev, I.: Surround haptics: tactile feedback for immersive gaming experiences. In: CHI 2012 Extended Abstracts on Human Factors in Computing Systems, CHI EA 2012, pp. 1087–1090. ACM, New York (2012)

5. Allison, R.S., Harris, L.R., Jenkin, M., Jasiobedzka, U., Zacher, J.E.: Tolerance of temporal delay in virtual environments. In: Proceedings of the Virtual Reality 2001 Conference, VR 2001. IEEE Computer Society, Washington, DC (2001)

6. Danieau, F., Fleureau, J., Guillotel, P., Mollet, N., Lcuyer, A., Christie, M.: HapSeat: producing motion sensation with multiple force-feedback devices embedded in a seat. In: Proceedings of the 18th ACM Symposium on Virtual Reality Software and Technology, VRST 2012, pp. 69–76. ACM, New York (2012)

7. Israr, A., Poupyrev, I.: Exploring surround haptics displays. In: CHI 2010 Extended Abstracts on Human Factors in Computing Systems, CHI EA 2010, pp. 4171–4176. ACM, New York (2010)

8. Karam, M., Fels., D.I.: Designing a model human cochlea: issues and challenges in crossmodal audio-haptic displays. In: Proceedings of the 2008 Ambi-Sys Workshop on Haptic User Interfaces in Ambient Media Systems, HAS 2008. ICST (Institute for Computer Sciences, Social-Informatics and Telecommunications Engineering), ICST, Brussels, Belgium, Article 8, p. 9 (2008)

9. Branje, C., Nespoil, G., Russo, F., Fels, D.I.: The effect of vibrotactile stimulation on the emotional response to horror films. Comput. Entertain. **11**(1), 13 (2014). Article 4

10. Karam, M., Russo, F.A., Fels, D.I.: Designing the model human cochlea: an ambient crossmodal audio-tactile display. EEE Trans. Haptics **2**(3), 160–169 (2009)

11. Product web site. www.tadsinc.com/products/spinaltad/

12. Product web site. www.x-rocker.co.uk

13. Product web site. www.assetstore.unity3d.com

14. Product web site. https://share.oculus.com/app/oculus-tuscany-demo

15. Product web site. www.optitrack.com/

16. Schubert, T., Friedmann, F., Regenbrecht, H.: Embodied presence in virtual environments. In: Paton, R., Neilson, I. (eds.) Visual Representations and Interpretations, pp. 268–278. Springer, London (1999)

17. Sauro, J., Lewis, J.R.: Quantifying the User Experience: Practical Statistics for User Research. Elsevier, Amsterdam (2012)

18. Gianaros, P.J., Muth, E.R., Mordkoff, J.T., Levine, M.E., Stern, R.M.: A questionnaire for the assessment of the multiple dimensions of motion sickness. Aviat. Space. Environ. Med. **72**, 115–119 (2001)

Autonomous Identification of Virtual 3D Objects by Visually Impaired Users with Proprioception and Audio Feedback

Erico de Souza Veriscimo[✉] and João Luiz Bernardes Jr.

School of Arts Sciences and Humanities – EACH,
University of São Paulo, São Paulo, Brazil
{ericoveriscimo,jbernardes}@usp.br

Abstract. The World Health Organization estimates that there are 285 million people with severe visual impairment worldwide. With the advent of technology, 3D virtual environments are being increasingly used for several applications. Many of these applications, however, are not accessible to visually impaired users, creating a digital divide. Our goal is to develop a novel and low cost 3D interaction technique to allow the identification of virtual objects with autonomy using only proprioception and hearing. We developed a prototype implementing this technique and conducted preliminary tests with it, first with sighted users, only to test the prototype's basic functionalities and implementation, and then with a blind user with very promising results since the user was able to correctly and quickly identify virtual objects.

Keywords: 3D interaction · Accessibility · Visual impairment

1 Introduction

With technological advances, new devices for three-dimensional (3D) interaction are being created or becoming more available and less costly, contributing to the popularization of Virtual and Augmented Environments (VAEs). An example of this tendency is the extensive and growing use of Microsoft's Kinect, not only for entertainment but in several other applications, including research in several areas [1–4]. Many of these VAEs, however, are not accessible to visually impaired users, creating a digital barrier and excluding these users from certain activities [5]. The World Health Organization estimates that there are 285 million people with severe visual impairment worldwide [6].

Like any other citizen, those with visual impairment also have rights. The United Nations established in 1975 a declaration of rights specific to people with some form of disability [7] and these rights include:

- The inherent right to respect for their human dignity. Disabled persons have the same fundamental rights as their fellow-citizens, which implies first and foremost the right to enjoy a decent life, as normal and full as possible;
- Measures designed to enable them to become as self-reliant as possible;

© Springer International Publishing Switzerland 2016
M. Antona and C. Stephanidis (Eds.): UAHCI 2016, Part II, LNCS 9738, pp. 241–250, 2016.
DOI: 10.1007/978-3-319-40244-4_23

- Right to education and other services which will enable them to develop their capabilities and skills to the maximum and will hasten the processes of their social integration or reintegration.

Sadly, there has not been much research done to improve accessibility to the visually impaired in virtual environments. There are works that attempt to minimize problems faced by visually impaired people, such as recognition of real objects using a camera (including that in a smartphone) as a sensor and augmenting the real environment with aural information about detected objects [7–9], for instance to help users when shopping and needing to identify products on a shelf. Section 2 of this paper discusses related work in more detail. This form of interaction can be replicated for virtual objects easily enough, but it removes autonomy from users, who are forced to depend on a third party (the system) to identify each object for them and provide information about it. Another issue with this automatic identification is that, if users do not already have a mental model of the real or virtual object, this form of interaction offers no aid in building one. If instead users are merely aided in identifying the object on their own they have greater autonomy and may being building a mental model of the object, which can be particularly helpful, for instance, for educational applications. While the sense of touch can be used for this with real objects, it is not so easily explored for virtual ones.

In this work, then, we propose, develop and evaluate a novel 3D interaction technique accessible to visually impaired users to allow the identification of virtual objects with autonomy, using only low cost, easily available and portable devices and exploring the senses or proprioception and hearing, without using the sense of touch, which would require some form of force feedback which, in turn, usually require more complex and expensive setups. The technique consists of allowing users to "touch" the virtual object with the tips of both index fingers, which are tracked in space using computer vision and registered in the same system as the virtual object, then giving 3D audio feedback when the object is touched, with a different tone for each finger, which allows users to trace the surface of the object with their fingers and use their position, sensed through proprioception, to build a mental model of the object and use this model to identify it autonomously. When one index finger or both are not near the virtual object (and are, therefore, not being tracked) a buzzing sound informs users so they can reposition the fingers. While initially the intention was to allow users to touch the object with all fingers and their palms, as they can do with real objects, preliminary tests showed that, without haptic feedback, this made identifying the point of contact with the virtual object very difficult, which is why only the tips of the index fingers may touch the object.

A prototype was built in order to investigate this technique, using the Leap Motion device to track hands and fingers and headphones for 3D audio feedback. Currently head position is not tracked by the prototype, so the system assumes the user is facing a specific direction to be able to provide proper directional sound cues, but adding head tracking would is a relatively simple improvement for future work. This prototype is briefly described in Sect. 3.

Before evaluating the system with visually impaired users, first the prototype was tested to make sure it functioned as specified and implemented the technique described above correctly. Then a preliminary experiment was conducted with a blind user. These tests and their results are discussed in Sect. 4 which is followed by this paper's conclusion.

2   Related Work and Visual Impairment

According to a Systematic Review about 3D interactions accessible to visually impaired users, also by Veriscimo and Bernardes [11], the greatest concern for accessible interaction appears to be to aid in the task of navigation (exploring and moving within an environment), particularly in real or augmented environments but also in some purely virtual environments. 21.6 % of all papers included in the review dealt with navigation and only 3.8 % with object recognition.

These 3.8 % are composed of the already mentioned works of a Al-Khalifa [8] and Nanayakkara [9, 10]. They have a common concern of aiding visually disabled people to recognize objects using cameras or smartphone cameras, for instance products on shelves when shopping. The camera captures images of the object of interest, which are processed to attempt to recognize the object. If the recognition is successful, the system uses sound and names the product, vocalizing the word "shoe" for instance. We have already discussed how this lack of user autonomy in the process of object identification may bring problems to the user (not so severe in real environments, where the user could alleviate some of those problems by touching the physical objects, but much more so in purely virtual environments), including the lack of opportunity to acquire a mental model of the object. In that systematic review we were unable to find systems exploring 3D interaction to recognize virtual objects with user autonomy and particularly with low cost devices. The review summarizes the main applications and techniques for accessible 3D interaction in this context and which senses and devices these techniques explore but this discussion is beyond the scope of the present paper.

Instead, to develop our accessible technique to provide user autonomy in this task, we must better understand visually impaired users and how they interact with the world. When referring to visual impairment in this paper, we mean people that cannot see at all or those with severe difficulty in seeing. To interact with the environment, they use the following senses [12]:

- Hearing;
- Proprioception or kinesthesia (the sense of relative position of parts of one's own body and effort employed in movement [12]);
- Sense of touch;
- Sense of smell;
- Sense of taste.

Any interaction technique aiming to be accessible to visually impaired people must use only or primarily these senses, then. In the systematic review mentioned previously [11], the senses most often explored for interaction were, by far, hearing and then proprioception.

3 Prototype

Hearing and proprioception are not only very important senses used in interaction by visually impaired persons and were the most frequently explored in accessible 3D systems [11], they can also be explored with relative simple and low cost devices, such as headphones or speakers to provide aural feedback and sensors to track the position of user body parts. It was with that in mind that we developed the technique already described in the introduction, using the Leap Motion device [13] to track user hands and serve mostly as an input device and headphones for audio feedback. It is with the Leap Motion that we explore the sense of proprioception which allows the user to be aware of the positions of the two fingertips he "touches" the virtual object with (thanks to the registration provided by Leap Motion). Figure 1 illustrates our interaction technique, with the sphere representing a virtual object and the sound waves representing the audio feedback when each fingertip touches it.

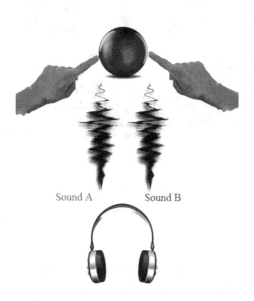

Sound A   Sound B

Fig. 1. Interaction Technique

This feedback uses 3D audio so the sound can originate in the point of contact, but since the two points are relatively close to each other for the size of the virtual objects we intend to use with this technique (limited also by Leap Motion's range of detection), the 3D position of the aural feedback is not always enough to identify which finger touched the object and we also need to use different tones for each. As mentioned before, we use a single fingertip from each hand to make it easier for the user to determine its position via proprioception, since earlier tests showed that using more fingers or the palm, as we had planned initially, makes this task much more complex, even though Leap Motion is capable of tracking all fingers, even when they occlude each other for brief periods of time during movement.

Because the user's fingers must be placed generally above the Leap device to be detected and because our target users cannot see the device's position, we use audio feedback to aid in that task as well. When sitting at a table they can either position the device themselves in front of them or be told generally where it is and the system emits a buzzing sound to inform the user if the sensor is unable to track one or both fingers for any reason (usually the hands being outside the sensor's field of detection) or if it is tracking more than just the two fingertips extended. The buzzing stops when tracking is properly resumed. Figure 2 shows some finger positions above the sensor illustrating one correct and three incorrect positions that would cause the system to emit the buzzing feedback.

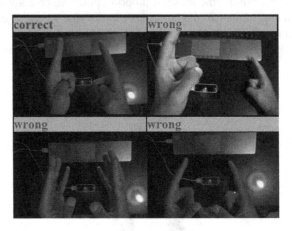

Fig. 2. Finger positions relative to the sensor

To aid in debugging, in the conduction of the tests with visually impaired users and in some preliminary tests with sighted users the system also has the option to render on a computer screen the virtual object and two small spheres representing the positions of the fingertips of each hand, as shown in Fig. 3.

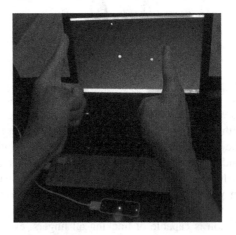

Fig. 3. Spheres showing fingertip positions

The prototype was developed in Java. The first version used JavaFx 3D rendering API [14], but this version of our system was discontinued because the API did not support 3D audio and we opted to continue development with a second version using the Java 3D API [15], which has native 3D sound support. This second version is the one that was used in the tests discussed in the present work.

Table 1. Participants

Participant	Gender	Age	Visual Impairment
A	Male	36	No
B	Female	61	No
C	Male	24	No
D	Female	19	No

4 Tests and Results

To test the prototypes basic functionalities before conducting experiments with visually impaired users, we first tested the system with four sighted participants. Since this was merely a test of basic functionalities and not of the interaction technique per se, we did not believe that the participation of sighted users to be a problem. Table 1 characterizes the participants in these first tests.

These initial tests were supposed to simply validate the following functionalities:

A. Whether the users can tell if their fingers are being correctly tracked or not and correct this situation so both are tracked. Users were blindfolded to simulate blindness and were asked to place their fingers over the sensor so both were detected correctly and keep them there for 30 s. The users were not shown the sensor or informed of its position and used only the buzzing feedback to accomplish this task, which was performed only once by each user.

B. Whether users can tell which finger touched the virtual object. As in the previous test, users were blindfolded (or the notebook was turned away from them) and were asked to explore the virtual environment moving their fingertips in 3D above the sensor until they could find an object. When that happened, they were asked which fingertip touched the object, based on the audio feedback with different tones for each fingertip. This time users were informed about the sensor's position before the test started. This task was repeated five times by each user with the virtual object in a different position each time, but the sensor in the same position.

Table 2 summarizes the results of these functional tests showing the time and success rate for each participant and each functionality. For functionality A, the time reported was the time until both fingers were detected correctly. The cumulative time shown for functionality B is the sum of the times necessary for the user to find the object with one fingertip all five times.

The results show that both functionalities are working properly in the prototype and that users could quickly find the sensor and virtual objects even when blindfolded. The time to find the sensor was between two and 4 s and averaged 2.75 s. Then, to find

Table 2. Functional test results

Participant	Functionality	Time	Success
A	A	3 s	100 %
B	A	4 s	100 %
C	A	2 s	100 %
D	A	2 s	100 %
A	B	15 s*	100 %
B	B	14 s*	80 %
C	B	13 s*	100 %
D	B	14 s*	80 %
*cumulative time			

the object, users averaged 2.8 s in the 20 trials. Out of those twenty trials, users could correctly identify which finger first touched the object 18 times.

Then we proceeded to conduct a preliminary experiment with a blind user. We were particularly worried at this point because, during the functional tests, sighted users reported difficulty in identifying or getting a mental model of the object they touched (which was a sphere), and even the authors had the same problem. This preliminary experiment with a visually disabled male participant happened in the following manner:

- The user was given two physical models of the virtual objects he should recognize, to make sure language would not be a barrier (the objects were a cube and a sphere, but the user referred to them as a rectangle and a circle during the experiment).
- He was then informed about how the technique worked, that he should place the tips of both index fingers above the area of the sensor, that it would stop buzzing when he did that and that a different tone would be played when each fingertip touched the object. He was also told that he could ask questions or abandon the experiment at any time. His participation was entirely and explicitly voluntary.
- He was not informed about the position of the sensor.
- There was no training, the first object presented to the user was already considered part of the experiment.
- The user had to differentiate between the virtual sphere and cube five times.
- The virtual object was selected randomly each time.

We were very pleasantly surprised with the results of this experiment. Out of the five times, with no previous training or even experience with the Leap Motion or 3D interaction in this way, the user got the object right four times. The only time he made a mistake was during the first interaction, perhaps due to lack of training and familiarity with the system. What happened in that instance was that, after finding the object with both fingers, the participant drew a shape with them crossing into the object instead of sticking only to its surface (and contact with the fingers was reported the whole time by the system), which was how he got the virtual object wrong. He was not informed that this is what happened, however, merely that he had gotten it wrong. This was enough for him to be more careful the next times and get all other objects right. Curiously, this user interacted the system in a substantially different way compared to the blindfolded, sighted users. While they would touch the object once, then pull back and touch it again in other spots, he ran his fingertips in continuous motions over the surface of the virtual object. The task only took him a few seconds each time. At one point the user said with some excitement "I know it is a rectangle!", suggesting the system provided the autonomy we were aiming for (and the user was not informed that this was one of our goals). We are not sure about whether he referred to the objects as two-dimensional figures due to a lack of concern for mathematical formalism in his communication, lack of knowledge of the terms or whether he did build a two-dimensional model of the objects, since they were simple shapes with regular cross-sections and the user was indeed moving his fingertips mostly in a plane (but we believe this hypothesis of a two-dimensional mental model to be unlikely, since the user did have contact with 3D physical models in the beginning of the experiment). The experiment was recorded with the participant's permission.

5 Conclusion

The development of 3D interaction techniques accessible to visually disabled people is necessary to reduce the digital and social exclusion with the growing use of 3D virtual and augmented environments. It is desirable that these techniques be accessible regarding cost as well, taking advantage of devices with lower cost. Sadly, there is still little exploration of this topic in the literature.

We contributed to this area with a simple technique, using low cost devices, to allow visually impaired users to recognize virtual objects with autonomy, taking advantage of the senses of proprioception and hearing, and hope that it can be improved and extended or even that it can inspire more work in this area to reduce the barriers faced by visually disabled people in virtual environments.

The results of the preliminary experiments discussed in the previous section not only show we have a working prototype but also that the technique appears to have indeed enabled a blind user to successfully, easily and autonomously indentify virtual objects. These results appear promising enough to demand further research.

At the time this paper was written we had already submitted a formal experimental protocol to our institution's ethics committee, which was analyzed and approved, and we are currently conducting more experiments with blind users to verify the effectiveness of our technique with a larger sampling of participants. We also modified the system as a result of the preliminary tests, so that now it gives audio feedback only when the fingertips touch the surface of the object but not when they penetrate it past a small depth tolerance, to avoid the issue with users sinking their fingers in the objects and still hearing that feedback while no longer being able to trace the object's shape. These formal tests with more users and the modified technique and prototype are happening in the same general manner as described in Sect. 4 but with a third simple object added to the set.

After this experiment is over and its results analyzed and published, however, we will still have some important questions left to be answered with more experimentation. To check whether participants build 3D or 2D mental models of the objects while using our technique, we plan to conduct an experiment asking them to identify different 3D objects that have the same cross-section, such as cylinders and spheres. We also intend to verify whether users can identify more complex 3D objects using this technique with a similar experiment. We very much would like to know how well users build this mental model of the virtual objects using our technique, but we are still having trouble designing an experiment to verify that. We also plan to build applications using this technique, the first of which will be an aid to teach 3D geometry for visually impaired students. Finally, it has been pointed out to us that this technique could be useful not only for visually disabled persons, but also to sighted users in situations where they cannot use sight to interact with 3D objects, be it because of darkness, for instance, or because they need to focus their gaze in some other direction but can interact with the virtual environment with their hands. We did notice a difference in how participants with and without sight used the system in our preliminary tests, inconclusive as they were due to the small number of participants, but we would also like to verify whether sighted users can be trained quickly to take advantage of this technique and how well they perform.

With all this we hope to add a small contribution in allowing visually impaired people to interact more with virtual objects and environments, be it for education, entertainment or professionally, to promote their inclusion in this context and greater social equality.

References

1. Lim, C.-K.: Application of kinect technology in the design of interactive products for chinese senior citizens. In: Stephanidis, C. (ed.) HCII 2013, Part I. CCIS, vol. 373, pp. 51–55. Springer, Heidelberg (2013)
2. Sousa, T., Cardoso, I., Parracho, J., Dias, P., Sousa Santos, B.: DETI-interact: interaction with large displays in public spaces using the kinect. In: Streitz, N., Markopoulos, P. (eds.) DAPI 2014. LNCS, vol. 8530, pp. 196–206. Springer, Heidelberg (2014)
3. Maike, V.R.M.L., Neto, L.S.B., Baranauskas, M.C.C., Goldenstein, S.K.: Seeing through the kinect: a survey on heuristics for building natural user interfaces environments in 8th international conference. In: UAHCI 2014, Held as Part of HCI International 2014, Heraklion, Crete, Greece, June 22–27, 2014, Proceedings, Part I (2014)
4. Rodriguez Esquivel, J.C., Meneses Viveros, A., Perry, N.: Gestures for interaction between the software CATIA and the human via microsoft kinect. In: Stephanidis, C. (ed.) HCI 2014, Part I. CCIS, vol. 434, pp. 457–462. Springer, Heidelberg (2014)
5. White, G., Fitzpatrick, G., McAllister, G.: Toward accessible 3D virtual environments for the blind and visually impaired. In: Proceedings of the 3rd International Conference on Digital Interactive Media in Entertainment and Arts. DIMEA 2008, vol. 349, pp. 134–141. ACM, New York (2008)
6. WHO, World Health Organization.: Global data on visual impairments 2010. Geneva, 17 p 2010. Web. 21 Nov. 2016. http://www.who.int/entity/blindness/GLOBALDATAFINAL forweb.pdf
7. UN, United Nations. Declaração de Direitos das Pessoas Deficientes in: Assembléia Geral da Organização das Nações Unidas. 09 Dez (1975)

8. Al-Khalifa, A.S., Al-Khalifa, H.S.: Do-It-Yourself object identification using augmented reality for visually impaired people. In: Miesenberger, K., Karshmer, A., Penaz, P., Zagler, W. (eds.) ICCHP 2012, Part II. LNCS, vol. 7383, pp. 560–565. Springer, Heidelberg (2012)
9. Nanayakkara, S., Shilkrot, R., Maes, P.: EyeRing: A finger-worn assistant. In: CHI 2012 Extended Abstracts on Human Factors in Computing Systems, 2012, pp. 1961–1966 (2012)
10. Nanayakkara S., Shilkrot, R.: EyeRing: a finger-worn input device for seamless interactions with our surroundings. In: AH 2013 Proceedings of the 4th Augmented Human International Conference (2013)
11. Veriscimo, E.S., Bernardes Júnior, J.L.: 3D Interaction accessible to visually impaired users: a systematic review in HCI International (2016)
12. Amiralian, M.L.T.M.: Compreendendo o cego. Uma visão psicanalítica da cegueira por meio de desenhos-estórias. São Paulo in Casa do Psicólogo, Fapesp (1997)
13. LEAP MOTION. Web. 06 Dez. 2014. https://www.leapmotion.com/
14. JAVAFX 3D. Web. 08 Dez. 2014. https://docs.oracle.com/javase/8/javafx/graphics-tutorial/javafx-3dgraphics.htm
15. JAVA 3D API. Web. 08 Dez. 2014, http://www.oracle.com/technetwork/java/javase/tech/index-jsp-138252.html

3D Interaction Accessible to Visually Impaired Users: A Systematic Review

Erico de Souza Veriscimo$^{(\boxtimes)}$ and João Luiz Bernardes Jr.

School of Arts Sciences and Humanities – EACH,
University of São Paulo, São Paulo, Brazil
{ericoveriscimo, jbernardes}@usp.br

Abstract. There is currently a large number of visually impaired people in Brazil and worldwide. And just as any citizen they have their rights, including in them the right to education and other services that accelerate the process of social. With advent of technology increasingly virtual environments in three dimensions are being used for various areas. But often these environments are not accessible to visually impaired becoming a digital divide. In this context, a review of interactions in three dimensions accessible to visually impaired people may facilitate the work of researchers and developers to build such accessible applications. This paper presents the results of such a systematic literature review.

Keywords: 3D interaction · Visual impairment · Virtual environments

1 Introduction

According to IBGE [1] there is a large number of visually impaired people in Brazil and in 2010 the World Health Organization estimates that, in the whole world, there are 285 million people with severe visual disability, out of which 39 million are completely blind [2].

Like any other citizen, those with visual impairment also have rights. The United Nations established in 1975 a declaration of rights specific to people with some form of disability [3] and these rights include:

- The inherent right to respect for their human dignity. Disabled persons have the same fundamental rights as their fellow-citizens, which implies first and foremost the right to enjoy a decent life, as normal and full as possible;
- Measures designed to enable them to become as self-reliant as possible;
- Right to education and other services which will enable them to develop their capabilities and skills to the maximum and will hasten the processes of their social integration or reintegration.

And with technological advances, new devices for three-dimensional (3D) interaction are being created or becoming more available and less costly, contributing to the popularization of Virtual and Augmented Environments. Many of these environments, however, are not accessible to visually impaired users, creating a digital barrier and excluding these users from certain activities [4].

© Springer International Publishing Switzerland 2016
M. Antona and C. Stephanidis (Eds.): UAHCI 2016, Part II, LNCS 9738, pp. 251–260, 2016.
DOI: 10.1007/978-3-319-40244-4_24

In this context, a review of interactions in three dimensions accessible to visually impaired people may facilitate the work of researchers and developers to build such accessible applications. The objective of this paper is to present a Systematic Review based on the method proposed by Kitchenham et al. [5] to identify 3D interaction techniques accessible to visually impaired users and the input and output devices and senses explored in these techniques.

2 Methodology

Before beginning to apply the method proposed Kitchenham et al. [5] we conducted an exploratory review of the related literature to identify the most frequent terms and keywords used in this context. We then proceeded to create a review protocol with the following information:

Our research questions were:

1. What are the existing techniques and applications of 3D interaction accessibly to visually disabled users?
2. What are the input and output devices used in these techniques?
3. How is feedback given to the user in these techniques and which senses does it explore?

The search was conducted in three databases relevant to the area: ACM Digital Library (http://dl.acm.org); IEEE Xplore (http://ieeexplore.ieee.org) and Springer (http://link.springer.com), using the following search string (adapted as needed to each engine): (("Interact 3D" OR "augmented reality" OR "Ambient Intelligence" OR "virtual reality") AND ("blind user" OR "visually impaired" OR "blind people")).

Papers returned by this string were then included in the review if they obeyed all of our inclusion criteria and none of the exclusion criteria. The inclusion criteria were:

– Full text available in English in the selected databases;
– Must conduct and discuss some sort of experiment with either visually impaired participants or somehow simulating such impairment.

And the exclusion criteria removed works that:

– Only discuss 3D interaction techniques not accessible to visually impaired users.
– Only discuss 2D interaction techniques, even if they are accessible.
– Discuss techniques are accessible only to users with other types of disability but not to visual disability.

One example of paper discarded due to these criteria is [6] because even though it discusses 3D interaction techniques accessible to visually disabled users, it discussed no experiments simulating their exploration by those users.

All papers returned by the search strings initially had their title and abstract read ub a first pass to verify whether they fit the inclusion and exclusion criteria. In a second pass, all remaining papers were read entirely until it was clear they did not match the criteria for inclusion. Finally the selected papers were read in their entirety and the relevant information was extracted from them and tabulated. Mendeley Desktop 1.12.4 was used to help organize the papers and references.

The information extracted from each selected paper was: bibliographic information, filename, country where the research was conducted, year of publications, user senses explored, application, input and output device, form of feedback and a summary of its contents, relevant to this review.

3 Results

The initial search in the databases returned 330 unique references, with 210 from ACM, 23 from IEEE and 97 from Springer. The databases were searched in that order. 181 of that total were discarded in the first pass, applying the inclusion and exclusion criteria while reading only title and abstract. Out of the 71 remaining papers, 39 were discarded in the second pass and 35 were left (27 from ACM, 6 from IEEE and 2 from Springer) from which information was extracted. Figure 1a shows the distribution of papers along the years and Fig. 1b shows the distribution by country. No papers were found before the year 2000. Papers came from many different countries and 27 different journals or conference proceedings, with most contributing only one or two papers and only CHI and SIGACESS proceedings having 3 papers found.

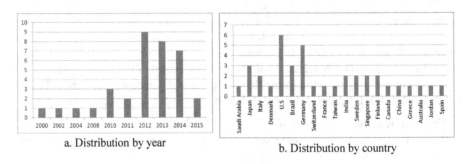

a. Distribution by year

b. Distribution by country

Fig. 1. Paper distribution

We classified the papers in 10 different types of application of accessible 3D interaction: navigation, finding objects, object recognition, object manipulation, object exploration and analysis, feeling the texture of objects, Braille reading, spatial perception and other applications. Figure 2 shows the total number and percentage of papers that mentioned each of these applications. Navigation was the most frequent concern mentioned in more than half the papers, particularly to augment the real environment to aid visually impaired users in navigating inside it. Interacting with virtual objects (or augmenting real objects with information) was the second most important concern in this review and we opted to subdivide this application further in more specific ways to interact with these objects. Each application and a few representative papers in each are summarized below.

Navigation: aiding visually impaired users to navigate indoor, outdoor or virtual environments was the main concern and application of 20 out of the 35 papers included in this review [7–26]. [24] actually proposes two different techniques for a total of 21 distinct ones. Jain [6] proposes an example of a system to aid in indoor navigation with two main components: modules to mark walls and one to represent a user, which includes a smartphone and a device attached to the waist. Vibration is used to inform the user whether he is following a correct path or not and information is also supplied to the user taking advantage of sound and the smartphone's text-to-speech functionality. The waist component communicates with the cellphone via Bluetooth and with the wall modules via infrared.

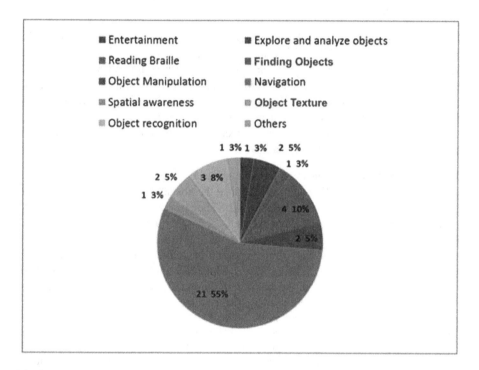

Fig. 2. Total number and percentage of papers mentioning each application (Color figure online)

Gallo et al. [7] describes an adaptation to the white canes used by visually disabled people with increased exploration range adding sensors (such as ultrasonic) to it and tactile feedback with vibration motors. An advantage of this system is that the way to use the cane does not change, so the user gains more exploration range without the need to relearn this skill.

Shangguan et al. [8] present an example of outdoor navigation system, to aid visually impaired users to cross safely along crosswalks using a smartphone's camera, orientation sensors and microphone as input devices and using voice audio messages as feedback.

Finding objects: out of the selected papers, 4 discuss some sort of solution to aid visually impaired users in finding objects around them or along their way [27–30]. Tang and Li [27], for instance, propose the use of a depth camera and spatial audio to locate objects and as feedback, respectively.

Object recognition: 3 papers attempt to aid in the problem of object recognition by visually impaired users [31–33]. Al-Khalifa and Al-Khalifa [31], for instance, identify objects using a smartphone camera and computer vision and add an augmented layer over physical objects of interest using sound. Pointing the smartphone to an object submits a query to a server requesting information about that object and the returned data is communicated to the user using audio telling what the object is and any other relevant characteristics.

Object manipulation: we found 2 works related to the manipulation of virtual objects by the visually impaired [28, 34]. Niinimäki and Tahiroglu [34] present a technique using Microsoft's Kinect as a sensor and providing both audio and haptic feedback using an active glove. All objects are surrounded by an exterior sphere and contain an interior cube. When users touch this sphere they begin receiving feedback, which increases in intensity as they approach the cube until they reach it. Once they are "touching" the object with both hands, Kinect tracks their position which is used to manipulate the virtual object in space.

Object exploration and analysis: 2 of the selected papers [35, 36] fit this classification. Ritterbusch et al. [35] attempts to reduce the obstacles a visually impaired user has in exploring certain objects, such as a map. They propose combining the feedback and input from a haptic device with 3D audio and show applications in three areas: architecture, math and medicine. Buonamici et al. [36] present a viability study for a novel system to map some work of art in virtual bas-relief and an audio description. User hand positions are tracked using Kinect while they explore this representation so the system can tell which part of the audio description to play. Kinect was also used as a 3D scanner to build the objects virtual representation.

Feeling object texture: this was the goal of 2 works included in this review. Ando et al. [38], propose a device placed under the nail of one finger to detect collision with virtual objects (or augmented real objects, such as a line drawing) and offer vibration feedback. Bau e Poupyrev [39] explore inverse electro-vibration, using weak electric signals on the user as feedback, to aid in the perception of texture of real objects, but these objects must be prepared beforehand.

Entertainment: Baldan [37] developed a virtual table tennis game accessible to visually disabled players that uses a smartphone as the paddle. While we are aware of a few other 3D games accessible to visually impaired users (including at least one first person shooter) our search of the literature did not return any of them.

Braille reading: Only Amemiya [10] described work in augmenting Braille text to aid in this task using a device called Finger-Braille that fits the fingers similarly to a glove that can aid both in Braille reading and navigation in an environment augmented with RFID tags and a camera.

Spatial Perception: Khambadkar and Folmer [40] use gesture-based interaction to aid visually impaired users in spatial perception, using a Kinect sensor attached to the user and synthesized voice audio feedback. The system is called GIST and has two modes of operation, mapping and gesture. In mapping mode it creates a map of the environment using color and depth information from Kinect, after which gesture mode is activated and the user is informed of it. Gestures are then used for different tasks, such as tell whether another person is present in the environment or identify how far objects are or their color.

Others: Hermann [41] proposes a system that helps identify head gestures directed to the user, such as shaking the head meaning "no". Its main contributions are two novel ways to represent these head gestures using sound: continuous sonification and event-based sonorization.

Besides these applications we also extracted more information from the selected papers, summarized in Fig. 3.

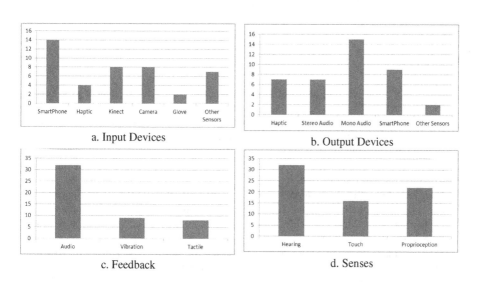

Fig. 3. Ocurrence of input and output devices, forms of feedback and explored senses

Figure 3a shows which input devices were used in the selected papers and how often, with the ubiquitous smartphones being used most often for both input and output (Fig. 3b), followed by other cameras and the Kinect sensors. While haptic devices and active gloves are very useful in many of these applications, their relatively high cost and low availability are probably the reason why they are not explored more often. Figure 3b shows the same for output devices. Mono audio was used most frequently by far, often as voice-based feedback, whether using synthesized or prerecorded voices, but other sound signals were frequent as well. Stereo audio was used often as well, particularly when exploring 3D sound. Haptic devices were more frequently used for feedback than for input. Figure 3c shows form of feedback independent of device, with audio being by far the most frequently used and Fig. 3d shows that hearing, of course, followed by proprioception were the senses most often explored in these accessible techniques.

4 Conclusion

We presented the results of a systematic literature review about 3D interaction accessible to visually disabled persons. Most of the research effort we found was aimed at the task of navigation, particularly to augment real environments with information and help users move through them. While we did find work to aid these users in exploring purely virtual environments, there is a clear deficit of research in this area. We hope that this review helps in some small measure to foment more research in this area, showing possible applications, research gaps to be filled and which senses and devices are more frequently and successfully explored aiming to help those who might want to get started in this sort of research.

References

1. IBGE, Diretoria de Pesquisas. Departamento de População e Indicadores Sociais. Rio de Janeiro (2010)
2. OMS, Organização Mundial da Saúde.: Global data on visual impairments 2010. Geneva, 17 p 2010. Disponível em. <http://www.who.int/entity/blindness/GLOBALDATAFINAL forweb.pdf> Acessado em: 21 Nov. 2014 (2010)
3. ONU. Declaração de Direitos das Pessoas Deficientes in: Assembléia Geral da Organização das Nações Unidas. 09 Dez (1975)
4. White, G., Fitzpatrick, G., McAllister, G.: Toward accessible 3D virtual environments for the blind and visually impaired. In: Proceedings of the 3rd International Conference on Digital Interactive Media in Entertainment and Arts. DIMEA 2008, vol. 349, pp. 134–141. ACM, New York (2008)
5. Kitchenham, B., Brereton, O., Budegen, D., Turner, M., Bailey, J., Linkman, S.: Systematic literature reviews in software engineering–a systematic literature review. Inf. Softw. Technol. **51**(1), 7–15 (2009)
6. Schätzle, S., Weber, B.: Towards vibrotactile direction and distance information for virtual reality and workstations for blind people. In: Antona, M., Stephanidis, C. (eds.) UAHCI 2015. LNCS, vol. 9176, pp. 148–160. Springer, Heidelberg (2015)
7. Jain, D.: Path-guided indoor navigation for the visually impaired using minimal building retrofitting. In: Proceedings of the 16th International ACM SIGACCESS Conference on Computers and Accessibility, pp. 225–232 (2014)
8. Gallo, S., Chapuis, D., Santos-Carreras, L., Kim, Y., Retornaz, P., Bleuler, H., Gassert, R.: Augmented white cane with multimodal haptic feedback. In: 2010 3rd IEEE RAS & EMBS International Conference on Biomedical Robotics and Biomechatronics, pp. 149–155 (2010)
9. Shangguan, L., Yang, Z., Zhou, Z.: CrossNavi: enabling real-time crossroad navigation for the blind with commodity phones. In: UbiComp 2014 - Proceedings of the 2014 ACM International Joint Conference on Pervasive and Ubiquitous Computing (2014)

10. Amemiya, T., Yamashita, J., Hirota, K., Hirose, M.: Virtual leading blocks for the deaf-blind: a real-time way-finder by verbal-nonverbal hybrid interface and high-density RFID tag space. In: IEEE Virtual Reality, pp. 165–287 (2004)

11. Berretta, L., Soares, F., Ferreira, D.J., Nascimento, H.A.D., Cardoso, A., Lamounier, E.: Virtual environment manipulated by recognition of poses using kinect: a study to help blind locomotion. In: 2013 XV Symposium on Unfamiliar Surroundings in Virtual and Augmented Reality (SVR), pp. 10–16 (2013)

12. Chuang, C., Hsieh, J., Fan, K.: A smart handheld device navigation system based on detecting visual code. In: 2013 International Conference on Machine Learning and Cybernetics, vol. 1, pp. 1407–1412 (2013)

13. Fallah, N., Apostolopoulos, I., Bekris, K., Folmer, E.: The user as a sensor. In: Proceedings of the 2012 ACM Annual Conference on Human Factors in Computing Systems - CHI 2012, p. 425 (2012)

14. Heller, F., Borchers, J.: AudioTorch: using a smartphone as directional microphone in virtual audio spaces. In: Proceedings of the 16th International Conference on Human-computer Interaction with Mobile Devices & Services, pp. 483–488 (2014)

15. Jain, D.: Pilot evaluation of a path-guided indoor navigation system for visually impaired in a public museum. In: Proceedings of the 16th International ACM SIGACCESS Conference on Computers and Accessibility, pp. 273–274 (2014)

16. Joseph, S.L., Zhang, X., Dryanovski, I., Xiao, J., Yi, C., Tian, Y.: Semantic indoor navigation with a blind-user oriented augmented reality. In: 2013 IEEE International Conference on Systems, Man, and Cybernetics, 2013, no. 65789, pp. 3585–3591 (2013)

17. Magnusson, C., Molina, M., Grohn, K.R., Szymczak, D.: Pointing for non-visual orientation and navigation. In: Proceedings 6th Nord Conference Human-Computer Interact. Extending Boundaries - Nord. 2010, p. 735 (2010)

18. Magnusson, C., Waern, A., Grohn, K.R., Bjernryd, A., Bernhardsson, H., Jakobsson, A., Salo, J., Wallon, M., Hedvall, P.O.: Navigating the world and learning to like it. In: Proceedings of the 13th International Conference on Human Computer Interaction with Mobile Devices and Services - MobileHCI 2011, p. 285 (2011)

19. Paneels, S.A., Olmos, A., Blum, J.R., Cooperstock, J.R.: Listen to it yourself!: evaluating usability of what's around me? for the blind. In: Proceedings of the SIGCHI Conference on Human Factors in Computing Systems, pp. 2107–2116 (2013)

20. Raposo, N., Rios, H., Lima, D., Gadelha, B., Castro, T.: An application of mobility aids for the visually impaired. In: Proceedings of the 13th International Conference on Mobile and Ubiquitous Multimedia - MUM 2014, pp. 180–189 (2014)

21. Ribeiro, F., Florencio, D., Chou, P.A., Zhang, Z.: Auditory augmented reality: Object sonification for the visually impaired. In: 2012 IEEE 14th International Workshop on Multimedia Signal Processing (MMSP), pp. 319–324 (2012)

22. Schneider, J., Strothotte, T.: Constructive exploration of spatial information by blind users. In: Proceedings of the Fourth International ACM Conference on Assistive Technologies - Assets 2000 (2000)

23. Soukaras, D.P., Chaniotis, I.K., Karagiannis, I.G., Stampologlou, I.S., Triantafyllou, C.A., Tselikas, N.D., Foukarakis, I.E., Boucouvalas, A.C.: Augmented audio reality mobile application specially designed for visually impaired people. In: 2012 16th Panhellenic Conference on Informatics, pp. 13–18 (2012)

24. Zollner, M., Huber, S., Jetter, H.C., Reiterer, H.: NAVI: a proof-of-concept of a mobile navigational aid for visually impaired based on the microsoft kinect. In: Proceedings of the 13th IFIP TC 13 International Conference on Human-computer Interaction - Volume Part IV, pp. 584–587 (2011)

25. Rodriguez-Sanchez, M.C., Moreno-Alvarez, M.A., Martin, E., Borromeo, S., Hernandez-Tamames, J.A.: Accessible smartphones for blind users: A case study for a wayfinding system. In: Expert Systems with Applications (2014)

26. Doush, I.A., Alshattnawi, S., Barhoush, M.: Non-visual navigation interface for completing tasks with a predefined order using mobile phone: a case study of pilgrimage. Int. J. Mobile Netw. Design Innov. 6(1), 1–13 (2015)

27. Tang, T.J.J., Li, W.H.: An assistive EyeWear prototype that interactively converts 3D object locations into spatial audio. In: Proceedings of the 2014 ACM International Symposium on Wearable Computers - ISWC 2014, pp. 119–126 (2014)

28. Vaananen-Vainio-Mattila, K., Suhonen, K., Laaksonen, J., Kildal, J., Tahiroglu, K.: User experience and usage scenarios of audio-tactile interaction with virtual objects in a physical environment. In: Proceedings of the 6th International Conference on Designing Pleasurable Products and Interfaces - DPPI 2013, p. 67 (2013)

29. Deville, B., Bologna, G., Pun, T.: Detecting objects and obstacles for visually impaired individuals using visual saliency. In: Proceedings of the 12th International ACM SIGACCESS Conference on Computers and Accessibility - ASSETS 2010, p. 253 (2010)

30. Dramas, F., Oriola, B., Katz, B.G., Thorpe, S.J., Jouffrais, C.: Designing an assistive device for the blind based on object localization and augmented auditory reality. In: Proceedings of the 10th International ACM SIGACCESS Conference on Computers and Accessibility - Assets 2008, p. 263 (2008)

31. Al-Khalifa, A.S., Al-Khalifa, H.S.: Do-It-Yourself object identification using augmented reality for visually impaired people. In: Miesenberger, K., Karshmer, A., Penaz, P., Zagler, W. (eds.) ICCHP 2012, Part II. LNCS, vol. 7383, pp. 560–565. Springer, Heidelberg (2012)

32. Nanayakkara, S., Shilkrot, R.: EyeRing: a finger-worn input device for seamless interactions with our surroundings. In: AH 2013 Proceedings of the 4th Augmented Human International Conference (2013)

33. Nanayakkara, S., Shilkrot, R., Maes, P.: EyeRing: A finger-worn assistant. In: CHI 2012 Extended Abstracts on Human Factors in Computing Systems, pp. 1961–1966 (2012)

34. Niinimaki M., Tahiroglu, K.: AHNE: a novel interface for spatial interaction. In: CHI 2012 Extended Abstracts on Human Factors in Computing Systems, 2012, pp. 1031–1034 (2012)

35. Ritterbusch, S., Constantinescu, A., Koch, V.: Hapto-acoustic scene representation. In: Miesenberger, K., Karshmer, A., Penaz, P., Zagler, W. (eds.) ICCHP 2012, Part II. LNCS, vol. 7383, pp. 644–650. Springer, Heidelberg (2012)

36. Buonamici, F., Furferi, R., Governi, L., Volpe, Y.: Making blind people autonomous in the exploration of tactile models: a feasibility study. In: Antona, M., Stephanidis, C. (eds.) UAHCI 2015. LNCS, vol. 9176, pp. 82–93. Springer, Heidelberg (2015)

37. Baldan, S., Gotzen, A., de Serafin, S.: Mobile rhythmic interaction in a sonic tennis game. In: CHI 2013 Extended Abstracts on Human Factors in Computing Systems on - CHI EA 2013, p. 2903 (2013)

38. Ando, H., Miki, T., Inami, M., Maeda, T.: SmartFinger: nail-mounted tactile display. In: ACM SIGGRAPH 2002 conference abstracts and applications on - SIGGRAPH 2002, 2002, p. 78 (2002)

39. Ba, O., Poupyrev, I., Goc, M.L., Galliot, L., Glisson, M.: REVEL: tactile feedback technology for augmented reality. In: SIGGRAPH 2012 ACM SIGGRAPH 2012 Emerging Technologies (2012)

40. Khambadkar, V., Folmer, E.: GIST: a gestural interface for remote nonvisual spatial perception. In: Proceedings of the 26th Annual ACM Symposium on User Interface Software and Technology - UIST 2013, pp. 301–310 (2013)
41. Hermann, T., Neumann, A., Zehe, S.: Head gesture sonification for supporting social interaction. In: Proceedings of the 7th Audio Most. Conf. A Conf. Interact. with Sound - AM 2012, pp. 82–89 (2012)

Haptic Virtual Approach: Biological Effect on Touching and Viewing

Atsushi Hoshina[1], Yoshiko Okada[1], Irini Giannopulu[2],
and Midori Sugaya[1(✉)]

[1] Shibaura Institute of Technology, Tokyo, Japan
{al12091,y-okada,doly}@shibaura-it.ac.jp
[2] Pierre and Marie Curie University, Paris, France
igiannopulu@psychoprat.fr

Abstract. The Digital Dollhouse we proposed enhanced traditional psychological play therapy with digital sensors and computer graphics combined together. It obtains significant difference in reaction of children that compared with normal dollhouse. We proposed the approach of connecting concrete object touching (Haptic), then the touching information of humans with several sensors and presents it for several representative image for the display as CG (Virtual). We assume this "Haptic Virtual" approach would have specific effect on improving the biological reaction for not only children, but also the adult, and try to conducted experiments with the proposed device and method implemented. From the preliminarily experimental, we obtained knowledge about the effect of the "Haptic Virtual" approach.

Keywords: Therapy device · CG· Biological information · Brain wave · Heat beat · Haptic virtual · Haptic · Virtual

1 Introduction

Imagine if you are having a device and monitor. If you touch specific part of the device, that action reflects to CG. Children might be fascinated more than just playing with ordinary device without action reflecting to CG. We have proposed a novel device that has this feature. The Digital Dollhouse (Fig. 1) enhanced traditional psychological play therapy with digital sensors and computer graphics on this mechanism [1]. It obtains significant difference in reaction of children that compared with normal dollhouse especially in taking the responsive actions are twice as much as the normal device, and for the abstract concept three times, the number of miss-communications are 80 % less than the normal one. Even more, children spent playing with this device twice as longer time as the normal device.

Based on the result, we, psychologists, brain scientist and human computer interaction researchers, have an assumption that there is a possibility for enhancing biological effect on collaboration of touching and viewing, compared with just touching, and just viewing. Based on this assumption, we define the cooperation of the action of touching the device (Haptic), and reflection of action to CG (Virtual) for viewing the

© Springer International Publishing Switzerland 2016
M. Antona and C. Stephanidis (Eds.): UAHCI 2016, Part II, LNCS 9738, pp. 261–270, 2016.
DOI: 10.1007/978-3-319-40244-4_25

Fig. 1. Digital Dollhouse and correspondence room [1]

result as a feedback of their action, and propose "Haptic Virtual Approach". It includes not only the haptic and virtual collaboration method, but also present the novel human-computer interaction technology that collecting touching information of humans with several sensors and present it for some representative image for the display. This immersive space should have lots of discussion that how to achieve the immersive play, real-time, virtual expression one-to-one mapping, and how to illustrate abstract image, and applications etc. In this paper, a first step of our research, we will present an experimental evaluation that uses biological responses of subjects with brainwave and heartbeat. We find out that our presented "Haptic Virtual Approach" has various results, different from each participant.

This paper is organized as follows. Section 2 explains related works. Section 3 explains our proposal. Section 4 shows system design and implementation. Section 5 introduces the experiment we conducted and the results earned from the experiment. Section 6 discusses about subjects we obtained from the experiment. At last, Sect. 7 draws the conclusion.

2   Related Works

There are several studies that apply the method of measuring biological information to estimate human's consciousness.

In the study of estimating "Wakuwaku (Japanese word mainly represents excitement)", Galvanic Skin Reflex (GSR), Electrocardiogram (ECG) and breathing rate are measured [2]. This study concluded that the use of heart rate, earned from ECG and GSR might have showed the measurement of "Wakuwaku" feeling.

In the study of measuring attention and relaxation, Electro Encephalogram (EEC) are used to measure these consciousness [3]. This study uses its own formula to calculate stress from values earned from brainwave sensor using. In this study, several experiments that are often used to generate stress deliberately were conducted and the brainwave was measured. From the results, the value of brainwave changes as the participants participated the experiment numerous times. From the results shown, participants generated lower stress as they participated on the experiment many times.

3 Proposal

Based on the preliminary experiment that had conducted with the Digital Dollhouse, we found out results that might be useful for therapy. For example, children who experienced the device increased the number of words spoken, comparing to normal device [1]. Somehow, the result was abstractive, and difficult to say that the device is suitable for enhancing speaking.

From the results, we presumed that combination of house-shaped device and CG enhanced speaking. From the control of concrete object and visualizing invisible and abstract information, we named the effect as "Haptic Virtual".

3.1 Combination of Touching and Viewing

We defined Haptic as controlling and touching concrete object, and Virtual as expressing the results of controlling and touching by changing information displayed on CG. Combination of these elements makes Haptic Virtual.

For example, there are functions to control character on the device. On the view of Haptic, person who experience the device control doll and placing it. On the view of Virtual, person will control the character inside CG. Combining these together to make Haptic Virtual, character inside CG can be controlled by using doll and placing it on the specific part of the device.

3.2 Use of Biological Information

To evaluate our interactive device, we consider the results earned from previous study that increase the number of speaking and the longer continuation on the device. We assumed that enhancing concentration and reducing stress were aroused from the device compared with the just only CG, touching the concrete object. To know the effect correctly, biological information as the measurement of stress and concentration can explain the background of these results. We measured heartbeat and brainwave to compare the effect between Haptic only, Virtual only and Haptic Virtual.

We used "WHS-1" for measuring heartbeat [6]. From this heartbeat sensor, we obtained LF/HF. This is a ratio of revitalization of the sympathetic nerve (LF), which revitalize when stressed and the parasympathetic nerve (HF), which revitalize when relaxed. This means that when the wearer of the heartbeat sensor feels more stress, the value of LF/HF increases [4].

Brainwave is obtained from "MindWave Mobile" [7]. From this brainwave, we obtained Attention, which is the value calculated with specific algorithm by this brainwave. Its value is from 0 to 100, and it is used to measure concentration [5]. In another word, the value will be lowered when the user with the sensor attached is having less concentration.

4   System Design and Implementation

To know the effect of the "Haptic Virtual Approach", we firstly focus on the topics that provided with abstract image, since we assume that virtual expression would be more effective with understanding the abstract things. Time and seasons has no actual things that can touch. However, it can be understanding only with the observable evidences that clock number and different color of leaves viewing in the window. We add the functions to change time and season. The other abstract thing, we present an emotion with displaying character, with moving around the actual doll in the house (Fig. 2). We also implemented the function to control temperature and brightness of CG, by using buttons and knob.

Fig. 2. Playing with Digital Dollhouse with design implemented

To compare the effect of Haptic only, Virtual only and Haptic Virtual, devices with Haptic only and Virtual only are required. We used the device we implemented with several functions changed to make these two devices. On device with Haptic only, there is no CG information, and user need to recognize the change of the situation by themselves. On device with Virtual only, there is no dollhouse to control, and user uses keyboard to control object.

5   Preliminary Experiment and Evaluation

We held a preliminary experiment to compare biological information earned from Haptic, Virtual and Haptic Virtual.

5.1   Objective

The experiment has held to know what kind of effect will appear not only on device with Haptic Virtual implemented, but also with Haptic implemented only and Virtual implemented only. There were 5 participants who participated on the experiment (Age of 21 to 22, Male: 4, Female: 1), and used biological information to evaluate the effect.

5.2   Method

The subject will proceed the experiment as follows.

1. Sit on the chair and attach heartbeat and brainwave sensor
2. Getting instructed the way how to control the device
3. Stay still for two minutes.
4. Experience devices with Haptic, Virtual and Haptic Virtual implemented, in order.

We started to measure biological information as soon as we started the process (3). We measured the biological information while staying still in the use to settling criteria value, since the biological information's value is going to be different by the individuals. We used this biological information to calculate the changing rate. The formula is listed below.

$$\textit{Changing rate of biological information while experiencing device}(\%)$$
$$= \frac{((\textit{Staying still}) - (\textit{device experiencing})) * 100}{(\textit{staying still})} \qquad (1)$$

This calculation method was used to calculate the changing rate of heartbeat at previous research [8].

After the experiment was held and calculating changing rate, we conducted hearing research to all participants who participated to the experiment. This research was conducted to know the influence between individual's thought and biological information. Content of the research was discussed by analyzing each participant's biological information recorded.

5.3   Environment

Experiment was held at silent room with only participants and explainer. We settled the situation to reject factors such as noises caused by human activities, participants getting strained from other person's existence to minimize an influence to biological

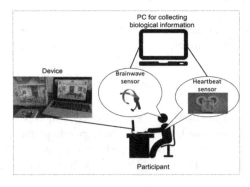

Fig. 3. System of experiment

information. Participants sit on a chair and attach heartbeat and brainwave sensor. They experience the device in that situation, and biological information is obtained (Fig. 3). Moreover, process of the experiment was recorded by video camera, to analyze the experiment in detail.

5.4   Result

Experiment was conducted as the way explained at Sect. 5.3. From these results, we compared the difference of biological information of Haptic (H), Virtual (V) and Haptic Virtual (HV). First, we analyzed the pattern of biological information's transition each participant recorded. Next, we analyzed the dimension of biological information each participant recorded. At last, we analyzed the summary of hearing research. The transition of biological information each participant recorded is listed on Fig. 4.

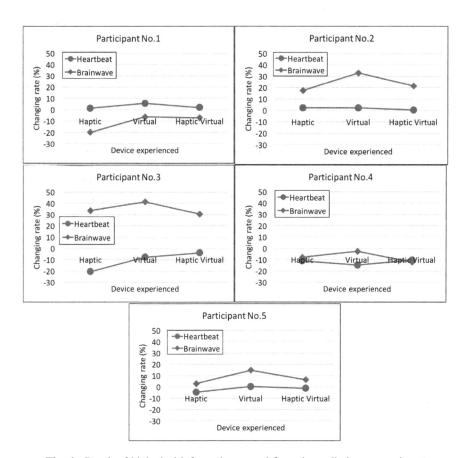

Fig. 4. Result of biological information earned from the preliminary experiment

As the result shown from all the participant's biological information on Fig. 4, we found out that transition of biological information showed some similar patterns with plural groups of participants. The pattern of these biological information is listed below.

(1) Measurement of LF/HF (stress) with heartbeat

There were three patterns of transition on heartbeat. One of the pattern was seen from participant 1, 2 and 5. The value of Heartbeat recorded from H to V increased its value, and the value recorded from V to HV decreased its value. From this result, participant 1, 2 and 5 increased LF/HF, or enhanced stress on V. Somehow, comparing to V, H and HV recorded lower LF/HF. This means that touching house-shaped device may had lead to decreasing stress. But just viewing at CG enhanced stress.

Participant 3 showed next pattern. The value of heartbeat recorded from H to V increased its value, same as first pattern. But the value of heartbeat recorded from V to HV also increased. We suggested that this participant may had increased stress, or enhanced stress because of time taking to conduct experiment. The longer the experiment held, more stress the participant may had enhanced.

Last pattern was seen from participant 4. The value of heartbeat recorded from H to V decreased its value, and the value of heartbeat recorded from V to HV increased its value. With the heartbeat recorded the lowest on V, elements which this participant only has might have lead this result.

(2) Measurement of Attention (concentration) with brainwave

All participants made the same pattern of transition on brainwave. They first experienced Haptic, and increased the value of the brainwave from H when experiencing V. However, value of the brainwave decreased from V when experiencing HV. From this result, we can suggest that V enhances the value of brainwave, meaning that displaying CG which changes enhances concentration. On the other hand, H and HV, which controls house-shaped device, couldn't have enhanced concentration enough, comparing to V.

Next, we analyzed the dimension of biological information. Dimension of heartbeat and brainwave each participant recorded is listed on Table 1.

Table 1. Dimension of biological information each subject recorded

Participants	Dimension of Heartbeat (LF/HF)	Dimension of Brainwave (Attention)
1	V > HV > H	V > HV > H
2	V > H>HV	V > HV > H
3	HV > V>H	V > H>HV
4	HV > H>V	V > H>HV
5	V > HV > H	V > HV > H

Same as transition of biological information listed on Fig. 4, there were several patterns of dimension appeared from Table 1. Here are the patterns that can be seen from this table.

(1) Measurement of LF/HF (stress) with heartbeat

The result from participant 1, 2 and 5, V was the device with the highest value of heartbeat recorded. Looking the result in detail, HV recorded the second highest value in participant 1 and 5. What we can consider about this result is that V, which controls and views CG information increases stress. And H, which only controls house-shaped device decreases stress. With Haptic Virtual, it recorded the intermediate value of H and V. As the result shown from participant 2, HV recorded the lowest value of heartbeat. This means, for participant 2, experiencing HV felt lower stress than experiencing any other devices.

As the result shown from participant 3 and 4, HV recorded the highest value of heartbeat. Looking the result in detail, heartbeat recorded from participant 3 increased its value as the participant experienced the device. Meaning that time elapsing may had caused the enhancement of stress. Participant 4 recorded the lowest value of heartbeat on V. Somehow, the value of heartbeat on HV, which also uses CG, recorded the highest value.

(2) Measurement of Attention (concentration) with brainwave

All participants recorded the highest value of brainwave on V. As the result shown from remaining H and HV, participant 1, 4 and 5, HV recorded higher brainwave than H. From this pattern of dimension, presence of CG may have enhanced concentration. Beside, presence of control of house-shaped device may have lead to cutting down concentration. We can assume that result earned from HV is a merge of results earned from H only and V only.

As the result shown from participant 2 and 3, HV recorded lower brainwave than H. What can be assumed from this result is that the participant might had felt tedious on experiment.

As we analyzed transition and dimension of biological information, some patterns were recorded. However, discussion about the result was completely subjective, and participant's impressions were required to substantiate the results earned from the experiment. For this problem, we conducted hearing research from all participants. The content of research was considered by results analyzed by the result shown from the transition and dimension of biological information. Several answers were earned as a result of the research. The correspondence of the result of the research and corresponding participants who answered the research is listed on Table 2.

Table 2. Summary of hearing research

Answer earned from hearing research	Participants corresponded
Likes playing with video games	1,2,3,4,5
Role-played character's role	2,3
Tedious experiment	1,4,5
Problems on Haptic device (Bared wires, uncertain control)	1,3

As the result shown from Table 2, four types of answers were mainly heard from five participants. The detail of the answer is that whether the participants like to play video games, role-played character's role, felt tedious on the experiment and felt some problems on the device. We analyzed the relationship between hearing research, and transition and dimension of biological information.

All participants answered "Likes playing with video games". Relevance of biological information and the answer appeared at brainwave. All participants recorded the highest value in V. This means that V, which controls and views the change of CG enhanced the attention of the participants, and their partial of playing video games may had lead this result.

Participant 2 and 3 answered "Role-played character's role". Relevance of biological information and the answer appeared at brainwave. Value of the brainwave was significantly high comparing to other participants. On the other hands, participants who answered "Tedious experiment", which was participant 1, 4 and 5, recorded lower brainwave than the one who answered "Role-played character's role". From this result, person who imagined the character's role enhanced attention. On the other hand, person who felt the experiment tedious, which was participant 1, 4 and 5, couldn't have enhanced the attention that much.

The answer "Problems on device" was heard from participant 1 and 3. Detail of this answer is that participant felt difficult to control the device because of bared wires and control with no descriptions. There was no relationship between the answer and biological information found. Somehow, both participants recorded the lowest heartbeat at H. This means that they felt the least stress through all the devices, even thought they felt that controlling the Haptic device was a problem.

6 Discussion About Experiment

From the experiment, value of biological information obtained from 5 participants showed several patterns. Haptic Virtual and other devices. Much as the result of hearing research, answers obtained from participant and the result of biological information showed specific relationship. Although, the method of the experiment we conducted was not well discussed. To obtain reliable and better data, more discussions about the method of the experiment is required. Here is the list of the problems that should be discussed at next experiment we're going to conduct.

(1) Experiencing order of the devices

At preliminary experiment, experiencing order of the device was constant to all participants. We are planning to prepare several patterns of experiencing order, to know the difference appearing by order of experiencing the devices.

(2) Inducting detailed questionnaire

From results earned from preliminary experiment, we earned the knowledge that elements each participants have may influence the results earned by experiencing the devices.

(3) Changing method of the experiment

We prepared a method to ask the participant to stay still at the beginning of the experiment. Somehow, while conducting the experiment, behavior while staying still was different by every participant. We're planning to involve the method to close their eyes and stay still during this situation.

(4) Ask participants to participate the experiment plural times

At experiment we're planning to held, we're going to ask some of the participants to participate the experiment plural times. This is to know the effect obtained from plural experiments.

7   Conclusion

In this paper, we examined "Haptic Virtual" as an approach that combines concrete object with sensors attached (Haptic) and CG (Virtual). With this combination, CG can be controlled by touching the objects inside the concrete device. We also discussed the way to evaluate "Haptic Virtual" by using biological information. From the result of the experiment, we found out that specific patterns were found on the transition and dimension of biological information. Hearing research also made progress to reveal the relationship between biological information each participant recorded and answer obtained from the research. To ensure the result earned from the preliminary experiment, more data is required. Furthermore, to obtain more reliable data, revision of the method of experiment is required.

References

1. Sugaya, M., Okada, Y., Osawa, H., Giannopulu, I.: Feel as agent: immersive dollhouse enhances sociality of children with developmental disorders. In: Proceedings of the 3rd International Conference on Human-Agent Interaction (HAI), Daegu, Korea (2015)
2. Ohkura, M., Hamano, M., Watanabe, H., Aoto, T.: Measurement of "wakuwaku" feeling generated by interactive systems using biological signals. In: KEER (2010)
3. Crowley, K., Sliney, A., Pitt, I., Murphy, D.: Evaluating a brain-computer interface to categorise human emotional response. In: IEEE, pp. 276–278 (2010)
4. Healey, J.A., Picard, R.W.: Detecting stress during real-world driving tasks using physiological sensors. IEEE Trans. Intell. Transp. Syst. **6**(2), 156–166 (2005)
5. Navalyal, G.U., Gavas, R.D.: A dynamic attention assessment and enhancement tool using computer graphics. Hum. Centric Comput. Inf. Sci. **4**, 11 (2014)
6. Heart Rate Sensor:: UNION TOOL CO. http://www.uniontool.co.jp/en/product/sensor/index.html
7. "MindWave". NeuroSky STORE. http://store.neurosky.com/pages/mindwave
8. Takatsu, H., Munakata, M., Ozeki, O., Yokoyama, K., Watanabe, Y., Takata, K.: An evaluation of the quantitative relationship between the subjective stress value and heart rate variability. T.IEE Japan, 120-C(1), 104–110 (2000)

Measurement of Lens Focus Adjustment While Wearing a See-Through Head-Mounted Display

Ryota Kimura[1], Kohei Iwata[1], Takahiro Totani[2], Toshiaki Miyao[2],
Takehito Kojima[1], Hiroki Takada[3], Hiromu Ishio[4], Chizue Uneme[1],
Masaru Miyao[1(✉)], and Masumi Takada[5]

[1] Department of Information Engineering,
Graduate School of Information Science, Nagoya University,
Furo-Cho, Nagoya, Chikusa-Ku 464-8601, Japan
kimura.ryota@h.mbox.nagoya-u.ac.jp,
miyao@nagoya-u.ac.jp
[2] Seiko Epson Corporation, 6925, Toyoshinatazawa,
Azumino, Nagano 399-8285, Japan
[3] Department of Human and Artificial Intelligent Systems,
Graduate School of Engineering, University of Fukui,
3-9-1 Bunkyo, Fukui 910-8507, Japan
[4] Department of Urban Management, Fukuyama City University, 2-19-1,
Minatomachi, Fukuyama, Hiroshima 721-0964, Japan
[5] Chubu Gakuin University, 2-1, Kirigaoka, Seki, Gifu 501-3993, Japan

Abstract. In recent years, many visual devices have been produced for consumers. The development of see-through smart glasses has attracted much attention. These glasses overlap virtually images by using Augmented Reality (AR) technology. Epson released the BT-2000 see-through smart glasses, which change distance of display by changing convergence. It is not confirmed that changing distance of display allow to change distance of lends accommodation. In this experiment, we measured lens accommodation of subjects viewing images displayed on see-through smart glasses. The results found that lens accommodation moved with the image position for over one hundred people. Therefore, our study verified that correct reaction occurred visual physiologically.

Keywords: See-through · Smart glasses · Lens accommodation · AR

1 Introduction

Various electronic devices equipped with an array of sensors have been made mobile by the down-sizing of electronic parts [1]. Devices designed to wear are termed wearable devices. In this study, we focused on an eyeglass-type device that is attached to the head, a see-through head-mounted display. See-through head-mounted displays are capable of superimposing information on one's view of the real world employing Augmented Reality (AR) technology [2].

© Springer International Publishing Switzerland 2016
M. Antona and C. Stephanidis (Eds.): UAHCI 2016, Part II, LNCS 9738, pp. 271–278, 2016.
DOI: 10.1007/978-3-319-40244-4_26

Studies on the use of see-through head-mounted displays to improve work support for users have recently been actively performed. In 2014, Makita et al. superimposed information on road damage on a head-mounted display and stated its usefulness [3], and Makibuchi et al. proposed a hands-free work support system using head-mounted displays in 2015 [4].

Work support systems using head-mounted displays are expected to proliferate in the future. On the other hand, the display position of contents on conventional head-mounted displays is fixed, but, for hand-related work in which the visual distance changes, the content display position should follow the hand position, otherwise an uncomfortable feeling may develop that influences the work. Thus, automatic modification of the perceived position in the depth direction of the content while using a head-mounted display may be significant for work support. One method to change the display position in the depth direction is changing the congestion focus position. In the visual function, when one sees a nearby object, lens accommodation occurs. The focus is adjusted by increasing the lens thickness in conjunction with convergence of the bilateral eyes toward the medial side, with which miosis of the pupils also occurs. These 3 reactions are termed the near reflex, and the occurrence of one reaction induces the others [5]. A lens accommodation response changes convergence, and this is termed accommodative convergence, while changes in convergence induce a lens accommodation response and this is termed convergence accommodation [6].

In this study, convergence accommodation was induced by moving the content display position in the lateral direction in a head-mounted display, and the influence on perceiving the depth direction of contents while using the display was investigated.

For the see-through head-mounted display, EPSON MOVERIO Pro BT-2000 was used. BT-2000 independently projects images for the bilateral eyes. In addition, it is capable of changing the center distance in the lateral direction. Thus, using an original application utilizing these 2 characteristics, the center distance was changed to alter the convergence, and the following of the convergence by an accommodation response was investigated. The head-mounted display used in this experiment, BT-2000, is presented as HMD (Head Mounted Display) below.

2 Materials and Methods

This study involved 128 subjects aged 14 to 88 years old (66 males and 62 females). Generally, the accommodative function starts to decline after the mid 40s [7]. Thus, the subjects were divided into those younger than 45 years old as a young group (58 subjects) and 45 years old or older as an older group (70 subjects). All subjects performed the experiment with naked eyes or wearing glasses and contact lenses usually used. As an ethical consideration, sufficient informed consent was obtained from the subjects before they participated in the experiment. This study was approved by the Ethics Committee of Graduate School of Information Science, Nagoya University. Lens focus adjustment was measured using an autorefractometer (WAM-5500, Shigiya Machinery Works, Ltd.). The temporal resolution of this device was 5 Hz. HMD and WAM-5500 used in the experiment are shown in Fig. 1.

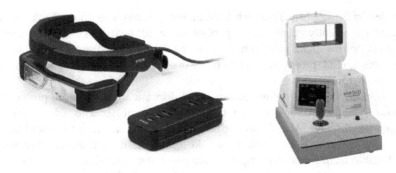

Fig. 1. Left: EPSON MOVERIO Pro BT-2000, right: WAM-5500

In this study, contents were displayed on HMD and a liquid crystal display (LCD), and lens focus adjustment was measured while viewing each content. The content position displayed on both devices was set at 1.43 (0.7 m), 0.8 (1.25 m), and 0.3 D (3.33 m) from the eyes of the subject. Diopter (D) is the unit of accommodative ability, and it is a reciprocal of the distance in meters (m). Using each device, the subjects viewed the contents for 10 s twice at each visual distance. Considering the order of the effect, the order of the device was alternately changed in each subject, and the visual distance was set in random order. The horizontal illuminance was 956 ℓx. The experimental environment and set-up are shown in Figs. 2 and 3.

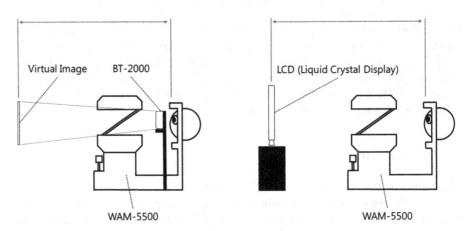

Fig. 2. Experimental environment

From time-series data of accommodation values collected in the experiment, 3-s time-series data were extracted because their distribution was the smallest in order to exclude factors, such as blinking, and the mean of the extracted 3-s time-series data was calculated as a representative value of the visual distance. When 3-s time-series data could not be extracted under any of the 6 conditions (2 device conditions with 3 visual distance conditions), the subject was excluded.

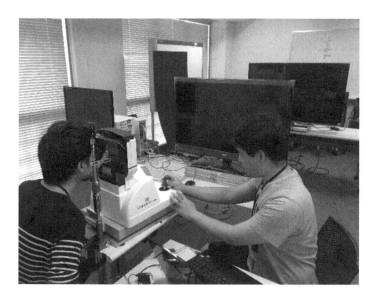

Fig. 3. Experimental set-up

The calculated representative values in each age group were subjected to 2-way layout analysis of variance with the device (LCD, HMD) and visual distance (1.43 D, 0.8 D, and 0.3 D) as factors, followed by the paired t-test regarding the absence of a difference in the population mean as a null hypothesis and multiple comparison. In addition, the paired t-test regarding the absence of a difference in the population mean as a null hypothesis was performed between the 2 devices at the same visual distance. The significance level was set at 5 % or lower.

3   Results

As an open-field-type device, WAM-5500, is capable of measurement under natural conditions while wearing glasses. However, this experiment required avoiding the image projection optical system (half mirror) of the see-through head-mounted display and projecting infrared light for measurement from an oblique. Thus, the measurement was contraindicated for some subjects even though the measurement range of WAM-5500 was 20° in the lateral direction in the front-open type. As a result, the numbers of the subjects were 15 and 26 in the young and older groups, respectively.

The results for the lens focus adjustment in the young and older groups are shown in Figs. 4 and 5. In the young group, when the content was displayed on LCD at 0.3, 0.8, and 1.43 D, the means were about 0.7, 0.9, and 1.2 D, respectively. When the content was displayed on HMD at 0.3, 0.8, and 1.43 D, the means were about 0.8, 1.0, and 1.1 D, respectively.

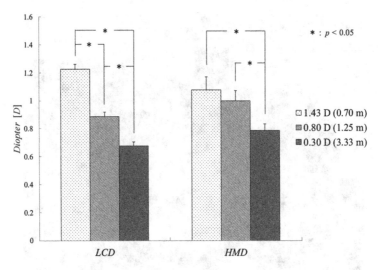

Fig. 4. Lens focus adjustment in the young group

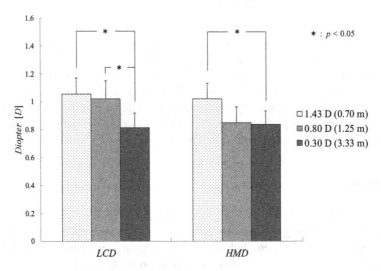

Fig. 5. Lens focus adjustment in the older group

In the older group, when the content was displayed on LCD at 0.3, 0.8, and 1.43 D, the means were about 0.8, 1.0, and 1.0 D, respectively. When the content was displayed on HMD at 0.3, 0.8, and 1.43 D, the means were about 0.8, 0.8, and 1.0 D, respectively.

The results for the young group were subjected to 2-way layout analysis of variance with the visual distance and device as factors. A main effect was detected when the factor was the visual distance, but no main effect was detected when the device was the factor ($p < 0.05$). No interaction was observed. Then, the results with LCD in the young group were subjected to the paired t-test. The mean significantly decreased at a visual distance of 0.8 D compared with that at 1.43 D ($p < 0.05$), at a visual distance of 0.3 D compared with that at 1.43 D ($p < 0.05$), and at a visual distance of 0.3 D compared with that at 0.8 D ($p < 0.05$). The results with HMD were subjected to the paired t-test. The mean significantly decreased at a visual distance of 0.3 D compared with that at 1.43 D ($p < 0.05$), and at a visual distance of 0.3 D compared with that at 0.8 D ($p < 0.05$).

The results for the older group were subjected to 2-way layout analysis of variance with the visual distance and device as factors. No main effect of either factor ($p < 0.05$) or interaction was noted. The results with LCD were subjected to the paired t-test. The mean significantly decreased at a visual distance of 1.43 D compared with that at 0.3 D ($p < 0.05$), and at a visual distance of 0.3 D compared with that at 0.8 D ($p < 0.05$). The results with HMD were subjected to the paired t-test. The mean significantly decreased at a visual distance of 1.43 D compared with that at 0.3 D ($p < 0.05$).

The values with the devices at the same visual distance were subjected to the paired t-test. No significant difference was noted at any visual distance between the results with LCD and HMD.

4 Discussion

Using EPSON MOVERIO Pro BT-2000, induction of an accommodation response in conjunction with convergence movement by changing the center distance in the lateral direction while using HMD was investigated. Convergence accommodation was induced while using HMD, confirming changes in the perception concerning the depth direction.

The mean lens focus adjustment deviated from the theoretical value, suggesting that the depth of the field increased due to the myopic tendency of the subjects and indoor lighting. The accommodation ability was decreased in the older group compared with that in the young group, and variation of the mean lens focus adjustment was small at all visual distances. On measurement of the lens focus adjustment during viewing the content displayed on HMD and LCD, a significant difference was noted in the mean lens focus adjustment between the visual distances of 1.43 and 0.3D while using HMD regardless of the age groups, confirming that the content displayed to the bilateral eyes changed the center distance of the content and induced an accommodation response.

On 2-way layout analysis of variance in the young group, no main effect was noted in either device, and a main effect was noted in the visual distance. Since the young group had sufficient accommodation ability, an accommodation response occurred corresponding to the visual distance, which may have caused transition of the lens focus adjustment. No significant difference was noted between the devices, confirming that visual-physiologically correct accommodation responses occurred while using HMD.

On 2-way layout analysis of variance in the older group, no main effect was noted with either the device or visual distance. The results with LCD and HMD confirmed that lens focus adjustment changed corresponding to the visual distance. It was confirmed that normal accommodation responses also occurred in the older group while viewing the content displayed on HMD.

5 Summary

With recent developments of mobile technology, various wearable devices have become available. Head-mounted displays are attracting attention as a new method of information presentation by superimposing information on one's view of the real world using AR technology. Omori et al., Hasegawa S. et al., and Hasegawa A. et al. measured lens focus adjustment while viewing 3D-images displayed on a head-mounted display [8–10]. However, these studies did not measure lens focus adjustment during viewing AR technology because a non-see-through head-mounted display was used. Makita et al. investigated the usefulness of displaying road information on a head-mounted display, and Makibuchi et al. performed a study on hands-free work support using a similar display. Improvements in work efficiency using head-mounted displays are expected. However, it is impossible to change the image display position in conventional head-mounted displays, and for hand-related work, an uncomfortable feeling may occur that reduces the work efficiency. Thus, using EPSON MOVERIO Pro BT-2000, which independently projects images for the bilateral eyes with a changeable convergence angle, we measured lens focus adjustment as a basic study for the improvement of work efficiency. The occurrence of accommodation responses corresponding to the visual distance was investigated by changing the content display position, and it was confirmed. Accordingly, it was also confirmed that visual-physiologically correct accommodation responses occurred when the content displayed on HMD was viewed, and it was suggested that the head-mounted display is useful for prolonged work.

References

1. Horikoshi, T.: Wearable devices: current features and future perspective. Mem. Shonan Inst. Technol. **49**(1), 65–73 (2015)
2. Shibata, F.: Augmented reality: application 1: mobile AR - AR systems based on location information. IPSJ Mag. **51**(4), 385–391 (2010)
3. Makita, K., Chou, K., Ichikari, R., Okuma, T., Kurata, T.: A fundamental study of an augmented reality system for road maintenance. IEICE-MVE 2014-34 **114**(239), 19–24 (2014)
4. Makibuchi, Y., Kobayashi, T., Kato, H., Yanagihara, H.: Handsfree remote work support AR system by HMD calibration and on-site learning. IPSJ SIG Notes 2015-AVM **88**(2), 1–6 (2015)
5. Nitta, M.: The Ophthalmologic Revision, 2nd edn. Bunkodo, Tokyo (1988)
6. Semmlow, J., Heerema, D.: The synkinetic interaction of convergence accommodation and accommodative convergence. Vision. Res. **16**, 1237–1242 (1979)
7. Uchikawa, K., Shinomori, K.: The Structure of the Visual System and Initial Function. Asuka Publishing, Tokyo (2007)
8. Omori, M., Hasegawa, S., Watanabe, T., Takada, H., Miyao, M., Ichikawa, T.: Study of lens accommodation in response to 3D images on a HMD. ITE Tech. Rep. **33**(16), 53–56 (2009)

9. Hasegawa, S., Omori, M., Watanabe, T., Fujikake, K., Miyao, M.: Lens accommodation to the stereoscopic vision on HMD. In: Shumaker, R. (ed.) VMR 2009. LNCS, vol. 5622, pp. 439–444. Springer, Heidelberg (2009)
10. Hasegawa, A., Hasegawa, S., Omori, M., Takada, H., Watanabe, T., Miyao, M.: Effects on Visibility and Lens Accommodation of Stereoscopic Vision Induced by HMD Parallax Images. Forma **29**, 65–70 (2014)

Changes of Potential Functions While Maintaining Upright Postures After Exposure to Stereoscopic Video Clips

Fumiya Kinoshita[1], Kohei Iwata[1], Yasuyuki Matsuura[2],
Masaru Miyao[1], and Hiroki Takada[1,3(✉)]

[1] Department of Information Engineering,
Graduate School of Information Science, Nagoya University, Furo-cho,
Chikusa-ku, Nagoya 464-8601, Japan
takada@u-fukui.ac.jp
[2] Faculty of Humanities and Social Sciences, Prince of Songkla University,
Muang 94000, Pattani, Thailand
[3] Department of Human and Artificial Intelligent Systems,
Graduate School of Engineering, University of Fukui,
3-9-1 Bunkyo, Fukui 910-8507, Japan

Abstract. Asthenopia and visually induced motion sickness (VIMS) is a well-known phenomenon in viewing video, playing video games and others. In previous studies, we pointed out peripherally viewing as a pathogenesis of the VIMS whose evidence was also shown and described the anomalous sway by using mathematical models. Stochastic differential equations are known to be a mathematical model of the body sway. We herein discuss the metamorphism in the potential functions to control the standing posture during/after the exposure to stereoscopic video clips.

Keywords: Style · Visually induced motion sickness (VIMS) · Stabilometry · Stereoscopic image · Stochastic differential equation (SDE) · Temporally averaged potential function (TAPF)

1 Introduction

Current 3D display mechanisms include stereoscopy, integral photography, the differential binocular vision method, volumetric display [1], and holography [2]. With these rapid progresses in image processing and stereoscopic technologies, images are not only available on television but also in theaters, on game machines, and elsewhere. Unpleasant symptoms such as asthenopia, dizziness and nausea have been observed in subjects viewing three-dimensional (3D) films in some individuals [3]. While the symptoms of general motion sickness include dizziness and vomiting, the phenomenon of visually-induced motion sickness (VIMS) is not fully understood. Currently, there is not enough knowledge accumulated on the effects of stereoscopic images on the living body and basic research is thus important [4].

At present, VIMS is explained by the sensory conflict theory [5]. In humans, the standing posture is maintained by the body's balance function that is an involuntary

© Springer International Publishing Switzerland 2016
M. Antona and C. Stephanidis (Eds.): UAHCI 2016, Part II, LNCS 9738, pp. 279–286, 2016.
DOI: 10.1007/978-3-319-40244-4_27

physiological adjustment mechanism referred to as the "righting reflex". In order to maintain the standing posture in the absence of locomotion, the righting reflex is initiated in the following sensory system and processed in the cerebral cortex. Sensory receptors, such as visual inputs, auditory, and vestibular functions, and proprioceptive inputs from the skin, muscles, and joints, are referred to maintain the body's balance function [6]. According to the sensory conflict theory, motion sickness is a response to the conflict generated by a discrepancy between received and previously stored messages. Variations are thus expected that may arise from acquired experiences. Contradictory messages originating from different sensory systems, or the absence of a sensory message that is expected in a given situation, are thought to lead to the feeling of sickness. Spatial localization of self becomes unstable and produces discomfort. Researchers generally agree that there is a close relationship between the vestibular and autonomic nervous systems both anatomically and electrophysiologically. The motion sickness is considered to be caused by the excess signal from the vestibular to the hypothalamus. This view strongly indicates that the equilibrium system is associated with the symptoms of motion sickness [7] and provides a basis for the quantitative evaluation of motion sickness based on body sway, an output of the equilibrium system.

Stabilometry is a useful test of body equilibrium for investigating the overall equilibrium function. Stabilometry methods are presented in the standards of the Japanese Society for Equilibrium Research and in international standards [8]. Stabilometry is a simple test in which 60 s recording starts when body sway stabilizes [9]. Objective evaluation is possible by the computer analysis of the speed and direction of the sway, enabling diagnosis of a patient's condition [10].

In previous studies, subjective exacerbation and deterioration of equilibrium function were observed after peripheral viewing of 3D video clips [11]. This persistent influence has been observed while subjects view a poorly depicted background element peripherally, which generates depth perception that contradicts daily life. Moreover, it has been mentioned on whether the sway values depend on the viewing period [12]. In this mathematical analysis, we examined the 3D viewing effect on systems of the equilibrium function to determine whether it is dependent on the exposure time.

2   Mathematical Models of Body Sway

In stabilogram, variables x (lateral direction) and y (anterior/posterior direction) are regarded to be independent [13]. The linear stochastic differential equation (Brownian motion process) have been proposed as a mathematical model to describe body sway [14–16]. To describe the individual body sway, we especially show that it is necessary to extend the following nonlinear stochastic differential equations:

$$\frac{\partial x}{\partial t} = -\frac{\partial}{\partial x} U_x(x) + w_x(t) \tag{1}$$

$$\frac{\partial y}{\partial t} = -\frac{\partial}{\partial y} U_y(y) + w_x(t) \tag{2}$$

where $w_x(t)$ and $w_y(t)$ are pseudorandom numbers produced by white noise [17]. The following formula describes the relationship between the distribution in each direction; $G_x(x), G_y(y)$, and the temporal averaged potential constituting the stochastic differential equations (SDEs);

$$U_x(x) = -\frac{1}{2}\ln G_x(x) + const. \tag{3}$$

$$U_y(y) = -\frac{1}{2}\ln G_y(y) + const. \tag{4}$$

The variance of stabilograms generally depends on the temporal averaged potential function (TAPF) with several minimum values when it follows the Markov process without abnormal dispersion. SDEs can represent movements within local stability with a high-frequency component near the minimal potential surface, where a high density at the measurement point is expected.

3   Materials and Methods

Sixteen healthy male subjects (mean age $\pm$ standard deviation: 22.4 ± 0.8 years) participated voluntarily in the study. We ensured that the body sway was not affected by environmental conditions. We used an air conditioner to adjust the temperature at 25 °C in the exercise room. The experiment was explained to all subjects and written informed consent was obtained in advance.

In this experiment, we conducted a stabilometry test with subjects peripherally viewing 2D and 3D images. The device used was a Wii Balance Board (Nintendo, Kyoto). The sampling frequency of the Wii Balance Board was 20 Hz. The subjects stood upright on the device in Romberg's posture. We conducted two types of measurements: (I) after resting for 30 s, the body sway of each subject was measured for one minute with opened eyes and for three minutes with closed eyes consecutively, and (II) after resting for 30 s, the body sway of each subject was measured for two minutes with opened eyes and three minutes with closed eyes consecutively. However, in the two-minute measurement test with opened eyes, we also collected data for a period of one minute after the test. Experiments were performed in a dark room to avoid irritation from sources other than the video. The 2D or 3D images were shown on a 3D KDL 40HX80R display (SONY, Tokyo) placed two meters away from the subject. In the image used in the experiment, spheres were fixed at the four corners, while another sphere moved around the screen. A comparison was then made with subjects who were asked to gaze simply at a point 2 m in front of them at eye level in the case where no image was displayed. The experiments were carried out in random order. Each experiment was carried out on a separate day.

(a)

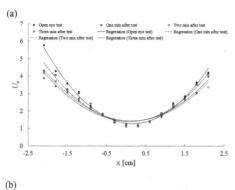

(b)

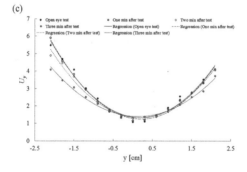

(c)

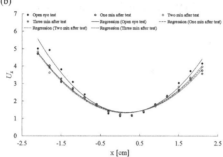

(d)

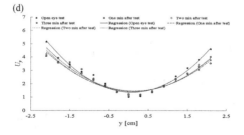

Fig. 1. Temporal averaged potential function derived from stabilograms during/after exposure to video clips; a 2D video clip (a), (c); a 3D video clip (b), (d). The TAPFs $U_x(x)$ in (a), (b) can be compared with $U_y(y)$ in (c), (d).

4 Results

The x-y coordinates were recorded for each sampled time point collected in the tests that were conducted with open and closed eyes, and the quantitative indices were calculated. The data were converted to time series and included the position of the center of gravity in the x (the right direction, designated as positive) and y (the anterior direction, designated as positive) directions in each of the open and closed eye tests.

Histograms of the stabilograms obtained from tests were prepared. Each stabilogram was processed by subtracting the series mean from each time-series to set the center of the stabilogram at the origin (0, 0). We compared histograms that were composed of all subjects' stabilograms and compared in the x and y directions, with eyes open and closed. The TAPFs in viewing 2D and 3D images were determined from the histograms using Eq. (3). The TAPFs were herein regressed by the following polynomial of degree 2 (Fig. 1).

$$\hat{U}_x(x) = a_x x^2 + b_x x + c \tag{5}$$

$$\hat{U}_y(y) = a_y y^2 + b_y y + c \tag{6}$$

5 Discussion

Constructing the nonlinear SDEs from the individual stabilograms in accordance with Eq. (2), their temporally averaged potential functions U_x, U_y have plural minimal points. However, a parabolic function is appropriate for the potential which is derived from all subjects' distribution (Fig. 1).

The following SDE could be obtained approximately as a mathematical model for the motion process with substituting an optimal regression polynomial (5), (6) to the first term of the right-hand side in Eqs. (3) and (4).

$$\frac{\partial x}{\partial t} = -(2a_x x + b_x) + w_x(t) \tag{7}$$

$$\frac{\partial y}{\partial t} = -(2a_y y + b_y) + w_x(t) \tag{8}$$

a_z and b_z are estimated as regression coefficients of the optimal polynomial of degree 2 by the least square method $(z = x, y)$. The second- order coefficient a_x in Eq. (5) decreased with eyes closed (Tables 1 and 2). Especially in the anterior/posterior direction y, the second-order co-efficient a_y in Eq. (6) decreased with eyes closed after the exposure to the 3D video clip (Table 2). Moreover, the coefficient of determination R^2 can be estimated to evaluate each regression. The value R^2 shows the suitability for the regression curve and the relative importance of correlations of different magnitudes [18]. The value 0.9 seems to be sufficiently large as a coefficient of determination R^2 because the correlation coefficient R attains to 0.95. In most cases, the coefficient of determination $R^2 > 0.9$ as shown in Tables 1 and 2. Fluctuations could be observed in the neighborhood of a minimal point. The variance in the stabilogram depends on the form of the potential function in the SDE; therefore, the SPD is regarded as an index for its measurement [19].

Table 1. Coefficients of TAPFs with eyes open for each component during/after the exposure to the 2D video clip for two minutes: the lateral direction x (a), the anterior/posterior direction (b).

(a)
component x

Two min 2D viewing	a	b	c	R^2
Open eye test	0.85	-0.28	1.30	0.92
One min after test	0.69	-0.15	1.41	0.97
Two min after test	0.58	-0.17	1.45	0.94
Three min after test	0.59	-0.10	1.42	0.98

(b)
component y

Two min 2D viewing	a	b	c	R^2
Open eye test	0.83	-0.33	1.36	0.90
One min after test	0.85	-0.35	1.28	0.89
Two min after test	0.76	-0.26	1.35	0.92
Three min after test	0.57	-0.15	1.41	0.95

We have examined whether the exposure to the 3D video clips affects the equilibrium function [12]. Conducting the stabilometry, we verified that 3D viewing the effect on our equilibrium function depends on exposure time. The SPD significantly increased after the exposure to the 3D video clip or the 2D video clip for two minutes. In these cases, sufficient loadings change the form of the TAPFs in the SDEs (1) and (2).

When viewing a 2D image, sway is increased depending on the viewing time [12]. Moreover, when viewing an image for two minutes, the area of sway and the total locus length were significantly smaller for the open eye test compared to the values elicited when the image had been viewed two minutes after the test. Therefore, we considered that after the image had been viewed, equilibrium function still remained. Moreover, regardless of the solidity images (2D/3D), the area of sway and the total locus length were significantly smaller in the open eye test compared to the values elicited in the case where these images were viewed three minutes after the test. The results of the control were the same as these. Accordingly, the reason for the sway increase in the case when the images were viewed three minutes after the test is not attributed to the effects of VIMS but to the effects of fatigue. Therefore, we considered that the change in viewing time affected the equilibrium function system, and that viewing a 3D image for two minutes affected the equilibrium function system for a period of two minutes after the images had been viewed.

Table 2. Coefficients of TAPFs with eyes open for each component during/after the exposure to the 3D video clip for two minutes: the lateral direction x (a), the anterior/posterior direction (b).

(a)

component x

Two min 3D viewing	a	b	c	R^2
Open eye test	0.82	-0.28	1.36	0.93
One min after test	0.68	-0.20	1.36	0.94
Two min after test	0.69	-0.17	1.34	0.96
Three min after test	0.66	-0.23	1.38	0.92

(b)

component y

Two min 3D viewing	a	b	c	R^2
Open eye test	0.81	-0.14	1.38	0.98
One min after test	0.59	-0.15	1.47	0.96
Two min after test	0.63	-0.14	1.42	0.97
Three min after test	0.64	-0.19	1.47	0.94

The sway value total locus length was increased after the exposure to these video clips, which might be caused by the diminution of the gradient in the bottom of the parabolic potential function (Fig. 1). We herein note that it is important to focus on the form of the potential function. We have succeeded in estimating the decrease in the gradient of the potential function by using the SPD. This tendency was enhanced by the exposure to the 3D video clip.

In this study, we observed the VIMS by conducting the stabilometry. The sway values were evaluated during/after peripherally viewing video clips. On the contrast, it is known that there are two different cortial streams (vental and dorsal). This division of visual information is traditionally separated into an object and spatial vision [20] or color/form and motion vision [21]. The later proceeds in an unconscious state, which may be corresponding to the 3D sickness induced by peripherally viewing. We will examine whether the exposure to sufficient loadings of 3D video clips affects the brain activity in the dorsal stream in the next step.

Previously, we evaluated body sway by conducting stabilometry studies with simply used of the analytical indices for stabilograms [12]. In this study, we furthermore obtained TAPFs in the SDEs as mathematical models of the body sway. We also examined whether there is remarkable metamorphism in the potential functions to control the standing posture during/after the exposure to stereoscopic video clips. As a result, we verified that 3D viewing effects on our equilibrium function depends on exposure time.

Acknowledgements. This work was supported in part by the Japan Society for the Promotion of Science, Grant-in-Aid for Scientific Research (B) Number 24300046 and (C) Number 26350004.

References

1. Suyama, S., Date, M., Takada, H.: Three dimensional display system with dual frequency liquid crystal varifocal lens. Jpn. J. Appl. Phys. **39, Part 1**(2A), 480–484 (2000)
2. Gabor, D.: A new microscopic principle. Nature **161**, 777–779 (1948)
3. International standard organization: IWA3: 2005 image safety-reducing determinism in a time series. Phys. Rev. Lett. **70**, 530–582 (1993)
4. Sumio, Y., Shinji, I.: Visual comfort and fatigue based on accommodation response for stereoscopic image. Inst. Image Inf. Telev. Eng. **55**(5), 711–717 (2001)
5. Reason, J.T., Brand, J.J.: Motion Sickness. Academic Press, London (1975)
6. Okawa, T., Tokita, T., Shibata, Y., Ogawa, T., Miyata, H.: Stabilometry: significance of locus length per unit area (L/A) in patients with equilibrium disturbances. Equilib. Res. **55** (3), 283–293 (1995)
7. Barmack, N.H.: Central vestibular system: vestibular nuclei and posterior cerebellum. Brain Res. Bull. **60**, 511–541 (2003)
8. Japan Society for Equilibrium Research: Standard of stabilometry. Equilib. Res. **42**, 367–369 (1983)
9. Kaptyen, T.S., Bles, W., Njiokiktjien, C.J., Kodde, L., Massen, C.H., Mol, J.M.: Standarization in platform stabilometry being a part of posturography. Agreessologie **24**, 321–326 (1983)
10. Hase, M., Ohta, Y.: Meaning of barycentric position and measurement method. J. Environ. Eng. **8**, 220–221 (2006)
11. Takada, M., Fukui, Y., Matsuura, Y., Sato, M., Takada, H.: Peripheral viewing during exposure to a 2D/3D video clip: effects on the human body. Environ. Health Prev. Med. **20**, 79–89 (2015)
12. Yoshikawa, K., Kinoshita, F., Miyashita, K., Sugiura, A., Kojima, T., Takada, H., Miyao, M.: Effects of two-minute stereoscopic viewing on human balance function. In: Antona, M., Stephanidis, C. (eds.) UAHCI 2015. LNCS, vol. 9176, pp. 297–304. Springer, Heidelberg (2015)
13. Goldie, P.A., Bach, T.M., Evans, O.M.: Force platform measures for evaluating postural control: reliability and validity. Arch. Phys. Med. Rehabil. **70**, 510–517 (1986)
14. Emmerrik, R.E.A., Van Sprague, R.L., Newell, K.M.: Assessment of sway dynamics in tardive dyskinesia and developmental disability: sway profile orientation and stereotypy. Moving Dis. **8**, 305–314 (1993)
15. Collins, J.J., De Luca, C.J.: Open-loop and closed-loop control of posture: a random-walk analysis of center of pressure trajectories. Exp. Brain Res. **95**, 308–318 (1993)
16. Newell, K.M., Slobounov, S.M., Slobounova, E.S., Molenaar, P.C.: Stochastic processes in postural center of pressure profiles. Exp. Brain Res. **113**, 158–164 (1997)
17. Takada, H., Kitaoka, Y., Shimizu, Y.: mathematical index and model in stabilometry. Forma **16**, 17–46 (2001)
18. Sokal, R.R., Rohlf, F.J.: Introduction to Biostatistics. W.H. Freeman and Company, San Francisco (1973)
19. Takada, H., Kitaoka, Y., Ichikawa, M., Miyao, M.: Physical meaning on geometrical index for stabilometry. Equilib. Res. **62**, 168–180 (2003)
20. Ungerleider, L.G., Mishkin, M.: Two cortical visual systems. In: Ingle, D.J., Mansfield, R.J. W., Goodale, M.A. (eds.) The Analysis of Visual Behavior, pp. 549–586. MIT Press, Cambridge (1982)
21. Van Essen, D.C., Maunsell, J.H.R.: Hierarchical organization and functional streams in the visual cortex. Trends in Neurosci. **6**, 370–375 (1983)

Metaphor and Storytelling in Interface Design for Virtual Reality

Andreas Kratky[✉]

Interactive Media Division, School of Cinematic Arts,
University of Southern California, 3470 McClintock Ave., SCI 201Q,
Los Angeles, CA 90089-2211, USA
akratky@cinema.usc.edu

Abstract. Virtual Reality has – again – become the target of substantial interest, research and industry growth. In the current market situation it is aimed at a general audience rather than expert users and therefore requires a fundamental rethinking of how we conceive of human computer interaction in Virtual Reality. In comparison to the established methods of designing interfaces for the desktop environment and for mobile applications numerous changes need to be considered. Even though the use of metaphors has become looser and more abstract, it is still the common way of providing an easily graspable conceptual model of the functions and behaviors of an application, be it an operating system or a task-oriented application. How do metaphors work in Virtual Reality? How does the relationship between the metaphorical environment and the environment of operation change? What kind of cognitive support structures are necessary for the perceptual situation of Virtual Reality? Drawing from an interdisciplinary set of theories we will address these questions through high-level analysis and develop methodologies to recast the design principles for the creation of user interfaces for Virtual Reality.

Keywords: Virtual reality · User interface design · Storytelling · Metaphor · Urban planning · Worldbuilding

1 Introduction

1.1 Evolution of Interface Metaphors

For the last thirty years the desktop metaphor has helped "the rest of us [1]" to use computers more easily and more efficiently. Interface metaphors are the dominant approach to communicate the conceptual structure of software applications and support the user in forming cognitive models of what a program can do and how to operate it. They are the backbone of how we conceive of computer human interfaces. When Apple introduced the first Macintosh computer in 1984 it was marketed as a computer for all those who were not specifically trained in the use of computers and who did not want to go through an extensive training. The marketing highlighted the ease of use and quick learning process realized through several new inventions, such as the Graphical User Interface, direct object interaction with the mouse, and the desktop metaphor. The desktop metaphor was intended to provide a conceptual framework for users to more

© Springer International Publishing Switzerland 2016
M. Antona and C. Stephanidis (Eds.): UAHCI 2016, Part II, LNCS 9738, pp. 287–300, 2016.
DOI: 10.1007/978-3-319-40244-4_28

easily understand the environment of the computer, its actions, and the options it offered. As all users were expected to be familiar with the office environment and the handling of documents and folders they could use this existing knowledge and transfer it to the computer operations. The metaphor was intended to accommodate an intuitive understanding of the objects and operations that can be expected in the computer. The idea of direct interaction with documents, the possibility to move them in and out of folders, copy them, throw them into the trash bin by dragging them with the mouse, was a way of getting around learning the complicated commands that were used so far to carry out this type of operation. Since the early days of personal computing, the desktop has been the standard of human computer interface design. After Apple introduced the concept to the market in 1984, Microsoft adopted it a year later with the Windows 1.0 platform and since then numerous implementations of the same idea have been produced. Today the metaphor seems an almost natural image for the use of computers. A closer examination, though, complicates this image.

Many activities carried out with a personal computer are revolving around documents and many people use them for text processing and table calculations in an office environment, but the mainstay of Macintosh users was in the creative field and graphic design rather than in professional office work. The office environment was dominated by IBM and computers running Microsoft operating systems and Apple did not get a significant market share in this field. Along with the first Macintosh software applications like *MacDraw* and *MacPaint* were released, which founded the strong position of the Macintosh in the design field. This software also introduced a metaphor-mismatch: A paint brush, canvas and paint bucket are not normally used in an office, they are icons of the creative design or art studio, which stereotypically is perceived as the counter-concept to the stiff and rigid office environment. The office metaphor made perfect sense in its original setting on the Xerox Alto and Xerox Star computers as these machines were conceived specifically to prototype "the office of the future [2]." The concept was intended to serve users who were focused on producing and managing reports and neither knowledgeable nor interested in computers. For these users the decision was to make the computer as invisible as possible [3]. This was to be achieved by allowing the users to transfer their existing knowledge about the office procedures to the computer. Familiar objects like paper, folders and file cabinets translated into digital icons were supposed to make this transfer easy. The system was made purely for document processing and all software applications were started with the system, so users only interacted with the documents themselves and did not have to care about launching applications for specific tasks [4]. What may seem limiting from today's point of view made sense for Xerox, the companies business was document processing and after having made millions with copying machines the company wanted to make sure its business grew into the new era of digital document processing. For other computers and other purposes, the desktop metaphor was at best only a partial match and inevitably brought inconsistencies with it. While it helped to explain file management to users, it was out of tune with applications like Adobe's *Photoshop*, which employs the metaphor of the darkroom to explain its tools for photo retouching and many other applications that implement operations from other domains.

The limitations of interface metaphors and the constraints they put on designers have been criticized [5] and various concepts for improvement have been devised.

In the 1990s several attempts were made to make the metaphor more specific and to extend it to other fields and spaces for specific activities. Systems like Microsoft's *Bob*, Apple's *eWorld* or General Magic's *Magic Cap* introduced multi-room environments that allowed the user to switch rooms according to specific tasks. The login-screen, for example, was presented as the front door, there was a hallway to start different applications, which, within the metaphor, meant to enter different rooms. Magic Cap had a "game room" to play games, a "store room" to store data etc. [6]. The idea behind these systems was to provide more detail and specificity to remedy metaphor mismatches and the perceived problem of abstraction. They were intended as virtual environments inhabited by the user and additional characters such as the friendly assistant *Rover*, a retriever dog, in Microsoft's *Bob*. None of these systems had success with the users, they were perceived as overly cluttered, too cute and unusable [7–9]. Instead, the movement went away from interface metaphors altogether.

1.2 Non-metaphoric Interfaces

While the desktop metaphor has remained as the basis of most current operating systems with a graphical user interfaces, new application types, such as mobile operating systems, do not use strong metaphors anymore. A turning point was the introduction of the iPhone in 2007, a smartphone that was able to carry out several tasks that, until then, were a domain of the desktop computer. The iPhone came with a specifically designed mobile operating system, Apple's *iOS*. A year later the first version of the Android operating system was released by Google and then Microsoft's *Windows Phone*. All of these operating systems do not use an explicit comprehensive metaphor like the desktop anymore. There were local metaphors for certain applications, like the wooden bookcase in *iOS* for the iBooks application or the notepad with torn-off paper edges trying to make the digital representation of the action of note-taking more relatable and "friendly." These references to material reality disappeared in later releases. In 2007, comprehensive metaphors were not needed anymore to explain the concept of devices like smartphones or tablets, which are taking over more and more of higher-level computing tasks from desktop machines, such as real-time 3d rendering, complex design tasks, text processing of long and complex texts etc. Many of the targeted users are familiar with digital devices and the basics of computing from a user point of view, these concepts do not need to be explained anymore with the help of metaphors. The metaphors, as mentioned in Apple's *iOS* interface guidelines, are reduced to simple gestures like the operation of switches through tapping, sliding, flicking through pages etc. [10].

The maturing of digital technology and the fact that most current users have either grown up with these technologies, or at least had enough exposure to have familiarity with their basic functions, has changed the interface design methods and the cognitive models users can apply to become familiar with new technologies. The desktop metaphor still dominates the user interfaces of desktop computers mostly for questions of 'backwards compatibility:' users have become accustomed to the desktop interface as the way of operating a computer and the prior knowledge activated to use such a system does probably not come from the actual office environment anymore but rather from the digital representation of it. How people use computer operating systems has changed: familiar with the way Google's 'one-box search interface dominates internet search, users have become accustomed to using a search tool like *Spotlight* to launch applications rather than navigating through the directory structure or using a launch bar.

Now functions established in non-metaphoric operating systems like iOS migrate back into the desktop systems. An example is the split view-feature, introduced in iOS 9 and then brought to OS X 10.11, where normally this idea would have been in conflict with the metaphor of overlapping windows, simulating the overlapping documents on a desk. The uses and the prior knowledge to be applied to learning and operating new technology have shifted with a generational shift. In early mobile operating systems like *MagicCap*, which was made for devices such as Sony's *Magic Link* or Apple's *Newton*, the room and desktop metaphor was still used, trying to build on the success of the desktop operating system. Besides the overemphasized metaphor, it also seems that the office environment did not fit to a mobile device. What was appropriate for the desktop computer, which in many cases indeed stood on a desk in an office environment, was out of tune with mobile devices, which could be used in many different environments. Having an explicit setting like the office environment would be in potential dissonance with the actual operating environment and a more abstract design allows the device to merge more seamlessly with the environment of operation. The effectiveness of an interface metaphor lives from an understanding of the environment in which a task is carried out and a translation of the main components and actions of this environment. Because an office environment and the related tasks were not suitable for the interface of the *One Laptop Per Child* project, which was intended to be a learning tool for children in developing countries, the so called Zooming User Interface was created, which uses the metaphor of a community, seen in different zoom stages from *Neighborhood*, to *Groups*, to *Home*. The zoom stages also represent the network environment of the computer and are indicative of the experience using the computer [11].

2 Problems of Interface Design for VR

From this evolution of the interface metaphor we can deduct a set of questions relevant to user interface design for Virtual Reality applications. These questions are becoming important as VR is moving into general usage. In contrast to the first wave of Virtual Reality in the late 1980s and early 1990s, which was producing research and products for task-oriented applications such as simulation, vehicular control and telepresence, the current wave of VR is targeted on entertainment. In this sector we are used to specific interface devices and control schemes from computer games, using game controllers or other custom tools, and do not expect general purpose interaction strategies as the WIMP (Window, Icon, Menu, Pointer) interfaces. But as the boundary gets blurred between entertainment and task-oriented applications carried out in a VR environment, the need for effective interface structures and efficient support for users to build cognitive models for what they are doing becomes important. We begin to see a variety of task-oriented applications emerging in VR. Specifically spatial tasks such as three-dimensional drawing in Virtual Reality promise a good match between task and the affordance of the VR environment. The application *Tilt Brush* provides a new and seemingly intuitive interface for spatial drawing [12]. The option to view immersive content in a web browser such as MozVR [13] or YouTube merges the experience of VR with that of the conventional web browser. Finally VR input device-maker *Control VR* [14] imagines users at work sitting on a normal desktop interface inside the Virtual Reality space.

A direct transfer of the desktop metaphor into Virtual Reality is probably not the best solution. The role and function of metaphors is different in Virtual Reality. The most obvious difference is in the environment structure. The screen-view is modeled on the framed window into a space, which is not shared by the user. Like in a painting the user remains outside of the depicted reality and is looking at it or into it. Despite 3-dimensional elements in traditional interfaces the visual paradigm is flat perspective projection in the style of Renaissance perspective [15]. The framed view has an inherent organization that structures areas like center and periphery and the stacking order of depth layering. Most traditional interfaces make use of these principles. They place the menu bar in the top-peripheral zone of the screen, other tools and information panels are generally also organized in peripheral zones to free the view to the center where the object of attention, the document that is being written or the drawing that is being made, resides. The center periphery structure is essential to most interfaces in both categories entertainment as well as task oriented applications. A related visual rhetoric is used for the stacking windows, which, simulating the overlapping documents on a desktop, can easily be navigated by the user based on the notion of a flat surface and a stacking order along one depth axis directly perpendicular to the screen surface.

The framed, flat surface of the screen is also used to negotiate the different kinds of information that needs to be communicated to users when navigating an entertainment experience: There is the information pertaining to the content of the experience and information necessary to operate it. Both are very different levels of address, the operating information is meant solely for the user and not accessible for characters in the experience. Integrating these two different layers in a seamless and compelling way has been traditionally a challenge in interactive entertainment. The metaphor of the fourth wall, which originally comes from theater, indicating the separation between the stage and the audience, has been used to achieve this integration [16]. For example heads-up displays (HUDs) are often used in computer games, simulating a helmet display or the information a pilot sees through instruments in his cockpit or in a projected HUD on the windshield of his plane [17]. The notion of the fourth wall, the canopy separating the pilot from the exterior, implies generally a degree of separation between the user and the experience as the framing of the view provides a means of orientation and structure of the information display. In a virtual environment this separation would go against the idea of full immersion.

In VR a perspective that is similarly "restricted" as the perspective window, exists, which is the field of view in which we see in focus. The normal field of view of human beings spans ca. 200° in horizontal direction and 150° in the vertical [18]. Current VR headsets have a span of ca. 100°, which could be seen as limiting the field of view in a similar way as the framed window does. But the peripheral areas of the field of view function differently – we could say in opposition – than the frame boundaries. While the frame boundaries are limiting the view and directing the attention to the center, peripheral vision scans the extreme edges of the field of view and directs attention outwards [19]. Peripheral vision is particularly suited to detect fast motion and visual cues while the observer is in motion [20]. This kind of scanning function is an important counterpart to the high-quality vision in the small area of foveal vision [21]. In contrast to the traditional screen-based interface it is the characteristic of VR experiences that the view can indeed be attracted outward and – similar to real vision – by turning the head and directing the foveal vision to phenomena that are not in front of the user a much wider range of space can be used for interaction. The immersive space extends far beyond the bounded space of the desktop – which has tremendous potential, while at the same time bringing new questions and problems to the interface design.

One of these questions is how users resolve inconsistencies in interface metaphors. The virtual environment, in order to support orientation in the wide immersive space, has to rely on a higher degree of consistency of how this space is represented and constituted. A user working in a desktop environment is perfectly aware of the two worlds separated by the 'fourth wall' of the screen surface, his own reality and the world of the task or experience. Inconsistent metaphors, such as switching between a virtual office environment for some parts of a task and a darkroom or painter's studio for other parts of the same task, can easily be resolved. In the immersive space of virtual reality the user has a harder time to reconcile this type of mismatch because he is cut off from his physical reality, which is therefore missing as a corrective. Disposing of two transparently coupled environments, the task environment and the environment of operation, allows to more flexibly negotiate between target and source environment of the metaphor [22]. To provide the necessary cucs for operation and navigation of the immersive space the conceptual models provided for the user have to be tighter and more comprehensive than the loose metaphors we are using in desktop interface design. Given this difference between the traditional desktop environment and VR we might even question if metaphors can work at all in VR.

It is clear, though, that support for the user to build a mental model of the system he is operating in and the task he is aiming to solve needs to be provided. This support, since the success of the desktop, is coming largely from interface metaphors. As Lakoff and Johnson argue, "the human conceptual system is metaphorically structured and defined [23]. A set of metaphors that is to effectively support a user in the operation of a virtual environment needs to be structured differently and has to include different considerations than the traditional design approaches. The design for such a metaphor will have to draw on multiple fields of research that have so far been considered independently and for different types of applications. In the following we will develop a heuristic for addressing the problems we elaborated here and how new methodologies for user interface design with specific consideration of the affordances of Virtual Reality environments can be formulated.

3 Interface Design Heuristics for Virtual Reality Environments

3.1 Physiological Aspects

The main characteristic of a Virtual Reality environment is that it provides a complete space which is shared between the user and the experience or the work area in which a task is solved. In contrast to the desktop interface the user's gaze in not fixed but can move around freely. In many of the current VR systems the user has to remain statically in one place and can only change the perspective by moving the head. Since the user cannot see the real space in which the interaction takes place it is very difficult to move around freely if the dimensions and potential obstacles of the virtual space and the real space do not coincide [24]. Remaining static has the downside that the user is less inclined to change the view. If seated in one position looking straight is the most comfortable direction, and the more the object of interest moves away from this central axis the less comfortable it is to look at it. Liberating the physical movement by not being seated in a chair makes the user significantly more mobile and use of the full environment more likely. Even though it is difficult to realize in the normal setting of a casual user, the first consumer VR systems with user tracking in space are approaching the market [25].

With a mobile gaze and eventually a mobile viewer the main organizational principle of the Virtual Reality environment is spatial and the design of it has to ensure that the user is able to navigate it with ease. Rather than stacking documents on a table and organizing them within a fixed frame information and interaction affordances are distributed in space. Designs that aim to support the user in constructing cognitive models of the VR application will have to focus on spatial orientation. The desktop environment mostly excluded the physical reality of the user and reduced orientation in the environment the user interacts with to rational and visual procedures. In the VR environment the physiological reality plays an important role and is part of the processes used for orientation and the construction of a mental model of the environment. We have to distinguish two categories of orientation in the case of VR, the first considering a static user, seated in a chair and only navigating by moving the head and upper body to a limited degree; and the second, considering a user freely moving within the bounds of a room in which user's movements are tracked and translated into the VR environment. In the first case the physiological senses involved into determining the body's position in space are visual cues and the vestibular system, and, to a comparatively smaller degree, proprioceptive cues stemming from the neck and upper body movement, and auditory cues [26]. In the second case the proprioceptive component as well as the tactile component play important roles. The cues from these different sensory systems are integrated into an internal model of the physical position in space [27] and they have to be considered in the design and orientational structure of the VR application. Disregarding these cues and their consistent integration can lead to feelings of motion- or 'cybersickness' and disorientation [28, 29].

The spatial organization of information and interactive affordances enables users to interact through gestures and body movement. In the case of a static user this will mostly be deictic gestures of pointing or looking in certain directions and at certain objects in the virtual environment. A Virtual Reality display in contrast to the traditional bounded-screen display is perceived as an extremely large display that exetends beyond the user's field of view. Large displays incite users to use more deictic gestures as part of their conceptual reference system regarding the displayed environment [30]. Gestures like these can be used for selecting, activating etc. functions in the environment [31]. In the second case this interaction vocabulary is extended to include movement through space, such as walking up to certain objects, revealing more information through a change of position.

In both cases self-perception of the user within the virtual environment is required. Already in the first wave of Virtual Reality research the data-glove was developed to provide a means to the user to be present and have manifest agency in the environment [32]. While this form of presence required complicated and cumbersome technology back then, today multiple tracking methods are available to track the user's hand movement and translate it into the environment [33]. Features of structuring an environment for predominantly visual navigation rely on visibility, salience and other visual cues allowing to estimate distance, order, occlusion etc.

In case of a mobile user the dominant ordering principles include, besides the described visual cues, multiple aspects of body movement. Gross body movement, such as movement through a tracked space, can be used to support the construction of mental models and support orientation of users in a virtual environment. Structuring this kind of movement through space in a meaningful way is part of the design aspects that need to be considered to support users in carrying out tasks in a virtual environment. Research in the relationship between gross body movement and cognitive processes has been done in several separate fields. The research threads that inform our set of questions most fruitfully are haptics and grounded cognition [34] on one side and choreography [35] on the other. Both fields reveal specific processes of building mental models and constituting memory distinct from other sensory modalities like vision, which can be used to structure the movement sequences and rhythms of traversing and interacting with objects in the virtual environment. The physiological involvement and its targeted design can leverage additional potential for meaning-making and retention of actions necessary to accomplish a task. In this respect a VR environment may be superior to the traditional desktop environment for certain tasks and entertainment purposes. In designing movements and gestures the designer has to be aware of physiological constraints of the human body and its biomechanics. Large gestures can be straining and causing fatigue and hyperextension of joints has to be avoided [36].

3.2   Conceptual Modeling Through Story and Metaphor

In order to successfully benefit from the physiological aspect of operating in a virtual environment and to benefit from the large space it can provide, the user has to be able to orient herself with ease within the environment. Head-mounted displays have a restricted field of view, requiring the user to be able to accommodate to the restrictions [37] and to develop a memory for the parts of the environment that are out of sight as user is moving and changing perspective. This locational memory is part of the mental model the user constructs when solving a task or going through an entertainment experience in Virtual Reality. It is in part achieved through the physiological memory acquired through body movement and in part through metaphors or other forms of conceptual modeling. As elaborated earlier, metaphors work well for the predominantly rationally structured operations of desktop user interfaces. To support the conceptual modeling of a virtual environment we need potentially more complex and comprehensive models.

Metaphorically structured models normally employ several different metaphors that correspond to separate aspects of the model. As Lakoff and Johnson write, metaphorical structuring is partial and relies on a form of lexicon rooted in language to resolve the individual metaphors and construct a higher-level model from them [23]. To provide the comprehensive structuring that is desirable in a virtual environment instead of using partial metaphors we can use elements of storytelling, which have a more specific and tighter structure.

Storytelling can work as a structure to organize both space and processes that take place in the space. Classic narrative theory distinguishes between two parts of a narrative text, the story, which refers to the actions that make up the story, and the discourse, the order of how the actions are communicated. The actions exist independently from the way they are relayed through words, images or other media forms [38]. They can, for example, be communicated in a different temporal structure than they actually happened, which enables different ways of organizing the same narrative content through effects like flash-backs and time inversions. Both story and discourse have a temporal structure as well as a spatial structure. The spatial structure of the story organizes all elements that are part of the story, lists them, describes and places them inside the space in which the story unfolds [38]. The existence and location of these elements is again independent from how relationships between them unfold over time. The discourse space, in contrast, is the order of how the story elements (also called "existents" [38]) are arranged in the flow of communicating them, i.e. which elements are visible, in which perspective they are visible etc. This fundamental structure of narrative indicates how it could be used as a method of structuring and communicating operations in a virtual environment. It can serve as an ontological structure providing all elements of an environment and within this space different temporal processes of task execution or entertainment can be devised. The discourse layer of the narrative structure can provide perspectives and selections for how a user perceives the environment and in response plans her interactions. Storytelling provides the foundational layers for an efficient structuring of the interaction flow in a virtual environment.

The methodology of 'worldbuilding' has become a popular tool to develop environment descriptions that focus on the story-space aspect. Inspired by the philosophy of possible worlds, which regards a given state of a world as just one possible state among many other alternative world descriptions contained in one larger, maximally inclusive world. The notion of possible worlds is an epistemic tool that considers situations as "simply structured collections of physical objects [39] " and aims to formulate the set of possible logical statements that are part of the maximally inclusive world. In storytelling the idea of possible worlds has been used as a speculative tool to design alternative worlds that could have been possible if certain historic events did not happen, or happened differently. Possible worlds are consistent within themselves and even if they do not correspond to reality as it is known they provide compelling descriptions of alternative realities. Worldbuilding is the act of constructing possible fictional worlds. It is a creative method used in writing as well as filmmaking and game design to create environments for possible stories. This approach of building narrative from the space-component is in contrast with traditional models of storytelling, which tend to construct the story from the chain of events rather than from the world in which the events happen. As Mark J. P. Wolf writes, storytelling and worldbuilding are often in conflict in that the latter produces digressions and descriptions that slow down the narrative flow [40]. In game design, for example, worldbuilding is a method of creating environments in which multiple stories can take place and different characters can be accommodated, in this sense allowing for a bandwidth of variations in gameplay. For our current set of questions worldbuilding offers a method to formulate consistent models of worlds that can help users to conceptualize the virtual environment they are operating in. Those descriptions can be in conflict with reality, as long as they provide a compelling and consistent description of the environment and enable the user to form expectations and concepts about the environment. An example for such a world-description could be Edwin A. Abbott's novella "Flatland [41]," which describes a world that exists in only two dimensions.

3.3   Patterns of Visual Organization

A method of investigation that merges the aspects of space, spatial perception and choreography in a unique way is Kevin Lynch's analysis of the modern cityscape. This method can serve as a model for the creation of environmental cues to facilitate orientation and mental mapping of users in a virtual environment and it provides a suitable complement to the conceptual modeling through metaphors and storytelling. The urban planner Kevin Lynch conceives of the city as a spatio-temporal construct, a large built environment that is experienced by its users over long time spans. His approach examines the city as not only consisting of its architectural units, but equally of the inhabitants moving across it and pursuing multiple activities in it. Each single inhabitant has a different experience and perception of the city depending on her interests, experiences, associations and memories, which makes for a double structure of the image of a city: the public image, shared by many inhabitants, and the private image, shaped by the specific perception of an individual. In this sense Lynch formulates a method that directly fuses with the narrative structure we discussed above as the basis for conceptual modeling techniques and delivers a suitable aesthetic and experiential heuristic to address the design of environment-based user interfaces for Virtual Reality. Through observations and interviews Lynch studied how people create a mental image of the city, elaborating principles for what he called the "legibility of the city [42]." The term legibility refers to organizational principles of the urban structure that facilitate recognition and memorization. He identifies five main properties that support imageability: paths, edges, districts, nodes and landmarks. These properties are the salient features of a city inhabitants use to structure their mental representation of their surroundings. Paths are the streets, transit lines and walkways people use to navigate the city. They structure the sequence in which places are perceived and form the orientational grid of the users. The edges are boundaries that delimit sections in the cityscape. These can be walls, canals, streets etc., not in their function as a pathway, but in their function as delimiters akin to the barrier a freeway poses to pedestrians. Districts are areas that are perceived as larger geometric units. These may coincide with neighborhoods but they can also be individually construed subsections. Nodes are places in which main pathways intersect, meeting points with high traffic frequency or different kinds of discernible concentrations. And finally landmarks are points of reference in a city that stand out such as high buildings, signs, mountains or other features of singular quality and visibility [42].

The legibility properties elaborated by Lynch can serve as both a vocabulary to construct virtual environments and deliberately integrate certain features, as well as a methodology of designing and evaluating interface designs. Lynch's approach to urban planning, even though it originated in a completely different field, can function as an extension of the methods of design ethnography and ethnomethodology that emerged in the late 1980s and 1990s, when the personal computer entered the workplace and the home at a large scale. Ethnography as a tool for user interface design developed at Xerox at the time when the company was working on the Alto and Star systems. Triggered by customer complaints about usability issues with copiers observational studies were used to understand the reasons for those issues. This approach was generalized and extended as a tool to systematically study the underlying conceptions about the nature of a task that inform the design of every tools made to support the task [43]. Design ethnography has since become an established component of systems design and human computer interaction, focusing on "studying work in the wild" to analyze potential mismatches between systems functionality and the methods employed by users to organize their interactions and do their work [44]. The notions of Lynch's studies are apt to extend the methods of design ethnography in a direction specifically relevant to the design of user interfaces for virtual environments.

4   Conclusions and Future Work

This paper brings together several threads of theory and design research from a heterogeneous set of fields that are normally considered completely separate from each other to formulate a heuristic for the design of user interfaces for Virtual Reality applications. The challenges that emerge in the task of creating interfaces and accommodating work and entertainment in Virtual Reality have distinctively different properties than the design principles in classic desktop interface design. As prominent aspects stand out the involvement of the physiological reality of the user as part of her interaction with a computer and the particular focus on spatial navigation and action. Drawing from linguistics, narrative theory, urban planning and ethnography we are giving a high-level overview over the specific problems of user interface design for virtual environments and develop a heuristic to address these problems. The heuristic is formulated with consideration of the requirements of task-oriented applications that start emerging in the realm of Virtual Reality, but the foundational principles promise to be applicable also for entertainment oriented experiences.

The perspective of this paper focuses on aspects of visuality and how it influences the construction of mental representations. As future areas of inquiry it will be necessary to investigate the role of haptics in this process. Given the importance of the physiological involvement, haptics play an important role and one of the drawbacks of current VR systems is that haptics are only addressed in a rudimentary way. It is imaginable that specifically designed interaction objects that can be imbued with varying functions and roles are suitable avenues to involve the haptic senses in a more controlled and developed way into the design process.

The perspective shifts and interdisciplinary inspirations described in this paper are apt to also provide useful correctives in the consideration of traditional and non-traditional user interface design. In particular in mobile and distributed user interfaces aspects of environmental properties and orientation come into play that can be approached with similar methods as developed here in the context of VR.

References

1. Apple advertisement campaign (1984)
2. Perry, T.S., Wallich, P.: Inside the PARC The information architects: Insiders who became outsiders describe the trials and successes of the Xerox Palo Alto Research Center as it sought to create the electronic office of the future. IEEE Spectr. **22**(10), 62–76 (1985). IEEE
3. Johnson, J., Roberts, T.L., Verplank, W., Smith, D.C., Irby, C.H., Beard, M., Mackey, K.: The xerox star: a retrospective. Computer **22**(9), 11–26 (1989)
4. Smith, D.C., Irby, C., Kimball, R., Harslem, E.: The star user interface: an overview. In: Proceedings of the National Computer Conference, AFIPS 1982, 7–10 June 1982, pp. 515–528. ACM (1982)
5. Gentner, D., Nielsen, J.: The anti-mac interface. Commun. ACM **39**(8), 70–82 (1996)
6. General Magic Inc.: Design and Magic Cap. Icras, Sunnyvale, CA, 24 April 2000
7. Hassard, S.T., Blandford, A., Cox, A.L.: Analogies in design decision-making. In: Proceedings of the 23rd British HCI Group Annual Conference on People and Computers: Celebrating People and Technology, BCS-HCI 2009, pp. 140–148. British Computer Society (2009)
8. Dvorak, J.: The bottom 10: Worst Software Disasters. PC Magazine (2004)
9. Newman, M.: Bob is dead; long live Bob. Pittsburg Post-Gazette (1999)
10. Apple Inc.: IOS Human Interface Guidelines: UI Design Basics. Apple Inc. (2015)
11. Sugar Labs: Human interface guidelines/the laptop experience/zoom metaphor. Sugar Labs (2009)
12. Cass, S.: Tiltbrush: The killer app for VR. IEEE Spectrum. IEEE (2016)
13. MozVR. http://mozvr.com/
14. Control VR- the future of virtual reality, animation & more by the control VR team – kickstarter. https://www.kickstarter.com/projects/controlvr/control-vr-motion-capture-for-vr-animation-and-mor/description
15. Friedberg, A.: The Virtual Window: From Alberti to Microsoft. MIT Press, Cambridge (2009)
16. Conway, S.: A circular wall? Reformulating the fourth wall for video games (2009). www.gamasutra.com, http://www.gamasutra.com/view/feature/4086/a_circular_wall_reformulating_the_.php

17. Iacovides, I., Cox, A., Kennedy, R., Cairns, P., Jennett, C.: Removing the HUD: The impact of non-diegetic game elements and expertise on player involvement. In: Proceedings of the 2015 Annual Symposium on Computer-Human Interaction in Play, CHI PLAY 2015, pp. 13–22. ACM (2015)

18. Steinicke, F., Bruder, G., Hinrichs, K., Kuhl, S., Lappe, M., Willemsen, P.: Judgment of natural perspective projections in head-mounted display environments. In: Proceedings of the 16th ACM Symposium on Virtual Reality Software and Technology, VRST 2009, pp. 35–42. ACM (2009)

19. Johnson, J.: Designing with the Mind in Mind: Simple Guide to Understanding User Interface Design Rules. Morgan Kaufmann Publishers, Elsevier, Amsterdam, Boston (2010)

20. McKee, S.P., Nakayama, K.: The detection of motion in the peripheral visual field. Vis. Res. **24**(1), 25–32 (1984)

21. Lachenmayr, B.: Visual field and road traffic. How does peripheral vision function? Ophthalmologe **103**(5), 373–381 (2006)

22. Khoury, G.R., Simoff, S.J.: Elastic metaphors: Expanding the philosophy of interface design. In: Selected Papers from Conference on Computers and Philosophy, CRPIT 2003, vol. 37, pp. 65–71. Australian Computer Society, Inc., (2003)

23. Lakoff, G., Johnson, M.: Metaphors We Live By. University of Chicago Press, Chicago (1980)

24. Greuter, S., Roberts, D.J.: SpaceWalk: movement and interaction in virtual space with commodity hardware. In: Proceedings of the 2014 Conference on Interactive Entertainment, IE 2014, pp. 1:1–1:7. ACM (2014)

25. Vive | home. http://www.htcvive.com/us/

26. Bortolami, S.B., Rocca, S., Daros, S., DiZio, P., Lackner, J.R.: Mechanisms of human static spatial orientation. Exp. Brain Res. **173**(3), 374–388 (2006)

27. Merfeld, D.M., Zupan, L., Peterka, R.J.: Humans use internal models to estimate gravity and linear acceleration. Nature **398**(6728), 615–618 (1999)

28. Davis, S., Nesbitt, K., Nalivaiko, E.: A systematic review of cybersickness. In: Proceedings of the 2014 Conference on Interactive Entertainment, IE 2014, pp. 8:1–8:9. ACM (2014)

29. Kitazaki, M., Nakano, T., Matsuzaki, N., Shigemasu, H.: Control of eye-movement to decrease ve-sickness. In: Proceedings of the ACM Symposium on Virtual Reality Software and Technology, VRST 2006, pp. 350–355. ACM (2006)

30. Bao, P., Gergle, D.: What's "this" you say?: The use of local references on distant displays. In: Proceedings of the SIGCHI Conference on Human Factors in Computing Systems, CHI 2009, pp. 1029–1032. ACM (2009)

31. Haffegee, A., Alexandrov, V., Barrow, R.: Eye tracking and gaze vector calculation within immersive virtual environments. In: 2007 Proceedings of the ACM Symposium on Virtual Reality Software and Technology, VRST 2007, pp. 225–226. ACM (2007)

32. Sturman, D.J., Zeltzer, D.: A survey of glove-based input. IEEE Comput. Graph. Appl. **14**(1), 30–39 (1994)

33. Leap motion | mac & PC motion controller for games, design, virtual reality & more. https://www.leapmotion.com/

34. Barsalou, L.W.: Grounded cognition. Annu. Rev. Psychol. **59**, 617–645 (2008)

35. McCarthy, R., Blackwell, A., de Lahunta, S., Wing, A., Hollands, K., Barnard, P., Marcel, A.: Bodies meet minds: Choreography and cognition. Leonardo **39**(5), 475–477 (2006)

36. Lin, J., Wu, Y., Huang, T.S.: Modeling the constraints of human hand motion. In: Proceedings of the Workshop on Human Motion (HUMO 2000), p. 121. IEEE Computer Society (2000)

37. Creem-Regehr, S.H., Willemsen, P., Gooch, A.A., Thompson, W.B.: The influence of restricted viewing conditions on egocentric distance perception: Implications for real and virtual indoor environments. Perception **34**, 191–204 (2005). SAGE Publications

38. Chatman, S.B.: Story and Discourse: Narrative Structure in Fiction and Film. Cornell University Press, Ithaca (1978)

39. Menzel, C.: Possible worlds. In: The Stanford Encyclopedia of Philosophy (2016)

40. Wolf, M.J.P.: Building Imaginary Worlds: The Theory and History of Subcreation. Routledge, New York (2013)

41. Abbott, E.: Flatland: A Romance of Many Dimensions. Penguin Books, New York (1998)

42. Lynch, K.: The Image of the City. MIT Press, Cambridge (1960)

43. Suchman, L.A.: Human-Machine Reconfigurations: Plans and Situated Actions. Cambridge University Press, Cambridge (2007)

44. Crabtree, A., Rouncefield, M., Tolmie, P.: Doing Design Ethnography. Springer, New York (2012)

Haptic Training Simulator for Pedicle Screw Insertion in Scoliosis Surgery

Maryam Moafimadani[1], Adam Gomes[1(✉)], Karl Zabjek[2],
Reinhard Zeller[3], and David Wang[1]

[1] Electrical and Computer Engineering, University of Waterloo,
Waterloo, ON N2L 3G1, Canada
adam_gom@live.com
[2] Department of Physical Therapy, University of Toronto,
Toronto, ON M5G 1V7, Canada
[3] Paediatric Orthopedic Surgery Division, Hospital for Sick Children,
Toronto, ON M5G 1X8, Canada

Abstract. Pedicle screw insertion is a common treatment in fixing spinal deformities in idiopathic scoliosis. This paper discusses the development of a haptic device which will aid in training for pedicle screw insertion surgery. By translating the rotational and linear effects of the surgery into tunable haptic parameters, a realistic haptic simulator is created. Over 10 surgeons of varying experience levels used the simulator, and were able to tune the device to what they felt was most realistic. They were also asked to judge the system based on its feasibility and usefulness. The results indicate the simulator is feasible for surgical education.

Keywords: Haptics · Scoliosis · Pedicle screw insertion

1 Introduction

Idiopathic scoliosis is defined as a lateral curvature of the spine greater than 10 degrees with unknown cause. The reasons for treatment include improving physical appearance, reducing back pain, promoting physical comfort, and preventing excessive spine curvature. In pedicle screw instrumentation, screws are placed through the pedicle and inside the vertebral body, and are then connected by a short rod which straightens the spine [1]. This type of surgery is often conducted using the free-hand anatomic technique and relies on visual and haptic feedback. Steps in pedicle screw insertion consist of identifying the entry point, removing the cortical cortex of the pedicle, creating the channel, palpation and placing the screws.

In the critical phase of channel creation, the probe is pushed through the pedicle and towards the vertebral body [2]. The required depth is different for different regions of the spine. The advancement of the probe should be smooth and consistent. A sudden change in resistance means that the probe is touching

© Springer International Publishing Switzerland 2016
M. Antona and C. Stephanidis (Eds.): UAHCI 2016, Part II, LNCS 9738, pp. 301–311, 2016.
DOI: 10.1007/978-3-319-40244-4_29

the pedicle wall or the wall of the vertebrae body. In such situations, a sudden downward motion (breach) can occur if the surgeon continues to apply force to the probe [3]. Many visual aids are difficult due to deformity of the bone, in other words haptics is key.

Creating a pathway through the pedicle by the free-hand technique is composed of two main degrees of freedom: rotation and linear (translational). Rotating the probe removes the soft cancellous bone and applying force creates linear translational movement along the pedicle axis. Optimal screw insertion relies on the experience of the surgeon and his ability to differentiate the tactile sensations associated with different textures in the bone when performing channel creation [4]. This is because the surgeon has limited visibility of the internal organs or spinal cord. Complications can occur due to an incorrect entry point, an incorrect trajectory, or failure to recognize wall breaches. The complications cause neurological issues, visceral organ's damage and/or problems with mechanical motion [1,5,6].

Although the accuracy of surgeons is not solely due to the surgeons' experience or lack of experience, studies showed that experienced surgeons have a significantly lower chance of having a medical breach than novices [7]. With the steep learning curve in the procedure, this haptic simulator can allow surgeons and residents to learn and practice the differentiation between proper and improper haptic signals. Among the current approaches in the education of surgeons, haptics simulators provide the trainee with the safest and most repeatable environment. Traditional surgical training includes supervised practice on live patients or cadavers. The former risks the comfort and safety of the patient, and also extends the time and cost of the operation in order to allow for corrections to be made. The latter is expensive and also imposes unrealistic physiological responses due to the embalming chemicals and lack of blood pressure in cadavers. Moreover, it is very difficult to assess the practitioners' proficiency through these techniques. Virtual reality simulators provide the trainee with unlimited practice with no time constraints and, by integrating sensors to the simulator, makes it feasible to assess skills [8]. Current simulators usually employ visual and/or touch modalities to replicate the real environment. A problem with many of the available haptic platforms is that they fail to create realistic effects due to device limitations. For instance, the haptic feedback related to a spine biopsy simulator remained limited to interactions with soft tissues since the haptic device being used was unable to provide high realistic force peaks [9,10]. Most available works focus on the visual aspects of the surgical education [11–13]. As well, most virtual reality simulators for bone tissue procedures involve power drill simulations and not the free hand technique [14,15]. This paper presents a customized simulator that is the first to be able to emulate the high forces created in the free-hand pedicle screw insertion technique. This work adds a linear degree of freedom to the rotary stage of previous work [16] and can simulate the haptic effects associated with the coupled two degrees of freedom involved in the pedicle screw insertion: rotation and linear progression. Haptic model parameters for a spine surgery with normal bone density are clinically tuned within this user study.

Although the proposed haptic techniques in this study are capable of simulating various anatomical scenarios, for the initial prototype, virtual clinical testing is only performed for healthy vertebrae with normal size and normal bone density as opposed to an older, osteoporotic bone or a high-density bone in a young patient.

2 Biomechanical Characteristics of the Surgical Procedure

The pedicle is composed of two types of tissue: cancellous bone, which is soft bone with a low density structure, and cortical bone, the harder, outer layer of the pedicle wall. The pedicle screw insertion procedure can be split into two degrees of freedom: rotational and linear progression. Probe rotation through cancellous bone causes vibrations, as well the sensation of going a series of bumps, similar to the scratching of a match across a surface. Probe rotation through the cortical bone, on the other hand, creates the sensation of viscous friction. Linear progression through the cancellous bone creates the sensation of moving over small bumps in a smooth and consistent manner. If linear progression is not performed correctly, perforation of the pedicle wall, or a breach, can occur. Breaches occur due to either the incorrect probe trajectory, or when the surgeon continually applies pressure when feeling high resistance on the probe. Images of correct and incorrect (breached) pedical screw insertion are shown in Fig. 1. Based on feedback from expert surgeons, the linear degree of freedom is composed of two system effects: linear motion and breach effects. These effects are dependant on the the anatomical characteristics of each patient, and as a result, the sensations are not consistent across all patients. The prototype for this study focuses solely on vertebrae with normal size and normal bone density, as would be found in healthy patients. Additionally, as will be explained in the further sections, breach effects will not be a focus of this study.

3 Experimental Platform

The rotary stage of the system was developed in an earlier iteration of the platform [16]. The mechanical component of this stage consists of a fabricated probe handle connected to the shaft of a non-geared DC motor. Connected to the motor is an encoder which measures the angular position of the probe. The hardware for the system interfaces with a PC using a data aquisition system (DAQ), and the haptic effects are programmed in MATLAB/Simulink and run at a sampling rate of 1000 Hz.

For the linear stage of the simulator, an electrical geared motor, with load capacity of 100 pounds, was chosen as the linear actuator for the system. This actuator is capable of supplying forces of over 100N. Delivering high forces is important for this application because surgeons typically exert extreme forces during the procedure. To measure the position along the axis of the linear actuator, a position sensor is used and is coupled to the rotary stage plate. Lastly,

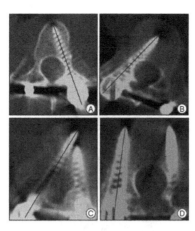

Fig. 1. Computed tomography (CT) scan of screws inside pedicle. (A) and (B) demonstrate a proper pedicle screw insertion. (C) shows the medial cortical breach and (D) shows a lateral cortical breach [2]

a tranducer is placed between the probe and the shaft of the motor to measure the user's force and torque. The entire experimental set up is shown in Fig. 2.

4   Control Structure and Design

The general control structure that is used in this work is shown in Fig. 3. It includes the rotary stage control scheme coupled with the linear stage control scheme. The rotary simulation model that was proposed in [16] consists of two main haptic effects: vibration effects and viscous friction effects. Vibration effects are modelled as a series of bumps through rotation and is simulated by using a derivative controller. The effects are felt as a resistive torque which increases in magnitude proportionally to the speed of rotation. In the rotary stage of the block diagram, shown in Fig. 3, the angle θ_d is the desired angular position and is generated using the trajectory planner block. This block uses Eq. 1 which is a function of the detent interval and the detent width (indicated by θ_i and θ_w, respectively).

$$\theta_d = \begin{cases} \theta', & \text{if } \theta' < \theta_L \\ \theta_L, & \text{if } \theta_L < \theta' < \dfrac{\theta_i}{2} \\ \theta_R, & \text{if } \dfrac{\theta_i}{2} < \theta' < \theta_R \\ \theta', & \text{if } \theta' > \theta_R \end{cases} \tag{1}$$

here, θ' is the remainder obtained if θ is divided by θ_i. The response torque is calculated using the PD controller in Eq. 2.

$$\tau_c(t) = k_p(\theta_d - \theta') - k_d \dot{\theta} \tag{2}$$

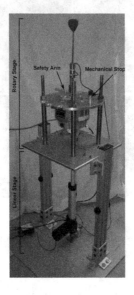

Fig. 2. Haptic simulator experimental setup

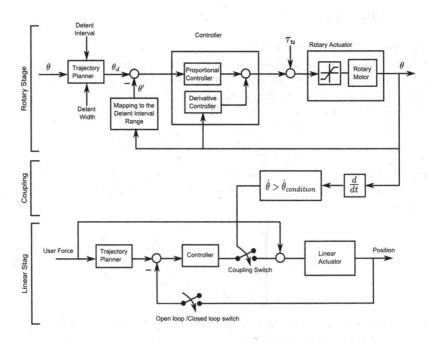

Fig. 3. General control diagram of the haptic training simulator

The proportional component of the controller creates a series of detents in the probe position. When the position of the probe lies in the first and last case in Eq. 1 , the response torque is zero. As the probe position moves away from θ_L, the controller creates an increasing torque similar to the feeling of a spring compressing. As the the probe passes the midpoint and gets closer to θ_R, the sensation is similar to that of a spring returning to its starting position.

All four haptic parameters for the rotational stage (detent interval, detent width, detent magnitude, viscous friction coefficient) are tuned to what surgeons feel is most realistic to the actual surgical scenario during clinical testing.

The second stage of the control scheme, shown as the linear stage in Fig. 3, simulates the linear dynamics of the system. The device used for simulating these effects should be able to replicate the vibration and resistance sensation felt as the probe proceeds through the pedicle. For simulating breach effects, the actuator must be able to deliver very large forces. Additionally, the device must use impedance control. For simulating the haptic effects of the linear stage, two control strategies are presented. One strategy employs a closed loop PID control technique, while the other strategy uses an open loop control scheme. For simulating linear progression, both control techniques simulate vibration by making step-wise motions whose progression speed is the control variable. Breach simulations involve simulating the dropping of the probe with a certain displacement in a short amount of time.

Through observations and discussions with expert surgeons it was found that rotation was a key factor in linear progression, i.e. the rotational and linear effects are coupled, shown in Fig. 3 as the coupling stage. To simulate this, the angular velocity of the probe rotation is used for determining how subtle rotation should be for linear progression. This is verified through a comparison block which controls the coupling switch between the linear and rotational stages.

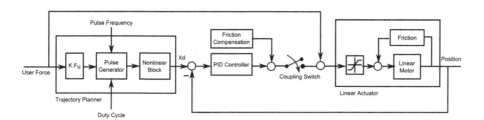

Fig. 4. Block diagram of the PID control scheme

4.1   Closed Loop PID Control

Although the closed loop control technique was not implemented for the final prototype, the following is a brief description of its design. For the control of the linear stage of the haptic device, a trajectory planner is used to generate the desired reference trajectory and a PID controller is used for driving the motor to follow the trajectory. A block diagram for this approach is shown in Fig. 4.

For linear progression, the trajectory planner uses three inputs to generate the desired trajectory. First, the user force is scaled by a factor of k, which determines how much force the user should put on the probe to get motion, and is then converted into a series of pulses. The pulse frequency and duty cycle are tuning parameters that can change the vibration sensation. The pulses are then passed through a nonlinear block where the current signal is added with its one-sample-delayed signal. This block updates the reference trajectory.

To simulate breach effects, the desired displacement, the user's force and a force threshold are used as inputs. When the user's force is greater than the force threshold, a step signal, with the size of the desired displacement, is injected into the nonlinear block mentioned earlier. This check remains idle for a short period of time to avoid multiple true conditions in the presence of noisy signals.

4.2 Open Loop Control

For open loop control, the displacement is no longer the main focus, instead, the speed of movement is controlled. The block diagram for this control scheme is shown in Fig. 5.

For simulating linear progression, vibrations can be achieved by simply feeding the actuator with a series of pulses. The user force is first measured and scaled by a factor of k to specify how resistive the motion will be. The frequency and duty cycle of the pulses determine the sensation the user feels. If there is friction inside the motor, part of the control signal is used to overcome the friction and move the actuator as intended.

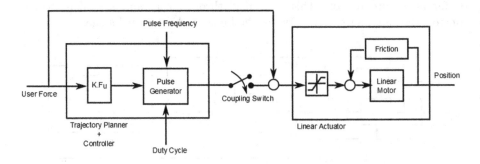

Fig. 5. Block diagram of the open loop control scheme

For breach simulation, the force condition is checked, just as in the closed loop control scheme. However, instead of feeding the signal into the Zero-Order-Hold block, a pulse of maximum input and specified duration is fed directly into the actuator. When the actuator is fed with the maximum input, the displacement of the actuator is controlled by the duration of the pulse. This relationship between the pulse width and actuator displacement can be approximated by a linear function.

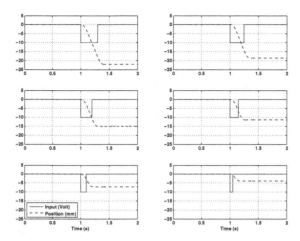

Fig. 6. Displacement of the actuator with maximum input voltage and six different pulse duration including 0.3, 0.25, 0.2, 0.15, 0.1 and 0.05 s.

Open Loop Control Design. In open loop control, as mentioned previously, it was found that there is a linear relationship between the input pulse width and the displacement of the actuator. Using a series of tests where displacements were measured from differing pulse widths, it was found that the ratio between pulse duration and displacement is 1 : 7.44 with a standard deviation of 0.17. The results of each test signal is shown in Fig. 6.

5   Clinical Tuning

To further refine the simulation model to more accurately simulate the biomechanical properties of the scoliosis procedure, model parameters were tuned with the aid of participating surgeons. For this study, 11 surgeons were recruited to define the model parameters for normal density bone. 8 participants were orthopedic surgeons and 3 were neurosurgeons. Among the orthopedic surgeons, one was senior, three were fellows and four were residents. The set of neurosurgeons consisted of one surgeon from each experience level. Senior surgeons had over 15 years of experience, fellow surgeons had 6–10 years of experience and residents had between 4–9 years of experience.

For the study, each participant stands beside the device and holds the probe with one hand, while holding the top plate of the device with the other. Prior to testing, each participant goes through a training session where the haptic effects are introduced. Each model parameter is changed over a wide range of values, allowing the surgeons to experience each sensation independently. After training, each surgeon is asked to tune the parameters so that the simulation is equivalent to feeling normal, healthy bone. Once all parameters are adjusted, the surgeons are given another chance to feel their tuning and perform any final tuning. After tuning, the surgeons are told to perform the procedure of probe channelling on the simulator while the force, torque, linear position and angular position are recorded. At the end of each trial, the surgeons complete a four question, five-point Likert scale survey probing how well the effects of haptic simulator compared to the real surgery. The survey consisted of the following statements: (1) The haptic sensations associated with the rotation of the probe was simulated realistically; (2) The haptic sensations associated with the linear progression of the probe was simulated realistically; (3) Overall, the simulator produced realistic haptic sensations felt during probe channelling; (4) The simulator could potentially be a useful tool for teaching pedicle screw insertion surgery.

5.1   Results

Although it is not feasible to find exact parameter values that generate the most realistic haptic sensations on normal bone, there is sufficient evidence to conclude that at least 50 % of surgeons can perform within 25 % tolerance of the average of the two senior surgeons' tuned values for five parameters. These parameters are detent interval, viscous friction coefficient, duty cycle, frequency and scaling gain [17]. The exact statistics for each parameter, for the senior surgeons, are shown in Table 1.

The survey results show that the simulator provided a realistic haptic simulation of rotation and linear progression. They also agreed considerably that the simulator can potentially be a useful tool for teaching pedicle screw insertion surgery. For all four questions, the fellow and senior surgeons either agreed or strongly agreed.

Table 1. Percentage of surgeons able to adjust the simulator parameters to within 25 % of the average of the two expert surgeons values (N = 9) [17]

	Parameter	Seniors' Avg.	Completion rate	Exact prob
Rotary stage	Detent interval	1.85	55.6 %	62.30 %
	Detent width	0.4	33.3 %	17.19 %
	Detent magnitude	0.85	44.4 %	37.70 %
	Viscous friction coeff	15	66.7 %	82.81 %
Linear stage	Duty cycle	0.7	88.9 %	98.93 %
	Frequency	8.25	77.8 %	94.53 %
	Scaling Gain	0.16	66.7 %	82.81 %

6   Conclusion

There are relatively few surgeons in Canada performing pedicle screw insertion. Therefore, participant recruitment was a major challenge for the clinical tuning of parameters. Moreover, not all surgeons perform the surgery regularly and most residents develop their surgical skill set on cadaver bones rather than the healthy bones of young patients, who comprise the highest volume of scoliosis surgical cases. Despite the small sample size, among the participants is a senior surgeon who performs a major proportion of all this type of surgery in Canada.

The participants' expertise were quite varied by multiple factors including their level of training, number of performed operations in operating room, number of performed operations on bony tissue, and the number of operations performed specifically for pedicle screw insertion. Some had more surgical experience with robotic tools. The neurosurgeons less often perform this procedure, performing them sometimes only once or twice a year.

According to the questionnaire, all of the senior and fellow surgeon participants found the haptic training simulator to be a useful tool in teaching probe channelling in pedicle screw insertion. The current device is capable of simulating the various force and torque effects a surgeon feels in this surgery. The current simulator is a first of its kind in the field of spine surgery, with the ability of replicating the haptic sensations in free-hand probe channelling through the bone with high-fidelity haptic feedback.

6.1   Future Works

As previously discussed, breach simulation is an important adverse event that surgeons should be aware of in pedicle screw insertion surgery. Breach simulations, however, were not very effective in this iteration of the simulator due to hardware limitations. Replacing the linear motor with a faster one, and incorporating lighter hardware, may make breach simulations feasible. Also, to increase realism for a more immersive simulation, a graphical interface is necessary. The apparatus can be overlaid by a visual interface that looks like a patient's body, thus, creating a more authentic feel to the simulation. Lastly, since the haptic simulator is planned to serve as a surgical training tool, future work includes determining appropriate training techniques for the surgery and investigating ways of performing surgical skill assessment.

References

1. Vaccaro, A., Rizzolo, S., Allardyce, T., Ramsey, M., Salvo, J., Balderston, R., Cotler, J.: Placement of pedicle screws in the thoracic spine. J. Bone Joint Surg. Am. **77**, 1200–1206 (1995)
2. Hyun, S.-J., Kim, Y.J., Cheh, G., Yoon, S.H., Rhim, S.-C.: Free hand pedicle screw placement in the thoracic spine without any radiographic guidance: technical note, a cadaveric study. J. Korean Neurosurg. Soc. **51**(1), 66–70 (2012)
3. Phillips, F., Khan, S.N.: Treatment of Complex Cervical Spine Disorders, An Issue of Orthopedic Clinics, vol. 43. Elsevier Health Sciences, New York (2012)
4. Sud, A., Tsirikos, A.I.: Current concepts and controversies on adolescent idiopathic scoliosis: Part i, Indian. J. Orthop. **47**(2), 117 (2013)
5. Wegener, B., Birkenmaier, C., Fottner, A., Jansson, V., Dürr, H.R.: Delayed perforation of the aorta by a thoracic pedicle screw. Eur. Spine J. **17**(2), 351–354 (2008)

6. Sud, A., Tsirikos, A.I.: Current concepts and controversies on adolescent idiopathic scoliosis: Part ii, Indian. J. Orthop. **47**(3), 219 (2013)
7. Samdani, A.F., Ranade, A., Sciubba, D.M., Cahill, P.J., Antonacci, M.D., Clements, D.H., Betz, R.R.: Accuracy of free-hand placement of thoracic pedicle screws in adolescent idiopathic scoliosis: how much of a difference does surgeon experience make? Eur. Spine J. **19**(1), 91–95 (2010)
8. Haluck, R.S., Marshall, R.L., Krummel, T.M., Melkonian, M.G.: Are surgery training programs ready for virtual reality? a survey of program directors in general surgery. J. Am. Coll. Surg. **193**(6), 660–665 (2001)
9. Ra, J., Kim, J., Yi, J., Kim, K., Park, H., Kyung, K.-U., Kwon, D.-S., Kang, H., Kwon, S., Kwon, S., et al.: Spine needle biopsy simulator using visual and force feedback. Comput. Aided Surg. **7**(6), 353–363 (2002)
10. Kwon, D.-S., Kyung, K.-U., Kwon, S.M., Ra, J.B., Park, H.W., Kang, H.S., Zeng, J., Cleary, K.R.: Realistic force reflection in a spine biopsy simulator. In: IEEE International Conference on Robotics and Automation, Proceedings 2001 ICRA, vol. 2, pp. 1358–1363. IEEE (2001)
11. Klein, S., Whyne, C.M., Rush, R., Ginsberg, H.J.: CT-based patient-specific simulation software for pedicle screw insertion. J. Spinal Disord. Tech. **22**(7), 502–506 (2009)
12. Eftekhar, B., Ghodsi, M., Ketabchi, E., Rasaee, S.: Surgical simulation software for insertion of pedicle screws. Neurosurgery **50**(1), 222–224 (2002)
13. Rambani, R., Ward, J., Viant, W.: Desktop-based computer-assisted orthopedic training system for spinal surgery. J. Surg. Educ. **71**(6), 805–809 (2014)
14. Schmidt, R.: Spinaltap: An architecture for real-time vertebrae drilling simulation. Department of Computer Sciences at the University of Calgary, Technical report (2002)
15. Luciano, C.J., Banerjee, P.P., Bellotte, B., Lemole Jr., G.M., Oh, M., Charbel, F.T., Roitberg, B.: Learning retention of thoracic pedicle screw placement using a high-resolution augmented reality simulator with haptic feedback. Neurosurgery **69**(Suppl Operative), 14–19 (2011)
16. Leung, R.: Design of a haptic simulator for pedicle screw insertion in pediatric scoliosis surgery, Master's thesis, University of Toronto (2013)
17. Moafimadani, S.: Development of a haptic simulator for pedicle screw insertion: a pilot study. J. Surg. Educ. (2015)

Automation of the Simple Test for Evaluating Hand Function Using Leap Motion Controller

Kouki Nagamune[1,2(✉)], Yosuke Uozumi[1], and Yoshitada Sakai[2]

[1] Graduate School of Engineering, University of Fukui, Fukui, Japan
nagamune@u-fukui.ac.jp
[2] Graduate School of Medicine, Kobe University, Kobe, Japan

Abstract. In the test to evaluate the upper limb function, there is Simple Test for Evaluating Hand Function (STEF). This test is performed for one subject by one examiner. When the subject moves to grab the object, it is evaluated with the accuracy and speed. However STEF has problems that takes labor and massive time. In addition human error happens due to huge data management. In order to solve these problems, this study proposes an automated system of the simple test for evaluating hand function using Leap Motion controller to conduct a STEF on the PC screen. Leap Motion controller is a sensor that focuses on only the finger and hand motions. The proposed system could automatically evaluat the hand motion of the subjects by moving virtual objects on the screen. As a future challenge, there is a need to evaluate attracting upper limb function disabilities.

Keywords: Rehabilitation system · Virtual reality · Occupational therapist · Hand motion

1 Introduction

The number of persons who has handicap or paralysis in the upper limb is increasing with year. As one of the reason, an increasment of the survival rate in stroke patients can be considered. In Japan, the survival rate was doubled in the past five decada. This results in that patients would have paralysis in the after-effect of the stroke. However, the paralisis has a variety. Thus, evaluation method for the upper limb function has been modified with the variety. As examples of the evaluation methods, there are two methods. The first one is manual function test (MFT) which aims for the comparative large number of handicapped person with upper limb [1]. The second one is simple test for evaluating hand function (STEF) which aims to evaluate the ability of agility of upper limb. All the tests are performed under an examiner and evaluated with judement of the examiner and performance time.

These test has four problems. First, the reliability is not high, because the performance is scored by the examiner visually. Second, the management of the data is tough task, beause the performance results is handled by manual. Third, comsumption labor and time in an occupational therapist is high, because they are required to example the test procedure equaly for all the patients. Fourth, the mental effect can happen in patients, because some patients strongly consider the relathionship between them and occupational therapists.

© Springer International Publishing Switzerland 2016
M. Antona and C. Stephanidis (Eds.): UAHCI 2016, Part II, LNCS 9738, pp. 312–319, 2016.
DOI: 10.1007/978-3-319-40244-4_30

To solve these problem, an evaluation system for rehabilitation with virtual reality (VR) has been researched, recently. Norio et al. developed telerehabilitation system based on VR with multi-sensory feedback [2]. Toshiaki et al. proposed a training system of upper limb with virtual emvironment [3]. These studies can solve the previous problems, however ignore grasping motion of the upper limb. Therefore, this study aims to develope a evaluation system for upper limb motion which is performed on the personal computer screen. In addtion, this study automated STEF which requires to score the grasping motion.

2 Preliminary

2.1 STEF

STEF is performed under one occupational therapist, and can evaluate agility and position of upper limb in comparing with normal person. In STEF, patients moves multiple objects from one position to another position. The motion can help to diagnosis the symptoms of the patients and improve rehabilitation and daily motion after this. STEF consists of ten examinations and uses ten instruments Fig. 1 [4]. One examination is scored from zero to ten ponts. Full marks means 100 points. The targets coveres all the patients who have upper limb function disorder regardless of the sympton types. However patients who has serious disorder cannot move objects, then the patients are excluded from the target.

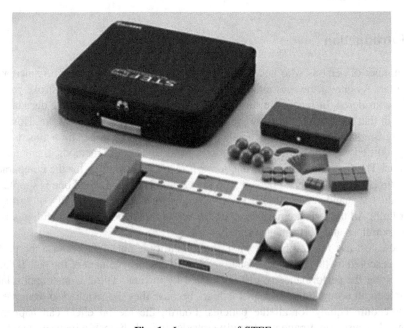

Fig. 1. Instruments of STEF

One examination to be considered in this study is exampled. The examination uses five big balls. Figure 2 shows a platform used in STEF. Each character from A to H means places where some objects move to by patients. In case of right hand evaluation, all the balles are placed on region B at first. Then, a patients moves five balls from region B to region A one by one (and vice versa).

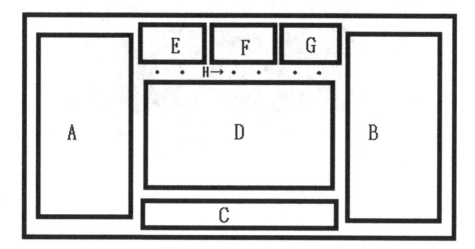

Fig. 2. Platform of STEF instruments

2.2   Leap Motion Controller

This study uses a motion sensor (Leap Motion Controller, Leap Motion Inc.) as shown in Fig. 3. This sensor focuses on only finger and hand motions. The size of the sensor is 30 mm (depth) × 80 mm (width) × 12.7 mm (height). The sampling speed is 90 to 150 fps.

This sensor can detect hand motion with resolution of 0.7 mm [5]. The detective area is 500 mm in one edge and spread out with upper position when the sensor is placed on the table as shown in Fig. 4. The range of height is from 25 mm to 600 mm [6]. Thefore, this study employs 500 mm as hand motion distance, which is corresponding with actual examination. The coordinate system is as follows. X, Y, and Z axes are right direction (positive), upper direction (positive), and drawing direction (positive), respectively. Although Leap Motion Controller can trace hand motion with the highest accuracy among the motion capture devices, the error along Y axis is large. Therefore, this study focuses on only X and Z axes motion.

Fig. 3. Leap Motion Controller

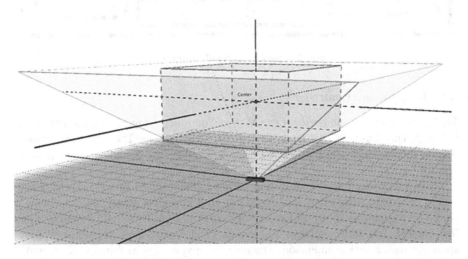

Fig. 4. Detective area of leap motion controller

3 Method

Subjects sit on a chair in front of a PC screen as shown in Fig. 5. Leap Motion Conroller is placed on a desk which is in front of the screen. The hand of the subjects is displayed on the screen with virtual ball objects. The subjects moves the virtual ball object from one place to another place on the screen. The grasping condition of the hand is recongnized by Leap Motion Controller and immeiately reflected on the virtural environment.

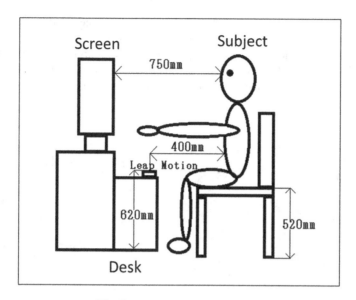

Fig. 5. Measurement environment

The starting condition on the virtual environment is shown in Fig. 6. This is an example for left hand examination. Five virtual ball are placed on the left. A grey line can be seen in the right. The subjects should move the all the ball over the line one by one. The blue box (center) is the start button on this panel. When pushing the start button the measurement starts.

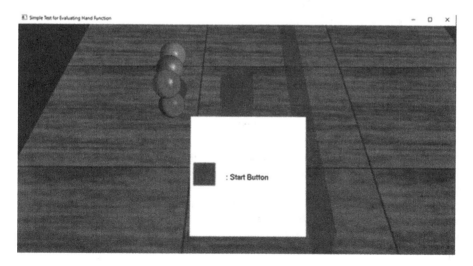

Fig. 6. Starting conditions (Color figure online)

In this system, subjects feels difficulty to comprehend the relathionship between ball and hand, because the ball is virtual object and cannot tell the contacting feeling. To overcome this problem, this study employs color coding to tell the hand condition for the subject as visual feedback. Here, the hand condition can be classified into three situations: non-contact, contact, and grasp. Each condition is colored seperately as shown in Fig. 7.

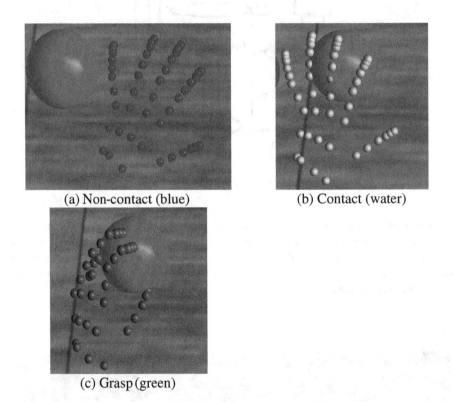

(a) Non-contact (blue)   (b) Contact (water)

(c) Grasp (green)

Fig. 7. Hand condition to the virtual objects. (Color figure online)

The five virtual objects are also colored as red, deep green, blue, yellowish green, and violet. When moving the virtual object over the goal line (grey line), color of the virtual object is changed as water to make it easy to understand the achievement. When finishing movement of all the virtual objects over the goal line, the measurement time was recorded automatically. The unit of measurement time is second.

The hand condtion can be recognized by considering the coordinates of the hand and balls. Here, the hand coordinate is F_x, F_y, and F_z. The center coordinate of the ball is M_x, M_y, and M_z. The distance d between the finger tip and the ball is calculated by Eq. (1).

$$d = \sqrt{(F_x - M_x)^2 + (F_y - M_y)^2 + (F_z - M_z)^2} \qquad (1)$$

When d is less than threshold value th, the hand is recognized as contacting the ball. th is set to be the radius of the ball. Leap Motion Controller can diagnose the bending angle of the fingers. When two or more fingers bend and contact the ball, the hand is recognized as grasping the ball.

4 Experiments

The number of subjects was six (Sex: six males, Age: 25 ± 3, Dominant hand: all right-handed). The evaluation method is ·to score the speed to move the objects as actual evaluation. In this study, the measurement time was compared. Ten trials were performed in left and right hands.

5 Results

The results of the measurment time is shown in Table 1. This results indicate that the right hand has higher agility than left hand.

Table 1. Measurement time in left and right hands.

Subject #	Performance Time (s)	
	Left	Right
#1	11.17 ± 2.70	9.70 ± 1.15
#2	13.23 ± 3.64	11.21 ± 1.50
#3	12.63 ± 3.48	12.50 ± 2.26
#4	9.82 ± 1.80	7.46 ± 1.18
#5	10.86 ± 2.40	11.39 ± 3.99
#6	9.69 ± 3.11	6.36 ± 1.17

6 Discussions

This study assigned ten trials to subjects. The performance time was improved with trials in all the subjects. The reason is a learning ability of the subjects for appropriate hand motion in this system. Therefore, it might be better to assign a constant training time for the subjects.

The measurement time of the right hand is faster than left hands in all cases. Perhaps, dominant hand effects this results. However there are no data to conclude that. Therefore, we have to apply this system to left-handed person.

7   Conclusion

This study proposes an automated system for STEF with Leap Motion Controller. The proposed system was applied to healthy six subjects. The measurement time is automatically recorded. Then, the proposed system could judge the hand condition which cannot be realized in conventional systems. Therefore, the proposed system is usefull for occupational therapists. As a future work is to apply this system to the handicapped person.

Acknowledgment. Authors would like to thank Mr. Aoki for making software in this study.

References

1. Maiko, K., Shin, M., Takahiro, K., Tomomi, H.: Evaluation of han. West Kyushu J. Rehabil. Sci. **5**, 63 (2012)
2. Norio, K., Toshiaki, T., Syunichi, S., Koichi, S.: Development and evaluation of a new telerehabilitation system based on VR technology using multisensory feedback for patients with strok. J. Phys. Ther. Sci. **27**, 3185–3190 (2015)
3. Toshiaki, T., Akira, K., Syunichi, S., Tkashi, I., Yusuke, M., Norio, K., Tomoya, M., Maureen, K.H.: A study of upper extermity training for patients with stroke using a virtual environment system. J. Phys. Ther. Sci. **25**, 575–580 (2013)
4. Sakai Medical Co., Ltd. http://www.sakaimed.co.jp/special/hand/hand03.html
5. Frank, W., Daniel, B., Bartholom, R., Denis, F.: Analysis of the accuracy and robustness of the leap motion controller. Sensors **6391**, 6380–6393 (2013)
6. Jože, G., Grega, J., Matevž, P., Sašo, T., Jaka, S.: An analysis of the precision and rehability of the leap motion sensor and its suitability for static and dynamic trachking. Sensors **3706**, 3702–3720 (2014)

Using Virtual Reality to Enhance Vision for People Who Are Blind in One Eye

Michael Ostrander and Tony Morelli[✉]

Department of Computer Science, Central Michigan University,
Mount Pleasant, USA
{ostralmj,tony.morelli}@cmich.edu

Abstract. People who are blind in one eye or have low vision in one eye have issues dealing with the lack of binocular stereoscopic vision and reduced peripheral vision. Current virtual reality hardware allows all visuals to be presented through a screen built into a headset. The idea presented here, utilizes two wide angle cameras affixed to the headset and presents the combined video feed to the user's better performing eye. A user study with 11 participants, including 3 participants who are blind in one eye, was performed to understand the feasibility of increasing the peripheral vision of a person with only one functioning eye. Three different types of image combination were tested and user preference and performance were recorded.

Keywords: Accessibility · Peripheral vision · Stereoscopic

1 Introduction

People who are blind or have low vision in one eye lose their stereoscopic binocular vision and they also have reduced peripheral vision. The loss of stereoscopic vision can result in a lack of knowledge about depth and positioning elements. People who lose vision in one eye can obtain this missing information through other visual clues such as shadows, lighting and size comparisons. People with stereoscopic vision also have better skills relating their body to the environment. Skills such as reaching and grabbing items, motor skills, and balance are more challenging when stereoscopic vision is not an option [10]. People who are without vision in one eye typically have a reduction in depth perception making acquiring items within three feet of the person difficult [8].

In order to make up for the lack of peripheral vision, people without sight in one eye make more lateral head movements [5]. This adaptive head motion allows people to regain some peripheral vision, however it is more time consuming than glancing. The reason this motion is considered adaptive is that it is more prevalent in individuals who are blind in one eye when compared to individuals who have vision in both eyes but cover one eye up for the sake of the experiment [2]. These head movements are especially used when looking at objects within an arms length of the subject [5].

People who are blind in one eye are typically able to fulfill the requirements for a driver's license in the United States. However several states including, Alaska, Pennsylvania, and South Carolina require people who have low vision in one eye to drive only vehicles equipped with side mirrors [7]. In addition to specifying additional

M. Antona and C. Stephanidis (Eds.): UAHCI 2016, Part II, LNCS 9738, pp. 320–328, 2016.
DOI: 10.1007/978-3-319-40244-4_31

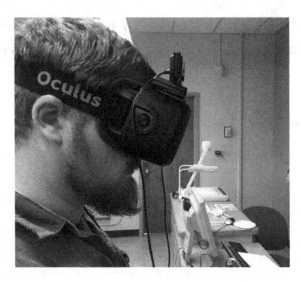

Fig. 1. User wearing peripheral vision enhancement

pieces of equipment for driving, driver's license regulations also contain minimum requirements for peripheral vision. The standards vary from state to state, some require 140° of vision, while others require 30° on either side of the point of focus. A pair of human eyes can see approximately 200° laterally. This is comprised of 120° seen by both eyes, and 40° on each side that is visible by only one eye [3].

Drivers who are blind in one eye statistically are more likely to be in car accidents [4]. Drivers who are blind in one eye must take time to move their head in order to scan the environment where a person with two functioning eyes can quickly scan the entire area by glancing. A formula one driver [11] with vision in only one eye was granted racing privileges for an entire season, and on a subsequent optical exam, his vision was determined to be unfit for competitive racing. As a result his professional license was revoked. His one season of racing contained no crashes, however there was one incident where he was unaware of a notification flag for seven consecutive laps that was being waved on the side of his functioning eye. It was felt that at such high speeds, even though there were no crash incidents, the chances of a crash incident initiated as a result of having vision in only one eye were high enough that the racing league did not want to put the other drivers in what they considered a dangerous situation.

The concept presented in this paper is an attempt to assist those who are blind in one eye. A virtual reality headset contains a screen that can display any necessary information. This dedicated screen is the only item that a user can see. This is different than augmented reality where a user can see directly with his eye and can also have a digital overlay. Using a virtual reality headset to show the video stream from two different cameras mimicking two human eyes on the built in screen may provide advantages for people who are blind in one eye.

2   Hardware Options

An Oculus Rift DK2 [6] was used to produce the virtual reality environment (Fig. 1). The DK2 contains a display that supports 960×1080 pixel resolution for each eye. It also contains a positional tracking camera to follow the movement of the player and use this movement to change the environment within the game. For this experiment, the positional tracking device was not needed. The live video feed from each of the cameras was projected down to one eye of the user on a constant basis. There were no changes to the display based on the position of the user's head outside of the video captured by the cameras.

The webcams used in this setup are the Genius WideCam F100 [1]. Each of these cameras contain $120°$ field of view and can capture video at 1920×1080 pixels per frame at the rate of 30 frames per second. The cameras were attached to the top of an Oculus Rift with velcro strips which allowed for the user to position the cameras where they felt the most natural. Also, the cameras contained a swivel mechanism which allowed the user to rotate the cameras across the horizon.

3   Methods

In order to test the feasibility of using virtual reality as an enhancement for peripheral vision, several different methods were used to test the hardware setup for usability.

The first test showed live video from one of the cameras to one of the eyes. This was meant to simulate having vision in only one eye. Although the headset contained two cameras mounted on it, for this test, only the camera on the side of the chosen eye was used. For example, if the participant requested for the experiment to be done using his left eye, then the video feed from the left camera was presented to the left eye for all trials. The 1920×1080 resolution of the camera was compressed into the 960×1080 resolution of one side of the DK2. The image was scaled to fit the entire width while leaving the height constant.

The second implementation (Split Screen) method (Fig. 2) projected both cameras to the requested eye piece. The images were placed side by side and were meant to have the functionality of the full field of view compressed into one eye. The left camera was presented on the left side of the eyepiece, and the right was presented on the right side. The native widths of these images were cut in half, while the height remained constant. This slightly exaggerated the height of the presentation, however it was decided to fill up the entire viewport with motion images from the cameras, instead of leaving black bars in order to keep proper proportions. Another option would have been to zoom in on a section of the camera feed such that the aspect rations remained natural and the entire video filled up the screen. This created an environment where each camera used 480×1080 resolution of space on one half of the DK2 display.

The third implementation (Slow Switch) presented the full view of both cameras in an alternating fashion. In order to overcome the issues found in the second implementation such as scaling, zooming, or compressing, this method alternated each camera to the requested side. The camera was set to alternate virtual eyes every one second. This would allow the participant to have the full view out of both eyes.

Fig. 2. Sample view of two cameras combined into one eye using Split Screen Method

The fourth implementation (Fast Switch) was identical to the third implementation, however the rate at which the cameras were switched was different. Instead of alternating once per second, the images were switched five times a second. The hope with this implementation was that the brain would automatically stitch together the fast switching in order to give the appearance of the field of view of two eyes.

All of these methods were implemented in Unity3D which allows for easy portability to different types of operating systems. All experiments performed for this research were performed on a MacBook Pro running OSX Yosemite with a Oculus Rift DK2 and two USB Genius F100 webcams.

4   Experiment

11 users performed the experiment in isolation with only an administrator present. The users were informed that the experiment was being performed in order to possibly help people who have no or low vision in one eye. Three of the participants were blind in one eye, and the other participants reported no severe visual impairments. Users who wear corrected lenses were asked to keep their prescribed glasses on during the experiment.

Users were first asked to choose an eye to use for the experiment. All methods were projected only to this eye, while the video contents of the other eye remained black. Users went through the experiments one at a time and always in the same order described in the previous section. For each method, users were asked to stand a distance of 10 feet from a wall that contained a standard eye chart [9]. They were asked to read each line from the chart. Users were shown the focus knobs on the lenses and were allowed to modify the focus as needed. If the user could not read the first line on the chart, they slowly moved forward until it could be read. Their distance from the wall was recorded. Then the user was asked to move closer and closer to the wall until the last line could be read. After the last line was read aloud and verified to be accurate, the final distance was recorded.

After the first method, and before the start of the second method, users were given the opportunity to adjust the orientation of the cameras. In this second method, users were presented with a scaled image containing both the right and left cameras. Users could modify the rotation of the cameras such that the resultant combined image was pleasing. They then continued on with the rest of the methods of the experiment with the cameras in these positions.

Following the conclusion of user study, users were asked to rank their preference of the methods. They were also asked to rate how useful they considered each method.

5   Results and Discussions

In total, 12 people participated in the user study. None of the users had used an Oculus Rift prior to this experiment. One of the participants was extremely uncomfortable with the Rift and chose to not participate after first placing the headset on his head. The results discussed here contain the results from 11 users (all male, Avg age: 24.1 SD = 12.0), three of whom self reported being severely visually impaired in one eye.

Table 1. User survey of techniques (1-Bad, 5-Great)

Type	Usability	Comfort	Potential
Split screen	3.40 (0.96)	3.2 (1.3)	3.6 (1.2)
Slow switch	2.7 (0.8)	3.1 (1.1)	2.8 (1.0)
Fast switch	1.3 (0.5)	1.7 (0.8)	1.9 (0.9)

Table 2. Distance from eye chart where bottom line was visible

Type	Average distance (In)
Split screen	8.6 (3.4)
Slow switch	11.29 (4.4)
Fast switch	13.56 (4.3)

At the conclusion of the user study, participants were surveyed (Table 1) on their preferences. Participants preferred split screen over the other choices and did not prefer the fast switch at all. Many participants were observed complaining about the fast switching mode. A large factor in the effectiveness of the fast switching mode was the difference in horizontal angles between the two cameras. A larger difference here makes a larger difference when the frame alternates. The alternating frames at 5 frames a second seemed to be very hard to deal with when the cameras were pointing in different directions. Participants whose cameras were pointing at the same angles seemed to complain less about the fast switching mode.

Table 2 shows the average distance from the eye chart that participants were in order to correctly read the bottom line on the chart. In order for a person to have 20/20 vision, the bottom line on the chart should be readable from a distance of 20 feet. These results show that participants were not anywhere near 20/20 vision even when wearing their prescribed corrective lenses. The average distance from the eye chart for the slow switching was better than the fast switch and both switching methods were better than the split screen. The resolution available to the switching methods for each camera was twice as much horizontally when compared to the split screen method. This can explain why those methods could see more at a further distance. The slow switch was better than the fast switch. This can be attributed to the disorienting feeling generated by the quick switching of the cameras in fast switch mode.

The results of the distance test may appear to be discouraging. Requiring the user to be within 1 foot of an object to see it as good as a person without any corrective lenses at 20 feet is a step backward. However, the limitations in this study may be do to the resolution of the display contained within the headset. When the display hardware matures, it may be able to avoid this requirement. The point to be taken away is that the switching method provides better results, however when the cameras are looking at drastically different objects it can be disorienting to the user, especially when it is switching at a fast rate. To increase the peripheral vision of a person who is blind in one eye using the switching method, the cameras must be pointed such that the entire range of vision is restored, and the rate of switching must be fast enough such that any delay does not result in a potential loss of information, yet slow enough that it avoids the disorienting side effects.

After various runs with the participants, it seemed as though allow them to adjust the angle at which the webcams were facing was a more limiting factor than a helpful one. One participant angled the webcams outwards, opposite of each other. While it extended the range of vision, it also caused much difficulty with both switching methods, as it showed nearly two completely different images. Participants also seemed to have slight trouble adjusting the camera, as they were unable to properly see the location of webcams and the output they gave at the same time. It may be more conducive to have the cameras permanently placed in a position that would directly emulate a set of human eyes.

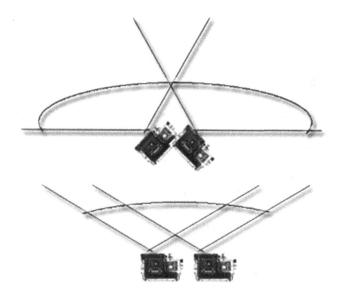

Fig. 3. Peripheral difference based on camera position

During the experiment it was discovered that the effective peripheral vision enhancement was based completely on the angles the cameras were adjusted to (Fig. 3). Initially scheduled to be investigated was the increase in peripheral vision, however participants wishing to increase their peripheral vision would twist the cameras such that they each were 90° rotated essentially giving the user eyes on the side of his head. Although this greatly improved the peripheral vision, it also greatly reduced the usability. The tasks defined in this user study were up close tasks. Figure 3 shows when the cameras are rotated outwards, there is a larger empty zone right in front of the user where neither camera captures any video. For tasks involving far away items, this may be OK, but because the user needed to be so close to the eye chart in this experiment, that empty zone becomes important.

Instead of performing a standard peripheral vision test, participants were asked to adjust the cameras to produce a comfortable view. These adjustments were done when the display was set to split screen. After the participant was satisfied with the location and orientation of the cameras, a picture was taken and later analyzed to show the angles the cameras were set to. For the purposes of these results, a positive rotation value indicates the camera was rotated in the clockwise direction, while a negative value indicates the camera was rotated in the counter clockwise direction. A value of zero indicates that the camera was not rotated and was pointed straight ahead. If a participant desired more peripheral vision, the left camera would have a negative rotation value and the right camera would have a positive rotation value.

The average rotation for the right camera was 8.18° (SD = 16.0) and the average rotation for the left camera was –6.2° (SD = 13.2). Three of the participants left both cameras pointed straight ahead. Two participants did not move the right camera, and moved the left camera counter clockwise. Four of the participants moved the left camera counter clockwise and the right camera clockwise. One participant rotated the right camera counter clockwise and the left camera clockwise, and one participant rotated both cameras an equal value (10°) in the counter clockwise direction.

6 Limitations

The experimental setup described in this paper does have several limitations that are important to consider. First, although this does increase the peripheral vision of a user, it may not increase the functional peripheral vision. For example, a user who is sighted in one or both eyes can move his eyes horizontally to increase the field of view without moving the head. In the case of the projecting the vision into the virtual reality headset, the user does not have this option. Moving only the eyeballs will not change what is visible as the images being presented to the user are based only on the mounted position of the cameras and the position of the user's head.

The limited resolution of the Oculus display is also an issue. Reading small print from a distance proved difficult for all users. While the cameras were able to pick up the details necessary for projecting the small font, the users were never able to actually see it. The viewing mode allowed for the user's viewport to be mirrored to the computer running the software, and it was observed that small text was clearly visible on the computer screen, yet the participant was not able to read the text. It is expected, however, that this type of technology will significantly improve and this limitation may not be an issue in the near future.

Another issue participants ran into was the amount of cabling required to use this technology. The Oculus Rift by itself requires two USB ports, an HDMI port and a standard wall power plug. With the addition of two USB cameras, the total required ports jumped to four USB ports. The laptop used to run the software contained only 2 USB ports, which then created the additional requirement of a USB hub, and its required power supply. As a result, the hardware setup for this experiment required 4 USB ports, 1 HDMI port, 1 USB hub and 2 AC power outlets. This is not a portable setup as motion was very difficult and if the participant was moving it was required to have an administrator present to move the wires and computer to wherever the user was going. Due to this limitation, certain methods had to be omitted, such as gauging the comfort level of walking short distances and different directions.

There was also an issue concerning the live feed from the webcams. There was a slight, yet still noticeable, delay between the webcam and the feed it returned. Movement shown through the webcams was slower than how they actually moved, which was slightly disorienting. However, because the methods used didn't require much movement, the issue was largely had no effect on the experiment. If the Oculus Rift were to be more portable and methods that focused on movements were used, this issue would have to be taken into consideration.

One last issue is about how the images were scaled to fit the display. The native resolution of the cameras was 1920 × 1080, however in the case of the side by side images, they were scaled to 480 × 1080. This results in the horizontal axis being one fourth of the original size while the height remained constant. This could have been part of the reason reading small text was difficult as the proportions of the letters were thrown off.

7 Future Work

The results presented here show some promise. Users were disoriented when the video display was switching between cameras too quickly. However, this test lasted only a few minutes. Our body may be able to adapt to handling visuals when they are presented in this method if given the time. Once the technology evolves to the point where basic tasks such as reading become possible, a longer term study should be completed to test the adaptability of this type of display.

8 Conclusion

This paper presented both a hardware and software implementation using a virtual reality headset to increase the peripheral vision for people with limited or no vision in one eye. A user study containing 11 adults (three with a visual impairment in one eye) compared three different methods of presenting visuals to one eye and found that the split screen method, where the images from the 2 cameras are scaled and placed side by side was preferred.

References

1. Genius, KYE Systems Corp. Genius (2015). http://www.geniusnet.com/genius/wsite/ct?xitem=53214ctnode=161
2. Goltz, H.C., Steinbach, M.J., Gallie, B.L.: Headturn in 1-eyed and normally sighted individuals during monocular viewing. Arch. Ophthalmol. 115(6), 748–750 (1997)
3. Henson, D.B.: Visual Fields. Butterworth-Heinemann Medical (2000)
4. Keeney, A., Garvey, J., Brunker, G.: Current experience with the monocular drivers of kentucky. In: Proceedings of the American Association for Automotive Medicine Annual Conference, vol. 25, pp. 215–221. Association for the Advancement of Automotive Medicine (1981)
5. Marotta, J., Perrot, T., Nicolle, D., Servos, P., Goodale, M.: Adapting to monocular vision: grasping with one eye. Exp. Brain Res. 104(1), 107–114 (1995)
6. Oculus VR. The all new oculus rift development kit 2(DK2) virtual reality headset-oculus rift – virtual reality headset for 3D gaming (2015). https://www.oculus.com/dk2/
7. Prevent Blindness. Low vision resources center; statevision screening and standards for license to drive (2015). http://lowvision.preventblindness.org/daily-living-2/state-vision-screening-and-standards-for-license-to-drive
8. Schein, O.D.: The measurement of patient-reported outcomes of refractive surgery: the refractive status and vision profile. Trans. Am. Ophthalmol. Soc. 98, 439 (2000)
9. Vision Source Member Support Center. Free eye chart- download, print, test jvision source (2015). http://www.visionsource.com/doctors/free-eye-chart-download/?it=patients/free-eye-chart-download/
10. Von Noorden, G.K., Campos, E.C.: Binocular Vision and Ocular Motility: Theory and Management of Strabismus, vol. 6. Mosby, St. Louis (1990)
11. Westlake, W.: Is a one eyed racing driver safe to compete? Formula one (eye) or two? Br. J. Ophthalmol. 85(5), 619–624 (2001)

3D Modeling of the Milreu Roman Heritage with UAVs

José Rodrigues[1(✉)], Mauro Figueiredo[1], João Bernardes[2], and César Gonçalves[1]

[1] University of Algarve – ISE, PT, Faro, Portugal
{jirodrig,mfiguei,cgoncal}@ualg.pt
[2] University of Algarve - CEAACP, PT, Faro, Portugal
jbernar@ualg.pt

Abstract. In this paper we present a methodology to build a 3D model of a roman heritage site in the South of Portugal, known as Milreu, covering a region of about one hectare. Today's Milreu ruins, a national heritage site, were once part of a 4rd century, luxurious villa-style manor house, which was subsequently converted into a thriving farm. Due to its relevance, it is important to make the 3D model of the Milreu ruins, to be available for the exploration in the Web and for virtual and augmented reality applications for mobile devices. This paper demonstrates the use of UAVs for the reconstruction of the 3D models of the ruins from vertical and oblique aerial photographs. To enhance the model quality and precision, terrestrial photographs were also incorporated in the workflow. This model is georeferenced, which give us the possibility to automatically determine accurate measurements of the Roman structures.

Keywords: 3D models · web3D · UAV · Digital photogrammetry · Cultural heritage

1 Introduction

Milreu ruins, located in Estoi, 7 Km from Faro (Fig. 1), were part of a larger complex that consisted of a villa, farm buildings, a Roman-style bath, a wine press, and a temple devoted to the aquatic deities. There are also signs that the Romans had a fairly evolved water supply-and-drainage system. One of the unique features of the manor house is the use of stones like marble and striking, patterned mosaics depicting marine life.

The creation of an archaeological virtual model is useful for different purposes such as preservation, reconstruction, as-built documentation and museum exhibitions [13] in which visitors can explore a 3D interactive and immersive environment, enhancing the exploration of the hidden history of Milreu. The three-dimensional virtual reconstruction of Milreu roman ruins, shows to the general public, in a more obvious way, the importance and the true scale that this archaeological site was for 1700 years ago.

© Springer International Publishing Switzerland 2016
M. Antona and C. Stephanidis (Eds.): UAHCI 2016, Part II, LNCS 9738, pp. 329–337, 2016.
DOI: 10.1007/978-3-319-40244-4_32

The 3D model in this work is the support to build a virtual model of the Roman villa to show the original buildings of this Roman site. The user can visualize the 3D virtual models in a Web browser or visit the Milreu site and explore, with a mobile device that shows the 3D models superimposed with the real word, using augmented reality.

The surveying of archaeological sites using drones has now become common due to its importance for preservation, reconstruction, as-built documentation and even museum exhibitions. The quality of processed measurements has reached a level of accuracy [10] sufficient to convince the cultural heritage community. Some applications has been made and are known in the bibliography such as presented by Rinaudo et al. [10] where the authors describe the process to generate the digital surface model (DSM) and orthophoto of a Roman villa archaeological site located in Aquileia (Italy), a well-known UNESCO WHL site. Identical approach was adopted by Seitz and Altenbach [16] but moreover than image mosaics, they also delivered a 3D model of in Germany and Cambodia. Fiorillo et al. [5] integrated photogrammetry and terrestrial laser scanning (TLS) acquisitions to produce digital 3D models, orthoimages, maps and other geometric representations useful for archaeological, architectural and communication needs. 3D reconstruction is often the preferred product to be delivered in archaeology and ancient building surveying.

In this work a detailed and reality-based 3D recording of the Milreu Roman ruins for documentation, conservation, preservation, restoration and visualization purposes were built from an imagery photo collection taken from a UAV. These models, accurate 3D data models and orthoimages, will be used to develop applications for: (i) interactive web3D navigations exploring the concept of gamification [1] and (ii) mobile devices superimposed with the real and virtual word, using virtual augmented reality.

The problems addressed in this paper are the reconstruction of the heritage site objects in the form of a realistically textured 3D model from areal and terrestrial images taken with uncalibrated cameras for the Web and mobile augmented reality platforms. The Sect. 2 presents the Milreu heritage site, Sect. 3 the UAV systems and image processing methods to produce 3D mesh models and point clouds. Section 4 is dedicated to show the results of the 3D modelling of the site and Sect. 5 the Web3d where the user can navigate the 3D model and the 3D point cloud in a browser. Finally, in Sect. 6 the results are discussed and the conclusions highlighted.

2   Milreu

The ruins of Milreu correspond to a Roman villa with a long period of occupation between the first and fifth centuries. It is one of the largest and best preserved Roman villas in the southwest of the peninsula, and is classified as a national monument since 1910, after the excavations of the 19th century carried out by the archaeologist Estácio da Veiga has revealed the archaeological importance of the site [15]. Since then, is a reference among the Portuguese archaeological

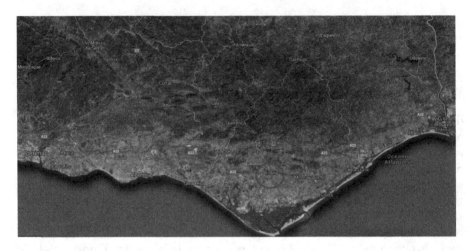

Fig. 1. Milreu ruins located in Estoi, 7 Km from Faro. (source: Google maps)

sites, and from the 70 s of last century has an extensive program of excavations coordinated Theodor Hauschild. It is then that is definitely placed in sight the residential part and richest of the villa, the pars urbana, which was acquired by the State and made visitable to the public. This part visitable today include the mosaics with marine motifs, the temple, the baths and the residential area organized around a peristyle and a atrium [7,11]. The pars rustica, i.e. the part corresponding to the agricultural dependencies, stables and accommodation for slaves organized around a courtyard, clearly visible in 19th-century plant raised by Estacio da Veiga (Fig. 2), remains today occupied by agricultural land.

The site of Milreu constitutes a remarkable example of continuity of occupation over 2000 years, which is not limited, as it turned out, the ruins of the different phases of the Roman period but also the human occupations of different times. It is thus understandable that it is not easy to musealization a site with these characteristics and that the interpretation and presentation to the public of all its ruins into a coherent discourse is a complex task, since often some structures are inserted, interrupt or overlap structures from various eras.

According to the 2014 activities report of the Regional Direction of Culture of the Algarve, more than 15,000 visitors annually visit Milreu, of which almost 80 % (78.6 %) are foreigners. Despite having a circuit with explanatory panels of different parts that make up the ruins, it is difficult for the ordinary visitor to imagine the different volumetric and understand the relationship between the various dependencies. Sometimes, due to the interleaving of structures from different eras or the disappearance of parts of them, it becomes impossible for a visitor to have a correct idea of what it would be like in Roman times the appearance of buildings belonging those ruins. The use of UAVs technologies, to rigorous survey of structures, and subsequent reconstructions of 3D models, can allow visitors the cabal understanding of how were those ruins or how was the evolution of the site over time. Indeed, and for the times when there are historical

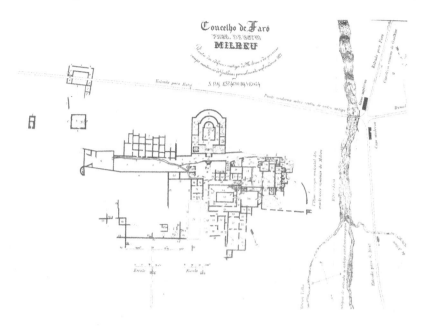

Fig. 2. 19th century plan of the Milreu Roman ruins [15].

and archaeological data, it is possible to reconstruct archaeological buildings or built sets, revealing that the ruins of a place like Milreu correspond, in fact, not one but several constructive realities that were happening and reflect our history of the last 2000 years.

This reconstruction from all the information available, in order to enable a better interpretation and reading of archaeological sites to visitors, is similar process to that of anastylosis, i.e. the re-composition of the dismembered parts of the historical monument, as already defined in The Athens Charter for the Restoration of Historic Monuments (October 1931). It is, however, a virtual anastylosis that, unlike the real one, can go further, to the total reconstruction of the building from unidentified elements but imagined, since the primary objective is to provide the visitor easy reading and closer to what the monument was (Fig. 3). And this, because the process is virtual, without ever compromising the identity and historical integrity of the object or reconstituted building.

3   UAVs

Unmanned aerial vehicles (UAV) or simply, drones are an emerging technology with autonomous navigation capability or remotely controlled, without human presence on the aircraft. Each vehicle includes several components including flight computer, sensors and actuators and payload such as cameras, thermal, multi- and hyper-spectral sensors or other equipment depending on the mission to accomplish.

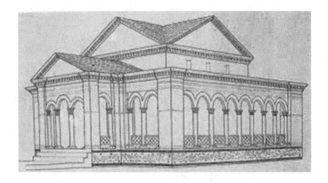

Fig. 3. Ancient Roman temple at Milreu [7].

The progressive miniaturisation capability made possible the production of high flexible mini- and micro-UAVs, equipped with navigation and autopilot systems that enable the independent execution of previously planned missions, assisted by a ground control station.

With these features, UAVs are good platforms for the acquisition of aerial images covering medium-sized areas, previously only accessible at higher costs and long planning cycles [6]. The versatility, the ease of operation, and the low costs of these small aircrafts enable its use in a large variety of applications such as agricultural and environmental applications, intelligence, surveillance, and reconnaissance, aerial monitoring in engineering, traditional surveying, conventional mapping and photogrammetry, and cultural heritage [3].

Traditional photogrammetric software requires a relatively intense human interaction, which is not suitable for processing large collections of photographs. To avoid such dependency, procedures such as structure from motion (SfM) [14] for automatic orientation of unordered image blocks obtained from UAV has been developed exploiting operators like SIFT [12] and SURF [2], which are invariant with respect to scale and rotations variations. Such methods are able to extract a set of manifold tie points to be used as observations in a photogrammetric bundle adjustment [4] to estimate camera parameters, whether or not the presence of GPS/INS (Global positioning system/Inertial navigation system) data. To select tie points these methods process pairs of overlapped and, since they consider all possible pairwise image combination in the block, $\frac{n(n-1)}{2}$ pairs of photos need to be processed. In this way complex image configurations and scenes can be dealt with, encompassing the use of convergent imagery, strong perspective deformations, lighting changes and so on.

Next step involves the dense reconstruction for generating point clouds from images and camera parameters and dense surface models for generating 3D mesh surfaces exploiting Multi-View Stereo techniques [17] combining computer vision and photogrammetry.

Usually, low-cost UAVs only carry sensors for position and orientation data (such as GPS and INS) with limited accuracy. Thus, for georeferencing the 3D meshes and point clouds accurately, the adopted techniques mainly rely upon ground control points (GCP), a well defined natural features or artificial marks surveyed with high precision.

4   3D Modelling of the Cultural Heritage Site

The adopted workflow to build the dense point cloud and the 3D mesh of the Milreu site starts with the planning of the flight and the selection of six well distributes GCPs in the area of the site.

The aerial photogrammetric survey to cover the site was realized by a DJI Phantom 3 Professional UAV system with an FC300X photo camera. FC300X is an RGB camera with 12 megapixels equipped with a f/2.8 lens, 94° of field of view and 3.61 mm of focal length. The stabilization of the camera is assured by a 3-axis gimbal mounted on the drone that also enables the system to take vertical and oblique photos.

The flights to collect photos had been done in October 2015, on a sunny day with some sparse clouds. The ruins were covered by a collection of 186 aerial near vertical photos with about 85 % strip overlap and of 65 % side overlap and pixel size of about 3.5 cm average. A second collection with 375 of very high oblique aerial photos around the ancient Roman temple was taken by the same UAV system. Finally, a third block of terrestrial photographs was taken with a Nikon D3000 SLR camera with an AF-S NIKKOR 18–55mm lens.

The three collected blocks of photos were processed by the SfM based software Agisoft/PhotoScan and Pix4D/Pix4Dmapper. These systems typically use GPS information for reconstruction initialization and apply an exhaustive matching approach for tie point extraction, which is needless for sequential imagery and computationally prohibitive for large image sequences due to its quadratic computational complexity. Both of the two software include in its workflows the ability to calculate the interior and exterior orientation parameters of each photo, produce dense point clouds, build a textured 3D mesh and produce georeferenced models using GCPs.

The Fig. 4 presents the textured point cloud obtained by the Agisoft/Photoscan with the aerial vertical and oblique photographs. The ruins of the ancient roman temple of Fig. 3 can be seen at the left upper side in the model.

Both software were able to produce georeferenced textured dense point clouds and dense meshes from blocks with aerial vertical and oblique photos and terrestrial photos. In general, the Agisoft/Photoscan workflow takes more time to complete the tasks than Pix4D/Pix4D Mapper but the global quality of the models compare favorable to Photoscan. Pix4D Mapper is more effective to produce results in less time, but it required the definition of manual tie points using features visible in vertical, oblique and terrestrial photographs.

Fig. 4. 3D model of the Milreu Roman - general perspective of the site

5   Web3D

As a consequence of advances in computer hardware and internet connection speed, Web3D sites that include three-dimensional models where users navigate and interact through a 3D graphical interface, are increasingly employed in different domains. The possibility to publish 3D data on the Web is of particular interest for enabling researchers and the general public to visualize, navigate and interact with three-dimensional data on a simple Web browser.

In this work, we propose a framework available at http://geomatics.no-ip.org/milreu that uses HTML5, WebGL, and SceneJS to enable users to visualize and navigate the 3D models of the Milreu site produced with sets of aerial and terrestrial photographs.

HTML5 is the new markup language version published on October 2014 by the World Wide Web Consortium (W3C) [8], used to structure content on the World Wide Web. With this new version, the web browsers have become platforms with advanced graphics technologies and Javascript language support. WebGL (Web Graphics Library) is a JavaScript API for rendering interactive 3D and 2D graphics within any compatible web browser that can be used in HTML5, without any plugins. Finally, SceneJS is an open-source WebGL-based 3D visualization engine from @xeoLabs [9] with plugins to import 3D models

Fig. 5. 3D model of the temple in a browser

from geometry definition file formats such as the Wavefront .obj file, which is an open and a universally accepted format adopted by other 3D graphics application vendors.

The Fig. 5 presents a 3D model of the actual state of the ruins of the ancient roman temple in the Milreu heritage site available for visualization and navigation in a browser.

6   Conclusions

In this work, a workflow to produce georeferenced textured dense point clouds and 3D mesh models of the Milreu cultural heritage site in Faro, Algarve (Portugal) was developed and applied. These models were obtained combining sets of aerial photos, vertical and obliques taken from a UAV system, and blocks of terrestrial photos. The integration of these three types of photos has enabled complete and accurate 3D models more than the ones obtained processing each set of photos independently.

A framework for 3D visualization of the Milreu heritage site was made available on the Web using HTML5, WebGL, and SceneJS. Such solution does not require any additional plugins. The availability of Milreu Roman heritage in a Web3D is interesting for the geospatial field. Researcher and the general public can navigate in this environment to visualize at different scales the whole site and its structures.

References

1. Baptista, E., Rodrigues, J., Figueiredo, M.: Culroute: Plataforma websig3d gamificada para seleção de roteiros turśsticos. Dos Algarves **26**(2), 5–22 (2015)
2. Bay, H., Ess, A., Tuytelaars, T., Gool, L.V.: Speeded-up robust features (surf). Comput. Vis. Image Underst. **110**(3), 346–359 (2008). Similarity Matching in Computer Vision and Multimedia
3. Colomina, I., Molina, P.: Unmanned aerial systems for photogrammetry and remote sensing: A review. ISPRS J. Photogrammetry Remote Sens. **92**, 79–97 (2014)
4. Engels, C., Stewénius, H., Nistér, D.: Bundle adjustment rules. In: Photogrammetric Computer Vision (PCV), September 2006
5. Fiorillo, F., Fernńndez-Palacios, B.J., Remondino, F., Barba, S.: 3d surveying and modelling of the archaeological area of paestum, italy. Virtual Archaeol. Rev. **4**(8), 55–60 (2013)
6. Gupta, S.G., Ghonge, M.M., Jawandhiya, P.M.: Review of unmanned aircraft system (UAS). Int. J. Adv. Res. Comput. Eng. Technol. (IJARCET) **2**(4), 1646–1659 (2013)
7. Hauschild, T., Teichner, F.: Milreu - ruínas. Roteiros da Arqueologia Portuguesa. Instituto Português de Museus (2002)
8. Hickson, I., Berjon, R., Faulkner, S., Leithead, T., Navara, E.D., O'Connor, E., Pfeiffer, S.: Html 5: W3c recommendation, october 28, 2014. Techniocal report, W3C, October 2014. http://www.w3.org/TR/2014/REC-html5-20141028/
9. Kay, L.: Scenejs tutorials. Technical report, xeoLabs (2016). http://xeolabs.com/articles/learning-scenejs/
10. Küng, O., Strecha, C., Beyeler, A., Jean-Christophe, F., D., Fua, P., Gervaix, F.: The Accuracy of Automatic Photogrammetric Techniques on Ultra-light UAV Imagery. In: UAV-g 2011 - Unmanned Aerial Vehicle in Geomatics (2011). http://www.pix4d.com/
11. Lancha, J., Oliveira, C.: Corpus dos mosaicos romanos de Portugal / Corpus des mosaïques romaines du Portugal: II, Conventus pacensis: 2, Algarve Este, vol. 2. Universidade do Algarve (2013)
12. Lowe, D.G.: Distinctive image features from scale-invariant keypoints. Int. J. Comput. Vision **60**(2), 91–110 (2004). http://dx.doi.org/10.1023/B: VISI.0000029664.99615.94
13. Remondino, F.: Heritage recording and 3d modeling with photogrammetry and 3d scanning. Remote Sens. **3**(6), 1104 (2011). http://www.mdpi.com/2072-4292/3/6/1104
14. Robertson, D.P., Cipolla, R.: Structure from Motion. Wiley, New York (2009)
15. Santos, M.: Arqueologia romana do Algarve, vol. II. Associação dos Arqueólogos Portugueses, Lisboa (1972)
16. Seitz, C., Altenbach, H.: Project archeye - the quadrocopter as the archaeologist's eye. In: ISPRS - International Archives of the Photogrammetry, Remote Sensing and Spatial Information Sciences XXXVIII-1/C22, 297–302: Conference on Unmanned Aerial Vehicle in Geomatics (UAV-g 2011). Zurich, Switzerland (2011)
17. Seitz, S.M., Curless, B., Diebel, J., Scharstein, D., Szeliski, R.: A comparison and evaluation of multi-view stereo reconstruction algorithms. In: 2006 IEEE Computer Society Conference on Computer Vision and Pattern Recognition, vol. 1, pp. 519–528, June 2006

Communicating Panoramic 360 Degree Immersed Experiences: A Simple Technique for Sketching in 3D

Frode Eika Sandnes[1,2(✉)]

[1] Oslo and Akershus University College of Applied Sciences, Oslo, Norway
Frode-Eika.Sandnes@hioa.no
[2] Westerdals Oslo School of Art, Communication and Technology,
Oslo, Norway

Abstract. Immersive three-dimensional environments can give test users a valuable first-person experience of design ideas. Trained designers can quickly create mock-ups using three-dimensional modelling software, but this task is very hard and time-consuming for individuals without three-dimensional modelling experience. This paper presents a simple sketching strategy that allows simple two-dimensional panoramic sketches to be rendered in pseudo-three-dimensions using panoramic viewers. This allows designers without three-dimensional modelling experience to represent their design ideas that can be explored from single points in space. The paper explores the properties of the projections, and illustrates how to represent spatial shapes.

Keywords: Sketching · 3D · Panorama

1 Introduction

Sketching is often associated with the design phase where the sketches represent ideas [1]. Sketching is usually performed before prototyping and user testing. The concept of a sketch is not limited to any particular representation or physical-visual genre, but in practice, it is usually associated with two-dimensional hand-drawn representations of graphical user interfaces [2]. Hand-drawn sketches look very unlike finished products and therefore do not give involved users and customers false expectations that a product is finished. From the developers' perspective, the sketch should be quick to render allowing "bad" ideas to be discarded quickly.

The value of sketching in two- or three-dimensions for conceptual design has been explored and documented [3]. Sketches of three-dimensional experiences can be used for the design of products that are to be used in the wild, such as mobile apps, wearable computing technologies, or ubiquitous and pervasive technologies embedded in the physical environment such as buildings and structures. There are several ways to make sketches to communicate such ideas. Simple three-dimensional static snapshot of the environment are quick to draw and indeed look like drawings. To make non-static sketches of an environment, that can facilitate immersed experiences, designers often rely on three dimensional design software where the environment is modelled

© Springer International Publishing Switzerland 2016
M. Antona and C. Stephanidis (Eds.): UAHCI 2016, Part II, LNCS 9738, pp. 338–346, 2016.
DOI: 10.1007/978-3-319-40244-4_33

mathematically. Such models allow users to view the environment from any angle, for instance using virtual reality technology. Another approach is to place sketched in a real physical environment and thus achieve a very realistic experience while at the same time communicating that the product is not finished.

This paper presents a novel approach to sketching three-dimensional immersed experiences while maintaining the impulsiveness and organic feeling of the pen-stroke [2]. Sketches are made by making panoramic, even hand-drawn, sketches in the equirectangular projected plane which is quite different from classic panoramic drawings and paintings. These sketches are later viewed using panoramic viewing software [4]. The idea of panoramic viewing has successfully been applied in Google street view [5] and other domain such as the communication of heritage and history [6]. This paper illustrates practical techniques for how to represent various spatial shapes directly in the equirectangular plane to achieve the desired effects. In particular, the representation of common spatial shapes and distance is discussed in detail. The sketches are displayed using the FSPViewer [7].

Fig. 1. An equirectangular panorama (top), from PanoTools wiki, GNU free documentation license 1.2. and two panoramic renderings using FSPviewer (bottom).

The ability to make quick and cheap three-dimensional sketches that gives the viewer an immersed experience of the end result opens up for new ways of working. For instance, in universal design there are techniques for involving users when designing in the physical domain and different techniques for working in the virtual domain. Architects and construction engineers typically work in the physical domain and computer scientists in the virtual domain. There bridging of the virtual and physical domain is less explored. The proposed sketching technique may be used to involve users earlier and more closely in the design process and perhaps the technique may even facilitate participatory design [8].

2   Sketching Method

The sketching method outlined herein relies on standard panoramic rendering software that will render equirectangular panoramic images at various viewing angles in real time. For example, Fig. 1 shows a heritage building with a spherical dome. This is a relatively complex environment. One characteristic that can be observed from the equirectangular panorama is that horizontal lines are relatively straight towards the vertical centre of the image and such lines become more curved as one gets further away from the horizontal midline. This is especially visible by observing the floor mosaic and the railings. However, the vertical lines are relatively straight throughout, for example, the vertical sides of the window and the squares on the wall. Another important characteristic is that the left side of the panoramic image ends where the right part begins, or vice versa. This allows the panorama to be viewed seamlessly from any angle.

Such panoramic images are typically captured using special camera equipment or special image stitching software that transform a set of regular images into equirectangular panoramas. The rest of this paper explores how to sketch in the equirectangular domain. The objective is not to achieve complete mathematically correct projections, but panoramas that give a sufficient experience of the spatial environment.

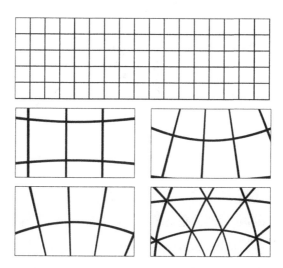

Fig. 2. Regular grid used as an equirectangular panorama and renderings of this panorama looking straight, up and down (sphere). Bottom left: rendering of a regular grid of triangles (dome).

The images in this paper are rendered using the FSPviewer, but most other panoramic renderers can be used. Note that these are still images. The interactive viewing experience of moving the view around with the cursor cannot be captured on paper in a fair manner. The interactive property of the panoramic viewers is the key advantage of the outlined method.

3 Sketching with Equidistance

An inspection of panoramic images published on various web-sites reveal that their aspect ratios vary from approximately 6:1 to 4:1, that is, the images are from four to six time as wide as they are tall. Equirectangular projections are also known as direct polar and spherical projection. Therefore, to represent all possible angles 360 degrees in the horizontal direction and 180 degrees in the vertical direction gives an aspect ratio of 360:180 or 2:1. This is analogous to latitude and longitude [9–11]. Equirectangular world maps therefore often have an aspect ratio of 2:1.

Figure 2 illustrates how a regular grid used as an equirectangular panorama is rendered. The viewing experience gives a perception of a sphere. This is because all the cross points are regularly spaced and becomes rendered as having the same distance to the viewer (equidistance).

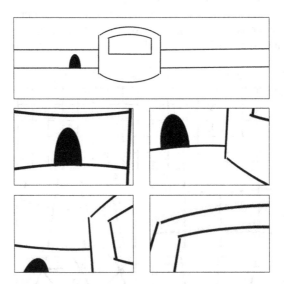

Fig. 3. A panoramic sketch of a circular hall with an entrance and a vending machine and four renderings of the panorama.

Figure 3 illustrates how the regular distance can be used to create the perception of a circular hall. Two horizontal lines are used to represent the walls of the hall. When rendered these lines become curved as one would see an actual circular hall. The vending machine in the middle has a straight horizontal line at the bottom of the screen and a curved line on the top of the screen. The straight line is located at the vertical centre of the view while the other horizontal lines are further away from the vertical centre. The horizontal lines at the top and bottom of the machine are even more curved. The renderings of the panorama shows that the curved lines on the vending machine are perhaps too curved.

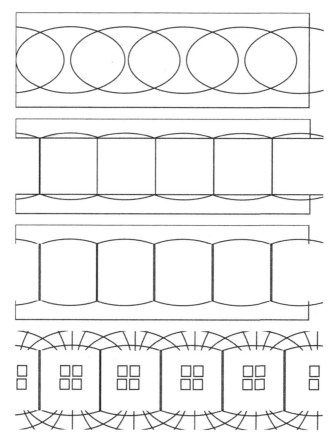

Fig. 4. Constructing a room in equirectangular space: (a) drawing overlapping ellipses, (b) adding straight vertical lines, (c) removing construction lines and (d) Adding windows and floor tiles.

4   Sketching Flat Faces

The sketching of flat planes is explored further in Figs. 4 and 5, which illustrates how to construct a pentagonal room. First, six overlapping ellipses are drawn to establish the horizontal lines of the walls of the room. The sixth ellipse is used to ensure that the left and right sides of the image overlaps smoothly allowing the image to be viewed completely around 360 degrees. Next, the straight vertical lines are drawn. Then, the construction lines are removed and finally windows and floor and ceiling tiles are added. The windows are drawn using regular squares since these are close to the horizontal midline of the panorama, while the lines indicating the floor tiles are further extensions of the ellipses. Hence, these lines become even more curved.

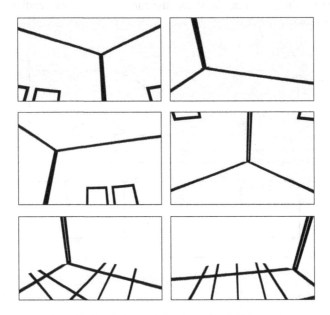

Fig. 5. Renderings of the panorama in Fig. 4(d)

Figure 5 shows several renderings of the result. As can be seen the lines that were curved has become straight, while the top of the window, which was straight, has become slightly curved.

Figure 6 shows how the technique of making curved horizontal lines is applied to the circular hall in Fig. 3 by making the room square. The four walls are thus

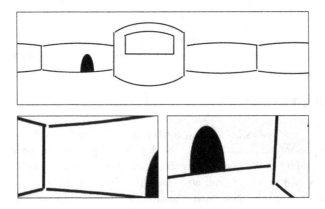

Fig. 6. Making the circular hall in Fig. 3 square

highlighted by adding the four vertical corner lines. Next, the top and bottom horizontal lines for each of the four walls are traced along the edge of an ellipse. Figure 7 shows this technique applied to an example where also colours are used. Note that the bottom three renderings are achieved with a 138 degrees field of view and the others are rendered with a 70 degrees field of view.

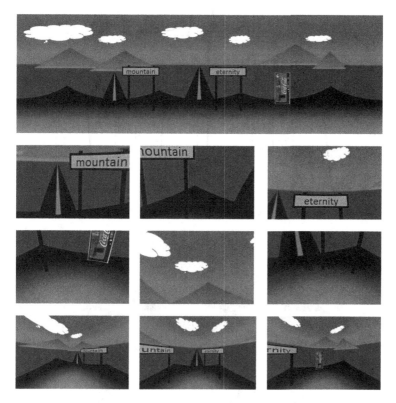

Fig. 7. A colour sketch with two signs and a coke vending machine

5   Diagonal Lines and Faces

Figure 8 illustrates how to sketch diagonal faces using diagonal lines. As shown by the panorama, the diagonal lines of the faces are straight. The resulting renderings show that the straight-line approximations give sufficient perception of straight lines although the rendered lines are actually curved. Figure 9 shows this technique applied in colour.

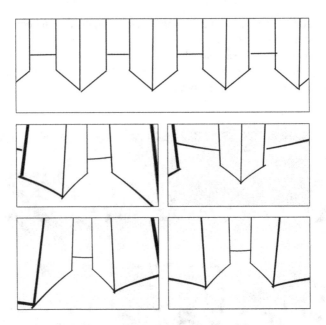

Fig. 8. Sketching diagonal lines and faces

Fig. 9. Sketching diagonal lines and faces in colour. (Color figure online)

6   Conclusions

A method for making interactive three-dimensional immersive sketches using off-the-shelves panorama viewing software was presented. The sketches are simple to make and can even be drawn by hand. Techniques for representing various spatial shapes have been presented using several examples. The technique can for instance be used to represent ideas about how virtual computer technology can be placed in the physical built environment. The technique can also be used to sketch and represent ideas and concepts for three-dimensional games. It may be valuable to study equirectangular panoramic images to develop ones' sketching technique.

References

1. Buxton, B.: Sketching User Experiences: Getting the Design Right and the Right Design: Getting the Design Right and the Right Design. Morgan Kaufmann, San Francisco (2010)
2. Sandnes, F.E., Jian, H.L.: Sketching with Chinese calligraphy. Interactions **19**, 62–66 (2012)
3. Israel, J.H., et al.: Investigating three-dimensional sketching for early conceptual design— Results from expert discussions and user studies. Comput. Graph. **33**, 462–473 (2009)
4. Dersch, H.: Interactive Java Viewer for HDR-panoramas (2003). http://citeseerx.ist.psu.edu/viewdoc/download?doi=10.1.1.122.5007&rep=rep1&type=pdf. Accessed 19 Nov 2015
5. Anguelov, D., et al.: Google street view: capturing the world at street level. Computer **6**, 32–38 (2010)
6. Kwiatek, K., Woolner. M.: Transporting the viewer into a 360 heritage story: panoramic interactive narrative presented on a wrap-around screen. In: 2010 16th International Conference on Virtual Systems and Multimedia. IEEE (2010)
7. Senore, F.: FSPViewer. http://www.fsoft.it/FSPViewer/. Accessed 20 Nov 2015
8. Muller, M.J., Kuhn, S.: Participatory design. Commun. ACM **36**, 24–28 (1993)
9. Sandnes, F.E.: Where was that photo taken? Deriving geographical information from image collections based on temporal exposure attributes. Multimedia Syst. **16**, 309–318 (2010)
10. Sandnes, F.E.: Determining the geographical location of image scenes based on object shadow lengths. J. Sign. Process. Syst. **65**, 35–47 (2011)
11. Gómez, J.V., Sandnes, F.S., Fernández, V.: Sunlight intensity based global positioning system for near-surface underwater sensors. Sensors **12**, 1930–1949 (2012)

Relationship Between Feeling of Presence and Visually Induced Motion Sickness While Viewing Stereoscopic Movies

Akihiro Sugiura[1,2(✉)], Takehito Kojima[2], Hiroki Takada[3],
Kunihiko Tanaka[1], and Masaru Miyao[2]

[1] Department of Radiology, Gifu University of Medical Science, Seki, Japan
{asugiura,ktanaka}@u-gifu-ms.ac.jp
[2] Graduate School of Information Science, Nagoya University, Nagoya, Japan
tkojima45@gmail.com, mmiyao@is.nagoya-u.ac.jp
[3] Graduate School of Engineering, University of Fukui, Fukui, Japan
takada@u-fukui.ac.jp

Abstract. Visually evoked postural responses (VEPRs) are postural changes induced by visual information. We focused on the change in VEPRs that better represents a feeling of presence or symptom of visually induced motion sickness (VIMS). We investigated the effect of stereoscopic vision on the change in the degree of feeling and VEPRs by simultaneous measurement of both feeling of presence, VIMS symptom, and body sway when viewing a movie showing a roundtrip sinusoidal motion. For the feeling of presence, significantly positive correlations between the body-sway indexes and visual analog scale value of the presence were observed. However, when the subject watched a two-dimensional movie, the correlations between the subjective and objective evaluation decreased. In contrast, no significantly positive/negative correlation between the body-sway indexes and the simulator sickness questionnaire scores was found. Therefore, performing objective assessments of the degree of subjective symptoms induced by VIMS by measuring body sway is difficult.

Keywords: Presence · Visually induced motion sickness · Visually Evoked Postural Response (VEPR) · Stereoscopic movie · Body sway

1 Introduction

Recent advances in audiovisual and virtual environment (VE) technologies have been employed to create high-accuracy virtual scenes. One of the aims of the VE technology is to provide a feeling of presence, defined as a feeling of "being there" [1].

VE technology is mainly based on the control of information input to a sensory organ. The control of visual input is most often used in VE technology because majority of information in daily life is visually obtained [2], and visual information affects human activity the most. Edwards reported that visual information has the most significant effects on human posture control and constitutes more than 50 % of all inputs [3]. Postural responses induced by visual information, such as motions or gradients, are called visually evoked postural responses (VEPRs) [4].

© Springer International Publishing Switzerland 2016
M. Antona and C. Stephanidis (Eds.): UAHCI 2016, Part II, LNCS 9738, pp. 347–355, 2016.
DOI: 10.1007/978-3-319-40244-4_34

VEPRs that are attributed to both video contents and visual environments occur when subjects are in VEs, which mainly consist of videos [5–7]. Ohmi et al. [8] and Freeman [9] proposed that objective evaluations of the feeling of presence can involve VEPRs measurements. In addition, they reported that subjective and objective VEPR assessments exhibit the same trends in various viewing conditions.

Viewing movies in VEs favorably affects the presence, but it can also cause complex symptoms that are similar to motion sickness as a collateral effect, which are generally called visually induced motion sickness (VIMS) or cyber sickness. Stanney showed that 88 % of VE participants developed VIMS when viewing virtual reality movies for 1 h [10]. VIMS is generally explained by the sensory conflict theory that suggests the presence of conflicts among the visual system, labyrinthus vestibularis, and the experience of a subject [11, 12]. However, the detailed mechanisms underlying the occurrence of VIMS are unclear. Similar to the assessments of the feeling of presence, both subjective and objective evaluations of VIMS have been proposed. One of the representative subjective assessments is the simulator sickness questionnaire (SSQ) [13]. For the objective assessments of VIMS, changes in the autonomic nerve activity are detected by measuring physiological factors such as sudation, blood pressure, and respiration. On the other hand, Smart et al. [14] and Villard et al. [15] reported that measurements of body sway while subjects are viewing a movie can detect VIMS.

We develop an interest in VEPRs when a human watches a global motion movie. In particular, we have investigated the change in VEPRs to better represent the feeling of presence or symptom of VIMS. In our previous study, we verified the degree of feeling, which is represented by VEPRs, by simultaneous measurement of both the feeling of presence, symptom of VIMS, and body sway by changing the viewing distance (viewing angle) [16]. Hence, we investigated the effect of stereoscopic viewing on the change in the degree of feeling and VEPRs using the same measurement procedure.

2   Materials and Methods

2.1   Stimulus and Apparatus

The visual stimulus that we employed consisted of a movie created by 3ds Max 2015 computer graphics software (Autodesk, Inc., San Rafael, CA, USA). A screenshot of the movie used in this study is shown in Fig. 1. The basic construction of the movie consisted of a large number of balls shown at random positions and a green cross shown at the center position as the reference point.

The motion in the movies was sinusoidal at 0.25 Hz in the depth direction (Z-direction) and was generated by moving camera-simulated ocular globes (the balls themselves did not move). The amplitude of the sinusoidal motion was set to 150 as the software setting.

To present the movie, it was projected onto a transmissive screen 200 cm in front of a standing subject using a domestic three-dimensional (3D) projector (EH-TW5100, Seiko Epson Corporation, Suwa, Japan). The maximum dive and maximum pull distances from the ocular globes in the 3D movies were 85 cm (parallactic angle, 2.5°) and 296 cm (parallactic angle, 1.8°), respectively, when the viewing distance was

200 cm. The subjects watched both the experimental 3D and two-dimensional (2D) movies, and 3D glasses (ELPGS03, Seiko Epson Crporation, Suwa, Japan) were used during the 3D movie viewing. To enable objective evaluation of the body sway, the subject stood on a Wii Balance Board (Nintendo Co., Ltd., Kyoto, Japan) adopting a Romberg's posture. To continuously measure the position of the center of pressure (COP), the FitTri ver. 1.1c self-build stabilometry software for the Wii Balance Board, which was created by Yoshimura, was used.

Fig. 1. Screenshot of the movie used in this study. A large number of balls were located at random positions, and the green cross was located at the center position as a point of reference in the movie space. The motion in the movies was sinusoidal at 0.25 Hz in the depth direction.

2.2   Procedure and Design

Eleven paid volunteers [five males and six females, age range: 20–22 years; motion sickness susceptibility questionnaire-short (MSSQ-short [17]) adult score: 7.20 (average) $\pm$ 5.83 (S.D.); total score: 16.3 (average) $\pm$ 12.2 (S.D.)] were employed in the experiment. They have no vision or equilibrium problem. Through the MSSQ-short accomplished by the subjects before examination, we confirmed that the distribution of participants did not have a sensitivity bias attributed to sensory conflict. The study was approved by the Research Ethics Committee of Nagoya University. Written consent was obtained from the participants after the purpose and significance of the study and the nature and risk of the measurements were explained both orally and in writing. In addition, the study was conducted in line with the 1964 Declaration of Helsinki and its later amendments or comparable ethical standards.

We performed the measurements in a controlled environment (illuminance: 5.9 lx, screen brightness 131.6 cd/m^2). The protocol followed is shown in Fig. 2. First, a subject watched a static (nonmoving) movie for 60 s as a pretest. Next, the subject watched a sinusoidally motion movie for 180 s. Finally, the initial static movie was shown again for 60 s. By treating this 240-task (except for the pretest) as one trial, two trials (3D and 2D movie viewing) were performed in a random sequence to avoid order effect. In the duration of the trials, body sway was continuously recorded. The trial interval was set to more than 5 min. Each subject watched all test movies in a day.

For the subjective measurements, the feeling of presence and VIMS symptoms were measured. The assessment of the presence in this study used words that precisely represented the presence because presence is a relatively unfamiliar construct to most nonexperts [18]. We expected that the viewing of the global motion movie would provide the viewer with the illusion of self-motion. Considering that presence is also a sensation caused by the motion characteristics in the movie, the degree of sensation of self-motion can serve as an assessment of the presence, which was limited to the viewing of the motion movie. Thus, in this study, the subjects orally reported their feeling of body sway every 30 s using a visual analog scale (VAS) that ranged from 0 to 100 after the sensory scale was explained (0: quiet stance to 100: rollover).

Next, for the VIMS symptom assessment, the subjects completed the SSQ, which has been used in a number of previous studies, before and after each motion movie viewing.

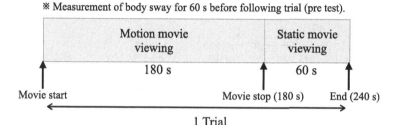

Fig. 2. Study protocol. A subject watched a static (nonmoving) movie for 60 s as a pretest. Next, the subject watched a sinusoidal moving movie for 180 s and then a static (nonmoving) movie for 60 s. By treating this 240-s task (except for the pretest) as one trial, two trials (2D and 3D movie viewing) were performed in a random sequence.

2.3   Analysis

The COP measurements were sampled at 100 Hz using the basic setting of the Wii Balance Board. In addition, a clinical test of the body sway was performed using a stabilometer at 20 Hz. The COP data were downsampled at 20 Hz and low-pass filtered at 10 Hz to adapt to the clinical standard.

The continuous COP data were separated by intervals of 60 s of viewing time to analyze each time segment. We reported the position of the COP moves in synchrony with the phase of the motion movie when the subjects watched movies with low-frequency global motion [19]. Thus, to evaluate the synchronization accuracy of the movie viewing, each separate data unit underwent a frequency analysis using a fast Fourier transform with a Hamming window. Moreover, the total locus length (TLL), area and the standard deviation of the COP data for the motion direction of the movie (SDz), which are general indexes of the body sway, in each separate data unit were calculated. Then, to examine the relationships of each of the body-sway indexes and the VAS value of the presence, the Pearson product–moment correlation coefficients were calculated for all time segment results.

For the SSQ, the total score and three subscores (oculomotor discomfort, disorientation, and nausea) under each condition were calculated (see [13] for the SSQ calculation methods). Then, the Pearson product–moment correlation coefficients were similarly calculated.

3   Result

The temporal changes in the indexes of the body sway and the VAS value of the feeling of presence while viewing each movie were analyzed, as shown in Fig. 3. The VAS value and all body-sway indexes showed similar results, and the VAS value and the amplitude component at 0.25 Hz (Amp. at 0.25 Hz) obtained from the frequency analysis also exhibited similar results. First, the increases in the motion movie viewing time increased all body-sway indexes, including the amplitude component obtained at 0.25 Hz from the frequency analysis and the VAS value. Second, when the motion movie viewing was stopped, all the index values decreased. Third, these tendencies increased when viewing the 3D movie compared with that when viewing the 2D movie.

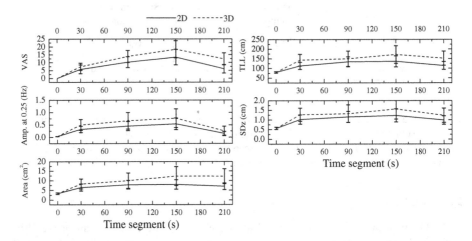

Fig. 3. Temporal changes in the body-sway indexes and the subjective measurements that configured the VAS of the presence. The solid line in each graph represents the average value, and the error bars represent the standard error.

Table 1(a) and (b) list the correlation coefficients between the body-sway indexes and the VAS value of the presence, including all time segment results. All body-sway indexes were strong and were significantly positively correlated ($0.76 > r > 0.98$, $P < 0.01$). In addition, difference in the correlations was not found in the viewing of the movie type. However, the relationship between the VAS value and the body-sway indexes differed from the relationships between each body-sway index. For the 3D movie viewing, the relationships between the VAS value and the body-sway indexes were significantly and positively correlated. On the other hand, for the 2D movie viewing, the correlation coefficient between the VAS value and the body-sway indexes show weak and positive correlations compared with that when viewing the 3D movie.

For the correlations between the subjective evaluation of VIMS (difference between the SSQ scores after and before viewing) and the objective evaluation (difference

Table 1. Pearson product–moment correlation coefficients of the relationship between the body-sway indexes and the VAS value of the presence. (a) 3D movie viewing. (b) 2D movie viewing

(a)

3D (Total)

Item	VAS	Amp. at 0.25 Hz	Area	TLL
VAS		0.65**	0.61**	0.66**
Amp. at 0.25Hz	0.65**		0.81**	0.89**
Area	0.61**	0.81**		0.93**
TLL	0.66**	0.89**	0.93**	
SDz	0.67**	0.9**	0.93**	0.98**

**: $P < 0.01$ $n=11$

(b)

2D (Total)

Item	VAS	Amp. at 0.25 Hz	Area	TLL
VAS		0.43**	0.45**	0.44**
Amp. at 0.25Hz	0.43**		0.76**	0.9**
Area	0.45**	0.76**		0.84**
TLL	0.44**	0.9**	0.84**	
SDz	0.45**	0.9**	0.92**	0.94**

**: $P < 0.01$ $n=11$

VAS: Visual analog scale, Amp. at 0.25 Hz: Amplitude at 0.25 Hz, TLL: Total locus length,
SDz: Standard deviation at Z-direction

between the body-sway index value calculated in the 120- to 180-s time segment to that in the pretest), no significant correlation was found under each viewing condition listed in Table 2.

Table 2. Pearson product–moment correlation coefficients of the relationships between the difference in the postscore and prescore SSQ scores and the difference in the body-sway index values between the 120- and 180-s time segment and that in the pretest.

Movie	SSQ category	Item ((180 s - 120 s) time segment - Pre test)			
		Amp. at 0.25Hz	Area	TLL	SDz
3D	Total (Main)	-0.07	0.08	0.07	0.02
	OD (Sub)	-0.15	0.05	-0.01	-0.05
	N (Sub)	0.33	0.43	0.43	0.4
	D (Sub)	-0.36	-0.17	-0.23	-0.3
2D	Total (Main)	0.13	0.35	0.06	0.15
	OD (Sub)	-0.03	0.3	-0.07	-0.01
	N (Sub)	0.18	0.19	0.15	0.21
	D (Sub)	0.17	0.31	0.05	0.15

$n = 11$

OD: Oculomotor Discomfort (Sub score), N: Nausea (Sub score), D: Disorientation (Sub score)
Amp. at 0.25 Hz: Amplitude at 0.25 Hz, TLL: Total locus length,
SDz: Standard deviation at Z-direction

4   General Discussion

With regard to the body-sway index during the motion movie viewing, the area, TLL, standard deviation of the movie motion direction (indexes of instability), and amplitude component at 0.25 Hz (calculated with the frequency analysis as an index of synchronization acuity to the phase of the motion of the movie) were calculated. The results of this study agreed with those of our previous study [19] in which the subjects watched sinusoidal reciprocating motion movies at 0.3 Hz. Both studies reported the same trends: the instability (increased index values) increased with the increases in the viewing time, and the stability (decreased index value) increased when the motion in the movie stopped Moreover, the instability while viewing the 3D movie was higher than that while viewing the 2D movie.

The relationships of the VAS value of the presence and the body-sway indexes indicated different correlation coefficients depending on the movie types. When the 3D motion movie was viewed, this relationship was significantly and positively correlated ($0.61 < r < 0.67$; $P < 0.01$). In contrast, the correlation coefficients during the 2D movie viewing were consistently lower than that while viewing the 3D movie ($0.43 < r < 0.45$; $P < 0.01$). Ideally, it is preferable that all the correlation coefficients are the same regardless of the movie types. However, the results of this study showed that the correlations between the subjective and objective evaluations were reduced under conditions of low instability for the body sway and low synchronization accuracy. This trend were also observed in our previous study [16].

With regard to the symptoms attributed to VIMS during the movie viewing, the subjects evaluated VIMS through the SSQ, and the body sway was measured as an objective assessment. SSQ is currently considered as the gold standard for the subjective evaluation of VIMS. For instance, Solimini [20] and Naqvi et al. [21] investigated the effects of stereoscopic viewing on VIMS using the SSQ.

For the correlations between the subjective evaluation of VIMS (difference between the SSQ score after and before viewing the movie) and the objective evaluation (difference between the body-sway index value calculated in the 120- to 180-s time segment and that in the pretest), no significant correlation was found in both 3D and 2D movie viewing (Table 2). The results in this study suggested that the relationships between each SSQ score and the body-sway index were small. Therefore, the relationships between the degree of symptoms induced by VIMS and the body-sway indexes were also small. These results were similar to our previous study results [16]. We have reported that VEPR is a response to correct the conflict conditions between the visual and equilibrium senses [22]. Moreover, we also reported that humans who are prone to motion sickness based on the sensory conflict theory are prone to body sway [22]. Thus, these findings suggested that we can only treat the occurrence of VEPRs as an indicator of the occurrence of VIMS. However, the VEPRs cannot directly represent the degree of subjective symptoms because the VEPRs are simply a conflict correction response.

5 Conclusion

We have verified the degree of feeling, which is represented by VEPRs, by simultaneous measurement of both feeling of presence, symptom of VIMS, and body sway while viewing 3D and 2D movies. The following results were demonstrated:

1. Significantly positive correlations between the body-sway indexes and the VAS value of the presence were recognized. However, when the subject watched the 2D movie, the correlations between the subjective and objective evaluation decreased.
2. No significantly positive/negative correlation between the body-sway indexes and the SSQ scores was found. Therefore, performing objective assessments of the degree of subjective symptoms induced by VIMS by measuring the body sway was difficult.

References

1. Philippe, F., Moreau, G., Pascal, G., Fuchs, P., Guitton, P., Moreau, G.: Virtual Reality: Concepts and Technologies. CRC Press, Boca Raton (2011)
2. Thau, A.P.: Vision and literacy. J. Read. **35**, 196–199 (1991)
3. Edwards, A.S.: Body sway and vision. J. Exp. Psychol. **36**, 526–535 (1946)
4. Bronstein, A.M.: Suppression of visually evoked postural responses. Exp. Brain Res. **63**, 655–658 (1986)
5. Bronstein, A.M., Buckwell, D.: Automatic control of postural sway by visual motion parallax. Exp. Brain Res. **113**, 243–248 (1997)
6. Meyer, G.F., Shao, F., White, M.D., Hopkins, C., Robotham, A.J.: Modulation of visually evoked postural responses by contextual visual, haptic and auditory information: a "virtual reality check". PLoS ONE **8**, e67651 (2013)
7. Nishiike, S., Okazaki, S., Watanabe, H., Akizuki, H., Imai, T., Uno, A., Kitahara, T., Horii, A., Takeda, N., Inohara, H.: The effect of visual-vestibulosomatosensory conflict induced by virtual reality on postural stability in humans. J. Med. Invest. **60**, 236–239 (2013)
8. Ohmi, M.: Sensation of self-motion induced by real-world stimuli. In: Proceedings of the International Workshop on Advances in Research on Visual Cognition: Selection and Integration of Visual Information, pp. 175–181 (1998)
9. Freeman, J., Avons, S.E., Meddis, R., Pearson, D.E., IJsselsteijn, W.: Using behavioral realism to estimate presence: a study of the utility of postural responses to motion stimuli. Presence Teleoperators Virtual Environ. **9**, 149–164 (2000)
10. Stanney, K.M., Kingdon, K.S., Kennedy, R.S.: Dropouts and aftereffects: examining general accessibility to virtual environment technology. Proc. Hum. Factors Ergon. Soc. Annu. Meet. **46**, 2114–2118 (2002)
11. Oman, C.M.: Motion sickness: a synthesis and evaluation of the sensory conflict theory. Can. J. Physiol. Pharmacol. **68**, 294–303 (1990)
12. Reason, J.T.: Motion sickness adaptation: a neural mismatch model. J. R. Soc. Med. **71**, 819–829 (1978)
13. Kennedy, R.S., Lane, N.E., Berbaum, K.S., Lilienthal, M.G.: Simulator sickness questionnaire: an enhanced method for quantifying simulator sickness. Int. J. Aviat. Psychol. **3**, 203–220 (1993)

14. Smart, L.J., Stoffregen, T.A., Bardy, B.G.: Visually induced motion sickness predicted by postural instability. Hum. Factors **44**, 451–465 (2002)
15. Villard, S.J., Flanagan, M.B., Albanese, G.M., Stoffregen, T.A.: Postural instability and motion sickness in a virtual moving room. Hum. Factors **50**, 332–345 (2008)
16. Sugiura, A., Ota, S., Shimura, M., Itou, Y., Takada, H., Tanaka, K.: Interpretation of visually evoked posture responses: representative of presence or visually induced motion sickness? Bull. Soc. Med. **33**, 35–47 (2016)
17. Golding, J.F.: Predicting Individual Differences in Motion Sickness Susceptibility by Questionnaire. Pers. Individ. Dif. **41**, 237–248 (2006)
18. Freeman, J., Avons, S.E.: Focus group Exploration of presence through advanced broadcast services. In: Proceedings of the SPIE, Human Vision and Electronic Imaging V, pp. 530–539 (2000)
19. Sugiura, A., Tanaka, K., Takada, H., Kojima, T., Yamakawa, T., Miyao, M.: A temporal analysis of body sway caused by self-motion during stereoscopic viewing. In: Antona, M., Stephanidis, C. (eds.) UAHCI 2015. LNCS, vol. 9176, pp. 246–254. Springer, Heidelberg (2015)
20. Solimini, A.G.: Are there side effects to watching 3D movies? A prospective crossover observational study on visually induced motion sickness. PLoS ONE **8**, e56160 (2013)
21. Naqvi, S.A.A., Badruddin, N., Malik, A.S., Hazabbah, W., Abdullah, B.: Does 3D produce more symptoms of visually induced motion sickness? In: Conference Proceedings of the IEEE Engineering in Medicine and Biology Society, pp. 6405–6408 (2013)
22. Sugiura, A., Tanaka, K., Wakatabe, S., Matsumoto, C., Miyao, M.: Temporal analysis of body sway during reciprocator motion movie viewing. Nihon Eiseigaku Zasshi **71**, 19–29 (2016)

Intelligent and Assistive Environments

A Universal Design Method for Adaptive Smart Home Environment

Silvia Ceccacci[(✉)], Lorenzo Cavalieri, Francesca Gullà,
Roberto Menghi, and Michele Germani

Department of Industrial Engineering and Mathematical Sciences,
Università Politecnica delle Marche, Via Brecce Bianche, 12,
60131 Ancona, Italy
{s.ceccacci,Lorenzo.cavalieri,f.gulla,
r.menghi,m.germani}@univpm.it

Abstract. Nowadays to design a product able to adapt to end-users with different needs and abilities it is necessary to manage a multitude of information coming from the analysis of different context of use. This means that we have to handle parallel and interdependent UCD multiple process. This research aims to define a methodology, which may apply this philosophy into design practice. In particular, it aims to provide tools to summarize the information needed to analyze user characteristics and needs, allows the designer to extrapolate the user's needs and support the selection of prototype technologies suitable to the user categories.

Keywords: Universal design · User centered design

1 Introduction

Universal Design (UD) addressed in this document is defined as "The design of products and environments to be usable by everyone, to the greatest extent possible, without the need for adaptation or special design" [1].

Its application requires conscious effort and awareness to consider the widest possible range of end-user requirements throughout the development cycle of a product or a service. The result of a UD design process should not be considered as a single project, but as a design space populated with appropriate alternatives to the specific characteristics of each user and context of use. In order to make the product easy to use, the adaptive features approach, based on ad hoc manner knowledge, is necessarily needed. A primary aspect of researching and developing adaptive system is to try and understand the behavior of those using the system itself. Being able to comprehend varies types of behavior gives us the basis to form strategies to adequately, effectively, and even adaptively aid user of the system [2].

Nowadays to design a product able to adapt to end-users needs and abilities it is necessary to manage a multitude of information coming from different context of use's analysis. This means that we have to handle parallel and interdependent UCD multiple process. To exhaustively define the project requirements is therefore necessary: first, systematically organize the information coming from the contest of use

© Springer International Publishing Switzerland 2016
M. Antona and C. Stephanidis (Eds.): UAHCI 2016, Part II, LNCS 9738, pp. 359–369, 2016.
DOI: 10.1007/978-3-319-40244-4_35

analysis, last but non least, synthesize the information so as to translate into design specifications, intelligible for the designer. Furthermore, to successfully implement a UCD design process, solutions must be tested. User involvement includes choosing appropriate prototyping technologies in the final evaluation. This ensures the prototypes accessibility so as to allow to perform the product analysis, depending on the user's class target identified.

This research work aims to define a methodology which may apply this philosophy in the design practice. In particular, it aims to provide tools to:

- Summarize the information needed to analyze characteristics and needs of all potential users;
- Provide a tool that allows the designer to extrapolate the users' needs and expand the product's performance in all possible contexts of use.
- Provide a method to support the selection of prototype technologies suitable to the user target categories.

2   Research Background

Universal design (UD) is the main method by which designers provide their products and services to be used by the widest possible audience, independently of age or ability. Initially defined by Mace [3], UD was conceptualized by a team of researchers organized in the Center for Universal Design at North Carolina State University, with the publication of the Principles of Universal Design [4]. These principles represented a tool by which determine and evaluate the usability of designed elements:

- Principle 1: Equitable Use
- Principle 2: Flexibility in Use
- Principle 3: Simple and Intuitive Use
- Principle 4: Perceptible Information
- Principle 5: Tolerance for Error
- Principle 6: Low Physical Effort
- Principle 7: Size and Space for Approach and Use

Each of these principles was then expanded in a set of guidelines [4] in order to guide the design process, to permit systematic evaluation of designs, and to help in educating both designers and consumers about the characteristics of more usable design solutions [5]. The principles are a first attempt to articulate a design method that embraces human diversity. These offer only a starting point for the UD process because they cannot analyze operation tasks and user requirements in detail.

To focus on user requirements, Cooper proposed a method that introduced the 'personas' into design process [6]. Personas are abstractions of a groups of real consumers who share common characteristics and needs. The introduction of personas allows product design teams to focus on the real needs of the target customers. Instead of talking about general 'users', personas bring the target consumers to life and help to integrate their needs as a central driver of design processes [7]. Goodwin has defined another method to help the designer in the definition of user profile [8]. He has utilized direct examination of users and their activities with different objects in a real ambient, and semi-structured interviews. By this, the designer can get a good understanding of the needs of the user.

Other researchers have developed methods to support the definition of the design solutions through the user task analysis. 'Hierarchical task decomposition' method [9], 'task-action grammars' method [10], and 'task-based design' method [11] have been developed and represent some example of the task-based design methods. These methods permit to the designer to decompose the user tasks in various levels and obtain an hierarchical structure of task. Sangelkar et al. [12] have proposed a method based on function-based approach. This method allows to highlight the differences between a universal and non product, through the graphical representation of action-function diagram. This formal user-product representation facilitates the design of universal products and the associated data management and collection.

However, these methods exclude the possibility to diversify and to represent design alternatives for the same task. The design outputs derive from only a specific instance of the design parameters, and they are outcome of a single task-based structure. Savidis et al. [13] have proposed to introduce on the hierarchical structure of design process, 'polymorphic task decomposition' as an iterative phase through which abstract design patterns become specialized to represent concrete alternatives suitable for the designated situations of use.

All methods analyzed are focused on only specific applications or product domains. Our work had been focused to create a new method in which designers could manage and use the all information about universal design in a more systematic way.

3   Proposed Method

Four iterative steps characterize the proposed approach, according to user-cantered perspective [14]: (1) context analysis; (2) definition of design solutions; (3) prototyping; (4) evaluation (Fig. 1). Context analysis consists of three interdependent activities: User Analysis (UA), Ethnographic Analysis (EA), Benchmark Analysis (BA) of available smart technologies. UA and EA respectively provide the definition and the collection of all information about end-user attributes and environmental and social factors, which are relevant for design purposes.

The output of UA consists in the definition of user target categories profiles and in their explanation through the definition of Personas [15]. To define the user profile, and in particular its abilities depending on its own physiological and psychological skills, we propose to use the International Classification of Functioning, Disability and Health (ICF). The EA consist of a user behavior analysis [15] and allows to identify the user actions which is necessary to support, according to the user profile defined in UA and on the available technology analyzed in BA. Moreover, the result of EA allows to refine Personas, and consequently the results of BA, in an iterative way.

Benchmark Analysis (BA) provides the collection of information related to the characteristics of suitable technologies (e.g. costs, flexibility, etc.) related to potential applications (e.g. safety monitoring, health and assistive application, interaction and

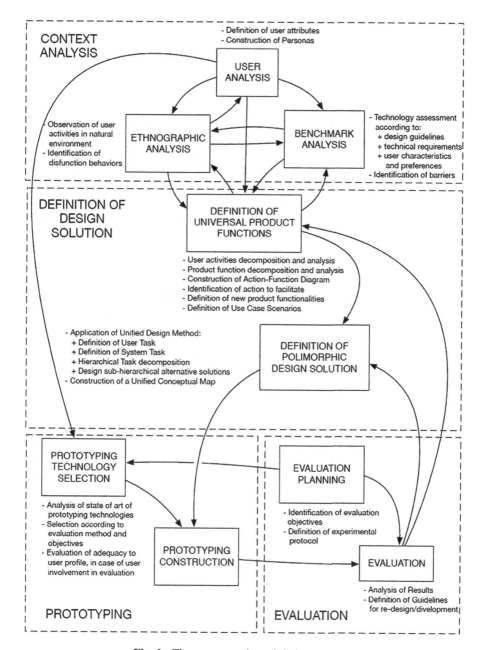

Fig. 1. The propose universal design process

communication, etc.) and aims to assess them in order to select the most adequate ones according to the design objectives. The evaluation is based on a Quality Function Deployment approach [16]. It takes into account design guidelines, technical requirements and user's characteristics, needs and preferences identified thanks to UA and EA.

The Design activity starts from the definition of the Universal Product Functions (UPFs) and ends with the definition of polymorphic design solutions.

In order to synthetize the knowledge acquired thanks to context analysis, we propose to use Action-Function Diagram (AFD) [12].

AFD allows representing and analyzing how a particular user interacts with a product/system/environment, according to his/her own capabilities. It is based on the Functional Modelling approach [17]. This research has developed a formal taxonomy which defines human flows in terms of the Body Functions and the Activities related to Mobility described by ICF. In this way AFD allows to represent the design context in terms of actions to be supported and to correlate them with system functionalities. The identified UPFs are explicated by defining use case scenarios.

In order to support the system design, which implements polymorphic solutions able to support different target user categories in different context of use, we propose to apply an approach based on the Unified User Interface Design Method. This method is able to support the definition of a "space populated with appropriate solution, along with their associated design parameters (e.g. user-and usage context, attribute values, etc.)" [13]. It stars from the definition of User Task (i.e., what the user has to do) and System Task (e.g. feedback, adaptation functions, etc.) and proceeds through a hierarchical task decomposition process until the design of sub-hierarchical alternative solutions.

In order to manage the output of such design process, we propose the implementation of a Unified Conceptual Map, which allows representing the relationship between User and System sub-task as well as the respective polymorphic design solution and the output data, which are necessary to manage adaptation functionalities.

Prototyping Construction is fundamental in order to assess design solutions. The Prototyping Activity starts with the selection of appropriate prototyping technology, according to method and objectives.

Finally, Evaluation is carried out in order to investigate the design process results and define guidelines for improvement.

4 The Case Study

The method here described has been applied to design a smart kitchen environment, providing support to three target user categories in cooking and kitchen management activities

4.1 Personas Method

To communicate the end-user's capabilities and needs to design team, so to encourage designer empathy and support identification of the main functionality that the system should have, the Personas method is used. The Personas method is a plain and effective tools to gather the strengths and objectives of the user profile for designer and developer. Through this method, according to data gather thanks to ethnographic analysis, we have defined three different target user categories: subjects with cognitive impairment, with dexterity problems and visually impaired. For each profile, we have identified: background, needs/limits, behavior and targets. For instance, the first identified profile, is reported in the figure below (Fig. 2).

	Background	John is a former metalworker, retired since 15 years ago. John is a widower and takes care of the housework and home activities. After his wife's death he has entered into a depressive state that partially compromises his cognitive status which includes degradation to maintain a good level of control and environmental organization in addition to an isolation form. His son lives far away and cannot effectively take care of his father daily needs.
Name: Mario	ICF Profile	• B(210-229).1 • B144.2
Age: 74	Needs/ Limits	• Initial cognitive impairment that prevents the use of common household appliances • Lack of knowledge and technology ability
Profession: Pensioner	Aptitude/ Behaviour	• The sense of inadequacy led him to not take care of himself and of his domestic environment
	How we can help	• Support independent living

Fig. 2. Example of defined personas

4.2 System Functionality

The kitchen environment chosen implements a home automation system able to detect and learn the user's behavior and to help him/her accordingly, through an adaptive user interface (Fig. 4). The interface is one of the most important modules of the entire architecture; this enables the system interaction and communication with the user. The Interface structure can be summarized in the following two aspects: graphic features, basic, i.e. standard features uniquely related to a disorder (color blindness, visual disturbances, etc.), and advanced features that represent all dynamic features about adapted interface items according to specific residual function consequent to a specific disorder and they are designed on a single user. Contents represent all interface items editable according to user's actions and the user acts on the interface with his own preferences and needs.

To this end, the interface supports the following functional areas:

– Meal preparation support: meal preparation will need information from refrigerator's food, user's profile and recipes.
– User interaction-appliance support: the system provides the ability to access the appliance control enabling the latter to set up, launch and monitor a given program.
– Environmental Comfort

In order to define the adaptive functions exhibited by the system, they have been defined various use cases.

This paper focuses on the user's interaction- appliance support, the oven in particular.

4.3 Project Interface Concept and Paper Prototype Implementation

A Unified Scheme Functional (SFU) was chosen, in order to manage the information needed to design the interface concept. It allows to represent in a single scheme, and in a simple and intuitive design, the entire of design space. Also the SFU is used to represent the full set of design variations depending on user's attributes and parameters that regulate adaptation mechanism. To this end, the SFU scheme is represented by five important points: the user actions (user task), the system actions performed by the system itself in order to provide the appropriate information to the user, the interface variants (physical alternatives) and services (Interface functions) that are associated with each user profile, at last, the adaptation and data management. The dynamic interface is represented by the subsequent follow:

- Logical and temporal follow, to connect user's action;
- Adaptation flow, to manage the adaptation mechanism;
- Data flow, to regulate data management.

The SFU defines all the interface design specifications, also it is used to manage the complexity in the development phase, so as to ensure compliance with the different projects specifications.

With the aim to support the end user to set cooking program execution two different modes of information presentation were assumed: using a common menu (Normal Setting) and through setting driven (Wizard Setting) process. The Wizard mode is designed to accomplish the task and minimizing the amount of information that the user should understand and manage. Consequently, this solution is suitable for users who have not familiarity with technology and/or have some cognitive dysfunction.

On the other side, the Normal mode, is designed to support user without cognitive dysfunction and characterized by a good technology attitude. Figure 3 shows the first menus screen concept, "Management Oven" in the two information channels.

As one can observe, during interaction with the interface, the user can change the information presentation mode by tapping on the proper button. Each transition from

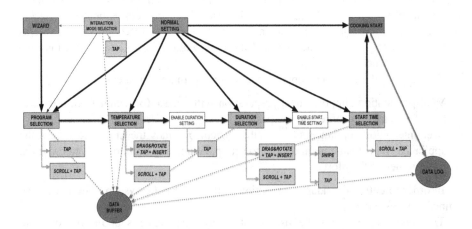

Fig. 3. A oven Unified Scheme Functional (SFU)

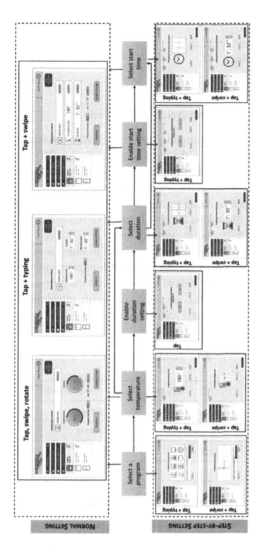

Fig. 4. The smart kitchen user interface: Example of polymorphic solutions related to oven functions.

one information mode to another is recorded by the system; the data collected are used to manage the interface's adaptive behavior.

In detail, when the probability of default mode information exceeds a certain threshold, the information mode presented by default for that specific user is changed.

To ensure access controls, depending on the motor skills and user's preferences, three different methods of interaction have been provided: (1) Tap-swipe-rotate; (2) tap-swipe; (3) tap-typing (Fig. 4). Depending on the user preferences, acquired by the system in the profile phase acquisition, the system will provide a specific interaction mode. To complete the "setting a cooking program" task of the oven, the user must perform the following tasks:

- Select a cooking program
- Select a program temperature
- Select a cooking time
- Select a start time

4.4 Heuristic Evaluation and Accessibility Test

A heuristic evaluation is a usability inspection method for computer software that helps to identify usability problems in the user interface design (UI) [18]. In particular, this evaluation was conducted using Jakob Nielsen's heuristics [19]: visibility of system status, match between system and the real world, user control and freedom, consistency and standards, error prevention, recognition rather than recall, flexibility and efficiency of use, aesthetic and minimalist design, help users recognize, diagnose, and recover from errors and lastly help and documentation.

A team of five experts with the following profiles conducted evaluation: two geriatricians, two psychologists and an expert in human computer interaction. Results, which are reported in the table below, highlight that the propose solutions are suitable for all the considered profile (i.e., profile 1, cognitive impairment; profile 2, dexterity problems; profile 3, visually impaired) (Table 1).

Table 1. Results of heuristics evaluation

		Profile 1	Profile 2	Profile 3
Nielsen's heuristics	*Visibility of system status*	Excellent	Excellent	Perception Problem
	Match between system and the real world	Excellent	Excellent	Excellent
	User control and freedom	Excellent	Excellent	Excellent
	Consistency and standards	Excellent	Excellent	The difference in the interaction mode (tap, swipe and rotate) could generate user frustration
	Error prevention	Excellent	Excellent	Excellent
	Recognition rather than recall	The amount of information about each program are probably too much to be correctly manage	The knob, used for oven temperature and duration changing, may not be intuitive for a inexpert user	- The knob, used for oven temperature and duration changing, may not be intuitive for a inexpert user - Some items may not be seen by the user
	Flexibility and efficiency of use	Excellent	Excellent	Excellent
	Aesthetic and minimalist design	Functional Design	Functional Design	Functional Design
	Help users recognize	No, there is no way to check for an error, but you can cancel any action.	No, there is no way to check for an error, but you can cancel any action.	No, there is no way to check for an error, but you can cancel any action.
	Help and documentation	Excellent	Excellent	Excellent

Related to "Recognition rather than recall" heuristic, the same minor usability issue has been identified for Profile 2 and Profile 3: the knob, used for oven temperature and duration changing, may not be intuitive for a inexpert user. Such problem may be solved by adopting a different interaction modality. In addition, for Profile 1 a relevant usability issue has been detected, as the amount of information about each program are probably too much to be correctly manage: this can be recover improving the wizard.

5 Conclusion

A methodology to support universal design of interactive products has been presented, which provides tools to summarize the information needed to analyze user characteristics and needs and allows the designer to extrapolate the user's needs and select of prototype technologies suitable to the user categories. It exploits Personas and implement a design approach based on functional modeling and on the Unified User Interface Design method.

This method has been used to design an innovative smart adaptive interface to support user with several disabilities (i.e., motor, cognitive, visual) in cooking tasks.

A preliminary expert evaluation, based on Nielsen's heuristics, was carried out to assess usability of the conceptual solution. Results highlight that the propose solutions are suitable for all the considered profile and allow to define design guidelines useful for improvements.

Acknowledgments. This work has been developed in the context of "D4All: Design for all" project, National Technological Cluster funded by the Italian Minister of University and Research.

References

1. ETSI EG 202 116: Human Factors (HF); Guidelines for ICT products and sevices; "Design for All" (2009)
2. Mathews, M., Mitrovi´c, T., Thomson, D.: Analising High-Level Help Seeking Behaviou in ITS (2008)
3. Mace, R.: Universal Design, Barrier Free Environments for Everyone, Designers West, November 1985
4. Connell, B.R., Jones, M., Mace, R., Mueller, J., Mullick, A., Ostroff, E., Sanford, J. et al.: The principles of universal design, Version 2.0, Raleigh, N.C., Center for Universal Design, North Carolina State University (1997)
5. Story, M. F., Mueller, J.L., Mace, R.L.: The Universal Design File: Designing for People of All Ages and Abilities, Raleigh, N.C., Center for Universal Design, North Carolina State University (1998)
6. Cooper, A.: The Inmates are Running the Asylum. Morgan Kaufmann, Indianapolis (1999)
7. Gulliksen, J., Georansson, B., Boivie, I., Blomkvist, S., Persson, J., Cajander, A.: Key principles for user-centered systems design. Behav. Inf. Technol. **22**(6), 397e409 (2003)
8. Goodwin, K.: Designing for the Digital Age: How to Create Human-Centered Products and Services. Wiley Publishing, Indianapolis (2009)

9. Johnson, P., Johnson, H., Waddington, P., Shouls, A.: Task-related knowledge structures: analysis, modeling, and applications. In: Jones, D.M., Winder, R. (eds.) Cambridge University Press, pp. 35–62 (1988)
10. Payne, S.: Task-action grammars. In: Proceedings of IFIP Conference on Human–Computer Interaction: INTERACT 1984, vol. 1. North-Holland/Elsevier Science, London/Amsterdam, pp. 139–144 (1984)
11. Wilson, S., Johnson, P.: Empowering users in task-based approach to design. In: Proceedings of ACM DIS 1995 Symposium on Designing Interactive Systems, MI, USA, pp. 25–31 (1995)
12. Sangelkar, S., Cowen, N., McAdams, D.: User activity e product function association based design rules for universal products. Des. Stud. **33**(1), 85–110 (2012)
13. Savids, A., Stephanidis, C.: Unified: designing universally accessible interactions. Interact. Comput. **16**, 243–270 (2004)
14. ISO 13407 Human-centred design processes for interactive systems (1999)
15. Kerr, S.J., Tan, O., Chua, J.C.: Cooking personas: goal-directed design requirements in the kitchen. Int. J. Hum. Comput. Stud. **72**, 255–274 (2014)
16. Park, T., Kim, K.: Technical note Determination of an optimal set of design requirements using house of quality. J. Oper. Manage. **16**, 569–581 (1998)
17. Mengoni, M., Ceccacci, S., Raponi, D.: An inclusive approach for home environment design. In: 2014 IEEE/ASME 10th International Conference on Mechatronic and Embedded Systems and Applications (MESA), pp. 1–6, 10–12 September 2014
18. Nielsen, J., Molich, R.: Heuristic evaluation of user interfaces. In: Proceedings of ACM CHI 1990 Conference (Seattle, WA), pp. 249–256, 1–5 April 1990
19. Nielsen, J.: Heuristic evaluation. In: Nielsen, J., Mack, R.L. (eds.) Usability Inspection Methods. Wiley, New York (1994)

A Deep Neural Network Video Framework
for Monitoring Elderly Persons

M. Farrajota[✉], João M.F. Rodrigues, and J.M.H. du Buf

Vision Laboratory, LARSyS, University of the Algarve, 8005-139 Faro, Portugal
{mafarrajota,jrodrig,dubuf}@ualg.pt

Abstract. The rapidly increasing population of elderly persons is a phenomenon which affects almost the entire world. Although there are many telecare systems that can be used to monitor senior persons, none integrates one key requirement: detection of abnormal behavior related to chronic or new ailments. This paper presents a framework based on deep neural networks for detecting and tracking people in known environments, using one or more cameras. Video frames are fed into a convolutional network, and faces and upper/full bodies are detected in a single forward pass through the network. Persons are recognized and tracked by using a Siamese network which compares faces and/or bodies in previous frames with those in the current frame. This allows the system to monitor the persons in the environment. By taking advantage of parallel processing of ConvNets with GPUs, the system runs in real time on a NVIDIA Titan board, performing all above tasks simultaneously. This framework provides the basic infrastructure for future pose inference and gait tracking, in order to detect abnormal behavior and, if necessary, to trigger timely assistance by caregivers.

Keywords: Design for aging · Design for quality of life technologies · Deep learning

1 Introduction

Deep learning methods have advanced greatly in recent years and they provide now the leading artificial vision framework for classification and categorization tasks. The deep learning architecture is inspired by the mammalian visual system, where simple processes are involved in the visual cortex through a recursive hierarchy [22]. Most deep architectures employ the multi-stage architecture studied by Hubel and Wiesel [11], composed by a hierarchy of layers where each layer consists of filtering, non-linearity and pooling stages.

In this paper we present a framework based on deep neural networks for detecting and tracking persons in a domestic environment, for telecare scenarios to aid elderly people at home, using one or multiple cameras. This framework is composed by three main tasks: (1) detection; (2) recognition; and (3) tracking. By employing a deep convolutional neural network (ConvNet) architecture for tasks (1) and (2), persons can be spotted using an algorithm for full-body

© Springer International Publishing Switzerland 2016
M. Antona and C. Stephanidis (Eds.): UAHCI 2016, Part II, LNCS 9738, pp. 370–381, 2016.
DOI: 10.1007/978-3-319-40244-4_36

pedestrian detection. A face recognition network allows to identify the persons in scenarios where multiple persons and their activities must be monitored.

Detection is done by using a sliding window search over the output features of the last convolutional layer in the network, where a classifier searches for persons and faces. To this end, a classifier scans for persons and faces over multiple scales of the feature map in parallel. This allows to process for arbitrary image region sizes in a single step over the network, thereby eliminating the need for feature computations over multiple scales. To recognize different persons, a Siamese network is used which compares detected faces retrieved from person detections against a database of faces belonging to all persons to be monitored in the specific domestic environment. After recognition, monitoring is reduced to tracking persons in consecutive frames by using another Siamese network which computes a binary matching classification between full-sized person detections in current and previous frames. Also, by computing image features only once and using them across the entire system networks, and by taking advantage of parallel processing of ConvNets on GPUs, the system runs in real time on a NVIDIA Titan GPU.

The main contribution of this paper is the integration into a single framework of detection, recognition and tracking tasks using a ConvNet model and to execute these tasks in a single, feed-forward pass over the network, thus reducing expensive, time-consuming computations in feature processing. This framework provides the basic infrastructure for future pose inference and gait tracking, to detect abnormal behavior and, if necessary, to trigger timely assistance by caregivers. In the next section we present the state of the art, followed in Sect. 3 by the framework, in Sect. 4 it is presented the experimental evaluation and finalizes (Sect. 5) with the conclusion and future work.

2   State of the Art

Deep convolutional neural networks (ConvNets/CNNs) have been used for many years [15] for tasks in category recognition of dominant objects in images: traffic signs [21], house numbers [19], handwritten characters [14], objects from the Caltech-101 dataset [12], or objects from the 1000-category ImageNet dataset [13,26]. These deep networks usually integrate low-,mid- and high-level features and classifiers in an end-to-end multilayer fashion [26] and the number of features (levels) can be increased by the number of stacked layers: the depth. The big advantage of ConvNets is that the entire system can be trained in an end-to-end fashion, from raw pixels to complex feature categories, therefore reducing or eliminating the need to handcraft suitable feature extractors, although this requires in practice a large amount of training data.

The latter aspect implies that accuracy on small datasets such as Caltech-101 has not been record-breaking, mainly because that such networks, with their millions of parameters, require more data in order to reduce over-fitting effects. A popular solution for such cases has been transfer learning: to use pre-trained features on much bigger datasets [17] and then to fine-tune the network on the smaller dataset in order to increase the accuracy. Recent works have shown how well deep networks can learn features from data in a supervised [13] or unsupervised way [25], and state-of-the-art results have been obtained using optimized back-propagation learning algorithms on huge datasets [13,23].

The detection of persons and pedestrians (and faces) is a very challenging task due to the large variability caused by different poses, abundant partial occlusions, complex/cluttered backgrounds and frequent changes in illumination. In recent years, considerable progress in the development of approaches and applications has been obtained concerning object detection [8] and class-specific segmentation [20] in tracking scenarios [24], pedestrian detection being of particular interest [4]. Many existing state-of-the-art methods use a combination of bio-inspired [6] or hand-crafted features such as HoG [2], Integral Channel Features [4] and other variations and combinations [7], along with trainable classifiers such as boosted ones [4], SVMs [7] or random forests [3]. Although low-level features can be designed by hand with good success, mid-level features composed by combinations of low-level features are difficult to engineer without resorting to some sort of learning procedure. Multi-stage classifiers that learn hierarchies of features can be trained end-to-end with little prior knowledge. ConvNets are examples of such hierarchical systems.

Face recognition in unconstrained conditions has been extensively studied due to the availability of LFW [10], a very popular dataset for face recognition and an algorithm benchmark. Although recently there have been significant advances in the field of face recognition [18], implementing face recognition efficiently presents serious challenges with current approaches. The currently best performing face verification algorithms [18] use a two-stage approach that combines a multi-patch deep ConvNets and deep metric learning. They extract low-dimensional but very discriminative features for face verification and recognition. Hence, using ConvNets for feature extraction is the best strategy for face recognition. Finally, many approaches have been proposed to perform long-term visual tracking [24]. Also in this area, deep neural networks trained for general-purpose applications have been proposed for long-term tracking [5]. This typically requires scale-invariant feature extraction when the object dramatically changes in shape as it moves in the scene.

3   Framework

As mentioned in the Introduction, the framework consists of three main tasks: (1) detection; (2) recognition; and (3) tracking. In the next sections these tasks will be presented in detail.

3.1   Detection

Persons and faces are detected using a sliding window method over the image, similar to many popular methods on a ConvNet, e.g. [20]; see Fig. 1b. The method consists of two steps: (i) convolve the entire image with the feature extraction layers of the ConvNet only once, thus avoiding expensive computations over multiple scales, and (ii) slide the classifier over the resulting feature map in multiple scales in order to detect persons and/or faces with different sizes. A fully supervised ConvNet model [13] is used for feature extraction and category (person/face/background) classification. The model is divided into two modules:

(a) *Feature extraction* is based on the convolutional features of an Alexnet. Each layer of the feature extraction consists generically of (a.1) convolution of the previous layer output (or, in the case of the 1st layer, the input image) with a set of learned filters; (a.2) passing the responses through the rectified linear function $ReLU(x) = \max(x, 0)$; and (a.3) max pooling over local neighborhoods. We use only the feature layers of the Alexnet before the first fully-connected classification layer, and we also exclude the last max-pooling layer in our network.

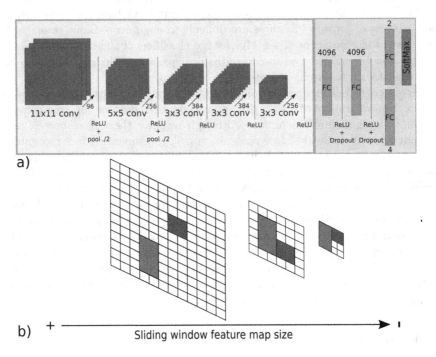

Fig. 1. Detection network architecture: (a) The network architecture used for classification/localization; (b) Sliding window scheme at multiple scales.

(b) For *Classification*, the top few layers of the network are conventional fully-connected (FC) networks and the final layer is a combination of a softmax classifier and a regression classifier during training. Those are converted to convolutional layers for normal system operation. The first two fully-connected layers have 4096 hidden units with 50 % dropout followed by the ReLU function. The output is connected to one FC layer with 2 outputs for classification, followed by a softmax layer and another FC layer with 4 outputs for bounding box estimation.

The convolutional layers accept arbitrary input sizes, and they also produce outputs of variable sizes. Since fully-connected layers require fixed-length vectors, they are replaced after training by convolutional layers. The result is that variable sized images can be processed in a single pass through the network, and computations are faster when evaluating the network.

Once the network is fine-tuned, detection amounts to little more than running a forward pass. The network takes as input a single-scale image, and several region proposals (RoI-region of interest; Fig. 1b color regions) are obtained after sliding the classifier over the last convolution layer (Fig. 1(a). The person/face ConvNet detector was designed for images of size 640 × 480 pixels. To classify/detect persons and faces, two classifiers with a fixed size are: one classifier window of 64 × 128 pixels for person detection, and 64 × 64 pixels for face detection. In order to classify/detect persons and faces at various sizes, the feature map is reduced and the previous classifiers are used. This is achieved by applying a 2 × 2 max pooling kernel over the feature map with a stride of 2 grid pixels, halving its size. This is done twice, resulting in probed regions by the classifiers of 128 × 256 and 256 × 512 pixels for person detection and 128 × 128 and 256 × 256 pixels for face detection. Feature maps smaller than the classifier are padded with zero values. This way, only one classifier needs to be trained, and scanning for larger faces and persons is quicker.

For each new image frame, the forward pass outputs a class posterior probability distribution and bounding box coordinates for each classifier, where all regions classified as background are then removed and non-maximum suppression to the output bounding boxes is applied in order to filter the strongest detections from the weakest (all bounding boxes which overlap at least 50 %). Although several classifiers are used for detection, their outputs are independent. Therefore, all classifiers can be applied in parallel when evaluating the network.

3.2   Recognition

For recognition we use two Siamese networks [1] to match detected faces and known persons. The two networks have the same architecture but are trained specifically for both tasks. Face recognition consist of matching detected faces in input images with face images from a database of known persons. Person recognition consists of matching a detected person in frames i and $i - 1$.

The Siamese network architecture (Fig. 2b) is composed of two networks with shared weights (Fig. 2(c) which are coupled at the top by two fully-connected layers to compute a binary (positive or negative) classification match between two inputs (see Fig. 2(a). Backpropagation is used to train the model using stochastic gradient descent and the negative log-likelihood loss. The networks are composed of the Alexnet feature extraction layers (Fig. 2b) as used in the previous section, followed by a spatial pyramid pooling layer (SPP) [9] with pooling windows of size 1×1, 2×2 and 3×3, and at the end two fully-connected layers with 4096 hidden units with 50 % dropout and ReLU regularization. The two networks are coupled with a matching module composed of two fully-connected layers, one with 4096 hidden units with 50 % dropout and ReLU regularization connected to another one with 2 outputs for classification, followed by a softmax layer. Because of the SPP layer, inputs images can have different sizes and aspect ratios.

Although the architectures for face and person recognition are identical during training, their implementation is different. For person recognition, detected patches are pooled in the feature map and those are fed to the SPP layer. Thus, by using the same convolutional features as in the detection process, features can be reused in the recognition process. Extra feature computations can be avoided and only the top layers (SPP, FC's and matching layer) of the Siamese network need to be applied. Detections in previous frames are stored, and matching consists of computing a forward pass through the last layers of the network with computed features in the current frame. This results in little computational overhead.

For face recognition, detected face regions are sampled from the input image and scaled to 128×128 pixels in order to be compared with the faces in the database which have all been normalized to this size. Then, pairs of images to be compared are fed into the Siamese network and the matching is computed. However, in order to reduce additional computations, ConvNet outputs of all faces in the database have been preprocessed and stored in memory. Therefore, only an input frame must be processed by the network, and because the detection features are reused, recognition is a very fast process.

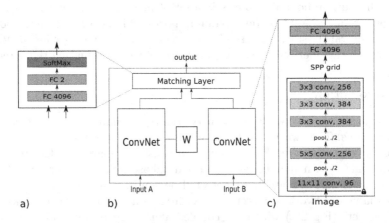

Fig. 2. Recognition architecture: (a) The Siamese matching layer; (b) The Siamese architecture for person/face recognition; c) Network architecture used for feature extraction.

3.3   Tracking

After a person has been detected and recognized, tracking only involved the detection window (bounding box). The procedure is as follows: (a) in frame i the person's bounding box is detected after the forward pass through the network and non-maximum suppression; (b) the person's features are matched with all detections in the previous frame $i-1$ using the Siamese network tuned to person matching, and the box with the highest but positive classification is selected; finally, (c) an additional constraint on the displacement between the current and the previous frames is applied. Only displacements smaller than a threshold are considered, and the average velocity and position of the detections are computed using the person's position in i, $i-1$ and $i-2$. This corresponds to the average trajectory and velocity of the person in the scene. This information also helps to keep track of occluded persons during several frames by predicting where the person may be located, assuming that the velocity remains constant. In case of mis-detections, i.e., occlusions or false negatives, the previous detections are used and the person's position is continually predicted up to a set number of frames (maximum 10), after which the detection windows stop being tracked and are discarded after that.

4   Experimental Evaluation

To train and evaluate the framework we used two datasets: (a) The Caltech pedestrian dataset [4] for pedestrian detection and tracking, and (b) the Labeled Faces in the Wild (LFW) dataset [10] for face classification and recognition.

4.1   Implementation Details

Pre-training: We used an Alexnet for feature extraction, which has been trained on Imagenet [17]. This is standard practice for deep networks, since the number of parameters is much larger than the available data for training a specific application and it provides a good starting point for the actual training. The network was trained on the ILSVR2012 [17] dataset with 1 million images of 224×224 pixels image.

Training: We used two datasets for person detection (Caltech) and face recognition (LFW). For detection, we used the Caltech typical category with 77,210 positive samples and 600 random negative samples for training, and 40,665 positive samples and 560 negative samples for testing. Of the LFW dataset, 10,000 faces were randomly sampled from the total of 13,233 faces for training, and the remaining 3,233 were used for testing. For the Caltech recognition training set, 10,000 pedestrian pairs were sampled from the dataset, 5,000 positive and 5,000 negative pairs. For testing we selected 2,000 pairs, 1,000 positive and 1,000 negative pairs. In case of the LFW dataset we followed the standard evaluation protocol defined for the "unrestricted" setting using no outside data. Here, the dataset was split into 10,586 training and 2,647 testing samples randomly.

Data generation: Data samples for training and evaluation were generated from ground truth bounding box annotations (Caltech) or images with normalized sizes (LFW). From the pedestrian detection dataset where ground truth bounding box annotations are available, sample regions with an intersect-over-union (IoU) [16] of at least 70 % overlap with the ground truth bounding box were used as positive samples. Those with overlaps ranging from 30 % to 50 % were used as negative samples. Additionally, negative samples with random sizes were randomly selected from a hard negative image set in order to scrutinize false positive rates. During training, we used a positive to negative data ratio of 1:2. Moreover, when a positive sample was selected, we applied a 50 % chance of flipping the sample label to negative. If a label was not flipped to negative (i.e., it stayed positive), we applied an additional 50 % chance of the sample having a full overlap with the ground truth bounding box plus additional padding with background pixels, or to have an overlap between 70 % and 100 % with the bounding box. Positive sample images with full overlap have a context ratio (padding) of the bounding box with the surrounding background. This context ratio ranges between 0 % and 100 % background padding: 0 % corresponds to no background pixels being added to the sampling region around the bounding box; 100 % corresponds to adding background pixels of half the height of the ground truth bounding box around the sampling region (top and bottom, left and right). In case of the LFW face detection/recognition dataset, there is no annotation information regarding ground truth bounding boxes. Since all face images are centered, the center pixels with $\{x_{min}, y_{min}, x_{max}, y_{max}\} = \{50, 50, 200, 200\}$ were used as ground truth coordinates, and the same positive and negative selection scheme as used for the pedestrian dataset was applied as well when training face classifiers. Random image crops were also used in the recognition task when generating data samples for training the Siamese network.

For face recognition, face samples were all resized to 128×128 pixels, and these were copied from images of 140×140 pixels with random shifts between 0 and 12 pixels, both horizontally and vertically. Color augmentation and image jittering were used to increase accuracy on all datasets. For color augmentation, we applied color casting to alter the intensities of the RGB channels in training data. Specifically, for each image, we randomly changed the R, G and B values up to ± 20 % with a 50 % chance. For image jittering, a 15-pixel maximum offset in the x and y directions was allowed, but this was only applied to samples with full overlap with a bounding box. For each image the global means of the R, G and B values were subtracted, after which the variances were normalized to 1.

Generated data containing bounding boxes of positive samples were used to train the bounding box estimation layer. We adopted the parameterizations of the four coordinates as in [8] for bounding box normalization: (1) $t_x = (x - x_a)/w_a$, (2) $t_y = (y - y_a)/h_a$, (3) $t_w = log(w/w_a)$, and (4) $t_h = log(h/h_a)$, where x, y, w and h denote the sampling window center coordinates and its width and height, whereas x_a, y_a, w_a and h_a denote the box's ground truth coordinates, and t_x, t_y, t_w and t_h are the normalized coordinates for regression.

Optimization Parameters: We used mini-batches of 256 samples, where positive and negative samples were randomly sampled with the same probability (50 % chance) from the training data. All network weights, which were not pre-trained on Imagenet, were randomly initialized and then updated using stochastic gradient descent with momentum of 0.9 and weight decay of 5×10^{-4}. The starting learning rate of 10^{-2} was reduced by a factor of 10 after the error converged (if it did not decrease further after 5 epochs) down to 10^{-4}. Dropout with a rate of 50 % chance was applied to the first and second fully connected layers of the classifiers. The detection classification layer was trained during 30 epochs with negative log-likelihood loss, and the regressor layer was trained during 100 epochs with mean-squared error loss. The Siamese networks for person and face matching were both trained during 100 epochs using the negative log-likelihood loss.

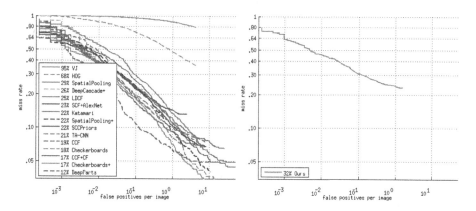

Fig. 3. Left, Available top-performing methods on the Caltech pedestrian dataset for large pedestrians benchmark [4], and (right) our method. Lower curves indicate better performance.

4.2   Results

The results were separated in pedestrian/person and face detection and recognition. Our person detection algorithm scores competitively against available top-performing algorithms specially tunned for pedestrian detection. Although not being amongst the top-performers, the trade-of between accuracy and speed necessary in our framework for fast detection of persons for tracking purposes minimizes this performance gap. In Fig. 3, a benchmark on the Caltech's pedestrian detection dataset [4] of our method ("Ours", burgundy line) against several available top-performing algorithms is shown.

In the case of face detection, our algorithm scores 93.1 % accuracy in the LFW dataset. Although this dataset was not designed for face detection benchmarking, the resulting accuracy shows our face detector's proof-of-concept. For our recognition algorithms, our face algorithm scores 94.89 % accuracy on the LFW dataset in the unrestricted, no outside data category and the person algorithm scores 93.22 % in the adapted Caltech dataset for person comparison. Note that a comparison of our recognition methods against others authors was not possible to perform due to the lack of available benchmarking data for this particular setups. Regarding our tracker's performance, moving persons were successfully detected and matched in domestic environments with multiple users in occluded and non-occluded scenarios. In cases of heavy, but temporary occlusions, the system was able to track persons robustly and recover from most situations when users continue in the same trajectory as in previous detections.

5 Discussion

In this paper we presented a framework based on deep neural networks for detecting and tracking people in known environments using one or multiple cameras. Deep neural networks (ConvNets) provide very expressive features for vision tasks. By feeding video frames into a ConvNet and using a sliding window detector, faces and upper/full bodies can be detected in a single forward pass through the network with good accuracy and speed. This is an important step: by computing a frame's features only once, and sliding a classifier on top of the last feature layer, persons and faces can be detected at about 10 fps in 640×480 pixel images using a NVIDIA Titan GPU. Moreover, the same features can be used for face/person recognition by computing a binary matching classification between two faces or persons using a Siamese network, without any considerable impact on performance. The developed framework provides the basic infrastructure for additional improvements to be added for a timely assistance and aid for elderly people in case of an accident or other problem.

Therefore, future work will focus on pose prediction and gait estimation. This will enable an early detection of health symptoms related to the gait and pose of a person.

Acknowledgements. This work was supported by the FCT project LARSyS: UID/EEA/50009/2013 and FCT PhD grant to author MF (SFRH/BD/79812/2011).

References

1. Chopra, S., Hadsell, R., LeCun, Y.: Learning a similarity metric discriminatively, with application to face verification. In: IEEE Conference CVPR, vol. 1, pp. 539–546 (2005)
2. Dalal, N., Triggs, B.: Histograms of oriented gradients for human detection. IEEE Conf. CVPR **1**, 886–893 (2005)
3. Dollár, P., Appel, R., Kienzle, W.: Crosstalk cascades for frame-rate pedestrian detection. In: Fitzgibbon, A., Lazebnik, S., Perona, P., Sato, Y., Schmid, C. (eds.) ECCV 2012, Part II. LNCS, vol. 7573, pp. 645–659. Springer, Heidelberg (2012)
4. Dollár, P., Tu, Z., Perona, P., Belongie, S.: Integral Channel Features, pp. 1–11. BMVC Press, Cambridge (2009)

5. Dundar, A., Bates, J., Farabet, C., Culurciello, E.: Tracking with deep neural networks. In: 47th Annual Conference CISS, pp. 1–5 (2013)
6. Farrajota, M., Rodrigues, J.M.F., du Buf, J.M.H.: Bio-Inspired pedestrian detection and tracking. In: 3rd International Conference on Advanced Bio-Informatics, Bio-Technology Environments, pp. 28–33 (2015)
7. Felzenszwalb, P.F., Girshick, R.B., Mcallester, D., Ramanan, D.: Object detection with discriminatively trained part based models. IEEE Trans. PAMI **34**, 1–20 (2009)
8. Girshick, R.: Fast R-CNN. In: IEEE Proceedings of the ICCV, June 2015
9. He, K., Zhang, X., Ren, S., Sun, J.: Spatial pyramid pooling in deep convolutional networks for visualrecognition. IEEE Trans. PAMI **37**, 346–361 (2015). IEEE
10. Huang, G.B., Ramesh, M., Berg, T., Learned-Miller, E.: Labeled faces in the wild: A database for studying face recognition in unconstrained environments. Technical Report 07–49, Uni. Massachusetts, Amherst, 49(07–49), 1–11 (2007)
11. Hubel, D.H., Wiesel, T.N.: Receptive fields of single neurones in the cat's striate cortex. J. Physiol. **148**, 574–591 (1959)
12. Jarrett, K., Kavukcuoglu, K., Ranzato, M., LeCun, Y.: What is the best multistage architecture for object recognition? In: IEEE Proceedings of the ICCV, pp. 2146–2153 (2009)
13. Krizhevsky, A., Sutskever, I., Hinton, G.E.: ImageNet classification with deep convolutional neural networks. In: NIPS, pp. 1–9 (2012)
14. LeCun, Y., Boser, B., Denker, J.S., Henderson, D., Howard, R.E., Hubbard, W., Jackel, L.D.: Handwritten digit recognition with a back-propagation network. In: NIPS, pp. 396–404 (1990)
15. LeCun, Y., Bottou, L., Bengio, Y., Haffner, P.: Gradient-based learning applied to document recognition. IEEE Proc. **86**, 2278–2323 (1998)
16. Nowozin, S.: Optimal decisions from probabilistic models: the intersection-over-union case. In: IEEE Proceedings of the CVPR, pp. 548–555. IEEE (2014)
17. Russakovsky, O., Deng, J., Su, H., Krause, J., Satheesh, S., Ma, S., Huang, Z., Karpathy, A., Khosla, A., Bernstein, M., Berg, A.C., Fei-Fei, L.: ImageNet Large Scale Visual Recognition Challenge. IJCV **115**(3), 211–252 (2015)
18. Schroff, F., Dmitry, K., Philbin, J.: FaceNet : a unified embedding for face recognition and clustering. In: IEEE Proceedings of the CVPR, pp. 815–823 (2015)
19. Sermanet, P., Chintala, S., LeCun, Y.: Convolutional neural networks applied to house numbers digit classification. In: Proceedings of the ICPR, pp. 3288–3291 (2012)
20. Sermanet, P., Eigen, D., Zhang, X., Mathieu, C., Fergus, R., LeCun, Y.: OverFeat : Integrated Recognition, Localization and Detection using Convolutional Networks. arXiv preprint, pp. 1–15 (2013). arXiv:1312.6229
21. Sermanet, P., Lecun, Y.: Traffic sign recognition with multi-scale convolutional networks. In: Proceedings of the International Joint Conference on Neural Networks, pp. 2809–2813 (2011)
22. Serre, T., Poggio, T.: A neuromorphic approach to computer vision. Commun. ACM **53**(10), 54–61 (2010)
23. Simonyan, K., Zisserman, A.: Very Deep Convolutional Networks for Large-Scale Image Recognition. arXiv, pp. 1–13 (2014)
24. Smeulders, A.W.M., Chu, D.M., Cucchiara, R., Calderara, S., Dehghan, A., Shah, M.: Visual tracking: An experimental survey. IEEE Trans. PAMI **36**, 1442–1468 (2014)

25. Vincent, P., Larochelle, H., Bengio, Y., Manzagol, P.: Extracting and composing robust features with denoising autoencoders. In: Proceedings of the International Conference on Machine Learning, ICML 2008, pp. 1096–1103 (2008)
26. Zeiler, M.D., Fergus, R.: Visualizing and understanding convolutional networks. In: Fleet, D., Pajdla, T., Schiele, B., Tuytelaars, T. (eds.) ECCV 2014, Part I. LNCS, vol. 8689, pp. 818–833. Springer, Heidelberg (2014)

The MOBOT Platform – Showcasing Multimodality in Human-Assistive Robot Interaction

Eleni Efthimiou[1(✉)], Stavroula-Evita Fotinea[1], Theodore Goulas[1], Athanasia-Lida Dimou[1], Maria Koutsombogera[1], Vassilis Pitsikalis[2], Petros Maragos[2], and Costas Tzafestas[2]

[1] Institute for Language and Speech Processing/ATHENA RC, Athens, Greece
{eleni_e, evita, tgoulas, ndimou, mkouts}@ilsp.gr
[2] Institute of Communication and Computer Systems–NTUA, Athens, Greece
{vpitsik, petros.maragos, ktzaf}@cs.ntua.gr

Abstract. Acquisition and annotation of a multimodal-multisensory data set of human-passive rollator-carer interactions have enabled the analysis of related human behavioural patterns and the definition of the MOBOT human-robot communication model. The MOBOT project has envisioned the development of cognitive robotic assistant prototypes that act proactively, adaptively and interactively with respect to elderly humans with slight walking and cognitive difficulties. To meet the project's goals, a multimodal action recognition system is being developed to monitor, analyse and predict user actions with a high level of accuracy and detail. In the same framework, the analysis of human behaviour data that have become available through the project's multimodal-multisensory corpus, have led to the modelling of Human-Robot Communication in order to achieve an effective, natural interaction between users and the assistive robotic platform. Here, we discuss how the project's communication model has been integrated in the robotic platform in order to support a natural multimodal human-robot interaction.

Keywords: Multisensory data · Multimodal semantics · Multimodal annotation scheme · Multimodal HRI model · Multimodal human-robot communication · Natural HRI

1 Introduction

The need to support mobility and vitality in our ageing society, as well as enhance independent living of elderly people and their quality of life [1] has inspired techno-logical solutions towards developing intelligent active mobility assistance robots for indoor environments, providing user-centred, context-adaptive and natural support [2–5]. The MOBOT project[1] addresses this need envisioning cognitive robotic assistants that act (a) proactively by realizing an autonomous and context-specific monitoring of human activities and by subsequently reasoning on meaningful user behavioural

---

[1] www.mobot-project.eu/.

M. Antona and C. Stephanidis (Eds.): UAHCI 2016, Part II, LNCS 9738, pp. 382–391, 2016.
DOI: 10.1007/978-3-319-40244-4_37

patterns, as well as (b) adaptively and interactively, by analyzing multi-sensory and physiological signals related to gait and postural stability, and by performing adaptive compliance control for optimal physical support and active fall prevention.

To address these targets, a multimodal action recognition system is being developed to monitor, analyse and predict user actions with a high level of accuracy and detail. Parallel to the enhancement of computer vision techniques with modalities such as range sensor images, haptic information as well as command-level speech and gesture recognition, data-driven multimodal human behaviour analysis has been conducted in order to extract behavioural patterns of elderly people. The aim here has been to import the basic elements of these behavioural patterns into a multimodal human-robot communication system [6], involving both verbal and nonverbal communication conceptually and systemically synthesised into mobility assistance models taking into consideration safety critical requirements.

By the end of the project, the different modules will be incorporated in a behaviour-based and context-aware robot control framework aiming at providing situation-adapted optimal assistance to users [7]. Direct involvement of end-user groups in various stages of the prototypes development has ensured that actual user needs are addressed by the functionalities and communication capabilities of the platform's prototypes. Thus, user trials have been conducted to evaluate and benchmark the overall system.

The next sections report on the technologies which have been integrated in the robotic platform's prototypes, the functionalities the latter provide, the HRI communication model adopted, as well as the various end user evaluation and usability studies conducted to ensure that the developed platform addresses actual user needs.

2 Platform Integrated Technologies and Functionalities

The development of the MOBOT platform has proven to be a rather ambitious experiment, since it envisioned integration and synergies of a wide range of technologies, which needed to reach a significant level of enhancement as a result of research work within the project, in order to reach the state of maturity required to meet the set targets in respect to functionalities and safety controls envisioned to be offered to the platform's end users.

We present next the various types of integrated technologies and the respective functionalities they support, in order to illustrate how the adopted multimodal HRI communication model makes optimal use of the available technological solutions.

At this point, it is also important to notice that the MOBOT multimodal-multisensorial dataset [8] has been exploited towards the enhancement of all technologies explored in order to be integrated in the MOBOT robotic platform (Fig. 1).

Fig. 1. The active rollator used at the first evaluation of the MOBOT rollator-type mobility assistant

2.1   The MOBOT Platform Technologies

Work on *visual action recognition* in continuous RGB-D video streams, captured by visual sensors on the MOBOT robotic platform [9], robust experimental results on *object detection* and advances in *human body pose estimation* have supported, in combination with other technologies, the detection capacity by the platform of human activity that denotes various user intentions such as to activate the robot [10, 11].

Exploitation of the MOBOT dataset in relation to research work in *action/gesture recognition*, provided the chance to apply the action/gesture recognition algorithms developed in the project to relevant data, where advancements in the field include (i) the development of an improved gesture recognition method that exploits specific articulatory points such as the arms and the hands of the subject, and (ii) the application and experimentation on actual MOBOT data, following research work with other datasets. The experimental framework concentrated mainly on HMM-type classifiers, using two visual cues for feature extraction: handshape (provided by the RGB stream) and 3D movement-position (provided by Kinect's depth stream and skeleton tracking) [12, 13].

For the processing of spoken commands, a *spoken command recognition system* is utilized, which in a first step uses a voice activity detector to detect in the audio stream the time segments with spoken commands and then in a second step trains a set of HMM models on these segments. Experimentation has taken place on the audio data from the benchmark dataset of the ACM 2013 Multimodal Gesture Challenge and also during work on developing a complete spoken command recognition system trained on MOBOT data and on integrating the corresponding software on the ROS platform with a MEMS microphone array to be used on the MOBOT active rollator prototype [14].

The adopted approach to *multimodal sensor fusion* for audio-visual gesture recognition exploits the color, depth and audio information captured by a Kinect sensor. Recognition of a time sequence of audio-visual gesture commands is based on an optimized fusion of all different cues and modalities (audio, movement-position, handshape). The methodology incorporates a generalized activity detection component, while extended experimentation and comparisons with several competing approaches have provided results which greatly outperform all other competing published approaches on the ACM 2013 benchmark dataset and achieve a 93 % accuracy, which corresponds to a 47 % error reduction over the best competing approach.

Processing of haptic data has been possible via the two force/torque sensors mounted on the two handles of the rollator type prototype. These sensors are used to detect and quantify haptic interactions between the robot and the user. Typical interaction patterns while standing up, sitting down and walking have been identified in this context [15].

Furthermore, *processing of physiological data* focuses on user fatigue, since this is considered an important physiological state that can strongly affect the human performance. Fatigue estimation is based on two specific features of the human heart rate and the total performed work. Moreover, available fatigue indicators suitable for elderly fatigue estimation [16] are extended in order to fit for their usage in the context of mobility assistive robots.

2.2   The MOBOT Platform Functionalities

The MOBOT platform has two prototype demonstrators: a rollator type robot for walking and sit-to-stand assistance and a nurse type robot for sit-to-stand assistance. The MOBOT rollator is an assistive device comprising the main frame, the actuated handles, active wheels, user interface, an electronic control unit and a number of environment and user sensors.

Various functions are foreseen to be implemented on the MOBOT rollator by the end of the project which are both related to the mechanical design and the collected user requirements. The MOBOT rollator's functions are grouped next according to their main characteristics as:

(i) those which are dedicated to perceiving the user and involve the device's capacity
  a. to localize the user with respect to the rollator exploiting 3D coordinates and the state in which the user is with respect to the rollator as regards the "distant", "close" and "in contact" variables
  b. to track the articulated human body
  c. to detect walking patterns
  d. to recognize user gestures
  e. to recognize and interpret the user voice commands
  f. to monitor the human performance and postural stability and to detect unstable configuration and falls
  g. to recognize the human physiological state

h. to recognize user actions

i. to recognize user plans and user intentions

(ii) those which are dedicated to detecting the environment, including the ability to detect obstacles, locomotion specific data (surface type, slip ...), environment specific data (e.g. slopes) and creation of a map of the environment

(iii) the ability of the device to localize itself within the environment map

(iv) the ability of the device to approach the user from a distance

(v) the ability of the device to assist the user by

a. providing physical assistance during sit-to-stand and stand-to-sit transfers and

b. assisting the user while walking in three ways which include following the user intention ("dock" to the user, accelerate, maneuver, decelerate, stop), balancing and stabilizing the user (fall prevention included), and assisting the user while passing through narrow passages and opening/closing doors

c. assisting the user while standing

d. assisting the user in proximity but in no contact mode

e. assisting the user by following him/her

f. assisting the user by providing sensorial assistance as when to avoid static and dynamic positive and negative obstacles, or assistance on slopes

g. providing cognitive assistance

h. assisting the user localization or guiding/navigating the user

(vi) the ability of the device to leave the user and go to parking position in autonomous mode, and finally

(vii) the ability of the device to perform autonomous charging

The features listed above, directly linked with the technological solutions in Sect. 2.1, have set the framework for the development of the platform's multimodal communication model.

3 The MOBOT Multimodal Communication Model

The technologies integrated in the MOBOT robotic platform enabled innovative synergies among modules towards the platform's target to provide walking and cognitive assistance to elderly users with slight walking and cognitive problems.

However, the potentials of the platform would remain unexploited, if there would be missing an adequate HRI communication model to support the most natural possible communication between the platform and its user, taking into account on the one hand the state of the integrated technologies, and on the other hand the ways the target user group communicate in their everyday activities.

Detection and interpretation of patterns of explicit interactional and behavioural cues may be a trivial task for humans, but it still remains a rather difficult -yet important to achieve- task for computer systems in view of the goal to realise a naturalistic, meaningful and engaging communication between humans and machines, including the performance of actions. Thus, building the HR communication model upon insights stemming from sets of acquired data allows for mining deeper into the semantics of human actions, their sequence and correlation during the interaction, so that a more detailed representation of the human action (speech, audio-gestural) model in this specific environment can be drawn.

In this line, the MOBOT dataset was exploited also in respect to the information provided as regards human-to-human communications between elderly individuals and their cares while performing everyday activity tasks. The study of this information enabled the spotting of a number of natural multimodal interactions which are accompanying the core activities of the addressed audience.

Furthermore, the underlying notion behind the part of data acquisition which entails the closed set of combinations of the MOBOT audio-gestural commands is that any system attempting to model human actions in terms of interactional behaviour, needs to have access to knowledge on structures of human actions. Specifically, assistive systems dealing with human-machine interaction must be able to decompose human behaviour activities into measurable and machine detectable features, so that they are able to make decisions and plan support actions on the basis of heterogeneous sensory data [6, 17]. To this end, a set of recognizable actions that are associated with specific forms of human behaviour needs to be identified to deduce information on underlying human intentions and needs.

The MOBOT human-robot communication model was built as a structured tree of possible multimodal action-reaction interactions engaging both audio and gestural signals, enriched with a number of cognitive assistance assertions from the part of the platform, which assimilate human reinforcement to elderly individuals while performing a trivial task. The platform may interact in three modes: (i) in hands-on mode, (ii) in following mode, and (iii) in stand-by mode, while user input focuses on developing a multimodal dialogue strategy, which takes into account the options of (a) communication via body posture in silence and thus complete absence of any other speech or gesture signal, processing information that can be linked with the platform's action recognition module, and (b) communication via speech and/or gesture signals, information that can be linked with the audio and gestural signal recognition.

The system's ability to learn how to navigate using a map is linked with a number of cognitive support messages which are sent to the user in the form of orally uttered questions or reinforcement messages, similar to those received from the part of human cares during natural human interaction.

The question type messages are linked with the activation and approach of the robotic device, decision making in respect to the route selected each time or obstacle avoidance situations, and demand some verification from the part of the user.

Reinforcement type messages help users be encouraged to complete a task successfully. Both types of messages are provided in a manner that prevents message generation from being part of a routine that does not help or even gets annoying for the receiver.

The scenarios of use, for which action trees are constructed, are extracted from real user needs as defined during preparation of acquisition of the MOBOT dataset and depicted in the scenarios actually used in creating the MOBOT corpus, and also through end user evaluation of the intermediate stages of the platform's prototypes.

4   MOBOT Platform End User Evaluation

The MOBOT platform functionalities and devices are steadily tested and evaluated by end user groups, since one main aim of the project has been to perform and carry out an overall benchmark verification of the developed intelligent mobility assistants via intensive evaluation studies involving end-users.

The first evaluation of the MOBOT rollator-type mobility assistant was conducted at the BETHANIEN-Hospital/Geriatric Centre at the University of Heidelberg from end of October 2014 to beginning of December 2014.

The subject recruitment procedure, the different test scenarios developed to evaluate specific functionalities of the MOBOT device, adequate quantitative and qualitative performance measures and preliminary results of this evaluation study are reported in detail in [18].

A detailed description of validation studies on existing devices by a systematic review, as well as a detailed account of the use cases included in the evaluation process, have been reported in [19] and have been updated in [20].

Use cases represent typical scenarios for the development of technical devices to guide technical development and allow validation of devices. The MOBOT project defined such use cases for the specified setting of geriatric rehabilitation and long-term care.

The exploited use cases identify tasks or situations which differ with respect to duration, frequency of activity and clinical relevance. Some use cases take only seconds while other may take minutes, while some situations occur frequently during a day while others may occur only once a year. However, some of the tested situations occur rarely but are crucial for the task of the device to support the motor stability of the user, thus, preventing injurious falls.

Technical functionalities were assessed with respect to accuracy, validity and reliability of technical function. Clinical evaluation targeted at the interaction between a human and the device.

The evaluation study was carried out with 36 participants who met predefined inclusion criteria and who were recruited from geriatric rehab wards of the BETHANIEN-Hospital, hospital-associated nursing homes and from a rehab sports club. The aim of the evaluation study was to validate the functionalities mounted on the MOBOT active rollator, which comprised the sit-to-stand assistance, sensorial assistance tested via obstacle avoidance, as well as basic walking assistance. To fit these functionalities, specific test scenarios and "tailored" assessment methods were developed including qualitative as well as quantitative performance measures. Most of the assessment procedure proved to be feasible and adequate for the needs of the testers. Furthermore this initial trial proved a valuable experiment for planning all following trials and evaluation studies. Most crucially, the gained results proved promising with respect to the tested STS assistance, the basic walking assistance, and the subjective user perception of the MOBOT device and its assistance systems.

5 Conclusion

In this work we discussed the integration of a multimodal communication model into the MOBOT robotic platform to support a natural multimodal human-robot interaction. The communication model was built through the analysis and annotation of acquired multi-sensory data of users interacting with mobility aids and their emerging multimodal human behavioural patterns. At the same time, the analysis of walking patterns and critical safety requirements in mobility assistance, as well as the detection of abnormalities were taken into account for the model development. Since the aim of the platform is to provide situation-adapted optimal assistance to users, the platform functionalities and communication capabilities have been initially tested by end user groups to evaluate and benchmark the overall system. This first trial was positively assessed in terms of feasibility and adequacy to the user needs (especially regarding the basic walking assistance, and the subjective user perception of the MOBOT device and its assistance systems), and it has served as a valuable experiment for planning all following trials and evaluation studies.

In parallel, a goal that has been addressed is the implementation of context-dependent instantiations and flows of the communication model following the different interaction states and user needs, successfully through the use of the audio and visual channels of communication with the device.

This Human-Robot Interaction model directly responds to the communication re-quirements as an integral part of an architecture towards monitoring, analysing and predicting user actions with a high level of accuracy and detail. The extension of the communication model with an enhanced set of audio-gestural commands as well as with device-initiated cognitive information regarding localization information and information of general interest (e.g. date, time, weather, patients' personal info, etc.) is currently work in progress. Moreover, the plans for the finalization of the communication scheme include an algorithmic flow diagram of all possible interaction states within the communication model. This flow will also specify the states implemented in the device at every step of the integration process together with the progress of the individual components of the spoken (audio-gesture) dialogue system (i.e. speech/gesture recognition, language understanding, dialogue management, communication with external system, response generation, speech output etc.).

An effective, natural interaction between users and the assistive robotic platform is a crucial step towards the development of safe hardware platforms for mobility aids which are tailored for indoor environments. Aspects of such platforms include software modules for robot navigation, human-adaptive and proactive robot motion control, and low-level active compliance control and shared control behaviours.

Intensive evaluation studies will keep being performed to include more end-users towards an overall benchmark verification of the developed intelligent mobility assistants.

Acknowledgements. The work leading to these results has received funding from the European Union under grant agreement n° 600796 (FP7-ICT MOBOT project).

References

1. Hirvensalo, M., Rantanen, T., Heikkinen, E.: Mobility difficulties and physical activity as predictors of mortality and loss of independence in the community-living older population. J. Am. Geriartric Soc. **48**, 493–498 (2005)
2. Chuy, O.J., Hirata, Y., Wang, Z., Kosuge, K.: Approach in assisting a sit-to-stand movement using robotic walking support system. In: IEE/RSJ International Conference on Intelligent Robots and Systems, China (2006)
3. Chugo, D., Asawa, T., Kitamura, T., Jia, S., Takase, K.: A rehabilitation walker with standing and walking assistance. In: IEE/RSJ International Conference on Intelligent Robots and Systems, Nice, France (2008)
4. Wakita, K., Huang, J., Di, P., Sekiyama, K., Fukuda, T.: Human walking-intention-based motion control of an omnidirectional-type cane robot. IEEE/ASME Trans. Mechatron. **18** (1), 285–296 (2013)
5. Hirata, Y., Komatsuda, S., Kosuge, K.: Fall prevention control of passive intelligent walker based on human model. In: IEE/RSJ International Conference on Intelligent Robots and Systems, IROS, Nice, France (2008)
6. Fotinea, S-E., Efthimiou, E., Koutsombogera, M., Dimou, A-L., Goulas, T., Maragos, P., Tzafestas, C.: The MOBOT human-robot communication model. In: Proceedings of 6th IEEE Conference on Cognitive Infocommunications (CogInfoCom 2015), Győr, Hungary, 19–21 October (2015)
7. Papageorgiou, X.S., Tzafestas, C.S., Maragos, P., Pavlakos, G., Chalvatzaki, G., Moustris, G., Kokkinos, I., Peer, A., Stanczyk, B., Fotinea, E.-S., Efthimiou, E.: Advances in intelligent mobility assistance robot integrating multimodal sensory processing. In: Stephanidis, C., Antona, M. (eds.) UAHCI 2014/HCII 2014 Part III. LNCS, vol. 8515, pp. 694–703. Springer, Heidelberg (2014)
8. Fotinea, E.-S., Efthimiou, E., Dimou, A.-L., Goulas, T., Karioris, P., Peer, A., Maragos, P., Tzafestas, C., Kokkinos, I., Hauer, K., Mombaur, K., Koumpouros, I., Stanzyk, B.: Data acquisition towards defining a multimodal interaction model for human – assistive robot communication. In: Stephanidis, C., Antona, M. (eds.) UAHCI 2014, Part III. LNCS, vol. 8515, pp. 613–624. Springer, Heidelberg (2014)
9. Trulls, E., Kokkinos, I., Sanfeliu, A., Moreno, F.: Dense segmentation-aware descriptors. In: Proceedings of IEEE Conference on Computer Vision and Pattern Recognition (CVPR) (2013)
10. Trulls, E., Kokkinos, I., Sanfeliu, A., Moreno, F.: Superpixel-grounded deformable part models. In: Proceedings of IEEE Conference on Computer Vision and Pattern Recognition (CVPR) (2014)
11. Boussaid, H., Kokkinos, I., Paragios, N.: Discriminative learning of de formable contour models. In: International Symposium on Biomedical Imaging (ISBI) (2014)
12. Pitsikalis, V., Katsamanis, A., Theodorakis, S., Maragos, P.: Multimodal gesture recognition via multiple hypotheses rescoring. J. Mach. Learn. Res. **16**(1), 255–284 (2015). http://www.jmlr.org/papers/volume16/pitsikalis15a/pitsikalis15a.pdf
13. Kardaris, R.N., Pitsikalis, V., Mavroudi, E., Katsamanis, A., Tsiami, A., Maragos, P.: Multimodal human action recognition in assistive human-robot interaction. In: Proceedings of 41st International Conference on Acoustics, Speech and Signal Processing (ICASSP 2016), Shanghai, China (2016)

14. Skordilis, Z.I., Tsiami, A., Maragos, P., Potamianos, G., Spelgatti, L., Sannino, R.: Multichannel speech enhancement using MEMS microphones. In: Proceedings of IEEE International Conference on Acoustics, Speech, and Signal Processing (ICASSP-2015), Brisbane, Australia, April 2015
15. Corredor, J., Sofrony, J., Peer, A.: Deciding on optimal assistance policies in haptic shared control tasks. In: IEEE International Conference on Robotics and Automation, pp. 2679–2684 (2014). http://dx.doi.org/10.1109/ICRA.2014.6907243
16. Ho Hoang, K.-L., Corradi, D., Mombaur, K.: Identification and classification of geriatric gait patterns - multi-contact capturability. In: French-German-Japanese Conference in Humanoid and Legged Robots, 12–14 May 2014, Heidelberg, Germany (2014)
17. Papageorgiou, X.S., Chalvatzaki, G., Tzafestas, C.S., Maragos, P.: Hidden Markov modeling of human normal gait using laser range finder for a mobility assistance robot. In: Proceedings of the 2014 IEEE International Conference on Robotics and Automation (ICRA-2014), Hong Kong, China, pp. 482–487, June 2014. http://dx.doi.org/10.1109/ICRA.2014.6906899
18. MOBOT Deliverable D5.3 - Report on performance metrics and first evaluation study. http://www.mobot-project.eu/userfiles/downloads/Deliverables/MOBOT_WP5_D5.3.pdf
19. MOBOT Deliverable D5.1: Preliminary report on use cases and user needs. http://www.mobot-project.eu/userfiles/downloads/Deliverables/MOBOT_WP5_D5.1_v1.5.pdf
20. MOBOT Deliverable D5.2: Report on use cases, performance metrics and user study preparations. http://www.mobot-project.eu/userfiles/downloads/Deliverables/MOBOT_WP5_D5.2_v1.5.pdf

Designing a Smart Scarf to Influence Group Members' Emotions in Ambience: Design Process and User Experience

Chen Guo[✉], Yingjie Victor Chen, Zhenyu Cheryl Qian, Yue Ma,
Hanhdung Dinh, and Saikiran Anasingaraju

Purdue University, West Lafayette, IN, USA
{guo171,victorchen,qianz,ma173,
hdinh,sanasing}@purdue.edu

Abstract. This paper presents the design rationale of a color-changing and olfactory scarf to affect people's emotional states in a group environment. The goal of the design is to cheer up depressed individuals or calm down those who are overexcited. Our design uses a heart rate sensor and a skin conductance sensor to detect and recognize emotional information. The scarf will change its color and emit an odor to enhance positive emotions or reduce negative ones. We went through a user-centered design process and discussed different forms of design. Given the wearability and comfort characteristics of scarves, we decided to choose scarves as the solution to regulate emotions.

Keywords: Design process · Wearable technology · Emotion regulation

1 Introduction

With the development of wearable sensors and textile technologies, wearable devices have been incorporated into our everyday life. Using unobtrusive and wearable technology as emotional assistance for wearers has been considered as an important research question in the field of Human-computer interaction (HCI). Not only is it essential to boost one's own emotional health, it also crucial to influence others' emotional states through interactions in a group environment. People are easily affected by the emotions and feelings among group members. For example, surrounded by people complaining about their situations, most likely you will feel depressed and sad. If your spouse comes home wearing a big smiling face, your mood can be dramatically affected and you will soon become happier. Researchers call this phenomenon "group emotional contagion" [1]. Affective devices should take into account the shared emotions occurring in groups and help their wearers to be aware of their bodily experience in depression or overexcitement and consequently help modify or pacify their emotions.

Designing for group emotional health with wearable technologies presents a new challenge to interaction designers. Wearable tech design should also be put in a group's context. It raises different issues and principles in addition to those of self-emotional awareness and regulation. Designers need to find the important touchpoints with users during the design process. This paper focuses only on people's bodily experiences in

© Springer International Publishing Switzerland 2016
M. Antona and C. Stephanidis (Eds.): UAHCI 2016, Part II, LNCS 9738, pp. 392–402, 2016.
DOI: 10.1007/978-3-319-40244-4_38

two extreme emotions: depression and overexcitement. After discussing existing design process and concepts within the wearable computing field, we conducted a phenomenological research to understand the aesthetic and technical needs of users for group emotional comfort. By comparing design alternatives and gathering feedbacks from users, our work extends current smart textile artifacts by proposing a scarf design concept aiming to assist in group emotional interactions.

2 Related Work

2.1 Quantified Self in Emotions

Quantified self is defined as the individual activities to track and monitor biological, physical, behavioral, or environmental information [2]. One recent trend in quantified self is that wearable technology is becoming more and more popular [3]. Humans are able to fabricate biosensors to detect physiological and mental changes. Many studies focus on how to monitor emotions and moods. Instead of using self-reports to measure moods, physiological signals, including heart rate, skin conductance, electrocardiogram, blood volume, and temperature, are broadly used to recognize them [4]. With an extensive survey of the work in emotion elicitation and recognition, researchers developed a multimodal affective user interface to monitor emotions via wearable computers and physiological signals [4]. To measure automobile drivers' stress, we used electrocardiogram, electromyogram, skin conductance, and respiration as metrics to classify their varied states [5]. Some researchers reported that five physiological signals, including blood volume pulse, electromyography, skin conductance, skin temperature, and respiration successfully extracted 30 features to recognize and classify emotional states [6]. Researches proposed that heart rate variability and skin conductance response were the dominant physiological signals to differentiate basic emotions such as happiness, sadness, indifference, anger, and stress [5, 7].

2.2 Affective Computing in Emotion Contagion

As an active research topic, affective computing aims to provide promising applications with computational technology to elicit and affect users' emotional experiences [8]. A few affective wearable products have been designed and created not only to modify emotional states of wearers, but also to transfer emotional states to others. SWARM is a wearable scarf to regulate wearer's emotions and to alert others' emotions through actuations [9]. The paper clearly presented the iterative, user-centered approach to address affective computing. The laughing dress supports social trust and enhances positive feelings among strangers by relating laughter to visual patterns of LED lights [10]. In the design concept, laughter is used as an emotional contagion to explore psychophysiological mirroring in HCI. Sensory Fiction is a wearable reading system to induce and evoke emotions of a person reading a book [11]. The paper reported that a social network was very powerful in altering people's moods through emotion contagion. It also proposed that affective computing and emotion monitoring should be regulated in the private sphere instead of face-to-face interactions and habitual emotional suppression [11].

2.3 Design Process in Wearable Computing

Wearable computing addresses product design problems from an interdisciplinary perspective that requires the close collaboration between textile designers and electronics engineers. Some researchers stated that design for wearables is not simply combing electronic components with fashionable clothing; it should include physical form, electronic components, GUI (graphical user interface), physical interface, and embodied product value [12]. The design process for wearable computing is also regarded as a set of procedures to solve a problem with various types of information [13]. Moreover, researchers developed a design methodology for wearable computing and indicated that authenticity may inform the design process [14]. Furthermore, they explored the role of the prototype in user-centered design processes for wearables. And some studies reported important design principles to guide such design decisions as aesthetics, affordance, comfort, contextual-awareness, customization, ease of use, ergonomy, wearability, and fashion [15].

3 Phenomenal Research to Gather Requirements

The purpose of our design is to help people become more aware of their emotions in a group environment and also to help them enhance positive emotions and mitigate negative ones. To understand the lived phenomenal experience of users, we have relied on phenomenological research to focus on user needs, especially IPA (Interpretative Phenomenological Analysis). The aim of IPA is to examine how users are experiencing and feeling in a group environment.

3.1 Participants

We recruited 12 participants through a snowball sampling method: 8 males and 4 females, 1 listed undergraduate student, 7 listed Master's students, 3 listed Ph.D. students, and 1 listed faculty member. Their ages ranged from the 20 s to the 40 s, and no participants were color-blind.

3.2 Data Collection and Analysis

The guided semistructure interview allowed us to understand and gather participants' descriptions of their lived phenomenal experiences, including feelings, thoughts, images, and memories. The essential open-ended interview questions were to learn user attitudes toward wearable objects and their emotional state within a group environment. We encouraged participants to describe what their bodies had experienced in terms of stressful situations, depressed situations, and over-excited situations in a group context and how their feelings had been affected in such a phenomenon. The interview felt like a natural exploratory conversation.

The interview questions are listed as follows:

- What are the things you wear that are able to cheer you up?
- What are the things you wear that are able to calm you down?
- What are the things you want to wear when feeling depressed or overexcited?
- Do you have any favorite wearable product? If so, can you describe the reason why you like it the most?
- Which materials below will make you comfortable? Woolen, cotton, nylon, fiber, silk, others?
- Can you describe a situation that would make you depressed or overexcited?
- Can you talk about how you shared or experienced emotions in a group environment?
- Will the mood of the group environment change your current feeling? How would the group environment affect you when you feel depressed or overexcited?
- Have you ever been in a group situation where you wanted to cheer up the group members or calm them down? How would you do that? How did your emotions affect the others' emotions?

After the interview, we read the transcripts and transformed the initial notes into emerging themes. A thematic analysis was applied to systematically classify the qualitative data. In the theme analysis, three researchers picked up the most prevalent and important issues that contributed most to the analysis and deleted some overlapping items. Researchers then referred back to the transcription to reach a consensus that those selective codes were the most important ones affecting the overall emotional experiences. In the end, researchers refined the final categories by combining some relevant subcategories.

3.3   The Main Findings

To set up the guidelines of our design, we concluded with the following three requirements based on the interview study.

Style: Wearable Products Should be Soft, Light, and Comfortable. Wearable products are the extension of human bodies and perceived as a second skin. Because of the close interaction with our body, physiological pleasure such as softness, lightness, comfort, and smoothness could affect people's choice of wearable products. Most participants loved cotton and woolen, which gives people pleasant sensations.

Participants cared about how other people perceive the product. One female student said, "When I am very excited, I wear a beautiful light dress. It makes me feel good and proud. I really care about how my friends perceive me. If I am judged harshly, my life will be miserable." Color is strong visual information and can relate to different perceptions and moods. This finding inspired us to create a comfortable cotton garment that can enhance psychological pleasure with color changing.

Aesthetic Emotions: Recognizing Emotions in an Aesthetic and Subtle Way Instead of Naked in an Emotional Expression. In the interview, a female user had this to say:

> "I was once angry with my roommate and totally out of control. I am not always aware of my negative emotions. I know it is important to understand and manage emotions, but I don't want to wear a band or a necklace to monitor my mood...it's like your inner state is exposed in public. Everyone will know your emotions. Why not influence my emotions directly?"

A male student told us that with this product he was concerned about looking like an alien to group members. He expected the product would be normal and acceptable.

Their words show that users may not be aware of their negative emotions and have the ability to control them, but they do care about the emotional states of their bodies. However, sometimes people want to hide their real emotions instead of showing them openly in public. They are more willing to silently influence their emotions rather than to translate emotional expressions frankly in a group environment. There are some privacy concerns about emotions. This inspired us to consider that people may want new technology to help them control their feelings in an aesthetic, subtle, and silent way.

Moreover, the smart wearable product should look normal to others, not obvious and strange. Fashionable products are also to be favored when they are able to convey their emotions subtly and unobtrusively.

Social Emotions: Emotional Empathy in Social Relations Makes People Feel Pleasure and Becomes a Distraction to Their Inner State. We asked participants several short questions pertaining to the phenomenon when they felt depressed or overexcited and what affected their experience of body in a group environment. Most were college students, and they admitted always feeling depressed because of exams, deadlines, presentations, singing, and win-lose situations. When they were depressed, they preferred a brighter environment rather than dim light. Some participants would like to go out and do something like shopping, singing, and drawing with their friends to distract their emotions. They also preferred a calm place with few people around. More people would cause more pressure.

Another interesting thing about negative emotions is that people usually dislike talking too much to the group members if they are in a depressed situation. They would rather talk less and create a relaxed environment so that their friends will feel good. These findings encourage us to explore a new interactive way to communicate non-verbal emotional expressions in a group. Emotions can be transmitted through a wearable garment and enhance social bonds among people without invading privacy.

All participants revealed that environment greatly affects overexcited emotions. One participant said, "When I am among excited people and talking about things I like, I'll get excited." Another one mentioned, "When I hang out with my friends or my family, we do too many things that make me laugh so much or make me lose control of my own laughing." People tend to express their excited emotions and are rarely aware of their harm. Before they reach the state of burnout, people want empathic interactions and let the other people feel the same way they do. They seek intimacy, attachment, and social interaction among people. This finding led us to use emphatic interaction to increase emotional wellbeing. Viewers' bodies are also an interface for the wearer. We can find ways to connect people and change people's emotions through other people's bodies. Emotional empathy in social relations makes people feel social pleasure and also become a distraction to people's inner state. A wearable garment can be a social medium to create new social interaction from private to public, intrapersonal to interpersonal.

4   Design Process

Given the interview results, we defined our design goals as using wearable and unobtrusive technology to affect their extreme emotions. The artifact needs to be physically and socially acceptable. We went through a series of brainstorming and sketching activities and came up with different concepts with regard to the wearable technologies and design forms.

4.1   Technology Options

Wearable Sensors. A wide range of technology options is available to detect emotional information. Emotion recognition using biosensors is an effective way to monitor human physiological signals, including heart rate variability (HRV), skin conductance (GSR), skin temperature, respiration, body volume pulse (BVP), and brain waves (EEG). As mentioned in the literature review, heart rate and skin conductance are the most reliable metrics to measure emotions. These sensors need not monitor wearers for a long time. The traditional way to measure heart rate is to attach wearable sensors to a person's chest. Previous work also demonstrated that it was possible to monitor the heart rate of an individual within one meter by use of the electric potential sensor [16]. Skin conductance is a highly important tool to measure emotional arousal. Studies indicate that feet, fingers, and shoulders were the most responsive positions of skin conductance [17]. We decided to use heart rate sensors and skin conductance sensors to measure emotions. The most important feature of the wearable sensors is reliable reading of body data and fast signal processing. The sensors should be also light in design and make wearers feel comfortable [18].

Wireless Communication. Wireless technologies have effectively infiltrated our everyday lives involve the transmission of data between different nodes over the air. There are four popular types of wireless technologies – infrared, Bluetooth, Wi-Fi, and Zigbee. Wi-Fi is mostly used for computer communications to access the Internet. Bluetooth is intended to support communications among connected devices, such as smartphones communicating to wireless headphones. Zigbee is ideal for low-power consumption and short-range communications. Infrared technology is widely used for device communications in short- and medium-range device communications. It can send or receive location information and decode signals. Considering the long transmission distance as well as the inexpensive cost, we chose the infrared receiver to receive the emotion data from the other wearers' sensors and to pass the raw data to the LilyPad controller for processing and analyzing the information.

Dynamic Output. Our concept is to influence people's emotions in a group environment. If one person is depressed or overexcited, the other individuals in this group will create a happy or calm environment with the use of wearable devices to affect his or her feelings. Bearing in mind the concept of group emotional interaction, we want to address emotions with sound, light, color, vibration, temperature, and olfaction. However, feeling the vibration and temperature are always from self to self instead of from others to self. They conflict with our design concept. Playing sound can make people feel happy or sad. Lighting in a room also has an effect on people's feeling. But these actuations are too obtrusive for wearers and may cause uncomfortable feelings. Thus we decided to use color and olfaction as the way to change emotions.

Color has psychological properties and conveys emotions biologically and culturally. Different colors are linked to different emotions. For example, blue may make people feel calm and peaceful; red is usually related to the feelings of optimism, energy, and passion. Olfaction is another powerful sense to enhance or reduce people's emotions. Smell plays an important role in social interaction and effectively triggers emotional memories deep inside the brain. The smell of lavender calms anxiety, and the scent of jasmine eases depression. The LilyPad controller will be used to process the raw emotion data from wearable sensors and display the visual and olfactory outputs in the wearable device.

4.2 Design Alternatives and Rapid Evaluation

After addressing the technology issues, we used brainstorming to generate ideas of design forms and proposed four possible solutions – a woolen vest, a plastic hairband, a cotton bracelet, and a cotton scarf (Fig. 1). All these four products will be incorporated with heart rate sensors and skin conductance sensors. Thus the devices will be able to monitor heart rate and skin conductance. In a group, if one wearer's smart object detects high heart rate and high values of skin conductance response (SCR) data, an infrared receiver in the device will send a signal to the other devices in this group. Once receiving the signal, the LilyPad controller of the other devices will process the data and determine the emotional index. Overexcitement usually raises heart rate and SCR values; depression is always associated with low heart rate and low SCR values. Once the extreme emotions are detected, the other individuals' smart devices will change their colors to cheer up or cool down the individual with negative emotions. In the meantime, the scent capsules of the other smart devices controlled by LilyPad Arduino will emit jasmine to cheer up or lavender to help calm down.

We presented the four low-fidelity prototypes to the same 12 participants recruited in the previous user study. The goal of the evaluation was to gather user feedbacks and investigate design improvements. Participants were asked to express what they felt about wearing the products. They had some concerns about the hairband and bracelet. No male participants wanted to wear a hairband, and it also seemed awkward for some female participants. The bracelet was simple and easy to wear, but it was not noticeable when worn. It was hard to detect the bracelet's color changes on people's wrists. Some participants were quite interested to see what the vest would look like to address emotions. They would be excited to wear such a vest to influence the other people's

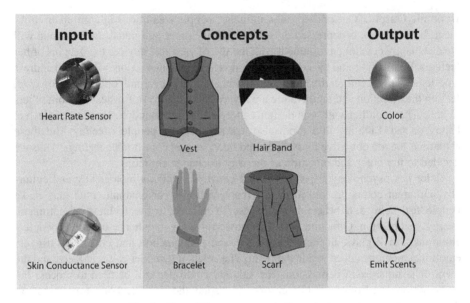

Fig. 1. Four different concepts of our design

feeling. However, a color-changing vest may draw too much attention, and they were worried about wearing it every day.

The cotton scarf concept received the more-positive feedbacks from participants. Participants felt comfortable when they wore a scarf every day. As a great accessory for both men and women, scarves are fashionable and affordable. They can be worn either indoors or outdoors. These findings led to the key insight that we would like to make a smart scarf that can change its color in a silent way based on people's negative emotions. Wrapped around the neck, a scarf is suitable for both men and women. It is usually accepted as part of our clothes. Therefore we decided to use a color combination (colors of scarves and clothes) for emotion regulation. Participants also mentioned that they wanted the smart device to influence their own emotions when they were alone. But the scarf concept will bring problems to self-regulation, since the wearer needs to look down to notice the changes.

During the interview, we also asked participants to connect their emotions to color. Blue was the favorite color for most male participants. Their preferences were mostly blue, navy blue, light blue, yellow, and light orange to cheer them up. Females preferred brighter and soft colors, such as light pink, red, orange, and yellow, to cheer them up. Concerning the favorite color to make people calm down, most males chose dark colors, such as gray, dark blue, green, and teal; the females loved blue, green, white, and light gray.

4.3   The Final Concept

We finally chose cotton scarf as the solution to transfer wearer's negative emotions to positive ones (Fig. 2). A heart rate sensor and a skin conductance sensor will be attached closer to the middle of the scarf. Wearers need to make sure the skin conductance sensor will touch the shoulder so that the responses will be more accurate. Sensors will send extreme emotion data to the IR transceivers in the group, and they will pass the raw data to the LilyPad controller. Then LilyPad will process the most negative emotion first and change the scarf's color to cheer up or calm down individuals. When the wearer is alone, the scarf will measure only his or her emotion to make people feel good.

IR Transceiver

Lilypad

Color Sensor

Skin Conductance Sensor

Heart Rate Sensor

Emit Scents

Fig. 2. The final concept of the smart scarf

In regard to color changing, scarves will be painted with thermochromics inks, which can change their hues with the use of electrical conductors heating up the surface. By controlling the temperature, thermochromics inks can show a wide range of colors. In general, we will use blue to cool down wearers and orange to cheer up them. In consideration of the unobtrusive appearance of scarves, their colors will vary to match wearers' clothes. Instead of passively perceived colors, wearers can actively change colors to affect different emotions.

5   Discussion and Conclusion

Using colors to change emotion is a valid solution. Wearers from different cultures interpret color differently. Sometimes misunderstanding may develop during group interaction. One possible solution to solve this issue is to create a mobile app connecting to the scarf. The app will ask the wearer to enter demographic information.

Wearers can also change scarf color settings. Thus the smart scarf is able to help customize the display color under user preference.

The limitations of heart rate sensors and skin conductance sensors may cause inaccurate readings. Moreover, the two sensors couldn't differentiate all of the body emotions. We may therefore consider using multiple channels, including respiration and blood volume pulse, to recognize emotions.

The purpose of our design is to regulate people's emotions in a group environment with the use of a wearable and acceptable product. As human beings, our emotions are easily affected by those of others. The user study shows that people don't want to be exposed to unwanted attention, and they do care more about emotional privacy. By taking advantage of emotional contagion, we designed the system hardware and proposed four different concepts to influence emotions. According to user feedbacks, wearing a scarf outweighs the other forms.

In future work we will conduct an evaluation with the high-fidelity prototype to refine the final design concept. We are also going to build a working prototype of the system with engineers.

References

1. Barsade, S.G.: The ripple effect: emotional contagion and its influence on group behavior. Adm. Sci. Q. **47**(4), 644–675 (2002)
2. Swan, M.: The quantified self: fundamental disruption in big data science and biological discovery. Big Data **1**(2), 85–99 (2013)
3. Fawcett, T.: Mining the quantified self: personal knowledge discovery as a challenge for data science. Big. Data **3**(4), 249–266 (2015)
4. etitia Lisetti, C.L., Nasoz, F.: Using noninvasive wearable computers to recognize human emotions from physiological signals. EURASIP J. Appl. Sig. Process. **2004**, 1672–1687 (2004)
5. Healey, J.A., Picard, R.W.: Detecting stress during real-world driving tasks using physiological sensors. IEEE Trans. Intell. Transp. Syst. **6**(2), 156–166 (2005)
6. Maaoui, C.M., Pruski, A.: Emotion Recognition through Physiological Signals for Human-Machine Communication, Sep 2010
7. Quazi, M.T., Mukhopadhyay, S.C., Suryadevara, N.K., Huang, Y.M.: Towards the smart sensors based human emotion recognition. In: 2012 IEEE International Instrumentation and Measurement Technology Conference (I2MTC), pp. 2365–2370 (2012)
8. Tao, J., Tan, T.: Affective computing: a review. In: Tao, J., Tan, T., Picard, R.W. (eds.) ACII 2005. LNCS, vol. 3784, pp. 981–995. Springer, Heidelberg (2005)
9. Williams, M.A., Roseway, A., O'Dowd, C., Czerwinski, M., Morris, M.R.: SWARM: an actuated wearable for mediating affect. In: Proceedings of the Ninth International Conference on Tangible, Embedded, and Embodied Interaction, New York, NY, USA, pp. 293–300 (2015)
10. Lee, S., Chung, (Wynnie) W.Y., Ip, E., Schiphorst, T.: The laughing dress: evoking prosocial interaction among strangers. In: CHI 2014 Extended Abstracts on Human Factors in Computing Systems, New York, NY, USA, pp. 2143–2148 (2014)

11. Heibeck, F., Hope, A., Legault, J.: Sensory fiction: a design fiction of emotional computation. In: Proceedings of the 2Nd ACM International Workshop on Immersive Media Experiences, New York, NY, USA, pp. 35–40 (2014)
12. Maeda, J.: The Laws of Simplicity. MIT Press, Cambridge, Mass (2006)
13. Clothing, S.: Technology and Applications, 1st edn. CRC Press, Boca Raton, FL (2009)
14. Kettley, S.: Crafting the wearable computer: design process and user experience: volume two. Ph.d., Napier University, Edinburgh (2007)
15. Motti, V.G., Caine, K.: Human factors considerations in the design of wearable devices. Proc. Hum. Factors Ergon. Soc. Annu. Meet. **58**(1), 1820–1824 (2014)
16. Harland, C.J., Prance, R.J., Prance, H.: Remote monitoring of biodynamic activity using electric potential sensors. J. Phys: Conf. Ser. **142**, 12042 (2008). 10.1088/1742-6596/142/1/012042
17. van Dooren, M., de Vries, J.J., Janssen, J.H.: Emotional sweating across the body: comparing 16 different skin conductance measurement locations. Physiol. Behav. **106**(2), 298–304 (2012)
18. Nag, A., Mukhopadhyay, S.C.: Wearable electronics sensors: current status and future opportunities. In: Mukhopadhyay, S.C. (ed.) Wearable Electronics Sensors. SSMI, vol. 15, pp. 1–35. Springer, Heidelberg (2015)

Wheelchair Users' Psychological Barrier Estimation Based on Inertial and Vital Data

Takashi Isezaki[1]([✉]), Arinobu Niijima[1], Akihiro Miyata[2],
Tomoki Watanabe[1], and Osamu Mizuno[1]

[1] NTT Service Evolution Laboratories, NTT Corporation, Tokyo, Japan
isezaki.takashi@lab.ntt.co.jp
[2] NTT, Tokyo, Japan

Abstract. Wheelchair users face many "barriers" that interrupt their movement outside. In order to support wheelchair users' comfortable movement, many studies use crowd-sourcing to understand the "barriers". However, barriers can be classified into physical barriers and psychological barriers, and many studies focused on only physical barriers. Psychological barriers disrupt the wheelchair users by increasing the level of stress. For example, too much traffic or inadequate visibility make the users anxious or stressed. It is important to understand psychological barriers to support wheelchair users' safe/comfort movement. We focus on the psychological barriers and propose a method for estimating the impact of such barriers. As the metric, we use "ride comfort". This paper gathers and processes inertial and vital data to propose a ride comfort estimation method.

Keywords: Wheelchair · Barrier estimation · Ride comfort

1 Introduction

Locomotion ability is diverse arise from several factors such as sex, ages and medical histories, and many people have to use wheelchair. Moreover, advanced personal mobility devices consisting of multiple wheels and computers are starting to enter daily life. It is presumed that the use of wheelchair type devices will only increase. The surface conditions of paths and roads such as roughness or inclines may interfere with wheelchair users' convenience while bipedal walkers experience no such difficulties. By gathering such surface information, we can improve movement ease for wheelchair users. MLIT(Ministry of Land, Infrastructure, Transport and Tourism) is distributing barrier information such as the existence of the roughness or gradients of roads [1]. Typical, barrier information is gathered by the office in charge of the facilities such as stations and parks. However, the amount of barrier information is insufficient, and much barrier information too old. In order to better support user movement, information must be gathered often from various areas and in more detail.

Many projects use the crowd-sourcing approach for collecting information about road surface state. For example, PADM(NPO Corporation) is running

© Springer International Publishing Switzerland 2016
M. Antona and C. Stephanidis (Eds.): UAHCI 2016, Part II, LNCS 9738, pp. 403–413, 2016.
DOI: 10.1007/978-3-319-40244-4_39

the project "Let's join together to create a Barrier Free Map" which uses smartphones to gather barrier information. This project won a grand prize in Google Impact Challenge [2]. As detailed in "Basic Program for Persons with Disabilities" which is published by the Japanese Cabinet, "Barrier" includes not only physical barriers such as roughness or slopes, but also psychological barriers such as a feeling of pressure or feeling of fear [3]. For example, areas that have cars passing nearby make wheelchair users afraid. Such areas represent a significant psychological barrier. Psychological barriers for wheelchair users are not considered by most researchers and most technologies focus on physical barriers such as road state.

"Ride Comfort" is commonly used as a metric related to psychological barriers [4,5]. Sawada et al. studied the ride comfort of wheelchair users in collaboration with medical and welfare institutions, and showed that ride comfort can be identified by terms such "Relief", "Safety", "Comfort", "Stability"[4]. In accordance with the findings of Sawada et al., we define "ride comfort" as the psychological barrier metric. Since many current technologies exist for gathering physical barrier information, our goal is to create a methodology for gathering psychological barrier information. This paper proposes a method that can estimate ride comfort based on inertial and vital data. It is confirmed by an experiment involving 12 subjects and 4 different courses. Our proposal will improve the comfort of wheelchair users by allowing physical and psychological barriers to be gathered and disseminated. In terms of HCI, user adaptive system is important. If user feels fear, computer should calculate and recommend different ways dynamically. The proposed method is expected to extract information for system's decision making. Therefore, this paper contributes to the user adaptive navigation or recommendation system.

2   Related Works

Many studies have focused on "Ride comfort" as a metric to evaluate physical and psychological factors and how they impact users. Liu et al. provided a factor analysis of the ride comfort of automobile users [5]. They found that ride comfort consisted of 3 groups of factors; vibratory stimulation factors such as vibration strength and frequency, physiological factors such as physical condition and alertness, and psychological factors such as mood and sense of stability. Sawada et al. studied the ride comfort of wheelchair users in collaboration with medical and welfare institutions, and introduced the semantic differential method which assesses ride comfort in terms of "Relief", "Safety", "Comfort", "Stability" [4,6].

Evaluating the surface state of roads, which is assumed to impact ride comfort, has been the goal of many researchers. Mounting acceleration sensors on wheelchairs and user responses are common techniques for evaluating the surface state of roads [7–9]. Some works tried to find barriers in urban areas by mounting acceleration and gyro sensors on wheelchairs [2,10,11]. Iwasawa et al. applied a learning support vector machine to acceleration data to detect roughness and slopes [10]. Kuwahara et al. showed how to detect road surface state with 85 % accuracy by applying the k-nearest neighbor method to acceleration data [11].

Some researchers have studied mental stress, which is assumed to be related to ride comfort. Mental stress estimation methods based on vital data have been proposed. Yokoyama et al. evaluate driver alertness from heartbeat rhythms [12]. Imai et al. proposed a way to quantitatively estimate the driver's mental workload from heart rate variability [11].

3 Ride Comfort Estimation Based on Inertial and Vital Data

This paper classifies barriers as physical or psychological, and proposes a method for estimating psychological barrier. As the ground truth of mental stress, we adopt the semantic differential method of Sawada et al. Wheelchair users have to respond to a questionnaire to assess the factors of "Relief", "Safety", "Comfort", "Stability". It is difficult for users to respond a questionnaire in real environments. Therefore, we propose a methodology for estimating ride comfort automatically, based on sensor data. The users are assumed to manipulate wheelchairs carefully, and to feel stress or fear in areas that impose high psychological burdens on the user. The burden is identified by gathering the physical movements of the wheelchair under the control of the user. Feelings of stress or fear are assumed to be reflected in the users' vital data such as heartbeat. Figure 1 shows the concept of the proposed method.

The ride comfort estimation method consists of a learning phase and an estimation phase. In the learning phase, sensor data vector $d = (s, acc, gyro, rri)$ is used; s is the degree of ride comfort, time-series 3-axis acceleration data acc, time-series 3-axis gyro data $gyro$, and RRI data rri. $acc = (ax, ay, az)$; time-series x-axis, y-axis, z-axis data is ax, ay, az, respectively. $gyro = (gx, gy, gz)$; time-series x-axis, y-axis, z-axis data is gx, gy, gz, respectively. From the heartbeat data we extract pulse shape, which includes P, Q, R, S, T waves. Time-series RRI data rri is obtained by calculating R wave intervals. x, y, z-axis acceleration data and x, y, z-axis gyro data are used as inertial data. Inertial features, shown in Table 1 are extracted from the inertial data. Statistical features(Minimum, Maximum, Amplitude, Median, Average, Standard deviation,

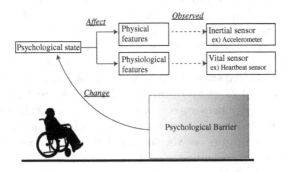

Fig. 1. The concept of the proposed method

Table 1. Inertial features

Feature	Explanation
min	Minimum
max	Maximum
ptp	Amplitude
median	Median
ave	Average
std	Standard deviation
amp0-1	0-1Hz freq intensity
amp1-2	1-2Hz freq intensity
amp2-3	2-3Hz freq intensity
amp3-4	3-4Hz freq intensity
amp4-5	4-5Hz freq intensity
amp5-6	5-6Hz freq intensity
amp6-7	6-7Hz freq intensity
amp7-8	7-8Hz freq intensity
amp8-9	8-9Hz freq intensity
amp9-10	9-10Hz freq intensity
amp10-11	10-11Hz freq intensity
amp11-12	11-12Hz freq intensity
amp12-13	12-13Hz freq intensity
amp13-14	13-14Hz freq intensity
amp14-15	14-15Hz freq intensity

Variance) and Frequency features(the intensity of the frequency of from 0 to 15[Hz] of 6-axis data at 1[Hz] intervals) are extracted.

Vital features are extracted as shown in Table 2. Bauer et al. investigated the relationship between heartbeat variability and the nervous system [14]. Heart rate variability(HRV) features are used as vital features.

mRR, SDNN, RMSSD, SDSD, pNN50, LF Norm, HF Norm, LFHF Ratio are calculated by following equations.

$$mRR = \frac{1}{N} \sum_{n=1}^{N} RRI_i \tag{1}$$

$$SDNN = \sqrt{\frac{1}{N-1} \sum_{n=1}^{N} (RRI_i - mRR)^2} \tag{2}$$

Table 2. Vital features

Feature	Explanation
mRR	Average of RRI
SDNN	Standard deviation of RRI
RMSSD	Root mean square of the difference between adjacent RRI
SDSD	Standard deviation of the difference between adjacent RRI
pNN50	Ratio of the difference between the adjacent RRI is equal to or more than 50ms
TotalPower	Frequency intensity lower than 0.4Hz
LF	Frequency intensity of 0.04-0.15Hz
LF Norm	Ratio of LF to TotalPower
HF	Frequency intensity of 0.15-0.4Hz
HF Norm	Ratio of HF to TotalPower
LFHF Ratio	Ratio of LF and HF
VLF	Frequency intensity lower than 0.04Hz

$$RMSSDN = \sqrt{\frac{1}{N}\sum_{n=1}^{N-1}(RRI_{i+1} - RRI_i)^2} \tag{3}$$

$$mA = \frac{1}{N-1}\sum_{n=1}^{N-1}(RRI_{i+1} - RRI_i) \tag{4}$$

$$SDSD = \frac{1}{N-1}\sum_{n=1}^{N-1}\{(RRI_{i+1} - RRI_i) - mA\}^2 \tag{5}$$

$$pNN50 = \frac{num(RRI > 50)}{num(RRI)} \tag{6}$$

$$LFNorm = \frac{LF}{TotalPower} \tag{7}$$

$$HFNorm = \frac{HF}{TotalPower} \tag{8}$$

$$LFHFRatio = \frac{LF}{HF} \tag{9}$$

144 dimension feature $\boldsymbol{f}$ is extracted from each datum $\boldsymbol{d}$, and each feature is normalized so that the average is 0.0 and variation is 1.0. Estimator $\boldsymbol{M}$ is created through machine learning, where the score(degree) of ride comfort, s, is the objective variable, and feature f is the explanatory variable. In the estimation phase, 144 dimension feature $\boldsymbol{f}$ is extracted from each datum $\boldsymbol{d}$. Ride comfort score s is calculated by using Estimator $\boldsymbol{M}$ and $\boldsymbol{f}$ as follows.

$$s = \boldsymbol{M}(\boldsymbol{f}) \tag{10}$$

4   Experiment

4.1   Purpose and Setup

The purpose of the experiment is to verify the accuracy of the proposed method. To verify the validity of the proposed method, Baseline1:only inertial data based method and Baseline2:only vital data based method were compared, 12 males participated (average age:28.3).

In order to collect a wide range of ride comfort scores, 4 courses were set as shown in Fig. 2. The environments were designed to alter each subjects psychological state. The narrow roads demand careful operation, while the uneven roads impose feelings of discomfort or disgust. In order to narrow course width while ensuring safety, we used paper cups. Subjects were asked not to damage/upset paper cups in Courses B and D. Woodblocks (height:4cm) and cable guards (height:3cm) were used in Courses C and D to impose a feeling of discomfort. Course D is shown in Fig. 3. Course A was designed to more clearly identify the psychological changes triggered by Courses B, C, and D.

In this experiment, WHILL(WHILL Corp.; max speed:6km/h, width:60cm) was used as a wheelchair. Acceleration and gyro data were acquired at 30[Hz] by

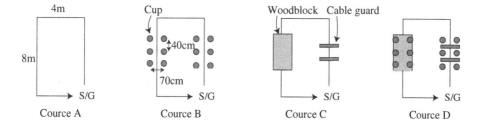

Fig. 2. Experimental environment

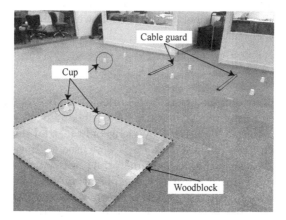

Fig. 3. Experimental landscape

Fig. 4. Axis coordination of the inertial sensor

Table 3. Questionnaire for ride comfort score

Number	Questionnaire
Q1	You felt stress?
Q2	You felt fear
Q3	You felt danger?
Q4	Had to take care?
Q5	Was it comfortable?
Q6	Were there uncomfortable shakiness?
Q7	Could you operate smoothly?
Q8	Could you follow the course?
Q9	Could you keep things stable?

mounting an Xperia A(Sony; Android OS 4.2) to the wheelchair with the axis setting shown in Fig. 4. RRI data was acquired by using myBeat(UNION Tool Corp.).

Table 3 shows the questionnaires used for acquiring ride comfort scores. Each subject drove around each course 3 times, and answered the questionnaires using a 7 point scale(6:very positive, 0:very negative) after circuit. The ride comfort score of each circuit, s, was calculated by the following equation, where s_k is the score of the k-that circuit.

$$s = \frac{\sum_{k=1}^{9} s_k}{9} \tag{11}$$

12 data sets d were obtained from each subject. Finally, 144 data $d_0, \ldots, d_{143}$ were obtained from all subjects. Features f described in Sect. 3 were calculated from each datum. Features obtained by using only inertial data $f_{inertial}$, and those obtained by using only vital data f_{vital} were used for Baseline1, Baseline2, respectively. In the learning phase, estimator M was created. The objective variable was the ride comfort score, s, the explanatory variable is the feature f. In the estimating phase, the correlation between obtained score and estimated score was determined by 10-fold cross validation. For learning, Random Forest

Regressor(Python Scikit-learn) was used, the number of trees in the forest was 10, the number of features to consider when looking for the best split was 10.

4.2   Results and Discussions

Figure 5 shows the averaged ride comfort score of each course. The courses (A, B, C, D) are shown in Fig. 2; the number is the number of circuits. For example, "Course C:3" is the 3rd circuit of Course C. The averaged scores of 3 times circuits are Course A:4.55, Course B:3.15, Course C:2.92, Course D:2.56. Comparing the scores of each trial of each course, the ride comfort score increased with the number of trials. As shown in Fig. 6, the differences on comfort score between the 1st trial and 3rd trial are Course A:0.78, Course B:0.96, Course C:0.80, Course D:0.43. The scores increased in later trials because the subjects became accustomed to the courses. This result showed that "ride comfort" alters with habituation. Of course, ride comfort is also assumed to depend on the road state. Course D was the most complex course and so the habituation effect was weakest in Course D.

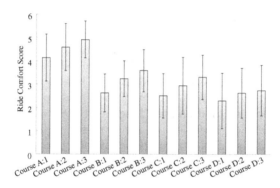

Fig. 5. Ride comfort score of each course

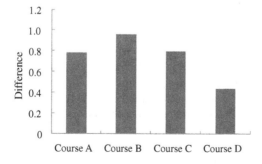

Fig. 6. Difference of the score of 1st time and 3rd time

Table 4. Correlation coefficient between obtained score and estimated score

Proposed method	Baseline1	Baseline2
0.759	0.684	0.543

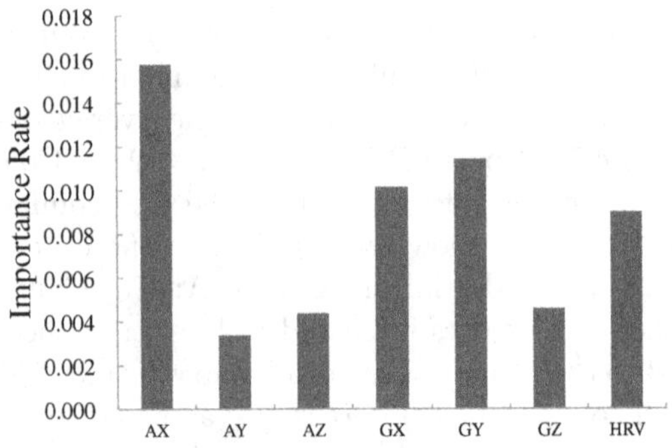

Fig. 7. Averaged importance of each features

Ride Comfort Estimation. In order to verify the validity of the proposed method, we determined the correlation between the obtained score and estimated score. As shown in Table 4, correlation coefficient of the proposed method was 0.759, that of the baseline1 was 0.684, that of the baseline2 was 0.543. We used bonferroni correction as a multiple comparison technique. There was a significant difference between the proposed method and the baseline2 according to the t-test($t(18) = 3.93$, $p < 0.05 / 3$). However, there was no significant difference between the proposed method and the baseline1 ($t(18) = 1.31$, $p > 0.05 / 3$). Although the correlation coefficient of the proposed method was higher than that of others, further studies are needed for validating the acceptable accuracy.

In order to investigate the contribution of each feature, the importance of each feature was calculated and compared by averaging each sensor type(x-axis acceleration, y-axis acceleration, z-axis acceleration, x-axis gyro, y-axis gyro, z-axis gyro, HRV). In the example of x-axis acceleration, the average of all x-axis features, shown in Table 1, was calculated. The result is shown in Fig. 7. "AX", "AY", "AZ" refer to the importances of x-axis, y-axis, z-axis acceleration data, respectively. "GX", "GY", "GZ" represent x-axis, y-axis, z-axis gyro importances, respectively. "HRV" is HRV importance. It can be seen that importance order is x-axis acceleration, y-axis gyro, x-axis gyro, and HRV.

We assume that there was no significant difference between proposed method and baseline1 because of the environment used in this experiment. As shown in Fig. 2, Courses C and D had rough surfaces to shake the subject. Such roughness mainly impacts the component of the x-axis gyro and y-axis gyro. Considering the high importance of the x-axis gyro and y-axis gyro in terms of ride comfort, x-axis and y-axis gyro highly contributed to estimation accuracy. As Courses B and D had limited width, many subjects adjusted their speed when entering and exiting the courses. Such manipulation characteristics altered the acceleration components on the front-back axis, which caused the high importance of x-axis acceleration. The importance of the HRV was next highest after the x-axis acceleration, x-axis and y-axis gyro. Further measurements and analysis are needed confirm why HRV features contributed to the estimation so strongly. The proposed method was validated by comparing the baselines, and the importance of both inertial and vital features was confirmed.

5   Conclusion

We classified the barriers facing users of personal mobility devices into physical and psychological barriers, and focused on the latter. As the psychological barrier metric, we adopted the "ride comfort" from Sawada et al. [4]. In order to obtain ground truth "ride comfort" data, the subjects had to reply to a questionnaire. Our goal is to estimate "ride comfort" from sensor data automatically so as to minimize users' burden. We hypothesized that the users' psychological state can be extracted from inertial and vital information, and we proposed an inertial and vital data based ride comfort estimation method. A verification experiment conducted with 12 subjects found that the proposed method had an accuracy of 0.75, higher than that of baseline methods that used only inertial or vital data. There was a significant difference between the proposed method and vital-data-based method. There was no significant difference between the proposed method and the inertial-data-based method because of the environment used in the experiment.

Some issues remain to be addressed. In this experiment, we used healthy subjects who do not normal use wheelchairs as the expected users of future personal mobility devices. The proposed method also can be applied to daily wheelchair users. It is unknown if the daily wheelchair users will exhibit the same psychological effects seen in the experiment. Further trials are needed with such subjects. In this experiment, the environments examined were artificial course constructed indoors. While it is difficult to perform extensive trials outdoors, such tests are necessary.

References

1. Ministory of Land, Infrastructure, Transport, Tourism: Barrier-free route search. https://www.hokoukukan.go.jp/routesearch/areaselect.html. Accessed 2 May 2016
2. PADM(specified non-profit organization): Let's join together to create a Barrier Free Map. http://enigata.com/data/minna_bmap.pdf. Accessed 2 May 2016
3. Office, C.: Basic Programme for Persons with Disabilities. http://www8.cao.go.jp/shougai/suishin/kihonkeikaku.pdf. Accessed 2 May 2016
4. Sawada, T., Kojima, Y., Kondou, T., Furusaki, T.: A fundamental study for sensual evaluation about orientation and ride of a wheelchair. Memoirs Tomakomai Techn. Coll. **39**, 81–85 (2004)

5. Liu, Z., Kubo, M., Aoki, H., Suzuki, T., Gotou, T.: Evaluative structure for riding feeling on moving automobile -development of a quantification by using the hierarchical fuzzy integral model. Bull. Japn. Soc. Sci. Des. **41**, 43–50 (1994)
6. Matsuo, Y., Kojima, Y., Ohashi, S., Kunisaki, M., Miyake, A., Sawada, T.: Comfortability and centroid fluctuation of wheelchair users during movements: -wheelchair travels on flat and rough surfaced roads-. Trans. Japn. Soc. Kansei Eng. **12**, 1–5 (2013)
7. Okamura, M.: Effect of joint of tile pavement on vibration of wheelchair and comfort of seated person. J. Jpn. Soc. Civil Eng. **14**, 189–194 (2008)
8. Ishida, T., Takemoto, H., Ishida, S., Kameyama, S., Himeno, K., Kashima, S.: Evaluation of sidewalk unevenness based on wheelchair traveling resistance. Trans. Res. Rec. J. Trans. Res. Board **1956**, 68–75 (2006)
9. Maki, T., Takeuti, Y., Matsuda, M.: A study for uneveness evaluation of sidewalk pavement. Doboku Gakkai Ronbunshuu **1**, 151–158 (1996)
10. Iwasawa, Y., Yairi, I.: Spatiotemporal life-log mining of wheelchair users' driving for visualizing accessibility of roads. In: 2013 IEEE 13th International Conference on Data Mining Workshops (ICDMW), pp. 680–687 (2013)
11. Kuwahara, N., Nishiura, M., Shiomi, Y., Morimoto, K., Iwawaki, Y., Nishida, N.: A study on a ubiquitous system for collecting barrier-free information of evacuation centers for wheelchair users. In: Proceedings of the 4th ACM International Workshop on Context-Awareness for Self-Managing Systems, pp. 36–39 (2010)
12. Takahashi, I., Yokoyama, K.: eDevelopment of a feedback stimulation for drowsy driver using heartbeat rhythms. In: Engineering in Medicine and Biology Society(EMBC), pp. 4153–4158 (2011)
13. Yokoi, T., Imai, M., Oguri, K.: Estimation of subjective mental work load level with heart rate variability by tolerance to driver's mental load. IEEJ Trans. Electron. Inf. Syst. **131**, 2051–2056 (2011)
14. Malik, M., Bigger, T.J., Camm, A.J., Kleiger, R.E., Malliani, A., Moss, A.J., Schwartz, A.J.: Heart rate variability Standards of measurement, physiological interpretation, and clinical use. Eur. Soc. Cardiol. **17**, 354–381 (1996)

Human Aware Robot Navigation
in Semantically Annotated
Domestic Environments

Ioannis Kostavelis$^{(\boxtimes)}$, Dimitrios Giakoumis, Sotiris Malassiotis,
and Dimitrios Tzovaras

Centre for Research and Technology Hellas, Information Technologies Institute,
6th Km Charilaou-Thermi Road, 57001 Thermi-Thessaloniki, Greece
{gkostave,dgiakoum,malasiot,tzovaras}@iti.gr

Abstract. In the near future, the seamless human robot cohabitation
can be achieved as long as the robots to be released in the market attain
socially acceptable behavior. Therefore, robots need to learn and react
appropriately, should they be able to share the same space with people
and to adapt their operation to human's activity. The goal of this work
is to introduce a human aware global path planning solution for robot
navigation that considers the humans presence in a domestic environment. Towards this direction, hierarchical semantic maps are built upon
metric maps where the human presence is modelled using frequently visited standing positions considering also the proxemics theory. During
the human's perambulation within the domestic environment the most
probable humans pathways are calculated and modeled with sequential,
yet descending Gaussian kernel's. This way, the robot reacts with safety
when operating in a domestic environment taking into consideration the
human presence and the physical obstacles. The method has been evaluated on a simulated environment, yet on realistic acquired data modeling
a real house space and exhibited remarkable performance.

Keywords: Human robot cohabitation · Safe navigation · Semantic
mapping · Metric mapping · Path planning

1 Introduction

The seamless integration of robots in human inhabited environments demands
the formation of strategies that allow them to navigate in a secure, appropriate and common manner among people. This provokes new research challenges,
where the concept of safe navigation attains wider dimensions and aims to facilitate human-robot cohabitation beyond the established safety strategies [1]. In
mobile robotics, mapping allows robots to construct a meaningful description of
their surrounding that endows them with the capacity to accomplish high-level
objectives. The emerging topic of human aware navigation deals with robots'
operating in complex environments, while considering the convenience of the

M. Antona and C. Stephanidis (Eds.): UAHCI 2016, Part II, LNCS 9738, pp. 414–423, 2016.
DOI: 10.1007/978-3-319-40244-4_40

humans being present. Therefore, the administration of space about humans and their reaction when interacting with each other need to be comprehended and modeled.

Environment modelling in terms of metric mapping comprises the cornerstone for the majority of the robotic applications. Specifically, in order for a robot to be able to navigate efficiently, a consistent metric map has to be built. In the last decades a lot of research has been conducted in the area of mobile robot navigation and mapping [2], yielding remarkable performance. With the purpose of accurately localizing themselves [3,4], mobile robots construct a consistent representation of the spatial layout of their working environment. The representative works described in [5,6] and [7] prove the necessity for an accurate representation of the robot's surroundings as well as the development of efficient mapping methods. More precisely, simultaneously localization and mapping (SLAM) provides solution to the problem, according to which a mobile robot placed at any unknown location in an unexplored area incrementally builds a consistent map of the environment while simultaneously determines its location within this map. Seeking to engineer an efficient solution to this problem, several successful research attempts have been carried out, an analytical summary of which is presented in a two-part review paper [8,9].

Albeit the advances in metric mapping, in order a robot to apprehend the environment in the way a human does, the formation of maps augmented by semantic attributes involving human concepts, such as types of rooms, objects and their spatial arrangement, is considered a compulsory attribute for the future robots. Semantic mapping [10] is a qualitative description of the robot's surroundings, aiming to augment the navigation capabilities and the task-planning, as well as to bridge the gap in human-robot interaction (HRI). A representative work where the semantic mapping is addressed with emphasis on HRI by using natural language is the one described in [11] and enables in the most direct way robots to socialize with humans. Moreover, it is an evidence that contemporary robots use to navigate in their environments by computing their pose within metric maps and, therefore, the vast amount of the semantic mapping methods reported in the literature use these metric maps to add semantic information on top of it [11,12].

The next step, after the construction of a map commonly apprehended by humans and robots, is the adoption of a human-aware behavior, while the robot performs navigation activities within the explored environment. However, during the robot's perambulation it is essential to consider navigation strategies that facilitate the convenience of the individuals being present and increase safety. One the one hand, safety can be achieved up to one extend using the on-board robot sensors for typical obstacle avoidance. One the other hand, the answer to the human's convenience during the robot's operation in a domestic environment stems from the social sciences, where the anthropologist Edward T. Hall [13] designated the Proxemics Theory. In accordance with this theory, the human comfort levels are influenced from their distance from other persons and, consequently, there are zones, i.e. proxemics zones, that determine the intimacy equilibrium model among human-human interactions. Robotics science adopted the Proxemics theory to model the human-robot interactions according to which the robots should be capable of perceiving proxemics and adopt their behavior accordingly [14]. Specifically, the work in [15] presents a navigation strategy in populated environments based on the prediction of people's movement and the level of discomfort as imposed by the proxemics theory. In a more contemporary solution, the work in [16] represent the social zones in terms of isocontours of an implicit function capable of describing complex social interaction. Such zones are shaped through non-linear probability functions which derive as solutions to a learning problem in the kernel space.

2   Proposed Methodology

2.1   Outline

In this work, a dense 3D metric map is firstly constructed processing the input images acquired from a RGBD sensor mounted on a mobile robot. On the top of the metric map a hierarchical semantic knowledge base is formed encoding all the high level information that describe the domestic environment in a human compatible model. In the knowledge database, information about the location of the large objects, the supporting surfaces and the human frequently visited standing positions are stored. The direction of human motion is constantly calculated among consecutive frames and the distance from the human and the standing positions is computed. Then, by minimizing those two parameters, the most probable path to be followed given his/her current position and the defined standing positions is calculated using a Dijkstra algorithm. In course of the calculated human path, Gaussian kernels of descending amplitude are defined, the parameters of which follow the proxemics rules. During the robot global planning, all the static obstacles of the metric map are top down projected and together with the sequences of the Gaussian kernels are used to form the map on which the D* Lite algorithm is executed to find an optimal path for the robot.

2.2   Metric and Hierarchical Semantic Mapping

The method we describe here uses a metric map in order to perform robot navigation activities. The metric mapping solution adopted, is the one presented in [17], yet enhanced in terms of memory and speed management in order to be operable for large scale mapping scenarios. This method utilizes the on-board RGBD sensor of the robot and performs incremental motion estimations along the robot's travel. Specifically, visual features (SURF) are matched among consecutive frames and by using the corresponding depth information, 3D matched features are produced. This set of matched features are fed into a Random Sample Consensus (RANSAC) algorithm [18] and the robot's motion estimation is calculated. Then, the robot estimated poses and the corresponding matched features are treated as graph, the optimization of which is performed using the

g^2o optimization algorithm [19]. Upon the metric map, the hierarchical model that contains semantic information is constructed. The latter is tree structure that retains the relationships among objects and places, the object supporting surfaces as well as the human standing position describing explicitly the domestic environment in terms of human concepts. The hierarchical mapping comprises a connection among the metric map and the human oriented concepts providing thus the robot with the capacity to apprehend the environment in a human compatible manner. Specifically, the semantic information is stored in an XML schema and comprises the following structure: the house environment is organised in rooms, the room types consist of large objects and frequently visited standing positions, the large objects are related with the robot parking positions and with small objects. The small objects are organized in terms of their attributes, their grasping points and their relations to other objects. Additionally, the room borders are connected with the metric map to define their coordinates, something that is also determined for the large and the small objects as well as the human standing and the robot parking positions. An illustrative example of the metric and hierarchical semantic mapping components is presented in Fig. 1.

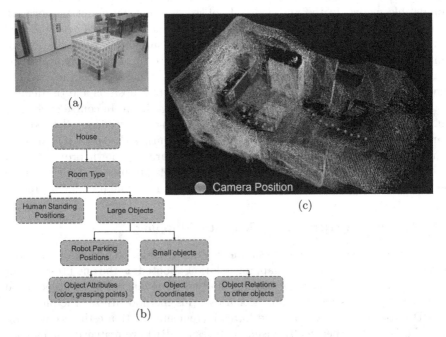

Fig. 1. (a) A reference image of a scene, (b) the hierarchical semantic model used for the annotation of the mapped environment, and (c) the 3D metric map

2.3 Human Motion Intention Modelling

Since all necessary information about the objects in the house has been modeled, this knowledge can be utilized from the robot to execute its navigation routines. Yet, the human presence needs to be considered during the robot's locomotion and, therefore, a human detection engine has been developed using the background information, by subtracting the current robot view from the 3D metric map. After certain optimization techniques on the subtracted frame, a rough human silhouette is extracted, the center of mass of which is utilized to calculate the intention of the human motion. In more detail, the direction of human motion is constantly calculated among consecutive frames and the distance from the human and the standing positions is computed. To model the short term human motion intention, the orientation deviation $\mathbf{d_r}$ from the current human pose to all standing position is calculated and the distance deviation $\mathbf{d_l}$ from the current human location to all the standing positions is also determined. Assuming that there are N human standing positions, the most probable one (P_i, i=1,..., N) that the human will move towards to, can be determined by minimizing the $P_{i=1}^{N} = argmin(\alpha\mathbf{d_r}_{i=1}^{N} + \beta\mathbf{d_l}_{i=1}^{N})$ where α and β are regularization parameters that control situations where the modelled environment is congested, i.e. with many furniture where the user has to follow curved paths to reach a standing position. The minimized values of the criterion are sorted from the most probable to the less probable one. All the human paths among his/her current location and the standing positions are calculated using a Dijkstra algorithm. For each point (location in the map) of the calculated human path sequence, an oriented Gaussian kernel is centered, the parameters $_x$ and $_y$ of which, model the personal space of the human. The amplitude A of the Gaussian kernels that form each human path is reverse proportional to the values of criterion $P_{i=1}^{N}$ indicating that the paths with less probability to be followed by the human have diminished weights. An example of the aforementioned strategy exhibited in the Fig. 2.

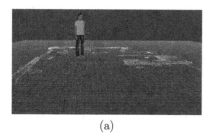 

(a)   (b)

Fig. 2. (a) Still human modelled with a single Gaussian kernel and (b) walking human with predicted paths modeled as a sequence of Gaussian kernels with retaining various amplitude A for the different paths.

2.4   Human Aware Navigation

Given the metric map of the domestic environment and the modelling of the human motion intention, the robot should draw a path in order to reach to its target location. The paper in hand examines the occasion of the global path planning where the robot has to find an optimal path that conjugates its current position to a goal one. Although the global planners typically work on static maps, the proposed strategy incorporates dynamically updated metric maps by modelling the human presence in the environment. Specifically, during the robot global planning, all the static obstacles of the metric map are top down projected and together with the sequences of the Gaussian kernels are used to form the map. The weighs of the sequential Gaussian Kernels (i.e. their amplitude A) are coded as weights in the metric map, while the respective points of the metric map are declared as lethal obstacles for the path planner. The utilize planning algorithm is the D* Lite [20] and is executed to find an optimal path for the robot. Following the Proxemics theory, parameterizations of the human presence using Gaussian kernel varies in occasions where the human is relatively still, i.e. standing or sitting, with the occasions where the person is moving. Following the proxemics rules, the personal space of the human is within the range of [0.45–1.2]m; in our method in order to increase safety during robot operations and to avoid unintentional collisions, we selected different social radius to model the human presence and, thus, we set the human personal space to 0.8 and 1.2 for moving and standing still, respectively. This selection was found to be descent compromise among, human comfort and natural robot motion under social constrained environments. A graphical outline of the steps for the proposed method is illustrated in the Fig. 3.

3   Assessment of the Proposed Method

The proposed method has been evaluated on realistic acquired data from a regular domestic environment. Firstly, the metric mapping of the house has been performed along with the hierarchical semantic mapping using manual annotations. Three logically inferred human standing positions have been determined within this map i.e. in front of the kitchen, near the sofa in the living room area and near the fireplace. Figure 4(a) illustrates the reference image from the modelled house, while Fig. 4(b) illustrates the constructed 3D metric map along with the standing positions. A human model has been rendered within this environment and its motion has been simulated to arbitrarily perambulate within the house. The robot was placed on specific parking positions in the house and by monitoring the human presence navigation commands where passed. The 3D metric map is considered as a static one and was top down projected while the Gaussian kernels where dynamically updated during the human motion. Once a navigation command was passed to the robot, the Gaussian weights were incorporated along with the top down projected map to form an occupancy grid, on which the global path planner operates. Multiple evaluation scenarios have been performed proving the ability of the proposed method to guide the robot

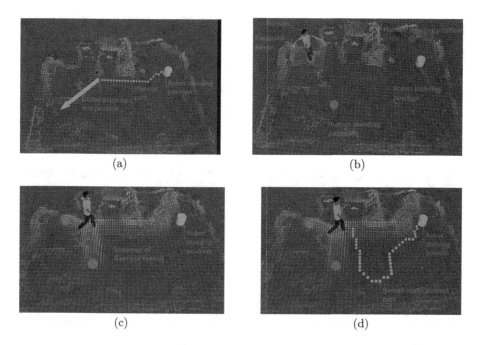

Fig. 3. A graphical outline of the steps of the proposed method; (a) the robot planning without human presence, (b) the model personal area of the human using a Gaussian kernel, (c) the sequences of the Gaussian kernels from the human current position to the standing positions and (d) a human aware planned path

in a away that avoids unexpected collisions with human, selecting thus the optimal path. Exemplar instances of the conducted experiment are summarized in Fig. 4, where the ability of the propose method human aware path planning is illustrated.

4   Discussion

In this work, a human aware robot navigation method has been developed. The robot apprehends its environment in a human conceivable manner and, moreover, adapts its navigation policies in accordance to the humans presence and activities. The method has been evaluated on a simulated environment, yet on realistic acquired data modeling a real house space and exhibited remarkable performance, toward facilitating human comfort during human robot cohabitation, naturalness of the robot behavior, sociability and safety during robot navigation.

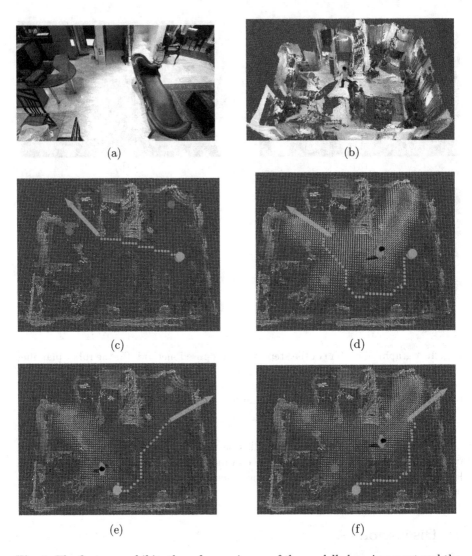

Fig. 4. The first row exhibits the reference image of the modelled environment and the 3D metric map along with the human standing positions. The rest two rows correspond to the experimental assessment of the methodology for various robot starting positions. On the left column the robot does not considers the human presence while on the right column the robot considers the human presence in order to draw a path.

Acknowledgments. This work has been supported by the EU Horizon 2020 funded project namely: "Robotic Assistant for MCI Patients at home (RAMCIP)" under the grant agreement with no: 643433.

References

1. Mitka, E., Gasteratos, A., Kyriakoulis, N., Mouroutsos, S.G.: Safety certification requirements for domestic robots. Saf. Sci. **50**(9), 1888–1897 (2012)
2. Thrun, S., Burgard, W., Fox, D., et al.: Probabilistic robotics, vol. 1. MIT Press, Cambridge (2005)
3. Filliat, D., Meyer, J.A.: Map-based navigation in mobile robots: I. a review of localization strategies. Cogn. Syst. Res. **4**(4), 243–282 (2003)
4. Meyer, J.A., Filliat, D.: Map-based navigation in mobile robots: II. a review of map-learning and path-planning strategies. Cogn. Syst. Res. **4**(4), 283–317 (2003)
5. Jian, Y.D., Balcan, D., Panageas, I., Tetali, P., Dellaert, F.: Support-theoretic subgraph preconditioners for large-scale slam. In: International Conference on Intelligent Robots and Systems, pp. 9–16. IEEE (2013)
6. Grisetti, G., Stachniss, C., Burgard, W.: Improved techniques for grid mapping with rao-blackwellized particle filters. IEEE Trans. Robot. **23**(1), 34–46 (2007)
7. Hahnel, D., Burgard, W., Fox, D., Thrun, S.: An efficient fastslam algorithm for generating maps of large-scale cyclic environments from raw laser range measurements. In: International Conference on Intelligent Robots and Systems. vol. 1, pp. 206–211. IEEE (2003)
8. Durrant-Whyte, H., Bailey, T.: Simultaneous localization and mapping: part i. Rob. Autom. Mag. IEEE **13**(2), 99–110 (2006)
9. Bailey, T., Durrant-Whyte, H.: Simultaneous localization and mapping (slam): Part II. Robot. Autom. Mag. **13**(3), 108–117 (2006)
10. Kostavelis, I., Gasteratos, A.: Semantic mapping for mobile robotics tasks: A survey. Robot. Autonom. Syst. **66**, 86–103 (2015)
11. Zender, H., Martínez Mozos, O., Jensfelt, P., Kruijff, G.J., Burgard, W.: Conceptual spatial representations for indoor mobile robots. Robot. Autonom. Syst. **56**(6), 493–502 (2008)
12. Pronobis, A., Jensfelt, P.: Large-scale semantic mapping and reasoning with heterogeneous modalities. In: International Conference on Robotics and Automation, pp. 3515–3522. IEEE (2012)
13. Hall, E.T., Hall, E.T.: The hidden dimension, vol. 1990. Anchor Books, New York (1969)
14. Takayama, L., Pantofaru, C.: Influences on proxemic behaviors in human-robot interaction. In: IEEE/RSJ International Conference on Intelligent Robots and Systems, IROS 2009, pp. 5495–5502. IEEE (2009)
15. Rios-Martinez, J., Renzaglia, A., Spalanzani, A., Martinelli, A., Laugier, C.: Navigating between people: a stochastic optimization approach. In: 2012 IEEE International Conference on Robotics and Automation (ICRA), pp. 2880–2885. IEEE (2012)
16. Papadakis, P., Spalanzani, A., Laugier, C.: Social mapping of human-populated environments by implicit function learning. In: 2013 IEEE/RSJ International Conference on Intelligent Robots and Systems (IROS), pp. 1701–1706. IEEE (2013)
17. Endres, F., Hess, J., Engelhard, N., Sturm, J., Cremers, D., Burgard, W.: An evaluation of the rgb-d slam system. In: 2012 IEEE International Conference on Robotics and Automation (ICRA), pp. 1691–1696. IEEE (2012)
18. Fischler, M.A., Bolles, R.C.: Random sample consensus: a paradigm for model fitting with applications to image analysis and automated cartography. Commun. ACM **24**(6), 381–395 (1981)

19. Kümmerle, R., Grisetti, G., Strasdat, H., Konolige, K., Burgard, W.: g2o: A general framework for graph optimization. In: 2011 IEEE International Conference on Robotics and Automation (ICRA), pp. 3607–3613. IEEE (2011)
20. Koenig, S., Likhachev, M.: Improved fast replanning for robot navigation in unknown terrain. In: IEEE International Conference on Robotics and Automation, 2002 Proceedings of the ICRA 2002, vol. 1, pp. 968–975. IEEE (2002)

Use of See-Through Wearable Display as an Interface for a Humanoid Robot

Shu Matsuura[✉]

Faculty of Education, Tokyo Gakugei University,
4-1-1 Nukuikita, Koganei, Tokyo 184-8501, Japan
shumats0@gmail.com

Abstract. This paper describes the development of a monitoring system for the NAO humanoid robot for speaking presentations. The dialog between the human and the robot is based on both a dialog list stored by the robot and its dynamic retrieval of information from an external topic map server. The stereoscopic 3D capability of a see-through wearable binocular-type display, i.e., the EPSON MOVERIO BT-200, is used to allow simultaneous observation of the robot and the retrieved information, and the distance between the side-by-side images is controlled to create a converged image overlaid on the robot's body. This image shift method is examined using simple line images with the see-through display, and the effect of pictorial cues of a real object on the generated images is discussed.

Keywords: See-through wearable display · Humanoid robot · Stereoscopic 3D

1 Introduction

Studies on education aided by humanoid robots with cognition function [1] have attracted interest for years. A humanoid robot has worked as a teaching assistant controlled by an instructional design tool in primary education [2]. An important characteristic of a humanoid robot for education is social interactivity with learners. A socially interactive humanoid robot in an educational environment can increase the efficiency of learning [3]. A fuzzy control system for robot communication has been proven effective in promoting self-efficacy in language learning [4]. A combination of educational robot and multimedia learning materials has been proven beneficial for increasing student motivation [5]. Furthermore, interactions with humanoid robots increase human creativity [6].

This study introduces the NAO humanoid robot (Aldebaran Robotics, SoftBank Group) for a principal's speech and presentation at an elementary school. NAO has programmable gesture and dialog capabilities, which enable cognitive interaction with humans based on recognition functionalities for speech, faces, and objects [7]. Educational researchers have utilized NAO for the instruction and care of children with autism [8–10]. The expressive and affective behaviors of the robot improve communication and reinforce learning [11]. Furthermore, future smart environments and ambient intelligence are expected to produce witty humor [12].

© Springer International Publishing Switzerland 2016
M. Antona and C. Stephanidis (Eds.): UAHCI 2016, Part II, LNCS 9738, pp. 424–433, 2016.
DOI: 10.1007/978-3-319-40244-4_41

Educational and therapeutic use of humanoid robots typically involves interactive relationships between humans and humanoid robots. In contrast, stage speeches or presentations are essentially one-way forms of communication, i.e., the audience is passive. A multi-robot system has performed *Manzai*, which is a Japanese-style comedy talk show, usually performed by two people, as a passive-social medium [13]. Hayashi et al. used a network to facilitate communication between robots performing *Manzai* rather than direct speech recognition between them because the sensing and recognition system was inadequate to create Japanese-style performance comedy. The humanoid NAO's recognition capability is satisfactory because the words it must recognize are pre-registered or pre-downloaded before the corresponding dialog occurs.

In this study, we examine a pilot system with the humanoid NAO that downloads keywords and related dialogs from an external e-learning server in which data are interconnected semantically and structured on the basis of topic map technology [14, 15]. To engage dialog between a humanoid robot and a person, it is necessary to know what topic words the robot has downloaded. For this purpose, a downloaded list of topic words is shown on a web page generated by the Internet server of NAO's operating system. A human presenter checks the list of candidate words using a see-through wearable display connected to an Android device while engaging the dialog. A stereoscopic 3D display was used to allow simultaneous observation of the humanoid robot and the retrieved information. This paper describes a simple stereoscopic 3D vision method to display the topic texts at an appropriate depth.

2 Method

Topic Map-based e-Learning Server. The author has created the "Everyday Physics on Web" (EPW) e-learning portal. The EPW system is based on topic map technology [16, 17]. Topic maps (ISO/IEC JTC1/SC34) represent information using a "topic," "association," and "occurrence." Topics represent subjects that are interconnected by various types of associations. An occurrence is a specific type of association that connects a topic and the actual information resources, such as text and web pages. The networked structures of topics are referred to as topic map ontology. Topic maps enable rich and flexible indexing based on semantics and increase the findability of information. Since one can edit the knowledge structure in the topic map tier, a topic maps-based web system is efficient relative to extensibility and manageability.

The EPW topic map was built using the "Ontopia" [17] topic maps server. Ontopia has its own topic map query language, "tolog," and the navigator framework, which consists of a set of tolog tag libraries, can generate JavaServer Pages. In addition, Ontopia has a web service interface, i.e., the Topic Maps Remote Access Protocol (TMRAP), which enables retrieval of topic map fragments from a remote topic maps server. By enabling TMRAP with EPW, one can utilize the topic map of the EPW server on the client. One can perform tolog queries from the client to retrieve any element of the EPW server.

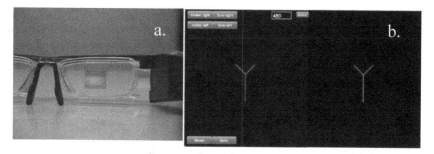

Fig. 1. a: BT-200 see-through display with supplemental lenses; b: side-by-side image of the S3D test application. Each of the side-by-side images is transformed from 8:9 to 9:16.

See-through Wearable Display. A see-through type binocular wearable display, i.e., the EPSON MOVERIO BT-200 (Fig. 1a), was used to monitor the topics of the humanoid robot's talk. The BT-200 has Wi-Fi and Bluetooth connectivity. In this study, the mirroring capability over Wi-Fi was used to show the PC display on the wearable display. In addition, the binocular dual displays work as a stereoscopic side-by-side 3D viewer. It has a 960×540 (pixel) area as the 2D display, and side-by-side 480×540 (pixel) areas are transformed into the whole area and shown to both the left and right eyes for 3D display. The distance between the left and right displays is 65 mm. In the 3D display mode, the image appears to be located approximately 4.5 m in front of the user.

Test Application. A simple Adobe Flash application was created to test the stereoscopic 3D (S3D) of text representation in the environment using the Papervision3D library. This application shows the same "Y-letter" as three lines connected at their edges in a plane parallel to the image plane (or screen), as shown in Fig. 1b. The same "Y-letter" lines were drawn in the centers of the side-by-side windows on a black background. These windows are movable in the horizontal directions by pushing the buttons. When this side-by-side display of the "Y-letter" is represented in the 3D mode, the left and right images exhibit a parallax, and the image appears at a distance of approximately 4.5 m from the user by default. The parallax of the image is changed by moving the right or left window. This application works on the Flash player on a PC. Then, the application display is mirrored to and controlled by the BT-200.

Test Process. We must be able to see the retrieved text while looking at and talking to the humanoid robot. Thus, the accommodation point of the user's eyes is primarily at the position of the robot. To observe the robot and the projected text simultaneously, the S3D position of the text must be moved to the appropriate position (i.e., depth) of the robot. For this purpose, the distance between the side-by-side windows of the application was reduced. When the accommodation and convergence agree at a position, we have clear focus. Some applications have been published on the MOVERIO application site [18, 19].

To test the effect of convergence on the cognition of the depth position and a possible illusion occurring during the display of the "Y-letter," two tests were conducted. The participants were asked to hold and focus on a cube as a target object, as shown in Fig. 2 (Tables 1 and 2).

Table 1. Test 1: Check stereo image and 3D illusion

Item name	Manipulation	Accommodation	Superimpose line
Stereo cognition	Participant sees the line images as a 3D object in space.	Line images	
At cube	The experimenter moves right side image to the left until the participant sees that the split lines converge.	Cube	
	Participant checks if the line image is seen at the same depth as the cube.	Line images	False/True
Closer than cube	The experimenter moves right side image to the left.	Line images	False/True
	Participant checks if the line image is seen closer to the participant.		
Farther than cube	The experimenter moves right side image to the right.	Line images	False/True
	Participant checks if the line image is seen beyond the cube.		

Table 2. Test 2: The movement of the side-by-side images

Image window movement	Cube object near the line image
Right image shifts to left	None
Left image shifts to right	None
Both side images shift closer	None
Right image shifts to left	Present
Left image shifts to right	Present
Both side images shift closer	Present

Test 1 checks if the depth of the line image is changeable by moving only the right side image. In addition, to consider how the projected image merges with the real scene, the illusion of line caused by the pictorial cues of cube edges.

In test 2, the participants were asked for their impressions about the effect of the different ways to converge the side-by-side images. We compared the impressions about the motion of the line images with and without coexistence of the cube near the line images.

NAO Humanoid Robot. An application of the NAO humanoid robot was created using its development environment, "Choregraphe." Note that the "NAOqi" programming

Fig. 2. Holding the cube

framework is capable of using external service APIs. In this study, URL TMRAP requests were sent to the EPW server to obtain a candidate list of topic names. When the person speaks one of the list items and when it is recognized by the speech recognition system, the dialog occurrence and topic list associated with the previous topic are again requested from the EPW. Then, using speech recognition, NAO speaks the dialog occurrence and waits for the person to speak. Thus, the person needs to know the candidate list of words retrieved by NAO. Then, when NAO obtains the topic name list, it generates a web page for the topic name list on its internal website. The person requests this page from NAO's URL, as if looking into the robot's mind. In this manner, the dialog between the humanoid and human can be developed dynamically using the knowledge structure of the EPW topic map.

Manzai **and Comic Frame.** Japanese comic performance has a common framework, i.e., *Furi, Boke, Tsukkomi,* and *Ochi. Furi* is a proposal or a suggestion for an interest, topic, and atmosphere of talk. *Boke* is speaking funny lines, and *Tsukkomi* is responding to the funny lines to make it impressive. The flow of *Furi, Boke, Tsukkomi,* and *Ochi* is a traditional framework of Japanese comic performance, such as *Manzai.* The speaking system with the humanoid robot in this work has the same structure. First, the human provides *Furi* from the topic list retrieved by the robot. Then, the robot presents the dialog occurrence, which is the main content of the talk. Finally, the human responds to the content shown by the robot. Again, the human can restart the frame choosing one of the related topics. If the talk is humorous, it is considered an effective representation of *Manzai.*

3   Results and Discussion

3.1   Topic Maps-Based Dialog

We conducted speech demonstrations, as shown in Fig. 3, based on the combination of topic map retrieval and the original dialog box of Choregraphe. Notably, the latter provides an exchange of rather humorous words. The former topic map talk was conducted to obtain knowledge about particular words. The human intermediates these knowledgeable parts in an entertaining discussion.

Fig. 3. Principal talking with NAO in an elementary school. The principal wears the BT-200 to talk with NAO.

NAO and the principal's talk began in autumn 2015. Many elementary school students appear to look forward to NAO's talk with the principal. From autumn 2015, a second-grade class began to play postal system as an activity in school. From then until January 2016, the principal received 46 letters from students; 70 % of the letters referred to NAO. In particular, the knowledgeable phrases that NAO spoke often encouraged the students to giggle or laugh. Students might feel a sense of incongruity when they see the humorous and expressive NAO speak intellectual words, and the principal admires this.

Verbal communication is more preferable for human–robot interaction than communication mediated by a computer. However, speech recognition as an interface is far from ideal. Thus, at least for now, humans require a visualization of the robot's "knowledge" or "brain." In addition, such a relationship is consistent with the human's role with *Tsukkomi*. NAO is not remote controlled, such as by a PC. In this sense, a see-through wearable type display with information retrieval from the robot's brain is preferable to remote control by PC.

3.2   See-Through Stereoscopic 3D Rendering in Space

Twenty-three subjects aged 19 to 21 years participated in the stereoscopic 3D line rendering experiments. Only two were female. If the participant wore glasses, they were asked to wear the see-through display over their glasses.

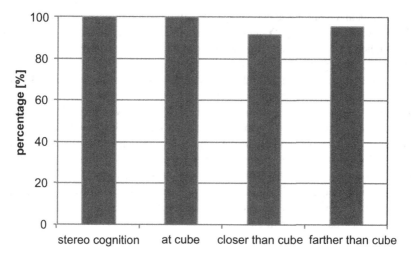

Fig. 4. Stereoscopic cognition of the position shift in test 1.

Figure 4 shows the percentage of participants who recognized a change in the position of the lines. Most participants felt that the lines were placed in the real space, and their positions shifted back and forth around the real cube held in front of their faces. However, a few participants saw the lines as split or shifted in the opposite direction. This was observed when the lines were shifted around the cube at a fixed position in space. Note that the shift motion was controlled by the experimenter rather than the participant. A more detailed investigation of the combination of accommodation and convergence for motion is required.

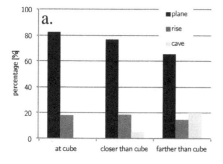 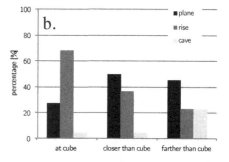

Fig. 5. Occurrence of 3D illusion on the lines rendered in the vertical plane. Participants were asked if the "Y-letter" shaped lines appeared "plane," "rising at the junction," or "caving at the junction." a: Lines were located around the cube arbitrarily directed in space; b: three lines were located to overlay the three edges of the cube.

Figures 5a and b show the percentage of participants who observed the 3D illusion on the projected lines. The "Y-letter" shaped lines were drawn on a vertical plane parallel to the eyes so that there is no parallax in the shape. In addition, since the shape is symmetric, it has particularly few cues for the emergence of the illusion. However, a possible visual illusion might be in the way that the junction of three lines looks raising toward the observer, or oppositely caving.

Figure 5a shows the results when the lines were observed around the real cube, which normally appears in 3D. Most participants felt that the lines were on a plane. However, as the lines moved around the cube, a few participants observed an illusion.

Figure 5b shows the results when the lines were overlaid on three edges of the real cube. The percentage of participants who observed the raising illusion increased significantly. Furthermore, as the lines shifted back and forth, the illusions decreased. In addition, it is intriguing that the rate of the cave-shaped illusion increased when the lines were observed on the real cube.

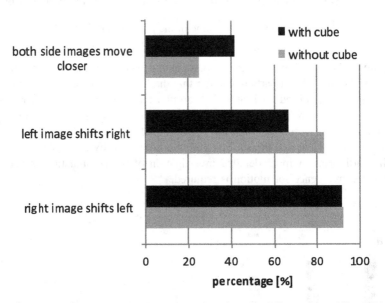

Fig. 6. Percentage of participants who observed horizontal shift motion while shifting the side-by-side images.

In test 1, the back and forth motion of the lines was generated by moving only the window of the right image of the lines to the left, while the left window was fixed. Even such asymmetric manipulation allows perception of motion in the depth direction. Only a few participants commented about the sense of asymmetric shift. Then, in test 2, the participants were asked if they could observe the right (for left window shift) or left (right shift) component of each shift with and without the cube.

Figure 6 shows the percentage of participants who observed right or left displacement of the lines. Even when both sides of the windows were moved simultaneously, 20-40 % of the participants indicated that they could observe right and left displacement separately (e.g., a zigzag-like motion) or the lines appeared split. Note that a few participants claimed visual fatigue after this test. Thus, frequent and quick manipulation of the convergence might be visually uncomfortable.

4 Conclusion

Human–robot paired dialog was performed using both a dialog list and dynamic retrieval of information from a topic map server. A binocular-type see-through wearable display, i.e., the EPSON MOVERIO BT-200, was used to monitor the information retrieval.

The stereoscopic 3D display was used to allow simultaneous observation of the robot and the retrieved information. The distance between the side-by-side images was changed to control the convergence and allow the image to be observed at an arbitrary depth in the view of field.

Acknowledgments. This study was funded in part by a Grant-in-Aid for Scientific Research (C) 15K00912 from the Ministry of Education, Culture, Sports, Science and Technology, Japan.

References

1. Vernon, D., von Hofsten, C., Fadiga, L.: A Roadmap for Cognitive Development in Humanoid Robots, Cognitive Systems Monographs, vol. 11. Springer-Verlag, Berlin Heidelberg (2010)
2. Chin, K.-Y., Wu, C-H., Hong, Z-W.: A Humanoid Robot as a Teaching assistant for primary education. In: Fifth International Conference on Genetic and Evolutionary Computing, pp. 21–24 (2011)
3. Brown, L-V., Howard, A.M.: Engaging children in math education using a socially interactive humanoid robot. In: 13th IEEE-RAS International Conference on Humanoid Robots, pp. 183–188 (2013)
4. Yorita, A., Botzheim, J., Kubota, N.: Self-efficacy using fuzzy control for long-term communication in robot-assisted language learning. In: IEEE/RSJ International Conference on Intelligent Robots and Systems, pp. 5708–5715 (2013)
5. Chin, K.-Y., Hong, Z-W., Chen, Y.-L.: Impact of using an educational robot-based learning system on students' motivation in elementary education. IEEE Trans. Learn. Tech. 7(4), 333–345 (2014)
6. Jo, D., Lee, J.-g., Lee, K.C.: Empirical analysis of changes in human creativity in people who work with humanoid robots and their avatars. In: Zaphiris, P., Ioannou, A. (eds.) LCT 2014, Part I. LNCS, vol. 8523, pp. 273–281. Springer, Heidelberg (2014)
7. Miskam, M.A., Shamsuddin, S., Yussof, H., Omar, A.R., Muda, M.Z.: Programming platform for NAO robot in cognitive interaction applications. In: IEEE International Symposium on Robotics and Manufacturing Automation, pp. 141–146 (2014)
8. Diaz, M., Nuno, N., Saez-Pons, J., Pardo, D.E., Angulo, C.: Building up child-robot relationship for therapeutic purposes. In: From Initial Attraction Towards Long-term Social Engagement, pp. 927–932 (2011)

9. Miskam, M.A., Shamsuddin, S., Abdul Samat, M.R, Yussof, H., Ainudin, H.A., Omar, A. R.: Humanoid robot NAO as a teaching tool of emotion recognition for children with autism using the android app. In: International Symposium on Micro-Nano Mechatronics and Human Science, pp. 1–5 (2014)
10. Bingbing, L.L., Chen, I-M., Goh, T.J., Sung, M.: Interactive robots as social partner for communication care. In: IEEE International Conference on Robotics and Automation, pp. 2231–2236 (2014)
11. Addo, I.D., Ahamed, S.I.: Applying affective feedback to reinforcement learning in ZOEI, a comic humanoid robot. In: IEEE International Symposium on Robot and Human Interactive Communication, pp. 423–428 (2014)
12. Nijholt, A.: Humor techniques: from real world and game environments to smart environments. In: Streitz, N., Markopoulos, P. (eds.) DAPI 2015. LNCS, vol. 9189, pp. 659–670. Springer, Heidelberg (2015)
13. Hayashi, K., Kanda, T., Miyashita, T., Ishiguro, H., Hagita, N.: Robot Manzai–Robots' conversation as a passive social medium. In: IEEE-RAS International Conference on Humanoid Robots, pp. 456–462 (2005)
14. Tsuchida, S., Yumoto, N., Matsuura, S.: Development of augmented reality teaching materials with projection mapping on real experimental settings. In: Stephanidis, C. (ed.) HCI 2014, Part II. CCIS, vol. 435, pp. 177–182. Springer, Heidelberg (2014)
15. ISO/IEC 13250:2002
16. Pepper, S.: The TAO of Topic Maps. http://www.ontopia.net/topicmaps/materials/tao. html#d0e632
17. "Everyday Physics on Web". http://tm.u-gakugei.ac.jp/epw/
18. Matsuura, S., Naito, M.: Subject-centric Computing Fourth International Conference on Topic Maps Research and Applications, TMRA 2008, Leipziger Beiträge zur Informatik: Band XII pp. 247–260 (2008)
19. "Ontopia". http://www.ontopia.net/
20. "MOVERIO Apps Market". https://moverio.epson.com/jsp/pc/pc_application_list.jsp
21. Yonemura, T.: A personal correspondence (2016)

Hybrid BCI Systems as HCI in Ambient Assisted Living Scenarios

Niccolò Mora[(✉)], Ilaria De Munari, and Paolo Ciampolini

Information Engineering Department, Università degli Studi di Parma,
Parco Area delle Scienze 181/A, 43124 Parma, Italy
{niccolo.mora,ilaria.demunari,
paolo.ciampolini}@unipr.it

Abstract. Brain Computer Interface (BCI) technology is an alternative/augmentative communication channel, based on the interpretation of the user's brain activity, who can then interact with the environment without relying on neuromuscular pathways. Such technologies can act as alternative HCI devices towards AAL (Ambient Assisted Living) systems, thus opening their services to people for whom interacting with conventional interfaces could be troublesome, or even not viable. A complete BCI implementation is presented and discussed, briefly introducing the customized hardware and focusing more on the signal processing aspects. The BCI is based on SSVEP signals, featuring self-paced calibration-less operation, aiming at a "plug&play" approach. The signal processing chain is presented, introducing a novel method for improving accuracy and immunity to false positives. The results achieved, especially in terms of false positive rate containment (0.16 min^{-1}) significantly improve over the literature. In addition, a possible integration of EMG signals in a hybrid-BCI scheme is discussed, serving as a binary switch to turn on/off the EEG-based BCI section (and the flashing stimuli unit). This can have positive impact on both the user's comfort as well as on the resilience towards false positives. Preliminary results for jaw clench recognition show good detectability, proving that such integration can be implemented.

Keywords: Brain Computer Interface (BCI) · Hybrid Brain Computer Interface (hBCI) · Steady State Visual Evoked Potential (SSVEP) · ElectroMyoGraphy (EMG) · ElectroEncephaloGraphy(EEG)

1 Introduction

A Brain Computer Interface (BCI) is an alternative, augmentative communication channel [1] which aims at providing the user with an interaction path based on the sole interpretation of her/his brain activity. In this sense, BCI can be viewed as a particular class of HCI devices, with different interaction requirements with respect to "conventional" HCI approaches. For the ease of discussion, but without loss of generality, let us focus on a possible use of BCI as a HCI, namely in Ambient Assisted Living (AAL [2]) system control [3, 4].

In order to be accepted and effective, such BCI-enabled HCI channel needs to be perceived as natural as possible; in other terms, BCI operation should be continuous

© Springer International Publishing Switzerland 2016
M. Antona and C. Stephanidis (Eds.): UAHCI 2016, Part II, LNCS 9738, pp. 434–443, 2016.
DOI: 10.1007/978-3-319-40244-4_42

and self-paced [5, 11], i.e. the device must be able to discern user's intentional control periods from nonintentional ones, providing reliable command decoding in the former case (since the user's interactions are quite sporadic, a major concern is being able to minimize false positive classifications). Furthermore, a "Plug&Play" approach is highly desirable in such application scenario, since complex and time-consuming "ad personam" calibration procedures, could be perceived as an excessive burden. In addition, the device's behavior should be uniform across different users, and fine performance tuning should be just limited to a few high-level parameters.

Previously, the need of false positive minimization was mentioned as capital for effective BCI-enabled control. This can be accomplished by exploiting multiple and different input channels, such as the (possibly minimal) residual motor ability: information on muscular activation could be picked up and monitored by means of ElectrMyoGraphy (EMG). In this case EMG signals could be integrated into a hybrid BCI (hBCI) framework and be used to switch on and off the SSVEP visual stimulation unit when not needed. This can improve user's comfort (less eye fatigue on the long run), as well as further reduce the BCI false positives (long inactive periods with SSVEP stimuli are excluded).

In the following the implementation of the BCI algorithms internals are discussed, focused on enabling effective AAL system control.

2 BCI Operating Paradigm and Infrastructure

Various paradigms are commonly exploited in BCI literature, including:

- Slow Cortical Potentials (SCP), i.e., potential shifts in the EEG waves voluntarily induced by user, who can learn to control them through biofeedback-like approaches [6].
- Event Related Desynchronization (ERD) and ER Synchronization (ERS) [7]: this paradigm exploits the brain response arising when preparing (or just imagining) to start a movement. In such conditions, neurons tend to de-synchronize from their idling state, to be allocated to motor processing, this reflecting in a decrease of spectral energy in the μ and β bands (8-12 Hz and around 20 Hz, respectively). After ERD, a pattern consisting in increase in the energy band after the completion of the motor task can also be observed (ERS).
- P300 [8, 9]: when a rare target stimulus is presented to the user during a sequence of repetitive, non-target stimuli, a characteristic pattern can be observed in the EEG signals, approximately after 300 ms from the target stimulus appearance.
- Steady State Visual Evoked Potential (SSVEP) [10, 13]: it is a periodic brain response elicited by a visual stimulus, flickering at a constant frequency; a peak in the brain power spectrum, synchronous with such frequency, can be produced just by looking at the visual stimulus.

Among the presented paradigms, SSVEP was chosen for core BCI operation. SSVEP has recently received much attention, especially in communication or control applications where fast, reliable interaction is needed and multiple simultaneous choices are presented to the user. SSVEP are regarded as robust features for BCI, given their inherently higher SNR (Signal to Noise Ratio) with respect to other paradigms (e.g., with respect to motor imagery, as discussed in [10]). Moreover, since it exploits involuntary response, SSVEP do not require, in principle, any specific user skill and thus involve no user training. In addition, the steady-state, repetitive nature of such potentials makes it possible to design calibration-free classification methods.

From the hardware point of view, our BCI solution is built on top of a custom, dedicated EEG module: it features 16 input channels in a small, 100×130 mm form factor, and can be powered by means of 4 AA alkaline batteries. Production costs are also contained, with respect to current, commercial EEG devices: in medium scale, device manufacturing amounts to, approximately, 300 €. The module communicates via a full-speed USB 2.0 link (12 Mbps), and can be controlled and set-up directly by a host computer.

Finally, the module was validated and compared against a reference, commercial EEG device (as discussed in [4, 13]), showing good performance and proving its suitability for EEG studies.

3 BCI Signal Processing

3.1 Classifying SSVEP in a Self-paced Scenario

Many algorithms exist in literature for SSVEP classification; among the most popular ones are: MEC [14] (Minimum Energy Combination), AMCC [15] (Average Maximum Contrast Combination) and CCA [16] (Canonical Correlation Analysis). A review of such methods goes beyond the scope of this article; the interested reader could refer, for example, to [12, 17]. Our implementation choice stems from a CCA-based approach, and proposes an extension in order to improve the system immunity against false positives.

CCA is a statistical method, generally used for finding the correlations between two sets of multi-dimensional variables. It seeks a pair of linear combinations (canonical variables, characterized by weight vectors $\mathbf{w_x}$, $\mathbf{w_y}$) for the two sets, such that the correlation between the two linear combinations $\mathbf{x_L} = \mathbf{w_x^T} X$ and $\mathbf{y_L} = \mathbf{w_y^T} Y$ is maximized:

$$\max_{w_x, w_y} \rho = \frac{E[x_L y_L^T]}{\sqrt{E[x_L x_L^T] E[y_L y_L^T]}} = \frac{w_x XY^T w_y}{\sqrt{w_x^T XX^T w_x w_y^T YY^T w_y}} . \tag{1}$$

Here X, Y are the input and the SSVEP reference matrix, respectively. Y is composed by N_h (sin, cos) couples representing a steady state sinusoidal response, with N_h representing the number of considered harmonics:

$$X = \begin{bmatrix} \sin 2\pi f t_1 & \cos 2\pi f t_1 & \cdots & \sin 2\pi N_h f t_1 & \cos 2\pi N_h f t_1 \\ \vdots & & \cdots & \vdots & \\ \sin 2\pi f t_{Nt} & \cos 2\pi f t_{Nt} & \cdots & \sin 2\pi N_h f t_{Nt} & \cos 2\pi N_h f t_{Nt} \end{bmatrix}, \tag{2}$$

Given the presence of a SSVEP in the observed EEG window, a classifier could pick the target frequency $f_{class} \in \{$flickering stimuli$\}$ which yields the largest correlation coefficient ρ_i:

$$f_{class} = \arg\max \rho_i . \tag{3}$$

However, in practical scenarios, the assumption of a SSVEP presence within the observed window does not hold true for any window: in other words, such simple classifier is not suitable for self-paced operation, where a "no SSVEP" class needs to be contemplated. A common solution to this problem is to smooth the classifier output, validating the classifier output only if n previous samples agree with the current one. In the following we adopt a different methodology, identifying a feature which could be used to assess the level of confidence in the prediction and that can be exploited to discern between user control and rest periods.

First, let us consider an offline 4-class SSVEP problem (i.e., each epoch contains a SSVEP in the {16, 18, 20, 22} Hz set) and introduce the notion of a confidence indicator for improving baseline CCA accuracy. We define such indicator as the absolute difference between the largest correlation coefficient and the second largest one as such indicator, from here on referred to as parameter d.

$$d = \max_{f \in Fstim} |\rho_f| - \max_{f \in Fstim \setminus \{fmax\}} |\rho_f| , \tag{4}$$

where ρ_f is the correlation coefficient yielded by CCA as described in Eq. (1), $Fstim$ is the set of possible stimuli frequencies and $fmax$ the frequency associated to the largest ρ_f.

Figure 1 allows to assess the usefulness of the introduced confidence indicator by reporting the distribution of correctly and wrongly classified epochs as a function of parameter d. Ideal behavior should associate all errors (black bars) to low values of d, with correct classification (light grey bars) associated to largest values instead. An optimal threshold, d^*, could then be easily determined and a rejection criterion set up to discard all epochs associated with low d values ($d \leq d^*$). However, since actual data show overlaps between the correct and wrong classification distributions, a tradeoff between prediction accuracy and data yield (i.e. the fraction of non-neutral epochs) is needed.

Figure 2 better explains such a tradeoff. In order to derive it, a d^* is fixed and classification performed using such value as decision threshold for the aforementioned rejection mechanism. Epochs not meeting the rejection criterion ($d \leq d^*$) are discarded, and accuracy is computed over the remaining ones; such computed accuracy, together with the corresponding fraction of rejected (*neutralized*) epochs, identifies a point in a 2D plane, and this procedure is repeated for different values of d^*. Figure 2 graphically summarizes this tradeoff with a scatter plot: in order to appreciate the improvement introduced by neutralization strategy, the performance achieved with no neutralization is also reported (grey solid line). Consistent improvement is achieved over the reference case, even at lower neutralization rates, i.e., without implying too relevant data loss. It is important to notice that the proposed confidence indicator method was evaluated over the whole subject population (four in this offline experiment), instead of relying on a per-user basis analysis: this is in line with our view of subject-independent approach.

The quality metric introduced above can also be exploited to effectively adapt the length of the observed EEG window. In particular, the SSVEP classification algorithm could start with a very short observation window, in order to maximize the system's responsiveness; in case the gathered waveforms do not support a reliable classification (the aforementioned rejection criterion is not passed), the observed EEG window length

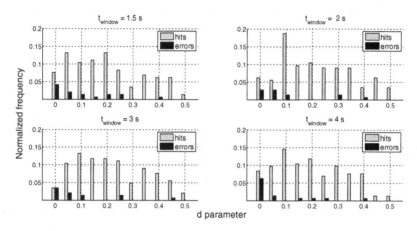

Fig. 1. Distribution of classifiers' hits and errors (light grey and black, respectively; each is normalized to the sample size) as a function of the parameter d. The distributions are also plotted for different EEG window lengths.

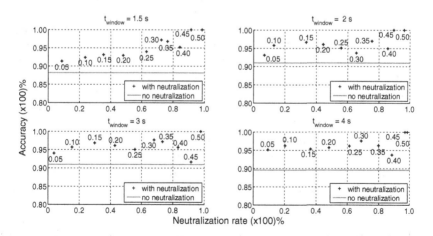

Fig. 2. Accuracy as a function of neutralization rate, at different values of threshold d^*. The solid grey line represents the original, "raw" accuracy level, without neutralization (i.e., $d^* = 0$). The graphs are plotted for different EEG window lengths.

Table 1. Online performance of the self-paced, 4-class experiment (10 subjects)

	False Positive Rate [min^{-1}]	True Positives [%]
Min	0.037	89.1
Max	0.489	100.0
Median	0.097	94.6
Mean	0.16	94.4
Std	0.13	4.2

is increased, looking for further evidence. This process continues until either a classification is attempted or a maximum pre-determined window length is reached. Such an adaptive mechanism gives more flexibility with respect to a fixed-window approach, where responsiveness and accuracy are more tightly coupled.

3.2   Real-Time, Self-paced Operation: Results

A self-paced, online BCI, exploiting a 4-class SSVEP paradigm was implemented and tested. Experimental setup is as follows: 4 visual stimuli (LED, organized in a rectangular pattern over a box) are shown simultaneously, with blinking frequencies equal to {16, 18, 20, 22} Hz; the subject is seated approximately 1 m away from the visual stimuli. Only 6 passive Ag/AgCl electrodes are used to acquire signals form scalp locations Pz, P3, P4, POz, O1, O2. The protocol associates a particular home automation task (namely on/off switching of a light and opening of a motorized shutter) to each stimulus, and the user is asked to perform several control actions, at his own pace and will. Moreover, in order to assess the immunity to false positive events, long idle periods are introduced on purpose, during which the subject does not make any intentional choice and is allowed to talk and, partially, move. A total of 10 healthy volunteers (age 24-61, 4 females) participated in this study, none of them with any prior BCI-control experience, nor was involved in any calibration/training phase.

The self-paced BCI has an update rate of 5 Hz, i.e. a classification is attempted every 200 ms. The optimal observed EEG window length is determined according to the adaptive criterion presented above. In this case, the minimum window length is set to 2 s, and it is allowed to grow up to 4 s in steps of 500 ms. In addition, in order to further improve immunity to false positives, a post-smoother is optionally added, which averages the last 5 classification outputs for each class (the 4 targets plus the neutral state): if the average for a class exceeds a given threshold, the classification is validated, otherwise a null output is assumed (i.e. no SSVEP detected).

Table 1 reports the online experiment results (mean and standard deviation), in terms of true positive, false negative and false positive rates. A very good performance is achieved, both in terms of true positive and false positive rates. In particular, false positives are kept to a very small amount (≈ 0.16 min^{-1} on average, i.e. approximately a false positive every 6'15"), improving over literature data [18, 19]. It is important to remark that such results were achieved without any subject-specific parameter tuning: in other words, all user share the exact same setup, this being in line with our subject-independent BCI approach.

Finally, the entire system was put to test in a relatively harsher environment, in the context of the *Handimatica 2014* exhibition. Here, high background luminosity, noise, electromagnetic interference, are not controlled as lab environments, and may potentially hinder the effectiveness of the solution. Furthermore, the subject was relatively free to move and speech, in order to interact with people. Overall, 6 live demos were performed, for the approximate duration of 30 min each. Although non-conclusive from a statistical point of view, promising results were achieved: the subject was able to successfully operate the BCI (controlling the on/off switching of a light and the opening of a mechanical shutter), and the false positive rate was as low as 0.14 min^{-1}. This encourages the transition of such technology also outside of lab environments.

4   An Auxiliary EMG-Based Input Channel

In the introduction, it was stated that a hybrid approach is sought for, looking to exploit different input channels other than pure EEG. A solution could be to sense the (possibly weak) residual motor ability via EMG. In this case, for instance, the EMG channel could be used as a binary switch for enabling the EEG signal analysis; when not enables, the visual stimuli unit could be turned off in order to improve user's comfort (long exposure to light flashing periods induces eye fatigue). Moreover, turning LED stimuli off when not needed could mean improving BCI robustness against false positives, since EEG peaks at the specific target frequencies are less likely to occur. Nonetheless, it is still important for the EEG-based BCI section to be able to make such a distinction on its own, since false activations could be triggered by the EMG part.

Two experiments are performed, exploiting different muscular activations: jaw clench and eye movements (vertical or horizontal). In the former experiment, EMG is acquired from the masseter muscle via a single, differential channel, whereas in the latter from the frontalis and orbicularis muscles. Sampling rate, in both cases, is set to 1000 SPS to pick-up relevant signal features.

After collection, the signal undergoes basic pre-processing. For the jaw clench case, a basic band-pass filtering is performed ([100-350] Hz bandwidth, optimized to extract the more significant signal features), followed by a squaring. Before extracting the necessary features, the observed signal window is inspected for potentially interesting peaks based on a percentile criterion. Based on this, two features are extracted from the isolated signals: the integral and the mean. Those features are then passed to a linear kernel SVM, which takes care of the classification between epoch with or without muscular activation. The ocular-based experiment, follows a similar path, with a basic low-pass ($f_{cut} = 200$ Hz) and notch (50 Hz) filtering, followed by a Savitzky–Golay smoothing stage (in order to preserve the signal shape). Temporal features are then extracted, based on mean and standard deviation and fed to a SVM classifier.

The training phase consisted of a series of 100 activations performed by a subject. Online, real-time performance was then assessed on two subjects, and no further subject-specific training was performed in both cases. In the first experiment, a real-time test session consisted of 50 attempts to achieve control by a slight jaw clench, performed in a self-paced fashion, with at least 6 s between consecutive activations. In this scenario, a false positive event represents a detected activation while the subject was not trying to achieve control, whereas a false negative is a missed activation attempt. In the second experiment, a subject follows the same protocol, but attempts to achieve control via marked horizontal/vertical eye movements.

Results are still preliminary but encouraging: in the jaw clench experiment, one subject (the one which performed the training phase) was able to achieve perfect control over the whole real-time test session; the other subject did achieve a very good performance too, with just one false positive (≈ 0.067 min^{-1}) and two false negatives (6 %). In the second experiment, false positives are kept within 0.1 min^{-1}, whereas false negatives were, on average less than 10 %. These findings are promising and encourage in moving towards a hybrid BCI architecture, fusing EMG and EEG information to achieve a more robust device. It is expected that the fusion of multiple input sources will further improve the performance in terms of false positives.

5 Conclusions

In this paper, a complete implementation of a SSVEP-based BCI was presented, and a proof of concept for a possible extension exploiting EMG as auxiliary input signal was discussed. This aims at a future hybrid BCI implementation, with possible positive impacts on system performance indicators such a s accuracy or false positives immunity.

First, the EEG-based BCI section was discussed, based on the SSVEP paradigm. A methodology for achieving online, self-paced operation was presented in detail, and the notion of a confidence indicator introduced to improve the BCI performance, both in terms of accuracy and false positives immunity. It is worth remarking that, given the specific application target (namely, BCI-enabled AAL system control), false positive immunity and robustness are primary concerns with respect to, for example, system responsiveness (data throughput). In fact, user's interactions are limited to a very small amount and sparse in time. Also, for this reason, undergoing long or periodical system calibration phases could be perceived as an excessive burden by the user (this spoiling acceptance and usability chances). Therefore, a calibration and training-free approach was pursued. Subject-independent operation was demonstrated, at the same time achieving remarkably good performance. The results achieved are very good and improve over literature in terms of false positives rejection (0.16 min^{-1} on average). Moreover, the entire setup was also replicated outside lab-controlled conditions, with very promising results, encouraging the adoption of such technology in more realistic contexts.

Also, a possible hybrid BCI architecture was discussed, exploiting EMG as an auxiliary input channel. A proof of concept of EMG as a binary switch was presented with two experiments, aiming at detecting jaw clenches or ocular movements. The use of EMG as a binary switch, turning off the EEG-based BCI section when not needed, can have two major implications: the first is an improved user's comfort (less exposure to flashing visual stimuli, which could otherwise lead to eye fatigue), the second is a better false positives rejection (EEG peaks at the specific target frequencies are less likely to occur with the stimuli unit turned off). Preliminary results show the feasibility of such an approach, encouraging the development of a hybrid BCI architecture.

References

1. Wolpaw, J.R., Birbaumer, N., McFarland, D.J., Pfurtscheller, G., Vaughan, T.M.: Brain-computer interfaces for communication and control. Clin. Neurophysiol. **113**(6), 767–791 (2002)
2. Bianchi, V., Grossi, F., De Munari, I., Ciampolini, P.: Multi sensor assistant: A multisensor wearable device for ambient assisted living. J. Med. Imaging Health Inf. **2**(1), 70–75 (2012)
3. Mora, N., Bianchi, V., De Munari, I., Ciampolini, P.: A BCI platform supporting aal applications. In: Stephanidis, C., Antona, M. (eds.) UAHCI 2014, Part I. LNCS, vol. 8513, pp. 515–526. Springer, Heidelberg (2014)
4. Mora, N., De Munari, I., Ciampolini, P.: Improving BCI usability as HCI in ambient assisted living system control. In: Schmorrow, D.D., Fidopiastis, C.M. (eds.) AC 2015. LNCS, vol. 9183, pp. 293–303. Springer, Heidelberg (2015)
5. del Millan, J.R., Mourino, J.: Asynchronous BCI and local neural classifiers: an overview of the adaptive brain interface project. Trans. Neur. Sys. Rehab. Eng. **11**(2), 159–161 (2003)
6. Hinterberger, T., Schmidt, S., Neumann, N., Mellinger, J., Blankertz, B., Curio, G., Birbaumer, N.: Brain-computer communication and slow cortical potentials. IEEE Trans. Biomed. Eng. **51**(6), 1011–1018 (2004)
7. Pfurtscheller, G., Brunner, C., Schlögl, A., Lopes da Silva, F.H.: Mu rhythm (de) syn-chronization and EEG single-trial classification of different motor imagery tasks. NeuroImage **31**(1), 153–159 (2006)
8. Nijboer, F., Sellers, E.W., Mellinger, J., Jordan, M.A., Matuz, T., Furdea, A., Halder, S., et al.: A P300-based brain–computer interface for people with amyotrophic lateral sclerosis. Clin. Neurophysiol. **119**(8), 1909–1916 (2008)
9. Carabalona, R., Grossi, F., Tessadri, A., Castiglioni, P., Caracciolo, A., De Munari, I.: Light on! Real world evaluation of a P300-based brain-computer interface (BCI) for environment control in a smart home. Ergonomics **55**(5), 552–563 (2012)
10. Cecotti, H.: A Self-Paced and Calibration-Less SSVEP-Based Brain-Computer Interface Speller. IEEE Trans. Neural Syst. Rehabil. Eng. **18**(2), 127–133 (2010)
11. Mora, N., De Munari, I., Ciampolini, P.: A plug&play Brain Computer Interface solution for AAL systems. Stud. Health Technol. Inf. **217**, 152–158 (2015)
12. Mora, N., Bianchi, V., De Munari, I., Ciampolini, P.: Simple and efficient methods for steady state visual evoked potential detection in BCI embedded system. In: 2014 IEEE International Conference on Acoustics, Speech and Signal Processing (ICASSP), pp. 2044–2048 (2014)
13. Mora, N., De Munari, I., Ciampolini, P.: Exploitation of a compact, cost-effective EEG module for plug-and-play, SSVEP-based BCI. In: 2015 7th International IEEE/EMBS Conference on Neural Engineering (NER), pp. 142–145 (2015)
14. Volosyak, I.: SSVEP-based Bremen-BCI interface - boosting information transfer rates. J. Neural Eng. **8**(3), 447–450 (2011)
15. Garcia-Molina, G., Zhu, D.: Optimal spatial filtering for the steady state visual evoked potential: BCI application. In: 5th International IEEE/EMBS Conference on Neural Engineering, pp. 156–160 (2011)
16. Lin, Z., Zhang, C., Wu, W., Gao, X.: Frequency recognition based on canonical correlation analysis for SSVEP-based BCIs. IEEE Trans. Biomed. Eng. **54**, 1172–1176 (2007)
17. Mora, N., De Munari, I., Ciampolini, P.: Subject-independent, SSVEP-based BCI: trading off among accuracy, responsiveness and complexity. In: 2015 7th International IEEE/EMBS Conference on Neural Engineering (NER) (2015)

18. Pfurtscheller, G., Solis-Escalante, T., Ortner, R., Linortner, P., Muller-Putz, G.R.: Self-paced operation of an ssvep-based orthosis with and without an imagery-based "brain switch:" a feasibility study towards a hybrid BCI. IEEE Trans. Neur. Sys. and Rehab. Eng. **18**(4), 409–414 (2010)
19. Pan, J., Li, Y., Zhang, R., Zhenghui, G., Li, F.: Discrimination Between Control and Idle States in Asynchronous SSVEP-Based Brain Switches: A Pseudo-Key-Based Approach. IEEE Trans. Neur. Sys. and Rehab. Eng. **21**(3), 435–443 (2013)

Accessibility of Cultural Heritage Exhibits

Nikolaos Partarakis[1], Iosif Klironomos[1], Margherita Antona[1(✉)],
George Margetis[1], Dimitris Grammenos[1],
and Constantine Stephanidis[1,2]

[1] Institute of Computer Science,
Foundation for Research and Technology – Hellas (FORTH),
N. Plastira 100, Vassilika Vouton, 700 13 Heraklion, Crete, Greece
{partarak,iosif,antona,gmarget,
gramenos,cs}@ics.forth.gr
[2] Department of Computer Science, University of Crete, Heraklion, Greece

Abstract. The global impact of the digital revolution in the cultural sector worldwide brings about the need to ensure the accessibility of physical exhibits, interactive digital exhibits, digital media and digital content for disabled people. The paper addresses the accessibility of CH resources, and the need for a new approach to accessible user interaction with CH exhibits.

Keywords: Accessibility · User interaction · Cultural heritage resources

1 Introduction

The impact of the digital revolution has resulted in the emergence of many and diverse opportunities for people to engage with culture also through the digital media. But are these opportunities granted in equal measure to all citizens? Although Cultural Heritage Institutions (CHIs) worldwide are developing strategies towards widening the public's interest through digitalization, while progressively paying increasing attention to the physical accessibility of their premises, there has barely been any discussion in the cultural sector worldwide about the accessibility of interactive digital exhibits, digital media and content for disabled people. An audit regarding the accessibility of museum web sites published in 2005 [26] has shown that disabled people face numerous potential stumbling blocks on the average cultural sector webpage. The idea that cultural venues, as a service to the public, have a responsibility to welcome all in inclusive settings is far from being universally embraced in the cultural sector. Only a few CHIs have planned access measures for casual visitors who are visually impaired, deaf or who have learning disabilities, whether or not digital media are deployed [3]. The accessibility of cultural venues is a complex and multi-dimensional reality. The creation of accessible cultural experiences requires a systematic approach. Accessibility and equality is not yet part of the script in cultural bodies worldwide, and the idea of equal access to cultural heritage for people with disabilities has not matured, although this right has been formally declared (see [5–7, 22, 23]). This paper provides an overview of the current trends in the CH digitalisation towards widening access to the public at large, followed by some scenarios of universally accessible digital cultural

© Springer International Publishing Switzerland 2016
M. Antona and C. Stephanidis (Eds.): UAHCI 2016, Part II, LNCS 9738, pp. 444–455, 2016.
DOI: 10.1007/978-3-319-40244-4_43

exhibits that are envisioned as feasible in the near future based on existing and emerging technologies. Finally, the paper concludes with a roadmap of further research and development required towards realizing the vision of accessible universally accessible digital cultural exhibits in the contemporary museum, focusing on issues related to software architecture.

2 Digital Experiences with Museums

Recent research on capturing and understanding the museum visiting experience focuses on conceptual and methodological approaches to planning, designing and assessing the integration and deployment of interactive technologies in the museum context. A study conducted on the use of multi-touch interfaces in museums [15] addresses methodological aspects and advocates the adoption of broader approaches targeting not only user performance, but also the user overall satisfaction and experience, also exploiting quantitative data of the museum visit provided by sensing technologies). [10] discusses engagement, appropriation and personalisation in experiencing digital arts, and supports the conclusion that empowering people to make an artefact their own lies at the centre of user-centred designed in domain of culture. Multidisciplinary co-design of cultural exhibits involving museologists, designers, computer scientists, domain experts, etc. is applied in [4] to the design of interactive exhibits based on Augmented Reality and Tangible Interfaces. The co-design process includes requirements definition, museum exhibit and interaction design, implementation and evaluation phases, thus covering the entire development from the earliest analysis phase until the final concrete installation. The formative evaluation of touch screen and table based interactive museum artefacts in real settings is discussed in [13], aiming at ecological validity and at understanding 'natural' group interaction involving users of different ages. Finally, [17] elaborates on design principles for museum exhibitions, identifying five main principles and exemplifying their applications through case studies. The principles are summarised by the keywords clarity, layering, engagement, authenticity and resonance.

Personalised Information in Museums. Nowadays museums strive to design and implement exhibitions that offer enjoyable and educational experiences. The provision of a personalised experience to the visitors may help alleviate the problem of limited time and may more generally enhance the experience of any visitor if properly customized. Personalised access to information is also essential for people with diverse backgrounds, physical abilities, knowledge and interests to seamlessly access cultural resources. For example, Museum Guide 2.0 is an eye-tracking based personal assistant for museums and exhibits. Visitors wear a head mounted eye tracker whilst strolling through the exhibition. As soon as gaze on a specific exhibit is detected, the application plays an audio file that provides additional information about the specific exhibit [21]. The AGAMEMNON project aimed at providing visitors of sites of historical interest with personalized, information enriched experience through 3G cell phones [27]. The Macrographia system [12], installed in the Archaeological Museum of Thessaloniki, presents personalised information to users based on their position and language. Virtual Digital assistants have been also been employed for providing personalised information to users. The virtual agent Max has a full-time job as a central exhibit at the Heinz Nixdorf Museums Forum since 2004. He welcomes and entertains visitors though text based and gestures based interaction [18].

Interactive Exhibits. Worldwide, a number of museums have installed, temporarily or permanently, interactive exhibits in their premises. The "Fire and the Mountain" exhibition comprised four hybrid exhibits aiming to promote awareness about the cultural heritage of the people living around the Como Lake [11]. ARoS, an art museum in Denmark, employed four interactive exhibits targeted in an exhibition of the Japanese artist Mariko Mori [16]. The Austrian Technical Museum in Vienna opened a digitally augmented exhibition on the history of modern media [13]. The Archaeological Museum of Thessaloniki hosts "Macedonia from Fragment to Pixels" [28], an interactive exhibition of prototypical interactive systems with subjects drawn from ancient Macedonia. The Panoptes system allows the browsing of artefact collections, while Polyapton offers multitouch, multiuser gaming experiences with archaeological artefacts [12]. The Art-E-Fact Project [14] has developed a generic platform for interactive storytelling in Mixed Reality that facilitates access to a knowledge base of objects of art and art history. One installation was placed in the Bargello Museum (Soprintendenza Speciale pei il Polo Museale Fiorentino).

Museum Mobile Applications. According to [9], existing mobile applications for museums fall into the following categories: 45% provide guided tours of permanent exhibitions and the museum in general, 31% provide guided tours of temporary exhibitions and practical information about the museum visit, 8% provide combinations of the first two, 8% are apps devoted to a single object or artwork from the collection, 4% offer content creation or manipulation from the user inspired by artists' work, and 3% are games based on the exhibits. Some of these applications are designed to be used during the museum visit to enrich the visitors' experience, and can be downloaded once the user enters the museum space (e.g., the TAP app from the Indianapolis Art Museum, [30]). The navigation of these apps is structured according to the spatial arrangement of the exhibits in the museum, include interactive or simple floor plans of the museum's exhibition spaces with the exhibits marked, or offer activities for enriching the museum visit, such as the Gallery Tag! [29].

Museum presence on the Web. As the World Wide Web is being widely used by a constantly growing number and variety of people and that technology has evolved in the area of digital culture and cultural heritage preservation, many museums have established some presence on the Web by creating their web sites. Probably the most important project aiming at making cultural heritage available online was not initiated by a museum, but established very strong collaboration with many art partners around the world. The Art Project [32] is collaboration between Google and 151 acclaimed art partners from across 40 countries. Using a combination of various Google technologies and expert information provided by our museum partners, Google has created a unique online art experience.

Museum Social Applications. Social media tools allow people to interact around ideas conveyed through images, video, audio, and animations. They have proven to be very effective not only in connecting audiences but also in engaging them, providing museums with real opportunities to dialog with their audiences in new conversations and learning experiences. Museums are trying to increase their use of social media for more two-way and multi-way communication strategies. The Brooklyn Museum uses a social media game (Freeze Tag!) to correct questionable tags that have been applied to its online collection [33]. The Victoria and Albert Museum's "World Beach Project" is an online global art project in which visitors upload photographs of patterns made with stones on beaches around the world. The photographs are linked to a map showing where they were taken [34].

3 Accessibility in the Cultural Heritage Sector

Despite the progress to date, cultural heritage fruition enabled by interactive technologies still presents considerable limitations, as: (i) the accessibility of existing interactive systems has not yet been considered by application providers (ii) current systems offer limited interactivity, personalisation and contextual grounding of the fruition experience, (iii) very few efforts are focused on exploiting the wealth of available digital content and specialised knowledge for the benefit of the public at large that would help further capitalise on significant investments in this area, (iv) there are no systematic technological solutions available for supporting museums and cultural heritage institutions in more effectively satisfying visitors' expectations. According to a Eurobarometer survey [30], culture is very important for the vast majority of Europeans (77%, including citizens educated to the age of 15 or below). While cultural expenditure in Europe is typically the preserve of wealthier citizens, modern ICTs have a significant impact on the way people interact and socialise, creating new practices and forms of cultural participation in step with technology, primarily the Internet (65% of Europeans had Internet connection in 2009 as opposed to 49% in 2006).

3.1 Accessibility of Cultural Heritage Resources

Accessibility in the context of individual applications and services has been defined as follows: for each task a user has to accomplish through an interactive system, and taking into account specific functional limitations and abilities, as well as other relevant contextual factors, there is a sequence of input and output actions which leads to successful task accomplishment [19]. The accessibility of cultural venues is a complex and multi-dimensional reality. It needs to be seamlessly integrated into all aspects of the museum experience: visitor information– including via digital media, the physical environment, signage, exhibitions, interpretation, and, more importantly, modern technology penetrating to the museum experience. The creation of accessible cultural experiences requires a systematic approach. The accessibility of public installations poses different problems and is more complex than currently available approaches to the accessibility of desktop or web applications and services, as these installations do not simply introduce a new technology, but an integrated set of technologies. Different levels of accessibility may be distinguished. A first level concerns accessibility of individual devices. Such devices need to be accessible in the first place to their owners according to their needs, but basic accessibility features should also be provided for other users with potentially different needs. A second level concerns the accessibility of the environment that should enable an equivalent access to content and functions for users with diverse characteristics, not necessarily through the same devices, but through a set of interaction options integrated in the environment in a dynamic configuration / ensemble.

Multimodality and the availability of alternative means of interaction is a key feature towards facilitating the provisioning of a personalisable museum exhibit that will be accessible by users with functional limitations and varying abilities and preferences. Different modalities can be used concurrently, to increase the quantity of information made available or present the same information in different contexts, or redundantly, to address different interaction channels, both to reinforce a particular piece of information or to cater for the different abilities of users. Although several interaction technologies, such as, for example, voice output, are already widely available, and others, such as, for example eye-tracking, are reaching a maturity stage where they can be robustly exploited for accessibility purposes, developing truly accessible solutions for CHIs is currently still very expensive in terms of time, effort, cost and required knowledge, and the results have often limited flexibility and reusability in terms of the accessibility of solutions and addressed target user groups.

3.2 Ambient Intelligence and Interaction Techniques for Enhancing Accessibility

The emergence of Ambient Intelligence (AmI) is leading to the elaboration of new interaction concepts that extend beyond current user interfaces based on the desktop metaphor and menu driven interfaces, thus driving a transition to more natural and intuitive interaction with everyday things [1]. Natural interaction refers to people interacting with technology as they are used to interact with the real world in everyday life, through gestures, expressions, movements, etc., and discovering the world by looking around and manipulating physical objects [24]. Typical examples are input techniques such as touch, gestures, head and body position tracking and manipulation of physical objects, which seamlessly integrate the physical and digital worlds and support the direct engagement of the user with the environment [1]. Augmented Reality (AR) allows virtual imagery to augment and enhance physical objects in real time. Users may interact with the virtual images using real objects in a seamless way [25]. Progress in computer vision approaches largely contributes to innovative interaction in AmI environments through techniques such as like image acquisition, image processing, object recognition (2D and 3D), scene analysis, and image flow analysis, which can be exploited for humans' and objects' recognition and tracking. At the same time, ICT components are embedded into everyday objects like furniture, clothing, white goods, toys, etc. [2]. Augmented objects can be used for providing implicit or explicit input to systems while their physical and mental existence as computational devices disappear. Ambient interaction merges real and virtual worlds to produce new environments and visualisations where physical and digital objects co-exist and interact in real time. Additionally, in Ambient Intelligence environments interaction is monitored and implicit input is also extended to include empathy to understand human's feeling or states. The centrality and role of user-centred design approaches in the emergence and development of Ambient Intelligence environments is discussed in [20]. The user-centred design process is analysed in the light of the requirements posed by AmI, focusing on emerging problems and potential solutions towards applying and revising existing methods and techniques or developing new ones. User experience factors which are considered as critical in such context include natural interaction, accessibility, cognitive demands, emotions, health, safety and privacy, social aspects, cultural aspects, and aesthetics.

4   Scenarios for Universally Accessible Digital Cultural Exhibits

The vision for universally accessible digital cultural exhibits can be better described through indicative scenarios. This section presents scenarios based on personas, i.e., virtual users with specific characteristics used to help defining their interaction with cultural heritage exhibits.

Persona: Nick, blind: Nick is 41 years old and has been blind since the age of eight. He is a lover of ancient Greece and spends his free time at museums. His main problem is that although he is familiar with public transportation and can easily travel within the city, when visiting museums he has to either visit with company or hire a guide. He would love to have the freedom of visiting by himself. He recently heard that the Archaeological Museum of Thessaloniki has upgraded its interactive exhibition to address the needs of all visitors including people with disabilities. This might be the only museum I could visit by myself he thought. While entering the museum at the reception a lady informs him that the museum has an easy-to-use device that could help him navigate through the exhibition. This device announces the user's location within the museum and can automatically understand exhibits so as to provide information. Nick takes the device and starts moving within the museum. He realises that while moving the device announces him his current location. For example, the device informs Nick that he is at the ancient pottery department and that on his right are the potteries found at the grave of King Phillip. Moving on the right and approximating an exhibit the device starts announcing information. He can also request for more information if he wishes so. When entering the interactive section of the museum, the device informs him that Macrographia [12] has been updated to support tactile interaction. I will be able to feel a real Wall Painting he thinks. He move towards the direction pointed by the device and encounters something like a kiosk. The device informs him that right in front of him is the tactile version of Macrographia. He touches the display to feel a fascinating experience. While interacting with the Wall Painting, the device tells him the story of The Royal Hunt of Philip the second. This unique sensory experience reveals him the history of ancient Macedonia.

Personas: Maria and John, reduced visual acuity and difficulty in adjusting focus: Maria and John are retired teachers. Being on their early seventies Maria and John are experiencing problems regarding their visual acuity and difficulty in adjusting focus for near vision. They both have an interest in Art and Archaeology and they spend a lot of time visiting museums and picture galleries. Today they have decided to visit the

Archaeological Museum of Thessaloniki. While on the reception they are informed that a section with interactive exhibits is available at the museum. The girl at the reception informs them that they could use their mobile phone to personalise the content provided by the exhibits to their advanced experience in Art and Archaeology, and helps them download the museum client and fill in their profile. They are tempted by the fact that the museum can provide personalised information to them so they decide to try. It's not too difficult they think, we have just to show our mobile phone to the exhibits. While entering a section of the museum Maria shows John a kiosk presenting a puzzle game with words. It is Cryptolexon [12], the hidden crossword, a game which combines entertainment with knowledge. The names of ancient gods and heroes are hidden within a matrix of letters for the visitors to discover. Maria shows her mobile phone towards the puzzle and gets notified that the game has entered an advance difficulty level (due to her experience) and fonts-contrast are adjusted so as to be more readable. At least I don't have to wear my reading glasses, she thinks. After playing for some time Maria and John sees people moving their hands in front of an informative display. This must present all the treasures in the museum they think but it seems quite difficult to keep your hand up for such a long time. They decide to give it a shot so they show their mobile phone to the exhibit. At the same time they are informed that they could use their eyes to interact with the display instead of waving their hands. Just by looking at different locations within the screen they can browse information. Having the desire to see the rest of the museum too they notice that small tablets are mounted on the sides of each exhibit. People are interacting and learning by these displays. What happened to the captions they think? When approaching one of these tablets Maria shows her mobile phone and she notices that fonts are increased, contrast has been changed and navigation arrows appear. It is like browsing a history book they think. Maria and John leave the museum after a couple of hours. "We should definitely return to see the rest" they think.

Persona: Luigi, elder, upper limb impairment. Luigi is 60 years old, retired and has lost the use of both his hands due to a car accident. Among his interests are painting (he had taken a number of classes on painting using his mouth to control brushes) and art in general. He is interested in technology but he faces difficulties due to his disability. Recently he was told that the Archaeological Museum of Thessaloniki has updated its section of interactive exhibits to address the requirements of all including people with disabilities. Visiting the museum with his wife, he enters the interactive section when the virtual character welcomes him. He also notices the existence of large push buttons that he could use to make questions to the character while also being able to ask questions orally. He tries both ways and the character responds well to both forms of interaction. He notices the existence a table, whose surface is covered by a printed map on which the location of various cities and other notable sites is projected. White paper tablets with a coloured frame are used by visitors to access information. Well I can't do that he thinks but decides to move closer. When in front on the table, museum staff informs him that he could use a HMD for gazing to the location within the map in order to access information. After wearing the device he notices that information is always located in front of him in order to have access and on the most distant POIs of the map. On another location of the museum he encounters a system called "Peridexion, the dexterous" [12]. Peridexion presents a masterpiece of 6th c. BC Athenian black-figured pottery, known as the Crater of Lydos, as well as three exceptional examples of Roman sculpture from the AMTh collection, all inspired by the legend of the hunt of a monstrous boar in Calydonia, Aetolia. The objects included in this presentation span eight centuries. He notices that people are interacting through touch while blind people use a device to announce them information about the exhibit and make selections. When approaching the exhibit, he notices that he could use it just by looking different areas of the screen. For selecting items, he just has to look a specific region of the artefact for a couple of seconds (a progress bar is filling while staring). When more than one pages of information is presented he can, in order to reduce interaction time, press the large buttons embedded on the exhibit. Luigi leaves the museum very pleased, as he was able to all exhibits without help from his wife.

5 Towards Accessibility of CHRs - Beyond the State of Art

Assistive solutions and accessibility technologies have so far supported the augmentation of the capabilities of the individuals and the adaptation of single artefacts for accessibility. Building on current approaches in the field, it becomes instrumental for accessibility to develop new interaction methods as they emerge in the context of interactive museum exhibits, taking advantage of multimodality.

5.1 Research Challenges

The provision of universally accessible multimodal solutions for Cultural Heritage Institutions is fundamental for offering equal access to cultural resources to all citizens including the elderly and people with disability. Thus, a number of challenges towards achieving accessibility for cultural heritage exhibits need to be addressed. These include:

Novel interaction paradigms for experiencing cultural heritage by developing pools of accessible, reusable interaction modules, which may constitute integral parts of a framework targeted to allow users to interact naturally with physical and digital artefacts in the museum and in living space environments, through various integrated devices.

Novel forms of UIs adaptation that are distributed in the environment responding also intelligently to context and situation changes.

New accessibility interaction techniques, designed for all, beyond the spectrum of the conventional computational devices need to be investigated, and an inclusive interaction model, addressing the needs of interaction with Cultural Heritage Resources within CHIs elaborated, encompassing both emerging and standardized techniques.

Alternative means of information display. Accessible augmented interaction with physical and digital artefacts should be supported by providing alternative means of information display through mobile devices, as well as ambient set-ups offering rich interaction techniques through mainstream devices such as Microsoft Kinect (http://www.xbox.com/en-GB/kinect/). Investigation and development of techniques for measuring various aspects of users' engagement and experience with Cultural Heritage by monitoring and capturing average time of visit, head orientation, etc.

Mechanisms for personalised retrieval based on user characteristics, annotation and presentation supporting individual users in shaping their interests and cultural heritage fruition experiences.

Personalised cross – domain smart assistive solutions to address the accessibility and usability needs of disabled and older users need to be designed and developed, building upon state-of-art solutions in voice interaction, scanning, visual layout adaptation, touch and haptics interaction, gestures, eye tracking, head pose interaction, sign language, persuasive and affective interaction, serious games and augmented reality. Improvement in specific existing technologies is also necessary:

- Both low-cost eye-aware appliances as well as high-end gaze tracking solutions need to be developed and tested in the context of interactive museum exhibits, with emphasis on making the solutions robust and safe, and ensuring that the solutions will adapt to different abilities, needs and preferences of individual users.
- Touch and gesture interfaces that allow people with visual impairments, or anyone in eyes-busy situations, to interact with cultural heritage resources should be further studied, and different modalities based on users' needs and preferences need to be offered.
- Both video and avatar -based representations need to be explored to assist deaf individuals in their interactions with museum exhibits. These should cover the needs of the different use cases and application scenarios, with properly coded linguistic resources to provide options for multilingual content maintenance and 3D representation editing.
- Interaction solutions to provide alternative input, output and information rendering modalities capable of addressing each individual's needs should be widely offered, supporting interoperability of assistive technologies and conventional computational devices (PCs, smart phones, etc.) with innovative high-end technology artefacts.

5.2   An Envisioned Architecture to Support the Accessibility of CHRs

This paper brings forward an approach to the development of multimodal accessible applications taking into account the majority of existing limitations of systems designed for all (a single interface designed for all results to reduced user experience for all). The most important aspects of accessible multimodal interaction such as the users, context and assignment of multimodal technologies are modeled in the form of ontologies to specific user and context. CH models can be developed to ensure the provision of appropriate cultural experience to all users taking into account aspects such as disability, functional limitations, technology, expertise and domain knowledge. When appropriate, these models could build on external knowledge such as existing domain standards to ensure maximum reusability and exploitation of results. Knowledge can be made available through a number of alternative end-point such as web-services, sparql end points and databases. For knowledge management by CHI personnel, an ontology manager can be created while curators have the option to form the visitors' experience through an exhibition designer. A number of sensors, assistive technologies, and smart and augmented objects can be made available through the "Sensor & Smart Objects & Assistive Devices Integration layer" (Fig. 1).

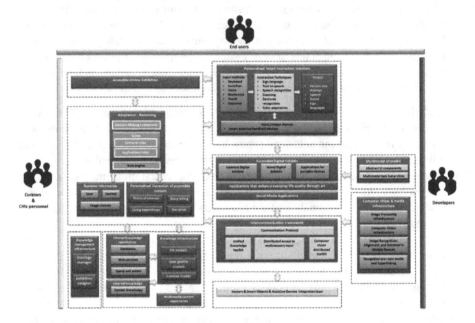

Fig. 1. Envisioned architecture

These technologies will be facilitated through the use of a common distributed service oriented Intercommunication Framework providing access to the sensory infrastructure, quick and inexpensive ways of knowledge retrieval, and the "Computer Vision & media infrastructure". This infrastructure offers a number of facilities for advanced interaction with CH resources including 3D models, image recognition and processing and at the same time can be used for offering visitor recognition and tracking facilities to be employed into complex space aware exhibits. The "Multimodal Interaction Toolkit" builds on these technologies to provide a unified ready to use solution for all interactive digital exhibits and applications. Additionally, the Adaptation – Reasoning components, employ "Runtime Information" gathered through interaction monitoring and the facilities for "Personalized Extraction of accessible content" to take decision regarding interface adaptation, modality selection and modality enhancement. Accessible Digital Exhibits can then be built on top of the aforementioned facilities and Personalized Smart Interaction Solutions for all to offer the optimal experience to end users.

6 Conclusion

Advanced interactive technologies have a significant role to play in enriching the fruition experience for all citizens, and unleash economic potential for new tools and services. Information and Communication Technology will have a profound impact on the means of interacting with Cultural Heritage Resources in the near future. Developing truly accessible ICT solutions CHIs is currently perceived as very expensive in terms of time, costs and required knowledge, and the results are of limited flexibility and reusability. To address this challenge, it is crucial to support the development of generic solutions effectively addressing accessible interaction with CHRs within CHIs, and make them available to designers, developers, and the industry, as well as to support the direct involvement of end users and facilitators.

Acknowledgments.   This work has been supported by the FORTH-ICS RTD Programme "Ambient Intelligence and Smart Environments".

References

1. Aarts, E., de Ruyter, B.: New research perspectives on Ambient Intelligence. J. Ambient Intell. Smart Environ. **1**(1), 5–14 (2009)
2. Alcañiz, M., Rey, B.: New Technologies For Ambient Intelligence. IOS Press, Amsterdam (2005)
3. Bell, J.A., Matty, S., Weisen, M.: MLA Disability Survey 2005. England: Museums, Libraries and Archives Council (2005). Web. http://www.nemo.org/fileadmin/Dateien/public/topics/Disability_and_museums/disability_survey_2005_summary_10447.pdf
4. Bortolaso, C., Bach, C., Duranthon, F., Dubois, F.: Co-design of interactive museographic exhibits: the MIME case study. In: Proceedings of Re-Thinking Technology in Museums (2011)
5. Council of Europe. Disability Action Plan 2006–2015 (2006). Web. www.coe.int/t/e/social_cohesion/soc%2Dsp/Rec_2006_5%20Disability%20Action%20Plan.pdf
6. Council of Europe. Recommendation R(92)6 of the Committee of Ministers to Member States on a Coherent Policy for People with Disabilities (1992). Web. www.handicapincifre.it/allegati/RECOMMENDATION_R(92)6.htm
7. Council of Europe. Resolution of 6 May 2003 on accessibility of cultural infrastructure and cultural activities for people with disabilities. Council of the European Union (2003). Web. www.rech2006.com/download_files/resolution_en.pdf
8. Dudani, S.A.: The distance-weighted k-nearest-neighbor rule 4. IEEE Trans. Syst. Man **6**, 325–327 (1976)
9. Economou, M., Meintani, E.: Promising beginnings? Evaluating museum mo-bile phone apps. In: Proceedings of Re-Thinking Technology in Museums (2011). http://www.idc.ul.ie/techmuseums11/index.php?option=com_content&view=article&id=15&Itemid=7
10. Flint, T., Turner, P.: The role of appropriation in the design of engaging artefacts. In: Proceedings of Re-Thinking Technology in Museums (2011). http://www.idc.ul.ie/techmuseums11/index.php?option=com_content&view=article&id=15&Itemid=7
11. Garzotto, F., Rizzo, F.: Interaction paradigms in technology-enhanced social spaces: a case study in museums. Proc. DPPI **2007**, 343–356 (2007)

12. Grammenos, D., Zabulis, X., Michel, D., Sarmis, T., Georgalis, G., Tzevanidis, K., Argyros, A., Stephanidis, C.: Design and development of four prototype interactive edutainment exhibits for museums. In: Stephanidis, C. (ed.) Universal Access in Human-Computer Interaction. Context Diversity. LNCS, vol. 6767, pp. 173–182. Springer, Heidelberg (2011)

13. Hornecker, E., Nicol, E.: Towards the Wild: Evaluating museum installations in semi-realistic situations. In: Proceedings of Re-Thinking Technology in Museums (2011). http://www.idc.ul.ie/techmuseums11/index.php?option=com_content&view=article&id=15&Itemid=7

14. Iurgel, I.: From another point of view: Art-E-fact. In: Göbel, S., Spierling, U., Hoffmann, A., Iurgel, I., Schneider, O., Dechau, J., Feix, A. (eds.) TIDSE 2004. LNCS, vol. 3105, pp. 26–35. Springer, Heidelberg (2004)

15. Kidd, J., Ntalla, I., Lyons, W.: Multi-touch interfaces in museum spaces: reporting preliminary findings on the nature of interaction. In: Proceedings of Re-Thinking Technology in Museums (2011). http://www.idc.ul.ie/techmuseums11/index.php?option=com_content&view=article&id=15&Itemid=7

16. Kortbek, K.J., Grønbæk, K.: Interactive spatial multimedia for communication of art in the physical museum space. Proc. MM **2008**, 609–618 (2008)

17. Leslie, M.: Applying basic design principles to technology in museums. In: Proceedings of Re-Thinking Technology in Museums (2011). http://www.idc.ul.ie/techmuseums11/index.php?option=com_content&view=article&id=15&Itemid=7

18. Pfeiffer, T., Liguda, C., Wachsmuth, I.: Living with a virtual agent: seven years with an embodied conversational agent at the heinz nixdorf MuseumsForum. In Proceedings of Re-Thinking Technology in Museums (2011)

19. Savidis, A., Stephanidis, C.: Unified user interface design: designing universally accessible interactions. Int. J. Interact. Comput. **16**(2), 243–270 (2004)

20. Stephanidis, C.: Human factors in ambient intelligence environments. In: Salvendy, G. (ed.) Handbook of Human Factors and Ergonomics, 4th edn. John Wiley and Sons, USA (2012)

21. Toyama, T., Kieninger, T., Shafait, S., Dengel, A.: Museum Guide 2.0 – an eye-tracking based personal assistant for museums and exhibits. In: Proceedings of Re-Thinking Technology in Museums (2011). http://www.idc.ul.ie/techmuseums11/index.php?option=com_content&view=article&id=15&Itemid=7

22. United Nations. Convention on the Rights of Persons with Disabilities. UN, came into force 8 May 2008. Web. www.un.org/disabilities/default.asp?navid=13&pid=150

23. United Nations. Universal Declaration of Human Rights. UN, 1948. Web. www.un.org/en/documents/udhr/

24. Valli, A.: The design of natural interaction. Multimedia Tools Appl. **38**(3), 295–305 (2008)

25. Van Krevelen, D.W.F., Poelman, R.: A survey of augmented reality technologies, applications and limitations. Int. J. Virtual Reality **9**(2), 1 (2010)

26. Weisen, M.: How accessible are museums today. Touch in Museums, Policy and Practice in Object Handling. Oxford & New York:Berg, 2008 Web

27. http://services.txt.it/agamemnon/

28. http://www.makedonopixels.org/

29. http://www.brooklynmuseum.org/community/blogosphere/2010/03/25/gallery-tag/

30. http://www.imamuseum.org/interact/tap

31. http://www.amnh.org/apps/explorer.php

32. https://www.google.com/culturalinstitute/u/0/project/art-project

33. http://www.brooklynmuseum.org/opencollection/freeze_tag/start.php

34. http://www.vam.ac.uk/collections/textiles/lawty/world_beach/00

Inclusive Smart City: An Exploratory Study

João Soares de Oliveira Neto[1(✉)] and Sergio Takeo Kofuji[2]

[1] Department of Technological and Exact Sciences (CETEC),
University of Recôncavo da Bahia (UFRB),
Av. Rui Barbosa, 710, Cruz das Almas, BA zip 44380-000, Brazil
jneto@ufrb.edu.br
[2] LSI - School of Engineering/Escola Politécnica, University of São Paulo,
Av. Prof. Luciano Gualberto, 380 – Butantã,
São Paulo, SP zip 05508-010, Brazil
kofuji@usp.br

Abstract. Smart City Projects are getting more and more attention from the academy, industry and government in a global scale. We investigate some problems People with Disabilities (PwD) face in the urban space; we also observed some improvements that assistive technology should have in order to assure autonomy and independency to each and every citizen. We walked along 1 km in the downtown area of São Paulo taking pictures and recorded a range of difficulties that impaired persons, elderly people, pregnant women and so forth can have while trying to orient themselves in metropolises. The results of this observation are the principles of a broader view of Smart Cities: Inclusive Smart Cities.

Keywords: Inclusive smart cities · Accessibility · Assistive technology · Smart cities · People with disabilities

1 Introduction

Technology has been strongly perceived as a key element in the daily life of contemporary cities. In recent years, municipalities have invested in Information and Communication Technologies (ICT) solutions in order to increase the efficiency and productivity of several local services/systems – such as transport, communication, water, business, city governance and others [1]. The offer of such services has transformed the way people interact with each other, with institutions and with the public space – namely, the city.

After the rise of several Smart City initiatives in different parts of the globe [2–5], the central point of this kind of initiatives has progressively changed to considering the role that citizens must play in a Smart City. Even considering this new approach, it is rare to find academic research and industry products that deal with accessibility issues, as is the employment of Information and Communication Technologies (ICT) to help persons with disabilities in the urban space. To be considered "smart", a city must reinforce the participations of everyone recognizing the diversity of citizens, struggle against the segregation of minorities, and try, as much as possible, to eliminate, not only physical but also digital, barriers. That is what we call Inclusive Smart City.

M. Antona and C. Stephanidis (Eds.): UAHCI 2016, Part II, LNCS 9738, pp. 456–465, 2016.
DOI: 10.1007/978-3-319-40244-4_44

This is an exploratory study on the challenges that people with disabilities face when they need to interact with the urban space and on how universal access and technology and can help them to move safely through and to better explore the city. Our main objectives are: (i) observing the urban space looking for opportunities make the urban space decipherable to PwD; (ii) looking at already installed assistive technology tools in the urban space trying to find opportunities to maximize their usability; and (iii) formulating some of the seminal principles of Inclusive Smart Cities.

This paper is organized as follows. First, we briefly discuss definitions and main features of Smart City projects. Then, we point out some aspects of accessibility in the urban space and the importance of assuring independence and autonomy to every citizen living in cities. Section 4 describes the methodology of our study and presents some relevant pictures and notes taken during the observation of the selected neighborhood. The findings are presented in Sect. 5 as well as some of the seminal principles of the Inclusive Smart City approach. Finally, Sect. 6 presents our conclusions.

2 Smart Cities

Finding a universal definition for the term "Smart City" is not a trivial task. This is a widely multidisciplinary subject. Therefore, different fields will conceive different definitions based on each different point-of-view and focusing in one or more particular aspects. [6] states that "Smart City" is not a static concept. It is rather a process – no end point -, a series of steps that will make the city more livable, resilient and ready to deal with new challenges. However, [6] underlines some aspects, which are strongly information-driven, which can better delineate some elements that Smart City projects should consider:

- A modern digital infrastructure to provide access to useful data enabling citizens to access the information they need, when and where they need it;
- Service delivery must be citizen-centered, meaning that citizens' needs must be in the forefront. City-administrators must collaborate with each other and share the information management in order to provide a coherent service and a consolidated view of data that, most of time, is spread over a multiplicity of silos;
- An intelligent physical infrastructure (computers, sensors and other Internet of Things components) to collect and to transport data supplying services and enabling those services to perform their tasks;
- An openness to learn from others and to experiment with new approaches and new business models; and
- Transparency of outcomes/performance to feedback citizens/ enterprises with data collected from the city and to enable citizens to compare and to challenge performance.

For the purpose of better management and control, urban systems are grouped in layers: natural environment (resources, environment, topography); infrastructure (utilities, buildings, roads); resources (minerals, oil, air); services (building services, transport, water, power); and social systems (people, policy, culture, commerce) [7]. Instrumenting cities with sensors and actuators allows citizens and city-administrators to access real time information on air quality conditions, traffic jams, natural disasters and emergency situations, health campaigns, job opportunities and so on.

However, the gain acquired with better transactions between citizens and local governments, as well as a better relationship between citizens and (public and non-public) service providers are not – or, at least, should not be – the major outcomes of Smart Cities projects [8, 9]. Since the context of Smart City projects is the city as a whole, such projects can mitigate the segregation of citizens regarding information access once the users of Smart City initiatives form, by definition, the wide variety of citizens living in the city.

3   Accessibility and the Urban Spaces

One of the key issues of contemporary societies, accessibility has brought together national and international organisms, governments and social movements around the needs of persons with disabilities. Concisely, the design (or redesign) of products, devices, services and environments [10] means a wide range of advantages to PwD: the ability to access - products, places, information, systems and so on – that were only previously accessible to people without disabilities. Assistive technology is mostly developed making use of Universal Design principles, in order to guarantee access to the widest possible range of abilities. Designing taking into account accessibility principles is designing for everyone.

The United Nations emphasize in their *Convention on the Rights of Persons with Disabilities* that accessibility has to "enable persons with disabilities to live independently and participate fully in all aspects of life, States Parties shall take appropriate measures to ensure to persons with disabilities access, on an equal basis with others, to the physical environment, to transportation, to information and communications, including information and communication technologies and systems, and to other facilities and services open or provided to the public, both in urban and in rural areas" [11]. This right to access concerns the physical layer (building, roads, and other indoor and outdoor facilities), such as to the digital layer (information, communications and other services, including electronic services and emergency services).

Cities continue to be one of the greatest obstacles for PwD: wheelchair users must deal with potholes; impaired–hearing persons must count mostly on their vision to compensate for the lack of sound; people with limited walking abilities have to move over sidewalks with changes in level; visually impaired have do deal with the lack of appropriate signs regarding places and objects. Specific laws and governmental regulations have treated part of these problems associated to the physical infrastructure of the urban space. In Brazil, for instance, number of municipalities have made it mandatory to adapt sidewalks equipping them with tactile floor indicators; buildings must be readapted with ramps, curb ramps and elevators – even old buildings are motivated to be retrofitted; parking lots must be reserved for elderly people and PwD; public spaces restrooms must fit PwD needs; buses must provide platform lifts, etc. As expected, those changes take time, but there have been advances and progress.

When the focus moves to the digital layer of the urban tissue (applications, systems, ICT services and electronic services), there is still a particular absence of digital services oriented to all diversity of citizens living in a city (including PwD, elderly persons, children, pregnant women, foreign people that do not speak the local language etc.). When discussing Smart City initiatives, accessibility and assistive technology, we rarely find options of services. Most applications in this field (route tracers, maps, emergency systems, sharing economy apps, ride-sharing programs, point of interest maps, bus tracker apps, smart parking and others) are not at all capable to interact properly in a non-excluding manner. Public administrators have more and more provided free Wi-Fi zones in squares and public buildings, but unfortunately, most PwD are not able to fully benefit from this service.

As most of our activities are becoming digital, providing digital services in an inclusive manner is to allow every citizen to occupy a place in a digital society and in a moving democracy era, potentially assuring the mitigation of the digital divide caused by the lack of full access to both urban physical and digital layers.

4   Methodology

This is a qualitative and exploratory research once the problem cannot be completely envisaged; it has not been clearly defined and has to be "discovered" [12]. One of the purposes of our research is to gain familiarity with the relationship between accessibility, urban spaces and Smart Cities, as background. Also, the exploratory approach helped us to gain experience in the difficulties faced by PwD in their daily routine when moving along streets, avenues, buildings, squares and other urban equipment. As the research subject is still new – namely, how Smart City initiatives could be inclusive – the exploratory research allowed us to learn while theories are still being formulated.

With 11.8 millions inhabitants, São Paulo – Fig. 1(a) - is a representative example of a contemporary megalopolis. We have chosen a 1-km route in São Paulo downtown

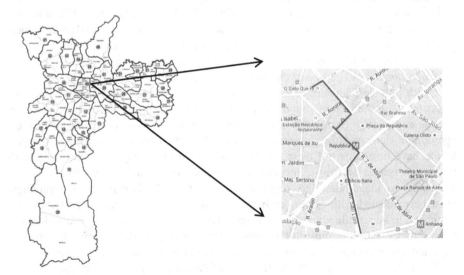

Fig. 1. Map of São Paulo and studied area in São Paulo downtown

Fig. 2. Overlapped information layers Urban landscape is made by layers of sensorial information (sight and hearing most of the time). These layers are overlapped in perspective.

depicted in Fig. 1(b) in order to explore (i) what kind of information is signed in a very confused area of a huge city, (ii) what kind of assistive technologies are found in the urban space, and (iii) opportunities for employing technology to adapt the urban digital layer so that the urban space can be more inclusive.

While walking, we have taken some pictures of obstacles and potential opportunities for developing assistive technology in the urban space; we also have written down some descriptive notes. The result of this documentation process can be seen in the following Figs. 2, 3, 4, 5, 6, 7, 8 and 9.

Fig. 3. Some very important information is not accessible to every citizen Extremely important information shown in the city is mostly textual. PwD, blind people, elderly persons and foreign people can not access this information at all or may have great difficulty in discovering what places and objects in the city are – as is the case of the information shown at bus stops.

Fig. 4. Low floor and tactile floor indicator Low floor and tactile floor indicator can be very useful for people with reduced mobility/wheelchair users and visually impaired people. Yet, as shown in Fig. 4, sometimes they float on the sideway: no signs show how to reach them – especially to blind people.

Fig. 5. Touristic places Low floor and tactile floor indicator can be very useful for people with reduced mobility/wheelchair users and visually impaired people. Yet, as shown in Fig. 4, sometimes they float on the sideway: no signs show how to reach them – especially to blind people.

5   Towards the Inclusive Smart City

The data collected and shown in Sect. 4 reinforces the hypothesis that cities still do not make very important information accessible – and that, in many cases, can be vital – to guide citizens in the urban space. Some aspects observed in the area selected determine that the urban space is a still more complex system concerning PwD needs. On the other hand, these aspects establish that cities are a source of research opportunities regarding the improvement of assistive technology already installed and/or the development of new products and services driven to PwD to allow them to fully use the urban space.

Fig. 6. Emergency situation warnings There are some places even the goodsighted are not able to find. Or places that deserve special attention such as touristic and historical places. These places have to be made reachable by PwD, too. Some well-known alert mechanisms concerning dangerous situations are mostly not accessible to PwD: warning sounds at the exit of underground parking can be misjudged due to street noises; textual messages addressed to escalator users cannot be accessed by impaired persons ("Keep left free" – in Fig. 6).

Hence, we propose an approach to deal with the observed lack of accessibility in the urban space and with improving the tools already offered to PwD in cities: the Inclusive Smart City. Inclusive Smart City is a new citizen-centered approach that combines pervasive technologies (hardware and software) and the Universal Design methodology in order to: (i) provide mechanisms that allow people with disabilities to interact with the urban space and to access geolocalized information and services; (ii) use ICT to mitigate the segregation of people with disabilities, creating innovative solutions or adapting some of those already in use but not available to everyone.

The urban space is a rich source of visual, audio and spatial data. People with disabilities have to face the obstacle of not perceiving one (or several) of these channels of information. A blind person, for instance, does not perceive what is drawn in a traffic sign a few meters away. If he/she does not know the place, he/she will probably not find where the public bathroom is (even though the place shows the appropriate sign). Thus, **the main feature of the Inclusive Smart City is the ability of identifying places and objects (or things) and making this information digitally available**. Once this information is available, it can be sent to devices that receive the information and personalize this information according to the disability of the user.

Fig. 7. Business opportunities Entrepreneurs are missing commercial transactions with PwD once holiday sales, renting and selling signs, as well as advertisement messages do not reach a significant part of the population that has valuable income. Another accessibility barrier is the identification of business and stores: PwD are simply unable to identify stores they are in front of, or to be "flaneurs"/wanderers in the streets and shopping malls.

Fig. 8. Urban common facilities Urban facilities – such as bus stops, taxi stations, police stations, hospital, restrooms – that are spread all over the city are not easily found by PwD. Most of these places are identified by signs and even by text written on the road.

Fig. 9. Subway station In large cities, the subway is a very important transport modality. The larger the subway station, the more confusing direction identification is. Finding information is a very hard task even for non-PwD., PwD usually depend on volunteers and subway personnel to help them to move inside these complex "universes".

6   Conclusions

A Smart City should enable every citizen to use all the services offered, public as well as private, in the way best suited to his or her needs. PwD are part of the city and have to take advantage to full access to products, urban equipment, services and information. They need independency, autonomy and safety. Based on the experiment held in a 1-km area of São Paulo downtown, we propose the Inclusive Smart City approach: a broader information digitalization, the use of Internet of Things, Pervasive Computing, Wearable Computing, Cloud Computing and other technologies to enhance the role of assistive technology already available in cities. We believe that the Inclusive Smart City approach can help PwD to explore neighborhoods and to know things and places by themselves.

References

1. IBM: "A vision of smarter cities," 23 Jun 2009. http://www-01.ibm.com/common/ssi/cgi-bin/ssialias?infotype=PM&subtype=XB&appname=GBSE_GB_TI_USEN&htmlfid=GBE0322 7USEN&attachment=GBE03227USEN.PDF. Accessed 24 Feb 2016
2. Gea, T., Paradells, J., Lamarca, M., Roldán, D.: Smart cities as an application of internet of things: experiences and lessons learnt in barcelona: In: 2013 Seventh International Conference on Innovative Mobile and Internet Services in Ubiquitous Computing (IMIS), pp. 552–557 (2013)
3. Mohammed, F., Idries, A., Mohamed, N., Al-Jaroodi, J., Jawhar, I.: Opportunities and challenges of using UAVs for dubai smart city. In: 2014 6th International Conference on New Technologies, Mobility and Security (NTMS), pp. 1–4 (2014)
4. Fortes, M.Z., Ferreira, V.H., Sotelo, G.G., Cabral, A., Correia, W.F., Pacheco, O.L.C.: Deployment of smart metering in the B #x00FA;zios City. In: Transmission Distribution Conference and Exposition - Latin America (PES T D-LA), 2014 IEEE PES, pp. 1–6 (2014)
5. Pla-Castells, M., Martinez-Durá, J.J., Samper-Zapater, J.J., Cirilo-Gimeno, R.V.: Use of ICT in smart cities. A practical case applied to traffic management in the city of Valencia. In: Smart Cities Symposium Prague (SCSP), pp. 1–4 (2015)
6. UK: Smart cities: background paper - Publications - GOV.UK. https://www.gov.uk/government/publications/smart-cities-background-paper. Accessed 24 Feb 2016
7. Harrison, C., Donnelly, I.A.: A theory of smart cities. In: Proceedings of the 55th Annual Meeting of the ISSS - 2011 Hull UK, vol. 55, no. 1, September 2011
8. Oliveira, Á., Campolargo, M., Martins, M.: Human smart cities: a human-centric model aiming at the wellbeing and quality of life of citizens. In: eChallenges e-2014, 2014 Conference, pp. 1–8 (2014)
9. Hollands, R.G.: Will the real smart city please stand up? City 12(3), 303–320 (2008)
10. "Accessibility," Wikipedia, the free encyclopedia, 05 December 2015
11. United Nations: Convention on the rights of persons with disabilities. http://www.un.org/disabilities/convention/conventionfull.shtml. Accessed 25 February 2016
12. HCI Models: Theories, and Frameworks: Toward a Multidisciplinary Science, 1st edn. Morgan Kaufmann, Amsterdam; Boston (2003)

A Study Exploring the Concept
of Virtual Windows for the Elderly

Kevin C. Tseng[1,2(✉)], Huu-Kha Hoang[1], and Po-Hsin Huang[1]

[1] Product Design and Development Laboratory,
Department of Industrial Design, College of Management,
Chang Gung University, Taoyuan City, Taiwan, ROC
ktseng@pddlab.org
[2] Healthy Aging Research Centre, Chang Gung University,
Taoyuan City, Taiwan, ROC

Abstract. Virtual windows could improve the elderly's health and emotional state. Therefore, this study aims to identify and understand the concept of the virtual window in the elderly's living environment. To achieve this purpose, this study summarizes the concept of the virtual window for the elderly's windowless living environment. Then, based on this concept, this study proposes syntheses of the virtual window. The concept of the three syntheses could assist the designers of the visual window in designing a helpful and realistic environment for the elderly and, thus, improve the elderly's health and emotional state.

Keywords: Elderly · Virtual window · Synthesis · Healthy and emotional

1 Introduction

A view from a window plays an important role in humans' physical and psychological well-being in indoor environments [1]. Moreover, windows allow sufficient illumination in a room, which is linked with good results related to the elderly's health [2]. In addition, the lack of window is associated with higher levels of anxiety, depression, and delirium [3]. A study showed that university dormitory environments with a window view of nature had a greater effect on students' grades and attention than those with a less natural view [4]. Thus, the window plays an important role in people's health, especially the elderly's health.

According to the research of Bernardo Schorr [5], in the future, people will have to live in a "windowless department". Therefore, many studies on virtual windows have been conducted in recent years [6]. Häkkilä et al. [6] examined the virtual window by connecting two locations through interactive public displays. Dowds and Masthoff [7] designed a mobile application (app) to bring live and recorded local events into the homes of the elderly.

Moreover, in recent years, several studies have demonstrated a relationship between the environment and health [8–10]. In addition, many studies have described the environment. First, views of nature have positively impacted individuals' psychological state [11]. Furthermore, according to Ulrich [12], viewing nature from a window has positive effects on physical well-being. The elderly's community is

© Springer International Publishing Switzerland 2016
M. Antona and C. Stephanidis (Eds.): UAHCI 2016, Part II, LNCS 9738, pp. 466–471, 2016.
DOI: 10.1007/978-3-319-40244-4_45

another important factor in their living environment. Moreover, according to the research conducted by Golant [13], an important environment surrounding the elderly's living space is the neighborhood. Therefore, the community is another factor that is important for the elderly's daily life. Finally, the urban environment could improve the elderly's social health through design [14]. Thus, the urban environment is also an important factor for the elderly.

This study conducts a review of the literature and integrates the concept of the virtual window with the natural, community and urban environments for the elderly. Then, based on the design concept, this study proposes virtual window syntheses for the elderly. The results could assist designers in designing a real virtual window for the elderly.

2 Literature Review

2.1 Virtual Window Environments

Nature provides an inner sense of serenity and peacefulness [15]. Several studies have reported the beneficial and restorative effects of views of a natural scene [4, 16].

First, Tennessen and Cimprich [4] explored the content of the window view and found that students who had natural views showed a greater capacity to sustain attention. In addition, another study revealed that exposure to natural settings could significantly reduce mental fatigue and improve self-esteem and life satisfaction [17].

Then, the results of Verderber's [2] study indicated that patients prefer hospitals with window views of nature. Moreover, for retirement home residents, passive involvement with a green environment through looking out of windows and taking excursions into outdoor recreational areas is an important factor in well-being and life satisfaction [18].

Furthermore, according to the Ulrich [12], the natural environment not only provides beauty and artistic elements but also is a factor that improves older people's health. In another study, Ulrich examined the restorative effect of natural views on post-operative recovery. The patients with a window view of vegetation spent less time in the hospital than those with the view of the brick wall [16].

In MacKerron's [19] study, participants rated the sea, mountains and woodlands as the happiest locations.

In a study of Berto [20], the results showed that hills and lakes were rated as more restorative, more preferred, and more familiar.

The research of Kaplan [21] and Talbot and Kaplan [17] showed that the elderly reported greater satisfaction with their neighborhood. A view of gardens or wooded spaces in the living area might have anti-stress effects on healthy citizens. Another kind of environment that surrounds the elderly's living space is the neighborhood. This environment is more important for the daily lives of elderly people because as their ability and/or willingness to move decreases, their activity space shrinks and their dependence on the local environment tends to grow [13, 22].

Viewing slides of nature had a more positive impact on psychical and mental states than viewing slides of urban scenes [12]. The results of Yung et al.'s [23] study demonstrate that urban spaces enhance the elderly's social interaction and active aging.

2.2 Concept of the Virtual Window

As shown in Sect. 2.1, many studies support the concept of the visual window environment presented in this study. The emergence of increasingly cramped living spaces will affect older people's health and emotion; thus, the abovementioned study was launched. This study will propose the design concept of the virtual window for the lives of the elderly in a windowless environment and focus on the virtual window element of the elderly's living space. Moreover, this study will further develop the concept of the virtual design window and place such windows in a windowless department. Thus, one objective of this study is to fully exploit the virtual window. Finally, the purpose of this study is to identify and understand the design concept of the visual window for the elderly's daily living environment.

Table 1 summarizes the concept of three visual window environments.

Table 1. The concept of three visual window environments

Environment	Concept
Natural environment	• Bringing beauty and artistic elements [16] Hills, lakes [20], the sea, mountains and woodlands • [19] were rated as more restorative, more preferred, and more familiar than other environments
Community environment	• The neighborhood is an important environment surrounding the elderly's living space [13] • A view of gardens or wooded spaces in a living area might have anti-stress effects on healthy citizens [24, 25]
Urban environment	• Enhancing social interaction and active aging [23] • The urban environment could improve the elderly's social health through elements of design [14] • The relationship between humans' health and well-being and satisfaction with their living space is a factor in building human society

3 Proposed Synthesis

Based on the above literature review, this study proposes the concept of the virtual window in elder people's living space to improve their lives and health. Based on recent developments in the concept, this study integrates three environment categories: natural environments (Fig. 1), community spaces (Fig. 2) and urban places (Fig. 3). The natural environment includes hills, the sea, mountains and woodlands. The community spaces are composed of gardens, neighborhoods and wooded areas. Finally, the urban place is composed of buildings.

Fig. 1. Natural environments

Fig. 2. Community spaces

Fig. 3. Urban places

4   Conclusion

Urbanization could lead people to live in windowless departments, and the lack of windows in a living space could affect people, especially elderly people's, mental, emotional and physical status, as shown in many studies. Therefore, this study integrates the recent developments in the concept of the visual window and proposes syntheses of three environments: natural environments, community spaces and urban places. The concept of the three syntheses could assist the designers of the visual window in designing a helpful and realistic environment that improves the elderly's health and emotional state.

A future experiment could be conducted to verify the effect of the three syntheses of the visual windows. The results of such a study could improve visual windows such that they more efficiently benefit people, especially the elderly.

Acknowledgement. This work was supported in part by the Ministry of Science and Technology, Taiwan, ROC under Contracts MOST 103-2628-H-182-001-MY2 and 104-2410-H-182-025-MY2, and by the Healthy Aging Research Centre, Chang Gung University (fund no. EMRPD1F0301, CMRPD1B0331, and CMRPD1B0332). The funders had no role in study design, data collection and analysis, decision to publish, or preparation of the manuscript.

References

1. IJsselsteijn, W.A., Oosting, W., Vogels, I.M.L.C., de Kort, Y.A.M., van Loenen, E.: A room with a cue: The efficacy of movement parallax, occlusion, and blur in creating a virtual window. Presence Teleoperators Virtual Environ. **17**, 269–282 (2008)
2. Verderber, S.: Dimensions ofperson-window transactionsin the hospital environment. Environ. Behav. **18**, 450–466 (1986)
3. Ochodo, C., Ndetei, D.M., Moturi, W.N., Otieno, J.O.: External built residential environment characteristics that affect mental health of adults. J. Urban Health **91**, 908–927 (2014)
4. Tennessen, C.M., Cimprich, B.: Views to nature: effects on attention. J. Environ. Psychol. **15**, 77–85 (1995)
5. Schorr, B. http://mixedreality.cc
6. Häkkilä, J., Koskenranta, O., Posti, M., Ventä-Olkkonen, L., Colley, A.: Clearing the virtual window: connecting two locations with interactive public displays. In: Proceedings of the 2nd ACM International Symposium on Pervasive Displays, pp. 85–90. ACM (2013)
7. Dowds, G., Masthoff, J.: A virtual window to the outside world: initial design and plans for evaluation. In: Proceedings of the 2015 British HCI Conference, pp. 265–266. ACM (2015)
8. Clarke, P., Nieuwenhuijsen, E.R.: Environments for healthy ageing: A critical review. Maturitas **64**, 14–19 (2009)
9. Tse, T.: The environment and falls prevention: do environmental modifications make a difference? Aust. Occup. Ther. J. **52**, 271–281 (2005)
10. Bind, M.A., Baccarelli, A., Zanobetti, A., Tarantini, L., Suh, H., Vokonas, P., Schwartz, J.: Air pollution and markers of coagulation, inflammation and endothelial function: Associations and epigene-environment interactions in an elderly cohort. Epidemiology **23**, 332–340 (2012)
11. Bonnefoy, X.R., Braubach, M., Moissonnier, B., Monolbaev, K., Röbbel, N.: Housing and health in Europe: preliminary results of a pan-European study. Am. J. Public Health **93**, 1559–1563 (2003)
12. Ulrich, R.S.: Natural versus urban scenes some psychophysiological effects. Environ. Behav. **13**, 523–556 (1981)
13. Golant, S.M.: The effects of residential and activity behaviors on old people's environmental experiences. In: Altman, I., Lawton, M.P., Wohlwill, J.F. (eds.) Elderly People and the Environment. Human Behavior and Environment, vol. 7, pp. 239–278. Springer, New York (1984)
14. Alidoust, S., Holden, G., Bosman, C.: Urban environment and social health of the elderly: a critical discussion on physical, social and policy environments. Athens J. Health **1**, 169–180 (2014)
15. Lyle, J.: Design for Human Ecosystems: Landscape, Land Use, and Natural Resources. Island Press, New York (1999)
16. Ulrich, R.: View through a window may influence recovery. Science **224**, 224–225 (1984)
17. Talbot, J.F., Kaplan, R.: The benefits of nearby nature for elderly apartment residents. Int. J. Aging Hum. Develop. **33**, 119–130 (1990)
18. Brascamp, W., Kidd, J.L.: Contribution of plants to the well-being of retirement home residents. In: XXVI International Horticultural Congress: Expanding Roles for Horticulture in Improving Human Well-Being and Life Quality, pp. 145–150 (2002)
19. MacKerron, G., Mourato, S.: Happiness is greater in natural environments. Global Environ. Change **23**, 992–1000 (2013)

20. Berto, R.: Assessing the restorative value of the environment: A study on the elderly in comparison with young adults and adolescents. Int. J. Psychol. **42**, 331–341 (2007)
21. Kaplan, R.: The role of nature in the urban context. In: Altman, I., Wohlwill, J.F. (eds.) Behavior and the Natural Environment, pp. 127–161. Springer, New York (1983)
22. Musil, J.: Changing urban systems in post-communist societies in central Europe: analysis and prediction. Urban Stud. **30**, 899–905 (1993)
23. Yung, E.H.K., Conejos, S., Chan, E.H.W.: Social needs of the elderly and active aging in public open spaces in urban renewal. Cities **52**, 114–122 (2016)
24. Kuo, F.E., Sullivan, W.C.: Environment and crime in the inner city does vegetation reduce crime? Environ. Behav. **33**, 343–367 (2001)
25. Rosso, A.L., Auchincloss, A.H., Michael, Y.L.: The urban built environment and mobility in older adults: a comprehensive review. J. Aging Res. **2011**, 1–10 (2011)

Author Index

Printed in the United States
By Bookmasters